MT. OLIVET CEMETERY

Baltimore, Maryland

Caretaker Records
Volume 1: Sections A through D

John J. Winterbottom

HERITAGE BOOKS
2011

HERITAGE BOOKS
AN IMPRINT OF HERITAGE BOOKS, INC.

Books, CDs, and more—Worldwide

For our listing of thousands of titles see our website
at
www.HeritageBooks.com

Published 2011 by
HERITAGE BOOKS, INC.
Publishing Division
100 Railroad Ave. #104
Westminster, Maryland 21157

Copyright © 1989 John J. Winterbottom

Other Heritage Books by the author:

Mt. Olivet Cemetery, Baltimore, Maryland, Caretaker Records
Volume 1: Sections A through D
Volume 2: Sections E through J
Volume 3: Sections K through S
and Single Interments

All rights reserved. No part of this book may be reproduced or transmitted in any form or by any means, electronic or mechanical, including photocopying, recording or by any information storage and retrieval system without written permission from the author, except for the inclusion of brief quotations in a review.

International Standard Book Numbers
Paperbound: 978-1-58549-598-6
Clothbound: 978-0-7884-8681-4

PREFACE

In the early 1970's I contacted twelve of the largest cemeteries in Baltimore City about the possibility of their records being microfilmed. As a result of these initial inquiries, the records of three of the twelve cemeteries were put on microfilm. Each cemetery was given a copy of the microfilm, while other copies were deposited in the libraries of the Maryland Historical Society and the Maryland Genealogical Society. It was further decided that at some time the records would be published by the Genealogical Society. However, as years went by this did not occur and eventually I decided to publish the material myself.

Mt. Olivet Cemetery was one of the cemeteries that had agreed to allow its records to be microfilmed. Using a rotary microfilming camera rented by the Maryland Genealogical Society, I started on the actual microfilming. Working every Saturday for about four months, I completed the Lot Books. The three sets of microfilm were made, and copies were deposited with the cemetery, the Maryland Genealogical Society and the Maryland Historical Society.

Because the records as microfilmed were unindexed, I decided to publish them in a more usable format. Purchasing a microfilm reader I set about the work of transcribing the records. Finally the records were typed and indexed.

My thanks to the following people who have supported me in making this publication possible.

To the board of Mt. Olivet Cemetery, without whose permission this material would not have been made available.

To Mrs. Wegand, superintendent of Mt. Olivet, whose cooperation and thoughtful consideration aided in the filming of this material.

To Henry R. Kelly, past treasurer of the Maryland Genealogical Society, without whose encouragement this work would not have been published and to the Maryland Genealogical Society for the rental of the camera and payment for the microfilm.

John J. Winterbottom

INTRODUCTION

THE CEMETERY

Mount Olivet cemetery, located at 2930 Frederick Road, Baltimore, was founded in 1845 and dedicated on 16 July 1849. It replaced an earlier cemetery located at Lombard and Paca Streets in downtown Baltimore. No records have survived from the old address, and no information about the original cemetery is known to exist.

Over the years, many bodies from other cemeteries have been moved to Mount Olivet, and some bodies have been removed from there to other cemeteries. No precise information on these removals is available, partly because many early records of the cemetery are missing. At the time the records were microfilmed, it was estimated that over 36,000 persons were interred in the cemetery.

Prior to the establishment of Mount Olivet Cemetery by the Methodist Episcopal Church, several cemeteries had been used by the denomination. These cemeteries are long gone, covered by the expanding city. Many of the persons buried there were removed to Mount Olivet. These earlier cemeteries were: 1) The Southern Burial Ground (referred to in the records as S.B.G.), apparently located in South Baltimore, probably between the current Pratt Street and the Hanover Street Bridge. It was removed when South Hanover Street was built. 2) Northern Burial Ground, probably located no father north than the area between North Avenue and 25th Street and occupying the current location of Lovely Lane Methodist Church; 3) Eastern Burial Ground, located east of the city on Philadelphia Road, where Pulaski Highway and U.S. Route 40 merge; 4) Western Cemetery, still in existence as a commercial cemetery. Located at Edmondson Avenue, the cemetery is believed to have records of the old S.B.G., although officials at the Cemetery say they do not have any such records; 5) U.B.G., is an abbreviation found in the records of Mount Olivet. Its meaning is not known unless it is an unclear rendering of N.B.G.

Mount Olivet Cemetery, covering an area of about 51 acres, is the property of Lovely Lane United Methodist Church. The Cemetery is divided into 19 sections (called Section A, B, etc.) plus an underground vault.

THE RECORD BOOKS

The Cemetery Office contains the following types of records: books listing burials in chronological orders; a card file of lot owners dating from the mid 1930's, and folders (in storage) covering each lot, and Lot Books. The folders would have been too costly to microfilm, and the burial books were bound, which would have required special equipment to microfilm.

The Lot Books, 20 in number, are each about one inch thick; measuring 8 1/2 x 12 1/2 inches. They give the only information known for the early interments. They are in looseleaf notebooks which are not in good repair, and which in the past were not always kept very well. Early pages were used for unofficial purposes. Other pages were torn, blotted, and written over. The first 10 lot records from Section A are missing.

A typical page in a lot book is divided into two sections. On the left hand side is a list of all those buried in the lot, and perhaps the date of interment. The right hand side of the page shows a diagram of the lot, with the actual number of graves in that lot. The names of those individuals buried in each grave are entered here.

Sometimes a lot was owned by two families, in which case there will be two lists of names on the left of the page. It should also be noted that when bodies were removed from one grave to another within the lot, the names may not have always been completely erased from the list of names or the diagram of graves, giving the impression that a lot contains more bodies.

Sometimes the researcher will find the same name in two different lots with two different dates. It is not always possible to tell if the first date was the original interment and the second date that of a reinterment, or whether the two entries refer to two individuals who died at different times, but who had the same name.

The list of names on the left hand side contains a series of boxes, each box supposedly containing data on a single burial, but such is not always the case. Some of the early burials are merely indicated as "Remains," or sometimes as "Adult" or Child." Sometimes it is possible to identify the individuals noted in these scanty references by using other records, such as those mentioned above, or in the interment records.

The Interment Books are large journals about 3 inches thick, and 14 by 10 inches in size. They are in good condition.

In transcribing the records I have indicated the names of the lot numbers. While every effort has been made to transcribe the records accurately and completely, researchers should use other sources, such as newspapers, church records, and public records to confirm names and dates. It should also be borne in mind that cemeteries are in the business of interring bodies, and are more interested in recording the date of burial, rather than the date of death. Whenever a date was clearly indicated as the date of death I have indicated it as such. Keep in mind that sometimes "dates of death" were entered that were copied from a tombstone, which itself may have contained errors in the carving.

The names which appear at the beginning of each lot, before the semi-colon, are the lot owners.

LOTS 1-A through 9-A: There are no records of these lots in the lot book.

LOT 10-A: Martha LEE, James FITZGERALD;
Jas. A. LEE, June 19, 1853 (date from stone reads Dec. 16, 1856); Remains, June 24, 1853; John T. LEE, May 11, 1869 (date from stone reads Apr. 29, 1869); Laura V. VAN ORDER, Jan. 4, 1871; Mary A. LEE, Aug. 12, 1879; Martha A. LEE, June 10, 1884; James R. LEE, June 13, 1916; Louis W. FITZGERALD, Sept. 10, 1852; Frank H. FITZGERALD, July 10, 1857; James FITZGERALD, June 20, 1864; Annie E. MUSHAW, Mar. 25, 1879; Mary MUSHAW, Apr. 13, 1880; Clara V. FITZGERALD, June 13, 1881; Fannie H. MUSHAW, Jan. 22, 1885; George MUSHAW, June 23, 1885; Lewis H. MUSHAW, June 11, 1892; Cath. E. MUSHAW, July 8, 1930; Wm. A. MUSHAW, Jan. 14, 1931; Elizabeth LEE, Mar. 16, 1843; Jean CALTON, Aug. 4, 1944; Caroline MEUSHAW, Oct. 28, 1939.

LOT 11-A: Jos. REASON, John WILLETT, Jos. WILKINSON;
Remains, Oct. 14, 1854; Mary WILKINSON, June 14, 1864; Wm. H. BRYAN, May 5, 1866; Joseph C. WILKINSON, Apr. 17, 1876; Margt. E. WILKINSON, June 25, 1881; Vermillion BRYAN, Sept. 19, 1881; Jos. WILKINSON, Dec. 19, 1891; John H. H. WILKINSON, Nov. 24, 1882; Hiram H. WILKINSON, Nov. 11, 1881; child, July 8, 1852; Wilber WESSELLS, July 15, 1868; Asa WESSELLS, Aug. 21, 1876; Elmira WESSELLS, Feb. 23, 1878; Wm. D. WESSELLS, Dec. 29, 1885.

LOT 12-A: Wm. BURTON, Wm. NASH;
Remains, May 5, 1852; George H. COOPER, Aug. 4, 1858; Dissenter Anne M. LAWTON, Oct. 8, 1862; Marion LAWTON, July 1, 1852; Laura V. COOPER, May 17, 1866; Wm. COOPER, Oct. 24,1868; Chas. COOPER, July 6, 1869; Margt. COOPER, Feb 21, 1870; George W. COOPER, Sept. 15, 1875; Margt. HIGGINS, Jan. 28, 1881; John W. BODINE, Oct. 31, 1889; Child, Mar. 16, 1852; Wm. F. BAILEY, July 12,1867; Elizabeth NASH, Sept. 7, 1767; Elizabeth C. NASH, Mar. 26, 1886; Annie L. JENKINS, Sept. 1, 1887; Saml. T. JENKINS, May 1, 1906; Dorothy SULLIVAN, Mar. 28, 1914; Mary K. JENKINS, Dec. 16, 1914; William SULLIVAN, July 26, 1915; James JENKINS, May 10, 1920; Chas. D. JENKINS, Mar. 13, 1931; John JENKINS, Apr. 1, 1935; Richard BURTON, Aug. 4, 1821; Mark JENKINS, (no date given); Richard W. KEYS, Aug. 30, 1935.

LOT 13-A: Mani WALTON, James TOWNSEND, David MITCHELL;
Calbaugh, July 21, 1861; Remains, May 15, 1858; Remains, Aug. 23, 1853; Child, July 17, 1856; Jane MITCHELL, Apr. 16, 1856; Child, Aug. 10, 1859; Two Twins, Dec. 13, 1859; Child of Settler, Apr. 1, 1864; Mathew WALLACE,Jan. 5, 1871; Jane MITCHELL, Feb. 15, 1875; Wm. H. MITCHELL, Apr. 5, 1875; Danl. C. MITCHELL, Mar. 22, 1886; George W. MITCHELL,Nov. 2, 1888; Rebecca TOWNSEND, Sept. 13, 1851; Lillian M. WELLS, Apr. 25, 1891; Sadie M. WELLS, July 7, 1902; Martha WALLACE, May 26, 1863.

LOT 14-A: R(itzen) BROWNING;
Remains, Oct. 27, 1852; John W. BROWNING, Dec. 22, 1852; Ritzen BROWNING, July 4, 1859 (also date of Jan. 3, 1859 is given from stone); Fannie HARRISON, Apr. 27, 1859; Mary J. BROWNING, June 16, 1862; Evelin BROWNING, Oct. 30, 1880; Louisa K. BROWNING, Sept. 19, 1882; Mary A. BROWNING, Apr. 11, 1883; Virginia BROWN- ING, Aug. 22, 1889; Mary B. DISNEY, Apr. 27, 1904; Susan BROWN- ING, Feb. 25, 1913; Mary J. BROWNING, June 15, 1862; Wesley

DISNEY, Apr. 6, 1933; Thomas H. DISNEY, May 19, 1942; There is a stone reading "Mary A., Apr. 21, 1899"; J. WESLEY and J. DISNEY names entered in one space.

LOT 15-A: Mary A. VICKERY;
Elizabeth VICKERY, Mar. 12, 1851; Mary A. VICKERY, Dec. 21, 1859; Elizabeth MC DOWALL, Mar. 18, 1876; Wm. S. WEDGE, Feb. 11, 1892; Emily WEDGE, May 16, 1895; Infant of G. and Lucy DEVERE, Dec. 21, 1904; Chas. MC DOWELL, Sept. 3, 1844; (Hazeltire) VICKERY, Dec. 21, 1904; Maryman VICKERY, Nov. 3, 1858; Thomas VICKERY, May 3, 1844; Stephen J. VICKERY, June 1841.

LOT 16-A: John RICKETTS;
Child, July 8, 1851; Remains, May 31, 1851; Child, June 1, 1857; Margt. M. RICKETTS, Jan. 1, 1862; David RICKETTS, Sept. 18, 1871; John RICKETTS, Jan. 23, 1875; Cora D. RICKETTS, Jan. 30, 1877; Emily RICKETTS, Feb. 10, 1877; Child of James L. CARMINE, June 15, 1878; Stillborn of FITZGERALD, Jan. 25, 1882; Mary RICKETTS, May (2), 1893; Blanch RICKETTS, Apr. 10, 1908; Carroll CARMINE, May 8, 1913; Removed from Southern Burial Ground, May 26, 1851; Mary D. RICKETTS, Apr. 14, 1887; Fannie RICKETTS, Feb. 18, 1918; J. L. CARMINE, Dec. 27, 1919; George FITZGERALD, May 25, 1928; Elizabeth D. CARMINE, Feb. 26, 1929; Mary M. FITZGERALD, Oct. 2, 1931; John RICKETTS, Nov. 9, 1933; Cremated remains of John Francis CARMINE, Nov. 20, 1948; Caroline SCHERER, June 27, 1956; Cremation of Clarence H. SCHERER, Oct. 25, 1965; Louise RICKETTS, Oct. 23, 1939.

LOT 17-A: James A. MAYNARD, HARTLOVE, and SIMPSON;
Remains, Nov. 17, 1852; Child, Aug. 23, 1855; Removed from St. Peter's Cemetery, June 28, 1873; (Entry crossed out, appears to read: A. E. HARTLOVE, Mar. 14, 1874); Mary N. MAYNARD, May 13, 1889; Wm. B. TURNER, (Nov. or Mar.) 1, 1918 (There is also what appears to be Wm. T. TURNER); Jas. M. TURNER, Dec. 19, 1933; (The word Geo. is lined out and Chas. inserted before E. WATERS, Jr., Oct. 16, 1954 (There is an entry - Charles E. WATERS, born Apr. 20, 1887, died Oct. 5, 1970, dentist; also an entry for Charles E. WATERS, Jr., Oct. 16, 1954; Remains, Sept. 17, 1853; Chas. F. HARTLOVE, Apr. 14, 1857; Annie SIMPSON, Dec. 1, 1858; Alice HARTLOVE, Nov. 4, 1863; Ada M. HARTLOVE, Oct. 25, 1871; Child, June 1, 1872; Annie E. HARTLOVE, Oct. 9, 1873; Bessie SCHAUM, Nov. 29, 1880; Benj. O. SCHAUM, Feb. 18, 1881; Eliza A. HARTLOVE, May 7, 1883; Chas. H. HARTLOVE, Aug. 16, 1898; Elizabeth HARTLOVE, May 7, 1897; Alice S. HARTLOVE, Sept. 28, 1899; Chas. P. BROWN, Aug. 2, 1909; Eleanor Maynard TURNER, Jan. 7, 1953; Elizabeth MAYNARD, July 1, 1811; Nancy MAYNARD, (no date given); _____ MAYNARD, Mar. 8, 1815 (This entry is preceded by 3 or 4 words. The first may be Catherine, the next 2 or 3 are illegible, the last possibly being "Nan").

LOT 18-A: B. F. BENNETT;
Sallie BENNETT, June 3, 1853; Kate H. BENNETT, Mar. 25, 1858; Sarah WARD, Nov. 17, 1873; Allen BENNETT, May 12, 1892; Kate H. BENNETT, May 12, 1892; Elizabeth H. BENNETT, June 25, 1906; Elenora A. BENNETT, July 17, 1885; Benj. F. BENNETT, Apr. 25, 1913; Mary Ann REESE, Jan. 5, 1914; Saml. WARD, Aug. 31, 18--; Sarah WARD, Dec. 31, 1852.

LOT 19-A: Edwd. J. WARD;
Remains, Mar. 1, 1852; Annie T. WARD, Aug. 12, 1854; Edwd. J. WARD, Apr. 19, 1873; Mary E. WARD, Apr. 29, 1873; Grace E. WARD, Mar. 19, 1890; Edwd. J. (or T.) WARD, Feb. 2, 1891 (possibly Jr.); Marion E. WARD, July 15, 1904; Edwd. T. WARD, Jan. 4, 1907; Eleanor Kate WARD, May 8, 1952.

LOT 20-A: George ZIMMERMAN;
Remains, July 9, 1851; Isabell ZIMMERMAN, July 25, 1855; Christian ZIMMERMAN, Aug. 24, 1866; Emma C. ZIMMERMAN, Oct. 14, 1870; Harry A. ZIMMERMAN, Jan. 14, 1890; George E. ZIMMERMAN, July 6, 1894; Mary E. ZIMMERMAN, Apr. 21, 1897; Rev. George ZIMMERMAN, May 27, 1897; Wm. ZIMMERMAN, June 24, 1898; George J. ZIMMERMAN, Dec. 9, 1879; Fannie B. HULL, May 2, 1917; Marshall MC ILHENNY, and 2 children, Mar. 14, 1934; Clara Belle MC ILHENNY, Oct. 26, 1946; (Hannah) C. (no surname given), June 16, 1845.

LOT 21-A: Lewis & Kate BRIGGEMAN, Spencer M. WARRING;
Carolina A. G. REED, Nov. 23, 1896 (This name, which is probably Reese, appears in various places as Reeol, Reeas, Reed); Wm. CAULK, Mar. 7, 1876; Robt. Lee BLEDSOE, (Nov.) 27, 1917 (entry crossed out); Margt. CORK, Aug. 9, 1859; John S. REE(OL), Feb. 23, 1894, moved Apr. 12, 1894; Lewis E. BRIGGERMAN, July 25, 1916 (entry crossed out); Stillborn of Nellie & R. BRIGGEMAN, Sept. 23, 1910; Mary E. REESE (or REEOL), May 15, 1920; Robert Lee BLEDSOR, Nov. 17, 1917; Susan TA(BBALBS), July 13, 1853 (There is an entry for this name and the following: "Don't know which lots they are in"); Susan BRIGHT, Aug. 13, 1858; Beulah E. BLEDSOE, July 23, 1964.

LOT 22-A: W. G. FOSBENNER, S. W. FOSBENNER, Ann FOSBENNER;
W. G. FOSBENNER, July 19, 1869 (There is an entry for Wm. G. FOSBENNER which may be the same person and the number 56); Elizabeth FOSBENNER, July 11, 1874 (There is the number 81 in one of the spaces for one of the Elizabeth FOSBENNER's); George RICHARDSON, Jan. 30, 1915; Chas. L. MEYERS, Mar. 28, 1913; Hester A. MEYERS, Mar. 27, 1929; Danl. F. FOSBENNER, Mar. 13, 18(57), age 67 years; Sarah WATTS, Feb. 21, 1852; Ann FOSBENNER, Apr. 6, 1885, age 83 years; Kate BURKHART, May 26, 1920; Wm. G. FOSBENNER, Mar. 28, 1912; Elizabeth FOSBENNER, June 8, 1912; (Daniel) J. FOSBENNER, Mar. 12, 1914 (first name may be Saml.); Remains, June 22, 1855; Henry MORTIMER, Dec. 22, 1852; Elizabeth BAKER, July 10, 1871, age 73 years; Susannah FOSBENNER, Nov. 30, 1836; Mary PATTERSON, Feb. 13, 1836.

LOT 23-A: James B. GOODHAND, Sarah A. WHEELER;
Child, Apr. 10, 1871; James HANER, July 21, 1854; Infant of M. & J. GOODHAND, Nov. 29, 1890; Infant of M. & J. GOODHAND, Dec. 23, 1886; Elizabeth GOODHAND, Jan. 9, 1891; Jos. B. GOODHAND, Mar. 7, 1896; Thos. B. GOODHAND, Feb. 6, 1893; (J.) Frank GOODHAND, May 6, 1904; John P. GOODHAND, Jr., Mar. 15, 1911; Jas. B. (or E.) GOODHAND, Aug. 7, 1917; Alice J. GOODHAND, Apr. 29, 1918; Sarah A. WHEELER, Aug. 14, 1900; Jas. WHEELER, Aug. 4, 1860; Elizabeth SIMMONS, Dec. 3, 1858; Infant of (J.) Frank GOODHAND; Martha G. GOODHAND, July 20, 1905.

LOT 24-A: Samuel CLAYTON;
Child, July 14, 1851; Elizabeth C. TWEEDY, and child, Apr. 30, 1851; Remains, June 14, 1858; Lelia A. CLAYTON, June 24, 1863; A.

MC HEAN, Dec. 24, 1865; Saml. CLAYTON, July 27, 1873; Ann CLAYTON, Feb. 25, 1878; Mary RICHARDSON, June 22, 1881 (1800); Augustus TWEEDY, Dec. 19, 1892; Cath. TWEEDY, (date not readable); Elizabeth TWEEDY, Nov. 1, 1850, also two children, Jas. & Eclea.; Saml. TWEEDY, Sept. 6, 1910; (There may be two Samuel CLAYTON's buried in this lot); (Celiea) Caroline TWEEDY.

LOT 25-A: George W. SUMUALT, George (A.) NICHOLS, and Archibald WATKINS;
Mary C. BOSNELL, May 4, 1881; Hardy RUSSELL, Oct. 23, 1883; Chas. B. WATKINS, Dec. 2, 1918; Mary E. (EYLEREY), May 12, 1896; Martha CONWAY, Mar. 16, 1903; Kate REYNOLDS, Oct. 10, 1892; Chas. F. BRANAGAN, Apr. 16, 1904; Lillian N. BRANAGAN, Mar. 21, 1904; Emma SANDERS, Aug. 3, 1920; Emma JACKSON, Jan. 6, 1921; Margt. L. MARCH (or MARSH), Dec. 25, 1853; Elizabeth MARCH (or MARSH), Aug. 10, 1854; Remains, Oct. (18), 1855; A. W. WATKINS, Dec. 7, 1857; Margt. & Elizabeth (MARSH), Apr. 8, 1887; Mary A. WATKINS, Oct. 14, 1889; Infant of (C.) B. WATKINS, Dec. 6, 1889; (K)ate (H.) WATKINS, May 29, 1879; Elizabeth WATKINS, Dec. 12, 1866; Elizabeth BROWN, Apr. 20, 1880; John BROWN, July 1, 1880; Allen FORD, June 21, 1894 (possible infant); ___ W. WATKINS, May 1, 1883; Elizabeth BENSON, Nov. 17, 1871; Jas. A. WATKINS, Oct. 1, 1894; John (Q.) A. WATKINS, --- --, 18(1)4; John Q. A. WATKINS, Nov. 15, 1894 (previous two entries possibly the same); Hellen E. BRICE, June 17, 1898; Mary C. WATKINS, June 5, 1899; Elizabeth A. WATKINS, June 1, 1907; John Q. A. WATKINS, July 3, 1914; Annie WATKINS, Dec. 27, 1945; John BROWN, Apr. 1, 1856; Archibald WATKINS, Apr. 30, 1883; Archibald WATKINS, Aug. 23, 1856; Hester RUSSELL; (Annie) A. RUSSELL, June 26, 1934; Martin MARCH; Geo. (G.) RUSSELL, Dec. 15, 1920; (illegible), July 20, 19(34).

LOT 26-A and 27-A: "Sacred to the memory of Dead whose Remains were removed from the Burial Ground of the M. E. Church N.E. Corner Lombard and Paca Streets. Remains buried in this lot September 1851. Monument erected by Baltimore City Station, May 1853". There are three "identified" graves. One has a "tablet" which is illegible. The other two are for: John BOWERSOX, Mar. 28, 1851; Hannah SUCKLEY, Sept. 11, 1798, age 26 years.

LOTS 28-A and 29-A: Joseph LEWIS;
Prisulla LEWIS, Nov. 11, 1871; Joseph E. LEWIS, Dec. 19, 1894; Thos. BROWN, June 28, 1851; Henry LINTHICUM, Sept. 9, 1851; Child of WOOTEN, Aug. 4, 1852; Frances Brown LEWIS, Dec. 16, 1856; Frances BROWNE, Oct. 20, 1857; John N. LEWIS, Jr., June 3, 1861; Wm. T. BROWNE, Oct. 18, 1861; Pricilla G. LEWIS, Apr. 5, 1862; Chas. R. LEWIS, Sept. 29, 1864; Thos. B. LEWIS, Oct. 18, 1868; Edwd. LEWIS, Sept. 7, 1891; Mary E. LEWIS, Aug. 3, 1916; Robert P. LEWIS, Aug. 25, 1928; Elizabeth LEWIS, Apr. 22, 1935; Jos. N. LEWIS, Mar. 26, 1859; Jno. T. LEWIS; Elizabeth LEWIS; Elya LINTHICUM; (Henry) LINTHICUM; Master ___ E. LEWIS; Chas. B. LEWIS; W. S. BROWNE; Thomas BROWNE, Nov. 2, 1802.

LOT 30-A: Single Interments;
J. F. STOTTELMYER, Nov. 26, 1934; James T. HARDESTY, Dec. 1, 1934; Joseph BATERMAN, Dec. 5, 1934; Nathan BEACHER, Dec. 22, 1934; Gladys F. THOMAS, Dec. 22, 1934; Joseph P. FORSYTHE, Dec. 31, 1934; Walter W. HOHLSYD, Jan. 7, 1935 (Entry is crossed out and Frank W. HOLYROOD, Jan. 7, 1935 is entered); Annie G. HUNT, Jan. 10, 1935; Joshua MORGAN, Jan. 11, 1935; Blanch B. (G.)

BROOKS, Jan. 18, 1935; Alice BUCKINGHAM, Jan. 23, 1935; Frank LADS (or LATTA), Jan. 25, 193(5); Frank SEBASTIAN, Jan. 30, 1935; Catharine M. SHIFLETT, Feb. 5, 1935; John (W.) H. (PEAR), Feb. 23, 1935; George ADAMS, Feb. 28, 1935; Ella M. (HORWITZ), Mar. 8, 1935; Isabel CRONMILLER, & Thos. CRONMILLER, 1853.

LOT 31-A: Patence BARKER;
Remains, Apr. 5, 1853; Elizabeth BUCKINGHAM, May 13, 1856; Cath. BUCKINGHAM, July 4, 1851; (James) P. CLARK, Mar. 30, 1891; Leah BARKER, Jan. 7, 1893; Leonard BARKER, July 4, 1908; William BARKER, Mar. 29, 1911; Sidney BARKER, Feb. 24, 1913; Patence BARKER, Apr. 2, 1914; Milton L. BARKER, Nov. 27, 1930; Annie M. BARKER, Dec. 22, 1932; Mary C. CLARK, Apr. 3, 1940; William L. BARKER, Jan. 26, 1946; Sarah JONES, Feb. 25, 1853; John JONES, Aug. 30, 1842; Ann JONES, July 17, 1843; Joshua COLE, Dec. 23, 1828; Ann COLE, (March or May 25 or 28, 1835 or 1838); Levi BUCKINGHAM, Apr. 14, 1831; Sarah COLE, Nov. 12, 1828, age 85 years; William L. BARKER, Nov. 13, 1912; Leonard BARKER, Apr. 19, 1951.

LOT 32-A: Dr. (C. or E.) P. IRONS, George HINDS, James ARMIGER, and WILLIAM HINDES;
ARMIGER (no first name, no date); Child of E. P. YOUNG, June 20, 1874; Thomas YOUNG, June 25, 1879; Wm. H. YOUNG, June 23, 1885; Lillie YOUNG, Aug. 6, 1872; Florence YOUNG, July 29, 1866; (G.) C. CARANTHEW, Mar. 14, 1866; IRONS; Elizabeth P. ATKINSON, Jan. 19, 1915; John P. ATKINSON, May 29, 1916; Wm. HINES, Apr. 16, 1853; Wm. HINES, Oct. 24, 1859; Remains, Sept. 19, 1855; John HINES, Aug. 25, 1880; Geo. Hines, June 14, 1893.

LOT 33-A: Thomas ASHTON;
Child of HARVEY, July 28, 1856; Henry C. BUCKINGHAM, Oct. 14, 1857; Thos. H. ASHTON, Dec. 17, 1859; Margt. BUCKINGHAM, Feb. 8, 1864; John E. BUCKINGHAM, Aug. 12, 1865; Thos. ASHTON, Sept. 14, 1878; Lydia E. BUCKINGHAM, (child underneath), Apr. 14, 1880; Elizabeth ASHTON, Apr. 17, 1881; Chas. E. (or A.) ASHTON, Nov. 16, 1896; John M. ASHTON, Sept. 5, 1867.

LOT 34-A: Bowen McG. AYLSWORTH;
George MILES, Mar. 16, 1851; Mary E. AYLSWORTH, Apr. 17, 1868; Annie R. AYLSWORTH, Jan. 20, 1877; Helen M. I. AYLSWORTH, Aug. 6, 1892; Stillborn of Oleie & Harry MINOR, Dec. 7, 1908; Carroll D. MINOR, Mar. 11, 1912; Chas. B. AYLSWORTH, Apr. 30, 1914; Alice L. MINOR, Apr. 11, 1919; Mary I. AYLSLWORTH, Mar. 9, 1905; (Hay C. or Nay E.) AYLESWORTH.

LOT 35-A: Single Interments;
Carrie KELLY, Feb. 9, 192(9); Elizabeth M. BUTTS, Feb. 28, 1929; Wads BURREGHT, Mar. 23, 1929; John L. WADE, Apr. 4, 1929; Florence WADE, Apr. 30, 1929; Mary L. LONG, Apr. 9, 1929; Anna Louise BENSON, July 10, 1929; Stillborn of SHELLOR, Nov. 5, 1929; Stillborn of SMITH, Nov. 12, 1929; (George RESTON, Nov. 29, 1929); Mary SHANT, June 7, 1978; Augustine SHAW, Feb. 12, 1946; Edith (SPNCET), June 17, 1936; (William) JACOBSON, July 12, 1929; John R. BAKER, July 18, 1929; Stillborn of L(?)ERSSON, Oct. 7, 1929.

LOT 36-A: Jos. & Thos. HERBERT to Lulla May SMITH;
Felix McCurley HERBERT, Apr. 6, 1871; Child, Oct. 26, 1871; Child of KAULKMAN, Feb. 7, 1863; Mary A. HERBERT, Feb. 17, 1867; Joseph

A. HERBERT, July 4, 1876; Mi(lch)or HERBERT, Dec. 19, 1913; Mary S. TURNER, Apr. 24, 1853; Alexander CHRISTA, Apr. 7, 1854; Miss HERBERT, June 20, 1858; Harry H. KALKMAN, Aug. 1, 18(69); Richard HERBERT, July 12, 1865; Rebecca HERBERT, June 17, 1858; Bertha V. SMITH, Jan. 2, 1947; Albert L. SMITH, Aug. 13, 1957; Alex. J. HERBERT, Dec. 28, 1910.

LOT 37-A: Kate BRALEY, N. W. CRAWFORD, and Mary REED;
Wm. H. JAY, Feb. 5, 1867; Thos. W. JAY, Sept. 30, 1870; Elizabeth JAY, Jan. 17, 1880; M. Joseph JAY, Dec. 26, 1881; W. H. BRALEY, July 6, 1922; Julius BR(UNIC)K, July 27, 1870 (name also spelled Brunnick or Brunck); Margt. REED, Sept. 24, 1878; Carl F. BRUNCK, June 21, 1907; Oscar BRUNCK, Apr. 15, 1870; Katherine BRALEY, Jan. 21, 1941; John W. JAY; (Ward) BRADY.

LOT 38-A: Anna H. MC CLINTOCK, Joseph CARNOX, W. L. JOHNSON (name crossed out), Seven BRITT;
Child, Oct. 25, 1851; Child, Feb. 14, 1855; Child, Apr. 8, 1860; Child of Jos. GARDNER, Nov. 14, 1873; Geo. D. CANNOX, Feb. 2, 1874; Lydia CANNOX, June 10, 1875; Jos. CANNOX, Oct. 4, 1878; Elmer E. MC CLINTOCK, Feb. 26, 1934; Remains, May 14, 1858; Robert L. BRITT, July 23,1859; Gainor BRITT, Aug. 1(4), 1867; Caroline WRIGHT, May 8, 1914; (There is a space reserved for Ida E. MC CAULEY); Severn BRITT, June 4, 1858; Caroline B. MC (GLUE), June 23, 1858 ("Removed from Light Street"); Annie H. MC CLINTOCK, Aug. 23, 1947; Sarah G. REESE, Dec. 24, 1938; Carrie S. WALL, Dec. 27, 1958; Chas. P. WALL, born Oct. 10, 1885, died Nov. 11, 1969, buried Nov. 22, 1969.

LOT 39-A: Wesley HARTLOVE;
William DOWNS, Aug. 30, 1867; Frances SPILMAN, Oct. 7, 1863 (may be the same as "Sergt. F. SPILLMAN, Co. G, 5th N.Y. I.N.F. (sic)" on stone.); Wm. HARTLOVE, Sept. 17, 1872; Wesley HARTLOVE, July 12, 1870; Elizabeth HARTLOVE, Feb. 25, 1873; Edwd. (S.) LEACH, Mar. 13, 1883; Geo. M. LEACH, Aug. 21, 1883; Joshua HARTLOVE, Mar. 13, 1884; John ST(EIN)FORD, May 15, 1885; Geo. W. DOWNS, Sept. 10, 1885; Infant of M. & I. STEINFORD, Jan. 2, 1886; Harry S. HARTLOVE, July 18, 1887; Elizabeth HARTLOVE, July 10, 1890; Saml. E. HARTLOVE, Dec. (10), 1890; Edith LEACH, Oct. 17, 1893; Mary E. HARTLOVE, Dec. 1, 1893; "Dissenter Walter - Mary (F.) HARTLOVE"; Benty (?), Nov. 3, 1908; Estell HARTLOVE, Sept. 25, 1908; Laura A. DOWNS, Oct. 10, 1911; John R. EWARD, June 16, 1922; Robert D. (LANG or LONG), Sept. 12, 1923; Joseph HARTLOVE, Jan. 5, 1855; Remains, Sept. 2(?), 1853; John HARTLOVE, Oct. 11, 1853 (also a John HARTLOVE, Oct. 30, 1853, probably the same person); Mary BORNELL, May 26, 1860; Mel(aire) R. EDWARDS, Mar. 29, 1927; Mar(g). E. HARTLOVE, Mar. 10, 1928; Arthur M. LEACH; James E. LEACH, Feb. 22, 1964; Caroline (M.) LEACH, Apr. 17, 1913; Emma V. LONG, Jan. 14, 1948; Wm. HARTLOVE, 1852; James HARTLOVE, May 26, 1848; Rozetta (no surname given), Dec. 11, 1839 (buried with Hartlove's); Wm. HARTLOVE, (no dates given; buried with Rozetta & James HARTLOVE).

LOT 40-A: James IVES, Mrs. Louisa N. WILCOX;
Remains of IVES family, July 4, 1852; Margt. IVAS, Aug. 13, 1855; Priscilla SHAW, Apr. 10, 1856; Jas. IVES, Apr. 12, 1857, aged 85 years; Saranna SMITH, Feb. 10, 1860; Mary J. IVES, July 29, 1889, aged 80 years; Elizabeth IVES, Aug. 12, 1853, aged 80 years; Emma I. WILCOX, Aug. 24, 1942; Louis N. WILCOX, Aug. 24, 1937; Martha

(Matie) D. WILCOX, born Dec. 13, 1882, died Nov. 20, 1968, buried Nov. 22, 1968.

LOT 41-A: Ella Hahn SHIPLEY, Otho A. SHIPLEY; Henry W. COTTRELL, July 28, 1860; Rose A. TAUGHINBAUGH, July 5, 1886; Mary E. COTTRELL, May 1, 1902; Chas. COTTRELL, May 25, 1859; Mrs. COTTRELL, Oct. 5, 1861; Ella Hahn SHIPLEY, Sept. 11, 1935; Wilma SHIPLEY, (no date given); Space "reserved for Otho A. Jr., son of lot owner"; "for Anne E. SHIPLEY"; Otho A. SHIPLEY, Apr. 26, 1949.

LOT 42-A: Sophia NEWTON, NEWTON & MILLER; Willie E. NEWTON, Mar. 9, 1861 (There is a marker which reads: Willie NEWTON, 1878); John W. NEWTON, Aug. 14, 1868; Alfred C. NEWTON, July 1, 1876; Stillborn of Alfred NEWTON, Aug. 17, 1879; Harry N. WICKERS, Oct. 23, 1899; Sophia STEIFFE, Oct. 30, 1915; Emma WICKERS, Oct. 18, 1933; Edward D. NEWTON, 1849; Susanna NEWTON, 1877; Thos. NEWTON, Nov. 1, 1881; Mary A. NEWTON, Nov. 18, 1886; Adolph MILLER, 1899; Remains of Peter and Sarah HOOVER and Mary ZIMMERMAN, Aug. 18, 1895; Carrie "8" NEWTON, Feb. 20, 1920; Laura A. (MILLER), Aug. 28, 1922; "Bodies in lot can't locate, Dec. 28, 1852, Remains Cornelius, Dec. 31, 1854, Jas. M(ORIE), Apr. 28, 1857, Saml. BURNETT"; Charles H. WICKERS, Oct. 23, 1952; Lot book reads: "Res. for Ruth STURGIS"; George W. (no surname given, but probably NEWTON), 1856.

LOT 43-A: John OREM, Elizabeth WOOLEN; Remains, Apr. 13, 1852; John (H.) OREM, June 17, 1854 (stone reads 1852); John OREM, Dec. 28, 1857; James WOLLEN, Mar. 26, 1852; Elizabeth WOLLEN, May 13, 1878; Louisa M. BARKMAN, Oct. 22, 1880; There is a stone which reads: Jas. WOOLEN, Feb. 29, 1852, 82 years; A stone also reads: Elizabeth, Oct. 5, 1837, and one reading: Mary A., Oct. (5), 184(3); Another stone reads: Sarah A. E. CARVER, Apr. 16, 1844.

LOT 44-A: Richard H. SMITH; Remains, June 30, 1852; Ellen SMITH, Apr. 8, 1853; Mrs. BRASHEARS, June 29, 1854; Geo. A. SMITH, Nov. 20, 1855; Child of SMITH, Dec. 19, 1865; Geo. Z. SMITH, Mar. 8, 1866; Child, Oct. 1, 1867; Child of CLOGETT, July 15, 1874; Child of CLOGETT, Jan. 20, 1874; Jane R. SNYDER, Feb. 28, 1876; Child of SNYDER, removed grave of Ellen SNYDER, Sept. 7, 1876; Ann E. SMITH, July 29, 1880; Margt. SNYDER, July 30, 1890; Sarah (Jane) SMITH, June 20, 1896; R. Henry SMITH, (2 children underneath), Jan. 13, 1913; Mary SNYDER, July 8, 1918; Child, Apr. 9, 1869; Ellen SNYDER, Apr. 16, 1854; Sarah BARLING, Apr. 5, 1850; Julia A. SMITH, Nov. 11, 1963; Dr. Peter SNYDER, June 3, 1845; Annette Smith BURGESS, Aug. 4, 1962; Richard H. SMITH, Jr., Apr. 19, 1949; "Geo. ARCHOR, Ann Eliza, Walter (WAY), Chas. WESLEY".

LOT 45-A: Home of Friendless; Remains, May 10, 1851; Alethea MC DANIEL, Sept. 2, 1854; Ida HUNTER, Mar. 7, 1876; Levi GODRICH, May 12, 1876; Fredk. NEWHOUSE, June 16, 1876; Willie WALLACE, Sept. 26, 1876; Cath. COLLINS, Feb 3, 1877; Eva KING, Mar. 15, 1877; Lettie WILSON, Apr. 12, 1877; Ann NETTLESHIF, Aug. 15, 1877; Leroy FRANKLIN, Aug. 13, 1877; Wm. H. WATERS, Jan. 27, 1876; Wm. H. MAYER, Mar. 29, 1879; Frank NEWHOUSE; Eva KING. (Also see Lot 83-A)

LOT 46-A: John C. SMITH;
Remains, June 27, 1851; Child, May 13, 1852; Susan E. SMITH, June 9, 1858; Lulia L. SMITH, Aug. 13, 1862; Wm. T. SMITH, Apr. 12, 1866; John C. SMITH, May 17, 1869; John D. NORIS, Oct. 20, 1870; Wallis T. SMITH, Mar. 29, 1875; Margt. NORIS, May 7, 1884; Mary J. SMITH, May 1, 1889; David SMITH, May 13, 1852; Walter (F.) SMITH, Dec. 17, 1865; Ella V. (no surname given), Aug. 9, 1865; John G. SMITH, Dec. 10, 1868; (V)erda (possibly MOORE), Aug. 15, 1837; Luly (possibly MOORE), May 19, 1855 (or 1858); Luly MOORE, 1829; Maber H. STRINGER, Dec. 27, 1970, age 92 years; Edwin STRINGER, July 16, 1962; Chas. (I.) SMITH, 1872; Margt. (WILLIAMS), Dec. 11, (1852).

LOT 47-A: R. PUMPHREY, Lloyd PUMPHREY, G. E. PUMPHREY;
Rachel PUMPHREY, May 5, 1880; Remains, Oct. 28, 1851; B. PUMPHREY, July 6, 1858; Lloyd P. PUMPHREY, Mar. 28, 1871; Rebecca B. PUMPHREY, Jan. 14, 1898; Lillie J. PUMPHREY, Dec. 11, 1859; Geo. E. PUMPHREY, July 15, 1879; Mary V. PUMPHREY, July 5, 1879; Geo. S. PUMPHREY, Jan. 14, 1884; Ruth V. PUMPHREY, June 22, 1886; Mary A. PUMPHREY, June 10, 1892; Lloydia PUMPHREY, June 22, 1943; Rachel, Jan. 1, 1842; Geo. Shipley, Nov. 11, 1857; Lillie G., Nov. 29, 1859; Following are inscriptions: Children of Geo. S. PUMPHREY; Annie E. SMITH, Nov. 19, 1858; Ebeneza, 1829; Wife Rachel, May 5, 1880.

LOT 48-A: John LATHAM, Peregrine SPENCER;
Laura LATHAM, May 31, 1857; John LATHAM, Mar. 9, 1881; Child, May 17, 1854; Susan SPENCER, Dec. 21, 1878; Anne H. THRIFT, Jan. 14, 1882; Elizabeth FATHAMS, Nov. 1853; Joht. TATHAM.

LOT 49-A & 50-A: Elias BROWN & Margt. HOGG;
Elizabeth HOGG, May 9, 1855; Mary E. HOGG, July 4, 1854; Mary DILLEHANEY, Sept. 26, 1855; Mrs. H. HOGG, Aug. 17, 1855; Rachel HOGG, June 1, 1858; Child, May 4, 1859; Ann BROWN, Aug. 25, 1862; Eliza A. HOGG., Mar. 5, 1869; Alice BROWN, Apr. 11, 1871; Clara HAMILTON, Nov. 22, 1877; Sarah J. BROWN, July 14, 1896; Eliza BROWN, Feb. 3, 1899; George C. BROWN, Jan. 26, 1907; E. A. HOGG, Feb. 28, 1904, Norfolk Lodge B.P.O.E.; Martha A. HOGG, Apr. 15, 1918; Laura H. BROWN, Apr. 6, 1971 (or 1921); Joseph HOGG, 1848; Sarah HOGG, 1820; Elizabeth A. HOGG, Mar. 17, 1855; Wm. H. HOGG, Aug. 8, 1855; Janie (no surname or date given); Ellen _____, July 28, 18(98); Sarah BROWN, Dec. 29, 1835; Emma BROWN, Jan. 12, 1855; Alice BROWN, Jan. 10, 1871; Josephine _____, Nov. 28, 1840; Ellen M. DONALD, July 8, 1829; Eliza _____, Feb. 27, 1850; Ann _____, April 6, 1847.

LOT 51-A: Ann STINCHCOMB, Julia A. STURGESS;
Levin MISTER, Oct. 29, 1866; Elizabeth MISTER, Mar. 31, 1853; Mary A. STURGES, Aug. 24, 1863; George R. MC LAUGHLIN, Sept. 10,1866; Mary (S.) MC LAUGHLIN, Dec. 26, 1877; Wm. E. MC LAUGHLIN, Mar. 15, 1878; Julia A. STURGES, Aug. 18, 1883; Oliver STURGES, July 5, 1889; Julia STURGESS, Aug. 18, 1874; Vida B. MC LAUGHLIN, Nov. 10, 1884; Edith DIXON, Aug. 17, 1883; Nancy STURGES, Nov. 9, 1865; Reuben STURGES, Nov. 13, 1849; Oliver STURGES, Dec. 5, 1848; John A. STINCHCOMB, July 2, 1874; Ann STINCHCOMB, Jan. 2, 1879; Saml. STINCHCOMB, Jan. 8, 185(?).

LOT 52-A: James J. WILSON;
Emma F. WILSON, July 23, 1855; Wm. CONNELLY, Nov. 9, 1857; George
H. WOOD, Feb. 22, 1858; Hester A. WOOD, July 20, 1869; Child of
George H. WOOD, Jan. 26, 1870; Hester G. WOOD, Sept. 17, 1874;
Wm. D. BOYD, Feb. 3, 1874; Stillborn of A. F. PATTERSON, July 11,
1879; Casandra BRICKHEAD, Sept. 14, 1884; George H. WOOD, June
24, 1889; Danl. P. WOOD, Feb. 18, 1892; Wm. F. BOYD, Sept. 13,
1895; Stillborn, Apr. 17, 1896; Wm. G. MARR, Mar. 6, 1913 -
G.A.R.; Dissenterel & Ren., June 11, 1913; Hester A. WOOD, Mar.
23, 1902; Emma G. POPP, Sept. 28, 1931; Janet (no surname or
date); Augustus E. WILSON, Nov. 1, 18(80).

LOT 53-A: Arminta GODMAN & Elijah BAILEY;
Eliza (or ELJAH) GODMAN, May 22, 1855; Child of WHITE, Dec. 27,
1872; Caroline CHAMBERS, Jan. 6, 1874; Child, July 17, 1875; Edna
L. WHITE, Aug. 15, 1897; Jas. E. GREGORY, Apr. 14, 1911; Mary J.
GREGORY, Oct. 1, 1914; George W. GREGORY, Oct. 27, 1927; Remains
Jan. 24, 1852; George W. THOMAS, Mar. 29, 1854; Mrs. SMITH, Aug.
11, 1855; Elijah BAILEY, Aug. 9, 1852; Josiah (or Jonah) BAILEY,
Sept. 19, 1879; Susan BAILEY, Oct. 29, 1889; Ann BAILEY, Oct. 7,
1864; James BAILEY, Oct. 5, 1850; Arminta GODMAN, (no date).

LOT 54-A: Ann SCOTT, Wm. K. BOYLE;
Mr. SCOTT, Oct. 30, 1859; Elizabeth MATTHEWS, Nov. 7, 1865; Mary
R. SCOTT, Jan. 24, 1876; Elizabeth SCOTT, Jan. 10, 1885; Ann
SCOTT, June 28, 1897; (Ang) C. EMERICK, July 28, 1897; Anna G.
EMMERLICK, June 13, 1906; Saml. G. M. SCOTT, Feb. 1, 1709
(possibly 1909); (Aug) EMMERICK, Nov. 22, 1912; Horace R. SCOTT,
Feb. 1905; Ruth Josephine LEINBACK, June 24, 1932, age 8 years;
Wm. K. BOYLE, Aug. 30, 1852; Remains, Sept. 18, 1852; Elizabeth
J. BOYLE, Mar. 13, 1853; George H. BOYLE, Apr. 16, 1857; Luther
R. SIMPSON, Oct. 17, 1877; Rich. B. BOYL, Jan. 26, 1864; John
(S.) BOYLE, Mar. 11, 1862; Frances A. BAGLY, Jan. 27, 1827;
Rebecca C. BOYLE, Dec. 25, 1840; Luttle L. (no surname, probably
BOYLE, no date), age 9 years; John S. BOYLE, Mar. (18), 1862.

LOT 55-A: Thos. WILKINSON, John H. DURAND (The name Thos.
WINKELMAN is lined through);
Angelina KELLER, Dec. 14, 1853; Willie WILKINSON, Feb. 22, 1865;
Twins of H. CRONBLY, Aug. 1, 1819 or 1889; Namia OLDHAM, Sept.
25, 1903; George T. WRIGHT, Jan. 2(8), 1905; Henry F. JOHNSON,
Mar. 3, 1909; Sarah T. WRIGHT, Oct. 25, 1816; Olivia R. HOLTZ,
Feb. 2, 1918; (V.) Benjaman ZIMMERMAN, Apr. 2, 1909; John A.
DURAND, Sept. 3, 1856; Rich. E. BRIDGE, Mar. 20, 1865; Lucretia
BRYAN, Oct. 19, 1865; Lilie M. JACKSON, Aug. 21, 1868; Wm. T.
DURAND, Jan. 21, 1871; J. M. JACKSON, July 11, 1872; Maggie S.
BRIDGE, Apr. 15, 1876; Mary J. DURAN, Jan. 21, 1882; Everett L.
BRIDGE, Nov. 21, 1884; John H. DURNAD, Nov. 7,1894; Amanda (J.)
BRIDGE, Nov. 15, 1894; Mollie BRIDGE, May 7, 1895; (Annie) B.
ZIMMERMAN, Aug. 7, 1930; Sadie M. HOLTZ, Aug. 21, 1939; Luke
JACKSON; Everet L. BRIDGE.

LOT 56-A: W. H. MEEKS, Chas. L. COUAY;
Child, June 24, 1854; Jas. E. HADAWAY, Mar. 2, 1858; Wm. H.
HADAWAY, Aug, 17, 1860; Child, July 22, 1864; Edwd. HADAWAY, Nov.
4, 1865; Child, July 6, 1868; Wm. L. FURLONG, Feb. 19, 1872; Wm.
MEEKS, Oct. 4, 1888; Louisa MEEKS, May 28, 1898; Chas. D. WIL-
LIAMS, Oct. 31, 1905; Eliza MEEKS, Dec. 3, 1919; Child, Feb. 16,
1860; Earl O. LANGFORD, Aug. 29, 1906; Mary L. LANGFORD, Nov. 24,

1909; John. F. POTTE, Dec. 14, 1911; Infant of LANGFORD, May 14, 1914; George A. POTTEE; Child, July 28, 1852; Child, Jan. 9, 1862; Michael ABEY, July 24, 1893; Elizabeth CONWAY, Feb. 20, 1894; James CONWAY, Oct. 20, 1912; Elizabeth CONWAY, Mar. 31, 1917 (Another entry reads Elizabeth CONWAY 1894); Elizabeth MC CURDY, Mar. 11, 1851; Sarah L.MOLEY,June 9, 1856; Child of HARTMAN, Aug. 11, 1863; Annie LINK, June 14, 1887; Cath. SELET, Mar. 29, 1886; Lena T. POTEE, Oct. 31, 1925; Mary E. POTEE, Feb. 20, 1976; Clarence DOVE, Mar. 28, 1946; Wm. W. MEEKS, 1888; Viola A. RUHLAND, Dec. 11, 1939; Frederick M. RUHLAND, Dec. 1, 1949; Conrad C. RUHLAND, Mar. 21, 1945; Earl LANGFORD (name crossed out).

There are no lots listed for Lots 57-A thru 71-A.

LOT 72-A: Jos. ROBERTS, John CONWAY;
David ROBERTS, Aug. 2, 1856; Child, Apr. 4, 1861; Lillian ROBERTS, Feb. 10,1893; Josphene ROBERTS, Feb. 13, 1883; Elizabeth ROBERTS, Oct. 22, 1888; Ellizabeth CONWAY, Jan. 7, 1863; Child, Aug. 3, 1869; Rachael CONWAY, Aug. 1, 1866; (Alice) (PANCOAST), May 21, 1879; Ida CONWAY, Apr. 1, 1866; Sallie STEIN, Dec. 18, 1874; Child, Aug. 2, 1851; Child, Apr. 1, 1872; Child, May 19, 1862; Louisa ROGERS, Apr. 10, 1885; Lilliam PANCOST, Aug. 9, 1899; John CONWAY, Aug. 26, 1897; Celestine CONWAY, Nov. 20, 1909; Maria (H.) RUA(RK), July 5, 1926; Alfred CONWAY, Mar. 14, 1855; Mary R. CONWAY, Aug. 1, 1851.

LOT 73-A: Mary DUDLEY, Jas. GARDNER, Wm. AMEY, M(eri)ns L. DUDLEY;
Joseph AMEY, May 7, 1851; Margt. E. AMEY, Apr. 16, 1857; Alonzo AMEY, Nov. 25, 1869; Child,Sept. 20, 1873; Rose A. AMEY, May 4, 1887; Wm. AMEY, Nov. 27, 1901; Adele AMEY, May 21, 1903; Rosa (V.) GARDNER, May 20, 1917, children underneath; Jas. GARDNER, Feb. 22, 1930; Remains, May 17, 1852; Rebecca DUDLEY, Apr. 28, 1854; Child, June 22, 1870; Rebecca EMMERSON, Apr. 4, 1871; Geo. H. FITZPATRICK, Aug. 24, 1872; Mary J. DUDLEY, July 24, 1897; Mary D. TOOY, Sept. 1, 1863; Mary (P. V.) TOOY, Dec. 19, 1871; Mary E. TOOY, July 29, 1872; Elizabeth FITZPATRICK, Sept. 9, 1895; Marcus TOOY, Sept. 15, 1894; Harry D. TOOY, Aug. 9, 1863; Levy AMEY, Sept. 2, (1918); Florence A. AMEY, April 18, 1866.

LOT 74-A: James ESSENDER;
Remains, Aug. 13, 1851; Amelia M. MURRY, July 6, 1858; Mary MURRY, July 31, 1858; Remains, Nov. 27, 1858; Louis ESSENDER, Sept. 12, 1862; Mary ESSENDER, Oct. 31, 1865; Cath. ESSENDER, Apr. 16, 1874; Thos. LAMBETEN (or LAMBDEN), Feb. 7, 1881; Cordelia M. ROBERTS,July 4, 1900; Isac G. ROBERTS, July 7, 1892; Jas. ESSENDER, Jan. 28, 1902; Mary ESSENDER, Nov. 4, 1904; Annie R. REVORE, Sept. 10, 1885; John ESSENDER, Jan. 8, 1854; John R. [ESSENDER], May 11, 1855; William (or Wil(ber)) [ESSENDER], Dec. 5, 18(11) (or 1828); Edward [ESSENDER], Dec. 25, 1821; Cadelia ROBERTS, July 4, 1890.

LOT 75-A: Ann SIMKIN, Herman WIEGAND, Thos. N. WOOD;
Ann S. WEIGAND, June 23, 1874; Paul WIEGAND, Dec. 26, 1876; George BURGMAN, Oct. 16, 1889; Wm. BURGMAN, Apr. 12, 1893 (or 1873); Edwd. WEIGAND, Aug. 22, 1895; Edna BURGMAN, Nov. 13, 1905; Elmer MENDELL, Aug. 10, 1911; George ____ SIMKIM, Oct. 17, 18(92), disinterred; Adeline G. SIMKIN, Feb. 13, 1916; Wm. J.

SIMKIN, May 13, 1937; Lemuel T. SIMKIN, Sept. 11, 1935; Thos. M. WOODS, Dec. 3, 1870; Sarah A. WOODS, Dec. 18, 1888; Josephine G. SIMKIN, Jan. 12, 1965; Elizabeth WOODS, Oct.14, 1832; Pracilla (E. or C.) WOODS, Mar. 12, 1832; Thos. WOODS, Aug. 3, 1819; Henry R. MATTHEWS, June 24, 1974, born Dec. 1, 1892, died June 21, 1974; Frederick W. BURKMAN, Jan. 15, 1963; Lena D. BURKMAN, Jan. 16, 1941; Ann WIEGAND, (no date given).

LOT 76-A & 77-A:
Edwin F. HANNA, Jan. 13, 1929; Vavina D. H. HANNA, Mar. 22, 1931; Christian (illegible), May 28, 1855; Harriet WILLIAMS, Sept. 3, 1867; Catherine F. HERBERT, July 13, 1892; Francis HERBERT, Oct. 18, 1870; Sarah A. HERBERT, Aug. 10, 1875; John H. HERBERT, Jan. 15, 1904; Harlan HERBERT, Feb. 27, 1912; W. F. HERBERT, Feb. 26, 1921; Jos. B. LOFLIN, Apr. 4, 1936; Laura HERBERT, Nov. 12, 1936; J. Herbert HANNA, Mar. 5, 1956; John P. BRECKENRIDGE, Feb. 3, 1960, Government marker; Vavina H. BRECKENRIDGE; Laura HANNA; Cowin Colson HANNA, Jr., Aug. 24, 1973, father R. F. HANNA (Jr.), mother Verine HERBERT, born Aug. 19, 1890, died Aug. 21, 1973; Mabel Hardy HANNA, Dec. 10, 1963; Margaret B. HERBERT; Mary Sawyer HERBERT; William Frank HERBERT; Virginia L. H. LOFLIN, Dec. 3, 1949; Sarah Ann HERBERT, 1901; Francis HERBERT.

LOT 78-A: Jacob TABLER, Mary FOS (or FOSS);
George FOSS, Sept. 9, 1852; Mary FOSS,Jan. 5, 1859; Elizabeth FOSS, Jan. 11, 1859; (Glemia) R. HOWARD, Dec. 22, 1922; Elizabeth MILES, Jan. 9, 1859; Stillborn; Stillborn of KENNY; Baby BLYON, 20 minutes old; Thelma ROHR; Mad(l)ine HAWK(S); (Baby) ROHR; Richard L. _____ EAILEY; Baby _____ RIEGLIVE; Baby GARLAND; Aviedo BROWN; Baby PEREGOY, July 8, 1923.

LOT 79-A: Robert SMILEY, James SMILEY;
Ann SMILEY, Nov. 30, 1855; Laura V. and M. M. SMILEY, May 4, 1886 (another date given for Laura V. SMILEY is July 14, 1858.); Margt. SMILEY, May 7, 1888; Jonth. P. SMILEY, Aug. 22, 1884; Infant of L. and Wm. SMILEY, June 23, 1894; Harry H. SMILEY, Nov. 28, 1099; Mary J. MC GRATH; Fannie PERRIG(O), Apr. 6, 1929; Remains, July 2, 1851; Ann SMILEY, Nov. 30, 1855; Fannie A. SMILEY, Nov. 19, 1877; Robert SMILEY, Mar. 9, 1886; Jas. (H.) HOUSE, Sept. 29, 1889; Grace A. BAILEY, Nov. 1, 1897; Isabell SMILEY, Jan. 31, 1902; James SMILEY, Feb. 22, 1911; Joseph SMILEY, Jan. 17, 1916; Peter Robert SMILEY, Feb. 11, 1860, member of Light Street Church 50 years; Joseph P. SMILEY, Aug. 27, 1889; (Maggie) SMILEY, Feb. 27, 1871.

LOT 80-A: Fred. HARTMAN, Philip HARTMAN;
Frederick HARTMAN, Dec. 5, 1853; Mary A. HARTMAN, May 17, 1862; Child, July 5, 1862; Ernest HARTMAN, Aug. 27, 1865; Child, Sept. 31, 1867; M. E. HARTMAN, Dec. 5, 1872; John HARTMAN, Apr. 9, 1875; Alfred (H.) LU(P)TON, Aug. 18, 1830; Frank HARTMAN, May 22, 1889; John T. STOELTZER, Mar. 10, 1904; (Tre)dena HARTMAN, Mar. 27, 1908; Infant of (WILSON), July 15, 1908; Harry HARTMAN, May 5, 1859; Philip HARTMAN, Apr. 23, 1885; Christian HARTMAN, Feb. 13, 1894; Barbara B(ICKLURARN), Jan. 16, 1925; Es(tella) E. GALLEON, Jan. 31, 1933; Fredk. HARTMAN, Oct. 17, 1908; Philip HARTMAN, 1849.

LOT 81-A: Amelia R. DAVIS;
Ebinezer PUMPHERY; Elizabeth REESIDE; R. PERRY; Wm. LACH, Jan. 7,

186(5); Wm. B. DAVIS, Apr. 15, 1895; Emelia DAVIS, Sept. 19, 1909; Saml. L. DAVIS, Mar. 24, 1931; Theodore PUMPHREY, Dec. 13, 1855; Eliz. A. METZDORF, Oct. 9, 1856; Elizabeth TOLLING, July 21, 1864; Alice V. PUMPHREY, Oct. 24, 1869; Rem(oved) from St. Peters, July 15, 1873; Mary A. PUMPHREY, Mar. 28, 1895; Isabell PERRY, Jan. 19, 1864; Ann C. ROSS, Mar. 26, 1878; Annie E. ROSS, Aug. 27, 1879; George W. ROSS, Apr. 18, 1881; Mary C. PERRY, Jan. 26, 1883; Ann E. PERRY, Oct. 8, 1881; Harry DILLON, Mar. 9, 1858; Frank DILLION, Oct. 13, 1863; Rachael TILLINGS, Mar. 11, 1868; Cath. TILLINGS, Jan. 13, 1869; Harry DILL, Mar. 19, 1879; Stillborn of PERRY, Mar. 13, 1881; Rachel A. PERRY, Aug. 20, 1898; Amelia DAVIS, Sept. 19, 1907 (could be same person as Emelia above); Ebenezer PUMPHERY, Ap. 28, 1884; Susie PUMPHERY, Oct. (4), 1881; Mary A. PUMPHREY.

LOT 82-A: George W. BOWER, Stephen PECK;
Barbara BOWER, July 27, 1858; Kate P. BOWER, Dec. 16, 1861; Isabell BOWER, June 12, 1899; G(loxia) Bell BOWER, Jan. 21, 1925; Walter COOPER, Oct. 17, 1927; Mary Ann BOWER, Feb. 8, 1928; Isabel Disney HICKS, Sept. 17, 1936; Stephen PECK, May 22, 1866 (also given as Feb. 26, 1866); Catharine PECK, Jan. 11, 1854; Harriet PECK, June 20, 1870; Elizabeth PECK, July 23, 1887; David V. J. PECK, Nov. 16, 1921; Ella L. PECK, Apr. 27, 1935; Barbara BOWER, July 22, 1887; Elizabeth PECK, July 22, 1858.

LOT 83-A: Margt. MOORE;
Child, July 2, 1852; Mary HOWELL, July 25, 1860; Geo. WAT(TS), June 26, 1876; Saml. H. MOORE, Dec. 6, 1877; J. WALTON, July 6, 1869; David MOORE, May 13, 1886; Arthur S. WOOD, July 16, 1892; Charlotte K. MOORE, Nov. 20, 1894; Margaret MOORE, Dec. 19, 1861, 74 years, (no location #4038); See Lot 45-A.

LOT 84-A: Ann PATTERSON;
Susan H. PATTERSON, June 2, 1866; Child of REESE, Sept. 16, 1870; Walter M. REESE, May 1, 1887; Child, Nov. 1, 1876; Ann PATTERSON, May 31, 1880; Bessie REESE, Oct. 30, 1880; Mary V. REESE, Mar. 23, 1888; Capt. Wm. PATTERSON, Mar. 27, 1851; Daniel M. REESE, May 19, 1891; William PATTERSON, June 11, 1851.

LOT 85-A: Wm. C. SHAFFNER, Danl. L. BUCKLEY;
Wm. H. SCHAFFNER, Apr. 22, 1852; William E. (or C.) SCHAFFNER, June 19, 1860; Rem(ains), June 29, 1860; Ella VAN WORT, Apr. 2, 1865; Isac TUCKER, Jan. 6, 1866; Jos. A. WELSH, Dec. 19, 1867; Mary E. SCHAFFNER, Dec. 12, 1876; Mary E. BEALE, Aug. 24, 1883; Mary RYLAND, Aug. 30, 1887; Sarah A. TUCKER, July 17, 1897; Arthur SCHAFFNER, Jan. 16, 1899; Infant of W. C. SCHAFFNER, Nov. 24, 1899; Child, Dec. 25, 1852; Sarah HORSEMAN, May 2(1), 1858; Child, Oct. 18, 1858; David BUCKLEY, July 26, 1864; Saml. W. GLOVER, Dec. 9, 1868; Mary E. HORSEMAN, Oct. 14, 1872; Josephine MORSEL, Apr. 5, 1879; Mary LANGLEY, Dec. 19, 1884; Alice J. DOLSON, Mar. 2, 1885; Pauline BUCKLEY, Dec. 16, 1889; Harriet P. BUCKLEY, Feb. 27, 1895; Thos. G. BUCKLEY, Aug. 28, 1895; Wm. F. (in BUCKLEY lot), Jan. 6, 1847; Elizabeth A. (in BUCKLEY lot), July 15, 1850; Elenor (in BUCKLEY lot), Dec. 23, 1852; Children of Danl. and May BUCKLEY (no date given); Sarah HORSEMAN, Feb. 3, 1851; Danl. Z. BUCKLEY, Oct. 18, 1858; C. R. HORSEMAN, 1st Md. L.A. G.A.R. (no date); Mollie MORSEL, Dec. 18, 1870; David Z. BUCKLEY, Apr. 11, 1850; John E. CONNELLY, Feb. 22, 1957; Thos. BUCKLEY, Apr. 11, 185(0); Elizabeth JONES, Mar. 4, 1862; Edwd. A.

CONNALLY, Mar. 31, 1926; Flora B. MILE(S), Mar. 4, 1936; Zas (WEBALS), no date; James P. CONNALLY, June 17, 193(5 or 8); Mary C. BLADE, (no date); Arthur BUCKLEY, (no date); Mary G(OVIOR) CONNELLY, May 13, 1935; Frances O. CONNALLY, Sept. 12, 1934.

LOT 86-A: John HANDY, James H. HOPKINS; R.E.L. DRIVER, July 18, 1868; Margaret M. DRIVER, Oct. 24, 1905; Two children, Apr. 12, 1858; Remains, June 23, 1853; Mrs. HOPKINS, July 16, 1853; James H. HOPKINS, Apr. 2, 1887; Child of J. H. HOPKINS, Aug. 5, 1863; Hettie M. HOPKINS, Jan. 4, 1919; Mary E. HOPKINS, Aug. 14, 1922; Stewart F. HOPKINS or F. Stewart HOPKINS, Mar. 23, 1930.

LOT 87-A: Eneas REYNOLDS; Edw. and Eliz. REYNOLDS, May 7, 1853; Mary (L.) BELL, Aug. 9, 1974, born June 5, 1887; died Aug. 6, 1974, father Joseph T. BELL, mother Laura REYNOLDS; Mrs. Emma STACK, (no date); Ethel C. BRADFORD, Mar. 4, 1957; Raymond W. REYNOLDS, (child), Apr. 20, 1896; Charles F. BELL, Sept. 19, 1930; Joseph T. BELL, Mar. 25, 1926; Harry C. REYNOLDS, Aug. 15, 1898; Laura V. BELL, Apr. 2, 1928; Jos. BELL, (child) Nov. 7, 1962; Thomas REYNOLDS, Aug. 3, 1893; James C. REYNOLDS, Dec. 30, 1891; Thomas R. BELL, June 5, 1940; Conrad A. MINNICK, July 9, 1875; Joseph T. BELL, July 19, 1889; Louisa (possible called Laura) MINNICK, June 14, 1909; Eneas W. REYNOLDS, Oct. 22, 1874; Louise C. (possible called Laura) REYNOLDS, Apr. 2, 1900; Bertha E. BELL, Jan. 2, 189(5 or 8); Roy F. BELL, (child) Aug. 27, 1890; George W. REYNOLDS, Sept. 26, 1904; Bessie E. BELL, Apr. 2, 1947; Harry BELL, Oct. 9, 1954.

LOT 88-A: Alex M. CARRIE, Jno. W. SHOEMAKER; Geo. D. CARRIE, Apr. 27, 1857; Daniel B. CARRIE, Dec. 5, 1867; Child of DUNLOP, Nov. 28, 1868; Cath. CARRIE, Feb. 15 (17), 1876; Rem(ains) of Peter CARRIE, May 5, 1886; Margt. A. DUNLOP, Apr. 11, 1891; Laura DUNLOP, Mar. 30, 1903; James CARRIE, Oct. 27, 1849; John T. SHOEMAKER, Feb. 21, 1874; Child of REYNOLDS, Jan. 14, 1870; Georgana SHOEMAKER, May 3, 189(3); Jno. H. SHOEMAKER, Dec. 6, 1892; Chas. A. SHOEMAKER, Sept. 14, 1905; Mary M. SHOEMAKER, Sept. 14, 1937; John H. SHOEMAKER, Nov. 4, 1964; John SHOEMAKER, Nov. 7, 1892.

LOT 89-A: John and Eliza SPIES, Robert M. RICHARDSON; Remains, May 4, 1853; Child, Oct. 29, 1859; Child, Dec. 17, 1859; Barton (AMS), July 5, 1860; Elizabeth SPIES, May 23, 1867; Lillie BATEMAN, June 23, 1882; Bridget BATEMAN, Nov. 19, 1895; Stillborn of Alice BATEMAN, May 7, 1907; Annie M. SOPER, Sept. 16, 1901; Geo. A. SOPER, Apr. 22, 1930; Elizabeth A. BATEMAN, Jan. 17, 1888; Remains, May 4, 1853; Robert RICHARDSON, Sept. 2, 1859; Rich. M. RICHARDSON, May 18, 1863; Maria B. MC DANIEL, Sept. 13, 1876; Wm. J. RICHARDSON, Jan. 7, 1877; Chas. MARINER, May 4, 1881; John L. RICHARDSON, May 10, 1883; Infant of RICHARDSON, Nov. 12, 1883; Wm. F. MC DANIEL, Dec. 29, 1883; Elizabeth RICHARDSON, Jan. 22, 1887; Sarah J. RICHARDSON, July 9, 1900; Stillborn of R. & F. RICHARDSON, Feb. 4, 1908; Robert RICHARDSON, Feb. 22, 1905; Thos. RICHARDSON, Nov. 22, 1902; John V. RICHARDSON, Mar. 10, 1919; Robt. RICHARDSON, Jan. 2, 1928; M(innie) RICHARDSON, Oct. 31, 1929; Ethel RICHARDSON, Dec. 29, 19(20); Elizabeth A. RICHARDSON, Nov. 25, 1847; Philip E. (RICHARDSON), Mar. 25, 1849; (Raba) RICHARDSON, baby (no date); Robert RICHARDSON, May 18, 1863; Marion F. MC DANIEL, (no date).

LOT 90-A: W. (D.) BAKER;
Wm. BAKER, Dec. 6, 1915 (the date 1905 is also given); Wilhelmina D. BAKER, Feb. 23, 1920; Meridith JANVIER, Jan. 23, 1936; Florence Baker JANVIER, Jan. 12, 1950; Blanche Baker FOLK, Aug. 28, 1957; Grace BAKER, Dec. 10, 1955; Arabella E. BAKER, Sept. 5, 1944; Emma M. BAKER, May 21, 1949.

LOT 91-A & 93-A: John DURHAM, Miss BULLOCK;
Remains, July 11, 1855; John DURHAM, Aug. 13, 1860; Isabell (no surname), May 5, 18(18); Sarah & Anna (no surname), Sept. 18, 1822; Jeremiah D. DURHAM, Apr. 10, 1847; Cath. DURHAM, Aug. 7, 1889; M. HARDESTY, June 14, 1862; Edwd. HARDESTY, Feb. 12, 1864; Rebecca G. SPICER, Mar. 18, 1860; Thos. SPICER, May 5, 1882; Cath. DURHAM, Aug. 8, 1889; Mary A. DURHAM, May 6, 1892; J. F. SICER, Sept. 21, 1901 (probably the same as J. Fenton SPICER, Sept. 20, 1901); John DURHAM, Apr. 27, 1903; Rebecca C. SPICER, Mar. 17, 1880; Thos. SPICER, Jan. 3, 1837 (or Jan. 9, 1838); Martha HARDESTY, Jan. 12, 1869; Elizabeth HUNTER, Mar. 11, 1814 native of England; Hester (PU)LTERSON, Mar. 14, 1826 native of Ireland; Mary A. DURHAM, May 4, 1892; Martha DURHAM, born Nov. 24, 1785, died Dec. 4, 1826, age 45 years "Confermed of 20th Child"; All stones in this lot said flat by order of Miss Emma M. BAKER.

LOT 92-A: Lewis and Katie F. BRIGGEMAN;
Lewis E. BRIGGEMAN, July 25, 1916; Kate F. BRIGGEMAN, Nov. 7, 1929; Raymond L. BRIGGEMAN, Mar. 1, 1941; Nellie B. BRIGGEMAN, Jan. 18, 1962.

LOT 93-A: See LOT 91

LOT 94-A: George COULTER, Nellie MC CORMECK;
Alexander HAMILTON, Dec. 11, 1855; George COULTER, June 14, 1866; Mrs. HAMILTON, Apr. 17, 1856; Saml. W. SARILLE, Sept. 26, 1908 (This and following surnames may be SAVILLE.); Wm. W. SARILLE, Dec. 21, 1855; Mary C. SARILLE, Aug. 8, 1856; Chas. A. SARILLE, Dec. 27, 1915; Frank SADILLE (sic), Apr. 17, 1935.

LOT 95-A: Gideon B. SMITH, Saml. W. CLEMENTS, Conrad SCHLOTT;
Elizabeth KIER(RIAN), June 21, 1854; Catherine SCHLOTT, June 29, 1879; Conrad SCHLOTT, July 17, 1868; Godfrey HUNTER, Jan. 11, 1878; Ella HUNTER, July 13, 1872; Remains, May 11, 1855; Susan SMITH, Jan. 9, 1856; Dr. GIRDEN (may be Geden) B. SMITH, Mar. 26, 1867; Rubie CLEMENTS, Apr. 27, 1897; Norman S. CLEMENTS, Jan. 25, 1901; Saml. W. CLEMENTS, May 9, 1916; Sallie CLEMENTS, Feb. 12, 1934; Elizabeth (no surname given), July 24, 1832; Gales (no surname given), June 2, 1835; Nelson (no surname given), Dec. 8, 1857.

LOT 96-A: James STIDHAM, Elija and Wm. JORY;
Ann STIDHAM, Mar. 14, 1856; Child, Feb. 1, 1865; James STIDHAM, Apr. 25, 1865; Jno. A. STIDHAM, Aug. 8, 1865; Edger J. STIDHAM, Oct. 21, 1871; Child, Oct. 25, 1872; Jane STIDHAM, Aug. 12, 1870; Saml. STIDHAM, Sept. 29, 1872; Geo. W. STIDHAM, Dec. 27, 1876; Sallie V. STIDHAM, Nov. 14, 1882; Nannie STIDHAM, Jan. 26, 1883; Annie B. STIDHAM, Apr. 2, 1899; Mary Ann JORY, June 5, 1856; Thos. HUCK, Apr. 1, 1856; Kalura HUDSON, Jan. 3, 1897; Stephen JORY, Aug. 26, 1898; B(irtie) PHILLIPS, Mar. 11, 1903; Fredk. PHILLIPS, Oct. 15, 1904; Adeline PHILLIPS, Aug. 28, 1906; Malco-

lin EISHELLUGER (may be same as Malcol(in) EIGELBERGER, Feb. 19, 1978); John W. EICHELLEGER, Jan. 20, 1865; Caroline JORY, Apr. 16, 1858; Rebecca STIDHAM, June 17, 1873.

LOT 97-A: Jno. T. SHIPLEY, Frances M. BAUGHMAN, Sarah J. MEARS; Cordelia E. SHIPLEY, June 18, 1855; Isah MERCER, Sept. 14, 1859; John T. SHIPLEY, Sept. 23, 1861; Jno. W. SHIPLEY, Sept. 2, 1889; John W. SHIPLEY, Nov. 16, 1936; John B. MEARS, Dec. 18, 1853; Remains, Sept. 4, 1852; Sarah J. MARSHALL, Nov. 5, 1869 ("Wife of Wm. J. Mi(c)hall"); Mary Ellen BAUGHMAN, May 27, 1855; Saml. GLA(L)DING, Sept. 2, 1848; Sarah (no surname given), Dec. 21, 1843; Sarah J. SHIPLEY, May 16, 1922; Mary J. SHIPLEY; Medora SHIPLEY, Mar. 11, 1942; (David C.) SMITH, Nov. 2, 1959; Florence B. SMITH, Mar. 7, 1963.

LOT 98-A: Cath. COLLINS, Mary A. BIRCH; Mary OLDHAM, July 21, 1853; George W. WHIPPS, July 15, 1859; Amelia CHANDLER, Jan. 27, 1864; David F. BIRCH, Apr. 29, 1870; John OLDHAM, Feb. 2, 1878; Ephran H. RAICHARDS, Dec. 30, 1895; Mary A. BIRCH, Aug. 10, 1894; Child OF DOLL, Feb. 24, 1857; Michal DOLL, Mar. 3, 1861; Mary C. DOLL, Dec. 12, 1861; Ellen F. COLLINS, Oct. 13, 1889; Eugene A. COLLINS, Nov. 4, 1863; C. W. WHILTON, Sept. 20, 1872; Child, Apr. 19, 1869; Frances T. COL-LINS, June 24, 1879; Lucretia YOUNG, June 5, 1894; Leuis ARGO, Aug. 15, 1865; Cath. ARGO, Jan. 8, 1867; Harry DULL, June 18, 1870; Ida DULL, June 16, 1877; Cath. KIRKWOOD, Dec 17, 1873; Cath. COLLINS, Mar. 11, 1898; Geo. COLLINS, (Jan. 5), 1853 (entry written over another entry which is illegible with date 1867); Cath. ARGO; Danl. COLLINS, Apr. 22, (1844 or 1884).

LOT 99-A: Washington STEWART, Julia PARROTT; Ann PARROTT, June 9, 1859; Sarah M. MAYDWELL, May 27, 1863; John. C. MAYDWELL, June 12, 1867 (also dates June 16 and Nov. 7); Child of Geo. WATTS, July 20, 1869; Nancy PARROTT, Dec. 7, 1875; Jas. W. PARROTT, Jan. 31, 1891; Margt. PARROTT, Aug. 12, 1892; Julia A. PARROTT, Aug. 10, 1899; Jas. F. PARROTT, May 7, 1901; "Jea & Ann PARROTT also Mary & Margt."; Jno. W. PARROTT; Sarah MAYDWELL, Nov. 21, 1862.

The following entries are very small and difficult to read. There are 33 of them in very careless script. 1. Stillborn "Com A. MAYNARD"; 2. Blyen or Mogeall; 3. Infant David (or Davis); 4. mna Burn(s); 5. Blushine; 6. Stillborn; 7. Douglas L(E)TT, (Sept.) 12, 1923; 8. (Rich.) UHLER; 9. F(?) M. G____; 10. Stillborn of L. & G. B(AG)LY); 11. Stillborn; 12. Stillborn of (illegible); 13. Morgan; 14. Thos. A. PARKS, May 25, 1929; 15. Helen PAN(COS), Sept. 26, 1923; 16. Edward H(ULSANT), Sept. 11, 1925; 17. Stillborn of PI(?); 18. (Prichart) Birth; 19. Margaret A. CAS(--); 20. Francis Wm. BULL; 21. Richard E. RICHE; 22. Stillborn of (illegible), Jan. 18, 1930; 23. Adal--- WALLS, Dec. 2, 1929; 24. Stillborn of HOFFMAN, Dec. 9, 192(9); 25. Charles HOWARD, Dec. 5, 1929; 26. Gordon H. MEYERS, Sept. 11, 1929; 27. Stillborn of (CARTASOUGH), Aug. 5, 1929; 28. _____ (SMITH----), Nov. 3, 1930; 29. Jos. J. RICE (Jr.), Mar. 8, 1930; 30. (Frank) COOPER, Mar. 3, 1930; 31. (Mildred) L. BAN(SET), Feb. 20, 1930; 32. (Sarah) M. (BABBITT), Jan. 22, 1930; 33. Stillborn of _____ (BRITTONS), Jan. 18, 1930.

LOT 100-A: Levin P. JONES, Zanetta JONES (also LOT 84-A);
Geo. B. JONES, July 8, 1859; Florence JONES, Aug. 7, 1869; Florence JONES, Oct. 14, 1866; J(ames) JONES, Aug. 18. 1875; Levin JONES, Sept. 5, 1875; Zanetta JONES, Mar. 28, 1906; Annie E. JONES, June 27, 1914; Levin (T. or F.) JONES, Sept. 20, 1914; Mary E. JONES, Apr. 17, 1922; Henrietta G. JONES, May (12 or 22), 1930; E. Newton JONES, Dec. 20, 1888; James JONES, Aug. 17, 1878; Florence JONES, Nov. 12, 1866; Levin JONES, Sept. 3, 1878; James & Sarah A. BOWERS (or BOWEN); Benj. WEST & wife Nance SPENCER; Dr. Walter JONES, Mar. 2, 1935; (Gresa) CLARK, Nov. 20, 1936; Mar. H. P. JONES, May 18, 1896. (See Lot 84-A)

LOT 101-A: John GUYER, (H.) LANCASTER, and Thomas (DAVIS);
Eliz. GUYER, Mar. 27, 1852; Mary E. KREAMER, July 30, 1852; Child, July 12, 1860; Albert GUYER, May 26, 1864; Mary SCOTT, Feb. 6, 1869; Thos. EDGAR, Mar. 23, 187(3); Mary EDGAR, Feb. 22, 1909; Thos. POTEET, Apr. 1, 1915; Geo. W. EDGER, Feb. 7, 1920; Mary POTEET, Aug. 7, 1936; Child, Aug. 3, 1851; M(in) DA(VI)S, Sept. 6, 1852; Child, Mar. 14, 1853; Child, Aug. 1, 1853; Ruth E. DA(VI)S, June 30, 1856; Wm. T. DA(VI)S, Apr. 13, 1861; Saml. C. (HUSH), Aug. 15, 1875 (possible infant); Infant of Anne DA(VI)S, Dec. 16, 1885; Chas. F. LANCASTER, Nov. 13, 1859; Remains, Oct. 23, 1872; Hannah LANCASTER, Dec. 5, 1885; Stillborn of OLLINGER, Nov. 12, 1897; Joseph LANCASTER; Chas. (FREDERICK), Nov. 12, 1859; Joseph OLIVER, Mar. 15, 1864; Ann M. FRANKLIN, Aug. 11, 1840; Isiah FRANKLIN, Nov. 3, 1843; William George POTEET, July 29, 1952; Albert GUYER, 1847; Anna Hall EDGER, Jan. 11, 1947.

LOT 102-A: Howard A. RIGGS, (Wm. K. TABB) transferred to Christopher W. TABB;
Longly B. CULLY, Jan. 19, 1863; Jessie A. RIGG, Sept. 28, 1885; Jessie (H)EATON, Nov. 17, 1885; Jessie (H)EATON, Dec. 28, 1885; Margt. RIGG, Apr. 19, 1892; Harriett HEATON, Oct. 20, 1888; Howard A. RIGG, Feb. 22, 1977; Isabel RIGG; (Charlisannia) RIGG, Feb. 24, 1932; Child, Nov. 25, 1868; Child of John KEYSER, June 29, 1871; Mary A. TABB, Apr. 22, 1873; Cora K. TABB, Sept. 13, 1877; Harriett A. HEATON, Oct. 20, 1898 (crossed out); Mary M. KESSLER, Feb. 10, 1890; (Wm.) K. TABB, Dec. 26, 19(0)4; Mary Dolores TABB, July 17, 1931; Child of Cora TABB; Christopher W. TABB, Mar. 10, 1959; Margaret KEASLER, Feb. 7, 1890, child; Wm. (azest (sic)), Apr. 15, 1854; (Ren CRANGLA), May 12, 1851; Child of CRANGLA, Dec. 12, 1856; (Dr. Taylor CRANGLE), Feb. 16, 1892.

LOT 103-A: Edward CONDEN, Charles ADAMS;
Isabella CONDEN, Aug. 15, 1851; Edward CONDEN, Dec. 14, 1869; Edward CONDON, July 19, 1872; John ALRAMS (probably ADAMS), Feb. 1, 1896; Wm. (H.) CONDON, June 22, 1913; John ALRAMS (ADAMS?) Mar. 22, 1910; J. (H.) CONDON, Oct. 22, 1922; Cath. DELEHAY, Mar. (3), 1854; John ADAMS, Nov. 26, 1855; (Mary) MEEKINS, Sept. 21, 1935; (Thomas A. MC DOWELL), Sept. 24, 1935; Wm. (SAWERS?), Sept. 26, 1935; Mary E. C???IAR, Sept. 30, 1935; Florence WARD, Oct. 1, 1935.

LOT 104-A: Mrs. Mary POWELL, John HARTMAN;
Chas. P____L, July 18, 1861; John HARTMAN, Nov. 25, 1864; M. E. HARTMAN, Aug. 21, 1868; Julia HARTMAN, Aug. 1, 1868; William HARTMAN, Jan. (12), 1876; William H. L. BROWN, Feb. 21, 1876; Oscar (H.) BROWN, Oct. 7, 1880; Margt. HARTMAN, Apr. 22, 1895; William O. BROWN, July 23, 1903; Chas. P. BROWN, Aug. 2, 1909;

Benj. C. BROWN, Sept. 10, 1918; Margaret BROWN, Feb. 23, 1924; John HARTMAN, Aug. 17, 1885; Julia HARTMAN, July 30, 186- (Possibly same as the Julia HARTMAN above.); Charles Philip BROWN, Dec. 15, 1952; Margaret Virginia BROWN, Dec. 24, 1940; Henrietta BROWN, Apr. 17, 1944; (Possible Danl. HARTMAN), Aug. __, 18__; Edward BROWN, Mar. 6, 1971, born Aug. 10, 1912, died Mar. 2, 1971, father Charles P. BROWN, mother Henrietta Rhode MC CUILY.

LOT 105-A: Lewis TYSINGER, Jas. M. CORRELL; J. M. CORRELL, Mar. 11, 1921; Child, Apr. 2, 1853; Mary TYSINGER, Jan. 11, 1862; Margt. S. MILLER, Nov. 6, 1871; Lewis TYSINGER, July 8, 1882; Margt. E. TYSINGER, Dec. 7, 1898; Chas. Osburn TYSINGER, Sept. 10, 1902; Wm. L. TYSINGER, Apr. 10, 1902; Alice E. TYSINGER, Apr. 17, 1908; Jas. Summerfield LAURENSON, Apr. 8, 1858; Margt. LAURENSON, June 11, 1840; Cora CORRELL, Jan. 6, 1962; Olivia Jane CORRELL, Nov. 14, 1938.

LOT 106-A: Geo. KNIGHT, Wm. H. GRANGER; Remains, June 4, 1855; Child, Sept. 21, 1852; Child of PHILLIP, May 11, 1863; Child of KNIGHT, May 29, 1864; Child of PHILLIP, Dec. 6, 1861; M. E. PHILLIP, Sept. 5, 1867; Mary SHANKS, Dec. 11, 1869; Geo. PHILLIP, June 7, 1876, disinterred; Annie KNIGHT, Oct. 30, 1875 (below entry is () is Ann Emily); Geo. T. KNIGHT, Mar. 29, 1889; Mary EWING & Geo. PHILLIP, Nov. 5, 1890; disinterred; Thos. KNIGHT, Nov. 5, 1890; Chas. KNIGHT, July 19, 18(9)4; Geo. KNIGHT, June 6, 1900; Elizabeth KNIGHT, Dec. 10, 1915; Jas. GRANGER, May 12, 1857; Sarah A. GRANGER, Oct. 13, 1853; Child, Mar. 26, 1859; Child, Dec. 14, 1859; Still born of H. & John GRANGER, Sept. 14, 1890; Henry K. GRANGER, Aug. 1, 1862; Afton CHILD, July 18, 1866; Emma GRANGER, Dec. 10, 1862; Harriett GRANGER, Dec. 3, 1869; Child, June 29, 1870; Wm. H. GRANGER, Feb. 22, 1875; Wm. GRANGER, Feb. 6, 1884; Albert GRANGER, Nov. 23, 18(73 or 93); Howard GRANGER, May 2, 1898; Child of GRANGER, June 7, 1898; Child, Feb. 24, 1900; Maggie GRANGER, May 16, 1866; M(aurice) Granger BARNES, Sept. 9, 1905; Roy HUBBARD, April 14, 1911; John W. GRANGER, Sept. 19, 1919; Mary GRANGER, Jan. 22, 1923; Mary E. H. (no date or surname given); William H. GRANGER, Apr. 26, 1945; Harriet Purdy GRANGER, Jan. 2, 1943; John GRANGER, (no date given); Wm. H. GRANGER, (no date given).

LOT 107-A: Stewart M. JOHNSON, Jno. C. BARRON; Lillie M. STEWART, Dec. 14, 1902; Merreen Q. STEWART, Mar. 5, 1903; Jas. C. KELLY, Mar. 13, 1914; Lula KELLY, Feb. 26, 1923; Helen M. KELLY, Nov. 17, 1919; Isabella BOHA(UM)ON, Dec. 15, 1937; John C. BARRON, May 21, 1855; Cath. BARRON, May 3, 1851; Bridget LENNON, June 17, 1859; Child of SPELLMAN, Aug. 20, 1861; Mary F. WATTS, Sept. 1, 1861; Child of REYNOLDS, May 1851; Child of REYNOLDS, Dec. 1, 1854; Mary E. WATTS, Dec. 1, 1862; Laura A. Stewart KELLY, March 19, 1940; John (H)AS(HIP), Apr. 12, 1863; (J.) W. S. BARRON, July 13, 1865; Child of WATTS, Dec. 9, 1868; Jno. W. SPELLMAN, Nov. 17, 1864; Chas. E. BARRON, July 16, 1872; George WATTS, Oct. 4, 1873; Child of (G.) W. BARRON, Feb. 2, 1875; Wm. C. BARRON, Jr., Jan. 29, 1875; Infant, Nov. 24, 1882; Still born of Thos. BARRON, Mar. 23, 1885; Cath. (HASHIP), Feb. 25, 1893; Lula HALL, (no date given); M(arion) D. (STEWART), (no date given). Letter from Stewart M. JOHNSON of Baltimore, Md. dated Dec. 13, 1932. Mr. JOHNSON requests grave be opened for remains of Isabel BOHANN(ON). Letter to be delivered by Mr. Harry ARMA(COS)T.

LOT 108-A: Mary Ann SUMWALT, Wm. MORSELL;
Mary SWEENY, July 9, 1861; (C. K. R.) SUMWALT, Aug. 30, 1876; 3 Children, July 27, 1878; Jas. H. SUMWALT, May 3, 1901; Mary A. SUMWALT, May 29, 1912; David SWEENY, June 27, 1854; Carrie M. SUMWALT, Oct. 30, 1922; Wm. (H.) MORSELL, Feb. 23, 1895; Elisha BRADY, Oct. 23, 1867; 3 Children of Wm. (H.) MORSELL, Sept. 27, 1879; Sarah R. MORSELL, Aug. 16, 1880; Freddy MORSELL, Apr. 24, 1884; Wm. (H.) MORSELL, Feb. 25, 1895; Chas. (H.) MORSELL, Apr. 21, 1908; Mary E. MORSELL, June 5, 1908; Wm. (H.) MORSELL, Feb. 11, 1869; Mary (F.A.) MORSELL, June 16, 1909; Cordelia P. SUMWALT, Sept. 29, 1948; Wm. H. MORSELL, Feb. 10, 1908 (or 9).

LOT 109-A: William H. HARMAN;
Child, Feb. 11, 1852; Child, Nov. 21, 1855; Child, Sept. 4, 1854; Henry G. GILES, July 3, 1866; Margt. A. GILES, Nov. 15, 1890; Wm. H. HARTMAN, Jr., June 28, 1888; Wm. H. HARTMAN, Aug. 14, 1868; Isabell HARTMAN, Apr. 9, 1886; Eliz. J. HARTMAN, Feb. 21, 1893; Wm. HARMAN, Aug. 10, 1845; Eliz. J. HARTMAN, (no date given).

LOT 109-A and 132-A: Joseph RUNDLE;
Remains, Sept. 3, 1851; Eloner RUNDLE, Aug. 5, 1854; Elizabeth RUNDLE, June 19, 1848; Jos. RUNDLE, Feb. 10, 1881; John S. RUNDLE, Feb. 12, 1892; Annie KELLY, July 25, 1895; Lucy COOK, Sept. 16, 1895; Chas. RUNDLE, July 22, 1898; Jos. RUNDLE, May 24, 1873; Sarah E. COOK, Mar. 4, 1876; Sarah RUNDLE, July 18, 1879; Geo. L. RUNDLE, Nov. 17, 1873; Jos. R. COOK, Jan. 29, 1934; John P. RUNDLE, (no date given).

LOT 110-A and 131-A: Eliz. J. FRY;
Child of Wm. BARNETT, Nov. 17, 1860; Remains, Sept. 19, 1851; Re(mains) ALLEN, Oct. 10, 1851; Caroline (V.) ARMSTR(ONG), July 20, 1852; Thos. GREENWOOD, June 1, 1854; Ann ARMSTRONG, July 31, 1855; Wm. MC MULLEN, June 23, 1856; Wm. A SPEDDEN, Dec. 9, 1860; Cath. ARMSTRONG, Sept. 16, 1862; Thos. SMITH, Feb. 22, 1869; Hannah A. ARMSTRONG, Mar. 27, 1866; Saml. ARMSTRONG, Dec. 8, 1870; Child of Ann HANNA, Jan. 3, 1875; Ann HANNAH, Feb. 27, 1870; Clara (V.) ARMSTRONG, Sept. 28, 1887; John M. ARMSTRONG, Oct. 3, 1878; Danl. ARMSTRONG, May 2, 1881; Mollie A. ARMSTRONG, Oct. 15, 1888; Wm. ARMSTRONG, May 18, 1891; Julia L. ARMSTRONG, Apr. 17, 1888; Morris ARMSTRONG, Dec. 3, 1882; Child of Chas. (WARMA (sic)), May 5, 1875; Cath. E. ARMSTRONG, June 15, 1850; Jno. M. ARMSTRONG, Sept. 7, 1878; Clara L. (ARMSTRONG), Aug, 28, 1877; Mary G. SUMMERS, Sept. 14, 1866; Caroline V. ARMSTRONG, July 4, 1852; (Janah SPICER), May 9, 1855.

LOT 111-A: Ceal C. HASSON, and David RONSRILLE;
Remains, Nov. 8, 1860; Rem(ains), Nov. 9, 1860; Caroline E. WATERS, July 20, 1885; Mary E. HASSON, Oct. 12, 1885; Remains, July 13, 1852; (Wm. F.) RONSARILLE, July 3, 1865; Dayton RONSARILLE, July 31, 1865; David G. RONSARILLE, Dec. 21, 1876; Sarah T. RONSARILLE, Dec. 26, 1875; Frank E. ARMSTRONG, Mar. 11, 1882; William RONSARILLE, June 27, 1865; Sarah CRON, July 19, 1847; Mary RONSARILLE, Oct. 22, 1840; David, C. RONSARILLE, (no date given); Sarah D. RONSARILLE, (no date given).

LOT 112-A: Thomas TITTLE, Maggie BALDWIN, and Henry N. KNIGHT; Child of SPENCER, Dec. 27, 1870; E. Virginia SPENCER, Sept. 26, 1871; Thos. TITTLE, June 2, 1877; Sarah A. TITTLE, May 20, 1904; Frederick BALDWIN, June 3, 1903; Margaret R. BALDWIN, Mar. 27, 1924; Wm. H. BALDWIN, Feb. 14, 1878; Ida E. (BORKKENS), July 19, 1926; Mary E. KNIGHT, Apr. 13, 1857; Henry N. KNIGHT, Nov. 14, 1883; Eliz. DURICKSON, Dec. 31, 1895; Mary C. KNIGHT, Sept. 22, 1873; Ann M. KNIGHT, Apr. 28, 1879; Ann M. KNIGHT, Apr. 6, 1883; Elizabeth DERICKSON, Jan. 2, 1896 (crossed out); Carrie M. (TRUDERNIVE), Mar. 12, 1895; Andrew (TRUDERNIVE), Sept. 24, 1886 (last two, surname possibly TRUDEWINE); E. A. SPENCER, (no date given); Margaret Retta BALDWIN, (no date given); Wm. H. BALDWIN, (no date given).

LOTS 113-A through 125-A appear to be missing.

LOT 126-A and 127-A: Single Interments; Disenterments, July 7, 1911; Mary O'Keefe B(ROSON), April 16, 1935; Thos. M. B(EROTT), April 22, 1935; John E. SMITH, April 26, 1935; Mary MILL, April 2, 1935; Elizabeth MEEK, April 29, 1935; Thos. TWEEDELL, April 31 (sic), 1935; Nellie F. E(IC)K, Jan. 30, 1935; Grace R. (ALT), March 9, 1935; Walter DAY, March 13, 1935; Enos W. FRANKLIN, March 23, 1935; Frank K(EARUS), March 25, 1935; S(ebastian) A. ADAMS, April 11, 1935.

LOT 128-A: John A. VERNON; 2 children of RAYMOND, April 11, 1851; John VERNON, May 13, 1856; Mrs. VERNON, May 13, 1858; Child, May 27, 1861.

LOT 129-A: Mrs. Pearl (Zepp) GA(RVER), and John STAUM, and Christian STAUM; Remains, July 30, 1852; Ida A. CRAWFORD, July 7, 1869; Ella May BENETT, Oct. 21, 1881; Clyde E. STAUM, Mar. 25, 1912; Elan E. STAUM, Apr. 23, 1927; Clyd Estelle STAUM, June 5, 19(2)6; Pearl E. GA(RVER), Jan. 23, 1931; Elizabeth STAUM, Aug. 12, 1851; Christian STAUM, May 8, 1866; Nellie LEWIS, Aug. 3, 1903; Nellie LEWIS, Oct. 15, 1913; Elan E. STAUM, Apr. 23, 1927 (crossed out); Reva E. DALE, Nov. 4, 19(14) (or 1974), born Aug. 14, 1889, died Nov. 3, 19(7?); John E. STAUM, Sept. 24, 1868; Christian STAUM, Nov. 25, 1865.

LOT 130-A: Claressa DONAVAN; Richard (I.) DONAVAN, June 24, 1853; Alfred M. (DONAVAN?), Sept. 21, 1852; (Isab)ella DONAVAN, Jan. 7, 1897; C(o)neli(a) DONAVAN, Dec. 19, 1898; Eliza A. DuMONT, Apr. 24, 1901; Clarissa DONAVAN, Dec. 31, 188(1 or 6); Julius DeMONT, (no date given).

LOT 131-A: Margaret KENNEDY; Lizzie KENNEDY, June 16, 1865; Fredk. KENNEDY, May 5, 1852; Wm. H. KENNEDY, Oct. 10, 1898; Remains of children, May 10, 1898; Stillborn of Eva LANGFORD, Jan. 7, 1897; Frank M. KENNEDY, Apr. 11, 1910; Jas. H. KENNEDY, May 5, 1911; Robert A. KENNEDY, Oct. 17, 1914; Margaret G. KENNEDY, Dec. 31, 1923; Chas. A. KENNEDY, Nov. 6, 1932; Ethel May KENNEDY, (no date given); Catherine Alberta KENNEDY, July 7, 1949; Jeremiah GARY, Jan. 7, 1828; Ann ELY, Apr. 28, 1828; Henrietta (no surname given), Apr. 19, 1828; Mary Anne (no surname given), Apr. 27, 1828; Margaret KENNEDY, (no date given); Nettie Margaret KENNEDY, Mar. 18, 1964.

LOT 132-A: Saml. PL(UMMER);
Remains, Sept. 17, 1871; Saml. P. HALL, Apr. 25, 1854; Gilbert DOWNS, July 27, 1898 (also date of 1878); George R. HALL, Nov. 2, 1906; John R. HALL, Dec. 26, 1906; Susan A. HALL, Aug. 30, 1809; J. Randolph DOWNS, June 26, 1917; Saml. P. HALL, July 10, 1895; John R. HALL, Feb. 14, 1942; There is a note on this lot which states: "deed to this lot claimed by both Mrs. Mary A. GIBSON, 1010 Roland Heights Ave., and Mrs. Randolph HALL, 4321 Old York Rd.

LOT 133-A: William F. BROWN, and William HISSEY, and Jno. BROWN;
Julia BROWN, Aug. 31, 1854; Ann E. HISSEY, June 28, 1871; Benj. D. BROWN, Nov. 30, 1880; Mary E. ALEXANDER, Dec. 4, 1880; Eliza Ann and John M. BROWN, Dec. 7, 1880; Sophia C. BROWN, Nov. 13, 1882; Stillborn of Wm. DARLY, Oct. 7, 1884; Wm. H. CARNEY, Dec. 31, 1838; Harry BROWN, May 4, 1891; 3 Remains, Apr. 24, 1851; Hannah HISSEY, Apr. 25, 1852; Wm. S. BROWN, Sept. 8, 1852; Franklin HISSY, Apr. 23, 1856; Penbrook BROWN, June 17, 1864; Julia C. LIENTLAND, Aug. 19, 1873; John A. CARNEY, Dec. 2, 1882; Julia BROWN, July 3, 1886; William HISSEY, May 17, 1889; Thomas CARNEY, (no date given); Wm. HISSEY, July 6, 1893; Jno. W. BROWN, May 26, 1894; Louisa CARNEY, June 22, 1897; Alex BROWN, July 15, 1899; Infant of George CARNEY, June 4, 1900; Julia (A. or O.) LEINTLAND, Aug. 1, 1901; Julia LEINTLAND, Jan. 28, 1902; John BROWN, Oct. 3, 1850; Hannah M. BROWN, Oct. 11, 1841; George W. BROWN, (appears to be erased), 1894; Mary ALEXANDER, (no date given); Benjamin BROWN, (no date given).

LOT 134-A: John VANZANT, and Robert MILES, (also the name Mrs. (W.) E. CASSETL);
Remains, Sept. 19, 1851; Caroline VANSANT, Nov. 4, 1851; Ellinor VANSANT, Aug. 26, 1855; John VANSANT, Jan. 13, 1837; Maggie WATSON, June 12, 1862; Child of WATSON, Apr. 19, 1862; Chas. WATSON, July 7, 1862; Margt. VANSANT, May 1, 1864; Frank VANSANT, Feb. 19, 1865; Mary E. FOWLER, Feb. 9, 1885; Josephine Amanda CASSELL, Feb. 17, 1944; Mary E. BEAVER, April 29, 1918 (or 1919); Frank (Y.) (BREWER), Oct. 9, 192(?); John MILES, Feb. 16, 185(5); Mary RATLIFF, May 8, 1850; Lydia MILES, Jan. 14, 1862; Robert MILES, Feb. 16, 1866; Emma MILES, June 27, 1877; Child of C. M. (HAMPT), June 24, 1878; (Mary TYLER) Child, July 1, 1878; Wm. R. L. MILES, July 23, 1885; (Wm.) MILES, Sept. 1, 1892; Cath. MILES, Aug. 27, 1895; Annie MILES, June 10, 1896; Margt. A. (LINGEY), March 30, 1915; Thos. MILES,Feb. 10, 1931; Wm. E. CASSELL, March 2, 1936; George R. MILES, Feb. 19, 18(57); John W. MILES, Nov. 17, 1854; Mary C. STANDIFORD, July 28, 1852; Caroline E. VANSANT, Nov. 12, 1857; Frank ____, (no date given); Lee G. (LUZEY), June 24, 1935; (Ell____) VANSANT, Aug. 25, 1855; Ronda VANSANT, Oct. 5, ____.

LOT 135-A: William T. SAVIN;
Remains, Sept. 26, 1851; Thos. L. SAVIN, June 15, 1856; Elizabeth SAVIN, July 27, 1909; F. W. SAVIN, Feb. 25, 1865; Wm. T. SAVIN, July 5, 1881; Eliza M. SAVIN, Aug. 25, 1894; Augustus SAVIN, May 6, 1899; Marcus D. SAVIN, Jan. 19, 1906.

LOT 136-A: David WHITSON and Eliza SHEETS;
Remains, Aug. 4, 1852; Child, Nov. 24, 1856; Rebecca SHEARS, Dec. 20, 1858; Jane A. WHITSON, Feb. 13, 1872; David WHITSON, Apr. 1, 1897; Jane WHITSON and Rebecca SHEARS, Oct. 7, 1882; Remains of

Almina WHITSON, Oct. 1, 1884; John WHITSON, Oct. 5, 1903; Remains, Aug. 4, 1852; John M. DORSEY, Nov. 15, 1859; George H. PARSON, Sept. 12, 1864; Eliz. SEYER, and John H. DORSEY, July 14, 1868; Bell ARENDT, Mar. 2, 1878; Frank ARENDT, Feb. 19, 1885; Emma C. ARENDT, Apr. 12,1888; Eliza SHEETS, Apr. 29, 1891; Child of George ARENDT, Oct. 6, 1894; Eliza ARENDT, Apr. 10, 1902; Kate ARENDT, Nov. 13, 1918; George M. WHITSON, Oct. 24, 1843; Mary WHITSON, Mar. 29, 1845; John SHEETS, (no date given); David WHITSON, (no date given). A letter found in the lot book addressed to a Miss Ronsaville gives the date of George M. WHITSON as OCt. 24, 1840, David WHITSON as Apr. 1, 1877, Benjamin WHITSON July 24, 1888, Remains Jan. 13, 1897 and Ida May MALLONEE, Dec. 7, 1912.

LOT 137-A: William H. HOLSTINE, and William E. CLEMM; Remains, Dec. 11, 1857; Wm. H. HOLSTEIN, Dec. 10, 1870; Remains, Dec. 7, 1871; Child, Sept. 20, 1852; John R. CLEMM, May 20, 1863 (GAR after name); William E. CLEMM, Aug. 20, 1885; Rebecca R. CLEMM, Aug. 20, 1891; Wm. E. CLEMM, Jan. 7, 1896; Carrie R. HEYDE, Jan. 23, 1917; Capt. Edw. HYDE, Apr. 3, 1917 (GAR after name); Rachel COLE, June 20, 1844; Lydia HOLSTINE, (no date given); Michael and Sarah B. (SALILDIENE (sic)), (no date given); Willie and Charlie CREMM, May 9, 1863; D. E. REESE, Aug. 17, 1849; Ruth REESE, Feb. 25, 1842.

LOT 138-A: Matilda CARTER, and Isaac POTEE; Child, July 21, 1864; Ruth CARTER, Nov. 9, 1869; Laban W. CARTER, Oct. 24, 1870; Ida (CARTER), Dec. 23, 1871; Sarah (?) CARTER, Jan. 13, 1872; Matilda W. CARTER, May 13, 1884; Wm. (T. or F.) CARTER, Sept. 28, 1927; Mary E. POTEE, Apr. 13, 1853; Child, Dec. 31, 1853; Child, May 5, 1856; Child, Feb. 12, 1857; Child, Aug. 21, 1866; Child of PERRY, June 3, 1870; Child, June 17, 1870; Edwin E. WHISTLER, May 3, 1895; Jas. E. JEFFRIES, June 2, 1906; William H. POTEE, Apr. 15, 1854 (The words "for Henry E. KRIES" are crossed out); Isaac POTEE, (no date given); Virginia Lee JEFERIES, July 13, 1960; Mary C. POTEE, May 4, 1852; Mary E. POTEE, Nov. 13, 1852; Elizabeth BROBST, Jan. 17, 1951.

LOT 139-A: Anne G. LANGRILLE, and Jemimah RHODES, and Mary (HEVALY); Remains, June 19, 1851; Ann E. LANGRILLE, Feb. 27, 1856; Mary E. MITCHELL, Dec. 9, 1858; Child, Dec. 5, 1859; Anne B. TUCKER, July 17, 1859; Grandchild of LONGLEY, Jan, 15, 1863; George W. MITCHELL, Dec. 17, 1863; Cath. MAXWELL, Aug. 1, 1864; Emma MITCHELL, June 25, 1865; Wm. H. LANGRILLE, Jan. 20, 1866; Mary E. LONGLEY, Jan. 25, 1868; Wm. SH(EC)KETS, Apr. 14, 1868 (surname possible SHERKETS or SHERCKEK); John JEFFERIES, Aug. 5, 1867; Wm. H. LANGRILLE, Aug. 20, 1870; John (T.) LANGRILLE, Aug. 23, 1871; Sarah E. FOREMAN, Apr. 7, 1879; Wm. H. LANGLEY, Mar. 28, 1880; Chas. R. LANGRILLE, Nov. 15, 1881; Wm. H. LANGRILLE, Sept. 29, 1887; (Jusna (sic)) of R. LANGRILLE, Aug. 1, 1898; Jemima LONG, Feb. 12, 1879; Daniel LONG, Apr. 27, 1870; Wm. LONG, (no date given); (Budie) BARTLETT, (no date given); Child of (ZELK) (no date given); Mary (SHICKSETS), (no date given); Maggie (ZELLIS), (no date given); (Possibly Mary and Sarah ZELLER), (no date given); Jefferson LANGRILLE, Oct. 9, 1844; Elizabeth LANGRILLE, June 23, 1883; Mary E. LANGRILLE, (no date given).

LOT 140-A: Eliza A. WINKELMAN, Susanna (WINKELMAN), and Chas. E. (WINKELMAN);
Remains, May 22, 1855; John WALLEN, Sept. 8, 1857; Remains of BROWN, May 30, 1851; Child, Sept. 3, 1860; 2 children, Apr. 25, 1851; Joseph ALLEN, May 1, 1858; Alice V. ALLEN, June 18, 18(9)1; (?) WINKLEMAN, Apr. 8, 1858; Elizabeth A. (HARRSON), Nov. 1, 1887; Chas. WINKLEMAN, Feb. 8, 1919; Elizabeth WINKLEMAN, Dec. 2, 1852; Keith (?) DARRS, Apr. 22, 1884; Rhods FALL, July 29, 1930; Susannah WINKLEMAN, Dec. 6, 1855; Child, Sept. 12, 1868; Child, Sept. 20, 1867; Chas. AMETT, Dec. 28, 1872; Child of Chas. WINKLEMAN, Feb. 22, 1876; Child, July 9, 1870; Ann E. WINKLEMAN, Jan. 17, 1873; Emily ALLEN, May 23, 1867; Peter R. ALLEN, May 28, 1878; Joseph ALLEN, Jan. 15, 1869; R. A. ALLEN, Apr. 2, 1861; Mary (FITZMORRIS), Mar. 13, 1923; Jas. ALLEN, Aug. 6, 1926; Stillborn, Sept. 10, 1884; Ann WINKLEMAN, Nov. 14, 1885; Annie WINKLEMAN, Feb. 14, 1892; Sophia WINKLEMAN, May 6, 1899; Child, Sept. 10, 1914; Chas. BARNETT, Dec. 28, 1872; Catherine H. DAVIS, (no date given); Charles Edward WINKELMAN, May 3, 1943; Peter ALLEN, (no date given); Joseph E. ALLEN, Apr. 13, 1956; Dora ALLEN, Nov. 1, 1972, born Apr. 26, 1884, died Oct. 25, 1972, father John L. KURTZ, mother Catherine WARD, F. H. Witzke; ALLEN, Twins of Peter, Aug. 13, 1954; Mary E. (FITZMORRIS), (no date given); Alice A. (WINKLEMAN or ALLEN).

LOT 141-A: John M. LOTZ (last name crossed out and SOLZE entered), and Thomas DORSEY;
Julius LOTZ, Nov. 28, 1851 (last name crossed out and SOLZE entered); Caroline S. LOTZ, Aug. 30, 1858 (last name crossed out); Caroline LOTZ, May 4, 1889 (last name crossed out and SOLZE entered); Robert NICHOLSON, Dec. 13, 1889; John LOTZ, Apr. 18, 1876 (last name crossed out and SOLZE entered); There is a note which states "see letter in file under Mrs. J. L. COTTON for source of above corrections. F.L.W., 9-30-72"; Thomas DORSEY, Aug. 1, 1853; Mary A. DORSEY, June 17, 1864; Mary E. DORSEY, July 15, 1815; John W. DORSEY, (?), 1846; Elizabeth DORSEY, Aug. (28), 1840; Wm. T. DORSEY, (J-- ?1), 1855.

LOT 142-A: Robert W. ROSS;
Maria DEMPSTER, June 25, 1852; Ida B. SUTTON, Feb. 1, 1860; John W. SUTTON, Apr. 14, 1860; M. R. SUTTON, Apr. 23, 1860; Margt. MITCHELL, May 30, 1867; Sarah E. ROSS, July 25, 1870; Rich S. ROSS, Mar. 5, 1872; Robert R. ROSS, Mar. 28, 1878; Child, July 18, 1878; Sarah E. ROSS, Aug. 2, 1878; Mary E. ROSS, Sept. 20, 1881; Bessie T. MITCHELL, Dec. 19, 1890; Georgia A. ROSE (or ROZE), Nov. 18, 1918; Mon(ro)e MITCHELL, Dec. 30, 1924; Susie Rose MITCHELL, Jan. 9, 1933; Sadie T. MITCHELL, Feb. 24, 1969, born Apr. 7, 1889, died Feb. 21, 1969; Charles R. MITCHELL, Aug. 24, 1956; Mary R. SUTTON, Apr. 24, 1861; Willie M. ROSS, Jan. (2)0, 1861; Mary (or May) ROSS, Dec. 15, 1832.

LOT 143-A: Charles A. DAVIS, and Elizabeth KNIGHT; (The earlier clerk has written DAVIS as DARIS, DARRS and DANS. However, clerks making entries after 1920 have clearly entered the name DAVIS. I have taken the liberty of spelling the earlier entries DAVIS.);
Emily DAVIS, Mar. 29, 1851; 4 children, Apr. 4, 1851; Child of KROUSE, Apr. 27, 1872; Chas. W. DAVIS, Sept. 10, 1888; James DAVIS, Oct. 29, 1883; Patrick CURRAN, Jan. 6, 1890; John W. DAVIS, Oct. 24, 1891; George W. DAVIS, Aug. 17, 1908; Elizabeth

DAVIS, Apr. 19, 1906; Arthur H. DAVIS, May 12, 1919; Remove, May 15, 1851; Ann KRETZER, June 25, 1856; Wm. KRETZER, Dec. 27, 1865; Elizabeth KRETZER, Feb. 8, 1882; Jacob B. KRETZER, Sept. 20, 1894; Franklin P. DAVIS, Oct. 1, 1895; Hannah KRETZER, Jan. 3, 1896; Mary HAMMEL, Jan. 25, 1897; Stillborn of HAMMELL, July 6, 1913; Chas. W. DAVIS, Jan. 13, 1920; Eliza J. DAVIS, Mar. 3, 1920; James DAVIS, July 29, 1964, died May 5, 1960, moved from Mt. Auburn Cemetery; Jno. W. DAVIS, (no date given); Chas. W. DAVIS, (no date given); Wm. HUT(Z)ER, (no date given); John B. KRETZER, (no date given); Emma J. CURN, Mar. 28, 1947.

LOT 144-A: Single Interments;
Chas. MOORE, May 9, 1851 (crossed out); Remains, Aug, 31, 1853 (crossed out); Annie DUCKETT, Dec. 24, 1929; John HIRSHFIELD, Mar. 1, 1930; Lucy E. CORBY, Apr. 28, 1930; Esther (V.) SLATER, May 2, 1932; Samuel B. WHITE, (Feb.) 9, 1932; John W. BENSON, Mar. 7, 1933; (Beatrice) WATTERS, Mar. 16, 1933; Lillie M. DAVIS, Nov. 24, 1934; Ellen Fleuheart CLOUGH, Apr. 8, 1941; L(?) E. COSBY, (no date given); (Mary, child), 1858; Mary MOORE, 1858; Clarence WHITE, Mar. 8, 1937; Annie K. MITCHELL, (sold to her Mar. 7, 1931).

LOT 145-A: John S. LEE, and Thomas MORTIMER;
Elizabeth LEE, June 17, 1853; C. W. LEE, Dec. 15, 1858; Mary LEE, Mar. 4, 1858; Eliza LEE, Apr. 15, 1861; John R. LEE, Sept. 18, 1889; Saml. B. MORTIMER, Dec. 11, 1877; Amelia G. MORTIMER, Aug. 31, 1866; Thos. MORTIMER, Nov. 29, 1887; Armeda (or Almeda) MORTIMER, Dec. 18, 1882; John H. MORTIMER, Mar. 13, 1900; (also possibly the same person is John H. MORTIMER, Mar. 11, 1890); Ella T. MORTIMER, Sept. 11, 1942.

LOT 146-A and 148-A: Rev. Solomon MULLEN;
Harriet A. MC MULLEN, Mar. 12, 1856 (also given as Dec. 25, 1855); M. S. MC MULLEN, Mar. 16, 1869; L. G. M. MULLEN, Nov. 15, 1867; Sarah A. AUSTIN, Dec. 21, 1865; Rev. S. MC MULLEN, (no date given); Margt. E. MC MULLEN, (no date given).

LOT 146-A: Langly B. CULLY;
Mary A. CULLEY, Nov. 18, 1868; Sarah AUSTIN, Dec. 21, 1865 (crossed out); John AUSTIN, Oct. 27, 1866 (crossed out); George CULLY, Sept. 29, 1873; Wesley CULLY, June 22, 1880; George L. CULLEY, Sept. 28, 1874; Langley B. CULLEY, Jan. 19, 1863; Albert (W.) CULLEY, Oct. 11, 1862; Armistead CULLEY, Feb. 17, 1859; Mary CULLEY, Sept. 25, 1849; Wm. R. CULLEY, Jan. 1(1), 1846; Mary Jane CULLEY, (no date given).

LOT 147-A: Sophia KNAPP, and Thomas BEASON;
Jos. D.KNAPP, Mar. 17, 1902; Milton C. COLLISON, June 6, 1908; Wm. W. COLLISON, Jan. 14, 1910; Henry KNAPP, Dec. 2, 1918; Burton E. KNAPP, Mar. 10, 1949; H. G. KNAPP, Feb. 26, 1925; Sophia L. TALBOTT, Feb. 5, 1940; Thomas M. BEASON, "member of Capt. Berry's Artillery Co. who nobly fell and the defence of Fort McHenry Sept. 15, 1811, 50 years old".

LOT 148-A: Sarah BLAKE;
Jno. W. BLAKE, June 10, 1868 (other entry states Apr. 3, 1868); Sarah A. BLAKE, Mar. 1(8), 1877; Space reserved for children.

LOT 149-A: Philip FOSTER, Mary A. FOREMAN, and Joseph DOWNS;
Hannah DORSEY, Apr. 10, 1853; Philip (GISTER - crossed out)
FESTER, Oct. 10, 1866; Ada F. LILLY, June 27, 1874; Eugene LILLY,
Sept. 13, 1895; Anna C. FOSTER, July 15, 1897; Blanch SE(RFS),
Dec. 22, 1898; Stewart N. FUNBAUGH, Dec. 2, 1912; Henrietta
FOREMAN, Apr. 27, 1854; John DILLEHEY, Aug. 31, 1854; Elizabeth
DOWNS, Feb. 25, 1888; Maggie DOWNS, Apr. 19, 1893; Joseph DOWNS,
Jan. 29, 1885; John J. DOWNS, Feb. 12, 1926; Charlotte DOWNS,
June 6, 1942; Mary A. FORMAN, Dec. 18, 1869; (There is a Philip
W. FOSTER, Oct. 4, --66, possibly the same as Philip FESTER
above. Also an Annie C. FESTER, probably the same as Anna C.
FOSTER above. There is a Henrietta FOREMAN, Feb. 22, 1854,
perhaps the same as the Henrietta FOREMAN above. And there is a
Hannah FOREMAN, Jan. 8, 1853, perhaps the same as Hannah DORSEY
above.

A "General Affidavit" found among the pages of the lot books and
headed "The Daily Record Print" reads as follows:
"State of Maryland, City of Baltimore, to wit: Be it remembered,
that on this 16th day of June A.D. 1919, before me the subscri-
ber, a Justice of the Peace of the said state, in and for the
city aforesaid, personally appeared Thomas Foreman, residing at
15 E. Centre St. Balto. Md. and made oath in due form of law that
he is the sole survivor of Mary Ann Foreman purchaser of N.E. 1/4
149 Area A in 1833 in Mt. Olivet Cemetery. Thomas Foreman.
Subscribed and sworn to before me this 6th day of June 1919.
David H. Lercche, Justice of the Peace, 528 W. Franklin Street,
Baltimore, Md."

LOT 150-A: John COULTER;
Remains, Oct. 31, 1851; Joseph KING, Mar. 18, 1852; Mrs. COULTER,
Aug. 14, 1866; Eliza J. KING, May 28, 1866; John COULTER, Dec. 1,
1866; Child of Robert COULTER, Mar. 28, 1871; Annie COULTER, Nov.
29, 1880; Infant of Robert A. COULTER, Dec.4, 1882; Stillborn of
R. A. COULTER, Nov. 18, 1883; Kate LEE, Jan. 9, 1884; (no name
given), Aug. 26, 1885; Infant of E. (?) LEE, July 5, 1887; Edwin
BRADY, Oct. 22, 1898; La(vor)a KING, Dec. 16, 1899; Robert A.
COULTER, July 17, 1911; Ellen L. COULTER, Apr. 15, 1914; Mary
KING, 1890; Mary COULTER, Oct. 19, 1861; John COULTER, Aug. 18,
1866 (could be the same as John COULTER above); Robert A. COUL-
TER, Nov. 28, 1880; Mary V. COULTE, Feb. 18, 1952; Ann COU, Oct.
1838.

LOT 151-A: Joseph SHANE;
Marie SHANE, Aug. 6, 1851; (Mrs.) Joseph SHANE, May 10, 1851;
Rev. Joseph SHANE, June 11, 1854; Catherine G. SHANE, July 21,
1854; Sussannah P. SHANE, July 17, 1855; George R. SHANE, Nov. 6,
1897; Joseph SHANE, Apr.25, 1885; Susan M. SHANE, Jan. 11, 1901;
Frances M. TAYLOR, May 17, 1907; Elizabeth A. MAULL, Sept. 30,
1916; Edward A. MAULL, Apr. 2, 1920; Marg. B. MAULL, Sept. 15,
1926; Amelia B. SHANE, Aug. 20, 1845; Saml. B. (no surname
given), Dec. 3, 1842; Elizabeth (no surname given), June 18,
1808; Elizabeth (no surname given), Sept. 1, 1849; Sussannah M.
SHANE, July 9, 1901; Mary B. MAULL, (no date given); Edward
A.MAULL, (no date given); Maria M. SHANE, July 29, 1851.

LOT 152-A: Jno. H. BARNES (name crossed out), DICKENS and TUCKER,
Henry T. and Mary I. (COLLENBY);
Jennie PARDO, Aug. 12, 1866; Child, Sept. 4, 1852; Mary TUCKER,

Sept. 13, 1856; Child of CUTTLER, June 11, 1861; Saml. JONES, May 26, 1865; M. A. SMITH, June 30, 1867; Child, Sept. 21, 1874; Mary A. DICKENS, May 2, 1877; Mary A. DICKENS, Apr. 4, 1877; Benj. TUCKER, Aug. 10, 1883; Elizabeth TUCKER, Apr. 4, 1890; George DICKENS, Jan. 24, 1914; Chas. M. BARNES, Sept. 17, 1847; Mary R. LUCAS, Sept. 14, 1944.

LOT 153-A: Mary DISNEY;
Remains, May 30, 1853; Saline BARNES, May 30, 1853; Mary DISNEY, Oct. 24, 1862; John W. ALLEN, Aug. 16, 1884; Jas. M. DISNEY, Sept. 28, 1841; Isabell (J.) DISNEY, Mar. 8, 1843; Salina BARNES, Apr. 9, 1853; Elizabeth ALLEN, Apr. 16, 1841; Wm. DISNEY, (inscription illegible).

LOT 154-A: Mary A. HOLMES, Thomas WILLIAMS, Mary J. WILLIAMS; Martha E. GODFREY, Feb. 24, 1862; Mary A. HOLMES, Apr. 6, 1866; Lenna GODFREY, Dec. 14, 1870; Martha E. GODFREY, May 7, 1903; James (crossed out) George HOLMES, June 30, 1851; George GODFREY, Mar. 7, 1916, G.A.R.; Mary A. GODFREY, Dec. 9, 1870; L(ottie) GODFREY, Feb. 20, 1930; Maria WILLIAMS, Nov. 27, 1865; Andrew WILLIAMS, Dec. 31, 1856; Wm. P. WILLIAMS, Mar. 9, 1860; Chas. E. WILLIAMS, Dec. 5, 1883; Edward T. (or F.) WILLIAMS, Oct. 1, 1896; Chas. C. WILLIAMS, Oct. 4, 1905; Louisa WILLIAMS, Dec. 13, 19(2)6; (Walter) WILLIAMS, Jan, 17, 1911 (First name may be Watts); Wm. LaFAYETTE WILLIAMS, Oct. 25, 1930; Mary J. WILLIAMS, Apr. 16, 1963; Grace Dixon WILLIAMS, Mar. 8, 1973, born Dec. 7, 1897, died Mar. 5, 1973, father Walter J. BARTON, Mother Cora FITTECH; F. H. Chenoweth; Samuel V. SMUCK, Jan. 25, 1950; Lillie G.SMUCK, Aug. 22, 1949; Mary A. HOLMES, (no date given, the name appears twice in lot and once in left margin); L. Merce SMUCK, born Oct. 12, 1899, died Sept. 11, 1969, buried Sept. 15, 1969.

LOT 155-A: Edward C. WHITE, and John H. LYNCH;
Mary A. WHITE, July 6, 1891; Virginia Way GIBSON, July 26, 1923; Edmond C. WHITE, Dec. 17, 1923; Jean M. GIBSON, Mar. 23, 1935; (Tramsall) LYNCH, Oct. 5, 1909; John H. LYNCH, Jan. 2, 1924; Annie R. KAHN, Dec. 13, 1927; Dr. William Seebert GIBSON, Aug. 21, 1928; Gustave KAHN, Aug. 5, 1937; Lois M. HOLLEY, ("for him"); Ella M. GIBSON, Aug. 17, 1942; Alice White SUTTON, Jan. 5, 1944.

Found between the pages of the lot book is an affidavit stating that William L. GIBSON sold a lot N 1/2 155 Sec. A to Mrs. Lois Anna Holley GILMORE, for the use of Lois M. HOLLY Apr. 28, 1958.

LOT 156-A: Thomas HENTHORN, and Samuel REDMOND;
Child, Sept. 20, 1853; Jos. H.HENTHORN, Aug. 15, 1855; James HENTHORN, Aug. 20, 1855; Frank G. GRAY, Mar. 10, 1883; Robert E. HENTHORN, Sept. 9, 1886; Infant of George W. GALLAWAY, Aug. 1, 1887; Stillborn of Geo. GALLAWAY, Dec. 2, 1894; Thomas HENTHORN, May 2, 1898; James E. ROGERS, (Mar.) 20, 1928 (entry crossed out); George Lee GALLAWAY, June 10, 1890; Elizabeth REDMOND, Jan. 15, 1864; ROGERS child, May 8, 1869; Saml. ROGERS, Mar. 10, 1873; John RODGERS, Nov. 7, 1873; Ann Rebecca REDMAN, Mar. 11, 1875; Saml. REDMAN, Aug. 28, 1882 (second entry looks like 1832); Infant of Joseph ROGERS, Nov. 3, 1896; Glades ROGERS, Feb. 28, 1900; Sarah E. JONES, Oct. 27, 1808; James E. ROGERS, Mar. 20, 1923; Elizabeth Rogers SMITH, Feb. 25, 1925; John W. RODGERS, Feb. 25, 1942; Elizabeth ROGERS, (no date given); Ann REDMAN, (no

date given); Gladys ROGERS, (no date given); William J. HENTHORNE, Feb. 10, 1958; Mary HENTHORNE, (no date given); Robert T. HENTHORNE, Mar. 3, 1938.

LOT 157-A: Ephram NASH;
Joabelle HITCHCOCK, June 17, 1851; Remains, Oct. 6, 1852; Elizabeth KING, July 19, 1852; Child, July 25, 1854; Annie E. NASH, June 15, 1859; Louisa NASH, July 8, 1864; Chas. NASH, June 17, 1867; George A. NASH, Mar. 20, 1874; Child of Chas. NASH, Mar. 23, 1874; Mary GREEN, Dec. 14, 1878; Caroline MEEKIN, Nov. 8, 1878; John L. CLEMENTS, July 19, 1880; Caroline KING, Jan. 28, 1886; Jacob MEEKIN, Jan. 28, 1889; James NASH, Dec. 18, 1896; Wm. A. NASH, Oct. 9, 1899; Benella NASH, May 2, 1906; Emma J. (HEIDERMAN), Feb. 24, 1921; Stillborn, Feb. 6, 1924; George M. (MESKEL), Dec. 16, 1873; Caroline V. (no surname given), Nov. 6, 1877; John H. (no surname given), Jan. 26, 1884 (or 1894).

LOT 158-A: Jonatha PARSONS, and Mary MC NIER;
John MC NEIR, Sr., Dec. 5, 1849; Mary MC NEIR, Aug. 16, 185-; Benj. R. HILLYARD, May 18, 1887; Martha E. HILLYARD, Mar. 23, 1880; Harriet HILLYARD, July 12, 1882; Remains, July 15, 1851; Benj. HYLLARD, Jan. 13, 185(1); Mary MC NIER, Aug. 26, 1859; Mrs. WALKER, Feb. 21, 1860; Mary B. PARSON, Oct. 14, 1862; Chas. PARSON, June 6, 1872; Jonathan PARSON, Sept. 6, 1886; Mary A. PARSON, June 7, 1850; Emma E. PARSON, Dec. 24, 1915; Child, Mar. 21, 1852; Child, Apr. 1, 1852; John and Ginnie (no surname given), (no date given); Cath. REED, (no date given).

LOT 159-A: Isaiah TERRY, and William A. ARMOR;
Florence NEWMAN, May 6, 1861; Jishella HITCHCOCK, June 17, 1851; Child of JEFFRIES, Oct. 1, 1852; Sarah TERRY, Oct. 11, 1861; Harry C. JEFFRIES, June 7, 1876; Margt. M. TERRY, June 12, 1905; Isaih TERRY, Oct. 10, 1861; John W. TERRY, May 7, 1890; Martha A. TERRY, Sept. 31, 1889 (date as written); Tho. W. TERRY, May 7, 1890 (entry crossed out); Wm. ARMOR, Dec. 6, 1853; John ARMOR, Oct. 14, 1859; Wm. ARMOR, July 11, 1861; Mrs. GUBY, Apr. 11, 1869; Jas. MC CAFFERY, May 20, 1879; Josephine Anderson TERRY, Jan. 24, 1941; Maynard ARMO(RIS), May 17, 1822; Sallie HITCHCOCK, May 15, 1851 (or 1857); Sarah TERRY, Mar. 18, 1841; Annie TERRY, July 3, 1848; Hannah TERRY, Sept. 10, 1850.

LOT 160-A: John C. R. B. CHAMBERLAIN;
Wm. F. CHAMBERLAIN, Apr. 16, 1857; John CHAMBERLAIN, Apr. 18, 1860; Hettie CHAMBERLAIN, Sept. 22, 1883; Rem(oved) FROM N.B.G., June 8, 1877; Hettie R. CHAMBERLAIN, Sept. 29, 1883; Annie R. REVERE, Sept. 10, 1885; Rebecca A. CHAMBERLAIN, Oct. 1, 1896; John C. R. B. CHAMBERLAIN, Apr. 8, 1898; Nicholas W. WATKINS, Feb. 8, 1905; Mrs. H. R. WATKINS, Nov. 24, 1899; Rebecca CHAMBERLAIN, May 6, 1857; Elizabeth A. STAKETT, Jan. 29, (no year given).

LOT 161-A: Wm. W. WOODWARD, and Millard F. ERDMAN;
Virginia (?) WOODWARD, Sept. 22, 1851; Ellen WOODWARD, Dec. 16, 1852; Wm. WOODWARD, Feb. 20, 1863; James WOODWARD, Dec. 4, 1855; Mary WOODWARD, Jan. 21, 1851; Sallie E. ERDMAN, Apr. 18, 1891; Child of ERDMAN, Mar. 29, 1852; John F. EREDMAN, Mar. 16, 1897; Mildred F. ERDMAN, July 13, 1897; Millard ERDMAN, Dec. 26, 1914; Annie T. ERDMAN, Jan. 14, 1909.

LOT 162-A: Wm. and Henry HELMLING, John MUSSELMAN;
Susan E. HELMING, Apr. 25, 1851; Cardelia HELMLING, Apr. 4, 1861;
Jno. HELMLING, July 23, 1865; Lectie Helmling MC DOWELL, Aug. 19,
1863 (middle name is lined through); Jas. HELMLING, Aug. 24,
1865; Jno. HELMLING, Dec. 5, 1865; Annie HELMLING, Oct. 18, 1868;
Gertrude HELMLING, July 24, 1873; George R. HELMLING, July 25,
1874; Wm. HELMLING, Nov. 13, 1876; Wm. H. HELMLING, July 23,
1874; Jas. E. HELMLING, Aug. 10, 1880; Florence MUSSELMAN, Apr.
5, 1851; George R.MUSSELMAN, May 1, 1874; Florence MUSSELMAN,
June 11, 1874; John MUSSELMAN, Jan. 19, 1875; Annie C. MUSSELMAN,
Mar. 6, 1880; Hiram D. MUSSELMAN, Feb. 25, 1904; Mary M. MUSSEL-
MAN, Feb. 12, 1906; Harriet MUSSELMAN, Apr. 20, 1915; Elizabeth
HAUSE, Aug. 4, 1925; Fannie MUSSELMAN, June 10, 1874; Annie C.
MUSSELMAN, Mar. 6, 1879; Florence MUSSELMAN, Feb. 27, 1851; John
HELMLING, (no date given);

LOT 163-A: John PEREGOY; (Deed and papers turned over to Mt.
Olivet with orders that no more interments to go in this lot.
Jan. 17, 1955);
Rem(ains), Oct. 6, 1851; Elizabeth (RENTT), Oct. 20, 1853
(surname could also be BUTT or BRITT); Jos. PEREGOY, Apr. 12,
1857; Althea PEREGOY, May 7, 1865; Archey PEREGOY, Aug. 27, 1877;
Joshua PEREGOY, July 24, 1869 (crossed out); Saml. S. BLACK, Mar.
25, 1881; Wm. ROSE, Sept. 27, 1888; Lelia M. BRADFORD, Mar. 12,
1894; Hannah N. PEREGOY, June 22, 1897; Jas. H. (BURON), Oct. 27,
1899; Laura E. BRIAN, June 7, 1900; Paul ROSE, Jan. 23, 1906;
Jos(ua) PEREGOY, Nov. 5, 1914 (possibly "taken to Loudon Park");
Wm. L. (BRALFORD), Mar. 11, 1892; Jacob SCHWERTZER, Mar. 5, 1852;
Rachel SCHWERTZER, Nov. 21, 1851; Florence V. BURROWS, Jan. 17,
1955; Paul ROSE, (no date given).

LOT 164-A: George BOOKHOLTS, and Annie B. FROST;
Elias W. FROST, Oct. 17, 1922; Annie B. FROST, Apr. 14, 1937;
Child, Aug. 9, 1852; Elijah SANKS, Aug. 1, 1855; Sarah R. BOOK-
HOLTS, Sept. 11, 1858; Annie SANKS, Apr. 25, 1864; Wm. H. BOOK-
HOLTZ, Dec. 24, 1880; Carroll BOOKHOLTZ, Feb. 5, 1891; Oliva S.
(TARR), Mar. 18, 1891; Sarah G. DOOKHOLTZ, Mar. 4, 1901; John G.
NEARY, June 20, 1914; John T. NEARY, Nov. 23, 1915; John PESINA,
Oct. 24, 1918; Mary V. HOGAN, (June) 17, 1924; C. Walter FROST,
May 8, 1962; Harry S. NEARY, born Nov. 10, 1899, died June 7,
1969, buried June 10, 1969; Sarah E. NEARY, Apr. 28, 1938.

LOT 165-A: Daniel ROSS and Charles PEREGOY;
Mary ROSS, May 4, 1853; Child, Dec. 23, 1854; Sallie MORSELL,
Apr. 10, 1867; Frances W. PASCA(L), Aug. 8, 1874; Child of Ann
PEREGOY, Mar. 2, 1852; Nicholas PEREGOY, July 6, 1869, and wife;
Walter T. PEREGOY, Aug. 24, 1878; Chas. PEREGOY, Oct. 9, 1883;
Hannah PEREGOY, June 22, 1897; Elizabeth ROSS, Apr. 15, 1855;
Mary ROSS, Dec. 25, 1852; Daniel ROSS, Aug. 14, 1863; Edwd. N.
PEREGOY, Jan. 24, 1848; Chas. C. (no surname given), Nov. 24,
1851; Wm. P. PEREGOY, Aug. 23, 1878; Chas. PEREGOY, Aug. 6, 1833.

LOT 166-A: Richard HUTCHINS;
Two children, Jan. 27, 1857; Mary I. BROWN, Sept. 12, 1862;
Amanda A. HUTCHINS, April 1, 1865; Richard HUTCHINS, March 17,
1879; Ann HUTCHINS, Aug. 23, 1886; Stillborn of Pauline CASEY,
April 23, 1914.

LOT 167-A: Abraham FISHER;
George F. FISHER, April 27, 1857; Child, Jan. 19, 1860; Albert M. FISHER, Oct. 17, 1862; Abraham FISHER, Oct. 19, 1881; Amanda FISHER, Aug. 27, 1886; Wm. H. DOXYON (also spelled DOXON), June 19, 1900.

LOT 168-A: George CLAGG;
David CARSON, May 26, 1879; Clara E. GLENDING, March 31, 1900; John GLENDENNING, April 20, 1929; Dora GLENDENNING, Nov. 5, 1955.

LOT 169-A: Pamelia MOORE;
Remains, July 18, 1854; Pamela MOORE, Oct. 11, 1864; Pamela MOORE, April 8, 1840.

LOT 170-A and 222-A: Marie E. STREET;
Child (of) HODGES, April 4, 1862; S. K. I. STREET, Feb. 18, 1879 (also given as Dec. 24, 1878); Maria E. STREET, Nov. 2, 1880; John H. BECK, Jan. 16, 1854; Maria E. BECK, Dec. 9, 1856; Peter R. HILDITCK, Nov. 1840; Mary Ann HILDITCK, June 6, 1876.

LOT 171-A: Joseph KIRBY;
Remains, June 14, 1854; Child, March 17, 1857; Child, Aug. 12, 1858.

LOT 172-A: John LEESON;
Jo(hn) LESSON, (hole in page) 1876, April 26, 1887; John LEESON, June 7, 1876; Jno. W. DAVIS, April 26, 1887; Elizabeth J. LEESON, April 29, 1853.

LOT 173-A: Robt. J. WEEKS;
Sarah WEEKS, March 28, 1853; Child of WEEKS, June 22, 1853; Levindas COULTER, Aug. 17, 1881 (disinterred, removed from cemetery April 14, 1882); S. F. WEEKS, July 25, 1882; Burley COULTER, Nov. 22, 1889; Lydia A. COULTER, Jan. 16, 1893.

LOT 174-A: Robt. HUTCHINSON;
Margt. HUTCHINSON, Dec. 16, 1852; Child, May 16, 1858; Robt. HUTCHINSON, Oct. 5, 1863; Infant, May 21, 1870; Child of Mr. BROOKS, April 3, 1872; Mary A. MASINGO, Sept. 7, 1874; Littie M. BROOKS, July 27, 1877; I. L. HUTCHINSON, Nov. 5, 1877; Sarah E. FENDLEY, Feb. 14, 1878; Stillborn, April 22, 1880; (Mary A.) HUTCHINSON, May 7, 1887; John W. HUTCHINSON, Jan. 22, 1890; Wm. M. BROOKS, April 15, 1890; Eddie BROWN, Sept. 8, 1890; Wm. M. BROOKS, April 15, 1890 (entry crossed out); Wm. HUTCHINSON, Jan. 22, 1893; Wm. C. HUTCHINSON, Sept. 21, 1896; Amanda R. BROOKS, (July) 12, 1874; Wm. H. HUTCHINSON, 1846; Wm. A. HUTCHINSON, Dec. 16, 1847.

LOT 175-A: Zacharias SMITH;
Ann SMITH, April 25, 1853; Sarah E. WALKER, Aug. 23, 1854; Wm. SMITH, Jan. 30, 1860; Sarah A. SMITH, Jan. 6, 1915.

LOT 176-A: Ephram MARPHLE;
Benj. FREENEY, Feb. 20, 1853; Chas. W. MASELL, May 20, 1877; Elizabeth J. MORSELL, Jan. 29, 1880.

LOT 177-A: Chas. DARYMPLE;
Remains, Oct. 12, 1853; C. F. DALRYMPLE, Oct. 21, 1857; Elizabeth DALRYMPLE, Dec. 20, 1861; Child of Chas. DALRYMPLE, March 23,

1863; J. A. DARYMPLE, Nov. 4, 1861 (also given as Nov. 14, 1860); Rev. C. W. DALRYMPLE, Jan. 8, 1861; Rev. J. W. DALRYMPLE, Jan. 8, 1861 (last two entries may be same person).

LOT 178-A: Robt. G. ARMSTRONG;
Mrs. BROOKS, April 15, 1853; John DAVIS, Feb. 28, 1853; Mary M. NOLAND, May 7, 1853.

LOT 179-A: Jos. GILES;
Child, July 23, 1855; M. F. GILES, April 14, 1862; Maggie E. GILES, Oct. 17, 1868; Jos. D. GILES, Nov. 20, 1872; Joseph GILES, Aug. 1, 1892; Joseph GILES, April 23, 1895.

LOT 180-A: Rachel SMITH;
Mary H. CROUCH, May 25, 1859; Rachel SMITH, March 17, 1863.

LOT 181-A: James MC CURDY;
Remains, May 20, 1851; Child of COLLIER, April 14, 1851; Mary ZIMMERMAN, April 21, 1851; Walter S. MC CURDY, June 30, 1891; Jas. MC CURDY, (no date given); Amanda J. MC CURDY, Nov. 7, 1887 (the year 1885 is also given).

LOT 182-A: Eliza TIMANUS;
Child, Apr. 20, 1852; Remains, June 19, 1857; Ida Wall HISSEY, July 14, 1858; Child of Jacob TIMANUS, Jan. 19, 1869; Child of Jacob TIMANUS, Jan. 24, 1870; Child of (illegible), May 15, 1873; Chas. H. HISSEY, June 17, 1874; B. M. HISSEY, Jan. 12, 1878; Frank E. HISSEY, Apr. 6, 1880; Frank E. TIMANUS, Aug. 26, 1885; Chas. B. HISSEY, Feb. 24, 1887; Jacob H. TIMANUS, Apr. 3, 1891; Ann M. HISSEY, Mar. 9, 1893; Frank E. HISSEY, Apr. 24, 1900; Henry GREEN, July 18, 1820; John TIMANUS, July 29, 1826; Eliza WALL, Aug. 21, 1876; Hannah WALL, Aug. 16, 1850; Jacob WALL, (no date given).

LOT 183-A: James CAULK, James CHAMBERS;
Fillmor CAULK, June 5, 1856; James (T.) CAULK, Aug. 9, 1864; John R. CAULK, Jan. 1, 1865; Child, Feb. 20, 1874; Elizabeth CAULK, Sept. 13, 1878; James CAULK, Mar. 16, 1866; Henry (T.) CAULK, Mar. 23, 1906; Wm. H. CAULK, Nov. 25, 1907; Mary S. CAULK, May 5, 1909; Mary C. CAULK, Feb. 8, 1911; Elizabeth COATE(S), Mar. 19, 1919; George T. CAULK, Jan. 4, 1935; Ann BLYZARD, Apr. 20, 1865; James CHAMBERS, May 13, 1872; Elizabeth CHAMBERS, Jan. 23, 1875; Child of Thos. (SIMICK), Dec. 29, 1877; Elizabeth CHAMBERS, Aug. 27, 1881; Robert J. A. CHAMBERS, Oct. 20, 1888; Mary M. CHAMBERS, Apr. 10, 1891; James CAULK, May 14, 1886; Margt. CAULK, (no date given); Harry CAULK, (no date given).

LOT 184-A: Basiel BURGESS, and Susan H. COOPER;
Ann BURGESS, Sept. 25, 1851; Miss A. MERRYMAN, Nov. 29, 1851; Basiel B. MERCER, Mar. 9, 1859; Basel BURGESS, Nov. 24, 1862; (an entry blackened out); Dissenter CHILD, Feb. 10, 1877; Jno. M. BURGESS, May 15, 1878; Infant of E. and F. BURGESS, Sept. 11, 1887; Infant of C. and O. BURGESS, July 2, 1889; Jno. M. BURGESS, Sept. 5, 1894; Harry L. BURGESS, Sept. 4, 1903; Milton BURGESS, Mar. 11, 1906; Wilk (or Wells) COOPER, Sept. 13, 1851; Rem(ains), June 10, 1854; Child, Mar. 10, 1859; Mary C. LANGHELD, Aug. 1, 1874; Susan A.H. RICHTER, July 11, 1876; Kanelia BURGESS, Mar. 24, 1915; Owen BURGESS, Nov. 17, 1899; Basil BURGESS, Feb. 25, 1859; Herbert BURGESS, (no date given); Florence Virginia BUR-

ROWS, Jan. 17, 1955 (entry crossed out); Lillian V. COLL(MAN), July 9, 1865; G. Frederick LANGHELD, Mar. 12, 1862.

LOT 185-A: Thomas DENNY, James R. BROWN, George F. SMITH, of Harrisburg, Pa.; Mrs. DENNY's child, May 20, 1853; Clinton DENNY, Aug. 2, 1858; Chas. DENNY, July 2, 1865; Thos. DENNY, Sept. 20, 1861; Child, Sept. 21, 1852; C. H. BROWN, July 10, 1861; Jas. R. BROWN, Aug. 17, 1899; Esther A. BROWN, Sept. 15, 1905; Hester BROWN, 1852 (or 1853); Chas. H. (BROWN), 1861; Chas. B. (BROWN), 1862; M. G. (BROWN), 1887; Emily R. SMITH, July 21, 1919; Wm. (Geo.) BROWN, Jan. 11, 1887; John H. SMITH, Oct. 17, 1931; Remains of CHAMBERS, Aug. 29, 1855; Alv(er)dd (DUN), Feb. 4, 1860.

LOT 186-A: Jacob W. MEYERS; R. Minerva MYERS, Dec. 3, 1901; Amelia MEYERS, June 27, 1902; Margt. D. MEYERS, Jan. 7, 1907; Wm. F. GOSNELL, Nov. 16, 1911; Jacob W. MEYERS, June 16, 1913; Chas. A. MEYERS, Apr. 13, 1914; Rachel A. MEYERS, May 12, 1915; Ellen Amanda MEYERS, Dec. 21, 1915; Sallie Ann MEYERS, Apr. 3, 1924; Jessie H. (or A.) MEYERS, June 4, 1924; Chas. MEYERS, July 4, 1923; Jacob (W.) MEYERS, Feb. 14, 1927; Eva E. MEYERS, Apr. 20, 193(4); Homer E. MEYERS, Nov. 11, 1954; Wm. T. GOSNELL, (no date given); R. Minerva MEYERS, 190(1) (possibly same as above. Appears twice in the record.)

LOT 187-A: Chas. PURPER (This name may be PURFER or PURSSER); Christian PURPER, May 24, 1852; 2 children of John CALTON, July 12, 1853; Chas. CORAN, Aug. 17, 1856; Hester CORAN, July 12, 1859; Mrs. CALLOW, Aug. 25, 1860; J. CORAN, Oct. 27, 1865; Chas. PURPER, Dec. 1, 1873; Ann C. BRAIN (or BRAN), Aug. 3, 1875; Jane QUINN, Aug. 11, 1875; Adelia WATKINS, May 29, 1879; Ann B. PURPER, Jan. 22, 1889; Annie KELLEY, July 15, 1895; Ann PURPER is shown in two different places; Elizabeth WISE, Mar. 26, 1867, age 94 years old.

LOT 188-A: Margt. PAMPHILON, Jane ROMNEY, and John H. PRICE; Ann Rel ROMNEY, Feb. 14, 1854; Child of Thos. LAUGHLIN, Nov. 7, 1871; A. H. LAUGHLIN, June 27, 1884; Thomas Henry LAUGHLIN, June 28, 1875; Wm. S. WHITAKER, May 28, 1872; Lavinia LAUGHLIN, Feb. 13, 1915; Remains, Sept. 29, 1854; Ida May RUMNEY, Apr. 5, 1860; Jane RUMNEY, Jan. 18, 1864; Child, June 30, 1865; Florence PAMPHILON, July 7, 1874; Ida PAMPHILON, July 2, 1877; Nicholas PAMPHILON, Sept. 9, 1887; John H. PRICE, June 30, 1851; Remains, July 3, 1853; Amelia M. PRICE, Jan. 29, 1856; Wm. TRAFFNBERG, Mar. 8, 1858; Eliza H. SEWELL, Mar. 13, 1886; Margt. PAMPHILON, Mar. 16, 1888; Wm. (G.) WHITAKER, Mar. 2(4), 1895; Margt. WHITAKER, Mar. 27, 1885; A. M. LAUGHLIN, (no date given); (Tho.) H. LAUGHLIN, (no date given); Wm. J. WHITAKER, Mar. 26, 1885; Sallie COPENHAGEN, Jan. 4, 1869; John SEWELL, Oct. 2, 1846; George H. WAIN, June 29, 1865;

LOT 189-A: Alvin M. WILLIS, John UNDERWOOD transferred to Irving B. and Helen LEDDON; Louisa J. UNDERWOOD, Oct. 3, 1853; Louisa UNDERWOOD, May 6, 1863; Elizabeth WALKER, Mar. 28, 1871; Children of WALKER, Aug. 22, 1874; Susannah HEIRING, July 24, 1865; Child of UNDERWOOD, Sept. 28, 1864; John UNDERWOOD, Apr. 26, 1883, disintered; Annie WALKER, Jan. 15, 1887; "(#18553)", May 2, 1905; Edward WILLIS, Dec. 2, 1913; Mary E. WILLIS, July 24, 1907; Geneva M. WILLIS, Nov. 5,

1930; Annie E. BLANCH, Nov. 9, 1886; Benjamin LEDDON, Feb. 10, 1926; Benj. LEDDON III, Feb. 5, 1940; Margaret (SHELDON), Jan. 11, 1910 to Louden Park Cemetery; Fannie and Willie (no date or surname given); Lillian B. WILLIS, May 28, 1932; Mary L. WILLIS, Feb. 13, 1937; Alvin M. WILLIS, Dec. 21, 1940; Tamsie W. WILLIS, Apr. 4, 1955; Sarah J. HARRIS, disintered to Louden Park Nov. 29, 18(?)9; Irving B. LEDDON, Jr., Aug. 18, 1961; Irving Benjamin LEDDON, May 4, 1974, born Jan. 8, 1889, died May 1, 1974, father Benjamin LEDDON, mother unknown; Helen C. LEDDON, Apr. 2, 1941.

LOT 190-A: Nicholas A. SHEPPARD, and Mary C. PARKS;
Remains, July 11, 1856; John T. SHEPPARD, Dec. 12, 1856; Mary J. SHEPPARD, June 29, 1859; Isabella SHEPPARD, Jan. 26, 1864; Child, Mar. 19, 1864; H. M. SHEPPARD, Aug. 1, 1868; N. A. SHEPPARD, June 5, 1869; Franklin A. SHEPPARD, May 27, 1870; Mary E. SHEPPARD, July 25, 1872; Infant of Ida SHEPPARD, Feb. 23, 1891; Edward SHEPPARD, Sept. 27, 1913; Ida W. SHEPPARD, (no date given); Mary E. PARKS, Apr. 12, 1857; Amanda LONGLEY, June 4, 1860; Margt. SMITH, May 11, 1863; James SMITH, Nov. 5, 1864; Child of WIL-LIAMS, Dec. 30, 1864; Sarah SMITH, Dec. 26, 1865; Sarah H. PARKS, Feb. 22, 1868; Elenora LONGLEY, July 3, 1879; John LONGLEY, July 28, 1877; Stillborn, Sept. 19, 1884; E. Florence PARKS, Dec. 23, 1891; Marion PARKS, Oct. 3, 1905; Lydia PARKS, Nov. 5, 1906; John A. PARKS, May 20, 1914; Mary C. PARKS, May 1, 1917; Nicholas SHEPPARD, (no date given); Edwin Thomas SHEPPARD, Nov. 1, 1952; Mary G. SHEPPARD, Aug. 23, 1969, born Sept. 24, 1875, died Aug. 20, 1969; George THOMAS, Dec. 7, 1838; Jennie SHEPPARD, Jan. 21, 1861; Wm. J. SHEPPARD, May 16, 1861; Emma Jane PARKS, Jan. 27, 1941; Elonora LONGLEY, July 2, 1869; Charles A. PARKS, Mar. 12, 1952.

LOT 191-A: John J. BROOKS;
(Annie) O. BROOKS, May 15, 1852; Edw. and Oliver BROOKS, Oct. 10, 1862; Edwin BROOKS, July 11, 1863; Mollie E. BROOKS, Feb. 17, 1877; Mary (G.) BROOKS, Aug. 31, 1876; John T. BROOKS, Apr. 9, 1891; Thos. BROOKS, July 22, 1887; Mary BROOKS, Apr. 29, 1889; Chas. H. BROOKS, May 13, 1916; Clara (N.) SPICER, Apr, 16, 1923; Florence U. BROOKS, Dec. 8, 1926; (Hiram) K. SPICER, Nov. 18, 1933; John T. BROOKS, July 30, 1937; Harris C. BROOKS, Oct. 4, 1947; John J. BROOKS, (no date given); Mary BROOKS (there are two: this one buried next to the above Mary BROOKS); John Thomas BROOKS, Mar. 20, 1974, born Oct. 28, 1904, died Mar. 15, 1974, father Chas. H. BROOKS, mother unknown.

Affidavit: Letter from John Thomas BROOKS to Mt. Olivet Cemetery, Nov. 19, 1970. Mr. Brooks states he is the sole surviving son of Charles H. BROOKS and wishes to be buried in Lot 191-A between Charles H. BROOKS and John T. BROOKS.

LOT 192-A: Wm. WOODS, Francis MARTIN, "transferred to WOLF only her Mrs. S. JONES";
Remains, May 15, 1852; Wm. WOODS, Oct. 16, 1852; Wm. O. WELCH, Aug. 1, 1860; D. WOODS, Oct. 21, 1862; Elizabeth WELCH, Jan. 21, 1866; Virginia F. COLEMAN, Jan. 7, 1897; Eliza WELSH, Dec. 30, 1896; Child, May 5, 1852; Frances MARTIN, Jan. 20, 1860; Geo. E. WOLF, Nov. 26, 1887; Wm. E. WOLF, May 21, 1906, disintered, died May 22, 1891 (The name Mary E. WOLF has been crossed out and Wm. E. WOLF written in); (Araminta) L. WOLF, Oct. 28, 1912 (the date 1892 is crossed out); Isaac T. WOLF, May 22, 1916, "disintered

June 5, 1916 and taken to undertaker to be buried in Jew cemetery mistake in deed / 550 22386"; Isaac T. WOLF, Jan. 8, 1926; Geo. H. WOLF, Feb. 10, 1930; Elizabeth WOODS, July 17, 1884; Wm. WOODS, Dec. 14, 1858; E. W. GOLDEN, (no date given); G. B. WOODS, (no date given); Daisy G. WOLF, Aug. 4, 1944.

LOT 193-A: Thomas WORTHINGTON, William WILHELM; Nicholas WORTHINGTON, Dec. 27, 1856; Wm. G. WORTHINGTON, Jan. 26, 1859; Sarah WORTHINGTON, Mar. 2, 1859; Harriett WORTHINGTON, Apr. 7, 1871; Henrietta WORTHINGTON, Apr. 7, 1871; O. O. JONES, May 5, 1874; Child of Danl. SHAFFER, Jan. 8, 1880; Chas. T. WORTHINGTON, May 22, 1885; Virginia BERNHARDT, Dec. 26, 1889; Willie A. WORTHINGTON, Mar. 6, 1885; Virginia D. WILHELM, Apr. 30, 1852; Susan A. WILHELM, April 27, 1863; Wm. WILHELM, Sept. 2, 1873; Thos. F. WILHELM, June 22, 1920; Virginia WILHELM, Dec. 20, 1856; John A. (no surname given), Oct. 24, 1851; Simon ERNST, Nov. 13, 1930; Thomas ARMACOST, (no date given); Clara M. BIERAU, Feb. 1, 1943; Ashes of Ludwig BIERAU, April 19, 1957; Thomas J. WORTHINGTON, Jan. 8, 1858.

LOT 194-A: Hester KING, Ann MILLS; Remains, June 17, 1851; Ann M. LEADLEY, Mar. 29, 1852; Jacob LEDLEY, Apr. 18, 1871, d. Apr. 17, 1871; William A. LEDLEY, Oct. 12, 1872; Margt. LEDLEY, Dec. 25, 1880; Alex. LEDLEY, July 6, 1882; Remains, June 5, 1851 (2 sets of remains buried on this date); Rev. Jacob KING, June 10, 1854 (Another reference in the record states "Rev. Jacob KING, Mar. 13, 1844, 85 years old); Elizabeth MILLS, (no date given); Mary MILLS, Jan. 25, 1841; Hester KING, Dec. 22, 1862; Alex CARTER, 1817.

LOT 194-A - 153-A: This lot is held in the name of Wesley DISNEY; Remains, Apr. 13, 1853; Margt. A. DISNEY, Feb. 1, 1859 (The date Jan. 9, 1859 is also given); Remains, July 1, 1851; Unknown, June 6, 1851, a child burial; Alexander T. WAUGH, July 5, 1872; Virginia R. MATTHEWS, Oct. 7, 1875; John Wesley WAUGH, Feb. 18, 1881; John W. WAUGH, July 5, 1890; Clara ALLEN, Aug. 26, 1875; Annie MILLS, July 24, 1897 (There is an entry which states "Ann MILLS, about 1885." There are also markers for persons named Virginia, Tomey and Carrie.); Margt. A. WAUGH, July 31, 1904; John MATTHEWS, Jan. 22, 1917; Kate F. WAUGH, Sept. 15, 1893; Ledie Waugh DUNNING, Nov. 16, 1929; Jas. DISNEY, Mar. 31, 1843; William B. WAUGH, (no date given); Wesley DISNEY, May 10, 1868; James ALEXANDER, May 31, 1836.

LOT 195-A: Ann E. MADDEN, Richard BARNUM, transferred to Frank T. TURNER; John F. MADDEN, Oct. 16, 1891; Louisa E. MADDEN, Jan. 18, 1890; Florence DAHNS, May 24, 1861; John MADDEN, Oct. 18, 1863; Unknown, Dec. 1, 1863 (a child burial); Upton SHORT, Oct. 4, 1882; Ann E. MADDEN, May 19 1884, d. May 17, 1884; (?) BARNUM, Oct. 15, 1859 (family of Dr. BARNUM); Stillborn, Aug. 30, 1879; Eliza BARNUM, Mar. 30, 1892; Chas. G. (WECKERSTENS), Oct. 10, 1911; Frank T. TURNER, Apr. 7, 1941; Lillie Pearl TURNER, Mar. 10, 1941; Re(beccs or Rehus) (HURST), March 1848; Caroline BARNUM, July 23, 1841; Louise E. MADDEN, Jan. 17, 1860; Elizabeth SNEED, Feb. 17, 1847; John F. MADDEN, 185(1).

LOT 196-A: Jacob H. MEDARY, Elizabeth GIBBS; Remains, May 12, 1853; Norman MEDAIRY, Apr. 27, 1861; Child, Oct.

28, 1861; Child of Jacob MEDARY, July 3, 1868; Rich. MEDAIRY, Sept. 15, 1880; Walter WOOD, Apr. 3, 1888; Infant of R. & S. MEDARY, July 29, 1889; John MEDARY, Sept. 11, 1857; John GIBBS, June 29, 1854; Ellen GILES, June 7, 1856; John GILES, Oct. 27, 1857; Emma GILES, Feb. 16, 1859; Munay BURTON, Dec. 19, 1810; John W. BURTON, Dec. 13, 1886; Mary BURTON, (no date given); Rachel MEDARY, Sept. 13, 1880; John GILES, July 12, 1835;

LOT 197-A: Thomas WARFIELD;
Mary WARFIELD, Dec. 30, 1860; Sarah A. WARFIELD, Nov. 3, 1862; Thomas WARFIELD, June 20, 1874; Elizabeth WARFIELD, Nov. 29, 1884; Ann WARFIELD, May 9, 1890; Rachel WARFIELD, Dec. 2, 1905 (A date of Jan. 1, 1905 is also given); Susannah WARFIELD, Apr. 23, 1908; Emily WARFIELD, Aug. 11, 1916; Alice E. WARFIELD, Nov. 7, 1899; Annie R. WARFIELD, Aug. 9, 1920.

LOT 198-A: Margt. A. SHAW and Mary A. MITCHELL;
John H. SHAW, Aug. 30, 1891; Sophia MC KELDIN, (no date given); Frank C. WALTON, Sept. 21, 1892; Mrs. D. R. KELLY, Aug. 18, 1898; Elizabeth WALTON, Mar. 14, 1899; Margt. A. SHAW, Dec. 29, 1920; Elizabeth MITCHELL, May 21, 1892; Mary L. MITCHELL, July 23, 1892; Mary WALKER, Aug. 1, 1900; Jos. B. MITCHELL, Feb. 11, 1908; Eloise K. MITCHELL, Dec. 4, 1907; Stillborn of Jos. F. O'SHEA, Mar. 15, 1949; Caroliner KINCAID, July 13, 1965.

LOT 198 1/2-A: J. R. LERRY;
Maria SEWELL, Feb. 24, 1873; Martha E. SEMMON, Sept. 7, 1874;

LOT 199-A: Edward C. BILLINGS, and Amelia R. HOLLINGSHEAD;
Child, July 29, 1864; Stillborn of BROWN, June 15, 1881; Stillborn of BROWN, Dec. 16, 1882; Sallie BILLING(ER), Aug. 29, 1900; Infant of H(AR)PER, May 15, 1903; Edud. N. BILLINGER, Aug. 9, 1854 (The date of the 19th is also given); Bradley GURNEY, Apr. 27, 1857; Nora BILLINGER, May 16, 1888; Lillian G. BILLINGS, Nov. 24, 1923; Laura V. BILLINGS, Aug. 20, 1877; Saml. O. HOLLINGS-HEAD, Sept. 18, 1872; Saml. O. HOLLINGSHEAD, Apr. 9, 1873; Amelia R. HOLLINGSHEAD, Dec. 19, 1877; Frank H. HOLBITGELL, Aug. 6, 1883 (This name may also be HOBLITZELL); Frank HOLLINGSHEAD, Apr. 22, 1891; Disinterment of a small box, Nov. 22, 1892; Mary E. (HOLT-GELL), May 15, 1896, d. May 12, 1896; John B. HOLLINGSHEAD, Jan. 14, 1898; Frances HOLLINGSHEAD, Nov. 12, 1855; Remains, Aug. 4, 1857; George F. HOLLINGSHEAD, Dec. 14, 1857; Mrs. Capt. HOLLINGS-HEAD, Jan. 25, 1858; George HOLLINGSHEAD, July 11, 18(67); Samuel OWENS, Sept. 17, 1872; Capt. Frances HOLLINGSHEAD, July 6, 1855; James HOLLINGSHEAD, 1833; M. Nettie HOBLITZELL, May 25, 1939; Capt. Frank HOLLINGSHEAD, Apr. 21, 1901.

LOT 200-A: George A. STEWART, Susan HAYES, Ann E. WINKLER, and (Lucelle ALLDERCICE);
George A. STEUART, Feb. 13, 1861 (The month of January is also given); Sarah FISHER, Feb. 12, 1871 (There is also a Sarah A. FISHER given with a burial date of Dec. 10, 1870.); Sarah STEUART, June 13, 1871; Edith A. STEUART, Oct. 18, 1880; John ALDERDIS, Jan. 14, 1888; Edith WILLIAMS, May 5, 1870; Stillborn, Sept. 21, 1918; Chas. E. WILLIAMS, Mar. 5, 1936; Mrs. WINKLER, July 13, 1852; Jos. ADERDIRE, June 9, 1854; Edwd. WINKLER, May 11, 1856 (There is an Edud. WINKLER buried Feb. 5, 1856.); John ALDERDISE, Oct. 11, 1869 (The date of Oct. 9 is also given); Sarah J. ALDERDICE, Sept. 18, 1899 (The date of Sept. 17 is also

given); William E. ALDERDICE, Sept. 21, 1901 (The date of Sept. 18 is also given); William T. WOOD, Nov. 28, 1893; Jennie (H.) ALDERDICE, Nov. 24, 1902; Jas. FISHER, Mar. 6, 1838; Charles E. ALTDERDISS, (no date given); Anne E. (no surname given), May 27, 1851 (The burial is with the Winkler's and Alderdice's.); Lucille F. ALLDERDICE, May 23, 1974, b. July 17, 1881, d. May 21, 1974, age 92 yrs., 10 mos. & 4 da., Father Ira FLEAGLE, Mother (G.) TROMAN, Funeral Home Schwab.

LOT 201-A: Jno. T. SNEED, & Jno. H. MILLER;
William SNEED, Dec. 10, 1861; Child, Mar. 22, 1863; Remains, Jan. 29, 1869; Sarah A. OULER, Dec. 1(9), 1867 (This may be the same as Sarah A. OUTTAN, Dec. 16, 1869; Child of M(ALLAN), June 12, 1871; Stillborn, Apr. 19, 1875; Child of Edud. MOLLOH(IN), Apr. 22, 1875; William E. MOFFITT, Dec. 6, 1888; Robert SNEED, Dec. 26, 1906; (Nellie) B. WHEELER, Mar. 14, 1900; Remains, June 14, 1851; Remains, Oct. 10, 1851; John H. MILLER, June 29, 1896 (Also given as Jan. 18, 1891); Eliza MILLER, June 27, 1890 (The date of June 22, 1890 is also given); Emily B(RI)DING, Apr. 19, 1885; Mary E. MILLER, June 4, 1920; Valentine A. MILLER, Mar. 26, 1921; William C. MILLER, Dec. 19, 1907; Danl. MILLER, Mar. 16, 1922; Ellen A. MILLER, Aug. 22, 1938; John T. MILLER, Sept. 12, 1858; Capt. T. SPRIGG, May 14, 1855; Mary WHEELER, Mar. 29, 1932; Elizabeth OU(LTAN), Jan. 1849.

LOT 202-A: Henry BROOME;
Mary ASH(VI)LLE, Apr. 4, 1851; Henry BROONE, Feb. 17, 1875, d. Feb. 16, 1875; Franzina BROONE, Sept. 26, 1878, d. Sept. 24, 1878; Henry BROONE, Nov. 1, 1881, d. Oct. 31, 1881; Rose E. BARNEWELL, July 4, 1892; Infant of BARNWELL, Jan. 19, 1913; Mary A. BROONE, Jan. 31, 1907, d. Jan. 4, 1907; John H. SLACK, Apr. 20, 1914; John (N.) BROONE, Feb. 12, 1916; Sallie A. BROOME, Dec. 19, 1917; Sarah Eugenia BARNEWELL, Aug. 6, 1925; Fannie T. BROONE, Oct. 13, 1927; Mary ASH(VI)LLE, Feb. 18, 1825; Jessie S. HARBOUR, Jan. 17, 1955.

LOT 203-A: Fred. SHEPPARD, and Jno. G. MEDINGER;
Chas. W. SHEPPARD, May 12, 1853; Child, Feb. 16, 1857; Margt. SHEPPARD, Aug. 22, 1880; John STEWART, Nov. 6, 1880; Willie STEWART, July 29, 1881; Margt. T. SIMMONDS, Nov. 13, 1882; Emma STEWART, Feb. 2, 1886; Infant of Frank SHEPPARD, Dec. 27, 1886; Albert SHEPPARD, Jan. 30, 1887; Blanch (C.) SHEPPARD, Oct. 19, 1889; Infant of E. & W. (MOCHLER), May 13, 1870; Child, May 6, 1853; Willa CHILD, May 27, 1853; Louisa MEDINGER, Mar. 29, 1859; Chas. W. LEOCHLER, Dec. 1, 1871; John (C. or G.) MEDINGER, Nov. 9, 1883; William H. MEDINGER, Nov. 6, 1885; Herbert (S.) MEDINGER, Jan. 10, 1888; Fredk. MEDINGER, June 14, 1900, d. June 11, 1900; Margt. MEDINGER, Apr. 29, 1918; (O. or C.) F. STEWART, Jan. 20, 1891; Chas W. KOEHLER, Oct. 22, 1892; Stillborn of SHEPPARD, Mar. 2, 1893; William SHEPPARD, Apr. 25, 1883 (or 1893); Viola SHEPPARD, Sept. 2, 1896; Charlie (no surname given), Oct. 27, 1871; Louisa (no surname given), Jan. 27, 1859; Caroline (no surname given), Nov. 1844; Elizabeth (no surname given), Dec. 28, 1844; Johnnie (no surname given), Mar. 10, 1858; Fred. SHEPPARD, (no date given); Margaret SHEPPARD (no date given); Chas. W. SHEPPARD, Feb. 21, 1855.

LOT 204-A: Margaret ENNIS, Elijah BISHOP, (Also message reading "Duplicate issued Jos. B. GRIFFITH".), and Harriet WOODS;

Peter B. BROOKS, Oct. 29, 1851; Remains, Apr. 30, 1852; Mary J. BROOKS, Dec. 6, 1853; Mary V. BROOKS, Sept. 6, 1854; Margt. MAY, Dec. 19, 1854; Child, July 23, 1857; Thos. EWELL, Dec. 8, 1857; Child, Feb. 20, 1859; Thos. EWELL, Sept. 11, 1862; Jacob BUCK, June 9, 1864; Child, July 30, 1870; Peter B. BROOKS, Apr. 4, 1881; Annie H. BROOKS, Dec. 11, 1899; Remains, Aug. 2, 1852; Elijah BISHOP, & daughter, Aug. 2, 1852; Child of George W. BISHOP, Dec. 22, 1872; J. J. BUCK, (no date given), W.S.N.; Rose D. GRIFFITH, (no date given); Joseph B. GRIFFITH, Aug. 23, 1944; Ann Maria buried with Annie H. BROOKS; Joseph WELLS (or WILK), ____ 9, 1827; Saml. BISHOP, Feb. 1810.

LOT 205-A: Dur(brow) DORSEY, and WOODS, also in the name of Temperance BIRCH;
Remains, Jan. 2, 1852; Joseph JOHNSON, Sept. 1, 1858; M. C. JOHNSON, Oct. 24, 1866; John C. DINBROW, Aug. 8, 1893; Eli(z or J.) WOOD, Jan. 9, 1869; Ann B. WOODS, Oct. 2, 1885; Chas. BIRCK, Aug. 6, 1879; Maria BURCH, July 4, 1910; Margt. B. BURCH, Jan. 28, 1916; Mary BURCH, Sept. 20, 1900; Henry B. BIRCH, Mar. 10, 1841; Margaret Davy BIRCH, Dec. 7, 1954; Elizabeth W. DURLROW, Jan. 9, 1869; Ann Berry WOODS, Nov. 29, 1813; William WOODS, Sept. 3, 1826; Mary HAGGAIT, Aug. 17, 1878; Ann HAMMOND, July 15, 1829; Elizabeth H. WOODS, Oct. 17, 1832;

LOT 206-A: Dorothy REITER;
Willie G. REITER, Jan. 9, 1863; A. (I.) REITER, Dec. 27, 1864; Peter REITER, Nov. 15, 1864; Emily REITER, Apr. 24, 1865; Child, Mar. 23, 1865; Abraham REITER, Mar. 30, 1873; Annie D. REITER, Jan. 24, 1881; Peter REITER, Sept. 3, 1851; James P. R. GOFF, Feb. 3, 1888; Dorothy REITER, Aug. 21, 1886; Annie E. FOX, Sept. 8, 1902; Mary J. REITER, Dec. 24, 1905; Remains, May 29, 1851; Peter REITER, May 25, 1852; Jno. W. MORTIMER, Sept. 25, 1852; James GOFF, July 8, 1856; Jessie B. REITER, May 30, 1880; Dorothy REITER, Sept. 22, 1886; James R. P. GOFF, Feb. 6, 1888; Conrad FOX, Mar. 31, 1923; Annie M. BRASS, Apr. 30, 1937; John W. BRASS, July 7, 1954.

LOT 207-A: Henrietta ENTZ, and Henry MORTIMER;
Harriett ENTZ, Mar. 19, 1883 (This entry is crossed out); Henrietta ENTZ, Mar. 17, 1883; Willemina T. MILLS, Feb. 9, 1914 (surname may be MILES); Elizabeth GRUBB, May 5, 1881 (The date May 7, 1881 is also given); Elizabeth (E.) GLOCKER, Jan. 23, 1925; Jessie MORTIMER, Oct. 5, 1851, d. Oct. 3, 1851; Remains, Nov. 17, 1851; Mrs. LASH, Dec. 28, 1861 (Apparently the same as Maria S. LASH); A. Maria MORTIMER, Oct. 3, 1887 (Also called Maria A. MORTIMER); Willie MORTIMER, Sept. 24, 1872; Harry MORTIMER, July 31, 1849; Henry H. MORTIMER, Dec. 20, 1852; Saloni GRUBB, Dec. 16, 1836; Andrew ENTZ, Aug. 30, 1851; Grace Miles DECKER, Feb. 11, 1955 (An item in the lot book states that Grace Estella DECKER died Feb. 9, 1955 in Hamiltonian Township, Adams Co., Pa. of arteriosclerotic cardiovascular disease.).

LOT 208-A: William PRESTON and John PRESTON;
Remains, Aug. 4, 1852; Henry PRESTON, May 7, 1857 (Apparently the same person as Harry Merrill PRESTON, May 6, 1857.); William F. GILSON, Nov. 4, 1862, d. Nov. 3, 1862; M. E. GILSON, Aug, 15, 1866; Mary GILSON, Sept. 23, 1814; Harry M. (or Henry M.) MERRILL, Mar. 29, 1886, d. Mar. 28, 1886; Mary MERRILL, Dec. 12, 1872; Agnes GILSON, July 15, 1891, d. July 14, 1891; Cath. PRES-

TON, Dec. 21, 1904, d. Dec. 20, 1904; Mary MERRILL, Dec. 9, 1887; Mary GILSON, Sept. 22, 1878; Laura PRESTON, Apr. 9, 1849; William PRESTON, Oct. 28, 1828.

LOT 209-A: Edud. S. PARRISH, "Transferred to Grace T. WELSH" (last entry crossed out and Emory T. WELSH inserted); Jacob J. PARRISH, Nov. 4, 1866; Edud. S. PARRISH, Feb. 16, 1871; William H. PARRISH, Dec. 24, 1854; (Laura Z.) PARRISH, Jan. 21, 1855; Ann C. FOWLER, Mar. 28, 1877 (Also listed is a child named Charlie); Maggie FOWLER, Sept. 23, 1866; Child of FOWLER, Apr. 14, 1862; Eliza PARRISH, Nov. 31, 1846.

LOT 210-A: Earnest W. BRIDING; Martha H. BRIDING, Aug. 18, 1849; Emily BRIDING, Apr. 16, 1855; Chas. E. WITENBAKER, June 4, 1884; E. W. BRIDING, Mar. 26, 1889 (At the right of the page is listed Ernest W. BRIDING, Jan. 2, 1889, who may be the same person.); G. A. HIEKEL, May 7, 1903 (At the right of the page is listed M. G. Adolph HICHEL, May 4, 1903, who may be the same person.); Annie M. BRIDING, May 23, 1904 (The date May 25, 1904 is also given); Emily M. HIEHLE, Apr. 8, 1922.

LOT 211-A: Chas. N. DAVIDSON, Philip PIPER, and William BROWN; Sarah PIPER, June 15, 1859 (May be the same as Sarah E. PIPER May 12, Philip PIPER, Feb. 10, 1860, d. Feb. 7, 1860; Chas. M. DAVIDSON, June 4, 1866; Kate PIPER, Apr. 20, 1880; Mary A. PIPER, June 25, 1894; Elizabeth PIPER, Feb. 8, 19(11); Mary PIPER, May 13, 1838; Jas. R. BROWN, Apr. 1, 1824; Elenor BROWN, (no date given).

LOT 212-A: John SULLAVIN, and Marion GODMAN; Remains, Oct. 21, 1853; John SULLAVIN, Nov. 5, 1857, d. Nov. 4, 1857; Abbie SULLAVIN, Nov. 28, 1872; Jane R. SULLAVIN, Oct. 7, 1898 (also given is Oct. 8, 1898); William M. SULLAVIN, July 9, 1900; Mary SULLAVIN, Jan. 21, 1910; William SULLAVIN, Sept. 19, 1902; Louise K. SULLAVIN, May 6, 1915; I. GODMAN, and children, Apr. 10, 1851; John GODMAN, Dec. 20, 1897 disinterred; Edward C. GODMAN, Feb. 3, 1860; Mary L. GODMAN, June 26, 1864; John GODMAN, Feb. 20, 1851; Mary A. GODMAN, May 19, 1883 (may also be the same as Ann M. GODMAN, May 19, 1883.); Katherene GODMAN, Jan. 17, 1907, disentered; Jno. & Cath. GODMAN, Apr. 24, 1907; Hariet SULLAVIN, Jan. 16, 1854; Abigil SULLAVIN, Nov. 26, 1873; William Mansfield SULLAVIN, Sept. 18, 1902; George M. SULLAVIN, July 7, 1900.

LOT 213-A: John JARRETT, Sarah JARRETT, and Mary JARRETT; Thos. JARRETT, June 15, 1854; Remains, Sept. 8, 1852; Fredk. JARRETT, May 1, 1873; Edud. (I.) JARRETT, Oct. 21, 1886; Christopher JARRETT, Feb. 23, 1903; Fra(ncie) JARRETT, June 4, 1901; Antionaitte SCH(ORCK)EY, July 9, 1926; Aaron M. JARRETT, July 24, 1931; Thos. JARRETT, Oct. 3, 1851; Ellen JARRETT, Apr. 11, 1852; Sarah JARRETT, Mar. 29, 1856; Mary JARRETT, Dec. 13, 1856; Anna Maire JARRETT, (no date given); Sarah H. JARRETT, Mar. 27, 1826; Mary JARRETT, Aug. 9, 1939; Clarense JARRETT, Mar. 13, 1956.

LOT 214-A: Thos S. ALLEN, and Fred. MYERS; Remains, Sept. 4, 1851; John RUSSELL, July 27, 1854; Jas. J. MILBURIN, Dec. 28, 1856; Thos. S. ALLEN, July 14, 1860 (The date July 11 is also given); Robert W. GRAY, June 28, 1861; Elizabeth ALLEN, Sept. 20, 1880; Francis MICHAEL, June 20, 1889 (The given name also appears as Frances.); Elizabeth A. MICHAEL, Feb. 1,

1930; Child, July 19, 1851; Fredk. MYERS, Apr. 30, 1852; R. J. MYERS, June 27, 1862; Elizabeth E. MYERS, June 23, 1877; Fredk. P. MEYERS, Oct. 20, 1880; Margt. D. MYERS, May 15, 1882, d. May 14, 1882; Franklin P. MYERS, Apr. 16, 1885; Fredk. MEYERS, Oct. 4, 1890, d. Oct. 3, 1890; Fredk. F. J. MEYERS, June 26, 1917 (The date of June 26, 1912 is also given); Zachariah ALLEN, Mar. 17, 1831; J. W. HYSON, (no date given. There is the following inserted: Co. A., S.P.H.B. Md. Inf. G.A.R.).

LOT 215-A: Cath. EARNEST;
Mrs. COULTER, April 30, 1851; Child of RICHARDSON, May 1, 1851; Cath. EARNEST, Oct. 10, 1862; Rhena ROSSEAN, May 4 (or 9), 1878; Susan KENLEY, Sept. 7, 1882 (also given as Aug. 8, 1882); Elizabeth EARNEST, April 7, 1863 (also given as 1868).

LOT 216-A: Geo. & Jacob SHINNICK; "See 1/4 272 for diagram."

LOT 217-A: Martha R. WHITE;
Wm. LATCHFORD, July 21, 1853; N(orman) ERB, Sept. 23, 1862; Saml. W. WHITE, May 29, 1901 (Aug. 5, 1872 is crossed out); Norris WHITE, March 23, 1920; Claire WHITE, March 30, 1930; Ma(ne)ta R. WHITE, April 21, 1920; Elaine WHITE, 9 mo. (no other information).

LOT 218-A: Mary A. LONG;
M. O. KEMBLE, April 28, 1862; Elizabeth LONG, Feb. 22, 1868; Eliza A. LONG, Aug. 5, 1872; Infant of Matilda & Jas. H. ALLEN, April 26, 1905.

LOT 219-A: Jno. W. PARKS;
Lydia PARKS, July 25, 1852.

LOT 220-A: James MATCHSET;
Mrs. MATCHETT, April 8, 1853; Mary J. MATCHETT, July 27, 1868; Elizabeth T. WILKINSON, May 12, 1928.

LOT 221-A: Maba LANG;
Mrs. HALL and child, Oct. 6, 1858; Ruth M. LANG, March 22, 1907, disinterred from 1/4 392-D and reinterred on N sied Oct. 7, 1914; Edward W. LANG, April 12, 1941; Alice LANG, May 7, 1959; (A faint message refers to Lot 269-A which I can not make out.); Reference is also made of a Mabel LANG.

LOT 222-A and 170-A: "See 170 for diagram" (The number 270 is lined through or vice versa).

LOT 223-A: Jno. G. R. ADAMS;
Child, May 2, 1859; Child, Aug. 9, 1855; Martha G. ADAMS, Aug. 29, 1864; Charlotte ADAMS, Jan. 30, 1868; Jas. Edw. ADAMS, July 26, 1876; Child of ADAMS, July 22, 1882; Infant of C. & E. ADAMS, Nov. 7, 1888; Stella M. ADAMS, April 9, 1892; Lucy B(RUCHEY), Oct. 4, 1895; Jos. C. ADAMS, June 22, 1896; J(o)s. BRUNCHEY, July 2, 1909; Danl. E. HEISER, July 17, 1907; Lucy B(RUNCHEY), Dec.24, 1902, reinterred into 174-F; Stillborn of Ella & Jos. B(RUNCHEY), Feb. 29, 1912; Jas. W. BR(UN)CHEY, May 2, 1913; Ellenor L. GRIFFITH, March 16, 1927, baby 4 hrs. old; Ella BRUNCHEY, Sept. 26, 1941.

LOT 224-A: Martha TATHAM, transferred to Henry JENKINS;
Wm. G. W. ADAMS, July 27, 1863; Ellen TAYLOR, Nov. 25, 1872;
Alice TAYLOR, Nov. 3, 1877; Martha TATHAM, Feb. 22, 1878; Sarah
BRUSHMILLER, Jan. 24, 1906; Chas. BRUSHMILLER, Jan. 16, 1916;
Dallas LEMUEL, Feb. 7, 1921; Lillian SUTER, March 15, 1923; Abel
ERICKSON (or ESIKSAM), Dec. 28, 1926; George R. SUTER, April 15,
1948; Madeline C. (no surname given), Oct. 21, 1965, age 62 yrs.;
Mary SUTER, Oct. 29, 1948.

LOT 225-A: Wm. LANCASTER;
Geo. W. T. LAANCASSTER, Dec. 16, 1906; Sarah LANCASTER, Jan. 15, 1929.

LOT 226-A: Thomas CRISWELL;
Child of SHAW, Feb. 19, 1857, disinterred July 23, 1859; John F. CRISWELL, Dec. 8, 1876; Mary B. CRISWELL, 1861.

LOT 227-A: Wm. JOHNSON;
Child, Aug. 22, 1856; Child of LANTRAM, Feb. 30, 1862; Rich. JOHNSON, JAn. 25, 1870; Wm.JOHNSON, May 10, 1873; Emma JOHNSON, Aug. 31, 1889; Julia JOHNSON, Oct. 17, 1892; Mary V. SCOTT, Aug. 13, 1891.

LOT 228-A: Wm. J. FLOYD;
Robt. McClary FLOYD, Sept. 5, 1856; Wm. BENNETT, May 17, 1863; Julia A. MC CLEARY, April 1, 1881; Camella ACTON, July 21, 1884; Geo. B. MC CLEARY, Nov. 29, 1920; Mary E. ACTON, Nov. 4, 1868.

LOT 229-A: Herman SHEARS;
Remains of FOXWELL, May 16, 1851; Remains of HILL, July 2, 1855; Wm. LAWTON, Nov. 26, 1856; Child, Jan. 27, 1857; Wm. DILLA, Dec. 13, 1858; Peter D. DALLION, Dec. 1, 1858; Susan SHEARS, April 21, 1864; C. M. SHEARS, Sept. 12, 1885; Emiel R. KOHILFHOFF, Oct. 23, 1899; Richard F. KOHLHOFF, March 2, 1934; Zeta KOHLHOFF, Feb. 26, 1947.

LOT 230-A: John NINER;
Chas. DAYTON, Dec. 5, 1876 (entry crossed out); John NINER, Dec. 17, 1915; Alice A. NINER, Oct. 27, 1939.

LOT 231-A: Paul RUST, and George W. SMITH;
Lucy RUST, Aug. 4, 1856 (The date Aug. 3, 1855 is also given); Jas. W. ALEXANDER, July 2, 1891; Nathan L. ALEXANDER, Nov. 27, 1886 (Child); Paul RUST, June 23, 1882, d. June 22, 1882; Cath. RUST, Nov. 4, 1889, d. Nov. 3, 1889; Alda G. SMITH, Aug. 5, 1850; Patience RUST, Aug. 9, 1850.

LOT 232-A: Frederick RICHLER, and John SHROTE;
Louisa VERTIN, Nov. 13, 1859; Robert H. JOYCE, Feb. 23, 1864; Sarah E. JOYCE, July 7, 1867; Ellen F. SHROTE, July 30, 1873; John SCHROTE, July 18, 1876; Ann E. SCHROTE, July 9, 1890 (This surname SCHROTE is crossed out and another surname inserted which may be SANDERS. However, the entry is not clear.); Sarah A. SCHROTE, Mar. 23, 1904; Edwin J. SCHROTE, Feb. 22, 1926; (Laura) I. SHROTE, Dec. 30, 1929; Elizabeth J. SHROTE, May 5, 1937; John J. BOWEN, Feb. 1, 1937; Remains, Jan. 2, 1853; Child, July 20, 1853; A. DIFFO(RY), June 29, 1856; S. C. TALBOTT, Nov. 2, 1857; Child of Thos. RICHLER, Nov. 5, 1857; Child of WOODALL, Nov. 15, 1862; Child of WOODALL, Jan. 15, 1863; Alfred WOODALL, Aug. 29,

1865; Ann E. MERRITT, Apr. 28, 1870; Mary M. RICHTER, Nov. 23, 1871; Margt. A. WOODALL, July 15, 1903, d.July 14, 1903; Henry (C. or E.) WOODALL, Dec. 21, 1909, d. Dec. 20, 1909; William E. WOODALL, Jan. 5, 1940; Fannie W. WOODALL, June 14, 1940; Samuel T. WOODALL, Jan. 12, 1943.

LOT 233-A: Jno. W. HAYS, and also contains single interments; Remains, Aug. 23, 1853; Stephen MYERS, Aug. 13, 1855; Jno. W. HAYS, Nov. 12, 1855; Child, Apr. 20, 1856; Jno. W. HAYS, Oct. 16, 1878; Sarah KOCHLER, Oct. 27, 1907; George W. HAYS, July 20, 1904, disinterred; George W. HAYS, Aug. 18, 1908; Jas. MEYERS, June 26, 1879; Hannah MYERS, Jan. 29, 1855; Chas. F. DIETZ, Oct. 9, 1934; (Horatio) (LEREAMOR), Oct. 9, 1934; Wallace E. B. HOWARD, Oct. 12, 1934; William C. BELL, Oct. 16, 1934; Victor P. TSCHUDY, Nov. 20, 1934; (Elenor) E. B(ER....), Nov. 20, 1934; William E. BURNHAM, Mar. 9, 1940; Harriet GRAVES, Mar. 21, 1938.

LOT 234-A: John Elwood MORRISON; John E. DA(VID)SON, Apr. 7, 1853; E. M. SANTRIGER, Oct. 31, 1854; Mary MORRISON, Nov. 9, 1858; Lockwood MORRISON, Nov. 19, 1858; Elizabeth W. MORRISON, Feb. 25, 1860; Child, Apr. 8, 1861; M. M. MORRISON, May 12, 1868; Susan MORRISON, Aug. 22, 1869; Wesley M. S. WASTENN, Apr. 6, 1871; William MORRISON, Apr. 9, 1872; Child of S. S. PLEASANT, Nov. 23, 1876; I. Elwood MORRISON, Oct. 20, 1885; Elizabeth STANTUZER, Sept. 11, 1888, d. Sept. 10, 1888; Sylvester W. MORRISON, Feb. 6, 1891; Henriette A. WARTHEM, Mar. 26, 1904; Clara M. PECK, May 25, 1909; Hannah MORRISON, Mar. 7, 1910; Virginia L. MORRISON, May 28, 1924 (Removed from Bonnie Brae Cemetery); J. Elwood MORRISON, July 31, 1930; Elwood MORRISON, Oct. 25, 1854; Elizabeth SAN(TMYER), Apr. 12, (1850).

LOT 235-A: William SUMMERS, and John S. MACHER (Deed is held by Mrs. R. Ernest STUARD); Child, Aug. 16, 1859; Rose L. SUMMERS, Oct. 28, 1866; Chas. T. KRAUSS, Oct. 14, 1919; Chas. Thos. KRAUSS, Sr., May 21, 1932; _____ MACHER, Mar. 27, 1851 (This is the burial place of J. S. MACHER's parents); Martha A. NAGLE, Apr. 4, 1854; Benjamin MACHER, Apr. 27, 1854; Emma Augusta MACHER, Sept. 29, 1854; Mrs. WOODALL, May 20, 1858; Child, June 17, 1862; Child, Mar. 19, 1867; Elizabeth MACHER, Aug, 3, 1881; Mary ELDERD(IRE), Dec. 7, 1867; Lillie A. RANDOLPH, Oct. 1, 1872; John T. TAYLOR, May 13, 1879; William H. HOOPER, Oct. 4, 1879; Anna M. KRAUSS, Apr. 12, 1938.

LOT 236-A: Con(dua) GATCH; Jas. E. GATCH, June 11, 1856; "Rem. from St. Retors NE 300", July 15, 1873 (This probably means remains from St. Peter's Cemetery.); Con(dua) GATCH, Nov. 10, 1881; Jane W. N. GATCH, May 31, 1889; Jane White GATCH, Dec. 31, 1896; Margt. A. GATCH, Apr. 21, 1911; Chas. H. GATCH, Dec. 5, 1917; Martha J. GATCH, Feb. 22, 1921; Edwd. L. GATCH, June 12, 1878; Mary (GATCH), (no date given); Lillian E. GATCH, Apr. 17, 1937.

LOT 237-A: Danl. WEAVER, Jennings BARTON; Danl. WEAVER, Nov. 20, 1870 (The date Nov. 22, 1870 is also given); Elena WEAVER, July 7, 1877, d. July 5, 1877; Mrs. Jennings BARTON, June 11, 1855; Jennings BARTON, May 9, 1889, d. May 7, 1889; Hannah R. WEAVER, June 11, 1850, disinterred; Hannah WEAVER, Nov. 11, 1900, disinterred and reinterred into Lot 46-F;

Ann PEACOCK, Aug. 15, 1900; Ellen WEAVER, July 8, 1850; Infant of Edurn. BARTON, (no date given); Hannah HIGH, Apr. 20, 1823; Jas. HIGH, Oct. 15, 1840.

LOT 238-A: Mary (A.) WALKER (BLEDSOE), Jacob SAUMEIG; Child, May 5, 1854; Alice SOMENIG, Mar. 26, 1856 (There may be another person buried with Alice SAUMENIG. The name is very faint, but appears to be Aupirict Vincent (sic).); Remains, Mar. 26, 1856; Jann SOMENIG, Nov. 28, 1867; Mary SOMENIG, Mar. 19, 1874; Jacob SOMENIG, Jan. 29, 1891; Edward SAUMENIG, Sept. 10, 1928; Mathias WALKER, Sept. 10, 1870; Robert (H. or M.) BLEDSOE, Sept. 1, 1870; Robert BLEDSOE, Dec. 26, 1879 (There is indication of two persons named Robert Lee BLEDSOE, one in space one and one in space 2. There is a Robert H. BLEDSOE, Jr. in space 3.); Jas. W. WALKER, Oct. 12, 1886 (May be the same as stone for Jas. B. WALKER, Oct. 11, 1886.); Harrison S. WALKER, Sept, 4, 1888 (This person may be the same as the one with stone for Harry WALKER, Sept. 2, 1888, G. A. R.); Mary WALKER, July 16, 1900, d. July 15, 1900; Robert BLEDSOE, Nov. 27, (1907); Disinterred. Matthias T. WALKER, July 12, 1863; Katherine V. BLEDSOE, Nov. 3, 1954; Margaret Jane BLEDSOE, Oct. 31, 1942 (was moved to another space Nov. 3, 1954.

LOT 239-A: William HOOPER, Ann STONE, Mary J. STEWART, George and Elizabeth M. STEWART (There is an authorization dated Dec. 10, 1907 for Mt. Olivet Cemetery to prepare a grave for G. W. STEWART in Lot 239-A. The request was made by George & Elizabeth M. STEWART and was signed by George D. STEWART of Ellicott City, Md.);
Child, Aug. 22, 1851; William STONE, Apr. 18, 1862; S. DONALDSON, Apr. 14, 1851; Mary J. STEWART, Dec. 23, 1851; Adult, Dec. 12, 1866; Lucretta YOUNG, June 5, 1894; George W. YOUNG, Apr. 16, 1897; Susan BOSWELL, 1824; George Washington STEWART, Dec. 11, 1937; Negro slave MANDAY, Dec. 12, 1866; Mary Elizabeth STEWART, Nov. 7, 1941; George D. STEWART, June 4, 1962.

LOT 240-A: C. W. KEATCH, Ann WATKINS, and Samuel GAITHER; Cyrus MEDAIRY, May 29, 1872 (This is only for a "lymb" of Cyrus Medairy); William M. H. ARDY, Jan. 26, 1850; Eliza Jane FITZ-GERALD, Nov. 14, 1853; Jos. WATKINS, Nov. 22, 1854; Ann WATKINS, July 4, 1865; William HARDESTY, Feb. 9, 1852; Mary DICKENSON, Oct. 18, 1860; William T. GAITHER, Sept. 6, 1868; Greenbury GAITHER, May 7, 1864; Cath. GAITHER, Nov. 25, 1870; Saml. GAI-THER, Apr. 14, 1912; Hettie GAITHER, Apr.25, 1879.

LOT 241-A: Jacob PENN, and George W. CHANDLER; Remains, May 10, 1851; William PENN, Aug. 26, 1854; Child, Aug. 27, 1856; John NEWHOUSE, July 9, 1858; Elijah PENN, Aug. 17, 1872; Emma V. PENN, Nov. 5, 1866, d. Nov. 3, 1866; Jacob PENN, Jr., Feb. 2(8), 1868; William PENN, June 25, 1870; Walter F. PENN, Aug. 1, 1873 (Also given is August 10, 1873); Henry PENN, Mar. 24, 1905; Jacob PENN, Apr. 16, 1883; Henry PENN, Apr. 21, 1885; John H. JOHNSON, Nov. 19, 1858; George W. JOHNSON, Nov. 29, 1865; William A. CHANDLER, July 1, 1868; Nancy A. CHANDLER, Sept. 6, 1870; Estell D. CHANDLER, Nov. 12, 1869; N. A. CHANDLER, Aug. 3, 1871; George S. CHANDLER, June 21, 1876; Hugh E. CHANDLER, July 27, 1877; Peter T. CHANDLER, Oct. 18, 1878; Sarah S. CHAND-LER, Aug.3, 1881; George CHANDLER, Sept. 7, 1881; Charlotte CHANDLER, Aug. 26, 1885; Margt. CHANDLER, Aug. 13, 1889; Mark W.

CHANDLER, July 25, 1891; Paul CHANDLER, June 24, 1909; Frank (H.) CHANDLER, July 4, 1891; Sarah L. CHANDLER, Jan. 21, 1905; William E. CHANDLER, Sept. 23, 1913; Da(niel) & Benjamin A. CHANDLER, July 7, 1880; Emma PENN, July 12, 1904; Elizabeth PENN, Aug. 17, 1802; Jacob PENN, Jan. 6, 1883 (The date Jan. 9, 1883 in the same space, different handwriting); Emma C. PENN, July 10, 1904; Harry (N.) PENN, Mar. 21, 1885; Ann PENN, (no date given); Hugh CHANDLER, (no date given) (In one grave are Hugh CHANDLER, Peter & Sarah R., some or all of these may be accounted for above.); Charlotte WOOD, Jan. 20, 1856; Ethel D. (CHANDLER), (no date given); George W. CHANDLER, Dec. 11, 1870; George CHANDLER, (no date given) (Also in one grave are George CHANDLER, Charlotte, Margt., Mark. No surnames given.).

LOT 242-A: Wm. D. REESE, Geo. C. PARKS;
Child, Apr. 29, 1853; Adult, child underneath, Apr. 25, 1866; Wm. D. REESE, Mar. 15, 1852; Ellan N. PARKS, Apr. 21, 1920; Geo. C. PARKS, Nov. 20, 1923; John E. PARKS, Sr., Mar. 26, 1958; John Edger PARKS, Jr., Feb. 1, 1972, b. Oct. 12, 1908, d. Jan. 28, 1972, father John E. PARKS, Sr., mother Anne E. LUCAS.

LOT 243-A: Mary H. SEWELL, Thomas H. SEWELL;
Anna MURPHEY, Nov. 13, 1862; T.H. QUINN, June 3, 1869; Thos. H. SEWELL, Sept. 29, 1871; Mary J. SEWELL, Mar. 22, 1886; Jas. F. SEWELL, May 7, 1889; Ruthanna QUINN, Feb. 16, 1903; Jas. A. COLEMAN, Oct. 27, 1903 (entry crossed out); Elizabeth A.KIR(L)Y, Oct. 27, 1903 (surname may be KIRBY); James MURPHEY, May 27, 1851; Edith M. LOWERY, July 10, 1873; Sarah A. SEWELL, Mar. 20, 1885; Elya P. SEWELL, May 7, 1886; Elizabeth R. NOLEN, July 22, 1898; Margt. S. LOWERY, Dec. 17, 1914; Dora (no surname given) (no date given); Child of FRANK, July 13, 1855; Margt. A. (FRANK), Sept. 10, 1854; Mrs. WHITE, Oct. 7, 185(8).

LOT 244-A: Benjamin CHANEY, Joseph H. AULD;
3 children, Apr. 7, 1851; James WILLIAMS, Mar. 13, 1853; Chas. H. TURNER, July 10, 1854; Susan CHANEY, Feb. 17, 1853; Louisa STOCKETT, May 7, 1860; Joseph T. STOCKETT, Sept. 1, 1862; Anne STOCKETT, Sept. 28, 1863; Emily L. STOCKETT, Sept. 7, 1865; Christian CHANEY, Jan. 29, 1881; Benjamin CHANEY, Nov. 30, 1881; Wm. CHANEY, Apr. 9, 1889; Moses N. MOGNESS, Apr. 26, 1903, disinterred; Moses N. MAGNESS, Nov. 10, 1903, Removed to Loudoun Park; Child, June 8, 1853; Child, Aug. 15, 1856; Child, Apr. 1, 1863; Jos. H. AULD, June 6, 1882; Margt. A. AULD, (June 6, 1882); Wm. W. ROWE, July 16, 1884, disinterred; Wm. E. ROWE, Oct. 30, 1888, disinterred; Carrie N. DUDLEY, Apr. 18, 1895; Margt. A. AULD, Apr. 30, 1882; Carrie N. DUDLEY, Nov. 16, 1916, disinterred and moved to "34.9.0"; Wm. TALL, Child, Apr. 31, 188(?); Emma V. AULD, Oct. 11, 1854; Fredk. DA(W)SON, May 10, 18(53); Jos. H AULD, Mar. 4, 1882.

LOT 245-A: Edud. (E.) THOMPSON, Wm. G. MORAN;
Child, Aug. 7, 1854; Edud. THOMPSON, July 18, 1861, G.A.R.; Aly STANLY, Oct. 24, 1861; Elizabeth THOMPSON, Sept. 31, 1884, 82 years old; Helen JOHNSON, June 10, 1887 (There are two persons buried in this lot named Johnson, first name of second illegible); Helen L. JOHNSON, July 20, 1896; Elizabeth A. STANLEY, June 7, 1899; Dollie THOMSON, July 17, 1909; Wm. W. STANLEY, Aug. 23, 1921; Remains, Oct. 5, 1851; Mary MORAN, July 23, 1872; Frank MORAN, Sept. 24, 1883; Wm. J. E. MORAN, Oct. 21, 1889, disin-

terred; Lilliam M. CROSS, Jan. 17, 1894; Maria MORAN, Apr. 1, 1850; Chas. H. MORAN, Jan. 29, 1810; Wm. G. MORAN, 1910; Mary (no surname given, buried with Wm. G. MORAN), 1872.

LOT 246-A: Chas. W. BARTLETT;
Chas W. BARTLETT, Mar. 22, 1866; Charlotte JOHNSON, Jan. 17, 1870, disinterred; Oliver JOHNSON, Jan. 1, 1870, disinterred; Margaret BARTLETT, Jan. 12, 1877; Chas. W. BARTLETT, Oct. 19, 1891; Cath. JOHNSON, (no date given).

LOT 246 1/2 and 247-A: John W. WATKINS;
Gassaway WATKINS, May 26, 1859; Frederick DITMAR, Feb. 18, 1818; Edward HEIMILLER, Nov. 16, 1942; Henry B.WATKINS, Sept. 20, 1935; Emma WATKINS, Jan. 16, 1929; M. Emily STEEL, June 22, 1878; John Wesley WATKINS, Sept. 19, 1887; Catherine L. WATKINS, June 21, 1867; Dr. William J. MC MINN, Nov. 15, 1943; Mortimer S. WATKINS, Jan. 26, 1897; Florence A. MC MINN, "Con. Boy", May 27, 1954; Maria WATKINS, Dec. 10, 1875; Harry W. WATKINS, May 15, 1893, child; Robert P. WATKINS, Feb. 10, 1854.

LOT 248-A: Wm. PRESTON;
John T. PRESTON, Mar. 3, 1853; Wm. PRESTON, Nov. 23, 1863; Child, Aug. 13, 1865; Elizabeth PRESTON, Sept. 7, 1874; Child, Jan. 28, 1874; Caroline PRESTON, Apr. 20, 1879; Ella PRESTON, Nov. 3, 1890; Elizabeth PRESTON, Aug. 26, 1871; Wm. H. PRESTON, Nov. 4, 1850; John PRESTON, Jan. 21, 1853.

LOT 249-A: Jacob LOVE, Philip AULD, Jos. H. AULD;
Senena LOVE, Aug. 1, 1870 (May be same person as Serine A. LOVE, July 30, 1870.); Mary A. LOVE, Apr. 11, 1887; Jos. K. LOVE, Jr., Mar. 27, 1881; Jas. K. LOVE, Mar. 27, 1901 (A stone reads Jos. K. LOVE, Jan. 5, 1901.); Remains, May 16, 1854; Emma V. AULD, Oct. 25, 1854; Joseph Da(m)son LOVE, Sept. 12, 1885; Child, Dec. 5, 1865; Albert A. AULD, June 11, 1866; Philip AULD, Oct. 21, 1881; Philip AULD, Jr., June 15, 1905, child; Edwd. C. AULD, Oct. 29, 1906; Margt. AULD, July 8, 1912; Edwd. M. AULD, Aug. 1, 1913; A. J. AULD, Jan. 5, 1922; Mary E. LOVE, July 2, 1849; Chas. LOVE, Jan. 19, 1840; Philip F. AULD, BR, b. Aug. 5, 1901, d. Sept. 9, 1969, buried Sept. 12, 1969; Joseph LOVE, Aug. 30, 1838; Sarah LOVE, Dec. 15, 1841; Alice Cordelia LOVE, Oct. 11, 1943; Danson AULD, July 13, 1844; Susan (no surname given, buried with Danson AULD, Dec. 11, 1834); Mary E. AULD, Nov. 2, 1847; Harry E. AULD, Jan. 6, 1956; Joseph DA(VAM), Sept. 1, 1835; Mary Ann LOVE, Dec. 11, 1886; Joseph K. AULD, June (13, 1844); S(illegible) D(illegible), Oct. 17, 1840 (entry crossed out).

LOT 250-A: W. F. BURNETT, Samuel BURNETT;
Remains of 3 children, May 3, 1866 ("3 children, Saml., Edgar & Susannah); Wm. T. BURNETT, Aug. 27, 1868, disinterred; Eddie BURNETT, July 24, 1874 (May be same person as Edgar BURNETT, no date); Saml. BURNETT, Jr., July 12, 1879; Saml. BURNETT, Aug. 6, 1877; Sarah BURNETT, Dec. 28, 1884; Wm. T. BURNETT, Jan. 5, 1915 (disinterred and moved to Loudon Park); Frank A. ZEGLER, Jan. 25, 1916; Geo. R. BURNETT, Feb. 13, 1922 (There are either two George R. BURNETT's or one was moved and record not corrected); El(aum) Va. WHITE, Sept. 25, 1926; Edna Rowe DUVALL, June 17, 1929; Edith M. ZEIGLER, Mar. 16, 1953. Letter found in Lot Book A dated Nov. 28, 1961 from Mt. Olivet Cemetery to Mr. E. P. Beachum mentions lot 250-A held in name of Sauel Burnett. Mentions Mrs. D. H.

Duvall of Baltimore City and Mr. W. T. Burnett, also of Baltimore City.

Letter from E. P. Beachum to Mt. Olivet Cemetery states E. P. Beachum is husband of Catherine D. Duvall. She possesses family Bible of Samuel Burnett, her great-grandfather. Her mother was according to it Edna Rowe Duvall. This letter is in reference to Lot 250-A.

LOT 251-A: Samuel HARRISS;
Sarah E. HARRISS, May 19, 1859; Thos. G. HARRISS, Oct. 14, 1844; Mary A. HARRISS, Dec. 7, 1840; Edud. G. CHRISTIE, April 5, 18(27 or 37); E. O. CHRISTIE, Dec. 9, 1887; Willye B. WARE, May (3, 1810 or 1910), disinterred; Willye B. WARE, May 11, 1916, disinterred and reinterred; Wm. B. WARE, July 19, 1918; Mary (Ida) WARE, Nov. 21, 1938; Julia Ware Reinhard GLOVER, Oct. 1, 1971, born June 19, 1892, died Sept. 28, 1971, Father Wm. B. WARE, mother Ida RIDGELY, funeral home Wm. E. Johnson; Elizabeth __. CHRISTIE, (no date given); "for Vertie HARRISON"; Harold Ware REINHARD, (no date given); Mrs. REINHARD, (no date given); M. Helen JOHNSON, Aug. 2, 1971, born Jan. 16, 1895, died July 30, 1971, Father Albert BIBER, mother Margaret ___, Funeral home Lorin Byers; Rev. George Bil. JOHNSON, June 16, 1943.

LOT 252-A and 253-A: David THOMAS;
Remains, April 7, 1853; Child, June 13, 1853; Thos. L. Jones, May 1(5), 1851 (entry crossed out); Susan B. Sweetser THOMAS, "S. side of David", Nov. 26, 1900; Daniel E. THOMAS, Oct. 18, 1864; Elizabeth (no surname or date given); Grace THOMAS, June 11, 1853; Ely THOMAS, July 7, 1838; Wm. B. THOMAS, Aug. 31, 18(3)7; Lena CASSELL, (no date given).

LOT 253-A: Thomas L. JONES;
Thos. L. JONES, May 13, 1851; Mary LONG, Nov. 29, (1851); Margaret MC COY, Sept. 11, 1869; Florence Jones BROTT, April 8, 1936; Charles W. BROTT, May 22, 1962; C. Melvin BROTT, May 10, 1939.

LOT 254-A and 255-A: Charles B. KEYWORTH;
Child of Rev. HAWTHORN, July 10, 1869; Child of Chas. E. KEYWORTH, Dec. 26, 1871; Child of C. E. KEYWORTH, Feb. 3, 1876; Mary E. CLARK, Jan. 9, 1897; Chas. B. KEYWORTH, March 7, 1897; Elizabeth KEYWORTH, July 23, 1870; Elizabeth LEMOUR, June 19, 1892; Danl. T. KEYWORTH, May 22, 190(3 or 5); Annie E. KEYWORTH, July 12, 1912; Jane W. STANSBERY, Jan. 19, 1915; 4 children (no further information); Charles B. STANSBURY, March 25, 1947.

LOT 256-A: Robt. R. LLOYD, Thos. D. SUMMERS, Jno. F. RICHARDSON; Robt. G. LLOYD, July 18, 1881; Robt. (crossed out and Annie written in) E. LLOYD, Sept. 7, 1916; Robt. R. LLOYD, Feb. 4, 1922; Wm. M. LLOYD, Dec. 11, 1935; Infant of Thos. D. SUMMERS, Sept. 12, 1914; Ruth A. SUMMERS, June 2(6), 1917; Thos. N. SUMMERS, Oct. 25, 1917; Thos. D. SUMMERS, (no date given).

LOT 257-A: Wm. and Joseph HIGH, Emma AHLSLEGER;
Child, June 24, 1852; Chas. S. HIGH, Nov. 26, 1853; Child of SMITH, July 5, 1859; Child, July 5, 1855; Susan HIGH, March 18, 1860; Ida E. HIGH, April 20, 1860; Child, Sept. 22, 1862; Benj. B. SMITH, June 26, 1865; Wm. T. HIGH, April 2, 1867; Benj. F. HIGH, March 21, 1871; Mary E. HIGH, Dec. 3, 1874; Wm. Thos. HIGH,

Oct. 6, 1900 (entry crossed out); Mary E. HIGH, Dec. 11, 1913; Mary R. ALSEGER, May 8, 1897; Charles SMITH, Oct. 23, 1853; Wm. F. HIGH, Feb. 14, 1867; Ann R. AHLSEGER, May 7, 1897; Joseph HIGH, Jan. 22, 1865; Kate SMITH, May 21, 186(9); William S. AHLSLEGER, Nov. 20, 1939; Emma AHLSEGER, May 24, 1939; Elizabeth HIGH, Sept. 2, 1849.

LOT 258-A: Jane V. BROWN, Amelia GOULD;
John BROWN, Aug. 19, 1852; John C. BROWN, March 20, 1860; Sarah E. BROWN, June 30, 1865; Child, Jan. 22, 1872; Lulu A. BROWN, Oct. 4, 1872; Jas. BROWN, Oct. 11, 1872; Wm. E. BROWN, Feb. 11, 1875; Jas. V. BROWN, July 12, 1897; Margt. B. BROWN, Jan. 23, 1879; Laura V. BROWN, Feb. 25, 1880; Jane MAGE, June 1, 1880; Jas. A. BROWN, child underneath, June 18, 1887; Child of M(ENE)FEE, Aug. 31, 1887; John B. BROWN, June 12, 1898; Hopewell CH(WERCEL), Dec. 2, 1892; Sarah BROWN, Jan. 18, 1899; John BROWN, July 17, 1872, War of 1812 at Fort (Hollingmenth), 74 years old; Margt. BROWN, Jan. 1858; Mary BROWN, Jan. 1858; Wm. (K. or H.) BROWN, July 5, 1849; Geo. M. BROWN, Feb. 4, 1920.

LOT 259-A: Osman A. DANAKER;
John DANAKER, Oct. 1, 1851; Jas. D. DANAKER, Sept. 15, 1853; Jos. D. DANAKER, April 16, 1869; Child of DAVIS, June 16, 1871; Charlotte H. DANAKER, July 2, 1874; Harry S. DANAKER, July 15, 1875; C. H. DAVIS, Aug. 24, 1882; Florence E. DANAKER, July 16, 1891 (name appears second at right of page); _____ H. DANAKER, July 5, 1893; Mary E. DANAKER, July 14, 1885; Daisey DANAKER, Oct. 6, 188(0); John F. (no surname given), Aug. 4, 1843; Oram OSBURN, Aug. 23, 1848; John C. DANAKER, Sept. 30, 185(1); Wm. H. DANAKER, (no date given).

LOT 260-A: Isriel RIGGIN;
Eliz. DYER, March 29, 1862; (I.) RIGGIN, May 2, 1862; Maggie S. RIGGIN, March 27, 1871; Sadie M. RIGGIN, July 18, 1878; Maria M. DANAKER, Sept. 27, 1901; Orman DANAKER, Oct. 10, 1902; Wm. I. RIGGIN, Nov. 10, 1847; Israel RIGGIN, May 25, 1862; Emily RIGGIN, April 25, 1865.

LOT 261-A: Wm. INGHAM, Thos. PARSONS;
Child, Sept. 24, 1851; Remains, April 30, 1852; Wm. INGHAM, March 24, 1885; Rachel INGHAM, Sept. 9, 1891; _____ INGHAM, July 4, 1901; Elizabeth D. INGHAM, Jan. 21, 1928; Susannah Virginia INGHAM, Feb. 12, 1936; M. Sophia INGHAM, Nov. 30, 1937; Mr. JOHNSON's child, Jan. 3, 1857; Gordan W. EDDY, June 12, 1878; Elizabeth PARSON, Dec. 27, 1894; Sarah A. WHITAKER, Dec. 9, 1903; Margt. FOWLER, Sept. 25, 1886; Wm. F. (no surname given), July 16, 1845; (Henry) C. (no surname given), May 27, 1845; Thos. PARSON, Oct. 15, 1849; William T. INGHAM, Nov. 14, 1958; Lurinda W. EDDY, Oct. 20, 1877; Geo. W. EDDY, April 10, 18(35); Charles M. WHITAKER, cremated (no date given); Margaret LINTHICUM, Feb. 19, 1962; Clara (torn page) LINTHICUM, Jan. 10, 1966, born Aug. 23, 1889, died Jan. 7, 1966; George INGHAM, (no date given).

LOT 262-A: Elizabeth BROWN;
Hester A. DAYTON, Jan. 16, 1857; Elizabeth BROWN, July 26, 1875.

LOT 263-A: Sarah A. DOUGHERTY;
Remains of HORN, May 5, 1851; (Mis or Mia) ALL(iam), May 12, 1851; Rem(ains), July 5, 1855.

LOT 264-A: Thomas BENDER;
Remains, Apr. 24, 1855; Thomas (DOUNEY), Feb. 25, 1861; Rebecca CULEMBER, Mar. 13, 1867.

LOT 265-A: Sarah A. MC KEEVER; No interments listed.

LOTS 266-A and 267-A: Lambden S. BUCK;
Remains, Feb. 5, 1854; Maria J. HALL, Sept. 5, 1854; Remains, Dec. 18, 1856; Wm. T. BRAMLEY, May 22, 1863; Mrs. MC CULLOUGH, July 17, 1864.

LOT 268-A: John C. GEDDES;
Remains, June 6, 1853; Jane GEDDESS, Oct. 22, 1864; Adult, Jan. 29, 1869; Mary GEDDESS, Apr. 28, 1878; George W. GEDDES, Dec. 12, 1882; Jas. P. GEDDESS, Apr. 25, 1904; Adelaide E. WARFIELD, Oct. 22, 1908; George GEDDESS, Dec. 23, 1913; John C. GEDDESS, Jan. 13, 1930; Kate GEDDES, July 20, 1943; Mary GEDDESS (no date given).

LOT 269-A: John GRAHAM;
John GRAHAM, Mar. 20, 1856; Margt. I. BARGER, Mar. 2, 1887, child buried underneath; Margt. I. BADGER, (no date given); Mary J. GRAHAM, Mar. 19, 1901, also Edw. GRAHAM; John GRAHAM, b. in Scotland, 1873; Margt. INGLIS, 1908, b. in Scotland; Edwd. GRAHAM, July 25, 1927; The monuments read: Mary J. GRAHAM, Jan. 22, 1901; Edw. GRAHAM, member of Fry's Battery, Confederate States (W. S.), July 25, 1927; Margaret I. Bager, Feb. 6, 1887; Margaret I. INGLIS, Jan. 20, 18(8)8 or 1808.

LOT 270-A: Nathaniel NEWTON;
George BOYER, Feb. 10, 1855; Child, July 15, 1852; Child, Sept. 15, 1853; Sarah E. NEWTON, July 10, 1856; Child, Feb. 23, 1857; Chas. E. NEWTON, Oct. 8, 1865; Child, Dec. 14, 1868; A. NEWTON, Jan. 20, 1872.

LOT 271-A: E. B. PETTYMAN;
Eliza B. PETTYMAN, Feb. 26, 1861; Emma PETTYMAN, Dec. 20, 1865; Wm. PRETTYMAN, July 23, 1875; Rev. Wesley PRETTYMAN, May 21, 1901; Penelope PRETTYMAN, (no date given). Stones read: Rev. Wm. PRETTYMAN, July 2(1), 1875; Emma A. PRETTYMAN, Dec. 13, 1865; Eliza B. PRETTYMAN, Feb. 26, 1861.

LOT 272-A and 216-A: George and Jacob SHINNICK;
Edwd. FREELAND, Jan. 10, 1872; Martha SHINNICK, Apr.22, 1877; Julia JOHNSON, Oct. 17, 1902 (entry crossed out); Blanch W. SHINNICK, Aug. 3, 1914 (child at bottom); Jacob A. H. SHINNICK, Nov. 25, 1877; Remains, Sept. 3, 1851; Thos. E. SHINNICK, Oct. 5, 1853; Rachel R(OSS)EAN, May 26, 1861; Margt. SHINNICK, Apr. 5, 1870; Jacob A. H. SHINNICK, Dec. 30, 1890; Walter H. SHINNICK, Dec. 3, 1897; Kenneth SHINNICK, Aug. 20, 1919; Jacob A. H. SHINNICK, Aug. 9, 1922; Grace C. SHINNICK, Feb. 18, 1927; Jacob A. SHINNICK, 1887; Jaocb A. H. SHINNICK, Nov. 25, 1877; Lillian SHINNICK, 1891.

LOT 273-A: Robert SMILEY;
Child, May 28, 1862; George T.KNIGHT, Nov. 19, 1863; Adult, Apr. 20, 1867; Child, July 8, 1870; Lucy A. HOWARD, Apr. 4, 1872; Robert SMILEY, Jr., Aug. 26, 1875; Cath. SMILEY, Mar. 1, 1862.

LOT 274-A: Andrew MC MAHON;
Mrs. ZIMMERMAN, July 5, 1851; Robert G. MITCHELL, Mar. 7, 1852; Jennie WHITEFORD, Sept. 1, 1887; Andrew MC MAHON, May 4, 1888; (Arlene) (SULLIVAN), Feb. 24, 1934; Jennie WARFIELD, Sept. 1887; Ida M. SULLIVAN, Feb. 1, 1944; Mary O'LARY, July 9, 1863; Fanny O'LARY, June 8, 1863.

LOT 275-A: Annie E. HARRISON;
Remains, July 26, 1851; Tobetha HARRISON, Sept. 13, 1853; Cornelius BOYD, Aug. 15, 1855; Annie E. HARRISON, June 14, 1858.

LOT 276-A: Mary KENNEALLY;
Mary KENNELLY, Jan. 21, 1855; Robert G. MITCHELL, Mar. 4, 1852; Remains, Oct. 3, 1870; Elizabeth MITCHELL, July 23, 1883, b. in Cork, Ireland, d. in Balto. July 1, 1883.

LOT 277-A: JACKSON - NEWTON;
George M. JACKSON, Oct. 26, 1853; Henry GROSLAND, July 12, 1879, Co. B., 1st Md.; Susanna DE KUBLER, Feb. 9, 1888; George W. JACKSON, Mar. 9, 1893; Catherine JACKSON, Aug. 14, 1924.

LOT 278-A: James E. CARNEY, Margaret T. ALLEWALT;
Remains, July 24, 1855; J. H. BECKMAN, June 19, 1861; Wm. L. DILLAHUNT, Mar. 13, 1863; Child of Jno. DILLEHUNT, Apr. 19, 1868; Ann BECKMAN, Apr. 17, 1868; Jas.CARNEY, Feb. 7, 1902; Mary A. CARNEY, Mar. 3, 1900; Mary M.CARNEY, Oct. 18, 1906; Stillborn of Wm. & Sarah KE(NNY), May 7, 1907. An authorization found in the lot books: May 27, 1953, Mt. Olivet Cemetery is authorized to inter Margaret J. Allewalt in Lot 278-A of James E. Carney. Margaret J. Allewalt signed authorization before Notary Public June 4, 1953.

LOT 279-A: Saml. B. MARTIN;
Clara V. MARTIN, Oct. 1, 1888 (also given as Sept. 1); Infant of A. & I. MARTIN, Sept. 3, 1889; Chas. MARR (or MARS), July 13, 1891; Clara J. ULLRICK, Oct. 21, 1918; Saml. B. MARTIN, Mar. 30, 1934.

LOT 280-A: Milcha WHITE;
Remains, July 26, 1852; P. G. BROWNING, Apr. 20, 18(1)6, 52 years old.

LOT 281-A: Ellen DILL;
Child, July 14, 1852; Child of WISE, May 16, 1853.

LOT 282-A: Margt. A. BOSWELL;
Mrs. BOSWELL, Apr. 26, 1853; Child, Dec. 4, 1862; Child of M. COOK, Jan 28, 1873; Ann M. COOK, Jan. 23, 1873; Elizabeth RICHARDSON, Sept. 27, 1881; Margt. A. RICHARDSON, May 1, 1900; John W. RICHARDSON, Apr. 10, 191(0 or 8).

LOT 283-A: John GADDESS; See Lot 268-A.

LOT 284-A: Henry P. THOMAS;
Remains, Dec. 4, 1854; Annie R. THOMAS, July 12, 1904; George W. WARFIELD, Dec. 31, 1906; Wm. SEELEY, Oct. 30, 1908; Chas. E. WARFIELD, Apr. 18, 1923; Mary E. WARFIELD, May 24, 1933.

LOT 285-A: Jos. W. BARKER;
Sophia A. BARKER, Oct. 29, 1861; Mary A. F. SINCLAIR, June 8, 1923; Luara A. CRAMER, Feb. 21, 1927; Louise A. SINCLAIR, Jan. 12, 1938.

LOT 286-A: Jas. SMITH;
Otho J. ZITTLE, Feb. 15, 1915; Vera A. WOODBURY, Sept. 28, 1915; Marlin S. ZITTLE, Nov. 28, 1921; Josephine ZITTLE, Mar. 22, 1926; Rae PEACH, Feb. 27, 1928.

LOT 287-A: George R. KENNELEY;
Sarah MC ELLANEY, Dec. 2, 1854; Sarah MC ELLANEY, July 25, 1859; Eliza KENNELY, Sept. 10, 1860; Mary A. KENNELLY, Oct. 27, 1888; Emily G. KENNELLY, Dec. 25, 1870; George KENNELLY, 1860.

LOT 288-A: Jas. BRADLEY (name crossed out and Single Interments Mt. Olivet Cemetery entered);
Child, July 27, 1855 (entry crossed out); June STAGMAN, Mar. 4, 1936; Dorothy GR(AUEY), Mar. 16, 1936; Alverta May STOKES, Nov. 18, 1936; Joyce P. STOKES, Nov. 3, 1952; Stillborn of BROWN, Dec. 30, 1936; Stillborn of DE (LANNEY), Jan. 4, 1937; Mary E. ESRICK, Jan. 16, 1937; Stillborn of TALBOTT, Jan. 21, 1937.

LOT 289-A: Myrtle STEGMAN (CORSE) (name crossed out and Alfred G. STOKES, Sr. entered);
Jeanette Catherine STOKES, Oct. 19, 1973, b. May 30, 1917, d. Oct. 15 1973, father Wm. E. SMITH, mother Grace T. JOHNSON.

LOT 290-A: Lloyd LE COMPT;
Child, May 29, 1856; Mrs. LE COMPT, Aug. 4, 1859; George LECOMPT, July 22, 1874; Walter J. LECOMPT, Feb. 5, 1877; Mandekla GRIFFIN, May 22, 1901; Jos. L. LECOMPT, Aug. 3, 1859; Emily LE COMPTE, July 21, 1890; David L. GRIFFITH, July 4, 1931; George LE COMPT, (no date given); William P. DICKEL, Oct. 23, 1942.

LOT 291-A: Joseph MASK;
Chas. W. MASK, Mar. 12, 1857; Henry W. WHITEHURST, June 5, 1866; Child of Wm. MASK, Feb. 17, 1868; Saml. E. MASK, Jan. 4, 1873; Franklin MASK, July 24, 1877; Ellen C. WHITEHURST, Apr. 19, 1880; Josephine MASK, Apr. 20, 1891; Infant of Patiance & John MASK, Feb. 11, 1901; George R. MASK, (no date given).

LOT 292-A: Boran W. DURR, Aug. 7, 1863.

LOT 293-A: Sarah A. LINDSEY;
Remains ROSWELL, Sept. 9, 1856; Kate TALBOTT, July 25, 1883; Sarah M. LINDSEY, Sept. 4, 1886; Child of Thos. TALBOTT, Dec. 20, 1876; John R. LINZEY, Apr. 9, 1928.

LOT 294-A: Jno. M. VANDERGRIF;
Mary A. VANDERGRIFT, Dec. 5, 1855; Ada E. VANDERFRIFT, Jan. 30, 1860; Benj. VANDERGRIFT, May 20, 1864; John M. VANDERGRIFT, Jan. 20, 1862; Carrie V. VANDERGRIFT, Mar. 25, 1868.

LOT 295-A: Clara A. WEST;
Remains SPALDING, Aug. 14, 1855; Clara W. WEST, July 18, 1881; Lucy A. WEST, Aug. 6, 1917.

LOT 296-A: W. R. DAVIS;
Child, July 29, 1855; Emma DAVIS, July 12, 1860; Annie E. DAVIS, Nov. 20, 1862; Susan R. DAVIS, Aug. 8, 1867; Wm. DAVIS, Apr. 19, 1909; Susan S. DAVIS, May 18, 1909.

LOT 297-A: Elizabeth KREBS;
Rem(ains), May 5, 1856; Elizabeth KREBS, Jan. 10, 1865; George M. KREBS, Mar. 19, 1801; Mary J. KREBS, Jan. 26, 1918; George KREBS, Mar. 18, 1901.

LOT 298-A: Robert F. BONSELL;
Remains, Aug. 31, 1854; Martha E. FOGLER, Nov. 20, 1855; John S. FOGLER, July 18, 1857; Child of Robert BONSELL, (no date given); Robert H. RUSSELL, Nov. 15, 1858; Jas. H. RUSSELL, Jan. 17, 1867; John FOGLER, July 26, 1867; Minnie J. RUSSELL, Apr. 4, 1871; Hester M. RUSSELL, Apr. 26, 1873; Ann FOGLER, Aug. 5, 1875; Child of Saml. G. BOSNELL, Nov. 22, 1875; Ida M. FOGLER, May 24, 1880; Chas. R. WINKLER, Nov. 10, 1887; Martha A. FOGLER, Aug. 30, 1890.

LOT 299-A: John EBORALL (entry crossed out and Single Interments entered);
Joseph O. MAILHOT, Apr. 30, 1935; Anthony SHAULIS, May 3, 1935; Lulabelle PRICE, May 6, 1935; Margaret M. KILDOSS, May 11, 1935.

LOT 300-A: Margt. SICKLINE;
Mrs. SICKLIN, Dec. 16, 1852; Wm. SICKLIN, Oct. 20, 1856; Sarah WILCOX, Jan. 27, 1879.

LOT 301-A: Frances A. WINSATT;
Remains, Apr.16, 1855; Columbus NORMON, Mar. 28, 1853; Child of EMORY, July 19, 1856; Mr. COSLEY, May 1, 1863; Rose BEAN, Feb. 28, 1872; Jennie HALL, July 4, 1872; Frances F. WINSETT, Aug. 6, 1881; Phoe(be) A.NORWOOD, Dec. 31, 1891; Ann HALL, Apr. 19, 1895.

LOT 302-A: Thomas J. HARRISS;
Remains, June 15, 1854; James HARRISS, July 3, 1835; Nancy (no surname given), June 9, 1851; Kate F. POSTE, Aug. 8, 1847; Thos. J. HARRIS, Jan. 16, 1854. Affidavit found in Lot Book: Mrs. Ida Davis states she is sole survivor of her family and claims Lot 302 1/4 Section A, purchased by Thomas J. Harris, uncle of deceased husband.

LOT 303-A: Julia A. LYHANT;
Remains, Dec. 1, 1851; Mary LYHANT, May 7, 1867; Cath. A. WOLF, Nov. 7, 1870; Arabella WOLF, May 2(?), 1871; Julia LYHANT, July 11, 1874; Robert B. MULLIKIN, Jan. 15, 1897; Robert J. MULLIKIN, Sept. 11, 1899; Joseph LYHANT, July 26, 1907.

LOT 304-A: William FOWLER;
J. W. H. FOWLER, July 7, 1852; Child, Dec. 3, 1867; William FOWLER, Aug. 29, 1870; Susanna FOWLER, Jan. 21, 1871; FIDGET, Apr. 10, 1872.

LOT 305-A: Elizabeth FOSTER;
Remains, Nov. 28, 1856; Saml. FOSTER, Feb. 14, 1868; Child of H(ES)BBARD, Apr. 24, 1868; Child of Saml. HOLLAND, July 11, 1869; Elizabeth A. FOSTER, Nov. 25, 1884; Mary A. FOSTER, May 13, 1903; Elizabeth FOSTER, Nov. 10, 1904 (Date of Mar. 3, 1904 also given.).

LOT 306-A: STEWART and BARNES;
Archabold STARLING, Feb. 23, 1859; Rich DAVIS, June 30, 1861; Saml. F. BARNES, July 20, 1861; Chas. J. HELMLING, Dec. 6, 1864; Martha H. STEWART, Aug. 11, 1865; Saml. BARNES and John DAVIS, Feb. 4, 1860; Bessie STEWART, July 21, 1868; Ellen R. BARNES, Nov. 6, 1869; Willie F. STEWART, Sept. 6, 1870.

LOT 307-A: Single Interments (name Jno. F. BURT(OO)M crossed out);
John T. MASON, July 1, 1935; George DYKES, July 19, 1935; Annie O. KUMMILL, Aug. 23, 1935.

LOT 308-A: Harriott J. CHANDLER;
Harriott J. CHANDLER, Aug. 12, 1861; John Harry WALKER, Apr. 27, 1943; Saml. CHANDLER, July 22, 1847; Eliz. M. WALKER, Apr. 20, (19)66.

LOT 309-A: Harriot G. E. SPRIGG;
Remains, May 14, 1854; Horace SPRIGG, May 23, 1858; Harriet G. C. SPRIGG, June 21, 1859; Child of LEWIS, Apr. 25, 1863; Roger REED, July 2, 1869; Child, Sept. 15, 1870; Nathaniel SPRIGG, Mar. 23, 1876; Annie E. HISSEY, Sept. 1, 1876; Jennie HESSEY, Feb. 20, 1878; Elinna G. H. Hasey, Sept. 16, 1879; Rebecca SPRIGG, July 13, 1908; John A. HISSEY, Dec. 13, 1913; Horace SPRIGG, Mar. 15, 1894; Saml. (name on monument illegible), Apr. 11, 1822, b. in London, 1751.

LOT 310-A: Elizabeth GARRETT;
Robert GARRETT, Mar. 19, 1857; Remains, July 23, 1857; Elizabeth MASON, Oct. 6, 1862; Julian H. GARRETT, July 7, 1874; Child of Wm. A. GARRETT, Mar. 14, 1875; Elizabeth GARRETT, May 4, 1878; Frank GEESE, May 9, 1878; Robert W. GARRETT, Dec. 19, 1856; Mary GARRETT, Jan. 25, 1833; R. F. GARRETT, Jan. 19, 1876.

LOT 311-A: Arthur SHAW;
Mrs. (or Mia) SHAW, July 26, 1851; Thos. SHAW, Feb. 11, 1852.

LOT 312-A: Davidge MC CUBBIN;
Elizabeth FLETCHER, Jan. 30, 1857; Hester PURRIS, Feb. 12, 1857; Remains, Oct. 17, 1857; Frances BAILEY, Nov. 16, 1857; James BAILEY, Apr. 8, 1858; Child, Oct. 14, 1859; Child of CROW, June 24, 1861; Henrietta ASHLEY, Aug. 2, 1839; Millicent ASHLEY, Aug. 24, 1845.

LOT 313-A: Jno. HITZELBURGER;
Hannah HITZELBERGER, May 22, 1854; John W. CLAZZ, July 1, 1854; Adult, Aug. 20, 1866; Sarah WILLIAMS, Apr. 21, 1881; Stillborn of Nellie and William SELLY, July 26, 1910; Mary A. BURTON, July 19, 1905; Elizabeth RUARK, May 16, 1916; John W. SELLY, June 20, 1916; John (A.) B. HITZELBERGER, Mar. 22, 1929; Jane C. SQUIRES, Mar. 31, 1959.

LOT 314-A: Jno. J. KIRKWOOD;
Child, July 27, 1852; Child, Aug. 27, 1855; Child, July 28, 1864; William J. KIRKWOOD, Apr. 20, 1876; Stillborn, Mar. 17, 1880; Julia A. KIRKWOOD, July 23, 1881; Stillborn, Nov. 22, 1883; John KIRKWOOD, Apr. 10, 1897; Ella M. MILLER, Aug. 21, 1897; George R. CLIFT, Sr., Apr. 24, 1934; Ella M. KIRKWOOD, (no date given); Annie E. CLIFT, Feb. 18, 1939.

LOT 315-A: Patrick MC KEE;
Louisa EDWARDS, Mar. 23, 1853; Ann DYSART, Jan. 28, 1875; Lousia EDWARDS, July 31, 1852.

LOT 316-A: Mary J. SPIRES;
Mary A. SPIRES, Oct. 19, 1854; Martha E. MORRIS, Apr. 9, 1921; Ann SPIRES, Sept. 15, 1854.

LOT 317-A: Sarah E. SHANAHAN;
Mrs. SHANNAHAN, Sept.8, 1854; Mary SHANNAHAN, Oct. 6, 1858; M. A. JACKSON, June 27, 1861; Sarah E. TAYLOR, Oct. 21, 1914.

LOT 318-A: Jos. S. WOODS;
Clintonia STOCKETT, Sept. 3, 1870; Child, Sept. 28, 1871; Bettie STOCKETT, Feb. 27, 1877; Bessie DULEY, Aug. 12, 1879; Georgana DULEY, Oct. 15, 1883.

LOT 319-A: Alex. R. MADERY;
Alexandra MADERY, Apr. 4, 1858; Cyrus MEDARY, Nov. 11, 1894; Kate MEDARY, June 6, 1904; Wm. H. MEDARY, Jan. 5, 1912; Lavenia MEDARY, Mar. 20, 1912.

LOT 320-A: Shipley LESTER;
Elizabeth WALTHAM, Aug. 9, 1855 (died July 31, 1855); William WALTHAM, Apr. 23, 1859; Nancy MC KENLY, Dec. 1, 1861; John WAL-THAM, Apr. 1, 1822.

LOT 321-A: Sarah HIGH;
Remains, Dec. 20,1855; S. HIGH, Aug. 8, 1861; Child of Henry HIGH, Feb. 7, 1874; George HIGH, Feb. 3, 1885; Jos. R. SUTTON, Feb. 26, 1891.

LOT 322-A: Saml. LINTHICUM;
Samuel LINTHICUM, May 13, 1886; Lillie S. LINTHICUM, July 23, 1886; Alice M. HURLEY, Apr. 4, 1886; Andrew HURLEY, July 7, 1890; Chas. H. LINTHICUM, Feb. 11, 1899; Wm. E. ASHLEY, Nov. 17, 1900; Edwd, E. LINTHICUM, Aug. 5, 1912; John QUAIL, Mar. 14, 1919; John QUAIL, Feb. 12, 1920 (One of these John QUAIL's was a child which died age 9 days old).

LOT 323-A: Annie E. ROBEY (entry crossed out and James W. ROBEY entered);
James F. ROBEY,Aug. 25, 1917; Stillborn of George NORTH, Mar. 13, 1922; Annie E. ROBEY, Apr. 27, 1927; Anna ROBEY, Mar. 4, 1961; James W. ROBEY, Apr. 14, 1952.

LOT 324-A: Unsold.

LOT 325-A: Cathrin LAWTON;
Child, May 20, 1856; Rem(ains) ARMSTRONG, Aug. 16, 1856; E. J. BOWEN, Jan. 2, 1869; Emily MADGRICK, Oct. 17, 1871 (surname also spelled MEDGRICK); Chas. H. LAWTON, Dec. 9, 1879; Mary E. LAWTON, Feb. 19, 1888.

LOT 326-A: Daniel SPEDDEN;
Remains, Dec. 13, 1855; Emily A. SPEDDEN, Apr. 14, 1857 (Date Jan. 17, 1857 also given); David B. SPEDDEN, Nov. 20, 1857 (Date Aug. 30, 1857 also given); Child of (DANVILLE), Aug. 4, 1860; Emma SPEDDEN, Nov. 25, 1855.

LOT 327-A: Margt. SEVERSON;
Sarah MC (CLUSE), Feb. 25, 1865; Eliza SEVERSON, Mar. 6, 1866; John SEVERSON, May 16, 1845; Maggie CAYER, May 5, 1845.

LOT 328-A: Jno. W. SUTTON, transferred to Chas. H. JONES, Jr., and wife;
Philener FLOYD, Mar. 14, 1861; Child of GRANGER, June 17, 1861; Saml. K. THOMAS, May 29, 1863.

LOT 329-A: Lydia MATHEWS;
Addie (I.) JONES, Oct. 2, 1917; Marie J. HAEFFNER, Oct. 6, 1919; Arthur JONES, Jan. 7, 1942.

LOT 330-A: Levin FREEMAN;
Rem(ains) STEWART, July 21, 1864; Lydia STEWART, Mar. 19, 1872; Levin FREEMAN, Feb. 22, 1898; Sarah I. FREEMAN, Jan. 9, 1899.

LOT 331-A: Benj. and Dorsey BERRY;
Remains, June 4, 1851; Sidney E. BERRY, Mar. 26, 1860; Ellen BERRY, Mar. 24, 1860; Benj. D. BERRY, May 8, 1866; Child of E. D. BERRY, Dec. 6, 1870; B. D. BERRY, Sept. 21, 1872; Mary E. BERRY, July 18, 1876; Edwd. Daisy BERRY, Apr. 8, 1879; Edwd. D. BERRY, July 12, 1880; Alice L. BERRY, Jan. 25, 1881; Elizabeth E. BERRY, Sept. 24, 1883; Benj. BERRY, Nov. 30, 1888; John A. HISSEY,Jan. 16, 1911. Authorization for burials in this lot are to be from Wm. J. Berry.

LOT 332-A: Matilda C. NEWELL;
Rem(ains) MARSH, Aug. 20, 1852; Cecelia NEWELL, Apr. 19, 1855; Jas. NEWELL, July 15, 1859; Child of RICHTER, Aug. 14, 1857; Mary E. NEWELL, Feb. 26, 1858; Mrs. FLOYD, Jan. 13, 1864; George MARSH, July 19, 1865; Child, June 18, 1867; Martha E. NEWELL, Jan. 20, 1913.

LOT 333-A: Jno. WILLIAMS;
George W. WILLIAMS, Jan. 26, 1853; Child, Feb. 7, 1866; Rebecca MILLER, Nov. 26, 1898.

LOT 334-A: Chas. RIDGLEY;
Wm. S. MUTH, Aug. 15, 1904; Stillborn of E. & H. SMITH, May 5, 1906; Stillborn of E. & H. SMITH, Feb. 15, 1907; Stillborn of E. & h.SMITH, July 6, 1909; George W. MUTH, July 25, 1932; Hortence E. MUTH, Mar. 15, 1933; Elenora M. KREBS, Oct. 14, 1947.

LOT 335-A: Nicholas RIDGELY;
Child of M(asker), Aug. 16, 1852; Nicholas RIDGELY, Mar. 2, 1860 (Date of Jan. 24, 1860 is also given); Casper WEAVER, Feb. 26, 1861 (Date of Feb. 3, 1862 is also given); Ann RIDGLEY, Nov. 22, 1875 (Date of Mar. 20, 1875 is also given); Mary RINGLAND, July 2, 1881.

LOT 336-A: James WHEELER;
Ellen CORMAN, July 16, 1851; Mollie E. WHEELER, Dec. 17, 1915; Jessie L. WHEELER, Aug. 28, 1878, also Maud and Maggie; Jas. A. WHEELER, Mar. 26, 193(0).

LOT 337-A: William HILL;
William HILL, Jr., Dec. 3, 1851; William H. H. HILL, June 17, 1856; Jos. HILL, Feb. 12, 1857; Elizabeth HILL, June 7, 1884;

Josephine BUFTER, May 26, 1888; William H. HILL, Aug. 30, 1900; Mary (H)ILL, Mar. 20, 1873.

LOT 338-A: Elarkin RAYMOND;
Benj. RAYMOND, Jan. 14, 1857; Lizzie RAYMOND, Feb. 1, 1876 (Date of Jan. 30, 1876 is also given); Annie E. RAYMOND, Nov. 13, 1902; One space reads "Wm. Wingate Harry Benj. Childs Raymond".

LOT 339-A: Sarah S. WALKER;
Chas. C. DUVAL, Aug. 14, 1865; Sallie S. SALISABURY, Oct. 15, 1870; Sarah R. WALKER, Mar. 26,1872; Ethel BARTHOMLEW, May 8, 1897 (surname also spelled BARTHOLMLEW); Saml. T.WALKER, Apr. 29, 1904; John H. WALKER, Mar. 15, 1905; Edith (I.) MANSTER, July 17, 1906; Georgie E. WALKER, Dec. 18, 1931.

LOT 340-A: John THOMPSON, Martin DEPELL;
Sarah THOMPSON, July 12, 1872; John THOMPSON, Aug. 27, 1877; Stillborn, Oct. 7, 1879; William REESE, Mar. 17, 1882; James C. ORR, (Oct.) 1, 1898; Edith ORR, Sept. 23, 1893.

LOT 341-A: David HAYS;
Emily HAYS, June 1, 1853; Frances V. HAYS, Aug. 16, 1855; Child, July 29, 1860; Chas. A. HAYS, Mar. 30, 1863; Chas. WOOLF, Sept. 9, 1863; Walter E. HAYS, July 11, 1864; Child, Oct. 16, 1866.

LOT 342-A: Jane TALBOTT;
Jane TALBOTT, Jan. 2, 1851; Joseph TALBOTT, Dec. 5, 1851 (or 1857); Mrs. LYONS, Jan. 24, 1852 (Probably the same as Nancy LYONS, Jan. 23, 1852).

LOT 343-A: William B. FRANK;
Child,July 21,1851; Mary A. FRANK, Aug. 18, 1851; Alverda FRANK, Dec. 26, 1851; Alice FRANK, Dec. 15, 1853; Wm. B. FRANK, Aug.25, 1859.

LOT 344-A: Jos. B. RICHARDSON;
Gennet(he) APPLE(GISTH), May 5, 1858; Jos. B. RICHARDSON, Apr. 1, 1859 ("Came to his death with a pistol shot"); Child, Mar. 24, 1860; Thos. RICHARDSON, Oct. 30, 1869; John C. RICHARDSON, June 4, 1880; Frances RICHARDSON, Dec. 19, 1893; Jos. C. RICHARDSON, Sept. 21, 1910; Calvin J. RICHARDSON, Apr. 23, 19(2)7; Dave (or Dora) RICHARDSON, Nov. 20, 1936; Joseph Vincent RICHARDSON, June 21, 1939; Thos. (O.) (nosurname given), Nov. 28, 1866; Ann M. (no surname given), Mar. 30, 1860; Joseph (no surname given), 6 weeks.

LOT 345-A: A. J. HOLTZMAN is crossed out and Single Interments is entered;
Michael J. FITZGERALD, Sept. 21, 1935; Child, Jan. 23 1853; Mrs. (HOPKINS), May 8, 1862; Violet SCHAMM, Sept. 9, 1935; Laura M. YOUNG, Aug. 31, 1935; Adolph MEYER, Aug. 2, 1935.

LOT 346-A: Hanson WALLACE;
Remains, Apr. 12, 1853; Hanson WALLACE, Sept. 14, 1859; Susan E. WALLCAE, July 17, 1866; Child, July 12, 1870; William WALLACE, May 28, 1872, U.S. Navy; George N. WALLACE, July 12, 1850; John A. WALLACE, July 11, 1874; John A. WALLACE, July 11, 1874 (Apparently there are two John Wallace's); Stillborn, Nov. 13,

1878; Susan WALLACE, Mar. 29, 1881; Merison WALLACE, Sept. 12, 1859; Stillborn of WALLACE, Aug. 1, 1885.

LOT 347-A: James W. SPRIGGS;
Child of HOLTYN, July 27, 1852; Henson W. SPRIGG, Dec. 5, 1853; Chas. H. SPRIGG, Aug. 31, 1854; Margt. R. SPRIGG, Aug. 9, 1859; Benj. DAVIS, July 21, 1869 (In same grave are Marion and Bazel, no surname is entered); Child of MILK, July 22, 1870; Jas. W. SPRIGGS, Apr. 22, 1891; Mary SPRIGG, Apr. 25, 1891; Margt R. SPRIGG, Oct. 15, 1892; (Si)ngleton SPRIGG, Aug. 20, 1917; Mary E. SPRIGG, Apr. 3, 19(2)6; Margaret R. SPRIGG, June 14, 1854.

LOT 348-A: Elmer E. CROUSE, Joseph M. HAWKINS, Mary A. TREMPER, and Almieda MICHAEN;
Lilitia A. HARDY, Oct. 12, 1854; Alminda MICHION, June 27, 1881; George MICHAEN, Sept. 21, 1882; Dr. Thos. (J.) MICHAEN, Mar. 11, 1895; Almindor, Thos. and George Michaen removed to Loudon Park Nov. 8, 1909; Cath. MICHAEN, Oct. 4, 1865; Herman TRIMPER, June 8, 1940; Estella May HAWKINS, Apr. 24, 1939.

LOT 349-A: George S. MARTIN;
Maria MARTIN, and child, Nov. 6, 1854; George S. MARTIN, Mar. 12, 1858; Elizabeth MARTIN, Mar. 8, 1858; Jos. WILLEY, Mar. 29, 1860; Mary MARTIN, May 1, 1862; George S. MARTIN, Nov. 25, 1864; Child, Jan. 1, 1867; Chas. BEAUCHAMP, Feb. 12, 1867; Chas. BEAUCHAMP, Aug. 6, 1870; Caroline BEAUCHAMP, Feb. 3, 1873; George A. BEAU-CHAMP, July 3, 1870.

LOT 350-A: Mary SUMMERS;
Mary SUMMERS, Aug. 1, 1860; Isaac HARLOW, Oct. 25, 1869.

LOT 351-A: Ellen JONES;
Remains, Oct. 11, 1854; James T. JONES, Oct. 14, 1890; Annie E. HARRISON, Nov. 3, 1894; Cath. STARLING, July 17, 1905; Ellen A. JONES, Sept. 6, 1907.

LOT 352-A: Mary E. SEGUIN;
Rem(ains), DAVIS, Dec. 10, 1855; 3 children disinterred from 2 graves Feb. 8, 1887; Mary E. DAYTON, Jan. 10, 1857; Removed from Cathedral (Cemetery), May 16, 1887; Mary E. SEGUM, Aug. 26, 1896; R. L. (J.) SEGUIN, June 13, 1904; Charles H. SEGUIN, July 22, 1941.

LOT 353-A: Zachues DURHAM;
Rem(ains), Dec. 20, 1855; Mary DURHAM, Sept. 1, 1863; Zachues DURHAM, Jan. 28, 1865; Assian WOODEN, Jan. 31, 1846; Mary DURHAM, Aug.30, 1863.

LOT 354-A: Harriott GILSON;
Ann E. GILSON, Oct. 20, 1856.

LOT 355-A: Unused.

LOT 356-A: Unsued.

LOT 357-A: Susan B. WILLIAMS;
Remains, May 26, 1856; Child, July 6, 1858; Susan WILLIAMS, Feb. 22, 1863; Wm. T. WILLIAMS, Dec. 28, 1867; (Illegible stone), Oct. 7, 1857.

LOT 358-A: William ROSS;
William G. ROSS, Nov. 16, 1859; Child of DURHAM, Sept. 8, 1860; George S. WRIGHT, Aug. 6, 1872; Frank ROSS, Jan. 8, 1908; Jas. A. BENNETT, Feb. 3, 1925; John H. BENNETT, Nov. 5, 1936; Wm. G. ROSS, Mar. 15, 1819.

LOT 359-A: Jno. H. JONES;
Child, May 9, 1855; Elizabeth TAYLOR, Jan. 15, 1858; Thos. STARLING, Feb. 16, 1859; John JONES, Nov. 7, 1868; Edwd. T.JONES, Nov. 15, 1881; John H. JONES, Oct. 27, 1888; Alice L. DAVIS, July 4, 1892; Mary JONES, July 13, 1893; Irene DAVIS, Sept. 10, 1894; Stillborn of A. L. and G. N. DAVIS, May 20, 1895; Chas. M. (J.) JONES, Dec. 8, 1902; John M. JONES, Oct. 26, 1959; John JONES, (no date given).

LOT 360-A: William STONE;
Child, Dec. 1, 1861; Johannah STONE, May 22, 1882; Carrie V. STONE, Jan. 14, 1887; Caroline STONE, Feb. 23, 1903; Wm. T. STONE, July 10, 1907; Wm. B. STONE, July 1, 1914; Joshua STONE, May 22, 1882.

LOT 361-A: Ann TAYLOR;
Remains, Dec. 30, 1854; Ann RENBLE, Jan. 13, 1854; Sarah J. FOUNCE, Oct. 27, 1866; Ann TAYLOR, Apr. 22, 1870; Chas. H. WALTON, Sept. 16,1871; John E. WALTON, Nov. 25, 1871; Child of (Wm.) ALLEN, Jan. 18, 1876; Carmelia ROSTMAN, June 14, 1879; Philip ROSTMAN, July 19, 1879; Clara D. WALTON, Nov. 15, 1883; Kate ROSTMAN, Nov. 15, 1883.

LOT 362-A: Chas. R. HARDESTY;
George WOODFORD, Apr. 12, 1857.

LOT 363-A: Elizabeth MARTIN;
Sophia HALL, Jan. 26, 1863; Mary HALL, Mar. 17, 1870; Wells A. ASH(CROFT), Oct. 22, 1879; M. M. ROCKFORD, Oct. 17, 1881; Joseph M. ROCKFORD, Apr. 22, 1885; Annie HALL, July 6, 1887; Herman (J.) MARTIN,Sept. 17, 1897.

LOT 364-A: Elizabeth WORKING;
Elizabeth WORKING, Feb. 19, 1855; Henry WORKING, Jan. 9, 1870.

LOT 365-A: William H. HIGDON;
2 children, Aug. 11, 1852; Lydia A. HIGDON, Nov. 1, 1863; Child, Apr. 29, 1871; Maggie HIGDON, July 9, 1879; William BROWN, July 13, 1886; Infant of HIGDON, Feb. 18, 1887; Infant of Annie and Wm. KELLY, Jan. 29, 1897; Elizabeth LATHE, Nov. 16, 1906; Mary J. HIGDON, Apr. 10, 1862; Zenobia HIGDON, Sept. 1, 1909; Wm. H. HIGDON, Aug. 23, 1890; Mary J. HIGDON, Apr. 10, 1862.

LOT 366-A: Elizabeth BLAKE;
Elizabeth BLAKE, Oct. 17, 1857; Saml. G. OWENS, Dec. 28, 1862; Saml. H. THOMAS, June 4, 1862; M. V. THOMAS, Jan. 7, 1862; Child, Nov. 3, 1866; Hester DAVIS, Feb. 24, 1874; Lilly M. WILSON, May 23, 1874; 3 children, July 13, 1877; Bell WILSON, Jan. 14, 1882; George W. SPINK, Oct. 4, 1913; Annie SPINK, Mar. 28, 191(1).

LOT 367-A: Jessie BROMLEY;
Child, Apr. 15, 1852; Mrs. BROMLEY, Nov. 20, 1854; Jos. BROMLEY, July 20, 1855; Wm. T. BROMLEY, May 3, 1864; Child, Jan. 11, 1872;

Stillborn of J. BROMLEY, Mar. 26, 1878; Zenobia (surname illegible), Sept. 1, 1909 (entry crossed out).

LOT 368-A: Jno. H. FOSS;
Elizabeth FOSS, July 24, 1859; Geo. T. KNIGHT, Nov. 21, 1863; Jacob FOSS, Apr. 17, 1871; John A. FOSS, Feb. 4, 1875; Wm. CROUCH, Jan. 7, 1879; William T. KNIGHT, Oct. 13, 1881; Jas. E. KNIGHT, Aug. 13, 1876.

LOT 369-A: Jno. WOODMAN;
Rhoda SEMISTON, Aug. 16, 1852; George BELL, June 17, 1861; Jno. W. WOODMAN, Oct. 7, 1863; Mary Ann WOODMAN, Oct. 7, 1863; John WOODMAN, July 17, 1874; Saml. MARTIN, Oct. 4, 1876; Sarah E. ZIMMERMAN, July 29, 1878.

LOT 370-A: Jane CROW;
Sarah STONE, Jan. 5, 1855; Child of WILLIAMS, July 30, 1855; Mrs. DAMAR, Mar. 22, 1861; Mrs. CROW, May 8, 1861.

LOT 371-A: John SEDDICUM;
Remains, Nov. 1, 1871; Edwd. T. SEDICUMB, June 28, 1859; Wm. G. SEDICUMB, Aug. 15, 1865; Rose CASTLEMAN, June 7, 1880 (Removed from cemetery Oct. 6, 1881); Elizabeth SEDICUM, Oct. 21, 1882; Matilda SEDICUM, Jan. 14, 1896; John S. SEDICUM, Jan. 16, 1908; Lum ANDEKIN, b. 1794, d. 1844.

LOT 372-A: Henry COLLIER;
Annie M. COHA, Jan. 1, 1855; Mary EARL, Aug. 6, 1856; Fredk. MERRITT, Sept. 22, 1871.

LOT 373-A: Frank BEEBEE;
Peter HOOVER, Dec. 18, 1863; Chas.E. NEWTON, Oct. 28, 1891; Chas E. NEWTON, Jan. 15, 1875; Harry W. BEEBEE, Mar. 27, 1897; Laura May BEEBE, Nov. 16, 1946; Frank C. BEEBE, June 18, 1940.

LOT 374-A: Elizabeth FURLONG;
Remains, June 27, 1851; Thos. FURLONG, July 3, 1851; Elizabeth FURLONG, Jan. 3, 1865; Elizabeth FURLONG, Apr. 14, 1865; Remains, Dec. 12, 1861; Eliza FURLONG, Apr. 3, 1880; Elizabeth FURLONG, May 5, 1887; Frances M. BANGS, Jr., Mar. 30, 1842.

LOT 375-A: John COULTER;
Mary COULTER, Jan. 23, 1857; Peter HOOVER, June 6, 1876.

LOT 376-A: Greenbury CARR;
Child, Jan. 8, 1852; Emma R. CARR, July 2, 1856; Jone V. WILLIAMS, July 13, 1866; Child, Oct. 20, 1867; Elizabeth CARR, Aug, 10, 1870; Child of Daniel ENSOR, Dec. 19, 1870; Child of J. T. WILLIAMS, Dec.5, 1872; Greenbury CARR, Mar. 7, 1881.

LOT 377-A: Jno. T. WALL;
Remains, May 9, 1851; Remains, May 14, 1852; John W. MILLER, July 22, 1910; John T. WALL, Nov. 6, 1922; Howard GARRISON, b. Apr. 26, 1901, d. Apr. 9, 1970, buried Apr.13, 1970.

LOT 378-A: Thomas HIGDON;
Child, Aug. 7, 1857; Amanda TAYLOR, June 19, 1853; Alelia TAYLOR, Jan. 14, 1858; Wm. TAYLOR, June 4, 1858; Ann TAYLOR, Dec. 28, 1863; Willie HIGDON, July 30, 1868; Elizabeth TAYLOR, Oct. 21,

1872, child beneath; Wm. F. HIGDON, Mar. 6, 1877; George W. HIGDON, Feb. 25, 1882.

LOT 379-A: Harriot HIGDON;
Child, May 28, 1858; Wm. T. HIGDON, Oct. 28, 1863; M. C. HIGDON, Feb. 13, 1869; Child, July 11, 1869; Wife of Jos. HIGDON, Dec. 11, 1869; Child of Jos. HIGDON, Nov. 15, 1869; Child, Mar. 24, 1871; Robert HIGDON, July 2, 1880; Mary HIGDON, July 27, 1880; Harriet HIGDON, May 21, 1871; Jos. HIGDON (no date given); Ralph HIGDON, Jun 6, 1858.

LOT 380-A: Irvin TAYLOR;
Child, Aug. 10, 1858; Prescilla ADAMS, Sept.12, 1860; Martha A. TAYLOR, Aug. 10, 1863; Child, Aug. 9, 1868; George T. TAYLOR, Jan. 14, 1870; Nancy P. TAYLOR, Aug. 18, 1890; Wm. HENTZE, Oct. 20, 1899; Irvin TAYLOR, June 5, 1908; Stillborn of Gertrude ZEULLIN, Aug. 18, 1908; Thos. TAYLOR, Aug.2, 1873; Wm. Elmer HUKE, July 14, 1877.

LOT 381-A: Thomas G. FLOOD;
Thomas A. FLOOD, Feb. 7, 1854; Martha VALIENT, July 2, 1882; Elizabeth FLOOD, Feb. 2, 1888.

LOT 382-A: Mary FURGERSON;
Wm. FERGERSON, Apr. 23, 1853; Mary FERGERSON, Aug. 6, 1860; Adult, Feb. 5, 1864.

LOT 383-A: S. and M. FISHBURN;
Sophia TAYLOR, Jan. 9, 1824.

LOT 384-A: Joseph COSTER (surname may be CORTER);
Maggie E. COSTER, May 7, 1859; Nora L. COSTER, Aug. 10, 1861; Wilber H. COSTER, Jan. 1, 1871; P. R. COSTER, Aug. 12, 1873; L. F. COSTER, July 26, 1873; George E. COSTER, Sept. 8, 1876; Frank E. COSTER, Mar. 13, 1878; Etta V. COSTER, Dec. 30, 1866; Mary E. COSTER, Nov. 6, 1859; Joseph L. COSTER, Jan. 19, 1861; Wm. Elijah COSTER, Nov. 29, 1868; Joseph COSTER, Mar. 23, 1881.

LOT 385-A: Leory C. ROSS;
Child of WRIGHT, Mar. 23, 1868; Lillie A. WRIGHT, Aug. 22, 1869; Child of S. WRIGHT, June 12, 1871; Charlotte ROSS, Feb. 18, 1874; Jos. W. BELL, June 22, 1875; Chas. S(U)KE, Feb. 28, 1879 (surname may be SICK or SICKE); Mary Ellen BELL, Dec. 18, 1880; WILLIAM H. BELL, Dec. 28, 1881; Leory C. ROSS, June 19, 1888; Laura V. WAITE, Apr. 22, 1886.

LOT 386-A: Sarah A. WATERTON;
Elisha DICKENSON, Aug. 11, 1856; George M. TAYLOR, Dec. 22, 1865; Grace TAYLOR, Feb. 7, 1876; Ann DEMPSTER, Jan. 17, 1883; Sarah Ann TAYLOR, Dec. 29, 1913; Sarah A. TYLER, Dec. 3, 1920; "Copied from monument: Mary Ann DICKERSON, Sept. 23, 1852; Mary Ann DICKERSON, July 3, 1944; Elisha DICKERSON, Sept. 25, 1843; Mary Ann DICKERSON, Sept. 15, 1844; Remains of previous 4 brought here Sept. 19, 1859." Ann G. TAYLOR, Feb. 6,1876; George WATERTON, July 11, 1841.

LOT 387-A: Empty lot.

LOT 388-A: Empty lot.

LOT 389-A: Perry BECK;
Remains, Nov. 28, 1856; Mary E. BECK, Feb. 17, 1870; Child, June 10, 1871; Emma V. BECK, Oct. 28, 1856; John E. BECK, Oct. 30, 1937.

LOT 390-A: John P. HOOPER;
Remains, Dec. 20, 1855; Caston LECOMPT, June 8, 1819; Mary V. (no surname given), July 30, 1838.

LOT 391-A: Amanda SARBAUGH;
Capt. J. SAUBAUGH, Sept. 14, 1862; Amanda M. TATHAM, Jan. 24, 1872; Amanda SLAUGHTER, Dec. 30, 1890; Anna H. BROOKS, Jan. 17, 1801 (or 1901); Chas. BROOKS, Sept. 9, 1902; Mary Ann WHITE, Mar. 7, 1904; George E. BROOK, May 16, 1905; Amanda SARBOUGH, (no date given).

LOT 392-A: Jno. F. BALDWIN;
William SCHWARTZE, June 8, 1856; Child of WELCH, Mar. 15, 1861; Rachel BURNS, Jan. 26, 1855; Edythe Ray HELLMANN, Apr. 23, 1951; C. Joseph HELLMANN, Oct. 31, 1958; Other names found in record not necessarily deceased are: Mrs. Richard WORTHINGTON, and Francis J. HELLMANN.

LOT 393-A: Alex P. BROWN;
Nicholas S. BROWN, Sept. 6, 1854; Rem(ains), May 18, 1854; Rachel BROWN, Dec. 14, 1854; E. TRAINOR, Feb. 5, 1883; John R. TRAINOR, June 5, 1865; Edna Lee WARD, July 15, 1886; Hattie B. WASHEY, May 22, 1889.

LOT 394-A: Robert GABLE;
Ann E. MARTIN, Oct. 30, 1864; Nicholas FORRESTER, Nov.2, 1873; Jas. MC CRACKEN, Mar. 27, 1874; Child of Robert CREIGHTON, Jan. 18, 1876; Ann E. FORESTER, July (23), 1877; Ida C. FORESTER, Oct. 29, 1879; Ida V. CREIGHTON, July 15, 1882; Wm. H. GALBE, Apr. 16, 1884; Child of Wm. CHANEY, Oct. 8, 1894; Robert G. FOSTER, Dec. 31, 1887.

LOT 395-A: William HOOFNAGLE;
Jos. R. HOFFNAGLE, Sept. 7, 1871; Robert GRABE, July 18, 1887; Owan D. BURGESS, Nov. 16, 1899; Risenard CLARK, Oct. 7, 1910.

LOT 396-A: E. E. ZEANNERET;
Child of STOCKMAN, July 3, 1852; Jane T. STOCKMAN, Aug. 12, 1857; Child, May 1, 1860; Child of STOCKMAN, May 4, 1861; Child, May 9, 1866; Child, Feb. 2, 18(78); Zelin ZENNERET, July 9, 1889 (Date of July 11, 1889 is also given).

LOT 397-A: Ellen PARSON;
Child, June 12, 1872; Child of John PARSONS, Aug. 16, 1873; Child, Aug.1, 1874; Joseph M. PARSONS, Mar. 8, 1883; Elmer PARSON, July 23, 1892; Wm. PARSONS, Dec. 23, 1895; Elenor PARSONS, July 23, 1892.

LOT 398-A: James WHEELER, Clara L. GERICK;
Rem(ains), Mar. 1, 1852; John H. KOSTER, Oct. 2, 1854; Benj. WHEELER, Oct. 6, 1858; Edwd. L. WHEELER, Aug. 30,1875; Sallie M. WHEELER, Feb. 25, 1875; Ella M. WHEELER, Apr. 4, 1876; Robert E. MACKINSON, July 17, 1917 (Surname possibly MAKINSON).

LOT 399-A: James F. DAVIS;
Child, Dec. 23, 1851; Elizabeth B. DAVIS, Mar. 28, 1935; Ella BURGESS, June 12, 1937; Ann D. BURGESS, Mar. 1, 1939.

LOT 400-A: Thomas J. MAYS;
Remains, June 23, 1851; Wala F. MAYS, May 17, 1856; Child of TAYLOR, Oct. 3, 1856; Vernon A. REDLFIELD, May 11, 1892.

LOT 401-A: William H. WOODWARD;
Frank M. WOODWARD, child, Feb. 9, 1859; Wm. H. WOODWARD, Jan. 10, 1887; Wm. W. WOODWARD, June 5, 1909; Julia A. WOODWARD, Aug. 2, 1909; Emma L. GORSUCH, Aug, 8, 1927.

LOT 402-A: Rebecca MOFFIT;
Rem(ains) DORSEY, July 9, 1851; Jas. B. DORSEY, June 23, 1853; Child, Dec. 1, 1872; Jos. MOFFITT, Dec. 5, 1883, from Ireland; Hannah KINSELLA, Nov. 27, 1905; Rebecca MOFFITT, Sept. 15, 1894; Chas. REANEY, July 30, 1906; Mary REANEY, Sept.16, 1906; Evelyn REANEY, Sept. 29, 1911; All REANEY children, Sept. 29, 19(26); Elizabeth DEHN, Nov. 1, 1887.

LOT 403-A: Elijah POTTER;
Remains, June 26, 1851; Elizabeth POTTER, Apr. 29, 1872; Elizabeth POTTER, May 23, 1891; Elijah POTTER, Apr. 27, 1872.

LOT 404-A: George BELL;
Henry W. DIDENHOVER, Apr. 24, 1909; Remains, Oct. 17, 1851; Almarilla LEE, Sept. 23, 1853; John BELL, Oct. 19, 1865; Sarah BELL, July 8, 1876; Clara A. BELL, June 17, 1878; Rem(oved) from Western (Cemetery), May 30, 1880; Elizabeth BELL, Oct. 4, 1890; Chas. B. DIDEDHOVER, Oct. 15, 1898; Margt. LONG, Mar. 21, 1900; Harry R. DIDENHOVER, July 1, 1901; Margt A. LONG, Aug. 24, 1904, removed to Washington; Ida Clara DIDENHOVER, Jan. 9, 1946; Chas. A. BELL, (no date given).

LOT 405-A: W. L. RICHARDSON;
Wm. V. RICHARDSON, Nov. 7, 1855; Child, Jan. 21, 1867; Emma Jane RICHARDSON, May 6, 1875; Wm. L. RICHARDSON, July 27, 1877; Julia A. RICHARDSON, Aug. 3, 1899.

LOT 406-A: Mary THOMPSON;
Remains, June 21, 1851; Elizabeth ARNOLD, July 6, 1872; John T. and Lewis ARNOLD, Mar. 4, 1878; Mary THOMPSON, Jan. 3, 1879.

LOT 407-A: John MITCHELL;
Remains, May 13, 1857; Margt. MITCHELL, July 18, 1863; Sarah BRATT, Aug. 27, 1868; Child of John BELSCHNER, Feb. 23, 1872; Saml. MITCHELL, Sept.13, 1875; John T. MITCHELL, Dec. 28, 1876; Child of BELSCHNER, Apr. 1, 1877; Stillborn, Apr. 10, 1880; Infant of Jno. MITCHELL, Mar. 21, 1883; George R. MITCHELL, Nov. 11, 1891; Saml. MITCHELL, Jan. 9, 1909; Sarah A. MITCHELL, Mar. 17, 1913; John R. MITCHELL, Nov.10, 1891; Wm. MITCHELL, (no date given); Frances MITCHELL, Feb. 20, 1844.

LOT 408-A: Mary C. COALMAN;
Saml. COLEMAN, Sept.19, 1851; Mary DENNY, July 13, 1901; Saml. COLEMAN, Apr. 25, 1847.

LOT 409-A: Michael HUSTON; No record of burials.

LOT 410-A: Margt. GALLGHER; Records for this lot in Lot 427-A.

LOT 411-A: Thomas H. PIERPOINT;
Child, May 14, 1864; Thomas S. PIERPOINT, July 7, 1865; Chas. SHINNICK, Sept. 16, 1867; Thos. S. CROSLY, July 30, 1872 (Surname possibly CROSBY).

LOT 412-A: Rich LINDSEY; Records for this lot in Lot 425-A.

LOT 413-A: John J. HARRORD (or HANORD); No records for this lot.

LOT 414-A: Sarah ELLIOTT;
Remains, June 15, 1858; _____ CHILDS, June 2, 1864; _____ CHILDS, Sept. 1, 1874; Gorden B. ELLIOTT, Oct. 6, 1890; Lillian (J.) ELLIOTT, Mar. 22, 1902; Edward (G.) ELLIOTT, Aug. 12, 1919; Saml. A. ELLIOTT, Oct. 6, 192(7); Gideon ELLIOTT, (no date given); Sarah E. ELLIOTT, (no date given); Allie F. ELLIOTT, Jan. 25, 1937.

LOT 415-A: William H. MALE;
Wm. H. MALE, July 25, 1865, Co. H, 5th Md. Inf.; Maggie HOLLAND, Jan. 17, 1881; Mary E. MALE, July 19, 1881; Jos. MALE, May 16, 1892; Elizabeth MALE, Apr. 24, 1893; Jeremiah SPAIGHT, July 15, 1902; Jos. J. RIGLY, May 10, 1824; Maggie HOLLAND appears twice.

LOT 416-A: Robert C. MILES;
Elizabeth WHELER, Nov. 26, 1861; Mary A. MILES, Jan. 3, 1867; Child, Aug. 12, 1867; Robert MYERS, June 18, 1868; Robert C. MILES, Aug. 25, 1875; The name Robert MYERS appears twice.

LOT 417-A: Marie LOANE;
Rem(ains), Oct. 19, 1855; Ann WATKINS, May 1, 1856; Mary A. DENBOREN, May 5, 1887 (Surname also spelled DENBORE); Mary A. DENBER, May 25, 1887; Julia A. DENBORE, Apr. 20, 1918; Abraham DENBOER, Oct. 29, 1820; Julia (no surname given), July 6, 1847.

LOT 418-A: William W. OUSLER;
Anna E. OUSLER, May 6, 1856; Curtis OUSLER, Mar. 23, 1872; Wm. W. OUSLER, July 14, 1893.

LOT 419-A: Jno. W. WOODS; See Lot 448 for information.

LOT 420-A: John CROUCH;
Bertamin ROBERTS, May 21, 1870; George ROBERTS, June 23, 1870; Eva B. CRAIG, May 1, 1877; Sarah E. ROBINSON, July 20, 1877; Carrie W. JOHNSON, Oct. 2, 1880; Eva KELLY, Apr. 25, 1883; Lenn CRAIG, Feb. 25, 1883; Mary CRAIG, Jan. 28, 1890; Calvin K. MIT- CHELL, Apr. 5, 1890; Frances SCHNAILL, Aug. 8, 1896; Ella M. RITCHIE, July 21, 1923.

LOT 421-A: James PAUL;
James PAUL, May 11, 1875; Mary T. PAUL, Oct. 16, 1880.

LOT 422-A: Fred. HAGNER;
Susannah HAGNER, June 28, 1854; Mary A. WESLEY, July 12, 1864; Mary HAGNERE, Nov. 19, 1864; Jno. HOLTZER, Oct. 10, 1865 (Surname possibly HOETZER); Wm. H. WESLEY, Apr. 29, 1872, child under- neath; Cath. WESLEY, Aug. 6, 1890; Ely SEWELL, Oct. 15, 1865;

Frank R. HAGNER, May 25, 1865; Adam HAGNER, July 19, 1920 (Adam also appears as Attam).

LOT 423-A: George D. DANAKER;
George H. DANAKER, May 4, 1855 (Date of Feb. 19, 1855 also appears); George H. DANAKER, June 29, 1854; Alvin CLARY, Jan. 27, 1898; John & George (children, no date or surname given).

LOT 424-A: Rev. JAMES A. MASSEY;
Remains, July 5, 1853; Mary P. PHOEBUS, May 10, 1894; Caroline MASSEY, Dec. 27, 1856.

LOT 425-A: Rich. A. LINDSEY;
Child of PHILLIPS, Nov. 19, 1856; Elizabeth STAZTON, May 1, 1868; James STATEN, Aug. 18, 1871 (Surname also spelled STANTON); John A. PHILLIPS, Aug. 3, 1877; Infant of John GILL, Mar. 12, 1881; David STAYTON, Mar. 2, 1854; Infant of A. & T. GILL, Apr. 7, 1883; Mary E. BOUNEY, Dec. 26, 1884; Infant of A. J. GILL, and Rev. John PHILLIPS, May 16, 1887; Archibold LINDSEY, Apr. 13, 1893; Michael E. NEA(VY), Apr. 20, 1936; Addie C. NEA(VY), Oct. 3, 1936; Barbara AGNES, Dec. 24, 1936; Ella A. BARRETT, Oct. 22, 1938; Jean STONE, Dec. 18, 1941; Stillborn of ANDREWS, Sept. 15, 1941; Joseph BORIS, June 10, 1941.

LOT 426-A: George W. NORRIS; No record of burials.

LOT 427-A and 412-A: Margt. GALLAGHER;
Margt. GALLAGHER, May 25, 1855 (Date of Mar. 9, 1855 also given); Margt. PARSONS, May 16, 1854; Mrs. PARSONS, May 1, 1860; Joseph PARSONS, May 10, 1881; John C. PARSONS, Mar. 26, 1859; Mary PERKINS, Sept. 18, 1896; Wm. H. PERKINS, Oct. 1, 1879; Priscilla PARSONS, May 5, 1913; Howard (M.) LYNCH, Dec. 3, 1924; Jos. PARSON, Jr., Oct. 31, 1865; Chancy M. ROBINSON, Dec. 20, 1952 (First name may be Chaney); Jos. PARSONS, Apr. 14, 1828; John H. PERKINS, June 5, 1845; John T. LYNCH, May 24, 1943; Sarah E. LYNCH, Aug. 4, 1949.

LOT 428-A: Lewis P. BROWN;
James BOYD, Nov. 12, 1857; Harriet M. BROWN, Aug. 25, 1903; Louis P. BROWN, Dec. 8, 1910; Fannie E. DOANE, Nov. 21, 1918.

LOT 429-A: John C. HEMMUK;
George HEMMUK, Dec. 1, 1851; Chas. R. HEMMUK, Oct. 13, 1851; Child of WOODS, Nov. 22, 1859.

LOT 430-A: Sophia GILLBEE;
Lydia CLINE, June 21, 1851; Child of CLINE, July 7, 1853; George BARKMAN, Feb. 4, 1876; Mother & cousin, July 19, 1864; Elizabeth M. GELBEE, Oct. 30, 1896; Isabel H. GILBERT, Aug. 25, 1856; Cath. GILBEE, Mar. 12, 1864; Sophia GILBEE, July 5, 1897; Catharine GILBEE, June 3, 1897.

LOT 431-A: John and Alex MC ELHANEY;
Alexandra MC ELHANEY, Apr. 23, 1857; A. MC ELHANEY, Dec. 29, 1857; Saml. MC ELHANEY, Mar. 16, 1858; John MC ELHANEY, Feb. 4, 1859; Sarah MC ELHANEY, Sept. 13, 1859; Cath. MC ELHANEY, Nov. 28, 1860; Ann MC ELHANEY, Nov. 2, 1861.

LOT 432-A: Carson NEWHOUSE;
Jane WOODS, Feb. 2, 1872; Thomas WILKINS, Aug. 17, 1872; George W. WILKINS, June 4, 1899 (Date of July 2, 1900 is also listed); James THOMPSON, June 20, 1876 (Entry crossed out); Sarah WILKINS, Jan. 18, 1915, child underneath; Thos. WILKINS, May 19, 1920.

LOT 433-A: Missoun CROTHERS;
Virginia CROTHERS, May 28, 1853; Missoun CROTHERS, Oct. 18, 1859; Illinois CROTHERS, Feb. 26, 1870.

LOT 434-A: Thomas LITTLE;
Rachel CULVER(E)LL, June 19, 1852; Stephen CULVER(E)LL, Jan. 23, 1856; John W. MARSHALL, Dec. 24, 1888; Stillborn of Chas. LITTLE, June 4, 1893; Rem(oved) from Philadelphia Road, June 4, 1894; Rem(ains) of Thos. LITTLE, June 14, 1894; Orlana R. LITTLE, Mar. 16, 1904; Chas. LITTLE, (no date given).

LOT 435-A: William JORDAN;
Martha JORDAN, Apr. 30, 1852; Martha KEFFLER, May 16, 1856 (Surname may be KESSLER. Date of Jan. 9, 1856 is also listed); Wm. JORDAN, Mar. 14, 1858; Adult, May 22, 1866.

LOT 436-A: Mark HILL, and Johana WILSON;
Alice HASLAN, Nov. 12, 1855; Kate C. HOWARD, Aug. 16, 1862; Ellen HOWARD, May 4, 1865; Agnes A. HILL, Apr.2, 1872; Ellen HILL, Jan. 2, 1879; W. G. N. HOWARD, Mar. 8, 1868; Walter Lee HALL, July 18, 1886; Stillborn, July 25, 1887; Elizabeth HILL, Nov. 28, 1888; Mark (J.) HALL, Sept. 20, 1899; Eliza HILL, July 17, 1848.

LOT 437-A: John FOUNCE;
John FOUNCE, Apr. 30, 1852; Robert FOUNCE, Sept. 2, 1853; Thos. RUSSELL, May 9, 1856; George SHAW, July 13, 1858; Wm. E. SHAW, Jan. 22, 1859; Mary FOUNCE, Mar. 10, 1889; Sarah E. MARTIN, Dec. 19, 1912.

LOT 438-A: William T, HARRISS;
Rem(ains), Oct. 23, 1851; Martha HARRISS, Feb. 27, 1856; Mary DAVIS, Nov. 30, 1895; Amos M. DAVIS, Jan. 16, 1896; Isabelle DAVIS, June, 1921; Elizabeth V. DAVIS, Mar. 20, 1926.

LOT 439-A: Mary GLANVILLE;
Harriet GLANVILLE, Apr. 23, 1853; Annie A. GOULD, Aug. 24, 1854; Adda GOULD, Aug. 24, 1859; Child, Aug. 23, 1865; Mary GLANVILLE, May 10, 1857.

LOT 440-A: Chas. H. BYROM and Charlotte POOLE (niece);
Chas. H. BYROM, Apr. 23, 1860; Child of LENNAN, May 11, 1861; Mrs. BRYAN, Sept. 22, 1862; Child, Sept. 4, 1865; Adult, Apr. 24, 1866; Mary C. HOWARD, (no date given); Stillborn of W. H. BRYAN, Oct. 1, 1882; Sarah (J.) HOPKINS, May 5, 1903; George H. ELLISON, July 17, 1962; Clara S. ELLISON, Apr. 16, 1951.

LOT 441-A: Jacob WEAVER;
Remains, July 28, 1854; Remains, July 18, 1857; Unknown man, killed on N. E. Road, July 7, 1871; Child, Jan. 15, 1873; Child, Jan. 23, 1875; James WALLACE, July 9, 1817.

LOT 442-A and 455-A: Robert B. BAKER;
George SAUTZER, May 28, 1853 (Surname may be SANTZER or SUTER);

Rem(ains), July 18, 1854; M. V. GILBERT, Sept. 8, 1861; Harriet WHALEY, Mar. 23, 1864; Robert B. BAKER, Sr., Jan. 28, 1874; Barbury A. BAKER, Oct. 15, 1879 (First name also spelled Barbara); Henrietta SAUTZER, July 10, 1885 (Surname may be SANTZER or SUTER); Stillborn, Apr. 12, 1922; Eliza SUTER, (no date given); George SUTER, May 22, 1853; Theodore BAKER, July 15, 1842.

LOT 443-A: Hester HALL;
Saml. C. MORTIMER, July 17, 1855; Franklin BAKER, Oct. 18, 1858; Levin HALL, July 14, 1818.

LOT 444-A: William WALLACE;
William WALLACE, Apr. 17, 1855; Cath. HANNING, Dec. 11, 1853; William WALLACE, Mar. 29, 1859; William WALLACE, Mar. 29, 1854.

LOT 445-A: Hannah LONG;
Child of SUMMERS, July 17, 1856; Saml. GRILLETT, Aug. 2, 1873 (Surname also spelled GILBERT); John F. LONG, Jan. 22, 1893; John LONG, Sept. 28, 1893; Susie T. LONG, July 31, 1893; Hannah A. LONG, Jan. 13, 1911; Infant of J. T. and L. R. LONG, June 3, 1891; John F. LONG, Jr., Jan. 19, 1893.

LOT 446-A: Mary STEVENS;
Heigh MC GOWAN, Nov. 29, 1856; Mary STEVENS, May 27, 1865; Elizabeth HIGNET, Aug. 24, 1866; Mary A. LUCAS, July 25, 1872; Elizabeth HIGDON, July 18, 1873; Margt. C. LUCAS, Jan. 27, 1882; Alice L. BURNAP, Feb. 5, 1940; Jas. A. STEVENS, Oct. 5, 1848.

LOT 447-A: Angeline WRIGHT;
Sarah JONES, Sept. 26, 186(0); Saml. WRIGHT, Aug. 15, 1865; Maggie PURCELL, Mar. 23, 1883; Stillborn, June 13, 1921; James P. FLEMING, Sept. 26, 1964.

LOT 448-A and 419-A: Jno. W. WOODS;
Mrs. SMILEY, June 24, 1851; Remains, June 15, 1858; Elizabeth M. WOODS, July 10, 1873; Myrtle ASHTON, May 22, 1895; Elizabeth A. WOODS, Aug. 2, 1877; Robert A. WOODS, Apr. 30, 1884; Mary E. Woods BUCKINGHAM, Apr. 20, 1918; George W. WOODS, Feb. 16, 1874.

LOT 449-A: John A. S. FINN;
Edwin A. FINN, July 23, 1852; Ella FINN, June 23, 1856.

LOT 450-A: Jno. R. JONES;
Rem(ains), May 8, 1856; George W. CHANDLER, Feb. 3, 1871; R. E. KING, Feb. 5, 1874; Mary E. KING, Mar. 9, 1878; John R. JONES, Apr. 20, 1903.

LOT 451-A: Edw. H. SAULSBURY;
Child of Edw. SAULSBURY, June 10, 1863; Harry CHRISTNER, Aug. 11, 1877; Harry E. CRESMIER, Dec. 22, 1882; George MC GREEVY, Sept. 3, 1884; Edw. H. SAULSBURY, May 18, 1887; Maggie L. SAULSBURY, Jan. 29, 1890; Elizabeth SAULSBURY, Sept. 22, 1908; Martha C. LOBER, Sept. 19, 1910; Edw. C. LITTLE, Oct. 19, 1918; Martha A. PATTERSON, Dec. 3, 1975.

LOT 452-A: Thomas STANP;
Thos. H. STANP June 23, 1854; Thos. STANP, Jan. 28, 1860; Wm. W.

STANP, June 13, 1862; Elizabeth STANP, Aug. 7, 1869 (Surname throughout this lot may be STAMS or STANSS).

LOT 453-A: Susan HAGNER; Adam HAGNER, Oct. 18, 1869; William T. HAGNER, July 15, 1881; William T. HAGNER, June 27, 1884; Fredk. J. HADNER, July 13, 1886; Infant of (H.) W. HAGNER, July 30, 1888; Maggie HAGNER, May 28, 1889; Susan HAGNER, July 21, 1897; Ethel WALLACE, June 4, 1910.

LOT 454-A: Samuel WRIGHT; Johanna WRIGHT, Feb. 18, 1861; Adult, Aug. 2, 1864; Child, Sept. 14, 1871; Walter E. WRIGHT, Mar. 30, 1887; James B. WRIGHT, Sept. 22, 1904; Saml WRIGHT, Sept. 26, 1904 (Saml. crossed out and Mildred entered); Child of George WRIGHT, Jan. 1, 1872.

LOT 455-A: See Lot 442-A.

LOT 456-A: Martha WILSON; James WILSON, Mar. 14, 1856; Martha V. MARTIN, Mar. 28, 1906; Emily S. COX, Apr. 17, 1900; James WILSON, Dec. 23, 1853.

LOT 457-A: Robert COGGINS; Child of George WRIGHT, Dec. 22, 1871; Child of Robert COGGINS, Dec. 7, 1872; William F. COX, Sept. 24, 1875; Robert COGGINS, Apr. 1, 1886; Clara B. COGGINS, Sept. 9, 1890; Ann May COGGINS, Dec. 24, 1877; Mary A. COGGINS, Oct. 20, 1911.

LOT 458-A: Joshua JONES, Hannah PASSAPAE; Saml. JONES, Oct. 18, 1851; Hannah PASSAPAE, Sept. 11, 1897 (Also entered as Hannah JONES, Sept. 10, and crossed out.); Monroe PASSAPAE, Mar. 5, 1919. Authorization for Burial found between pages of Lot Book A stating that "Cecellie PASSAPAE (Cecelis Boisseau PASSAPAE)" is to be buried in Lot A 458 "standing in the name of Joshua JONES", July 30, 1951.

LOT 459-A: Mary Ann PIERPOINT; Remains, Oct. 10, 1851; Adult, Apr. 14, 1866.

LOT 460-A: Catherine FOXWELL (Name crossed out and Single Interments entered.); Child, Sept. 27, 1855; Dollis BE(U)ZLEY, June 11, 1935; Claude WALKER, June 14, 1935; (Hatck) COOK, June 18, 1935; William F. BE(U)ZLEY, Oct. 8, 1936; John CAROLAN, May 29, 1935.

LOT 461-A: Jno. T. WILSON; Clarence E. TAYLOR, Dec. 25, 1922; Chas. E. MUTH, Apr. 3, 1929; Chas. MUTH, June 12, 1929; Urnie Belle MUTH, Mar. 9, 1942.

LOT 462-A: William HISSEY; Ketty WEST, July 3, 1861; Child, Feb. 20, 1860; Caroline HESSEY, Feb. 26, 1870; Mary HESSEY, Nov. 16, 1872; Hannah (VOYCE), Oct. 10, 1872; Elizabeth J. BERRY, June 27, 1892; Saml. A. HESSEY, June 20, 1936.

LOT 463-A: Edward J. WARD (Name crossed out and Herman ROSSBERG entered.); Robert J. WARD, Oct. 17, 1854; Washington B. WHALEN, June 16, 1863; Herman ROSSBERG, Aug. 20, 1951; Clara B. ROSSBERG, June 23, 1958; To be used for Carl W. ROSSBERG; Burkh(ore) N. ROSSBERG, Oct. (10), 19(75).

LOT 464-A: Single Interments; Cora Lee (SHORT), June 27, 1935; (Tsang) (Ian) CHIN, June 29, 1935 (A person of Chinese ancestry); Alice MC DO(illegible), July 18, 1935; Lor(a)n JOHNSON, Mar. 14, 1938.

LOT 465-A: John SMITH; John SMITH, July 25, 1851; John M. SMITH, May 17, 1852; Remains, Sept. 25, 1855; John B. GRAY, Jan. 22, 1863; Mrs. GRAY, Dec. 8, 1864; Sarah HYDE, Aug. 1, 1865; Wm. J. SMITH, Nov. 4, 1840; Martha J. SMITH, Feb. 21, 1848.

LOT 466-A: Elizabeth ALLISON; George HIGDON, Nov. 27, 1856; Alexander HIGDON, Apr. 9, 1857; Child, June 5, 1870; Child of J. B. HIGDON, Mar. 24, 1877; Baptist HIGDON, Dec. 7, 1891.

LOT 467-A: Rebecca DUBLIN; Mrs. DUBLIN, Aug. 19, 1859; Rebecca DEULIN, Nov. 18, 1895; Gertrude STRIGEL, Sept. 16, 1898; Laura STRIGEL, Oct. 5, 1898; Laura CALWELL,July 14, 1904; Lilly DEULIN, Aug. 18, 1859; Jonathan J. E. CONNER, Jan. 24, 1931; Ann C. CONNER, June 28, 1947.

LOT 468-A: William S. ORAM; Remains, Apr. 23, 1856; Child of OREM, June 20, 1861; Keziah OREM, June 6, 1865; Wm. OREM, June 4, 1866 (on monument date reads June 4, 1865); Cornelius FRENCH, July 8, 1867; George C. MILES, May 22, 1872; Infant of J. and C. SEACHMAN, July 10, 1886; Chas. W. SEACHMAN, May 6, 1887.

LOT 469-A: Elizabeth M. O'RILEY; Remains, Oct. 8, 1851; George ROBINSON, Apr. 4, 1857; George F. FLYNN, Aug. 31, 1876; Jennie ELLISON, July 7, 1881; Florence C. ELLISON, Apr. 25, 1912; Ida V. ELLISON, June 6, 1882; Ann C. FLYNN, Aug. 3, 1917; Jno. W. AULL, Sept. 14, 1825.

LOT 470-A and 413-A: Marie H. PATRICK; Remains, Dec. 20, 1851; Elsie C Nov. 28, 1856; John MOORE, Mar. 12, 1849; Margt. MOORE, Mar. 28, 1840.

LOT 471-A: MC KELDRA - STEWART; Rebecca MC KELDRY, June 1, 1852; Isabell STEWART, June 12, 1875; John D. STEWART, Aug. 18, 1875; Annie K. STEWART, Mar. 30, 1886; Martha STEWART, July 12, 1876.

LOT 472-A: George A. BAKER; Jennie E. PINE, Apr. 17, 1872; Mary E. BAKER, Feb. 9, 1889; Elmer E. BAKER, Dec. 8, 1890; George A. BAKER, Mar. 11, 1901 (Feb. is crossed out.).

LOT 473-A: Lewis GRAY; Mary Eliza CARROLL, Oct. 21, 1853; Margt. GRAY, Sept. 13, 1856; Margt. A. LEORY, Aug. 4, 1857 (Surname may be LEONY); Child of TAYLOR, Feb. 1, 1859; Margt. ALLEN, Mar. 9, 1859; Esther MATTESON, Aug. 23, 1878.

LOT 474-A: Sarah MC CRA; John MC CRAY, July 8, 1854; George PERRY, Nov. 2, 1867 (Another entry reads Nov. 12, 1807.).

LOT 475-A: Rebecca BRO(W)N; Ida Kate MANN, Aug. 22, 1868; Stillborn, Nov. 25, 1879; Edwd. RILEY, Oct. 16, 1880; Jas. MANUS, Oct. 3, 1883; Stillborn of MITCHELL, Nov. 8, 1883; Stillborn of T. B. MITCHELL, Dec. 23, 1890; Mary T. MC KEE, July 21, 1892; Eliza E. MANN, June 7, 1912; James B. MITCHELL, Apr. 16, 1920; Henrieta M. MITCHELL, Apr. 30, 1926.

LOT 476-A: Chas. A. HARVEY (Entry crossed out and Chas. A. HANEY entered); Remains, May 29, 1855; Chas. M. HARVEY, June 9, 1869; Frank HARVEY, Dec. 5, 1872; Harry M. CHANEY, Sept. 29, 1877 (First name also given as Howard); Mary A. HARVEY, Apr. 29, 1890; Fielding M. HARVEY, Dec. 23, 1891; Allen KAHN, Apr, 8, 1892; John A. MC CORD, Apr. 8, 1892; Lilly M. MC CORD, Aug. 1, 1892; Chas. R. MC CORD, July 25, 1894; Wm. BURMINGH(AM), (no date given).

LOT 477-A: Sarah HOLLINGSHEAD; Mary R. LAVILLE, May 1, 1871; Margt. FOWLER, Mar. 4, 1882; Rebecca DORSEY, Sept. 17, 1889; Rebecca DORSEY, Nov. 24, 1893; Sarah HOLLINGSHEAD, July 12, 1904.

LOT 478-A: Sarah HOLLINGSHEAD; Rebecca A. DORSEY, Nov. 24, 1893; Rebecca A. DORSEY, Sept. 17, 1889 (These may be the same person).

LOT 479-A: There are no burials in this area. It has been made into a road.

LOT 480-A: James M. CLATCHEY; Hannah M. CLATCHEY, Nov. 29, 1870; Reuben H. LAKE, July 4, 1877; Sarah P. CLATCHEY, Dec. 9, 1879; Thos. L. CLATCHEY, Aug. 11, 1880; Jacob CLATCHEY, July 9, 1886; Rich. H. CLATCHEY, Apr.22, 1889; Wm. S. CLATCHEY, Apr. 27, 1890; Thos. T. CLATCHEY, Jan. 3, 1896; Stillborn of Sarah PHILIPS, Feb. 13, 1897; Infant of Sarah PHILIPS, Jan. 13, 1898; Chas. S. CLATCHEY, May 4, 1874.

LOT 481-A: George TOLSON; Alice FUGLER, May 24, 1855.

LOT 482-A: Frances A. ELLIOTT; Jos. ELLIOTT, May 30, 1853; James ELLIOTT, Sept. 27, 1855; Frances A. ELLIOTT, June 16, 1857; Sarah WARRY, Sept. 29, 1861; Thos. S. WHARRY, Jan. 12, 1884; Gideon A. ELLIOTT, May 28, 1885; Infant of John T. WARRY, Mar. 12, 1886; Amanda M. WHARRY, Oct. 29, 1904; Chas. S. WHARRY, Jan. 14, 1884 (Entry crossed out); Wm. T. ELLIOTT, July 12, 1879.

LOT 483-A: George M. ROBERTS; Child of LEWIS, May 11, 1853; Francis TAYLOR, Nov. 29, 1856 (Year of 1854 also given. There is a note written in: "died at Ft. McHenry".); Rich. H. TAYLOR, July 24, 1857.

LOT 484-A: Washington H. HOBBS; Wm. HARTLOVE, Feb. 17, 1853; Child of W. H. HOBBS, Feb. 19, 1853; M. L. HOBBS, May 28, 1861; Edw. HOBBS, Nov. 2, 1855; Lydia SPENCE, July 21, 1887; Margt. A. HOBBS, July 15, 1886; Ananuphalus WEBER, Sept. 18, 1886; Guyon WEBER, Feb. 26, 1890.

LOT 485-A: Thomas RUCKLE; Thos. RUCKLE, Sept. 5, 1853, "Defender in Balto. 1814"; Rosa M. RAUCKLE, Nov. 26, 1857; Elizabeth A. RUCKLE, Mar. 29, 1887; Thos. C. RUCKLE, Dec. 19, 1891; Jno. T. RICHARDSON, Apr. 14, 1897.

LOT 486-A: Lewis GLENN; Remains, July 27, 1852; Louisa GLENN, Dec. 10, 1852; Chas. H. SHELDON, Mar. 12, 1860; John SHELDON, May 22, 1872; James SHELDON, Feb. 21, 1898; Maria L. SHELDON, Jan. 11, 1901.

LOT 487-A: Philip MARCH; Martha A. MARCH, July 31, 1851; Willie MARCH, Oct. 9, 1862; Albert BRECKHAUSER, July 10, 1877; Ellen L.

MARCH, June 23, 1880; Infant of Jacob MARCH, June 28, 1889; Stillborn of (P.) and (J.) MARCH, Apr. 11, 1893.

LOT 488-A: Daniel WEAVER; Remains, Dec. 12, 1852; George W. ARMSTRONG, Dec. 9, 1855; Josephine L. ARMSTRONG, Dec. 15, 1888; Ann BAUER, May 7, 1824; Robert JAMES, July 13, 1835; Mary JAMES, Jan. 4, 1835.

LOT 489-A: Adam SNIVERLY; Ann SNIVERLY, June 24, 1851; Jacob SNIVERLY, Jan. 7, 1860 (Also given on stone Dec. 28, 1859).

LOT 490-A: Mary J. PARKER; Child, June 8, 1853; Strange Woman, Apr. 22, 1854; Mary J. CARR, May 6, 1879; Harry (or Henry) BYRD, Oct. 12, 1895; Robert PARKER, Nov. 3, 1908; Jas. M. BYRD, July 25, 1930; Annie C. BYRD, May 1, 1967, b. Oct. 9, 1884; d. May 2, 1967.

LOT 491-A: Henry HORN; Eliza Ann JENNINGS, Jan. 21, 1834; Angelia Mary BAKER, Sept. 19, 1838; Saml. K. JENNINGS, Dec. 27, 1825; Almira HORN, Jan. 30, 1839; Theodore SNETHEN, Feb. 26, 1830; Henry HORN, Aug. 18, 1857; Hannah HORN, Oct. 12, 1871.

LOT 492-A: Rowland ROGERS; Remains, May 22, 1852; Mary ROGERS, Mar. 13, 1865; Rowland ROGERS, Mar. 13, 1866; Mary A. ROGERS, June 5, 1910; Sarah T. ROGERS, Feb. 18, 1816.

LOT 493-A: Sarah ABELL; Thos. J. ABELL, Apr. 17, 1852 (Date of Feb. 26, 1852 also given); Wm. E. ABELL, Apr. 17, 1857 ("Killed at the Baltimore (Fire) April 14, 1857"); Sarah E. SMITH, Aug. 15, 1874; Samuel ABELL, May 10, 1904; Sarah E. ABELL, July 30, 1871; Saml. ABELL, Mar. 1, 1846.

The final pate in Lot Book A is entitled A Single Graves. The page is torn, taped, and has holes punched through the entries. The handwriting is sloppy.

There are 8 columns of graves grouped into pairs, making 4 sets. Each column is 12 places long. The first column of the first set reads top to bottom:
Geo. MILLER / Child of Jas. RIDGLEY; Chas. E. LINDER; Carrie MORRIS; Jacob TAYLOR; (A.) MC LAURIN; Mary F. HUBBA(?)RD; Nathan POLECK; Thos. BOLSTER; Wm. H. SADLER; Child of John SHIPLEY / Child of C. S(HIP)LEY; Mary TAYLOR / John (?)MAS; Peggy GOEE / Pe(?) GOTE.

The second set in the first column reads top to bottom:
Jos. NISE; Mark (D----VIN) (paper torn); (M)ORITZ (paper torn)ARK; M(paper torn)ASON; Thos. L(paper torn)AER; Charlot(paper torn) E. (paper torn)MITH; _____ LAUGHTON; J. M(AEWER); _____ E. R_____; Dixon (SERAL?); Francis (----ELLY); (M)ary (SHER).

The second set, column 1, reads:
Katie E. WEBB; (illegible entry) Allen GUTMAN; Geo.LEWIS / Saml. A. FIELDS; Samuel (W.) HOFFMAN; _____ HEGSELL; Julia MALCOM; Maria HERN; _____ Philis (CASDORF); Christian STEINWEDIC; Eliza MARSH.

Set 2, column 2, reads:
Jas. L. COLLINS; Ann HULL; Julia HULL; (Danl.) STEPHENS; Ida

BOOZE; Servant girl of Rev. Thos. SEWELL; Hennrieta COLEMAN / Wm. M. DAMMER; Joseph BROWN; Wilmer MARCH.

Set 3, column 1, reads:
Christian STAUM; (Hester) MARSH.

Set 3, column 2, reads:
Elizabeth FALKNER.

Set 4, column 1, reads:
(Kabacor) (Iraney HILL); Robert & Harriett WELSH; John D. KNOX.

Set 4, column 2, reads:
Elizabeth FIELDS; (Wm.) FIELDS; Elizabeth (C)OWARD.

There are several pages listing lot owners but as these have been placed at the head of each lot in the information above, they will not be repeated here.

SECTION B

A loose paper found in the lot book reads: Rev. S. J. SMITH died March 26, 1913 age 58 years, 7 months, 9 days. H. BOR(D)LEY June 4. John MORROW May 13, 1891.

Preachers Lot Section B
Bishop Francis ASBURY, 1816; Bishop Enoch GEORGE, 1828; Bishop Beverly WAUGH, 1858; Jessie LEE, 1816; Robert STRAWBRIDGE, 1781; Wilson LEE, 1804; Rueben ELLIS, 1796; Edward OREM, 1821; Leonard CASSELL; Bishop John EMORY, 1835; Hamilton JEFFERSON, 1821; John HAGERTY, 1823; James SMITH, 1826; William P. MC DOWELL, 1827; Samuel MC PHERSON (no date given); Edward MATTHEWS, 1833; Edward HUBBELL, 1836; Oliver BEALE, 1836; Nathan RICHARDSON, 1846; Joseph PLOTNER, 1847; John W. RICHARDSON, 1850; Joseph L. MORRIS, 1851; Joseph WHITE, 1851; Henry B. FURLONG, 1853; John M. JONES, 1855; John A. COLLINS, 1857; Samuel B. DUNLAP (no date given); William WICKES, 1862; William HIRST, 1862; Henry SMITH, 1862; James SEWELL, 1866; T.T.S. RICHARDS (no date given); Isaac COLLINS, 1870; R. C. HASLUP (no date given); Hezekiah VAN ARSDALE, 1876; William H. HALLIDAY, 1878; Abner NEAL, Apr. 14, 1821; Daniel STANSBURY, Nov. 10, 1860; Gerard MORGAN, Mar. 17, 1864; Robert EMORY, Aug. 5, 1851; Samuel BRISTON, Oct., 1853; Henry FARRING, Nov. 28, 1855; Horace S. HOLLAND, Dec. 7, 1855; Thomas S. BUSSEY, Sept. 30, 1852; R. H. HOLLAND, (Dec.) 7, 1855; Thomas BASSFORD, Apr. 20, 1863; T.H.W. MONROE, July 28, 1864; John ROBB, Mar. 2(6), 1869; G. K. KANE, October 27, 1869; Philip LIPSCOMB, Jan. 6, 1870; George C. M. ROBERTS, June 21, 1870; R. Spencer VINTON, (Jan.) 31, 1870; Lyttleton A. MORGAN, June 11, 186(?); John PUE, (Rice Lot) (no date given); Francis A. MC CARTNEY, October 7, 187(5); N. J. B. MORGAN, Apr. 6, 1872; John A. GERE, (June) 3, 1874; Daniel M. REESE, Apr. 8, 1875; Dabney BALL (no date given); Henry BALL, July 4, 1878; John COGGINS, Feb. 4, 1881; Samuel REGISTER, October 19, 1881; William H. WILSON, Aug. 25, 1884; John RICE, October 27, 1872; Tillison A. MORGAN, Apr. 25, 1887; Elisha PHILLIPS, Apr. 26, 1887; Alexander W. MC LEOD, Dec. 2, 1891; David FEELEMEYER, Oct. 15, 1894; George R. CROOK, Feb. 20, 1897; George W. FEELEMEYER, Jul. 20, 1885; William A. LONG (no date given); G. W. MORGAN, Aug. 20, 1900; George W.

COOPER, June 23, 1902; William A. MC DONALD, (June) 16, 190(2); J. W. START, Feb. 11, 1911; Watson CASE, Nov. 15, 1911; H. R. SAVAGE, Feb. 15, 1915; S. J. SMITH, Mar. 26, 1913; George W. EVANS (no date given); Joseph FRANCE, July 27, 1889; H. H. WESTWOOD, Sept. 26, 1921; H. S. (FRANCE), Jan. 27, 1955; Samuel W. COE (no date given); Charles (T.) TIPPETT, May 7, 1867; William KREBS, Sept. 26, 1870; John L. REESE, Sept. 19, 18(7)1; Aquila REESE (no date given); Thomas M. REESE, Mar. 27, 1882; James BRADS, Dec. 18, 1887; M. L. FORBES (no date given); J. T. STANSBURY (no date given); Christopher BROOKS (no date given); George TEAL (no date given); Nicholas A. WATKINS, (Aug.) 1, 1858; Jacob LARKINS (no date given); Dennis H. BATTEE, Mar. 9, 1865; John H. MARKS (no date given); Ellis S. TEALE; Samuel KRAMER, Aug. 18, 1891; J. W. PARKS, Sept. 23, 189(4); John F. BAGGS, (March) 9, 1921; John MARROW, May 13, 1871; William J. FLOYD, Feb. 15, 1902; Charles O. ISAAC, Mar. 20, 1920; Isaac W. CARTER, Aug. 20, 1921; Louis R. JONES, Mar. 30, 1914; John SWAHLEN, Aug. 30, 1898; Edward C. MINNER, June 1, 1859; Richard BROWN, Feb. 21, 1911; John POISAL, June 24, 1852; George W. DEEMS, July 30, 18(70); Henry FURLONG, (July), 18(72); John MILLER, Oct. 11, 1878; John H. C. DOSH, Apr. 16, 1881; Thomas MC CORMICK, Feb. 20, 1883; William T. D. CLEMM, (July) 21, 1895; I. M. HAWLEY, Aug. 12, 1895; J. W. HEDGES, May 27, 1907; William H. CHAPMAN, Apr. 8, 1908; B. G. W. REID, Sept. 6, 1908; W. R. GWYNN, Mar. 13, 1908; Samuel P. JOHNSON, Apr. 21, 1911; William EVANS, May 7, 1887; E. E. BLOUNT, Jan. 5, 1904; Samuel H. CUMMINGS, June 2, 1914; Jacob KING, Feb. 13, 184(4); D. E. REESE, Aug. 17, 1849; Joseph SHANE, (June) 11, 1854; C. W. DALRYMPLE (no date given); Solomon MC MULLEN, (Feb.) 15, 1867; Samuel CORNELIUS (no date given); William PRETTYMAN (no date given); Charles B. KEYWORTH, Mar. 7, 1897; Charles L. AVARD (no date given); Beverly DAUGHERTY, May 1, (18)77; Lewis D. HERRON, Apr. 5, 189(2); David S. MONROE, Nov. 17, 1910; Edwin DORSEY, 1887; J. N. SPANGLER, Dec. 21, 1887; William H. PITCHER, Dec. 26, 1883; Bernnett H. SMITH, Dec. 30, 1902; Charles A. JONES, Apr. 2, 1909; Henry NICE, Sept. 6, 1921; John J. GREEN, Jan. 29, 1879; C. C. CRONAN, May 18, 1891; J. J. WEBSTER, Apr. 8, 1892; W. M. OSBORNE, Nov. 6, 1908; M. B. J. RICE, Jan. 18, 1918; Charles E. SIMMONS, Aug. 24, 1915.

Affidavit: Berton A. BROMWELL declares he is sole surviving heir of Dwight L. BROMWELL, signed Jan. 26, 1967.

Rev. S. J. SMITH d. March 26, 1913, age 58 yr., 7 mo., 9 days. John MORROW, May 13, 1891 in 248-I.

LOT 1-B: William FLAXCOUCH;
Adult, May 22, 1864; William FLAXCOUCH, July 6, 1877; Harry FLAXCOUCH, Aug. 6, 1877; Mary FLAXCOUCH, Mar. 11, 1877; Jas. C. GARRETT, June 19, 1879; Ella WHEKOM, June 6, 1903; (Thelius) WHEKOM, Nov. 2, 1905; (Clement) WHEKOM, Nov. 17, 1910.

LOT 2-B: Elizabeth STANSBURY;
Joseph R. STANSBURY, April 27, 1858; Elizabeth H. STANSBURY, June 3, 1858; Sarah BRYEN, June 24, 1859; Daniel R. STANSBURY, Feb. 14, 1860; Charles F. STANSBURY, Jan. 24, 1865; Joseph C. STANSBURY, Jan. 17, 1894; Ann Eliz. STANSBURY, Feb. 23, 1900; Samuel STANSBURY, Dec. 7, 1904; James C. STANSBURY (no date given); Ann E. STANSBURY (no date given).

LOT 3-B: H. EARECKSON;
Thomas J. COLE, Nov. 13, 1852; William A. COLE, Feb. 15, 1853; Child, May 11, 1853; Mary A. COLE, Aug. 4, 1866; Julia A. EARECKSON, Dec. 6, 1906; Carrie D. COLE, May 10, 1919; Mary EARECKSON, May 18, 1865; Hennrietta EARECKSON, May 15, 1872; Federal EARECKSON, Jan. 7, 1852; Hennreitta EARECKSON, Jan. 4, 1904; Riza EARECKSON, Nov. 12, 1942; 2 children of Mollie & Phil.

LOT 4-B: Philip EVLON;
Philip EVLON, Nov. 18, 1859; Mary (GRAFFLER), May 14, 1859; William C. LYNCH, July 26, 1872; Catherine LYNCH, Aug. 10, 1877; Naomi E. SELLERS, Feb. 22, 1888; Mary LYNCH, June 17, 1907; George R. LYNCH, Nov. 21, 1912; Maria Emily SELLERS, Apr. 24, (1850); Sidney LYNCH (no date given); Joseph WILEY (no date given); Naomi LYNCH (no date given); John LYNCH (no date given); Sidney NORRIS (no date given).

LOT 5-B: Rev. U. J. B. MORGAN;
2 Children, April 24, 1850; Rosana H. MORGAN, May 24, 1858 (Also Dec. 31, 1858); Mary E. MORGAN, Aug. 19, 1862; Rachal PHELPS, Mar. 13, 1868; Rev. U. J. B. MORGAN, Apr. 8, 1872; Wilbur D. MORGAN, Aug. 24, 1877; Rev. Wilber P. MORGAN, Dec. 22, 1922; Rev. G. (C.) MORGAN, Mar. 17, 1846; "Virginia MORGAN, our children, Apr. 18, 1850".

LOT 6-B thru 7-B appear to be missing.

LOTS 8 & 9-B: George ROGERS & Mrs. Jane Margery COOK;
John J. ROGERS, Mar. 7, 1846; Carrie ROGERS, Oct. 14, 1854; Cara R. Kellinger THOMAS, July 26, 1946; Elizabeth R. KELLINGER, June 4, 1912; William J. KELLINGER, Aug. 20, 1900; George ROGERS, Dec. 9, 1862; Caroline ROGERS, Nov. 25, 1883; Rosalie ROGERS, Feb. 7, 1910; Sidney THOMAS, Sept. 19, 1910; George Poe ROGERS, June 22, 1884; George H. ROGERS, Oct. 15, 1925; Mary E. ROGERS, Dec. 31, 1932; Florence G. ROGERS, Jan. 30, 1937; Charles R. ROGERS, Feb. 18, 1942; Emma May ROGERS, Apr. 7, 1939.

LOT 10-B: Henry BUSCH, Jos. CRAGG;
(Wm. JANES), July 3, 1857; Saml. W. CRAGG, July 29, 1895; Annie R. CRAGG, Feb. 2, 1858; Cath. R. CRAGG, Feb. 14, 1858; Emma CRAGG, Aug. 11, 1859; Jos. CRAGG, June 4, 1890; Katherine CRAGG, Apr. 18, 1928; Margaret E. CRAGG, Feb. 9, 1933; George BUSCH, Feb. 11, 1862; Annie LEFFLER, Aug. 1, 1864; Walter J. REYNOLDS, Oct. 14, 1871; Hester A. LEFFLER, Apr. 4, 1872; Elizabeth BUSCH, Jan. 22, 1877; George D. LEFFLER, Oct. 9, 1891; Mary C. BUCH, Apr. 12, 1911; Henry BUSCH, Mar. 15, 1912; Jas. CRAGG, June 4, 1891; Flossie BUSCH, Dec. 25, 1907; Mary C. BUSCH, Oct. 14, 1871; John LEFFLER, Dec. 8, 1889; Andrew J. LEFFLER, Dec. 8, 1875. The name LEFFLER may be LEFFLES.

LOTS 11 & 12-B: missing.

Lot 13-B: Catherine KIRBY & Rev. Dabney BALL;
Mary D. BALL, Apr. 25, 1877; Rev. Dabney BALL, Feb. 16, 1878; Lillian N. BALL, Dec. 7, 19(24); (Isabel) (STEWART) KER, Feb. 14, 1929 interred Apr. 20, 1929, brought from (?); Adeline ROSENBROCK, Aug. 9, 1857; Virginia W. BALL, Dec. 22, 1859; Dabney W. BALL, Apr. 15, 1853; Chas. C. BALL, Feb. 27, 1852; Ludwig NECOLAI, 1819; Herbert KER, Jr., cremated remains, Apr. 10, 1943.

LOT 14-B: Rachel MADDOX, transferred to Raymond K. & M. E. JUSTICE;
Rachel MADDOX, Nov. 11, 1863 age 77 years; Mary C. HAMMELL, Oct. 15, 1895; Edward MADDOX, Feb. 9, 1835 age 55 years; Ann Rebecca (CURLETT), Feb. 18, 1846; Rachel Ann SANFORD, Sept. 13, 1860 dau. of Rachel, age 5 (7) years; M. Rebecca MADDOX, May 14, 1857; Imogene GRAHAM, May 24, 1903; Eliza Jane SCOTT, Apr. 20, 1903; (Marg.) E. WALTON, Nov. 14, 1873; Edwd. J. MADDOX, Aug. 1, 1887; Jas. F. MADDOX, Dec. 21, 1891; John G. SCOTT, Jan. 30, 1931; Mary A. (WYANT), June 19, 1842.

LOT 15-B: Mary & Rebecca YUNDT;
Leonard YUNDT, June 15, 1825; Ann JEFFERIS, June 20, 1841; Leonard YUNDT, July 3, 1850; Sarah M. YUNDT, March 14, 1857; Mary YUNDT, May 23, 1859; Rebecca YUNDT, Jan. 15, 1867; Samuel YUNDT (no date given); Sarah JEFFERIS (no date given).

LOT 16-B: Ellen S. OLDSON;
(H.) G. OLDSON, Feb. 8, 1892; John B. W. OLDSON, Dec. 22, 1933; (Clarence) H. OLDSON, Dec. 28, 1833; (Homer) H. OLDSON, Jan. 20, 1934; (Buck) M. MILLER, May 8, 1835, (could be Bessie); Ella S. OLDSON, June 3, 1935.

LOT 17 & 18-B: Missing.

LOT 19-B: Sarah HAWKINS & John E. OREM;
Eliza A. OREM, Sept. 28, 1863; John E. OREM, May 3, 1882; Chas. W. OREM, Feb. 23, 1893; Biddy J. OREM, Feb. 19, 1923; Sarah HAWKINS, Apr. 24, 1879; Maude B. RICHARDSON, Apr. 30, 1889; Sarah WILSON, Mar. 24, 1857; Samuel HAWKINS, Jan. 12, 1849; John C. HOPKINS, July 7, 1849; Sarah C. BUSH, Sept. 1, 1899; George C. RICHARDSON (no date given); Kate WILSON, Jan. 30, 1930; George P. HAWKINS (no date given).

LOT 20-B: Randolph MORGAN & Marg. ALTER;
Walter A. ALTER, June 24, 1880, (entry crossed out); Rose (ALLEN) MORGAN, Feb. 28, 1890; Randolph MORGAN, July 2, 1891; Elizabeth A. MORGAN, Nov. 8, 1884; Edwin KRAFT, June 27, 1892; Elizabeth M. ALTER, Mar. 21, 1896; George W. ALTER, Jan. 5, 1877; Mau(ida) KRAFT, Mar. 2, 1916; Marg. L. ALTELR, Apr. 11, 1912; Walter A. ALTER, June 24, 1880; Howard MORGAN, 1874.

LOT 21-B: Elavious CARTER;
Cath(arine) CARTER, Feb. 23, 1874; Remains from (U. B. G.), (Catherine) DYS(ART), Feb. 18, 1874; John H. (IRWIN), Jan, 1881; Chas. M. (IRWIN), Jan 6, 1882; R(uth) HARE, July 23, 1884; Eva-lious J. CARTER, Oct. 9, 1903; (Catherine) R. CARTER, Mar. 27, 1911; Emma V. (IRWIN), Oct. 22, 1923; (Harry) C. (IRWIN), Jan. 16, 1930; Ca(tharine) DYS(ART), (Oct.) 25, 1872; Mary Elizabeth IRWIN, Aug. 3, 1971, born Dec. 16, 1886, died July 24, 1971.

LOT 22-B: Vallura STARR;
George STARR, Nov. 17, 1879; Emma C. COLLINGTON, May 14, 1883; Emory W. STARR, May 9, 1884; Vallura STARR, July 12, 1890; Wm. N. ASKEW, June 20, 1913; Isabella ASKEW, Aug. 7, 1917; Dr. George E. STARR, Oct. 12, 1929.

LOT 23-B: Theopolius GILL & T. L. MATTHEWS;
Geo. MATTHEWS, Oct. 27, 1884; Grace MATTHEWS, Mar. 11, 1909;
Thos. L. MATTHEWS, Feb. 11, 1916; C. Starr MATTHEWS, Dec. 28,
1933; Theofilus P. GILL, Jan. 30, 1914; Willie SULLAVIN, Jan. 31,
1875 (or 8); Georganna MATTHEWS, Oct. 27, 1884; Ethel MATTHEWS,
June 16, 1951; Mary Elizabeth GILL, Dec. 9, 1944.

LOT 24-B: Single Graves;
James DONOVAN, Feb. 6, (1902) disinterred & reburied Jan. 18,
1917; John OLIVER, Feb. 18, 1903; Jerry L. RIGBY, Feb. 24, 1903;
John W. GEORGE, Mar. 22, 1904; Albert (V. BORAT), Mar. 2, 1905
(or BOIST); Isaac M. IRLAND, July 25, 1909; Pearl E. GEORGE, Apr.
8, 1910; Albert LEACH, July 27, 1910; George T. MASON, Aug. 9,
1910; Raymond R. WOOD, Sept. 5, 1910; Margt. E. LUTZ, Jan. 5,
1911; Margt. LUTZ, Mar. 13, 1911; Margt. OLIVER, Dec. 19, 1911;
Annie SEEVERS, Dec. 19, 1916; Nellie GEORGE, (no date given);
George MASON, (no date given); Hugh E. (IRELAND?), (no date
given).

LOT 25-B: John SULLIVAN;
Nancy SULLIVAN, Feb. 19, 1895.

LOT 26-B: John COGGINS & Richard COGGINS;
John COGGINS, Feb. 4, 1881*; Bessie BOLTON, (Feb.) 27, 1884;
Dorothy CRAWFORD, June 29, 1905; Mary E. HOWE, Dec. 21, 1882;
Harry M. BOLTON, July 9, 1888; Marea COGGINS, May 25, 1891; John
COGGINS, (Mar.) 18, 1896*; George E. COGGINS (no date given);
(Ensous) Howe COGGINS (no date given). *One of these is a
Reverend.

LOT 27-B: Rev. A. M. COURTNAY;
Infant, Mar. 3, 1882; Mary F. COURTNEY, Oct. 25, 1897; Mildred W.
COURTNEY, Feb. 27, 1903; Thos. E. COURTNEY, Sept. 9, 1875; Ellen
W. COURTNEY, Aug. 20, 1938; Reginald COURTNEY, (no date given);
Chas. COURTNEY, (no date given).

LOT 28-B: John R. WALL & W. W. ADDISON;
Child of John R. WALL, Aug. 20, 1872; Child of John R. WALL, Jan.
23, 1879; Child of John R. WALL, Aug. 18, 1879; Child Apr. 13,
1881; Eddie WALL, Sept. 26, 1887; Child, Aug. 4, 1882; Lena WALL,
Nov. 27, 1908; Saml. S. ADDISON, July 19, 1882; Walter A. ADDI-
SON, Nov. 9, 1888 (or Nov. 8, 1883); Susan ADDISON, Apr. 21,
1898; Bertha BUCK, Aug. 17, 1906, (entry crossed out); Leana
WALL, Nov. 27, 1808, (entry crossed out); John R. WALL, Dec. 10,
1919; Laura V. ADDISON, Mar. 23, 1922; Disinterred Bertha BUCK,
Oct. 22, 1921; Wm. W. ADDISON, June 24, 192(3).

LOT 29-B: Wm. F. MINNICK & Wm. H. KENNARD;
H. A. BOGART, June 27, 1866; Child, June 25, 1870; Chas. E.
MINNICK, June 19, 1872; Wm. T. MINNICK, Dec. 12, 1885; Clarence
G. MINNICK, Nov. 24, 1888; Wm. H. MINNICK, Aug. 17, 1891; Infant
of Sarah & Robert HUGHES, July 12, 1898; Mary E. HUGHES, Oct. 1,
1900; Maria A. MINNICK, Jan. 17, 1914; Louisa E. GRIENER, Oct.
10, 1878; Eliza GRIEVER, Jan. 30, 1901; Wm. H. KENNARD, May 26,
1914; Ada A. KENNARD, May 9, 1923; Wm. DURHAM (still born), Apr.
11, 1939; Florence E. KENNARD, Apr. 10, 1948; Louisa S. KENNARD,
Nov. 20, 1942.

LOT 30-B: Jane MORROW & T. Henry REI(SS);
Mary SMITH, Nov. 24, 1896; Mary L. SMITH, July 11, 1898; Jos. L.
REIP, Feb. 11, 1901; Lollie RHOLEDER, Nov. 5, 1906, disinterred &
removed to Louden Park May 2, 1910; Willie & Annie, May 28, 1890;
Mary G. REI(P), Feb. 3, 1900; Thos. H. REI(P), Sept. 6, 1917;
Partick MORROW, Apr. 1, 1860; John R. MORROW, Nov. 18, 1860; Jane
MORROW, Mar. 26, 1890; Fred B. HELLER, Jan. 11, 1919; Wm. MORROW,
Feb. 19, 1820; Carrie MORROW, June 11, 193(6); Ida Louise MORROW,
Aug. 2, 1955; Annie L. REIP, Jan. 2, 1889; William P. REIP, Jan.
23, 1886; Bessie M. MC LAIN, Jan. 24, 1957; Patrick MORROW, Jan.
16, 1860; Daisy M. REIP, July 15, (18)66.

Letter found in lot books addressed to cemetery office from Mrs.
A. SALTMARSH regards lot known as "Lot #S 1/2 of 30" in the name
of Jane MORROW. Mrs. SALTMARSH claims the lot belongs to her
family & that her great aunt Mrs. Bessie MC LAIN is buried there
with her late husband Fred B. HELLER. She states the stone on
the grave should be marked "Bessie M.". The letter is dated
Sept. 8, 1956.

LOT 31-B: Richard COCHRAN;
Elizabeth COCHRAN, Mar. 9, 1854; Thomas H. DURY, Mar. 24, 1858;
James R. SCOTT, Jan. 16, 1873; Mary COCHRAN, May 7, 1873.

LOT 32-B: William F. & Ann E. BOURKE;
Phetillah BOURKE, Mar. 21, 1858; Child, Oct. 7, 1868; Wm. T.
BOURKE, Aug. 27, 1884; Nellie CANECK, Mar. 18, 1904; Wm. H.
BOURKE, Mar. 23, 1904; Mary BOURKE, July 24, 1914; Wm. H. BOURKE,
Sept. 27, 1924; Tobias BORKE, (no date given). [There may be 2
Wm. H. BOURKE buried here. It is not clear if a third Wm. BOURKE
has the middle initial F. or T. Also the name appears as BOORKE
as well as BOURKE.]

LOT 33-B: Christian SIMERING & Mrs. Katherine SUWALL;
Alice SIMERING, Dec. 11, 1855; Christian SIMERING, Jan. 23, 1858;
Amelia SIMERING, Aug. 3, 1860; Child of Simering, May 3, 1876;
Stillborn, Feb. 19, 1895; J. C. SIMERING, Jan. 21, 1858; Margt.
SIMERING, Sept. 29, 1879, also Edwd. C., Almia F., & Amelia A.;
Rose D. SIMERING, June 19, 1887; M. Kate SIMERING, Oct. 11, 1918;
Florence Simerine HOOPER, Dec. 20, 1954; Wm. K. HOOPER, Oct. 5,
1955; SIMERING, Sept. 6, 1833.

An afidavit states Mr. Wm. K. HOOPER to be buried in Lot 33B
"standing in the name of" Christian SIMERING. It is signed Wm.
D. HOOPER, grandson Oct. 2, 1955.

LOT 34-B: Saml. HASLAN & John PEDDICORD;
Fayette D. CARPENTER, Feb. 11, 1857; Imines ANTHONY, Mar. 14,
1861; Rebecca HASLAN, Feb. 15, 1855; Charles HAUBACK, Dec. 6,
1864; (may be same as Chas. A. HANBACK); Nellie HAUBACK, Dec. 10,
1870; Chas. WILKENS, Nov. 2, 1871; Anna HASLAN, Apr. 4, 1892;
Chas. A. HAUBACK, Apr. 21, 1873; J. S. HAUBACK, June 12, 1874;
Saml. HASLAN, Sept. 14, 1881; Mary R. (F)ANTON, Nov. 6, 1903;
James HIGDON, Sept. 20, 1920; Emily J. HASLAN, Jan. 21, 193(0);
Wm. HIGDON, Mar. 8, 1932; Earl ANTHONY, 1896; Fitzhorn L. ANTHO-
NY, 1904; John HAUBACK, (no date given); Micajah G. MITCHELL (no
date given); Abevilla MITCHELL (no date given); Lawrence HIGDON,
Sept. 4, 1954; Ernestine HIGDON, July 30, 1954.

LOT 35-B: Samuel THOMAS;
Samuel THOMAS, Jan 23, 1873; Rebecca JONES, Jan. 25, 1851; Mrs. Samuel THOMAS, Nov. 25, 1855; S. Daw (or Dew) THOMAS, Apr. 23, 1868; Georgia A. THOMAS, Jan. 14, 1921; Mary A. THOMAS, Aug. 31, 1850; Benj. P. BOWERS, Feb. 15, 1855; S. D(ewa) or D(awa) THOMAS, May 30, 1868 (entry crossed out); Millicent G. THOMAS, Nov. 21, 1855; George R. THOMAS, May 22, 1881; Mary Adeline THOMAS, Aug. 31, 1850.

LOT 36-B: Francis L. LAWRENCE;
L. King LAWRENCE, Nov. 23, 1853; Francis LAWRENCE, Jan. 29, 1859; Louis A. LAWRENCE, Jan. 29, 1859; Edw. D. LAWRENCE, May 3, 1860; Lubries H. LAWRENCE, July 9, 1863; Geo. W. LAWRENCE, Aug. 17, 1866; Hammond D. LAWRENCE, Nov. 10, 1884, (Other entry gives date of 1844 "Father"); 3 Children, Apr. 20, 1886; Louisa L. LAWRENCE, May 18, 1858 (mother); Larkin H. LAWRENCE, Nov. 22, 1854; Caleb Van Buren LAWRENCE, July 12, 1850.

LOT 37-B: George J. KUHN & Sophia BLUMENAUR;
Geo. J. KUHN, Nov. 28, 1927; Kara K. KUHN, June 1, 1931; Still born of (Elica) KUHN (no date given); El(mer) KUHN, July 27, 1914; Sophia BLUMENAUER, Sept. 23, 1972, born Dec. 16, 1891, died Sept. 21, 1972, father Frank CHETELAT, mother Mary DARLING; Louis A. BLUMENAUR, Oct. 24, 1950.

LOT 38-B: John L. ALLEN & Benj. M. BIXLER;
Sarah ALLEN, Oct. 12, 1854; John L. ALLEN, Aug. 25, 1865; Leona L. ALLEN, July 12, 1877; Laura ALLEN, May 4, 18(9)1; Edw. T. ALLEN, Sept. 18, 1899; Mary ALLEN, Apr. 8, 1913; John L. HARRISON, Oct. 24, 1859; Bryon ALLEN, Mar. 4, 1868; Mary M. PATTERSON, July 9, 1921; Remains, Apr. 18, 1861; Wm. H. BIXLER, Dec. 25, 1875; Daniel BIXLER, Dec. 22, 1882 (father); David BIXLER, June 16, 1865; Harriet BIXLER, Aug. 5, 1859 (mother); Danl. BIXLER, Jr., Sept. 6, 1921; Marie Louise BIXLER, Sept. 8, 1881 (or 7). Other names - in 1922 Louis A. BIXLER & Louis A. BIXLER hold lots.

LOT 39-B: Thomas H. FREELAND;
T. FREELAND, Mar. 26, 1861; Dan D. IRELAND, May 26, 1866; El(uona) FREELAND, Sept. 28, 1867; Ellen MILLER, Dec. 5, 1892. The date Aug. 15, 1876 is given with no name indicated.

LOT 40-B: Felix MC CURLEY;
Child, May 5, 1853; Child of WATERS, May 25, 1871; Annie C. WATERS, June 18, 1878; Felexana PHILIPS, Apr. 19, 1878; Ann R. MC CURLEY, Apr. 7, 1882; Fannie WALTERS, Apr. 7, 1882; Felix MC CURLEY, Mar. 10, 1891; John L. WATTERS, June 18, 1895.

LOT 41-B: Saml. PILSON & Robert PILSON, Isabel R. D. SHAFFNER;
Easter TRAUGHT, May 24, 1856; Robert PILSON, Aug. 24, 1860; Mrs. M. ENGLISH, Nov. 11, 1864; Rebecca SHAFFNER, Dec. 20, 1875.

LOT 42-B: Henry BELL;
Isabella (MARRON), Jan. 24, 1878; Henry BELL, July 4, 1878; Mary KIRK, July 30, 1892; Gertrude KIRK, July 26, 1895; Sarah J. GIBBS, Nov. 20, 1899; Jane BELL, and Henry BELL, June 20, 1883; Martha H. KIRK, Jan. 17, 1895; John WATTERS, Mar. 9, 1843; George CARSON, Aug. 28, 1858; Eliza CARSON, Mar. 21, 1858; Rev. Joseph

W. KIRK, Dec. 15, 1943; Gertrude BRATT, Apr. 8, 1944; Mary WATTERS, Jan. 11, 1816.

LOT 43-B: Jos. OLDHAM, Mary A. ROOKER;
Josephine OLDHAM, May 20, 1838; Jos. OLDHAM, May 10, 1873; Jos. D. OLDHAM, (June) 8, 1874; Wm. M. OLDHAM, Dec. 13, 1886; Katherine WALTON, Aug. 12, 1924; Susannah L. OLDHAM, Aug. 27, 1894; Thomas D. WILKENS, Dec. 18, 1937; Samuel BOOKER, Sept. 7, 1852; B(ereuiet) THOMAS, Oct. 12, 1911; Margt. A. THOMAS, Feb. 1, 1932; Henrietta C. WALTON, May 10, 1945; Daniel W. WALTON, Feb. 27, 1951; Alice THOMAS, Jan. 16, 1956; Samuel ROOKER, b. 1799, age 54 years; Samuel OLDHAM, (no date given); Elizabeth HUNTER, (no date given); Mary Alice THOMAS, (no date given).

LOT 44-B: Wm. ULLRICK and David ANDERSON;
Ann DOBBS, Oct. 3, 1851; George (M.) ANDERSON, July 22, 1866; James ANDERSON, Nov. 2, 1871; David ANDERSON, Aug. 20, 1873; Margt. ANDERSON, July 30, 1874; still born, June 19, 1877; James K. ANDERSON, Dec. 17, 1879; Gussie PARSONS, Feb. 26, 1880; Eliza ANDERSON, Aug. 5, 1880; Kate R. ANDERSON, Nov. 10, 1882; Rose PARSONS, Oct. 3, 1885; Theo. PARSONS, July 26, 1887; Wesley W. PARSONS, Aug. 22, 1921; Wm. H. ULLRICK, Apr. 2, 1852; Christen ULRICK, Sept. 14, 1870; Wm. ULLRICK, Mar. 29, 1886; Frances W. WARNER, Apr. 11, 1886; Wm. H. ULLRICK, Apr. 29, 1856; Christen ULLRICH, July 11, 1894; A. Mary ULLRICK, Jan. 25, 1910; William Webster PARSONS, Jan. 11, 1945; Janie A. PARSONS, Mar. 20, 1944; Rudolph SLADKY, June 4, 1941; Catherine PARSONS, Aug. 11, 1965.

LOT 45-B: Thos. BALDERSON and John G. CHAPPELL;
Mary P. BUCKINGHAM, Apr. 22, 1895; Chas. W. BUCKINGHAM, May 13, 1908; Thos. BALDERSON, July 28, 1919; Clara V. BALDERSON, Feb. 6, 1928; Mabel B. YOUNG, Aug. 4, 1930; Child, Aug. 29, 1855; Child, Sept. 22, 1855; Rebecca CHAPPELL, Mar. 19, 1873; Annie P. CHAPPELL, Apr. 7, 1884; Priscilla E. CHAPPELL, Oct. 17, 1891; Philip CHAPPELL, June 20, 1892; Rachel M. CHAPPELL, Jan. 20, 1925 (or 1933); C/Philap/Edmond CHAPPELL, June 18, 1892; Grace M. CHAPPELL, Apr. 12, 1950; Rebecca I.M.A. CHAPPELL, June 1, 1854; Child, Oct. 6, 1855; M. T. CHAPPELL, Apr. 25, 1854; John C. CHAPPELL, May 19, 1856.

LOT 46-B: Joseph BARLOW, Mrs. Clara M. CHRISTEIN, Mrs. Anna BURGESS;
Ambrose ANDERSON, May 18, 1885; Williams ANDERSON, June 2, 1885; Child of Frank Jas. BARLOW, Nov. 22, 188(0); Edward SCHAFFER, Dec. 23, 1889; Rose ANDERSON, Nov. 29, 1889; Louis A. BARLOW, Sept. 9, 1895; Gladys BARLOW, Sept. 17, 1900; William F. ENSOR, Jan. 18, 1912; Frank BARLOW, Mar. 1, 1919; Mary C. BARLOW, Feb. 9, 1927; Frank W. BARLOW, Feb. 19, 1927; "for Louise Barlow STANFIELD, "for Clara M. CHRISTEIN," Anna A. BURGESS, Oct. 14, 1952; "for Harvey BURGESS."

LOT 47-B: John BLACK, Robert GORSUCH;
Eleandor BLACK, Feb, 1853; Thos. H. S. GORSUCH, Apr. 5, 1853; Robert GORSUCH, June 1, 1865; Roboert GORSUCH, Oct. 20, 1888; (Jophianna) GORSUCH, Aug. 15, 1892; Sarah A. HEAD (or HEARD), Oct. 7, 1873; Jas. S. GORSUCH, Nov. 8, 1934; Lieutenant Robert MC INTYRE, May 16, 18(44).

LOT 48-B & LOT 49-B appear to be the same lot, of Moses G. HINDES; William (T.) HINDES, Aug. 29, 18(51); Theodore HINDES, June 8, 185(3); Benjamine F. HINDES, 1873; John B. HINDES, Apr. 13, 1904; Child, June 10, 1871; Rebekah HINDES, 1874; John J. HINDES, Sept. 19, 1853; Fanhine (or Jahine) B. HINDES, July 26, 1856; Mary A. HINDES, Dec. 31, 1867; Mary A. HINDES, Sept. 25, 1877; William HINDES, Mar. 4, 1898; Emeline T. SIMMS, Oct. 17, 1900; Francis S. PRICE, Jan, 8, 1909; Rebekah HINDES, July 23, 1874; Jacob H. HINDES, Jan. 16, 1903; John HINDES, 1874.

LOT 11 & 50-B: John C. NAIRN; John C. NAIRN, Apr. 25, 1866; Francis T. NAIRN, Oct. 8, 1852.

LOT 51-B: Jas. H. STINCHCOMB, D. AARON, Mary BOSTON; Mary J. LECOMPT, July 26, 1869; Cynthia LECOMPT, May 26, 1869; M(arscellus) AARON, Feb. 14, 1874; D(oractry) AARON, Juliy 11, 1870; J. A. BOSTON, (possible 1846); (L.) E. BOSTON, 1842; M. F. BOSTON, 1849; John J. WRIGHT, Nov. 25, 1882; LaRue V. DORRETT, Aug. 2(7), 1877; Hooper LECOMPT, Mar. 3, 1936; Isabella STINCHCOMB, Sept. 24, 1877; Rebecca FRIZZELL, Jan. 10, 1883; (Aaron A.) STINCHCOMB, May 17, 1892; Emeline STEWART, Nov. 23, 1895; Jas. H. STINCHCOMB, May 23, 1896; Je(ssie) R. STEWART, Feb. 26, 1907; Josephine LIESTER, (no date given); J. T. AARON, (no date given); "D. H. of AARON" (no date given); Thos. F. LECOMPTE, May 26, 1869.

LOT 52-B: Chas. TOWSON; Remains from St. Peter's May 11, 1873; Peter KNIGHT, June 2, 1893.

LOT 53-B: Wesley MASON, John STINCHCOMB, James STINCHCOMB; (Len) STINCHCOMB, Oct. 15, 1858; Child of N. WILLIAMS, July 5, 1869; Child, Dec. 16, 1861; Susan STINCHCOMB, Aug. 22, 1873; Mary A. STINCHCOMB, Oct. 11, 1892; (Mos) MASON, Nov. 15, 1852; Rachel SHELDON, Sept. 12, 1853; Wm. T. B. HOPKINS, Aug. 22, 1874; Wesley MASON, Aug. 10, 1882; Maria A. E. MASON, July 16, 1891; John W. MASON, Apr. 15, 1902 (or 4); Fred. (BODENSICK), Dec. 10, 1858; Jacob (HENKEL), June 24, 1867; Robert MASON, Dec. 9, 1858; Maria MASON, July 15, 1891; Richard M. MC CLURE, Sept. 20, 1954; Eliza MASON, Oct. 9, 1852; Sarina MASON, (no date given); Almira MASON, (no date given); John W. MASON, (no date given); Virce MC CLURE, May 10, 1854; Richard MC CLURE, Nov. 1, 1944; Susan A. STINCHCOMB, May 22, 1914.

LOT 54-B: Louis C. MARPOE, Wm. BROOKS, Mrs. Susan FOX; Child, Apr. 14, 1851; Marg. A. MARPOE, July 28, 1879; Francis MARPOE, July 29, 1879; Mary C. BROOKS, Oct. 16, 1856; John BROOKS, June 10, 1858; Willie WHITE, Oct. 28, 1853; Mary C. BROOKS, July 15, 1858; Sarah C. WHITE, Apr. 27, 1865; Wm. BROOKS, May 25, 1874; Susan RICHARDS, Aug. 15, 1874; Annie L. RICHARDS, Jan. 3, 1876; Margt. BOOKS, Oct. 23, 1880; Sarah E. WHITE, June 27, 1882; still born Jan. 30, 189(1); J. (Emory) BROOKS, Mar. 17, 1894; Mary E. MARPOE, (no date given); Joseph MARPOE, Feb. 22, 1851; William H. WHITE, (no date given); Mary E. WHITE, (no date given); Sarah WHITE, (no date given); Jerimiah BROOKS, (no date given).

LOT 55-B: Sarah RICE transferred to John Thomas RICE; John Thomas RICE, June 9, 1937; Ada M. RICE, Sept. 20, 1929; John T. RICE, Jr., Jan. 23, 1908; John T. RICE, Feb. 23, 1887; Eliza RICE, Feb. 14, 1906; Sarah S. RICE, Nov. 1, 1909; Sarah RICE, Oct. 28, 1872; Rev. John RICE, Oct. 26, 1872.

LOT 56-B: Wm. ADDISON; Remains, Oct. 19, 1859; Mary A. ADDISON, May 23, 1877 (also Dec. 6, 1877); Elizabeth THOMAS, (no date given); Peter ARMSTRONG, Jan. 1, 1857; Elizabeth A. DOUGLAS, May 22, 1877; still born Apr. 14, 1884; Wm. ADDISON, Jan. 27, 1891; Taylor ADDISON, Feb. 10, 1916; Katherine W. ADDISON, May 24, 1918; George W. ADDISON, Feb. 8, 1896; Wm. WOOD, Feb. 8, 1889.

LOT 57-B: Tillison M. MORGAN, and N. P. MORGAN; Elizabeth MORGAN, Apr. 23, 1852; Lyttelton B. MORGAN, June 13, 1860; Rev. T. A. MORGAN, Ap. 26, 1887; Susan A. MORGAN, July 17, 1911; Caroline D. MORGAN, Feb. 26, 1913; Frances R. MORGAN, Jan. 16, 1917; Ann W. MORGAN, Aug. 17, 1862; J. A. MORGAN, Nov. 30, 1879; Susie MORGAN, Apr. 14, 1862; Cath. A. MORGAN, Feb. 17, 1863; Susan J. MORGAN, July 16, 1911; Frances C. MORGAN, Feb. 23, 1913.

LOT 58-B: Rev. Saml. REGESTER and Saml. BRISON; Child, May 16, 1853; Child, Oct. 20, 1858; Child, Apr. 12, 1861; Rev. Saml. REGESTER, Oct. 19, 1881; Annie E. REGESTER, Feb. 16, 1880; Ada G. REGESTER, Jan. 23, 1882; Annie E. REGESTER, Jan. 30, 1882; Paul REGESTER, Apr. 28, 1888; Fannie L. LAWRENCE, Oct. 17, 1895; Geo. E. LAWRENCE, March 6, 1903; Rev. Samuel BRISON, Oct. 13, 1858; Mary M. BRISON, Jan. 2, 1853; Margt. A. LAWRENCE, May 3, 1904; Fannie Gray REGISTER, Dec. 11, 1900.

LOT 59-B: John MC FARLAND; Ellen MILLER, Feb. 8, 1853; Annie M. MC FARLAND, Aug. 19, 1875; John MC FARLAND, Jan. 15, 1886; Wm. MC FARLAND, June 3, 1881; Mary MC FARLAND, Jan. 20, 1902; Sarah J. MC FARLAND, Jan. 7, 1905; Annie E. MC FARLAND, Oct. 10, 1911; Mable A. MC FARLAND, Apr. 21, 1881; Kava A. MC FARLAND, Oct. 26, 1908; James H. MC FARLAND, June 25, 1921; John MC FARLAND, Oct. 13, 1924; Franc(?)s MC FARLAND, Jan. 25, 1926; Harry MC FARLAND, June 11, 1937; Fanny MC FARLAND, (no date given); William MC FARLAND, (no date given); John MC FARLAND, (no date given).

LOTS 60-B through 65-B are missing.

LOT 66-B: E. P. PHELPS, Mrs. Mary P. MITCHELL; Eliz. (KIDIA), Apr. 9, 1851; Mary W. PHELPS, July 24, 1867; Elisha P. PHELPS, Apr. 26, 1887; Chas. M. H. PHELPS, Feb. 18, 1913; E. Cordelia R. PHELPS, May 29, 1851; Mary J. PHELPS, May 14, 1925; Herbert F. MITCHELL, Aug. 29, 1962; Thomas W. S. PHELPS, Aug. 27, 1938.

LOT 67-B: Susannah M. ROBERTS; Susan M. ROBERTS, Nov. 20, 1869; Chas. E. ROBERTS, Feb. 17, 1877; Nancy THOMAS, Nov. 27, 1880.

LOT 68-B: George W. ROBERTS; George C. M. ROBERTS, Jan. 15, 1870; George C. M. ROBERTS,

(1851); Elizabeth ROBERTS, (no date given); Amelia ROBERTS, (Jan. 12, 1865); Susanna ROBERTS, (Jan. 21, 1869?).

LOT 69-B: Edward S. HOUGH;
Edw. S. HOUGH, Mar. 28, 1881; Susan A. HOUGH, Apr. 12, 1886; Harrie HOUGH, Oct. 27, 1922; Hamilton F. BROWN, Aug. 20, 1923; Harre ROBBINS, May 28, 1932; Children of Edw. & Susan (no date given); Nannie Whiting Hamilton HOUGH, July 13, 1940; Edward Hamilton HOUGH, Mar. 8, 1952; Harre H. ROBBINS, b. Nov. 29, 1915; d. Oct. 25, 1969, bur. Oct. 27, 1969; Nannie L. ROBBINS, Sept. 30, 1966; Isabella Gregory Hough BROWN, July 31, 1940.

LOT 70-B: George R. CROOKS, and Katherine EMORY;
Rev. CROOKS, Feb. 1, 18(60, 66 or 68) and children; Rev. George R. CROOKS, Feb. 20, 1897; Katherine M. CROOKS, Dec. 22, 1916; George (no surname or date); Henry SELLERS, Feb. 4, 1857; "Our Little Babe" (no surname or date); George Richard (no surname), Jan. 28, 1860; Reober EMORY, Aug. 5, 1857; S. Frances Emory CROOKS, Nov. 5, 1877, dau. of Rev. John EMORY and wife of George R. CROOKS; Nellie CROOKS, Dec. 22, 1945.

Inscription on monument, Rev. Robert EMORY, D.D., President of Dickenson College, born July 27, 1814; died May 18, 1848.

LOT 71-B: Isaac MITCHELL, Wm. H. BIXLER;
Remains, (no date given); H. Elizabeth BIXLER, May 29, 1889; Wm. H. H. BIXLER, Mar. 5, 18(?)7; Carrie BOYER, Nov. 30, 1949; "Remains of John T. BOYER, 1923 and Infant of Divine 1926, Dec. 16, 1949" from St. Mary's Cemetery; Joan M. HOPKINS, Mar. 15, 1955; Wm. H. H. BIXLER, Sr., (no date given); Grace BIXLER, and John BIXLER children; Elizabeth M. ROBINSON, June 24, 1964; James E. ROBINSON, May 29, 1965; Elizabeth MITCHELL, Mar. 19, 1841; Julia G. BIXLER, June 13, 1966, b. Oct. 7, 1877, d. June 11, 1966, age 89 years; Dr. William H. H. BIXLER, Jr., June 21, 1951.

LOT 72-B and 77-B: Chapin A. HARRIS;
Va. BANKER, Mar. 28, 1894; Rich. H. JAMES, Dec. 10, 1896; Lillian M. JAMES, Apr. 3, 1898; Chapin A. HARRIS, Oct. 8, 1860; Libbie HARRIS, 1854; Darwin B. HARRIS, 18(3)7; Mary C. HARRIS, 1837; Irwin L. HARRIS, 1837; James HARRIS, 1835; Elizabeth HARRIS, 1805; Chapin B. HARRIS, 1861; Alfred H. (BLANDY), (no date given); Lucy H. (BLANDY), (no date given); Albert B. (BLANDY), (no date given).

LOT 73-B: John H. MILLER, Ruth A. SANKS, George MC LEAD;
Remains of child (disinterred) Mar. 29, 1873; Anne T. SANKS, Apr. 1, 1857; William SANKS, Apr. 5, 1862; Sarah J. MILLER, Feb. 10, 1875; Adeline MILLER, June 16, 1883; Ruth MILLER, Sept. 14, 1896; Maggie MILLER, Dec. 11, 1886; John A. MILLER, July 22, 1887; John T. MILLER, Feb. 21, 1908; George ROBERTS, Jan. 27, 1879; George H. MC LEAD, July 21, 1890; Alex W. MC LEAD, Dec. 2, 1891; John H. MILLER, Aug. 22, 1918; Mrs. Frederick Wm. WRIGHT, (Nova Scotia), (no date given); Sarah Truman MC LEOD, (no date given); Ge(os)ett MC LEAD, (no date given); Isabella C. BRANT, Jan. 25, 1850; John BRANT, Aug. 3, 1844; Georgina Hulse MC LEOD, (no date given).

LOT 74-B: George COOPER, Wm. YOUNG, Jr.;
Wil(li) WILLING, May 19, 1851, (could also be Wilba, Willia or Wilbr); Eliz PATTON, Aug. 24, 1856; Elizabeth NORTH, Oct. 9,

1863; Jane LAU(CK), Mar. 31, 1891; Flora SKIRVEN, Sept. 12, 1892: Wm. YOUNG, (no date given); George STONE, (no date given); Emma SKIRVEN, Mar 13, 1911.

LOT 75-B: Elizabeth DEAVER;
Elizabeth Ann DEAVER, (child), (no date given); John Lucas DEAVER, (child), (no date given); John Talbott DEAVER, (child), (no date given); Dr. Clarence S. GORE, Jan. 26, 1942; Dr. Albert P. GORE, Apr. 28, 1923; Fannie S. GORE, Jan. 20, 1919; Emmanuel Kent DEAVER, July 27, 1844.
This is a twelve-space lot. In space one is written "There is no boody here. Burial to take place in England, order of Miss Frances E. GORE, 84 Burton Ct., London SW 3 Chelsea 45X, England."

LOT 76-B: George HALTZMAN;
Kate HATLZMAN, Oct. 14, 1876; Sarah DEEN, Nov. 19, 1876; Eliz. ALLSWORTH, Dec. 24, 1864; M. C. HALTZMAN, July 13, 1866; Margt. HALTZMAN, Apr. 25, 1884; Willie J. WOOD, Sept. 24, 1886; Anna HALTZMAN, Mar. 1, 1904; Sarah Ann HOLTZMAN, (no date given).

[See LOT 72 for LOT 77]

LOT 78-B: Henry CHRISTLIFF;
(Mrs.) CHRISTLIFF, Apr. 1, 1864; Frances CHRISTLIFF, Dec. 14, 1872; George Henry CHRISTLIFF, Mar. 2, 1864; Sarah CHRISTLIFF, Apr. 6, 1870; Henry CHRISTLIFF, Nov. 26, 1866; Margt. A. CHRSITLIFF, Nov. 18, 1890; still born of Lom. CHRISTLIFF, Aug. 1, 1896; Susan F. CHRISTLIFF, Oct. 13, 1901; Adele F. CHRISTLIFF, May 20, 1930; Sarah, Thomas, Mattie ____.

LOT 79-B: Albert W. HONEYWELL, O. J. HONEYWELL, Susan H. DUNN; Eliza COOK, July 18, 1881; Sarah PARKER, Nov. 27, 1888; Charles B. HONEYWELL, Feb. 7, 1903; "This grave formally assigned to James (B.) HONEYWELL, by Kate HONEYWELL; Mamie H. HOBBS, Aug. 31, 1878; Children of DOUGHERTY, June 2, 1878; Susan H. RINGOLD, Mar. 18, 1904; B. B. HOBBS, Dec. 13, 1878; Emma E. HOBBS, June 29, 1879; Kate HONEYWELL, Oct. 27, 1945; Albert W. HONEYWELL, Feb. 3, 1887; Malina HONEYWELL, Dec. 30, 1882; Caleb COOKE, and ---- SWAN, Sept. 5, 1832; Jeanette L. DOUGHERTY, May 19, 1923; Georgianna DOUGHERTY, Aug. 2, 1940; Warren DOUGHERTY, Aug. 10, 1948.

LOT 80-B: Isabella CAMPBELL & Lydia WELSH;
Elvina CAMPBELL, Dec. 3, 1888; Isabella CAMPBELL, Sept. 10, 1900; Nicholas HOGAN, May 5, 1853; Horatio BEALL, Aug. 27, 1857; Horatio BEAL, Jr., (no date given); Levina Beall OFFUTT, Dec. 9, 1935; Charles (I.) WELSH, Dec. 4, 1862; Lydia CURRY, Nov. 12, 1870; Lydia WELSH, Dec. 12, 1871; John CURRY, Dec. 7, 1868; Leona W. BRIGHT, May 4, 1887; Elizabeth Evaline OFFUTT, Nov. 23, 1940; [Mrs. (G.) Frank WEATH(ER)LY of Mt. Washington, Baltimore, MD, claims usage of lot].

LOT 81-B: James R. SCOTT, Isaac JONES;
Anna E. SCOTT, Apr. 25, 1870 (or 1871); Jas. R. SCOTT, Jan. 14, 1873; Walter M. SCOTT, July 18, 1890; Maggie A. SCOTT, Apr. 21, 1903; Wm. R. SCOTT, Jan. 20, 1917; Leroy FETHERS, Jan 9, 1918; Walter L. FETHERS, Mar. 10, 1919; Wm. (W.) SCOTT, July 13, 1934; Isaac JONES, Mar. 2, 1895; Catherine JONES, Dec. 4, 1854; Isaac

W. JONES, Aug. 14, 1856; Emma TOWNSEND, Mar. 2, 1857; Willie
JONES, July 6, 1857; Mary BELL, June 15, 1866; Child, Aug. 20,
1866; George JENNINGS, Jan. 22, 1869; Mary JENNINGS, Mar. 23,
1870; Anna E. FORD, Ap. 19, 1879; George JENNINGS, Feb. 13, 1879;
Franklin C. FORD, June 5, 1876; Nellie M. JENNINGS, June 28,
1890; A. L. ACTON, July 13, 1892; Howard M. THOMAS, Apr. 20,
1885; (An K. ELAPANB [sic]), (no date given); Frances J. SCOTT,
July 10, 1907; Serg(n)t JONES, WSN, (no date given).

LOT 81 1/2 - 86-B: Aged Men & Women House, Calhoun & Lexington
Sts.
Elizabeth (COMSTARET), Sept. 22, 1934; (Jowet) JOHNSON, Jan. 2,
1934; (See LOT 86-B:)

LOT 82-B: Adam SNIVELY and Christian CLOSE;
Susannah CLOSE, June 19, 1857; Christian CLOSE, May 19, 1865;
Barbara CLOSE, Sept. 3, 1896.

LOT 83-B: Charlotte BAKER and George W. TERRELL;
Mary E. TERRELL, May 18, 1879; Wm. S. JEFFARES, Mar. 1, 1918
(entry is scratched through, George W. (LENCLL [sic]) is inserted); John A. SELBY, Nov. 2, 1926; John T. SELBY, Mar. 29, 1933;
Wm. E. BAKER, Jan. 1, 1859; Emily BAKER, Nov. 27, 1856; Charlotta
BAKER, July 6, 1857; Wm. BERRY, Mar. 3, 1864; Annie R. BERRY,
Apr. 16, 1872; Mary E. TERRELL, Feb. 1, 1897; Alice T. SELBY,
Feb. 12, 1937; Isaac BAKER, May 25, 1852; Wm. R. BERRY, Dec. 30,
1858; Frank B. BERRY, Jan. 25, 1859; Charlotte BERRY, Aug. 15,
1944; Ann Rebecca BAKER, Apr. 25, 1872.

LOT 84-B: Baltimore Orphan Asylum. The name Mrs. Andrew
WRITRIDGE is associated with this lot.
Child, July 17, 1859; Child, Oct. 31, 1856; Annie MARSHAL, Mar.
17, 1860; Charlotte LILLY, Mar. 22, 1860; Child, June 9, 1865;
Saml. TAYLOR, July 15, 1859; (Wm. DARR's [sic]), Dec. 26, 1862;
Thomas (?EDWARDS), Jan. 9, 1875; Walter W. GEORG(US), Jan. 19,
1875; Lillie (L.) TARR, (no date given); (Geo. TAYLER), Feb. 13,
1875; (Eunice CHRINGTON), Feb. 26, 1875; Carroll (FISHER),
(March) 30, 1875; Clara DANGERFIELD, Dec. 23, 1876; Rose BAILEY,
May 10, 1875; Kate ZIMMERMAN, (Jan.) 19, 1886; Theresa COLLINS,
June 28, 1886; Bertie WHITE, June 17, 1887; Lucy JONES, July 8,
18(7)1; Willis JOHNSON, Dec. 16, 1871; Lottie HANCOCK, ---- 7,
1910 (moved to Louden Park); Chas. E. WILLIAMS, Apr. 4, 1911;
Kath. WATTES, Jan. 14, 1918; Edna M. LEVY, Nov. 18, 1919; Emma
SEGARS, Feb. 14, 1922.

LOT 86-B: Aged Women's and Aged Men's Home, Calhoun & Lexington
Sts., (see LOT 81 1/2-B: also);
Harry OADES, May 11, 1942; John Lee KRIDER, Apr. 22, 1942; Daniel
SHEA, Feb. 11, 1941; Nathaniel MEEKINS, Jan. 7, 1941; Florence
TUCKER, Nov. 26, 1943; Jennie LEARY, Dec. 24, 1943; Robert Lee
MILBURN, Oct. 24, 1945; Leonard C. TREHERNE, Feb. 2, 1946.

LOT 88-B & 89-B: Aged Men & Women's House, Calhoun & Lexington
Sts.;
(Albert) B. (GRANBURY), July 23, 1925, (Also given as GRANBERRY);
Alice V. TAYLER, Aug. 20, 192(5), (Also given as TYLER); Chas.
(H.) BILL(EGHS), Jan. 14, 1926, (possible BILLAFES); (Jeamie) A.
SCOTT, Mar. 3, 1926; Laura V. GARLAND, May 10, 1926; (Resvell)
MARTIN, July 6, 1926; Geo. E. LEACH, Jan. 3, 1927; Samuel GRAY,

(May) 27, 1927; David COLLINS, Nov. 1(6), 1927; Ba(rney) DE CO(RSE), Dec. 14, 1928; Kate KELLAN, Jan. 23, 1929; Carl PIEPGRAS, Mar. 13, 1929; Elizabeth (SASC)HARD, July 21, 19(36); Mary J. REID, Mar. 12, 1932; Belle MC KENZIE, Mar. 12, 1932; John ANDERSON, July 9, 1932; John E. HOMER, Apr. 10, 19(??); John C. HORNER, Ap. 10, 1934; Georgia BARNETT, Oct. 13, 1934; James PURNELL, Jan. 3, 1935; Sallie HOPKINS, Feb. 2, 1935; Alexander VINCENT, Aug. 13, 1936; Giorgeanna SLOCUM, Dec. 1, 1936; Elmer C. SCHOPPERT, Sept. 11, 1965; Lloyd RUPPERT, Dec. 19, 1940; Anna S. WRIGHT, May 25, 1940; John B. SULLIVAN, Feb. 3, 1940; Harry MORTIMER, Sept. 5, 1939; Laura V. HORNER, (no date given).

LOT 87-B: David BALL;
Ann (PERRICIE), Dec. 6, 1870; David E. BALL, Dec. 25, 1875; 2 Children of J. T. TALBOT, Aug. 20, 1874; David BALL, JUne 18, 1877; Sarah BALL, Mar. 2(8), 1885; Walter BALL, Mar. 15, 1886; Carrie BALL, Sept. 10, 1888; John S. BALL, Nov. 1891; Al(eai)sta V. BALL, Apr. 23, 1892; H. Clay BALL, Jan. 4, 1899; Geo. C. BALL, Feb. 2, 1883; Harriett L. BURST, Sept. 26, 1927; Frank M. BURST, Apr. 23, 1934; David BALL (no date given).

LOT 89-B: John H. CHANDLER;
Susan CHANDLER, Aug. 19, 1874; Sarah R. TAYLOR, Dec. 8, 1875; John H. STRIDE, July 18, 1881; Ann Jane HARVEY, Dec. 2, 1889; Mary ALEXANDER, May 6, 1902.

LOT 90-B: Aged Women's Home, Calhoun & Lexington Sts., (See 81 1/2-B to 90-B LOTS). Also the name of Wm. REISINGER associated with lot;
Marion V. REISINGER, Mar. 26, 1867; Mary L. LITTING, Nov. 19, 1889; John S. RICHARDSON, Feb. 9, 1891; Nellie J. LETTING, Feb. 5, 1894; Wm. RIESINGER, Ap. 1, 1895, (child at foot); J. Harman (SNIAT), May 1, 1903; Mary A. REISINGER, Feb. 4, 1911; Bertha Mc Keever VON LINDENBURGER, July 13, 1972, born Apr. 28, 1904, died July 10, 1972. Father Caris W. RICHARDSON, mother Hattie ZELL, (Funeral Home) Hubbard; Mary A. REISINGER, (no date given); Helen R. SMITH, Nov. 30, 1943; Bertha J. RICHARDSON, Dec. 19, 1938; Caris W. RICHARDSON, Feb. 13, 1952.

LOT 91-B: Hester Ann BROWN and Howard GREENTREE;
M. Z. GREENTREE, Apr. 13, 1867; Wm. H. GREENTREE, Apr. 29, 1867; Eliz GREENTREE, May 7, 1867 (entry crossed out); Florence D. GREENTREE, Aug. 12, 1875 (also a burial Florence W. GREENTREE, possible it's same person); Ester A. GREENTREE, Apr. 18, 1891; Harriett R. GREENTREE, March 12, 1898; Howard GREENTREE, June 9, 1909; Rebecca (S. or A.) GREENTREE, Feb. 10, 1930; (Jno. GRAVES), May 7, 1866; Charlotte SODLER, Jan 11, 1875; Susie (I.) WATERS, Jan. 15, 1876; Jos. W. BROWN, Mar. 24, 1887; Philip H. MASON, July 9, 1887; Hester A. BROWN, May 7, 1896; John J. BROWN, Feb. 17, 1912; Chas. H. BROWN, Apr. 26, 1884; Harriett GREENTREE, (no date given).

LOT 92-B: John CALVERT;
Child, Sept. 12, 1859; John A. ALDRIDGE, Apr. 13, 1868; Sarah CALVERT, July 4, 1868; Child, Jan. 25, 1869; Jno. A. CALVERT, Nov. 15, 1869; Florence V. CALVERT, Sept. 4, 1871; Sadie C. HALBEY, Dec. 11, 1875; John G. CALVERT, June 14, 1876; Kate C. CALVERT, Apr. 7, 1876; (Leonard) T. HA(LLEY), Aug. 31, 1925; John (B.) CALVERT, Jan. 22, 1878; Chas. J. CALVERT, Sept. 3, 1880;

Edith C. HALLEY, July 17, 1871; Franklin T. HALLEY, Feb. 3, 1881; Stillborn, Oct. 20, 1881; Mary CALVERT, July 5, 1893; Mary M. HALLEY, Dec. 18, 1893; Amy CALVERT, June 27, 1895; Mary A. CALVERT, June 19, 1896; (Ebert) CALVLERT, Sept. 11, 1896; Gertrude MORGAN, Jan. 24, 1883; Mary (E.) CALVERT, June 12, 1890; (Vitue) H. CALVERT, Dec. 8, 1894; Stillborn of Jas. YOUNG, Nov. 20, 1916; Lilly L. CORNISH, May 15, 1922 (Possible MC CORNISH); Jos. B. CALVERT, Apr. 26, 1924; T. N. HAILEY, May 21, 1924; Kate C. HALLEY, Nov. 10, 1924; Mary L. CALVERT, May 2, 1932; Edward B. CALVERT, Feb. 22, 1972, born Dec. 22, 1888, died Feb. 18, 1972, father J(a)s. B. CALVERT, mother Molly BLAIR; Elizabeth V. CALVERT, Apr. 5, 1972; Fredk. HALLEY, (no date given).

LOT 93-B: William SMITH and John T. LAWSON; --------, July 4, 1867; Susan A. BOWER, Feb. 7, 1878; Emma S. SMITH, Aug. 2, 1879; Wm. R. BROWNING, Aug. 20, 1890; Wm. E. A(NI)GEN, Nov. 8, 1896; Elijah B. SMITH, June 4, 1906; Annie O. CRISPEN, Oct. 13, 1908; J. BROWNING, Apr. 11, 1922; Jos. N. (MAKOLING), Oct. 10, 1927; Child, Apr. 28, 1860; Rev. W. A. LONG, June 26, 1865; Florence V. LAWSON, Sept. 11, 1874; Wm. L. LAWSON, Mar. 24, 1928; Wm. SMITH, (no date given); Mrs. Wm. L. LA(W)SON, (no date given); Leanord V. LAWSON, Sept. 17, 1940; J. Frank LAWSON, (no date given); Emma Virginia LAWSON, July 2, 1952; Ada WARREN, June 2, 1954; William D. SCHOLMAN, Aug. 19, 1938.

LOT 94-B: John R. KENEAM & Thos. EDGAR (The KENEAM surname is poorly written throughout the lot record & its identity here is, after the K, purely speculation); Geo. EDGAR, June 2, 1864; child of T. EDGAR, July 19, 1864; Susan EDGAR, Jan. 14, 1876; Thos. EDGAR, Oct. 26, 1889; Harold EDGAR, Dec. 15, 1910; Child, July 16, 1872; Saml. D. KENEAN, July 11, 1873; John R. KENEAM, May 25, 1876; Laura V. KENEAN, June 22, 1885; Anna J. KENEAM, Sept. 5, 1885; Susan Jeanett EDGAR, May 15, 1973, born Mar. 10, 1894, died May 12, 1973, father James W. EDGAR, mother Florence E. TUCKEY; Harold EDGAR, (no date given); James W. EDGAR, Feb. 18, 1948; Florence Evelyn EDGAR, Nov. 7, 1956.

LOT 95-B: Genevieve BATHGATE, Mary W. TRIPP and Lillian Ray WESTWAY; Genevieve BATHGATE, Sept. 12, 1959; Daisy A. PURNELL, May 16, 1942; Mary M. PURNELL, July 17, 1934; Sarah E. BATHGATE, Jan. 19, 1954; Edward T. PALMER, Feb. 14, 1862, remains from S.B. ground, Mar. 8, 1852; William PALMER, Jan. 7, 1871; William P. PALMER, July 29, 1908; Lillian C. (Ray) WESTAWAY, May 4, 1973, b. Jan. 18, 1899, died May 1, 1973, father Robert CROWSON, mother Rachell GEALORD; Harry J. WESTWAY, Sept. 2, 1929; Mary W. TRIPP, Feb. 19, 1871.

LOT 96-B & 4 1/2 of 135-B: Home of Aged M.E. Church, Fulton & Franklin Sts., all burials in top; Sarah E. CLEMUS (or CLEMONS), June 12, 1922; Jane E. PAYNE, May 25, 1923; Mary E. H(IR)CORNE (could be HURCORNE), June 30, 1923; Susan SCHOENBORN, July 11, 1923; Dora L. RIRTGEWAY (also spelled RIDGEWAY), Jan 15, 1924; Rachel KALLER, Jan. 31, 1924; Madeline BENNING, Nov. 8, 1924; Susan COP(ER)Y (may be COPING), Mar. 12, 1923; Elizabeth PENN, Mar. 24, 1925; Ella NORMAN, Mar. 26, 1928; Ella FOOKE, Nov. 20, 1925; Eliza HILLEDGE, JUne 14, 1926; Annie HARDING (may be HATHING), Aug. 7, 1926; Josiah DICKINS, Sept. 21,

1926; Maria ERIKSON, Dec. 27, 1926; Axel ERCKSON, (July) 24, 1927.

LOT 96-B Continued. All of the following are reburials.
Mary DAVIDSON, June 9, 18(9)1; Mary CROSS, Apr. 26, 1880; Unknown, Mar. 9, 1892; Mary C. PEANINGTON, Sept. 8, 1880; Margaret DE FOREST, May 4, 1892; Frances SMITH, Dec. 17, 1883; Margaret BAKER, June 3, 1886; Ann CRAWFORD, Maya 4, 1873; Mary FAITH, Oct. 4, 1875; Ruth GOODWIN, June 13, 18(7)6; Sarah KEELSEY, July 13, 1876; Mary BAILEY, Sept. 17, 1879; Hannah SATTERFIELD, July 24, 1876; John FEAZARE, Nov. 25, 1876; Elizabeth WILLIAMS, Dec. 20, 1877; Margt. GAFFARD, May 9, 1878; Hannah WROTEN, July 29, 1878; Eliza RYAN, May 28, 1879; Eliza ASKEW, July 10, 1879.

LOT 96-B: Annie DURAND, Annie RAUSCHENBERG, Chas. E. CLARKE, Chas. A. MATTAX;
John B. DURAND, Aug. 28, 1934; Annie DURAND, (Jan. or July) 15, 1935; Carl H. RAUSCHENBERG, Sept. 4, 1904; Helen A. CLARKE, and baby Aug. 1, 1929; Ann M. MATTAX, Mar. 28, 1936; Anna RAUSCHENBERG, Jan. 5, 1948.

LOT 97-B: Alexander YEARLEY;
Alexander YEARLEY, May 1, 1853; Anne YEARLEY, June 27, 1864; John T. YEARLEY, Feb. 13, 1869; Saml. I. YEARLEY, Dec. 18, 1879; Aramenta YEARLEY, Jan. 9, 1889.

LOT 98-B: Mary PURDEN, John FRITZ, Cassinda FRUSH (may be FRNSH or FINSH);
Sarah FITZ, Aug. 22, 1871; Edna May ANDERSON, Sept. 4, (1918); Samuel S. MC CAULEY, July 2, 1929; Ada EADER, Oct. 11, 1920; Mary P(INDIN), July 22, 1858; Child, Oct. 9, 1860; Mary A. PURDEN, Dec. 25, 1869; Mary P. MILES, Jan. 22, 1917; Joseph H. MILES, Feb. 20, 1936; Elizabeth Ann MC CAULEY, Apr. 22, 1948; A. Leslie SAFNER, May 5, 1954; Mary PURDEN, July 18, 1887; Florence I. MULES, born Jan. 8, 1881, died Feb. 16, 1967, bur Feb. 20, 1967; Mary V. EADER, (no date given); John FITZ, July 25, 1854.

LOT 99-B: Beverly WAUGH;
Eliz. WAUGH, Mar. 2, 1859; Mary D. WAUGH, Dec. 19, 1859; John W. WAUGH, July 17, 1881, moved to LOT 194-A; A. T. WAUGH, July 5, 1890; Alex H. WAUGH, Mar. 24, 1894; Mary E. WAUGH, Mar. 20, 1916; Sgt. Beverly R. WAUGH, (no date given); Beverly WAUGH, Feb. 9, 1856; Catherine WAUGH, Mar. 22, 1865; Mary V. WAUGH, (no date given); Jas. B. WAUGH, (no date given).

LOT 100-B: Isaac P. COOK;
Child, May 14, 1854; Mary COOK, Oct. 28, 1863; Sarah CAULTER, May 12, 1868; Car(men) A. BIDD, Apr. 17, 1873; Sarah J. BLAKE, Sept. 10, 1900. There is a "Sarah Jacob BRICK", this may be the same as "Sarah J. BLACK" but buried in a brick grave. The record is not specific. John R. BLAKE, June 14, 1882.

LOT 101-B: Algernon WEBSTER and Moses L. EDMONDSON;
Child, July 13, 1854; 3 Children, Apr. 3, 1851; Algernon WEBSTER, Apr. 10, 1865; Florence _____ WEBSTER, Aug. 14, 1875; Alice WEBSTER, June 22, 1877; Saml. H. WEBSTER, May 18, 1881; Annie L. WEBSTER, Mar. 10, 1897; Stillborn of (Bertha) and Jos. WEBSTER, Dec. 15, 1904; Moses WEBSTER, Jan. 5, 1912; Harriet E. WEBSTER,

July 27, 1935; Jos. WEBSTER, July 2, 1936; Mary L. WHEELER, June 28, 1966; George E. WEBSTER, Dec. 13, 1949.

LOT 102-B: Rev. Robert S. VINTON; Juliet M. VINTON, May 24, 1872; Robert S. V. PERKINS, July 12, 1873; Rev. R. S. VINTON, July 31, 1870; Henry M. PERKINS, Jan. 5, 1880; Edith R. PERKINS, May 12, 1884; Marianna PERKINS, Jan. 5, 1915; Anna B. PERKINS, Aug. 10, 1916, 9 years old; Millard L. PERKINS, Sept. 27, 1922; Daniel D. BERRY, July 4, 1845; Olivia (probably BERRY, buried with above), Nov. 11, 1845; Jno. W. BERRY, July 24, 1859; Juliet VINTON, Mar. 21, 1846; Jeannette Vinton PERKINS, NOv. 15, 1948.

LOT 103-B: Wm. H. FRESHOUR and George W. KING; Catherine FRESHOUR, Feb. 28, 1861; Mable CLARK, Dec. 8, 1870; ___ M. CLARK, Spet. 2, 1882; D. W. CLARK, May 10, 18(84); (Ann) CLARK, July 13, 1889; (Daniel) CLARK, May 10, 1884; (Mrs. D. W.) CLARK, Aug. 4, 1928; (first seven entries disenterred & removed to Druid Ridge Cemetery); Elizabeth FRESHOUR, Apr. 15, 1892; Greenberry FRESHOUR, Mar .24, 1865; Anne M. LITTLEFIELD, May 4, 1905; John FREELAND, Jan. 18, 1869; Child of George W. KING, July 1, 1870; George D. FREELAND, July 21, 1870; George W. KING, Dec. 11, 1880; Edith (E.) FREELAND, Dec. 13, 1880; Sarah KING, July 22, 1882; George (W.) KING, May 17, 1890; Annie E. FREELAND, Aug. (5), 1911; Wilbur K. FREELAND, May 19, 1947.

LOT 104-B: Henry CARTER; Child, Feb. 14, 1861; Henry CARTER, Apr. 16, 1867; John CARTER, Jan. 22, 1868; George H. HYNSON, Nov. 3, 1875; Stillborn (Mr.) STOCKET, June 27, 1877; Jos. A. P. PENTZ, Sept. 13, 1877; J. R. and (G)eo. H. HYNSON, disinterred, Apr. 1, 1834; Ada V. CARTER, July 25, 1896; Mollie B. CARTER, Aug. 10, 1922; Susan J. CARTER, Nov. 20, 1901.

LOT 105-B: John P. MURRY and John DODD; John DODD, July 30, 1856; Eliz MC ALLISTER, Mar. 10, 1873; Henry F. BLACKBURN, Oct. 16, 1874; Emma L. DODD, Apr. 3, 1874; John DODD, May 25, 1864; Jane DODD, Nov. 28, 1887; Mary A. (STUMP), Oct. 21, 1914; John DODD, Mar. 1, 1891; Elizabeth J. BLACKBURN, Mar. 26, 193(?); Mary E. MURRAY, Sept. 16, 1854; Thos. C. MURRAY, Mar. 1, 1858; Clarence M. ARMSTRONG, Jan. 18, 1874; John P. MURRAY, Jan. 3, 1889; Cath. B. MURRAY, Feb. 13, 1890; Thomas O. MURRAY, (no date given); Sallie R. DODD, Oct. 17, 1901; Ella V. DODD, Sept. 7, 1934.

LOT 106-B: Daniel REESE; Ida V. GRAY, Apr. 8, 1858; Child, Oct. 22, 1866; Bertha GRAY, Jan. 19, 1867; Child of Chas. GRAY, July 25, 1870; Rev. Daniel M. REESE, Apr. 8, 1875; Children of E. I. REESE, Nov. 23, 1883; Ann REESE, Dec. 24, 1907; Fannie E. REESE, Feb. 11, 1933; W. Clarence STEWART, Jan. 2, 1937; Howard R. STEWART, Feb. 14, 1942; Ida R. STEWART, Mar. 4, 1946; Fannie Reese STEWART, (no date given).

LOT 107-B: Robert FISHER and Vincent P. SPEDDEN; Mrs. SPEDDEN, May 15, 1856; Rebecca SPEDDEN, Feb. 7, 1870; Wm. H. C. SPEEDEN, Dec. 25, 1871; Vincent P. SPEDDEN, July 13, 1872; Alfred E. SPEDDEN, May 11, 1881; Vincept P. SPEDDEN, May 4, 1886; Rebecca FISHER, June 24, 1855; Roboert FISHER, Jan. 28, 1893; Wm. W. FISHER, Aug. 25, 1921; Charles W. BAUMGARDNER, Apr. 22, 1974,

born May 29, 1902, died Apr. 18, 1974; father Amos BAUMGARDNER, mother Daisey SPILLMAN.
Letter from Lilyan M. WELLS to Mt. Olivet Cemetery declares she is heir to lots of her aunt, Annie M. BARNES (nee FISHER). Lilyan M. WELLS states she is selling three graves to Charles W. BAUMGARTNER on May 12, 1969. Letter dated May 12, 1969.

LOT 108-B: George LATCHFORD;
Eliabeth VERMILLER, June 11, 1856; Lydia F. HARVEY, June 4, 1878; Alice LATCHFORD, May 7, 1884; George LATCHFORD, Jan. 8, 1889; Andrew HARVEY, Mar. 30, 1904; Mary C. HARVEY, Jan. 22, 1918; Margaret DANIELS, (no date given); Alice DANIELS, (no date given); A. Edgar HARVEY, Feb. 28, 1920; V. Hau(es) WARD, Oct. 30, 1935; Alces L. STERLING, May 30, 1936; Annie C. WARD, Dec. 14, 1942.
Letter dated Sept. 29, 1964 to Mt. Olivet Cemetery. Harvey BOUNDS states his great-grandfather George LATCHFORD, and wife Alice LATCHFORD, were buried in Mt. Olivet Cemetery. He about 1889 and she possible 1884. Mr. Bounds' residence is given as Newark, Delaware (Ref. 108-B).

LOT 109-B: Philip D. LIPSCOMB and Edw. W. TEVES;
Bettie LIPSCOMB, May 1, 1855; Philip LIPSCOMB, Nov. 12, 1864; Philip D. LIPSCOMB, Jan. 6, 1870; Marie LIPSCOMB, Feb. 9, 1884; "Mrs. WILSON, child," Nov. 12, 1864; Elizabeth LIPSCOMB, (no date given, may be same as Bettie above); Wm. CA(RRIE), (no date given); George Edward William TEVES, Mar. 29, 1950; Wm. TEVES, (no date given).

LOT 110-B: John P. WALL and Wm. P. GETTIER;
Jacob GETTIER, Mar. 22, 1864; Children of RAY, Oct. 29, 1869; Margt. GETTIER, Aug. 13, 1875; Mary GETTIER, Mar. 21, 1876; Wm. P. GETTIER, Mar. 16, 1884; Mary E. WALL, Mar. 2, 1857; Elizabeth WALL, Sept. 9, 1871; Chas. BROOMFIELD, July 20, 1872; Ellen WALL, Jan. 9, 1884; John P. WALL, Aug. 4, 1884; Wm. F. WALL, Oct. 18, 1900; Ella Virginia GETTIER, 1856.

LOT 111-B: John S. MACHER;
John S. MACHER, May 20, 1858; Child, Apr. 2, 1866; Elbert MACHER, July 23, 1869; Chas. E. HAHN, Jan. 8, 1876; Kate E. MACHER, July 15, 1870; Anna E. MACHER, June 14, 1894; John S. MACHER, May 24, 1895; (Jas.) P. MACHER, (Oct.) 28, 1862; Mary E. MACHER, Apr. 16, 1865; Robt. T. EMORY, July 2, 1863; Benjamin MACHER, Mar. 29, 1880; Mrs. (Frances) E. MACHER, J(an.) 6, 1862, wife of J. S. M.; A. C. Ridgeway MACKER, 1894; Margaret J. MACKER, Oct. 21, 1928.

LOT 112-B: M. F. RUMNEY and Harriett BROOKS;
Wm. BROOKS, Sept. 8, 1858; Henrietta BROOKS, Nov. 2, 1869 (also given as Oct. 14, 1869); Robt. BROOKS, May 4, 1872; Sara A. BROOKS, Aug. 10, 1875; Brokie STOVER, July 22, 1878; Geo. W. BROOKS, Feb. 16, 1860 (also given as limb of, Nov. 28, 1861); Emily RAY, Feb. 16, 1889 (also given as Feb. 17, 1888); (Ruth WALTER), Sept. 12, 1935; Howard D. RUMNEY, Jan. 13, 1900; Earnest BELL, Aug. 16, 1902; Wain BELL, Jan. 24, 1908; John W. RUMNEY, Feb. 10, 1914; Frances RUMNEY, Aug. 23, 1915; Edwd. (A.) RUMNEY, July 8, 1918; Millard F. RUMNEY, Dec. 16, 1927; John RAY, May 7, 1863; Elizabeth RUMNEY, Feb. 2, 1937.

LOT 113-B: John G. KIRBY and Wm. LISH;
John E. KIRBY, June 3, 1881; Infant of E. & C. M. KIRBY, Mar. 29, 1886; Dr. Edwd. C. KIRBY, May 11, 1915; (Amah) J. KIRBY, Dec. 17, 1929; Clarence A. KIRBY, Dec. 17, 1929; L. F. V. LISH, June 24, 1865 (may be same as Lititia F. LISH); (Dr.) A. R. J. LISH, Sept. 26, 1874; Wm. LISH, M.D., Aug. 10, 1878; Bailey LISH, Mar. 21, 1884; Wm. B. LISH, Oct. 11, 1902 (may be same as Wm. Bruce LISH); Marie L. LISH, Aug. 13, 1903; Eliz M. LISH, May 8, 1915. (See also paragraph between LOT 117-B and LOT 118-B.)

LOT 114-B: James MOORE;
Remains from St. Peter's, June 28, 1873; child of MC LAUGHLIN, Sept. 1, 1875; James MOORE, the lot owner, has the number 1908 after his name, but does not appear in the diagram of burials. (See paragraph between LOT 117-B and LOT 118-B.)

Lot 115-B: Gideon SUNDERLAND;
Harriett BARNETT, Oct. 26, 1880.

LOT 116-B: Cordelia H. WILSON;
Robert and Hannah EDWARDS, July 16, 1884; Cordelia Howard WILSON, Aug. 18, 1908.

LOT 117-B: Henry W. MOORE & others;
James H. CADELE, Jan. 14, 1872; Stillborn of M. & Jos. (AWAS or AMOS), March 22, 1886; Margt. A. WINDER, Dec. 3, 1904; Martha J. MOORE, Aug. 6, 1907; Wm. A. MC LANAHAN, Sept. 12, 1923; Martha J. MC LANAHAN, Feb. 8, 1929 (probably same as Martha Johnstone MC LANHAN); Robert C. MC LANAHAN, Feb. 26, 1932; James J. MOORE, June 3, 1944; Ellen Jane MOORE, Apr. 3, 1945.
The back of the page has some very faint entries which appear to read as follows: 1. Pranrie SIMPSON in center of lot; 2. Burial; 3. Burial; 4. Dr. E. B. CURBY; 5. Wm. B. LISH; 6. Elizabeth LISH; 7. Letitia V. LISH; 8. Dr. R. R. J. LISH; 9. Dr. W. LISH; 10. Maria LISH; 11. Emily MOORE; 12. Margaret MOORE; 13. Mary & Sarah MOORE; 14. Mary S. MOORE. (Note: Numbers 4 through 10 probably refer to individuals buried in Lot 113-B. Numbers 11 through 14 should be in Lot 114-B, based on owner's name.)

LOT 118-B: Wm. A. WYLIE, Zelda (or ZELOLA) KLECH;
Francis SIMPSON, Sept. 14, 1886.

LOT 119-B: William B. PHILLIPS;
William Benjamin PHILLIPS, Jan. 6, 1880; John Robert PHILLIPS, Jr., Feb. 11, 1874; Gustavus A. BRIDE, Marh. 23, 1883; Harriet VEEDER, July 10, 1893; Eliza BRIDE, July 20, 1893; Alexander Crawford PHILLIPS, June 7, 1912; Williams B. PHILLIPS, Feb. 14, 1910; John R. PHILLIPS, Jan. 10, 1910; Mary E. Dalrymple PHILLIPS, Feb. 5, 1885; For Molly Dalrymple PHILLIPS, (no date given); Harriet J. BARBER, Dec. 29, 1893; Nancy Phillips MOORE, Nov. 3, 1938.
Letter from Louise Phillips STANG, Jr., to Mt. Olivet Cemetery regarding illness of his Aunt, Molly Dalrymple PHILLIPS, dated Oct. 30, 1964. Reference is made to funeral home of John O. Mitchell & Sons, Inc., mailed from Breinigsville, PA 18031.

Letter dated Sept. 2, 1964 from Mrs. Louise Phillips STANG, Jr. of Breinigsville, PA, to Mt. Olivet Cemetery. Mrs. STANG states her father is Harry D. PHILLIPS, formerly of Barrington Road,

Baltimore, MD, "but now of" Turner St., Allentown, PA. Harry D. PHILLIPS is son of John R. PHILLIPS, and nephew of Wm. B. PHILLIPS. John R. PHILLIPS had a daughter named Molly D. PHILLIPS. "Miss PHILLIPS is now 79 years old." Mrs. STANG also states her grandfather died in 1909 or 1910. She signs the letter Mrs. August STANG Jr.

LOT 120-B: John H. BRIDE;
Ralph BROWN, Dec. 14, 1860; Susan W. BROWN, Mar. 3, 1861 (may be same as Susannah W. BROWN); Child of BRIDE, Oct. 27, 1861; Ralph BROWN, Dec. 14, 1864; Jane H. PHILLIPS, Sept. 28, 1865; Eliz BRIDE, July 18, 1866; Caroline PHILLIPS, Nov. 2, 1869; Jane REYNOLDS, Jan. 20, 1871; Walter J. REYNOLDS, Oct. 16, 1871; (Therane) JONES, June 30, 1871; John H. BRIDE, Sept. 18, 1890; Wm. BROWN, Dec. 19, 1902 (entry crossed out), June 20, 1931 disinterred & moved to Louden Park Cemetery.

LOT 121-B: John A. W. PEARCE and Henry HOWARD;
John W. PEARCE, May 15, 1861; Nelson ROSHER, Aug. 6, 1867; John A. W. PEARCE, Jan. 16, 1888; Ruth A. PEARCE, Apr. 15, 1889; Jos. ROSHER, Aug. 15, 1869; Wilbur PEARCE, May 3, 1894, (an entry reads: "wife of Wilbur to go here."); Wilbur T. PEARCE, Jan. 1, 1918 (or 1917); Remains of John (illegible); P. G. MC CLENDISH, Jan. 26, 1921, (Phylis G. MC CLANDISH probably same person as above.); David G. EMMART, Mar. 4, 1925; Beal HOWARD, Jan. 29, 1848; Christopher HOWARD, May 6, 1852; Maria L. DUNGER, Dec. 22, 1859; Beal HOWARD, Jan. 30, 1861; Henry HOWARD, Jan. 7, 1887; Debora HOWARD, Feb. 16, 1874; Mary HOWARD, Feb. (20), (1915); Margt. A. DAVIS, Feb. 17, 1920; Ann HOWARD, June 20, 1848; Dorothy P(RUI)GTON, June 17, 1926; Jas. G. PEARCE, May 12, 1928; Wilford CADE, Apr. 24, 1934; Emma Pearce EMMART, Aug. 13, 1838; Edna Mae PEARCE, Jan. 21, 1973, born Apr. 6, 1905, died Jan. 17, 1973, father Chas. PEARCE, mother Emma SCHULTE.

LOT 122-B: Thomas A. CRANBLETT and Mrs. Wm. BURTON, daughter of CRAMBLETT;
Emma CRAMBLETT, June 6, 1863; Child, July 5, 1867; Child, Sept. 17, 1868; Catharine CRAMBLETT, Nov. 12, 1888; Arthur W. SHIPLEY, Nov. 9, 1892; Thos. A. CRAMBLETT, July 2, 1895; Infant of Cara & J. W. OHLEADORF, Mar. 16, 1896; Wm. BURTON, Mar. 19, 1923; Geo. W. CRAMBLETT, Jan. 22, 1926; Wm. CRAMBLETT, Oct. 8, 1929; Mary V. BURTON, June 25, 1932; Cora A. OHLENDORF, July 23, 1938; John W. OHLENDORF, Nov. 2, 1956.

LOT 123-B: Ann M(E)LLOR and John W. MC CAULEY;
Benj. MALLOW, Dec. 23, 1858; Ann MALLOW, Feb. 2, 1883; Child, Aug. 16, 18(65); Child, Apr. 23, 18(61); Augustus R. SCHOTTA, Aug. 25, 1874; Bertha C. PETERS, June 13, 1890; August SCHOTTA, Apr. 9, 1914; Sarah (S. or H.) SCHOTTA, July 29, 1812; Robert H. MELLOR, Aug. 25, 1874; Sarah May MC CAULEY, Apr. 25, 1869 (could also be 1864 or 1868); Willie SHIPLEY, June 18, 1874; Child, Aug. 12, 1878; Mary L. MC CAULEY, Sept. 14, 1881; (Harrie or Marrie or Harriet) E. MC CAULEY, Mar. 29, 1883; John W. MC CAULEY, Feb. 18, 1918; Mary M. MC CAULEY, Sept. 24, 1934; Sallie A. SCHOTTA, Aug. 14, 1865; Rachel (FISSEL), Feb. 7, 1863. There is a memorial stone for James MC CAULEY stating he was killed "overseas."

LOT 124-B: Wm. Emory MURRAY and Elizabeth RICHARDSON;
Howard L. MURRAY, June 28, 1882; Wm. R. MURRAY, (no date given);

Stillborn of (J. P.) MURRY, May 4, 1907; Ann R. MURRY, July 4, 1911; still born of J. P. MURRY, Dec. 3, 1915; Annie Barbara MURRAY, Feb. 14, 1925; Charles A. METZEL, Jan. 23, 1951; Kate Murray METZEL, May 28, 1947; W. Emory MURRY, (no date given); Joseph RICHARDSON, Oct. 5, 1865; Sophia RICHARDSON, May 30, 1882; Carrie C. RICHARDSON, Dec. 3, 1896; Mary E. RICHARDSON, July 7, 1897; Edith V. RICHARDSON, April 18, 1899; Wm. L. RICHARDSON, Dec. 23, 1919; Virginia A. RICHARDSON, Feb. 11, 1935; Florence M. SALMON, Feb. 7, 1940.

LOT 125-B: Local Preachers Lot;
Mary VANORSDALE, Feb. 24, 1880; Hezekiah VANORSDALE, May 4, 1876; Rev. Nathan RICHARDSON, (no date given).

LOT 126-B: Wm. H. WIGHTMAN and Daniel DODD;
Thos. DODD, Nov. 24, 1857; John FARSLEY, Mar. 3, 1863; Helen DODD, June 14, 1865; Martha DODD, June 21, 1823; Daniel DODD, May 11, 1875; John DODD, Dec. 19, 1876; Daniel DODD, Jr., Jan. 10, 1877; Robt. DODD, Feb. 2, 1880; (Saml.) DODD, Mar. 19, 1868; Child of Wm. B(U)K, Apr. 11, 1870; Annie Belle BOYD, (Oct.) 14, 1884; Child of Jos. (PASAPIE), Nov. 9, 1876; Robert DODD, Dec. 14, 1862; Ellen DODD, May 24, 1865; Daisy BOYD, Feb. 2, 1885; Henrietta WIGHTMAN, Mar. 12, 1856; Fannie WIGHTMAN, Apr. 29, 1869; Grace WIGHTMAN, Feb. 6, 1892; Jane WIGHTMAN, Jan. 24, 1887; Geo. WIGHTMAN, Mar. 19, 1887; Mary C. STEWART, July 21, 1898; Alice B. WIGHTMAN, Feb. 1, 1935.

LOT 127-B: Elizabeth FARRING and James E. ALFORD;
Rev. Henry FARRING, Nov. 28, 1855; Ely FARRING, Mar. 15, 1861; Annie E. ZIMMERMAN, Mar. 22,1926; Wm. L. ZIMMERMAN, Dec. 1, 1926; Mrs. EDMONSON, May 30, 1856; Mary M. ALFORD, June 9, 1865; Child of EAST, Apr. 5, 1871; Child of EAST, July 16, 1874; Thos. A. B. EAST, Mar. 12, 1879; Fredk. C. EAST, Apr. 8, 1881; Adam KING, Aug. 30, 1881; Stillborn of Harry EAST, April 7, 1884; still born of Harry EAST, May 1, 1885; Abigal EAST, Apr. 10, 1897; Henry EAST, June 26, 1918; Susanna EDMONDSON, 1856; Clifton W. RITER, Apr. 30, 1938; Emma R. RITTER, Oct. 24, 1939; Marie L. PARRISH, May 24, 1938; William E. LOWMAN, Apr. 26, 1952; Annie L. LOWMAN, Feb. 19, 1958.

LOT 128-B: Wm. H. SPEDDEN and James WRIGHT;
Mary G. SPEDDEN, Apr. 24, 1869; Maggie (buried with above, could be same as Maggie E. SPEDDEN, below); Margt. G. SPEDDON, Sept. 7, 1876 (may be same as Margaret J. G. SPEDDON); Lydia SPEDDEN, Mar. 25, 1878; Clarence SPEDDEN, Sept. 2, 1881; Annie WRIGHT, June 26, 1865; Child of Wm. H. CONWAY, Sept. 13, 1871; Annie S. WRIGHT, Jan. 20, 1868; Matilda GEORGE, Nov. 26, 1870; Chas. A. WALL, Feb. 15, 1888; Carrie L. WALL, July 15, 1918; Wm. A. SPEDDEN, Sept. 11, 1860; Maggie E. SPEDDEN, Jan. 9, 1865; Clarence C. SPEDDEN, Aug. 31, 1881; Carrie Wright WALL, Apr. 12, 1952.

LOT 129-B: Rev. John A. GERE;
Rev. Abner NEAL, Apr. 19, 1824; Barbara NEAL, June 18, 1834; Sarah NEAL, Oct. 8, 1840; Rev. John A. GERE, June 3, 1874; Joseph NEAL, Sept. 29, 1886; Harold C. THOMAS, June 3, 1898; Edwd. C. THOMAS, June 1, 1895 (also May 30, 1895 given); Laura N. THOMAS, April 15, 1861 (reads "false grave only for memory"); Mary G. THOMAS, June 19, 1915; Sarah GERE, Dec. 13, 1891; Mattie H.

THOMAS, Aug. 11, 1925; Sadie G. THOMAS, May 2, 1929; Carrie C. THOMAS, Sept. 25, 1931.

LOT 130-B: MONROE & WARD;
Emma L. MONROE, June 12, 1871; Philip G. W. WARD, Aug. 30, 1874; Rev. T. H. W. MONROE, July 28, 1864; Child of Warfield MONROE, Nov. 10, 1870; Sarah A. MONROE, Mar. 15, 1888; Laura V. LEWIS, Aug. 13, 1891; Virginia MONROE, Aug. 16, 1904; (A.) Warfield MONROE, Mar. 1, 1907; Mary V. MONROE, Aug. 15, 1904; Margt. LEWIS, Feb. 9, 1894.

LOT 131-B: John MATTLINGLY;
Goellive K. KANE, (no date given); John MARRINGLY, Mar. 14, 1861; John T. MATTINGLY, Aug. 1(6), 1865; Cath. MATTINGLY, Jan. 10, 1880; Eliza M. FRIDAY, May 19, 1888; Joseph B. GARMAN, Dec. 20, 1912; Margt. KANE, Aug. 1, 1873; Rev. G. KANE, Oct. 27, 1869; Sarah K. SUMWALT, Jan. 26, 1892; Eliza SEMMIS, Sept. 15, 1914 (may be SIMMEOUS or SIMMONS); Frank G. SIMMONS, June 22, 1923; Sarah M. SIMMONS, March 9, 1927.

LOT 132-B: Thomas BASSFORD and John F. MOFFITT;
Richd. MOFFITT, Apr. 5, 1851; Richd. (F.) MOFFITT, Oct. 9, 1862; Albert E. BASSFORD, Apr. 13, 1866; ANNA MOFFITT, JUNE 7, 1869; John F. MOFFITT, Feb. 22, 1883; Mary C. R. MOFFITT, Mar. 30, 190(7); Thomas B. BASSFORD, Apr. 20, 1863; M. E. SCHWARTZKOFF, Jan. 7, 1896.

LOT 133-B: Adam SHUCK;
Adam SHUCK, Dec. 4, 1857.

LOT 134-B: C. D. GROVES, W. W. WOODALL and Mary PATTERSON;
Alonza ROBERTS, Dec. 13, 1871; Cath. D. GRAVES, Sept. 23, 1873; Sarah GROVES, Oct. 3, 1873; Geo. TANELEY, Feb. 2, 1857; Eliza EDWARDS, Sept. 13, 1865; Child, Jan. 10, 1852; Jas. WOODALL, May 10, 1855; Geo. F(AWBANTA), Sept. 27, 1856; Rose WOODALL, Aug. 1866; Mary C. WOODALL, Oct. 15, 1874; Walter L. BROWN, July 30, 1877; Washington WOODALL, Nov. 3, 1879; Walter L. BROWN, July 17, 1879; Washington WOODALL, Nov. 3, 1879; Luella BROWN, Sept. 4, 1878; Eva LANCASTER, Sept. 24, 1880; John WOODALL, Nov. 28, 1868; Edith WOODALL, Mar. 21, 1882; Harry W. WOODALL, Feb. 3, 1883; Sarah E. JACKSON, Mar. 2, 1883; Wm. J. WOOD, Aug. 24, 1886.

LOT 135-B and North 1/2 of 153-B, (see also lot 95-B):
Samuel GUEST; Mrs. EDMONSON, July 7, 1865; Mary L. (GUEST, surname written over), Nov 18, 1876; Saml. C. (C?OAR) [entry crossed out], Apr. 2, 1884; Georgiano WILLIAMS, Feb. 12, 1855; Rich. G. GUEST, Sept. 28, 1851; Rebecca GUEST, Apr. 11, 1856; Sallie GUEST, Oct. 26, 1876; M. C. GUEST, Nov. 9, 1872; Richard (no surname given), Sept. 18(8)9, age 84 years; Dosoctes (no surname given), Apr. 5, 1829, age 63 years; Rich'd. W. (no surname given), Mar. 1843, age 51 yrs., Samuel, (Arthur), (Ellen), (Clare), (Augustus); all persons with no surname in the same grave; Rich'd. (SAUSIN), Aug. 11, 1851; Susan GUEST, Dec. 2, 1845, age 42 years, wife; (Rebecca) GUEST, Nov. 11, 1855, age 54 years; Sarah B. C(illegible), (entry crossed); Susan K. EDMONDSON, July 5, 1866, age 58 years; Sallie GUEST (possible same as Sallie GUEST above), (no date given); Sarah C. GUEST, Oct. 25, 187(4), age 40 years; Sarah B., Susan's Daughter (Sallie GUEST, Sarah C. GUEST & Sarah B. all buried in same grace); Samuel GUEST, July 9,

1879, age 76 years; Mary L. GUEST, (no date given); M. C. GUEST, (no date given).

LOT 136B: Charles A. SMELTZER, George BODENICK and Mrs. Wm. E. WEAVER;
Chas. SMELTZER, Nov. 7, 1853; Chas. A. SMELTZER, Oct. 1, 1856; Eliz. JAMES, Sept. 21, 1863; Wm. E. BARGE, Oct. 28, 1863; Mr. BARGE, Jan. 23, 1866; Clara E. SMELTZER, Aug. 1, 1884; Fredk. BODENSICK, Dec. 16, 1858; Jas. O. BROWN, Jan. 16, 1872; Wm. E. BROWN, Mar. 27, 1872; Saml. BROWN, Apr. 1, 1872; Wm. T. BROWN, Aug. 22, 1885; Geo. BODENSICK, Apr. 19, 1886; Auguste M. BODEN-SICK, Mar. 9, 1887; Margt. BROWN, Jan. 9, 1890; Child of BROWN, Jan. 8, 1895; Co(rnelius) (A.) BROWN, Dec. 27, 1897; Co(rnelius) E. BROWN, June 24, 1902; Stillborn of BROWN, June 29, 190(?); Wilhelmina BROWN, Jan. 2, 1905; Ada BROWN, (Apr.) 23, 1907; Eliza (S.) BROWN, Feb. 9,m 1920; "for Richard BROWN," (no date given).

LOT 137-B: Eliza MC GILL and Wm. D. WATERS;
A memo on "Harford Fire Insurance Co." stationery of Harford, Conn., states as follows: "John A. VAN SANT, 62 years at death, died Mar. 27, 1924. Emma L. VAN SANT, died Feb. 24, 1944 at age of 81 years. Marie V. DUKE, died Aug. 13, 1958 at age of 72 years." Elizabeth MC GILL, Aug. 8, 1869 (could be Sept. 7, 186(9); Geo. T. MC GILL, July 22, 1882; Maria DUYER, July 1, 1887; Frank P. DUYER, Nov. 8, 1889; Maria DUYER, Nov. 8, 1889; Catherine MC GILL, Dec. 17, 1891; Daniel C. DWYER, Dec. 2, 1926; Child of Wm. ARMSTRONG, June 25, 1863; Child, Sept. 13, 1866; LAWTOM Child, Aug. 1, 1861; Sarah WATERS, Aug. 16, 1869; Laura THOMAS, Dec. 24, 1900; Laura WATERS, Sept. 22, 1906; Wm. H. WATERS, Mar. 16, 1907; Chas. C. DUKE III, Jan. 20, 1917; John R. VAN ZANT, Jr., Mar. 27, 1924; Emma R. VANZANT, Feb. 24, 1944; Marie V. DUKE, Aug. 13, 1958; Matthew W. S(EMONOIDS), Aug. 28, 1823, also in same grave is Susanna A. (no surname given), Feb. 28, 1843.

LOT 138-B: Samuel B. CROSS;
Eliz. CONNOR, May 1(0), 1859; J. R. CROSS, Apr. 15, 1869; (removed from Light St., Apr. 28, 1869); Geo. (W.) CROSS, Aug. 10, 1882; Carrie S. CROSS, Dec. 10, 1889; Saml. B. CROSS, Aug. 24, 1890; Wm. H. CROSS, Jan. 20, 1891; Eliz. HANCOCK, Nov. 1, 1892; Margt. J. SH(RO)TE, Jan. 2, 1894; Wm. H. CROSS, Feb. 4, 1901; S. R. CROSS, (no date given); Sophia CROSS, Aug. 19, 1940; Saml. B. CROSS, Ap. 2, 1884.

LOT 139-B: Thos. MAGNESS, Eliz. WHALEN, Mary W. DAWSON, Rachel HIGH;
Susan B. MAGNESS, Apr. 30, 1884; Mary MAGNESS, Sept. 14, 1891; Charlotte STEWART, Feb. 6, 1873; Oliver P. WHELAN, Oct. 24, 1870; Eliz. WHALEN, Feb. 16, 1891; Rachel HIGH, Oct. 10, 1880; David GRAVE, Oct. 8, 1898; Sarah HIGH, July 1, 1909; Wm. A. DAWSON, Apr. 22, 1916; Rachel B. GRAVE, May 30, 1924; Wm. HIGH, (no date given); Ashes of Mary W. MELNS, Apr. 30, 1966; Brian W. BIEMAN, Sr., June 20, 1975; born Dec. 11, 1943; died June 16, 1973, father Geo. Wm. BIEMAN, mother Charlotte EADER.

LOT 140-B: C. V. EIGELBERNER, Fannie C. SHARBACHER and A. V. CHENOWETH;
Thomas A. EIGELBERNER, Oct. 13, 1892; Catherine V. EIGELBERNER, Dec. 11, 1915; Anna Mary EIGELBERNER, Jan. 23, 1920; Ellenor V.

EIGELBERNER, Feb. 4, 19(29); Eliza A. MC VEY, Jan. 1, 1902; James MC VEY, May 27, 1890; James M. MC VEY, July 3, 1904; Mabel EIGELBERNER, Feb. 10, 1966, age 85 years; Ashes, Georgiana D. SARBACHER, Dec. 11, 1937; Joseph C. SARBACHER, Aug. 9, 1957; Elmer Webster SARBACHER, (May) 21, 19(71), (ashes). A Certificate of Cremation from Cedar Hill Crematory, Washington, D.C. -- Elmer Webster SARBACHER, age 77, died May 18, 1971, cremated May 19, 1971.

Certificate of Crematory-West Coast Crematory, Inc., remains of Mary W. MELIUS to B. Marion Reed Co., Platt & Plant Avenue, Tampa, Fla. Certifies that Mary W. MELIUS, age 92, died Apr. 8, 1966 and was cremated St. Petersburg, Florida on Apr. 12, 1966.

LOT 141-B: Carrie REYNOLDS and James HENTHORN; Robert E. HENTHORN, Oct. 7, 1886; Mary E. HENTHORN, Sept. 9, 1903; Stillborn of Edna & (I. F.) CRISP, (no date given); Sarah E. HENTHORN, Mar. 10, 1922; James H. HENTHORN, Apr. 2, 1941; Chas. E. REYNOLDS, Aug. 20, 1885; Edw. C. REYNOLDS, Apr. 18, 1913; Ethel REYNOLDS, Oct. 27, 1913; Margaret REYNOLDS, Mar. 20, 1924; Joseph S. CLAYTON, Mar. 29, 1928; Carrie CLAYTON, Mar. 20, 1931.

LOT 142-B: Wm. H. STEMBLER and Geo. W. STEMBLER; Ecelia STEMBLER, July 1, 1918; Percy S. HOLLAND, Dec. 24, 1896; Wm. B. STEMBLER, Mar. 16, 1922; Sarah (A.) STEMBLER, Apr. 16, 1927; Maggie G. STEMBLER, Oct. 8, 1878 (Heavily crossed out entry reads "Moved Maggie G. STEMBLER, Oct. 8, 1878" and in light pencil "for John E. KERR, May 4, 1971." Mary C. (or E.) STEMBLER, Jan. 13, 1892; Geo. W. STEMBLER, Aug. 10, 1907; Ella G. STEMBLER, June 29, 1943; Ella G. STEMBLER, June 29, 1943; John M. KERR, July 24, 1946; Rose A. KERR, Jan. 6, 1971, born Nov. 8, 1888, died Jan. 3, 1971, father Chas. STEMBLER, mother Emma FAGER; Maggie G. STEMBLER, May 4, 1971; Ecelia EGGELSTON, (no date given).

LOT 143-B: Sarah J. MARLEY and E. M. GILL; James MARLEY, Mar. 26, 1894; George W. MARLEY, July 7, 1896; Elsie M. MARLEY, Nov. 19, 1911; Herman M. MARLEY, July 27, 1909; Sarah J. MARLEY, Feb. 18, 1915; Geo. W. MARLEY, Apr. 6, 1935; Remains of Children from 1/4 103-I, Oct. 24, 1892; Estella M. GILL, Nov. 18, 1896; William M. GILL, July 20, 1950; Anna H. GILL, June 20, 1951; William J. GILL, July 25, 1911. Funeral Director Joseph B. Cook memo states "April 6, 1935 permit request for interment of George W. MARLEY in lot N 1/2 143-B in name of Sarah J. MARLEY.

Certificate from J. J. HARTENSTEIN Mortuary states Rev. F. X. MOORE was buried in New Freedom Cemetery on Sept. 7, 1950 and his wife, Lillie M. MOORE was buried in New Freedom Cemetery on Oct. 25, 1952.

LOT 145-B: William GISRIEL; Mary Beulah GISRIEL, Mar. 22, 1892; James Mercer FAIRBANK, Mar. 22, 1941; Emma FAIRBANK, Oct. 17, 1956; William GISRIEL, Aug. 14, 1935; Martha W. GISRIEL, Nov. 27, 1920; Priscilla CORNELIUS, Dec. 22, 1893; Newman C. HOLMES, Mar. 19, 1940; Cora G. HOLMES, June 5, 1965.

LOT 146-B: Margaret A. COALMAN and Nathan ALEXANDER;
Alex COLEMAN, Feb. 27, 1894; Alex COLEMAN, Dec. 31, 1894; Minnie
V. TAYLOR, Aug. 8, 1899; Amelia SEMONT, Sept. 30, 1902; James A.
COLEMAN and 3 children, Oct. 27, 1903; Margaret A. COLEMAN, July
3, 1904; Warren G. COLEMAN, (no date given); Winfield FORRISTON,
May 21, 1900; Stillborn of WATKINS, Dec. 1898; Nathan Leroy
ALEXANDER, Nov. 26, 1880; Mary E. ALEXANDER, Dec. 4, 1880;
Removed from N 1/2 231-A 3 children, Mar. 15, 1892; Nathan E.
ALEXANDER, Nov. 14, 1928; Emma P. ALEXANDER, Oct. 22, 1932; Mary
E. SIMMONT, July 29, 1907; Sadie SWAN, Mar. 12, 1911; Josephine
BURGESS, Oct. 28, 1919; Emma J. B(OWERMAN), Feb. 12, 1936; Jas.
William (no surname given), July 1, 1871; Harry E. ALEXANDER,
Feb. 16, 1940.

LOT 147-B: Sarah E. BAILEY, Sarah DOWNS and Sallie A. (no surname given);
Ethel B. DOWNS, Nov. 30, 1895; Willard W. DOWNS, June 23, 1900;
Henry O. DOWNS, Nov. 12, 1913; Wm. F. DOWNS, Nov. 20, 1914;
Pauline BEALL, Aug. 8, 1923; Anna M(ARRAGOR), May 17, 1910; Geo.
A. FI(SCKER), about 1891; Wm. A. FISCHER, June 25, 1929; Willie
BAILEY, May 12, 1891; Sarah E. BAILEY, Dec. 18, 1895; W. L.
BAILEY, Feb. 7, 1900, (may be same as William L. BAILEY); Clinton D. BAILEY, Aug. 31, 1903; Wm. B. BAILEY, Mar. 20, 1923;
Margt. J. FISCHER, Mar. 26, 1932; Wm. G. BAILEY, (no date given);
Virginia Marion BAILEY, Apr. 29, 1942; Sallie A. BEALL, Oct. 16,
1942; Eugene E. BEALL, Feb. 8, 1940.

LOT 148-B: Chas. SHAFFER and Geo. A. CHRISTHIFF;
Frances SHAFFER, Sept. 5, 1893; Geo. E. SHAFFER, Sept. 28, 1917;
Chas. C. SHAFFER, Dec. 21, 1922; Frances E. CHRISTHIFF, July 17,
1893; Infant of Susie (COOPER), Mar. 17, 1899; Geo. S. CHRISTHIFF, May 22, 1914; Laura O'Dell CHRISTHIFF, Jan. 14, 1918; Henry
B. CHRISTHIFF, Oct. 21, 1919; Frances Adell CHRISTHIFF, Jan. 1,
1932; Grace E. SHAFFER, Nov. 1, 1952; Thos. S. GREENWALT, Jr.,
June 7, 1963.

LOT 149-B: Edith LARRABEE, W. H. SHELLHAUSE, CONWAY and LIVINGSTON;
Susan A. CASSELL, Sept. 8, 1838 (also given as April 11, 1896);
Margery CASSELL, Mar. 24, 1906; Morris Douglas CASSELL, (no date
given); Wm. G. CASSELL, 1839 (also given as 1911); Child of E.
LIVINGSTON, May 10, 1871; Child of W. CONWAY, Sept. 13, 1871;
Lillie W. CONWAY, Sept. 18, 1876; Mary CROSS, Apr. 26, 1880;
Frances MC DANIEL, Apr. 11, 1867; Child, Mar. 3, 1868; M(aiue)
LIVINGSTON, Dec. 21, 1868; Child, Aug. 29, 1869; Ada CONWAY, Feb.
20, 1882; Infant of Alexander MARSHALL, Mar. 27, 1897; Mary
SHELLHAUS, Feb. 27, 1901, (name crossed out & wirtten in looks
like Harry); Stillborn of SHELLHAUS, Jan. 9, 1910; Clara M.
SHELLHAUS, May 21,1914; Child, Nov. 6, 1866; Wm. H. SHELLHAUS,
May 6, 1925; (Anna) F. SHELLHAUS, Apr. 12, 19(32); John Wesley
LIVINGSTON, Apr. 26, 1947; Amelia LIVINGSTON, Mar. 11, 1947;
Martha LIVINGSTON, (no date given).

LOT 150-B: Rich FRAZIER;
John FRAZIER, Nov. 8, 1863; Lillian Estell FRAZIER, June 29,
1871; Adeline FRAZIER, Dec. 13, 1879; Julia A. VOGEL, Dec. 26,
1885; Mary E. FRAZIER, Mar. 8, 1913; Harry F. FRAZIER, Aug. 29,
1882; Alverda E. FRAZIER, July 29, 1899 (or 1889); Mary Helen
FRAZIER, Feb. 14, 1902; Rich M. FRAZIER, Sept. 9, 1916 (or Rich

H. FRAZIER); H. A. FRAZIER, July 8, 1922 (could be same as Harriett A. FRAZIER).

LOT 150-B: Fredk. BAAS, (South 1/2 of 190 Plat); Mary BAAS, Sept. 21, 1863; Fredk. BAAS, Feb. 9, 1868.

LOT 151-B: Wm. G. WILLS; Sarah NEWTON, Jan. 3, 1888; Adella OSBORN, Oct, 3, 1900; Wm. G. WILLS, Dec. 29, 1896; John Thomas WILLS, Jan. 18, 1861; Anna Jane WILLS, Jan. 24, 1859; Emily WILLS, Nov. 3, 1920.

LOT 152-B: Evelyn T. HAVILAND and Zachariah MAGNESS; Mrs. MAGNESS, Apr. 22, 1865; A. MAGNESS, Jan. 4, 1868; Fredk. BASS, (no date given); WHALENS children, Apr. 4, 1868; Ida WHALEN, Apr. 14, 1869; Two Boxes of remains from old ground, June 9, 1873; Zachariah MAGNESS, July 15, 1875; Wesley MAGNESS, Mar. 27, 1884; John H. NAGLE, Aug. 9, 1884; (Emma) NAGLE, Aug. 9, 1888; Maria BRA(UDE), Feb. 5, 1872; A. W. SMITH, July 3, 1868; Thos. SMITH, Mar. 6, 1869; Ann SMITH, Sept. 14, 1869; Infant of WESLEY, Apr. 29, 1876; Thos. F. SMITH, July 24, 1880; Sallie E. SMITH, May 9, 1893; John J. HILTON, Oct. 27, 1878; Georiana C. WILLIAMS, Nov. 5, 1851; Mad(ola) Christian GUEST, Nov. 8, 1852; Child of W. MAGNESS, Jan. 14, 1868.

LOT 153-B: Jos. D. BRUFF; Martha BRUFF, Sept. 25, 1851; Harold BRUFF, Apr. 27, 1864; Child of E. WILLY, Mar. 21, 1871; Susan WILLEY, Apr. 8, 1871; Saml. G. BRUFF, Oct. 19, 1877; Jos. C. BRUFF, (Feb.) 21, 1887; Annie M. BRUFF, Feb. 21, 1887; Jos. D. BRUFF, June 8, 1887; Beulah M. BRUFF, Nov. 12, 1890; Inft. of GEGL(UIE), Nov. 28, 1899; Walter E. LYNCH, Dec. 18, 1906.

LOT 154-B: James S. (MORROW) and James HAYES; Hugh L. MORROW, July 17, 1889; Glanville MORROW, July 2, 1891; Child, Aug. 13, 1855; Chas. FOGELMAN, Aug. 13, 1855; D(ISTES) Child, Feb. 24, 1863; Ida HAYES, Sept. 2, 1866; Child of DAVIS, July 4, 1872; Annie E. WILDER, July 7, 1874; Jos. L. HAYES, (no date given); Ruth WILDER, Feb. 11, 1893; Sarah C. KNIGHT, Apr. 15, 1895; Charity HAYES, Jan. 11, 1900; Mabel M. WILDER, Dec. 12, 1905 (Middle initial may be W.); (Mynete) WILDER, Sept. 23, 1906; Carroll M. SILVER, Nov. 24, 1908; Stillborn of GIBSON, Jan. 20, 1909; Martha B. LAUMAN, July 23, 1910; Maria RICE, Feb. 26, 1911; Elsie E. WILDER, July 21, 1911; (Oli and Lauele), Sept. 22, 1911 (May also be Olie LAUPE); Joseph Edward CONWAY, Sr., June 24, 1942; Edna M. LAMEY, July 26, 1968, born Apr. 17, 1902; died July 22, 1968; Lawrence H. CONWAY, May 22, 1970, born Aug. 2 (3), 1900, died May 19, 1970; William E. ZIEGLER, May 21, 1949; Margaret CONWAY. Certification - Joseph Edward CONWAY is the grandson of James HAYES.. Interment of Margaret CONWAY, widow of Lawrence H. CONWAY. The later interred in N/2 154-B. Date given is April 21, 1975.

LOT 155-B: Wm. F. MC CONN and David HIPBURN; Clara M. MC CANN, Aug. 24, 1888; Chas. B. MC CONN, Mar. 23, 1916; Louis HEPBURN, Feb. 17, 1888; Jos. M. WRIGHT, Nov. 23, 1824; Alueta (or Aluera) HEPBURN, Oct. 11, 1901; David H. HEPBURN, Nov. 23, 1931.

LOT 156-B: Ruel SHAW and Ann E. KENDALL;
Lucy SHAW, Oct. 28, 1933; Ernest SHAW, July 12, 1867; Callie SHAW, Sept. 15, 1874 (child); Sarah BEESEY, May 26, 1888; Mary L. SHAW, Oct 7, 1895; Bessie L. SHAW, July 25, 1876 (child); Edward SHAW, Dec. 14, 1870; Silvanus SHAW, July 27, 1868; Elizabeth SHAW, Dec. 11, 1873; Ruel M. SHAW, Nov. 29, 1876 "from Baltimore Health Dept. (Record) family believe this Rachel is really Ruel in this grave."; Mary A. GLAPSCOCK (or GLASSCOCK), Nov. 15, 1867; Rachel SHAW, Dec. 1, 1876; Thomas K. HUTCHINSON, Sept. 15, 1931; Chas. Meredith FORNEY, July 28, 1906 (child); Susan HUTCHINSON, Aug. 27, 1894; Grace HUTCHINSON, July 22, 1918 (child); Hilda K. FORNEY, July 13, 1938; Gaither HUTCHINSON, Dec. 7, 1916 (child); Florence H. HUTCHINSON, Feb. 25, 1904 (child); J. H. HUTCHINSON, May 19, 1902 (the date 1885 is penciled in); Charles M. FORNEY, Oct. 24, 1942; Elizabeth HUTCHINSON, July 29, 1915 (child); Harry L. KENDALL, Jr., Apr. 2, 1875 (child); Harry L. KENDALL, May 14, 1873; Eliza D. HUTCHINSON, May 7, 1921; Mary KENDALL, Dec. 29, 1858; "Thomas R. HUTCHINSON?", (no date given); Ann E. KENDALL, Nov. 17, 1892; Mason Edwin FORNEY, "J-18-70," Nov. 8, 1913, May 13, 1970. Also below this entry are the words ORSBURN, Stewartstown, Pa.

LOT 157-B: John T. EMMICK;
Albert EMMICK, July 25, 1854; Remains of Nicholas & Eliz. EMMICK, Aug. 24, 1876; John V. EMMICK, Apr. 10, 1880; Wm. LAUMAN, July 5, 1897; Ma(n)iella LAUMAN, Sept. 12, 1903.

LOT 158-B: Maria EMORY;
Maria EMORY, Sept. 25, 1869; Ann L. EMORY, Dec. 26, 1889; Frances EMORY, Jan. 9, 1912; Sue EMORY, July 29, 1912; Margt. EMORY, Oct. 4, 1915.

LOT 159-B: Wm. H. WILSON and Sarah N. BUSEY;
Rev. Wm. H. WILSON, Aug. 25, 1884; (Mrs.) M. R. WILSON, Jan. 2, 1892; Wm. H. WILSON, May 30, 1882; Ida ROSELLA, Oct. 9, 1853; Wilbur WILSON, May 7, 1856; Rev. Thos. BUSEY, Apr. 30, 1856; Emma BUSEY, Aug. 30, 1870; Willie A. BUSEY, Dec. 21, 1872; Chas. and Nellie BUSEY, Aug. 29, 1879; Sarah N. BUSEY, May 26, 1888; Lethe R. BUSEY, Mar. 13, 1908; Dr. J. J. WILLIAMS, Mar. 8, 1918; Betty Busey WILLIAMS, Jan. 4, 1946.

LOT 160-B: Mary COOKE;
Louesa M. BIBB, Jan. 25, 1866 (child); Carmen A. BIBB, Apr. 17, 1873; Bently S. BIBB, May 5, 1888; Amanda M. BIBB, June 10, 1891; Bently C. BIBB, June 25, 1894; S. Louesa WILSON, July 10, 1917; Mary M. MACCARTNEY, Aug. 22, 1884; Margt. R. WILSON, Sept. 17, 1880; Mary L. WILSON, Aug. 25, 1898; Cath. C. MAGARTNEY, Apr. 23, 1880; Rev. Frances MAGARTNEY, Oct. 7, 1873; John MAGARLEY, June 6, 1861; Mary MACARTNEY, Mar. 3, 1864; Kate MACARTNEY, Nov. 14, 1881; Henry WILSON, June 29, 1880; Kate V. MACARTNEY, Apr. 14, 1882; Malvina MACARTNEY, Aug. 25, 1884; Malvina MACARTNEY, Oct. 9, 1884; Sarah JARRETT, May 7, 1880; Miliah D. WILSON, Mar. 5, 1884; Robert COOK, Sept. 25, 1821; Cath. COOK, Oct. 13, 1881; Mary COOK, Oct. 2, 1863.

LOT 161-B: Walter BALL;
Lloyd O. BALL, Apr. 10, 1857; Mary KING, Apr. 17, 1858; Ella BALL, July 20, 1876; Walter BALL, Oct. 5, 1889; Mary L. RIDGLEY, Dec. 18, 1877; Walter BALL, Sept. 25, 1863; Mary BALL, June 25,

1865; Herbert BALL, Dec. 10, 1863; Ellen R. BALL, Apr. 8, 1909; Walter R. BALL, Oct. 7, 1927 (Probably same as Walter Randall BALL).

LOT 162-B: Elizabeth ALLEN;
James M. ALLEN, May 23, 1857; Remains, Apr. 14, 1861; John TREE, June 2, 1874; Henry C. PARLETT, July 13, 1874; Jane ALLEN, Jan. 28, 1881; Mary R. SHERWOOD, Feb. 14, 1882; Mrs. M. J. SHULTZ, Apr. 18, 1882; John T. SHULTZ, May 12, 1882; Stillborn, Aug. 2, 1882; Della LUSBY, May 27, 1885; James W. ALLEN, Nov. 14, 1887; C. J. ALLEN, Nov. 22, 1888; Infant of A. & C. HURLOCK, Jan. 2, 1890; Infant of E. & L. ALLEN, Sept. 3, 1891; Ruth A. COLE, July 8, 1892; Lawrence (W.) S. Allen, Feb. 6, 1899; Mary TREE, June 17, 1870; Stillborn, Jan. 15, 1921; Eliel ALLEN, June 5, 1860; Permelia ALLEN, June 13, 1861; Blanche E. STEIN(HAUSER), Jan. 31, 1921; Elizabeth ALLEN, July 1, 1935; Child of E. & L. ALLEN, (no date given); Ruth A. COLE, (no date given); Edna Marie ALLEN, May 2, 1970, born June 1, 1889, died Apr. 30, 1970.

LOT 163-B: Maggie D. MATTOX and James ANDREWS;
Mary E. CARSON, May 7, 1866; John E. CARSON, May 7, 1866; L. (S.) BENNETT, May 10, 1884; Susan HINDMAN, Sept. 5, 1894; Edith M. MATTOX, Mar. 16, 1896; Eliza BENNETT, July 17, 1900; Chas. H. L.BRANNAN, June 26, 1909; Margt. M. BRANNAN, Dec. 30, 1908; Emory CARSON, July 16, 1870; Alonzo D. MATTOX, Dec. 19, 1919; Maggie D. MATTOX, Aug. 2, 193(?); James ANDREWS, Mar. 9, 1872; Mary HOFFMAN, July 10, 1897; Mary A. ANDREWS, July 11, 1899; Harry HOFFMAN, Mar. 12, 1906; Stillborn, Feb. 10, 1921; Geo. W. (SILBERZAHN), Dec. 22, 1924; Martin C. BRANNAN, Jan. 27, 1942; (Entry erased, looks like Eliza ANDREWS); May SILBERZAHN, Oct. 25, 1947.

LOT 164-B: Margaret A. WILLIAMS, David B. FOSTER and Joseph ZIEGLER;
Harry (E.) FOSTER, July 2, 1866; James FOSTER, (no date given); Ida L. FOSTER, Feb. 7, 1867; Mary FOSTER, Mar. 21, 1877; Bertha A. FOSTER, Sept. 15, 1881; Eliza P. FOSTER, Jan. 19, 1880; Adele M. FOSTER, Jan. 9, 1888; David B. FOSTRER, Sept. 3, 1896; Mary M. FOSTER, Feb. 16, 1916; Child of WILSON, April 15, 1871; Annie M. WATERWORTH, Apr. 15, 1879; Jennie WATERWORTH, Mar. 29, 1880; Jas. M. WATERWORTH, Apr. 3, 1890; James S. WATERWORTH, Apr. 18, 1903; Samuel WATERWORTH, Aug. 4, 1877; Mary E. ZIEGLER, May 29, 1921; Nannie J. ZIEGLER, Oct. 4, 1870; Margaret A. WILLIAMS, Apr. 11, 1932; Hamilton WILLIAMS, Nov. 28, 1930; Harry E. CRAWFORD, Feb. 26, 1941; Jane WATERWORTH, (no date given). Note on page states Henry (S.) WILLIAMS is a son of Margaret and Hamilton WILLIAMS of Leo St.

LOT 165-B: Elizabeth J. ABBOTT, LITTLEFIELD and MADDOX;
Noal (Noah) ABBOTT, Oct. 27, 1870, (child at bottom); Lillian B. ABBOTT, Mar. 7, 1872 (entry crossed out); Gertrude W. ABBOTT, Jan. 16, 1884 (entry crossed out); Jos. W. ABBOTT, Aug. 5, 1887; Eliz (SPIDDEN), July 5, 1892, (Abbott entered after); Chas. E. SPIDDEN, Nov. 23, 1892 (entry crossed out); Walter W. ABBOTT, Dec. 31, 1883; John F. ABBOTT, Nov. 19, 1885; Mary (or Margt.) Ann MADDOX, Jan. 19, 1877; Geo. MADDOX, July 8, 187(8); John (H. or W.) LITTLEFIELD, (Apr.) 3, 1894; Wm. J. NORTH, Jan. 6, 1898 (entry crossed out and entered again); Sallie Byrd LITTLEFIELD, July 22, 1868; Mary B. LITTLEFIELD, Oct. 4, 1935.

LOT 166-B: Clara B. GREENFIELD, Geo. and Mary MC DANIELS;
Leona M. MC DANIELS, May 16, 1867; Geo. W. MC DANIELS, Aug. 7,
1868; Cora MC DANIELS, Mar. 29, 1873; Chas. B. TILYARD, Aug. 9,
1906; Clara B. GREENFIELD, Dec. 30, 1919; (Wm.) E. GREENFIELD,
Nov. 29, 1921; Chas. R. GREENFIELD, Oct. 10, 1936; Nora Greenfield TILYARD, Jan. 18, 1943; Clara HAINES, June 8, 1943.

LOT 167-B: Benjamin J. PARLETT and John T. MOFFITT;
(Mrs.) PARLETT, July 14, 1867; Minnie F. PARLETT, Dec. 7, 1875;
Matilda G. PARLETT, Feb. 23, 1881; Walter (S.) PARLETT, Apr. 7,
1885; disenterred 2 large bodies, Nov. 19, 1885; Benj. J. JUSTSICE, Feb. 11, 1890; Rebecca PARLETT, Feb. 6, 1893; Eliza E.
PARLETT, Mar. 22, 1894; Benj. J. PARLETT, Feb. 9, 1906; Benj. F.
PARLETT, July 10, 1911; Child, Nov. 29, 1858; Wm. H.MOFFITT, Nov.
26, 1853; John MOFFITT, Apr. 16, 1860; Child of John MOFFITT,
Feb. 6, 1864; Wm. R. MOFFITT, Apr. 15, 1869; Rachel MOFFITT, Apr.
20, 1876; Mable S. WATSON, Oct. 27, 1822; John (T.) MOFFITT, Mar.
3, 1914; Sophia MOFFITT, Apr. 5, 1921; Margaret STEWART, June 26,
1882; Rachel PARLETT, (no date given).

LOT 168-B: Isabel CANFIELD and James R. WALKER;
Ira C. CANFIELD, June 7, 1906; Isabell H. F. CANFIELD, Feb. 1,
1906; Walter Bliss CANFIELD, Feb. 1, 1927; Margt. (S.) WALKER,
Mar. 20, 1871; Maggie W. WALLACE, Jun3 22, 1871; Patience (T.)
WALKER, Nov. 18, 1872 (name crossed out and WHEELER written in);
Jas. R. WALKER, Jan. 26, 1872; Ellen J. WALKER, Apr. 16, 1875;
Annie (T.) WALKER, Apr. 25, 1875; (Henry) G. (UPMAN), Oct. 8,
1881; Sallie E. (UPMAN or EIPMAN), Oct. 28, 1882; (infant) of O.
C. (MARTOIST), Aug. 14, 1885; Edw. P. WHEELER, May 18, 1887; Ella
M. WALKER, July 17, 1882; Hannah S. WHEELER, June 11, 190(0);
Louis (UPEMAN), (no date given); (Salvina) WALKER, (no date
given); Isabel CANFIELD, Mar. 1, 1937.

LOT 169-B: Wilbur F. MATHEWS;
Mary Ann (?ARARK), July 25, 1875 (entry crossed out); Wilbur L.
MATTHEWS, Feb. 15, 1895; Wilbur (T.) MATTHEWS, Dec. 4, 1904; Mary
J. MATTHEWS, Nov. 8, 1921; Eliza B. MATTHEWS, Jan. 6, 1923;
Margaret (name erased), June __, (1882?); Mary Ellen MATTHEWS,
Oct. 12, 1956; James Scott MATHEWS, Sept. 16, 1950.

LOT 170-B through 171-B do not appear in the lot book.

LOT 172-B: George A. BRANNON;
Clarisa BRANNON, Nov. 28, 1869; Sarah BRANNON, Nov. 8, 1893;
George A. MEEKS, Nov. 9, 1893; John (KAV)DRASSLE, Dec. 6, 1870.

LOT 173-B: Benjamin C. BRICK (also appears as Benj. G. BUCK);
Jessie S. ARMIGER, Aug. 17, 186(9); Chas. Aug. 22 Jessie [sic],
Aug. 12, 18(55); Benj. J. BUCK, Apr. 25, 1895; Emily (A.) BUCK,
Dec. 18, 1905; Chas. C. BRICK, June 14, 1920. This name may be
BUCK, BRICK, BREEK. The handwriting is not clear enough to
determine.

LOT 174-B: Mary E. DECUS and Jas. H. M. LEMON;
John DECUS, Aug. 28, 1886 (name lined through); Ja(mes) DECUS,
Aug. 28, 1866; Maggie LEMON, July 8, 1867.

LOT 175-B: Elizabeth M. CONNOR and John KELLER;
J. J. H. CONNOR, Nov. 1, 1867; Eliz CONNOR, Oct. 29, 1869; Child

of J. T. WHITE, Sept. 16, 1871; Sarah J. ROATAN, Sept. 28, 1872; J. T. WHITE, Mar. 28, 1872; Laura M. (DRESDLET?), Jan. 3, 1881; Julia A. JONES, May 4, 1895; (Maranda) E. CONNER, Mar. 10, 1885; Child, Dec. 10, 1867; Child of D(ETTUS), Oct. 30, 1871; Child of D(ETTUS), Oct. 14, 1872; Hester L. D(ITTUS), Sept. 2, 1873; Child of D(ITTUS), Sept. 30, 1873; Hester KELLER, Dec. 18, 1873; Harriet KELLER, Nov. 21, 1884; Goldie G. KELLER, Jan. 6, 1930; John T. KELLER, Dec. 21, 1931; Mary A. ISAACS, Feb. 14, 1942; Paul(ine) E. KELLER, born July 21, 1919, died Feb. 16, 1969, buried Feb. 19, 1969; "For Thos. (P.) KELLER."

LOT 176-B: Jas. J. CAMPBELL and Sallie Sluting SADLER; Marion HAYES, Jan. 16, 1883; Lula W. CAMPBELL, Mar. 7, 1903; Jas. J. CAMPBELL, Jan. 1, 1898; Martha A. CAMPBELL, Mar. 22, 1910; (Minnie) A. CAMPBELL, Nov. 14, 1931; Sallie S. SADLER, Oct. 20, 1933.

LOT 177-B: Mary CADELL, Geo. PEREGOY and Mrs. Mary GREEN; Mary B. CADDELL, June 20, 1883; Eliza A. CADDELL, Sept. 23, 1885; Viola M. MORAN, Sept. 28, 1894; Raymond CADDELL, Dec. 16, 1895; Mary E. MORAN, Feb. 11, 1911; Wm. H. MORAN, Oct. 17, 1910; Laura V. PEREGOY, Aug. 22, 1871; Jennie PEREGOY, June 2, 1894; Virginia PEREGOY (disinterred), Aug. 29, 1894; Geo. PEREGOY, Oct. 31, 1911; Edward GREEN, Nov. 15, 1920; Margaret J. PEREGOY, Died Jan. 29, 1869; Ernest PEREGOY, Sept. 19, 1960 "not here"; Mary GREEN, Apr. 24, (1918); Stillborn of MORAN, Aug. 3, 1940; Kathleene WOLLSLAGER, May 7, 1958.

LOT 178-B: Samuel COULTER and Ann Rebecca SPEDDEN; Jane COULTER, (Mar.) 3, 18(?)2; Child, Apr. 29, 1878; Stillborn, Feb. 15, 1881; Samuel COULTER, Apr. 20, 18(8)8; Louis P. LONG, Oct. 4, 1896; Hannah A. COULTER, Apr. 15, 1910; Thomas SPEDDEN, July 25, 1866; Ann R. SPEDDEN, Nov. 17, 1869; Thomas H. SPEDDEN, Oct. 26, 1870; Edward P. SPEDDEN, Aug. 17, 1874; Infant of M. and J. SPEDDEN, Jan. 20, 1890; George HEART, May 8, 1893; Z. Taylor SPEDDEN, Oct. 27, 1914; Franklin PEDRICK, Oct. 6, 1923; Martha PEDRICK, Nov. 17, 1923; Laura Coulter LONG, Dec. 21, 1943; Eva P. COULTER, April 20, 18(8)8.

LOT 179-B: W. J. HINDMAN, Fannie ESHAM and Sarah BRANNON; 2 children, May 16, 1857; Child of HINDMAN, Nov. 23, 1881; Peter HINDMAN, July 22, 1888; Sarah R. CHAMBERS, Jan. 19, 1889; Emily HINDMAN, Feb. 26, 1890; Blanch HINDMAN, Jan. 9, 1893; Chas. R. HINDMAN, Aug. 11, 1893; Kate HINDMAN, Oct. 5, 1894; Peter M. HINDMAN, Nov. 4, 1891; Child, Sept. 8, 1861; G. B. BOON, Jan. 18, 1862; Margt. E. BOON, (Feb.) 7, 1862; Va. RICHARDSON, Sept. 15, 1863; D. BRANNAN, Oct. 23, 1864; Remains in box, Aug. 7, 1866; Fannie WATRKINS, May 6, 1905; Eliza J. BRYNE, May 12, 1919 (could be BRGNE, BRYNE, BYONES); Frank A. ROUSSELL, Feb. 15, 1932; Child of C. A. BRANNAN, Sept. 10, 1874; Sarah D. BRANNAN, Mar. 22, 1877 (There is a Sarah W. BRANNON who may be the same as this person. No date given for Sarah W.); Child of BRANNAN, July 2, 1879; D(remorl) BRANNAN, Oct. 11, 1881 (child); W. J. E. BUSH, July 2, 1872; Child of BUSH, Oct. 22, 1878; Grover C. BUSH, June 22, 1885; B(enj.) BOONE, May 7, 1891; Chas. A. LIPSCOMB, Aug. (7,) 1902; Carroll A. BUSH, Oct. 11, 1905; Matthew BYRNE, 1816; Annie BYRNE, 1851; Herman L. ESHAM, 1849; Augusta R. ROUSSELL, Dec. 28, 1937.

LOT 180-B: John ROBB;
Acksah ROBB, May 24, 1860; Mrs. RIDGLEY, Feb. 10, 1877; John ROBB, Mar. 30, 1869.

LOT 181-B: John ADDISON and Henry WEBSTER;
Edw. P. ADDISON, Dec. 11, 1858; Sarah D. ADDISON, Apr. 6, 1887; John W. ADDISON, Apr. 18, 1887; Nancy ADDISON, Sept. 29, 1899; Virginia ADDISON, Mar. 5, 1912; Martha WEBSTER, Apr. 19, 1862; M. L. H. FISHER, Jan. 9, 1872; Ann WEBSTER, Sept. 26, 1872; Eunna E. WEBSTER, Sept. 20, 1874; Stillborn, Nov. 9, 1877; Henry WEBSTER, May 10, 1878; Susan COLING, Dec. 3, 1879; Wm. WEBSTER, Fe.b 25, 1883; Emily MC CART(ING), Dec. 9, 1899; Wm. MARBURG(ER), May 13, 1890; Luke K. JONES, Jan. 9, 1911.

LOT 183-B: David FEELEMEYER, "all family dead--no more burials--deed returned to cemetery."
Geo. ANDERSON, Mar. 17, 1858; Geo. W. FEELEMEYER, July 20, 1865; Child, June 27, 1865; Mary FEELEMEYER, Aug. 22, 1879; Annie FEELEMEYER, Feb. 25, 1880; David FEELEMEYER, Oct. 5, 1894; Wm. M. FEELEMEYER, Mar. (3 or 5), 1896; Ch. FEELEMEYER, Nov. 22, 1901; Geo. W. FEELEMEYER, Nov. 28, 1904; Emma FEELEMEYER, Nov. 28, 1904.

LOT 183-B: Ama HOLLAND and Chas. MC KINZIE;
Rev. (Horas) HOLLAND, Apr. 28, 1856 (another entry reads Dec. 7, 1855); Amanda HOLLAND, Nov. 15, 1899 (or 1879); Chas. HOLLAND, Sept. 6, 1913; Holland MC CLEARY, placed in vault Oct. 25, 1916, buried Sept. 29, 1915); Richard (H.) HOLLAND, June 11, 1862; Mary E. Holland MC CLEARY, July 16, 1928; Martha A. IRLAND, Dec. 22, 1859; Geo. W. MC KENZIE, Aug. 24, 1866; Chas. MC KENZIE, July 20, 1876; Deborah MC KENZIE, Jan. 3, 1884; Maggie (no surname given, but probably HOLLAND), 1846.

LOT 184-B: Mary Ann BAKER and Jas. and Lewis HERRON;
Remains from N. B. G., May 24, 1877 (probably means Northern Burial Ground); Rachel H(ENNABURG), Dec. 25, 1870; Mary T. GREEN, Nov. 25, 1874; Frances B. REESE, June 10, 1884.

LOT 185-B: Leonard CASSELL, Edwin CASSELL, Geo. R. CASSELL and John D. CASSELL;
Saray LYTLE, May 2, 1870; Mary (J. PIPER), Sept. 5, 1872 (partly illegible entry lined out); Leonard CASSELL, July 3, 1891; Eliz CASSELL, Aug. 25, 1906; Ruby R. (LIPINSKY), June 25, 1913; Chas. B. (HASTY), Jan. 7, 1929; Fredk. CASSELL, July 4, 185(4); Frank CASSELL, Dec. 15, 1853; Mary J. D(ear) CASSELL, Sept. 10, 1872; Emily V. CASSELL, (no date given); Thos. PARSON, Mar. 11, 1872; Geo. R. CASSELL, Feb. 14, 1895; Ann (E.) CASSELL, Feb. 28, 1896; Elmer E. COLEMAN, Mar. 22, 1932; Ada R. COLEMAN, Nov. 18, 1936; Joseph CASSELL, Dec. 3, 1866; Walter R(EIGN), and son Walter, Mar. 13, 1884; Rebecca CASSELL, Mar. 11, 1894; Margt. E. CASSELL, Nov. 30, 1857; (My)nette (A. or F.) HARTY, Aug. 18, 1931 (first name may be Myrtle); (Heias or Aelas) R. HALL, Jan. 18, 1933 (Other first names given for apparently same person are Aties or Alies and Annie); John O'BRIEN, Oct. 5, 1942; Edwin CASSELL, (no date given).

LOT 186-B: Eliza WATKINS, Abel CASSELL and Wm. TAYLOR;
Abraham CASSELL, Mar. 30, 1869, 58 years; (Nora) P. BENSON, July 9, 1883 (May be Neva); Rebecca CASSELL, Sept. 1, 1884; Eliza

TAYLOR, Mar. 16, 1889; Chas. TAYLOR, May 11, 1898; Florence (I.) IRWIN, Sept. 1, 1902; Wm. S. TAYMOR, Mar. 4, 1895; Fannie WATKINS, Apr. 6, 1929; Rebecca CASSEL, (no date given, child); Washington WINTERSON, Mar. 9, 1884; Grace W. OWENS, Dec. 21, 1963; Rebecca CASSELL, (no date given); Betty TAYLOR, July 18, 1893; Sarah R. HAMILTON, June 20, 1939. Letter found in Lot Books from William W. OWENS to Mt. Olivet Cemetery. The first paragraph in part "... on Feb. 15 you, Mr. MERKEL, and I went to Lot 186-B and found you had buried my mother, Grace W. OWENS, on Dec. 19, 1963 . . . " (in the grave of Betty TAYLOR). She is to be removed to lot next to "her father Washington WINTERSON." The entry "moved to #10 Feb. 19, 1964" is written on the letter which is dated Feb. 17, 1964 and was posted from New York City.

LOT 187-B: Uriah JONES and Glina A. ROWE;
Franklin FORD, Oct. 19, 1859; Uriah JONES, Oct. 24, 1859; Franklin FORD, Aug. 1, 1860; Mary E. JONES, Feb. 10, 1877; Ann JONES, Dec. 19, 1877; Philip R. JONES, April 2, 1881; Annie FORD, Apr. 18, 1879; Jos. H. JONES, July 29, 1893; Charles E. F. COOK, May 3, 1861; E. E. MC GRADEY, Dec. 20, 1861 (In both places the R in MC GRADEY is crossed out. In one other place it is not. This would make the name MC GADEY.); Chas. W. S. COOK, Mar. 1, 1864; Joseph ROWE, July 10, 1869; Magdelene CARTHERS, Mar. 28, 1899 (There appears to be an attempt in one place to insert an O into this name to make it CAROTHERS.); Edmond COOK, Feb. 25, 1891; Jennie G. MC GRADEY, (no date given).

LOT 188-B: WILLIAM BRUNDIGE;
Baby Henry, June 23, 1856; Baby Clarence, June 23, 1856; Samuel B. BRUNDIGE, Mar. 1, 1867; Sallie BRUNDIGE, May 5, 1884; Sarah BRUNDIGE, Mar. 1, 1861; Rebecca BRUNDIGE, Apr. 2, 1883; William BRUNDIGE, Dec. 27, 1902; Annie R. ELLICOTT, Sept. 6, 1923; Flora Belle BRUNDIGE, Feb. 17, 1943; Joseph WILLEY, (no date given).

LOT 189-B, Pt. I: Wm. H. COX and John C. QUAY;
Ann COX, June 8, 1877; Harry C. COX, Dec. 16, 1896; Eugene COX, Oct. 18, 1899; Mary J. COX, Oct. 5, 1914; Amelia KENNARD, Dec. 1, 1883; Wm. H. COX, Oct. 10, 1887; Annie E. COX, Apr. 28, 1859; Remains, May 7, 1859; Walter COX, Aug. 2, 1863; W. COX, Aug. 2, 1865; Isaac COX, Nov. 8, 186(7); Mary A. QUAY, Aug. 17, 1868; John C. QUAY, Nov. 29, 1875; Chas. H. QUAY, July 24, 1900. (There is an Annie M. COX, who is probably one of the above.)

LOT 189-B, Pt. II: On this lot page is the entry "See previous page." The lot owners here are given as Benjamin F. WELSH and Wm. H. COX;
(Celestor or Calester) LA CROSS, Jan. 21, 1864; Benj. F. WELSH, Nov. 12, 1870; Isabell WELSH, Aug. 9, 1872; J. Henry (MEDENING), Aug. 20, 1875; Kate M. A(N)GELL, Oct. 26, 1878; J. Harry MED(EN)ING, June 6, 1890.

LOT 190-B: Wm. T. DAVIS;
Esther DAVIS, Apr. 12, 1879; Wm. T. DAVIS, Sept. 27, 1897; Ellen R. CONRADE, Dec. 4, 1899 (or 79); Percy M. DAVIS, Mar. 19, 1903; Nannie B. DAVIS, Jan. 2, 1920, age 75 years, 9 months, 7 days.

LOT 191-B: Charles L. BROWN and Geo. B. TYLER;
Chas. L. BROWN, Sept. 6, 1912; Saml. C. BROWN, Dec. 20, 1898; Grace C. CHESTER, July 14, 1913; Ella M. CHESTER, Jan. 5, 1914;

Grace FORD, Jan. 14, 1914; Mary E. BROWN, June 5, 1916; Marion M. BROWN, Feb. 16, 1928; Wilbur J. BROWN, Feb. 9, 1893; Ella M. TYLER, Mar. 20, 1886; Geo. B. TYLER, Sept. 5, 1897 (on stone is date Oct. 4, 1897); Isabella TYLER, Oct. 25, 1919; Blanche TYLER, born Oct. 26, 1882, died Feb. 7, 1967, buried Feb. 11, 1967; Isabelle TYLOR, born Feb. 24, 1889; died Oct. 17, 1967, buried Oct. 20, 1967.

LOT 192-B: James FREEMAN and Laura CHAMBERS; Herbert B. FREEMAN, Jr., July 22, 1918; Walter R. FREEMAN, Oct. 3, 1918; "For Grace FREEMAN," born Oct. 26, 1882, died Apr. 23, 1968, buried Apr. 27, 1968; Charles S. FREEMAN, Dec. 3, 1938; A. G. FREEMAN, June 28, 1892; Alexander HAMBLETON, May 15, 1915; Esther DOWDEN, May 9, 1916; James FREEMAN, July 1, 1917; Mary A. FREEMAN, Jan. 25, 1938; Wm. SIMMERING, Sept. 28, 1901; Arthur CHALMERS, June 23, 1892; Virginia FREEDENBERGER, July 7, 1915 (child); Rawlins CHALMERS, Oct. 13, 1956; Charles J. CHALMERS, 84 years, Oct. 25, 1938; Harry CHALMERS, 54 years, Oct. 18, 1938; Wallace J. WHITE, Jr., buried Mar. 17, 1971, born. Oct. 31, 1922, died Mar. 15, 1971, aged 48 years in Washington D.C. - R. A. Pumphrey Funeral Home, D. C. to Loring Byers Funeral Home, Randallstown, MD. Father W. J. WHITE, Sr., mother Evelyn CHALMERS.

LOT 193-B: Wm. H. ANSTINE and Walter Z. MITCHELL; Henry E. ANSTINE, July 13, 1911; Amanda A. ANSTINE, June 18, 1921; Wm. Henry ANSTINE, Jan. 8, 1926; Chester C. ANSTINE, July 15, 1948; Ida B. ANSTINE, Oct. 3, 1942; Henry M. MITCHELL, Apr. 3, 1893; Ann SCHOFIELD, May 1, 1905 (entry crossed out); Henrietta WHITEFORD, May 31, 1905; Walter Z. MITCHELL, Nov. 8, 1929; Octavia M. MITCHELL, Feb. 7, 1930; Grace S. SULLIVAN, Nov. 19, 1946.

LOT 194-B: Oscar HELWIG, Alex W. BROWN and Pauline MAYER; Ellen HALLWIG, Jan. 27, 1883; Edw. O. HALLWIG, Mar. 2, 1899; Oscar E. BURT, Aug. 14, 1902; Leonard BURT, May 5, 1905; Nellie L. BURT, May 19, 1905; Carroll BURT, Oct. 11, 1905; Mary HALWIG, Mar. 28, 1916; Oscar HALLWIG, Aug. 5, 1921; Delia A. BROWN, Sept. 15, 1883; Ida E. BROWN, Sept. 20, 1883; Alex BROWN, June 9, 1919; Mary L. BROWN, Apr. 4, 1935; Geo. Ewing BROWN, Jan. 14, 1957; Emma B. BROWN, Apr. 30, 1962; Bessie C. BROWN, Jan. 29, 1964. Letter from Pauline MAYER to Mt. Olivet Cemetery dated Oct. 23, 1952 in reference to Lot 194 N-2 Area B. Original owner Oscar HALLWIG. Transferred to Wm. HALLWIG, son to Pauline MAYER, granddaughter, May 1927.
Item From the Stewart & Mowen Co. Funeral Directors to prepare for interment of Mrs. Mary Lavinia BROWN on Apr. 4, 1935 in 194-B Lot. Signed Emma B. BROWN and Bessie C. BROWN. The back of the item shows a sketch of six spaces in the lot with Alex W. BROWN, June 9, 1919, and Mrs. Alex W. BROWN. Another item from the same company asks to prepare to inter (Mrs.) George Ewing BROWN, Jan. 14, 1957 in 194-B. The reverse side shows six spaces. Space 1 empty, 2 M.L.B., 3 Alex B., 4 Julia, 5 Ida, 6 Ade B. Misses Emma & Bessie BROWN are sisters.

LOT 195-B: Alexander S. HOGG; A. Upshur MAPP, Oct. 19, 1901; Upshur W. MAPP, July 26, 1909; Douglas W. MAPP, Jan. 2, 1923; Florida Wellbourne MAPP, Nov. 21, 1936; Florida WELLBOURNE, July 29, 1881; Charles S. BOUGHMAN,

Feb. 26, 1879; Virginia M. HOGG, Dec. 28, 1883; Alexander S. HOGG, Apr. 4, 1901; John E. WELLBOURNE, May 18, 1896; Lucy H. WELLBOURNE, April 14, 1921.

LOT 196-B: John TOFT and John and George DEMPSTER; Grace A. DEMPSTER, Nov. 29, 1877; Thos. DEMPSTER, Sept. 14, 1892; (Mister) BARNEY, Mar. 6, 1895; Geo. E. DEMPSTER, May 15, 1895; Mary A. DEMPSTER, May 21, 1912; Hattie M. DEMPSTER, Feb. 5, 1945; Mary M. DEMPSTER, Dec. 12, 1961; Child, Aug. 10, 1875; Child, Oct. 27, 1857; Ellen TOFT, May 11, 1864; Cath. TOFT, Jan. 26, 1874; Fannie E. TOFT, Mar. 28, 1874; Alice T. TALBOTT, July 18, 1888 (N.W. at foot); Jas. A. C. TALBOTT, July 20, 1899; Richard W. SHECKELS, July 30, 1912; Sarah E. SHECKELS, Nov. 15, 1926; Alice T. TALBOT, Oct. 18, 1932.

LOT 197-B: Matilda RECKERT; John RECKERT, May 14, 1864; Matilda RECKERT, Feb. 7, 18(67); H. E. RECKERT, Feb. 4, 1867; Geo. RECKERT, Dec. 8, 1871; Florence RECKERT, July 22, 1871; Florence M. RECKERT, July 21, 1871; Chas. A. RECKERT, July 11, 1891; Hester A. RECKERT, Jan. 13, 1885; Mary A. (or H.) RECKERT, Jan. 9, 1894; Stillborn of Mary A. RECKERT, Jan. 21, 1895; Mary (or May) E. RECKERT, Nov. 15, 1910; Chas. A. RECKERT, disinterred Jan. 24, 1916; Chas. A. RECKERT, disinterred and removed to Louden Park, Sept. 14, 1916; Elizabeth C. BROWN, Mar. 25, 1918; Chas. H. PORTER, Nov. 25, 1935; Lillie E. PORTER, Oct. 15, 1938.

LOT 198-B: Wm. H. COCKEY and Jeremiah HENNING; Margt. HO(RN), Dec. 10, 1857; Mary MC G(?)G(AR), Mar. 15, 1875; Blanch (MOOR or MOON), Sept. 16, 1876; Mary E. HENNING, May 15, 1882; John T. HO(RN), (Apr.) 22 or 28, 1884; Kate HO(RN), Nov. 11, 1899; Eddie MC COLGAN, Sept. 13, 1895; David HORN, Jan. 13, 1897; Willie HORN, Sept. 27, 1897 (First name may be Nellie); (Josephine) MC COLGAN, July 27, 1926; (Emma) COCKEY, Feb. 1, 1858; Wm. H. COCKEY, Mar. 18, 1903; Evelyn COCKEY, Mar. 18, 1905; Andrew J. MC COLGAN, Dec. 15, 1931; Ida K. COCKEY, Mar. 11, 1958; William H. COCKEY, Sept. 25, 1944; Ivy (no surname), 1933 (buried with Andrew J. MC COLGAN); Thomas W. HOHN, Jan. 24, 1948; Evelyn E. HOHN, Mar. 4, 1947; Florence E. HOHN, June 10, 1958.

LOT 199-B: Wm. L. MORSE and John MANLEY; Margt. VEASEY, July 24, 1858; Walter COX, Aug. 2, 1863; John MANLEY, Dec. 26, 1863; Chas. R. VEASEY, July 27, 1866; Melvin H. WORTH, Aug. 11, 1866; John M. VEASEY, Oct. 22, 1866; Naomi MANLEY, Sept. 8, 1891; Hannah HORN, Nov. 12, 1859; Chas. C. MOORE, Apr. 3, 1866; 3 children, July 6, 1867 (Chas. M., (Minnie D.), (Gertrude P.) children of J. KEE(UN). These are probably the 3 children referred to above.); John H. KEEN(ER), Aug. 7, 1872; Gertrude KEEN(ER), Oct. 8, 1872; Wm. L. MORSE, Oct. 20, 1885; Sarah A. MORSE, July 15, 1890; Francis M. F(RENCH), May 10, 1906; Martha J. KEEN(ER), Feb. 27, 1916; Mary MORSE, Nov. 20, 1919; Martha J. MANLEY, (no date given).

LOT 200-B: Mathias LINTHICUM; Annie E. LINTHICUM, May 29, 1856; Thos. LINTHICUM, June 29, 1865; Matthias LINTHICUM, Nov. 23, 1866; Chas. E. LINTHICUM, Sept. 6, 1867; Mathias LINTHICUM, Jan. 17, 1880; Carrie M. LINTHICUM, Mar. 23, 1880; Annie L. ELKINS, July 9, 1885; Sarah C. ELKINS, Sept. 27, 1902; Mary L. LINTHICUM, Aug. 10, 1909; Chas. E. ELKINS, Nov.

18, 1918; Katherine HILGARTNER, Mar. 14, 1957; Cremated remains of Agnes LA CROIX, July 17, 1951; Nannie C. ELKINS, July 8, 1885.

LOT 201-B: Isiah MERCER;
Virgil T. MERCER, Apr. 26, 1906; Mary E. MERCER, Jan. 13, 1908; Margaret A. MERCER, Feb. 27, 1920; Ann A. SCHOFIELD, May 31, 1905; Herbert S. EBAUGH, Sr., May 16, 1950; Belle Mercer EBAUGH, Aug. 11, 1938; Beverly H. EBAUGH, Feb. 20, 1920 (male child); Charles H. MERCER, Oct. 7, 1913; Mary Emma MERCER, Oct. 16, 1859; Isiah MERCER, Sept. 13, 1859; Harriet A. MERCER, Jan. 29, 1856.

LOT 202-B: Wm. S. QUIGLEY and Girdeon A. JARRETT;
Wm. QUIGLEY, Apr. 25, 1879; John QUIGLEY, Sept. 23, 1866; Fannie E. QUIGLEY, Feb. 4, 1866; Ann C. QUIGLEY, Apr. 3, 1876; Wm. (S.) QUIGLEY, Aug. 24, 1894; Martha W. QUIGLEY, Apr. 4, 1896; Elizabeth QUIGLEY, Oct.t 3, 1902; Geo. WEBSTER, May 9, 1859; John WEBSTER, Apr. 2, 1869; Geo. WEBSTER, Feb. 24, 1873; Child, July 20, 1874; Emma JESSOP, July 18, 18(8)9; Girdeon A. JESSOP, Mar. 26, 1901; Geo. H. JESSOP, Oct. 11, 1907; Sarah J. JARRETT, Jan. 7, 1888; Ella M. JESSOP, Sept. 4, 1915; Chas. L. JESSOP, Jan. 22, 1920; James M. JESSOP, Aug. 18, 1923; Annie C. JESSOP, Feb. 14, 1946.

LOT 203-B: Geo. T. PRICE and John H. JOHNSON;
Wm. T. PRICE, Oct. 11, 1877; Sarah B. PRICE, Nov. 16, 1877; Eliza PRICE, Apr. 27, 1897; Clarence PRICE, Feb. 21, 1898; Geo. T. PRICE, Apr. 9, 1904; Geo. D. PRICE, May 24, 1888; Redman JOHNSON, Dec. 13, 1872; Emily HAND, Mar. 24, 1886; Robt. JOHNSON, July 12, 1889; John H. JOHNSON, July 12, 1893; Charlotte JOHNSON, Mar. 5, 1897; Elijah R. JOHNSON, July 30, 1923; Joseph H. V(OR)STEG, Nov. 23, 1936; Robert Lee PRICE, Dec. 19, 1951; Ada A. PRICE, Apr. 15, 1955; John H. JOHNSON, Apr. 1, 1950.

LOT 204-B: Columbus SHIPLEY and Marion VE(RN)EY (this name very difficult to read);
John VERNEY, July 2, 1869; Elisha T. VERNEY, May 1, 1870; Child of Jas. SMITH, Sept. 25, 1871; Lola M. VERNEY, Aug. 10, 1874; L(ottie) VERNEY, June 18, 1884; Jas. E. VERNEY, Apr. 25, 1891; Margt. A. VERNEY, Feb. 25, 1895; David VERNEY, Mar. 17, 1916; Columbus SHIPLEY, Oct. 26, 1863; Child of H(OUSE), July 11, 1871; Leroy SHIPLEY, July 16, 1897; Maud SHIPLEY, Feb. 20, 1902; Rem. of E. SHIPLEY, Apr. 28, 1903; Owen H. SHIPLEY, Apr. 17, 1906; Clarence SHIPLEY, May 5, 1914; Sarah SHIPLEY, Mar. 31, 1863; Francis M. SHIPLEY, Oct. 16, 1975; Mary E. SHIPLEY, Oct. 7, 1931; Child of (KRAUSE or HOUSE), (no date given); Ida Adair SHIPLEY, Apr. 7, 1942.

LOT 205-B: Geo. W. MITCHELL;
Saml. MITCHELL, Jan. 14, 1868; Ella May MITCHELL, Nov. 9, 1870; Walter E. MITCHELL, Sept. 12, 1900; Geo. W. MITCHELL, Feb. 18, 1904; Lillie C. MITCHELL, June 10, 1884; Ella FITZPATRICK, Mar. 10, 1923; Annie MITCHELL, Mar. 13, 1926; Florence I. HAWKINS, Mar. 7, 1956.

LOT 205-B: South 1/2 and LOT 217-B: J. R. and Henry ARNOLD;
Mary ARNOLD, Dec. 4, 1897; Wm. ARNOLD, July 6, 1867; Sarah A. ARNOLD, June 12, 1872; Wm. H. ARNOLD, Mar. 9, 1881; Miss I. M. DUVALL, Dec. 4, 1919; Mary A. ARNOLD, Mar. 4, 1923; Anto(nia) M. ARNOLD, Sept. 17, 1926; Martha E. ARNOLD, (no date given); James

R. ARNOLD, (no date given); Henry P. ARNOLD, (no date given). There are stones for another Mary A. ARNOLD, also for W. H. A., and Mary J. ARNOLD.

LOT 206-B: Alice M. RICKEY and Francis BALDWIN; R. M. BALDWIN, Sept. 3, 1866; Robert D. BALDWIN, Nov. 27, 1876; Thos. M. BALDWIN, Jan. 18, 1891; Thos. P. BALDWIN, Oct. 29, 1892 (or 72); Fannie M. BALDWIN, Sept. 20, 1900; Rachel M. BALDWIN, Aug. 30, 1907; Geo. S. BALDWIN, Mar. 14, 1935; A. Maud RICKEY, Oct. 11, 1893; Albert RICKEY, Aug. 11, 1900; Alice M. RICKEY, Oct. 5, 1927; Edna M. LANGSTON, Feb. 2, 1971, born Sept. 30, 1885, died Jan. 30, 1971, father Chas. T. RICKEY, mother Alice M. JONES; John R. LANGSTON, Nov. 6, 1951.

LOT 207-B: Charles R. PUE and Margaret SEATON; Susan BAYLEY, Feb. 8, 1871; Wm. (S.) SEATON, Oct. 6, 1872; Mary SMITH, Apr. 16, 1872; Annie SMITH, Sept. 1, 1875; Minnie E. JOHNSON, June 9, 1877; Mary T. SEATON, Sept. 12, 1877; Pumphrey (W.) BURHAM, July 25, 1895 (In another place on the record this name is spelled BUONHAM); Nancy BLUNT, Apr. 24, 1871; Sallie PEREGOY, Jan. 25, 1873; Matilda R. PUE, July 13, 1878 (Matilda R. POE, 1878); Chas. R. PUE, June 30, 1879 (Charles Rigley POE, 1879); Chas. R. PUE, Feb. 1, 1905; Frank R. PUE, Nov. 6, 1905; Matilda R. REED, Dec. 10, 1907; Chas. R. PUE, Sept. 20, 1905; Mary E. BURNHAM, (no date given); Hazel L. BURHAM, (no date given).

LOT 208-B: David HEPBURN and John H. HALL; (Rev.) E. HALL, Sept. 26, 1871; Everet HALL, Jan. 7, 1873; John H. HALL, July 17, 1875; Dorothy Mae LEE, June 16, 1925 (entry crossed out), disinterred Aug. 21, 1948; Child, Sept. 26, 1871; Harry HEPBURN, July 2, 1859; Clara V. HEPBURN, Dec. 7, 1878; Clara A. H. GARDNER, Feb. 12, 1879; Everet GARDNER, May 18, 1880; Arthur B. HEPBURN, July 17, 1882; David HEPBURN, Apr. 20, 1885; Jas. HEPBURN, Apr. 26, 1912; (Re?) P. Hall, (no date given); Vergie E. GAITHER, Sept. 29, 1973, born Dec. 21, 1892, died Sept. 27, 1973, father Milton HALL, mother Estelle EARP. Witzke Funeral Home; Harry C. GAITHER, Sept. 20, 1945.

LOT 209-B: Gertrude L. LE(VEE), Margaret E. LANDON and Henry GUEST;
Geo. LANDON, Apr. 11, 1868; Child, July 24, 1869; Minnie LANDON, Nov. 6, 1869; Child of George LANDON, Apr. 22, 1873 (or 1875); Hennrietta L(EWIS), Mar. 15, 1877; Frances O. MILLER, Sept. 16, 1906; (Rev. C. LYNCH, Dec. 27, 1876; Josiah LANDON, Mar. (10), 1875; Minnie E. LANDON, June 14, 1928; Alice M. GA(W)THROP, July 25, 1931; Harry GUEST, Mar. 10, 1897; Mary Ann GUEST, July 1906; Emma GUEST, Aug. 13, 1928; Alice E. ROWE, (no date given); Henry GUEST, June 30, 1943.

LOT 210-B: SANDERS & BAUGHMAN, W. E. WHITE;
James DICKSON, Nov. 20, 1867; Martha DICKSON, Feb. 10, 1870; Maggie BAUGHMAN, Apr. 1, 1871; Chas. A. BAUGHMAN, Feb. 26, 1879; Annie V. BAUGHMAN, Feb. 7, 1881; Elizabeth A. BAUGHMAN, Feb. 14, 1884; Christian BAUGHMAN, Oct. 26, 1911; Mary A. CRO(PP)ER (or CROFFER), Mar. 19, 1918; Saml. W. BAUGHMAN, Sept. 17, 1923; Arthur D. (GREEN), July 4, 1871 (disinterreed written across this and next two entries); John (GREEN), Jan. 30, 1879; Ida A. (GREEN), May 30, 18(8)7; (Beulah) WHITTER, Feb. 1(6), 1892;

102

Stillborn of W. & J. WHITTER, Dec. 3, 1915; Wm. E. WHITTER, Mar. 25, 1927; Irene A. WHITTER, Aug. 24, 1929; Clarence P. B(URDS), June 2, 1934; Robert J. BAUGHMAN, July 12, 1946; Grace Irene BURNS, June 13, 1956; Mary WHITTER, Nov. 12, 1947; Crofton S. WHITTER, May 1, 1948.

LOT 211-B: Jessie ARMAGER;
Jessie (S.) ARMAGER, Aug. 17, 1869; Julia A. ARMAGER, Oct. 27, 1872; Jessie ARMAGER, Jan. 12, 1877; A. Margaret ARMAGER, Nov. 30, 1917; (Lore & J. Reese) ARMAGER, May 7, 1931.

LOT 212-B: Asa B. FARGO;
Mary V. FARGO, Mar. 6, 1897; Willie, Bessie and Elmer, Dec. 1, 1897.

LOT 213-B: Lancaster OULD; (no burials recorded in this lot.)

LOT 214-B: Robert HOLMES;
John HOLMES, Oct. 28, 185(3); E. STE(NAC)KER, May 10, 1861; Mary JOHNSON, Oct. 18, 1866; (Annita) SHEPPARD, Jan. 30, 1868; H. W. STE(NA)CKER, Oct. 25, 1870; Eliz A. SEABROOK, Aug. 13, 1872; Child of Robt. HOLMES, Aug. 29, 1876; Child of (Hen STENACKER), July 28, 1871; Wm. HOLMES, Apr. 19, 1879; Wm. R. Lloyd HOLMES, Mar. 12, 1879; Sarah J. HOLMES, May 19, 1879; Annie HOLMES, Jan. 30, 1885; Isabel HOLMES, Feb. 23, 1886; Thos. HOLMES, Apr. 10, 1897.

LOT 215-B: John H. BRADY and Robt. R. MACARTNEY;
Greenbury BRADY, Feb. 9, 1868; Martha L. BRADY, Feb. 1, 1874 (stone reads, Martha L. BRADY, Jan 11, 1874); Emma J. MILLER, Feb. 3, 1876, (stone reads Emma J. MILLER, Feb. 1, 1874); Wm. A. MILLER, Sept. 1, 1876 (Also called Willie A. MILLER, Aug. 30, 1876 apparently, from stone.); Mary BRADY, Apr. 16, 1885; John H. BRADY, Aug. 22, 1917; Robert H. MACARTNEY, Nov. 23, 1857; Rebecca K. REESE, Feb. 9, 1911; Robt. P. REESE, Jan. 8, 1912; Eliz. Magartney, Dec. 0, 1889; Robt. MACARTNEY, Mar. 18, 1880.

LOT 216-B: Wm. A. NOEL, Christopher KEHL and Mrs. John ZENTGRAF (of Ft. Pierce, Florida);
Ella S. NOEL, May 23, 1867; Geo. M. NOEL, July 14, 1875; Grace R. NOEL, Oct. 19, 1878; Sadie NOEL, Aug. 4, 1880; Frank M. NOEL, Oct. 22, 1886; Edw. G. NOEL, June 1, 1895; Sarah E. NOEL, Jan. 28, 1922; Child of (A. C.) KEHL, Apr. 10, 1876; Wm. KEHL, May 24, 1880; Lemie C. SEEBO, May 26, 1902; Christopher KEHLE, Dec. 29, 1895 (In parenthesis below this entry is "Aug. 51."); Katherine E. KEHLE, Sept. 28, 1926; Lelia Noel REDDER, June 29, 1940; Wm. Lee PADDY, Mar. 16, 1967, born Oct. 4, 1937, died Mar. 13, 1967.

LOT 217-B: Annie JONES;
F(leoance) JONES, June 30, 1871; Martha A. HOPKINS, June 25, 1875; Geo. T. ELLIOTT, Apr. 29, 1884; Elizabeth GREEN, Apr. 7, 188(7); Louisa CONWAY, Dec. 10, 1904; Anna E. HURLEY, Dec. 2, 1929.

LOT 218-B: Josephine MONTAGUE and David J. FORSYTH;
Child, Mar. 13, 1893 (entry crossed out); Annie FORSYTH, June 28, 1897; David FORSYTH, Mar. 29, 190(0); Josephine FORSYTH, Feb. 9, 1894; Josephine FORSYTH, Mar. 13, 1916; Lillie M. FORSYTH, Aug. 10, 1933; Susanne A. FORSYTH, Apr. 11, 1936; Wm. W. MONTAGUE,

Apr. 20, 1867; Wm. H. MONTAGUE, Apr. 11, 1874; Thos. GILBLELRT, Apr. 7, 1876; Loretta VEASEY, Apr. 18, 1879; Chas. V. MILLER, June 16, 1888; Rose VEASEY, Aug. (24), 1879; Josephine MONTAGUE, July 20, 1888; Edwd. R. YOUNG, Nov. 12, 1912.

LOT 219-B: Margaret BOLAND and Everhard KUHN; Margt. BOLAND, Mar. 28, 1867; Margt. A. BOLAND, Apr. 13, 1892; Gertrude H. HOLLAND, Jan. 12, 1903; John H. MISSELMAN, Jan. 15, 1913; M. Cassander MISSELMAN, May 1, 1923; John KUHN, June 25, 1867; Frances KUHN, June 25, 1868; Chas. E. KUHN, June 25, 1867; Eliza KUHN, June 21, 1884; Leibrecht KUHN, Jan. 23, 1888; Eberhart KUHN, Aug. 12, 1897; Frank B. KUHN, Apr. 12, 1899; Baby ZINKER, July 7, 1923; Dr. (Algie) L. KUHN, Oct. 10, 1934 (May be D. and Annie KUHN.).

LOT 220-B: Geo. and Ann LEFFLER; Ann L. LEFFLER, Oct. 25, 1866; Chas. LEFFLER, Aug. 29, 1870; Geo. R. LEFFLER, July 12, 1875; Robert S. LEFFLER, April 23, 1879; Mary A. JONES, Apr. 16, 1881; Chas. V. COLLINS, Dec. 8, 1890; Albert LEFFLER, Nov. 19, 1892; Helen W. GILL, Oct. 14, 1908; Dr. Saml. H. GILL, Mar. 9, 1917; Georgeanna LEFFLER, Dec. 11, 1910; Cremated ashes of Virginia A. EGERTEN, Dec. 10, 1917; James (C.) EGERTON, Aug. 10, 1920; Terese J. GILL, Oct. 3, 1935; Cremated remains of Walter C. EGERTON, Dec. 10, 1948; Cremated remains of Maud EGGERTON, June 12, 1950.

LOT 221-B: Charles R. MYERS; Wm. F. MYERS, Jr., Aug. 29, 1903; Mary J. MYERS, June 4, 1865; Geo. W. MYERS, June 10, 1860; Rebecca MYERS, Nov. 5, 1894; (Chas.) E. MYERS, July 11, 1866; Conrad R. MYERS, Mar. 11, 1858; Chas. R. MYERS, Nov. 15, 1900; Mary MEYERS, May 27, 1889; John E. MYERS, Mar. 8, 1898.

LOT 222-B: George YOECKEL and Philip WEHN; Geo. WEHN, July 20, 1857; Chas. H. WEHN, July 26, 1857; Philip WEHN, Mar. 2, 1882; Elizabeth WEHN, Nov. 30, 1894; Geo. YOECKEL, Feb. 19, 1877; Geo. W. CASH, May 17, 1877; (Mrs. RAENER), July 25, 1877; Fannie YOECKEL, Sept. 18, 1886; Wm. ROSA, Dec. 18, 1886; Sarah ROSS, Oct. 24, 1885.

LOT 223-B: Susan WILLIAMS and Adams A. NICOLL; Stillborn of LAMBIN, Feb. 8, 1897; Susan WILLIAMS, July 14, 1905, next to Edward WILLIAMS; Edward WILLIAMS, (no date given); Catherine NICOLL, Aug. 4, 1894; Adam A. NICOLL, Mar. 6, 1903; Herbert and Edith, April 25, 1895 (no surname given); Mary A. LINDSAY, Feb. 12, 1897 (There is a stone for a Mary E. LINDSAY); Adam A. NICOLL, March 15, 1921; Louisa W. NICOLL, Oct. 9, 1923.

LOT 224-B: WOOD and HALE, Wm. B. LYON; Charlotte R. WOOD, June 18, 1890; John E. HALE, June 21, 1935; Annie E. EVANS, Oct. 3, 1867; Mary A. WRIGHT, Aug. 15, 1869; Frances M. HALE, (no date given); John E. HALE, (no date given); Helena S. HALE, Nov. 20, 1968; Walter F. WOOD, (no date given); John O. WOOD, (no date given); Eleanora WOOD, (no date given); John C. WOOD, (no date given); "_____ HALE", (no date given); Anna G. HALE, (no date given); Charles W. HALE, (no date given).

LOT 225-B: J. R. MAGURIE, Mary (J.) MYER, Mrs. F. (Gracey) MURRAY; Martha SULLIVAN, Apr. 21, 1867; Stillborn, Jan. 14, 1884; Stillborn, Mar. 16, 1883; Mary J. MYERS, July 20, 1886; D. W. MYERS, June 11, 1895 (In the same grave are listed Daniel and Hester, no surname given.); John PETERSON, Oct. 18, 1901; Emma C. MYERS, "B & F Feb. 18, 1932, aged 66 years, 5 months, 2 days"; Charlotte C. MURRAY, (Dec.) 16, 1935; (The next eight entries, these bodies removed Aug. 10, 1896.); Stillborn, Aug. 1, 1887; Ann M. MEAD, Oct. 27, 1857; Wm. H. MEAD, Feb. 10, 1860; Chas. O. B(O)SS, June 10, 1862; Geo. MEAD, Jan. 22, 1866; Child, Apr. 7, 1866; Child of FOXWELL, Feb. 8, 1865; Annie E. FOXWELL, Aug. 3, 1872; Louis C. MAGURE, Apr. 19, 1897; Mildred MAGUIRE, July 31, 1899; Mary R. MAGUIRE, Apr. 10, 1919; Jas. R. MAGUIRE, June 2, 1933; Geo. W. MYER, Mar. 6, 1880.

LOT 226-B: Wm. BRONWELL and Chas. BAUSMITH; Margt. A. BONWELL, Apr. 18, 1872; Child, Sept. 4, 1878; Wm. R. BRONWELL, Mar. 22, 1887; John T. BRONWELL, Apr. 11, 1908; Fannie BROMWELL, Oct. 18, 1840 (entry crossed out); (hole in page) BROMWELL, Nov. 18, 192(?) (Entry at another point just below reads "Died (Feb.) 13, 1933"; (Francis) BROMWELL, Feb. 14, 1933; Joseph D. BROMWELL, (Mar.) 20, 1935; Nora BAUSMITH, Aug. 10, 1881; Clarence BAUSMITH, Jan. 20, 1881; Geo. W. BAUSMITH, Nov. 11, 1886; Chas. BAUSMITSH, Mar. 18, 1895; Chas. BAUSMITH, Oct. 31, 1899; Ella F. BAUSMITH, July 7, 1909; Julia A. BAUSMITH, Nov. 5, 1917; Walter BAUSMITH, Mar. 6, 1926; Georgia BROMWELL, (no date given); Estelle BAUSMITH, Apr. 20, 1961.

LOT 227-B: Jas. GIRDWOOD and Wm. H. WEHN; Mrs. E. J. PRICE, Mar. 11, 1876; Augusta GIRDWOOD, Feb. 26, 1877; Jessie B. GIRDWOOD, Mar. 29, 1877; Margt. C. GIRDWOOD, Apr. 14, 1877; Josephine GIRDWOOD, Feb. 2, 1915; (Jas.) GIRDWOOD, Apr. 20, 1918; Christine O. GIRDWOOD, Feb. 4, 1927; John G. (PICHTER), Mar. 12, 1890, disenterred Dec. 20, 1906 to Louden Park; Clara E. WHEN, Oct. 13, 1897; Willie WHEN, Dec. 20, 1880; Georganna WHEN, Apr. 24, 1911; Wm. H. WHEN, Aug. 17, 1899.

LOT 228-B: Walter RALEIGH and Louisa M. BRASS; Wm. E. RALEIGH, Apr. 22, 1886; Car(no) RALEIGH, Mar. 2, 1879; Tabitha W. RALEIGH, May 10, 1895; Walter RALEIGH, Mar. 12, 1878; Susanna A. BUSHEY, Oct. 22, 1923; (Page torn, name missing), Sept. 17, 1927; James H. BRASS, Dec. 10, 1891; Lucy and Minnie BRASS, Dec. 26, 1901; Cara BRASS, July 30, 1902; Louisa M. BRASS, Aug. 15, 1925; Andrew J. BRASS, Dec. 11, 1931; Katherine R. BROOKS, (no date given); Walter A. RALEIGH, June 21, 1957; James T. BRASS, Mar. 5, 1942.

LOT 229-B: William J. SMITH, Arthur H. SCHELHAUS and Annie M. KIEHLMAN; Julia MALONE, July 25, 1924; Florence G. SMITH, Aug. 9, 1910; Isabella (Page torn, name missing), Nov. 16, 1899; William P. SMITH, Aug. 14, 1896; Margaret JUENER, Oct. 17, 1895; Harry T. OLER, July 15, 1905; Howard A. JUENER, ("no record" written on the page of the lot book for this entry and all of the entries that follow; Julius MILLER; W. E. MILLER; Henry KUHLMAN; Mary JUENER.

SECTION C

LOT 1-C: Mercy B. PEFFER and Thomas A. VAN SANT; Clifton K. YEARLEY, May 19, 1964; Fanny V. YEARLEY, Dec. 10, 1968; Benjamin F. VAN SANT, June 1, 1948; Charles C. PEFFER, Nov. 30, 1942; Mercy B. PEFFER, Aug. 10, 1956.

LOT 2-C: Harry and EDITH CR(UM); No burials shown in this lot. There is an illegible death notice from newspaper for SULLIVAN.

LOT 4-C: Frederick C. SULLIVAN, James A. SKIRVEN, Louis BOYD and John H. FERGUSON; Frederick C. SULLIVAN, Dec. 11, 1969, born Feb. 14, 1903, died Dec. 9, 1969; Estella SULLIVAN, Nov. 9, 1966; William H. BENTON, Jan. 5, 1944; Louis L. BOYD, Aug. 9, 1952; Mary A. BOYD, Nov. 2, 1932; James A. SKIRVEN, May 1, 1954; Eva SKIRVEN, Removed from #6, 223F, June 16, 1954; John H. FERGUSON, Sept. 28, 1948; Clara L. FERGUSON, Feb. 8, 1966, born July 10, 1878, died Feb. 1, 1966. Authorization to Mt. Olivet to remove remains of Mrs. Eva G. SKIRVEN from #6, LOT 2(2) 3, Section F. to #4, Section C, next to her husband James A. SKIRVEN. Signed by Charles D. SKIRVEN, Thomas (K)ELL(OGG) and Mildred SKIRVEN, June 16, 1954.

LOT 5-C: George N. DURHAM, George H. and Alta May TURNER; Katie E. DURHAM, Feb. 14, 1935; Lillian C. DURHAM, June 18, 1949; George H. TURNER, Oct. 16, 1954. Grave Opening Permission for #5 lot, Section C, for body of Harry John REED of Baltimore, Md. Interred date Aug. 23, 1962. Next of kin, Mary M. REED, dated Aug. 21, 1962.

LOT 6-C: Edith M. MAHR, William T. LUTZ, Geo. M. MOORE, William L. LUTZ and Peter A. LUTZ and Mrs. Edna M. JACOB; Margaret E. LUTZ, Jan. 27, 1936; Edith M. MAHR, Apr. 24, 1954; Harry J. REED, Aug. 23, 1962; Mary M. REED, Aug. 22, 1967; Frederick W. JACOB, Oct. 15, 1963; William T. LUTZ, Sept. 2, 1940; Margaret E. LUTZ, Jan. 27, 1936; Peter A. LUTZ, Jan. 21, 1957; Mary Ellen LUTZ, May 18, 1944; Stillborn of LUTZ, Sept. 25, 1946; George M. MOORE, May 10, 1965; Louisa K. MOORE, Jan. 19, 1955. Letter from Arthur A. ANDERSON, Jr., attorney at law, regarding lots owned by deceased client Edith M. MAHR. Lots are 6 in section C. Edith M. MAHR left in a will all her property to Ruth B. DISNEY. Letter dated May 10, 1957.

LOT 7-C: Robert A. and Gladys A. LEHNERT, Thomas J. BURY, Mrs. Alice K. BLEDSOE, Thomas H. and Elizabeth K. SWANN and Mrs. Dora POWELL; Milton POWELL, Jan. 27, 1970, moved from single row Oct. 23, 1969. Born May 14, 1908, died Oct. 20, 1969; Irene L. BURY, Feb. 7, 1970, born July 7, 1901, Funeral Home of J. J. Cowan & Sons; Harry C. BLEDSOE, June 13, 1955; Filice K. BLEDSOE, Jan. 14, 1969, born July 7, 1881, died Jan. 11, 1969; Thomas Hadden SWANN, Feb. 6, 1971, born July 6, 1898, died Feb. 3, 1971. Born in Illinois, died in Rochester, New York. Jenkins Funeral Home, Baltimore, Md. Parents were John N. SWAN and Jane DURFFIELD; Elizabeth Baker SWAN, June 26, 1973, born Sept. 21, 1898, died June 22, 1973. Parents were J. W. KIRK and Gertrude BRATT, Jenkins Funeral Home.

LOT 8-C and 9-C, no record in lot book.

LOT 10-C: Wilbur L. CHARLTON;
Clara R. CHARLTON, May 16, 1956; Wilbur L. CHARLTON, Mar. 24, 1960.

LOT 11-C: David J. & Hally C. (or M.) CARVER;
Hally M. CARVER, Dec. 24, 1973, born Nov. 15, 1886, died Dec. 21, 1973. Parents were Rev. V. H. COUNCILL and Margaret MORAN. Jenkins Funeral Home; Dr. David J. CARVER, Mar. 28, 1969, born Aug. 12, 1882, died Mar. 26, 1969.

LOT 12-C: Harry W. MOORE and Edith B. MURPHY;
Harry Wilson MOORE, Jan. 4, 1946; Louis C. MURPHY, Oct. 11, 1940.

LOT 13-C: James Clinton COOKE, J. Edmund SCHUELER, Mrs. Wm. A. COOPER, John J. SCHAFER of Toronto, Canada;
Laura F. COOPER, Dec. 4, 1974, born Dec. 24, 1897, died Nov. 29, 1974. Mother Laura RIBBON. Funeral Home of J. J. Cowan; William A. COOPER, Aug. 1, 1969, born Aug. 23, 1894, died July 28, 1969. Funeral home of J. J. Cowan & Sons; Matilda E. COOKE, Nov. 7, 1947; James Clinton COOKE, Mar. 21, 1956; Space for Lydia M. EDGAR; Ida E. SCHUELER, May 11, 1950; J. Edmund SCHUELER, May 3, 1951.

LOT 14-C: Thomas E. GATTEN, Rev. Harry R. WILKES and Jennie MULLER;
Anna WILKES, July 5, 1940; Rev. Harry R. WILKES, Nov. 2, 1959; Theresa M. WILSON, Nov. 25, 1940; Audrey Muller TRAVIS, Aug. 27, 1938; Jennie MULLER, Mar. 26, 1951; Warren MULLER, Sept. 17, 1930.

LOT 15-C: Blanche K. COOKE, Benjamin P. ALRICH, Mrs. Harry I. SHIPLEY (Maude R. SHIPLEY) and Miss HOKHUACHEN;
James C. COOKE, Jr., July 15, 1940; Edward P. FORD, Aug. 12, 1964; Harry I. SHIPLEY, Apr. 14, 1970, born Feb. 9, 1906, died Apr. 11, 1970. Funeral home of G. Truman Schwab; Cortrude E. BLASINI, Dec. 13, 1974, born Mar. 9, 1906, died Dec. 10, 1974. Parents Harry D. WALTER and Gertrude F. HUGHES. Funeral home of G. Truman Schwab; Benjamin P. ALRICH, Apr. 27, 1936; Julia B. ALRICH, May 18, 1949; "(B. Don)" Benjamin ALRICH, Apr. 21, 1973, born Apr. 6, 1901, died Apr. 18, 1973. Parents Benj. P. ALRICH and Julia BROWN. Funeral home of Ullrich; Chao Ming CHEN, Nov. 1, 1961.

LOT 16-C: Grace M. OSTOVIT and Emma NORBURY;
Gordon J. OSTOVIT, Jan. 2, 1936; Grace M. "(OSTOVIT)", Oct. 14, 1952; William E. OSTOVIT, Dec. 12, 1947; Walter NORBURY, Sr., June 5, 1934.

LOT 17-C: W. Elliott BEST, Rev. Asbury SMITH, Reserved for Rev. E. M. AMOS. No burials recorded for this lot.

LOT 18-C and 19-C: No record found in lot books for these lots.

LOT 20-C: Earl Vernon EBER and Eliz. Mildred EBER. No burials recorded for this lot.

LOT 21-C: Mildred ____ PATTON; Roland A. PATTON, Dec. 2, 1952; Mildred Leo PATTON, cremains, Nov. 18, 1971, born Aug. 15, 1897, died Nov. 8, 1971, San Diego, Ca.

LOT 22-C: William B. and Margaret SPILLMAN; Andrew J. SPILLMAN, June 6, 1944; Matilda A. BAKER, May 6, 1950; William B. SPILLMAN, Oct. 8, 1946; Marguerite SPILLMAN, Jan. 18, 1954.

LOT 23-C: Madelon LANGVILLE, Estelle CROWN, Margaret J. MEETH (the name MEETH lined out and MADILL inserted, with note remarried 1960), Margaret C. WOCKENFUSS; George C. LANGVILLE, Apr. 25, 1940; Marion A. CROWN, Aug. 11, 1938; Estelle CROWN, Jan. 22, 1963; Elmer MEETH, 54 years, 11 months, 27 days, Apr. 22, 1939; William E. WOCKENFUSS, Sept. 8, 1939.

LOT 24-C: Ida M. ROBERTS and Dr. Henry M. WALTER; Clarence E. ROBERTS, Mar. 26, 1938; Mary Elizabeth ROBERTS, Jan. 28, 1972, born Apr. 6, 1926, died Jan. 25, 1972. Parents Clarence Elmer ROBERTS and Ida Martha WOCKENFUSS, Cvach funeral home; John J. GIBSON, Oct. 7, 1963; Mabel F. GIBSON, June 21, 1958; Emil WOCKENFUSS, Apr. 4, 1939; Margaretha WOCKENFUSS, Mar. 19, 1946; Guy S. STURTZ, Jan. 8, 1963; Harry O. WALTER, May 30, 1941; Gertrude WALTER, Mar. 1, 1938.

LOT 25-C: M. Ellen BUJAC, Howard F. WHEELER, Gladys M. JORY and Robert B. WHEELER; William J. BUJAC, Sept. 5, 1938; M. Ellen BUJAC, July 1, 1950; Robert Allen WHEELER, Dec. 24, 1940; Howard F. WHEELER, Jan. 16, 1960; Maude C. WHEELER, June 24, 1939; M. Vernon JORY, Aug. 22, 1940; Stillborn child of M. Vernon JORY III, Feb. 24, 1947; Gladys M. (JORY) MOMBERGER, May 4, 1971, born May 26, 1899, died Apr. 30, 1971. Parents John LA BARRE and Elsie CONWAY. Funeral home McCully.

LOT 26-C: Jennie (Virginia) L. GRIFFIN, Wm. H. BEST, Odna PRICE and William S. CAUDILL; Wm. A. GRIFFITH, Oct. 30, 1936; Courtney L. PRICE, Apr. 8, 1937; Lula M. FELLER, Jan. 20, 1971, born Nov. 12, 1894, died Jan. 17, 1971. Parents Geo. V. FELLER and Methilda THON. Hubbard Funeral Home; Courtney L. PRICE, (no date given); Odna L. TARR, Dec. 24, 1942; William R. GRIFFIN, (no date given); Virginia L. (Jennie) GRIFFIN, June 21, 1974, born Nov. 23, 1890, died June 18, 1974. Parents Geo. FELLER and Mathilda THON. Hubbard Funeral Home; Ethel L. CAUDILL, Feb. 13, 1941, from grave #82 Olivet; Wm. H. BEST, July 17, 1958; Mary Elliott BEST, June 16, 1958.

LOT 27-C: Anna L. PARLETT and daughters and Mary L. BESSLING; Mary E. PARLETT, Jan. 19, 1949; Anna L. PARLETT, Feb. 22, 1934; Nellie S. PARLETT, June 30, 1931; May Estelle PARLETT, Mar. 28, 1959; Edward Gardner PARLETT, Sept. 8, 1971, born Jan. 3, 1890, died Sept. 6, 1971. Parents Benjamin PARLETT and Ann Louisa BROWN. Funeral home of Stewart & Mowen; Albert W. BESSLING, Jan. 1, 1941; Mary L. BESSLING, July 25, 1961; "For John M. BESSLING, second husband of lot owner;" Earl E. HARMAN, Nov. 13, 1958.

LOT 28-C, 29-C, 30-C, and 31-C: There is no record in the Lot Books for these lots.

LOT 32-C: Thomas P. JOHNSON (name lined out), Elmer E. HOPWOOD and Harry WOODALL;
Edna M. JOHNSON, Mar. 1, 1960; Dorothy M. WOODALL, moved here 1950; Harry WOODALL, Sept. 11, 1957.

LOT 33-C: Mary Elizabeth SCOTT, Sr. and Edgar Arthur SCOTT And Dorothea E. SCOTT;
Mary E. SCOTT, July 11, 1953; Charles Edward SCOTT, June 6, 1949; Dorothea E. SCOTT, Mar. 25, 1975, born Oct. 29, 1883, died Mar. 25, 1975. Parents Henry HELLBACK and Emilie SCHWANEBACK. Funeral home of Mitchell-Wiedefeld; Joseph W. SCOTT, Feb. 17, 1945; "Remains of (1905) Rosanna SCOTT and Benjamin F. SCOTT, (1909)", Mar. 9, 1945.

LOT 34-C: Helen A. HUTCHINSON, Grace A. ALEXANDER and Dorothy L. (ROSS) now PROBST;
Thomas I. FLAHERTY, Apr. 20, 1972, died Apr. 15, 1972, Hubbard Funeral Home; John Franklin HUTCHINSON, July 19, 1944; William Dewey PROPST, Feb. 3, 1972, born Sept. 24, 1899, died Jan. 31, 1972. Parents John PROPST and _____ NELSON, Gonce Funeral Home; Brooke F. ROSS, Aug. 17, 1944; Grace Lorraine MEEHAN, June 16, 1971, born Dec. 23, 1927, died June 13, 1971. Parents Samuel I. ALEXANDER and Grace BE(?)CROFT (or DE(?)CRAFT; Grace ALEXANDER, Nov. 17, 1971, born Sept. 30, 1894, died Nov. 14, 1971. Parents Perry BECREAFT And _____ WINKS, Funeral home of Seitz; Samuel I. ALEXANDER, Feb. 17, 1943.

LOT 35-C: Elizabeth J. HUTCHINS and Mary A. CASEY. Also Lots for Church of The Messiah;
Elizabeth Jane HUTCHINS, May 23, 1942; Mary A. CASEY, Aug. 18, 1939.

LOT 36-C: Mrs. Edna M. TALBOTT, Frank FREUHSOROGER, Helen J. CHILDS, Malinda CONNELLY, graves transferred to TALBOT;
Walter B. TALBOTT, Feb. 22, 1958; Marie FRUEHSORGER, Sept. 10, 1937; 2 stillborn babies, died Jan. 9, 1936 from grave #30; Frank FRUEHSORGER, Dec. 21, 1962; Clarence Elmer TALBOTT, June 3, 1955; William D. CHILDS, June 1, 1937; James E. CONNELLY, May 31, 1960; Malinda A. CONNELLY, Mar. 28, 1941; Michael CONNELLY, Aug. 2, 1937. Notes dated July 1,1955 state lot sold to Mrs. Mary M. TABBOTT number 36, Section C, in the name of Helen J. Childs STEIN, June 2, 1955.

LOT 37-C: Mae Fee BRINKMAN, Elizabeth A. WRIGHT, George E. SMITH and Grace O. DOVE;
Mattie R. MC GEOY, June 21, 1939; Charles J. MC GEOY, June 21, 1939, from grave 332; Esther Brown CRONE, July 26, 1939; Emma V. BECKER, Dec. 12, 1945; Ethel Belle SMITH, Dec. 9, 1953; Elizabeth A. WRIGHT, Apr. 25, 1942; Wilbur T. WRIGHT, Apr. 21, 1936; Clara E. FARSON, Oct. 18, 1943; Katharine G. SMITH, Dec. 26, 1963; George E. SMITH, Aug. 10, 1946.

LOT 38-C: Ruby FURL, George L. and Geo. E. MC DANIEL, Mildred M. GENTRY and Allen B. HELLER;
for Toner FURL, (no date given); for Ruby FURL, (no date given); George E. MC DANIEL, Oct. 9, 1934; George W. GENTRY, May 30,

1934; Ella May MC DANIEL, June 28, 1933; George L. MC DANIEL, Mar. 29, 1958; Samuel H. MINOR, Dec. 26, 1956; Mary Alice HELLER, Oct. 30, 1933; Allen B. HELLER, Oct.t 27, 1950. Letter dated Aug. 10, 1972, affirms that the widow of George E. MC DANIEL and daughter-in-law of George L. MC DANIEL is Ruby MC DANIEL FURL, the rightful owner of Lot 38C. Grave #5 is reserved for her and #4 for her husband Toner FURL.

LOT 39-C: Thomas E. MC CAUSLAND and Elinor HARDESTY;
Thomas E. MC CAUSLAND, Jr., May 2, 193(5); James T. HARDESTY, June 3, 1936; Thomas E. MC CAUSLAND, Dec. 26, 1974, born May 7, 1902, died Dec. 22, 1974. Parents Thomas MC CAUSLAND and Elizabeth JONES.

LOT 40-C: No record in lot book.

LOT 41-C: Walter and Viola STANLEY (under this surname is written GUNTHER);
Howard R. ALEXANDER, Nov. 13, 1959; Carolyn H. BURLEW, Jan. 28, 1971, born June 8, 1881, died Jan. 25, 1971, Parents John BURLEW and _____ CHENNGE, funeral home of Cook-Zannine; Walter S. GUNTHER, July 2, 1960; Viola Stanley GUNTHER, Aug. 15, 1953. Letter dated Jan. 26, 1971 from Robert E. ALEXANDER states that he is the son of Walter S. GUNTHER. He (Robert) was adopted by his maternal grandmother. He further states he has a twin brother named Raymond GUNTHER and that the two now own lot 41-C. This letter was notorized in Baltimore City, Jan. 26, 1971.

LOT 42-C and 43-C: No record in lot books.

LOT 44-C: Lawrence C. and Margaret E. TASE;
Lawrence C. TASE, Jan. 2, 1970, born Sept. 20, 1901, died Dec. 29, 1969. Funeral home of Schimuner.

LOT 45-C: Stanley P. and Leona FREEMAN, Mrs. Bernice P. HEDRICK, Mrs. Theo. T. SCARBOROUGH, Raymond J. MANANOWSKI;
Mary Alice TARR, Jan. 17, 1974, born July 22, 1893, died Jan. 12, 1974. Parents Robert WILDE and Alice Ann TICKLE, funeral home Burgee. (In margin with arrow from this burial are the words - "M. Mary HARRIS, F. James Edw. FREEMAN, Disinterred - Jan. 11, 1972 to Dulany Valley." (Dulany Valley is in Baltimore County, Md., north of TOWSON); Frank B. HEDRICK, Sr., Nov. 25, 1955; Theodore SCARBOROUGH, Aug. 4, 1969, born Mar. 3, 1900, died Aug. 1, 1969; Myrtle M. MAZANOWSKI, Nov. 20, 1957.

LOT 46-C: Amos P. and Elise M. WRIGHT, Nellie G. FREEMAN and Charles H. MEDINGER;
Gordon H. FREEMAN, Jan. 19, 1951; Charles H. MEDINGER, Apr. 2, 1962; James Edward FREEMAN, Oct. 5, 1944; Amos P. WRIGHT, Nov. 16, 1965 (There is also the date Sept. 16, 1902, age 63 years); Elsie M. WRIGHT, May 1, 1972, born May 13, 1903, died Apr. 27, 1972. Parents Jos. ROBINSON and Laura BLUNT. Funeral Home E. K. Seitz.

LOT 47-C: Margaret HERPEL, Katherine D. LEONARD, John F. TREADWELL and Fred. P. HUBER;
Paul Benson LEONARD, July 25, 1952; Katherine D. LEONARD, Feb. 10, 1975, born Mra. 5, 1887, died Feb. 6, 1975. Parents John DIETER and _____ BICHE, funeral home, Jenkins; Michael O. HERPEL,

Sr., Mar. 8, 1948; Margaret HERPEL, Jan. 2, 1965; Hilton F. TREADWELL, Jan. 17, 1975, born July 18, 1914, died Jan. 13, 1975. Parents John TREADWELL and Jennie GRAHAM, funeral home of J. A. Moran; Gladys I. HUBER, Feb. 23, 1959; John F. TREADWELL, Dec. 23, 1947; Jennie TREADWELL, Dec. 6, 1938.

LOT 48-C: Jennie FARSON, Edward W. SOAPER, George F. YEAGER, Jr. and George F. YEAGER, Sr.;
Percy L. FARSON, Feb. 25, 1939; "For Jennie FARSON;" George F. YEAGER, Jr., Apr. 20, 1942; Estelle R. YEAGER, Apr. 4, 1974, born Nov. 6, 1896, died Apr. 1, 1974. Parents, John NAGEL and Minnie HINKEL, funeral home of Hubbard; George F. YEAGGER, Sr., July 28, 1952; Elizabeth M. YEAGER, Oct. 1, 1956; James H. BROWN, Feb. 22, 1958; May Belle BROWN, Dec. 27, 1960; Edward W. SOAPER, Dec. 3, 1962; Helen Ruth SOAPER, Sept. 26, 1938; "For Myrtle SOAPER."

LOT 49-C: Bessie E. HABERKAM, Virgil HOBBS, Mary M. CLAY, Fred. J. JACOBS, Margaret Eva CLAY and husband John W. CLAY; George M. SCHNEPF, Dec. 3, 1947; Carrie SCHNEPF, May 9, 1956; Mrs. Virgel G. HOBBS of Arbutus, (no date given); John H. CLAY, Apr. 14, 1938; Mary M. CLAY, June 3, 1959; William HABERKOM, Mar. 28, 1938; Bessie E. THOMMA, Mar. 30, 1966; Edna Marie JACOBS, Dec. 10, 1946; Margaret E. BURMAN, July 1, 1964.

LOT 50-C: E. Wilbur STOLL;
E. Wilbur STOLL, July 31, 1970, born Dec. 19, 1970, died July 29, 1970, removed from #3 Nov. 18, 1970; Rev. Samuel W. COE, Aug. 28, 1935; Laura B. COE, Dec. 12, 1935. Both COEs disinterred from Lot 49-G. There is also a note one are of monument in lot book - "See Mar. 11, 1938."

LOT 51-C: Ellen L. MESSERSMITH;
Ashes of Ellen M. MESSERSMITH, died July 27, 1963, Aug. 1, 1963; Ella McKay LINSLEY, Dec. 24, 1949. Certificate of Cremation for the remains of Ellen M. MESSERSMITH age 52 years, died July 27, 1963. Cremated same day at Greenmount Crematorium, Baltimore, Md.

LOTS 52-C, 53-C, 54-C, 55-C, 56-C and 57-C: There are no records in the lot book for these lots.

LOT 58-C: Mr. and Mrs. Chas. J. MENDEL;
Roland M. and Esther M. STEFFE; Charles G. MENDEL, Nov. 16, 1954.

LOT 59-C: BAST(?), POETZOLD, Gilbert R. ELLIOTT and John A. FISCHBECK;
Charles F. TRAVERS, Nov. 27, 1963; "for wife of Franke Augusta BAST"; Grace A. POETZOLD, Oct. 10, 1958; Ernest R. POETZOLD, Mar. 22, 1973, born Mar. 27, 1880, died Mar. 19, 1973, J. T. Stansbury Funeral Home; "For Gilbert R. and wife."; Frank E. BAST, June 26, 1954.

LOT 60-C: Oliver GALLION and George R. CLIFT;
Wm. E. GALLION, Jan. 28, 1959; John D. GALLION, Jan. 11, 1949; Esstella E. GALLION, Apr. 18, 1955; William E. GALLION, Nov. 7, 1935; Mary GALLION, Oct. 20, 1936 (Last 2 entries July 10, 1942, from south half of lot 2N); Mary Edith CLIFT, Oct. 22, 1938; George R. J. CLIFT, April 24, 1934; George R. CLIFT, Aug. 31, 1970, born Dec. 27, 1883, died Aug. 28, 1970.

LOT 61-C: Herbert L. WEAVER and Grace A. WARD;
Daisy W. PICKETT, June 11, 1952; Reserved for Virginia T. WEAVER
per H. L. WEAVER, Jr.; Myrtle V. WEAVER, Feb. 15, 1939; Herbert
Lee WEAVER, Nov. 20, 1950; Capt. Robert R. WARD, born Dec. 9,
1884, died May 1, 1968, buried May 4, 1968. Letter dated Aug.
18, 1961 to Rev. Herbert L. WEAVER of Lexington Park, Md. regarding Lot 61-C. A reply by Rev. WEAVER states his sister is Miss
Virginia WEAVER of Glen Burnie, Md. Permission to bury Virginia
Thomas WEAVER in Lot 61-C from John L. WEAVER, Jr., dated June 7,
1968.

LOT 62-C: Andrew and Charlotte E. SMITH, Wilbert A. FOWBLE,
William M. and Clara B. LEASE;
Maud E. SMITH, Feb. 7, 1955; Louis Albert REDFORD, Aug. 21, 1973,
born Jan. 10, 1890, died Aug. 16, 1973. Parents Thomas REDFORD
and Clara HOPKINS, funeral home - Kaczorowski; Anna Hart REDFORD,
Mar. 10, 1969, born May 30, 1897, died Mar. 7 1969; Lilia FOWBLE,
Jan. 11, 1958; Wilbert A. FOWBLE, Sept. 24, 1968, born Apr. 1,
1887, died Sept. 21, 1968; "For Mr. HOLLANS;" Clara B. LEASE,
Feb. 21, 1956; Wm. M. LEASE, Sr., Apr. 3, 1953. Letter dated
June 25, 1968, Charlotte E. POOLE gives permission for burial of
Anna Hart REDFORD, wife of Louis Albert REDFORD in 62-C.

LOT 63-C, 64-C, and 65-C: No record of these lots in the lot
books.

LOT 66-C: Mollie COLEMAN;
Mollie COLEMAN, Aug. 25, 1952; Alice L. JUMP, Feb. 28, 1941.

LOT 67-C: Chas. H. and Florence G. SIMPSON;
no burials recorded in this lot.

LOT 68-C: Mrs. Clarence STONER and Ralph W. RUSHWORTH;
George W. DONALDSON, Jan. 20, 1931; Stillborn of DOGGE, Sept. 3,
1942; Lily Mae DONALDSON, Mar. 9, 1960; Clarence F. STONER, Sept.
23, 1949; Grace G. STONER, Mar. 7, 1964; Ralph Walker RUSHWORTH,
Sept. 18, 1972, born Aug. 18, 1896 in England, died Sept. 14,
1972. Parents Jos. P. RUSHWORTH and Mary WALKER, Truman-Schwab
Funeral Home; Esther W. RUSHWORTH, Apr. 20, 1957; Henry C. LANG,
Mar. 19, 1945; Emma Virginia LANG, Sept. 28, 1948; John B. RIDGEWAY, Mar. 26, 1929.

LOT 69-C: Maurice RUSHWORTH, Mary R. HOWARD, Hasson HILTNER,
John H. KLERLEIN, Luther M. BRILL and Mary BRILL;
Joseph W. HOWARD, Oct. 22, 1948; Hasson E. HILTNER, Oct. 6, 1973,
born Nov. 19, 1908, died Oct. 3, 1973. Parents John HILTNER and
Margaret _____, funeral home of Hubbard; John J. RUSHWORTH, Oct.
7, 1929; Mary RUSHWORTH, Dec. 2, 1957; Luther M. BRILL, Apr. 29,
1967, born Jan. 31, 1(884), died April 26, 1(967); Lula Virginia
BRILL, Sept. 9, 1933; Mary BRILL, Nov. 9, 1966; Blanche V. KLERLEIN, May 6, 1957; John H. KLERLEIN, Mar. 8, 1962.

LOT 70-C: William YOUNGER, Walter A. GRENZ and B. Ormon HOBBS;
George YOUNGER, May 9, 1953; Charles W. YOUNGER, Oct. 29, 1962;
"for Walter A. GRENZ;" Maude Alma GRENZ, Feeb. 22, 1945; Anne
Rebecca HOBBS, Apr. 24, 1945; William YOUNGER, Aug. 10, 1973,
born June 1, 1882, died Aug. 6, 1973. Parent George YOUNGER;
funeral home - Hubbard; Bertha E. YOUNGER, Oct. 17, 1969, born
Nov. 18, 1884, died Oct. 14, 1969.

LOT 71-C: Harriett E. LETCHER, John A. FISCHBECK, Sr., John A. FISCHBECK, Charles and Nora WHITE; Henry L. LETCHER, Sept. 18, 1948; Harriette E. LETCHER, Mar. 2, 1971, born Sept. 8, 1902, died Feb. 26, 1971. Parents Gary HO(V)ADER and Florence ____, funeral home - Cowan; Samuel A. RICHARDSON, Mar. 2,1962; Nora C. RICHARDSON, Nov. 15, 1947; John A. FISCHBECK, Jan. 10, 1956; Agnes S. FISCHBECK, June 25, 1948; Scott J. FISCHBECK, Nov. 26, 1952.

LOT 72-C: Charles P. SPEDDEN, John and Lawrence CHARD, Anna KOENIG, Joseph S. and Florence S. HILL, Mrs. A. G. SOLISBURN; George Miller BECKER, Jr., Dec. 26, 1974, born Jan. 15, 1907, died Dec. 23, 1974. Parents Carl BECKER and Agatha MILLER, funeral home - Witzke; Ethel A. BARNES, Feb. 14, 1962; Charles W. KOENIG, May 10, 1951; Charles P. SPEDDEN, Apr. 2, 1960; Annie E. SPEDDEN, July 25, 1942; John Crane CHARD, June 25, 1974, born Oct. 16, 1880, died June 21, 1974. Parents Samuel CHARD and Victoria CRANE, funeral home of Watson in Seaford, Del.; Hattie B. CHARD, Apr. 27, 1942.

LOT 73-C: William R. and Milcah M. HODGES, Bertha M. WAGNER and William C. MYERS, Sr.; Lula May ARNOLD of North Garland, Md., July 15, 1974, born July 18, 1897, died July 12, 1974. Parents Wm. R. HODGES and Milcah ____, funeral home - Singleton; Joseph G. MEYERS, Jan. 12, 1949; Mildred Grace MEYERS, June 2, 1972, born Oct. 22, 1907, died May 29, 1972. Parents Wm. C. MEYERS and Crissie D. FOREMAN, funeral home - Ruck; William R. HODGES, Mar. 2, 1956; Milcah M. HODGES, June 14, 1948; George A. WAGNER, Feb. 10, 1941; Martha Louisa HOFFMAN, Dec. 14, 1953; Bertha M. WAGNER, July 15, 1963; William C. MEYERS, Sr., Jan. 29, 1944; Crissie D. MEYERS, Dec. 30, 1938.

LOT 74-C: Alma Lillian WILKINSON, Ralph G. and Margaret D. PLUMMER; James L. WILKINSON, Sept. 27, 1943; Jerome S. WILKINSON, Dec. 20, 1946; Ralph G. PLUMMER, Jr., June 26, 1967, born Aug. 17, 1919; died June 23, 1969; Margaret P. HURD, Nov. 14, 1941; Albert N. WILKINSON, June 9,1945; Alma L. WILKINSON, May 23, 1968, born Juy 11, 1885, died May 21, 1968; Livingston L. DELEVIE, Dec. 19, 1959; (Atunnonn BORRINCER), (no date given); Alma Estella DELIVIE, (no date given); Ralph G. PLUMMER, Sr., Mar. 14, 1968, born July 17, 1886, died Mar. 12, 1968; Margaret Ellen PLUMMER, Sept. 5, 1972, born Mar. 12, 1892, died Aug. 31, 1972. Parents Wm. DE SHIELS and Margaret JONES, funeral home - Lane, Church Hill, Md.

LOT 75-C: George Roy AIST and Carlton W. AIST, Wm. P. IHRIE; Laura V. JONES, June 7, 1961; Edith J. IHRIE, Dec. 5, 1946; William P. IHRIE, July 15, 1967, born Aug. 4, 1884, died July 13, 1967; Isabel AIST, Nov. 22, 1965, 70 years of age, born Dec. 9, 1894; Arthur L. AIST, Dec. 26, 1939; Ella Rebecca AIST, Jan. 16, 1959; Betty Lou AIST, Sept. 10, 1957; Annie May AIST, May 2, 1966, born Apr. 17, 1891, died Apr. 29, 1966; George Roy AIST, Dec. 6, 1972, born Aug. 29, 1894, died Dec. 3, 1972. Parents Arthur E. AIST and Ella JONES, funeral home Buchanan, Owings, Md.

LOTs 76-C, 77-C, 78-C, 79-C, and 80-C: There is no record of these lots in the Lot Book.

LOT 81C, Miss Lois CROSBY (the name Lawrence E. IRELAND is lined out);
Bessie May CROSBY, July 6, 1960; Fannie May BAKER, July 7, 1949; Howard B. BAKER, Aug. 13, 1949.

LOT 82-C: Catherine E. OWINGS, Myrtle L. WEAVER, Gertrude Alice SERIO and Elsie KELLNER;
Frederocl T. WEAVER, Jr., Died April 23, 1971 in Mississippi, aged 6 months. Parents F. T. WEAVER, Sr. and Patricia Ann (CARE), funeral home - MacNabb; Catherine E. OWINGS, Apr. 1, 1969, born Oct. 13, 1903, died Mar. 29, 1969; Howard M. OWINGS, July 18, 1949; Frederick WEAVER, Mar. 21, 1944; Gertrude A. SERIO, June 19, 1964; Frank SERIO, Apr. 14, 1949; Julius W. KELLNER, June 11, 1963.

LOT 83-C: E. Stanley JONES, Mrs. Eunice J. MATHEWS, Charles and Irene KLEIN. "Dr. E. Stanley JONES is to be buried in grave in Bishop's Lot, Section B. To be selected by officials of Lovely Lane, Jan. 14, 1963." Letter dated Oct. 25, 1966, Atlanta, Ga., Affidavit transferring Lot 83-C north half from E. Stanley JONES to Mrs. Eunice JONES. There are no burials recorded in Lot 83-C.

LOT 84-C: Walter W. TOMPKINS, Walter W. TOMPKINS, Jr., Margaret Tompkins PFAFF;
Walter W. TOMPKINS, Jr., Aug. 24, 1968, born. May 27, 1909, died Aug. 22, 1968; Edwin W. PFAFF, Oct. 28, 1974, born Nov. 29, 1904, died Oct. 24, 1974. Parents Henry PFAFF and Catherine HILMILLER, funeral home - Jenkins; Annie E. TOMPKINS, Mar. 18, 1944; Walter W. TOMPKINS, Sr., Mar. 9, 1944.

LOT 85-C: Frank Walter FARINHOLT, Mary SCHROTH, John W. NACE, Carrie M. NACE, Leola EINWICH;
Paul Berry FARINHOLT, Sept. 26, 1942; Joan C. B. GILDEN, Oct. 20, 1971, born Nov. 26, 1936, died Oct. 17, 1971. Parents Francis V. EINWICH and Leola C. DIETER, funeral home - Sterling; Amelia J. SCHROTH, Oct. 27, 1958; Charles G. SCHROTH, Dec. 27, 1960; Mary SCHROTH, Feb. 4, 1956; Irene SCHROTH, (no date given), child; George J. SCHROTH, July 3, 1943.

LOT 86-C: Edward J. FAIDLEY "(dec'd - buried in Louden Park) (Witzke 4-24-62)";
Flossie May FAIDLEY, Apr. 26, 1962; John W. FAIDLEY, Aug. 22, 1942; Robert S. FAIDLEY, Dec. 12, 1962.

LOT 87-C: Adah HALL, Ralph G. PLUMMER, Margaret D. PLUMMER, Margaret HOOK, LaRue H. JONES;
Adah S. HALL, Apr. 9, 1969, born Mar. 28, 1888, died Apr. 7, 1969; Charles A. HALL, May 7, 1942; Edward C. TOMPKINS, Dec. 9, 1965, age 68 years, born Nov. 29, 1897; Royston Paul JONES, Sept. 12, 1921, age 1 month; Della Plummer ELLIS, Mar. 3, 1942; Margaret L. PLUMMER, Aug. 19, 1949; Maude M. PLUMMER, June 28, 1954; Margaret HOOK, Apr. 23, 1942; Samuel J. HOOK, Feb. 28, 1955; Royston L. JONES, Sr., May 27, 1942.

LOT 88-C: William C. WEBER and Maye B. VOLZ;
George A. KRANZ, Jan. 20, 1944; Bertha Maye VOLZ, Oct. 4, 1971, born May 1, 1891, died Oct. 1, 1971. Parents Wm. I. WOLF and Anne F. FALK, funeral home - Eckhardt; Anthony F. VOLZ, Nov. 27, 1941; Cecil WEBER, Sept. 24, 1956; William C. WEBER, Mar. 6,

1969, born Jan. 19, 1886, died May 2, 1969; Myrtle WEBER, July 7, 1971, born July 23, 1893, died July 4, 1971. Parents were _____ KRANZ and _____, funeral home - Witzke.

LOT 89-C: Mrs. Doris M. WARD; Preston C. WARD, July 26, 1965.

LOTS 90-C, 91-C, 92-C, and 93-C: There is no record of these lots in the Lot Books.

LOT 94-C: Harvey E. REANEY; Remains of John L. KIDWELL, Sept. 25, 1908, moved from 71-D, Jan. 13, 1955; Lillie May KIDWELL, Jan. 13, 1955.

LOT 95-C: Harvey E. REANEY; Susan Carol REANEY, infant, Mar. 8, 1946; Harvey E. REANEY, May 5, 1965; "Reserved - N. J. KELLNER."

LOT 96-C: William Edward SMITH, Joseph N. COOPER and Maude A. COOPER; William SMITH, Oct. 30, 1953; William E. SMITH, Sr., July 5, 1962; Sarah E. SMITH, Feb. 12, 1945; Joseph N. COOPER, Jan. 29, 1958; Maude Amelia COOPER, July 6, 1973, born Jan. 28, 1878, died July 2, 1973. Parents John HUBER and Mary Elizabeth GERMAN. Funeral home of Wm. Cook-Brooks, Towson, Md.

LOT 97-C: Nellie Ida SCHMIDT, Mary Elma SHEPPARD and Mamie O. HUGHES; Jacob L. MILLER, Sept. 29, 1958; Henry SCHMIDT, Aug. 21, 1950; George G. HUGHES, Mar. 24, 1952; Mamie O. HUGHES, Nov. 1, 1968, born Aug. 31, 1889, died Oct. 28, 1968.

LOT 98-C: William Robert MARVEL, Hattie MARVEL, Tallie E. MORRIS and Edith B. WEDEMAN; Jane Ann MARVEL, Mar. 19, 1946, child; Madeline J. SLUSS, Dec. 4, 1970, born July 18, 1927, died Dec. 2, 1976, funeral home - Schimonek; Charles Edward MARVEL, Sr., Feb. 20, 1946; Hattie Lee MARVEL, Dec. 13, 1950; Tallie E. MORRIS, Apr. 17, 1969, born Apr. 23, 1882, died Apr. 14, 1968; Samuel J. LOYETT III, Feb. 15, 1971, stillborn, funeral home of Truman-Schwabb; Rebecca Ann MORRIS, Nov. 13, 1951, reinterred Aug. 20, 1954. Letter dated Aug. 17, 1954, Tallis E. MORRIS, lot owner of Lot 98-C, refers to the remains of his late wife buried in said lot, Rebecca Ann MORRIS.

LOT 99-C: Howard Arthur ECKMAN, Isabella H. GUNDRY, Charles R. HARGETT; Thelma Mae ECKMAN, Oct. 7, 1950; Howard A. ECKMAN, Nov. 12, 1952; William Pressman GUNDRY, Feb. 5, 1946; Isabella H. GUNDY, Oct. 17, 1967, born Oct. 22, 1885, died Oct. 12, 1967; Rachel S. HARGETT, Feb. 1, 1946.

LOT 100-C: James E. PADGETT, Emma J. WALTERS and John R. SHEC-KELLS; Vernon E. SHECKELLS, May 29, 1958; James E. PADGETT, Jr., June 4, 1945; Charles R. SHECKELLS, Mar. 9, 1950; Annie M. SHECKELLS, July 21, 1952; William WALTERS, Apr. 27, 1948; James E. PADGETT, Sr., Oct. 23, 1965; Molley B. PADGETT, July 9, 1964. Letter dated Dec. 17, 1958 from John R. SHECKELLS, Robert L. SHECKELLS and Charles W. SHECKELLS regarding their deceased brother, Vernon E. SHECKELS. Vernon's wife has had her name cut into the stone. Her name is not mentioned in the letter. All the above brothers are stated to be the children of Mr. and Mrs. Charles R. SHECKELLS of Baltimore, Md.

LOT 101-C: Thomas H. CLIFT and Verdie M. BREWER; Wilhelmina K. MUELLER, May 23, 1962; Herman Ernest MUELLER, disinterred from 43-F, June 8, 1944; Alfred T. BREWER, June 2, 1944.

LOT 102-C: William H. VAN SKIVER, Margaret H. FINK and Tyler C. WIRT; Edward VAN SKIVER, Dec. 24, 1957; Roland Edward BENTON, June 3, 1947, infant; Kathryn VAN SKIVER, Jan. 25, 1964; William L. FINK, July 30, 1946; Charles W. FINK, Aug. 18, 1942; Margaret H. FINK, Jan. 6, 1943; Annie Elizabeth VAN SKIVER, June 8, 1939; Doris A. VAN SKIVER, Aug. 9, 1941; Tyler C. WIRT, Mar. 3, 1964; Evelyn Pearl WIRT, Aug. 31, 1933.

LOTS 103-C through 110-C, there is no record of these lots in the Lot Book.

LOT 111-C: Annie H. HILL, Henry L. and Cora E. RONNENBERG and Arthur B. GARDNER; James B. HILL, Mar. 7, 1960; Cora E. RONNENBERG, Oct. 20, 1938; Henry L. RONNENBERG, Sept. 25, 1961; Katherine GARDNER, Jan. 20, 1964, disinterred to Druid Ridge Cemetery Aug. 13, 1973; Arthur B. GARDNER, Dec. 19, 1962, disinterred to Druid Ridge Cemetery Aug. 13, 1973.

LOT 112-C: Frank W. and Elizabeth W. FAIRMAN and EZELL; "for Max ALLENDER," per Mrs. EZELL; "for Virgie May FAIRMAN" per Mrs. EZELL; Frank Willard FAIRMAN, Oct. 27, 1950, aged 83 years; Elizabeth Jane FAIRMAN, Jan. 16, 1945; Robert W. FAIRMAN, Nov. 28, 1929.

LOT 113-C: Lillie Jane WHITE and Weightell M. WHITE, Mary E. SCHELHAUS, Helen Mary HOLLAND, Ruth S. NOFSINGER, daughter of SCHELHAUS and Charles DECK; Mary E. DECK, Apr. 9, 1956; Charles DECK, Apr. 8, 1958; Lillie Jane WHITE, Mar. 9, 1971, born May 31, 1888, died Mar. 5, 1971. Parents John OREM and Elizabeth FOSTER, funeral home - Hubbard; Weightell M. WHITE, June 13, 1953; Mary E. SCHELHAUS, May 8, 1975, born Nov. 6, 1888, died May 5, 1975. Parents Wm. SQUIRES and Mary GEISLER, funeral home - McCully; John C. SCHELHAUS, Dec. 12, 1952; John Alvin HOLLAND, Apr. 16, 1954; Warren H. NOFSINGER, Oct. 8, 1962.

LOT 114-C: George E. BOND, Elsie May BELL, Gertrude M. TALBOT; Mary E. ROBERTS, Jan. 26, 1960; Brantley E. ROBERTS, Feb. 3, 1953; Elsie May BELL, Mar. 4, 1963; Benjamin E. BELL, July (1), 1953; George E. BOND, Jr., July 10, 1953, disinterred to Belair, Md. (infant); hold for Gertrude (Mrs.) TALBOT."

LOT 115-C: Herbert Daniel HATFIELD, Mary M. POWELL, Edward L. VOGELMAN and James Cordy VICK; Mary A. HATFIELD, June 12, 1953; Herbert R. HATFIELD, Sept. 21, 1967, born Mar. 31, 1882, died Sept. 18, 1967; Mary Margaret

POWELL, Sept. 14, 1972, born Oct. 18, 1902, died Sept. 11, 1972. Parents John Tillman CHANCE and Emma R. BROWN, funeral home - McGilly, Brooklyn, Md; Keith M. POWELL, Feb. 2, 1953; Mary F. VOGELMAN, Dec. 11, 1952; Emma B. VICK, Jan. 20, 1972, born Nov. 2, 1883, died Jan. 18, 1972, father Charles BULL, funeral home - Jenkins; James Cordy VICK, Apr. 26, 1958; Edward L. VOGELMAN, Sept. 9, 1953.

LOT 116-C: Audrey KROEGER and Conrad KROEGER; Anna Bell KROEGER, Jan. 31, 1959; Conrad KROEGER, Dec. 18, 1962.

LOT 117-C through 125-C: No record in Lot Books for these lots.

LOT 126-C: Nannie G. HOLLAND; Edward H. HOLLAND, Feb. 15, 1937; Nannie G. HOLLAND, Aug. 16, 1944; Nelson O. HOLLAND, Mar. 28, 1960.

LOT 127-C: Carroll H. HOLLAND, Ethel L. SHRODES, Robert H. and Myrtle CHANDLER, J. E. and Ida K. MEYERS; Edgar D. SHRODES, Aug. 6, 1949; Ethel L. SHRODES, Apr. 10, 1970, born Jan. 6, 1895, died Apr. 7, 1970, funeral home - Loring Byers; Jacob E. MEYERS, Feb. 7, 1964; Ida K. MEYERS, Apr. 14, 1972, born June 5, 1891, died Apr. 11, 1972, parents Charles FRITZ and Carrie KRIETZ, funeral home - Hubbard.

LOT 128-C: John M. and Grace V. DREXEL, Chas. W. and Lena D. SHECKELLS; "This grave sold CHANDLER and MEYERS, see Lot 127-C, #5 grave to 127." Caroline ROHSIEPE, June 3, 1974, born Jan. 10, 1891, died May 31, 1974. Parents Henry Otto SPOERKE and Anna _____, funeral home - Zannino. John McMahon DREXEL, Aug. 14, 1971, born Sept. 22, 1900, died Aug. 10, 1971. Parents Richard DREXEL and Mary O'RILEY, funeral home - Walters; Magdalene SHECKELLS, Feb. 15, 1969, born Mar. 17, 1903, died Feb. 12, 1969.

LOT 129-C: Robert E. REID, Geo. and Laura SEYMOUR and Dalton and Anna HARN; Lillian REID, Jan. 20, 1971, born Feb. 23, 1899, died Jan. 15, 1971. Parents Wm. CRUTCHLEY and Lillian CROSBY, funeral home - Witzke; Dalton L. HARN, June 23, 1959.

LOT 130-C: Mary E. SPIGNER and Dorothy Jean FLINT (name lined out); Alice E. REID, Feb. 8, 1957.

LOT 131-C: John R. FEE, Dr. H. C. HYDE, Milton and Bertie FEE, John G. MC DERMOTT and Joan Luetta WRIGHT; Florence B. CREMEN, Oct. 25, 1969, born Apr. 3, 1902, died Oct. 22, 1969; William R. CREMEN, Dec. 9, 1953; Herbert M. FEE, Aug. 4, 1948; Dr. Harry C. HYDE, Nov. 21, 1959; Mary Kate HYDE, May 10, 1952; Lawrence A. FEE, Aug. 11, 1931; William MC DERMOTT, Jan. 28, 1937; Milton FEE, Dec. 15, 1947; Bertie V. FEE, May 31, 1943; John Russell FEE, Aug. 9, 1969, born July 20, 1910, died Aug. 5, 1969; Luetta C. MC DERMOTT, Sept. 10, 1946.

LOTS 132-C through 139-C: No record of these lots appear in the lot book.

LOT 140-C: Mrs. Barbara HARRISON, Viola (N.) RIDGELL, Charles F. HOFFACKER; William O. HARRISON, June 23, 1967, born July 20, 1906, died June 20, 1967; John W. RIDGELL, Dec. 19, 1970, born Dec. 19, 1900, died Dec. 16, 1970. Parents Charles RIDGELL and Missouri HALL, funeral home - McCully; Annie W. HOFFACKER, Aug. 14, 1964; Charles F. HOFFACKER, July 16, 1951.

LOT 141-C: No record of this lot in Lot Book.

LOT 142-C: Sarah YEWELL, Georgia WOLFSHEIMER; Norma F. BOIES (the surname YEWELL is lined through), Feb. 17, 1959; Sarah Georgiana YEWELL, Aug. 5, 1954; Thomas Oliver YEWELL, Sept. 29, 1949; Georgia B. WOLFSHEIMER, Jan. 24, 1935; Joel H. WOLFSHEIMER, Dec. 28, 1931.

LOT 143-C: Thelma L. SIM, Delphine C. PARKER, Wm. R. PATTERSON, ROBERTS and PATTERSON; Ray E. ROBERTS; William A. PARKER, Sr., Feb. 5, 1957; Arthur SIM, May 6, 1964; Sallie M. ROBERTS, Oct. 11, 1955; Raymond E. ROBERTS, July 3, 1965.

LOTS 114-C through 146-C: There is no record of these lots in the Lot Book.

LOT 147-C: Mrs. Ruth B. MATTHEWS and Miss Mary R. BELT; Mary Roberta BELT, May 17, 1974, born Oct. 29, 1903, died May 14, 1974. Parents Samuel H. BELT and Mary Ann ROSE, funeral home - Gasch, Hyattsville, Md.

LOTS 148-C through 153-C: There is no record of these lots in the Lot Book.

LOT 154-C: Clayland A. WILLIAMS; Gertrude M. J. WILLIAMS, Dec. 22, 1948.

LOT 155-C: George W. SANFORD and Harry F. MEYERS; Mary E. BARTLETT, Feb. 13, 1934; Mrytle L. MEYERS, Feb. 6, 1934; Fannie M. SANFORD, Aug. 2, 1954; George W. SANFORD, July 1, 1943; Lelia H. MEYERS, Nov. 3, 1954; Myrtle L. MEYERS, (no date given).

LOT 156-C: Emil J. and Rose E. LOETZ and Arthur BURTON; Emil J. LOETZ, Dec. 3, 1966, born Aug. 21, 1891, died Nov. 30, 1966; Robert J. BURTON, Feb. 20, 1933; Annie Elizabeth BURTON, Sept. 23, 1940; Arthur BURTON, Dec. 21, 1955; Isabella K. BURTON, Jan. 29, 1929; Edward J. CHANON, Jr., Oct. 7, 1939 (child).

LOT 157-C: Helen Lee BURTON, Norris W. and Ida M. SNELLING, Mrs. Susan R. BURTON, Roscoe EMINIZER, Morris G. and Bernice JORY; Robert R. BURTON, Nov. 29, 1946; Helen Lee BURTON, Oct. 23, 1961; Robert E. BURTON, Feb. 5, 1962; Bessie M. EMINIZER, June 23, 1960; Ida Mae SNELLING, Feb. 4, 1974, born Dec. 7, 1912, died Feb. 1, 1974. Parents Robert BURTON and _____, funeral home - Witzke, Catonsville, Md; Francis E. BURTON, Apr. 13, 1960; "For Sue BURTON;" Morris G. JORY, Sept. 26, 1962; Bernice E. JORY, June 2, 1964.

LOTS 158-C and 159-C: No record in the Lot Book.

LOT 160-C: Sophie HAGNER;
Earl F. HAGNER, June 6, 1932; Sophie HAGNER, Dec. 31, 1934; John T. HAGNER, June 20, 1932; Kimberly O. HAGNER, May 27, 1968, infant.

LOTS 161-C through 163-C: There are no records in the Lot Book for these lots.

LOT 164-C: John E. FABIAN, Sr. (son of Sarah A.) and Elizabeth W. FABIAN and Sadie REYNOLDS;
Wm. (S.) REYNOLDS, Oct. 24, 1933; Jas. FABIAN, Jan. 13, 1934; Caroline FABIAN, Nov. 10, 1960 (over this entry is written BOHOMILY); Sarah A. REYNOLDS, Sept. 4, 1954.

LOTS 165-C and 166-C: No record in the Lot Book.

LOT 167-C: James H. REVIS;
Evelyn Mae REVIS, Aug. 5, 1933; Della C. REVIS, Dec. 30, 1957; James H. REVIS, Sept. 15, 1953.

LOT 168-C: Wm. J. MINTON;
Robert Leon MINTON, May 1, 1967, reinterred from Moreland Park Cemetery.

LOT 169-C and 170-C: No record in the Lot Book.

LOT 171-C: Mrs. Myra KOETHER;
Emil A. KOETHER, Sr., Feb. 1, 1956; Myra(b Bette) KOETHER, Oct. 19, 1972, born May 6, 1893, died Oct. 15, 1972. Parents Myer STRAUSE and Hannah BERLINER. The Hoffman funeral home, Cornwolls Hts., Pa.

LOT 172-C: Leida HAUS;
Kenneth Lee HAUS, June 14, 1974, born Oct. 23, 1908, died June 12, 1974. Parents John HAUS and Leida _____, the Mitchell-Wiedefield funeral home; Leida F. HAUS, Jan. 12, 1952; Eileen deChantel HAUS, July 8, 1970, born Mar. 2, 1904, died July 5, 1970, the Armacost Funeral Home; Anita KAPFER, May 29, 1941; Ulo W. SCOFIELD, moved from 69-R, Dec. 27, 1933. Died July 17, 1928.

LOT 173-C: Edna V. M. MANN, Kenneth L. MANN, Howard F. and Grace M. RAPPOLD;
Cecil S. MANN, June 10, 1948; Howard Franklin RAPPOLD, Aug. 13, 1973, born May 4, 1890, died Aug. 9, 1973. Parents John Henry RAPPOLD and Elizabeth RODGERS, the McNabb Funeral Home; Grace Margaret RAPPOLD, Apr. 30, 1973, born Feb. 16, 1891, died Apr. 26, 1973. Parents August C. SPIEKERMAN and Emma MADDOX, McNabb Funeral Home.

LOTS 174-C through 177-C: There are no records of these lots in the Lot Book.

Lot 178-C: Mrs. Anna M. LEWIS; There is no record of any burials in this lot.

LOT 179-C: Mrs. Anna M. LEWIS, Mrs. Sarah (the surname MILLER is lined out and) TONTZ (is entered below it), and Mrs. Nellie E. DAVIS;
Mary M. PORCELLA, Nov. 18, 1963; Gordon L. LEWIS, Dec. 7, 1963;

Leroy J. MILLER, May 13, 1960; Edward Tensall SOCKRITTER, Sept. 18, 1974, born July 21, 1946, died Sept. 15, 1974. Parents Edw. SOCKRITTER and Sarah DAVIS, "(SOCKRITTER MILLER TONTZ)," The McCully Funeral Home, Brooklyn, Md.; Frank E. DAVIS, Nov. 30, 1959; Nellie V. DAVIS, May 10, 1974, born July 6, 1904, died May 7, 1974. Parents Edward BUCK and Sarah E. EMERSON, the Ruck Funeral Home.

LOT 183-C: Miss Alice E. GRONEWELL and Irene BAVE; (Part of entry within unphotographed curl in page) " . . . 9, 1(9)37, (Rem)ains of (L.) C. BAVE) . . . "; Alice E. GRONEWELL, Nov. 20, 1958; Hannah E. ESPEY, Mar. 22, 1964, born July 19, 1904, died Mar. 19, 1968; Irene BAVER, May 2, 1961; Robert C. BAVER, (may be same as "stillborn of BATTON, Aug. 2, 1943"); Carl B. J. BAVER, Dec. 9, 1936.

SECTION D

LOT 1-D: Jas. A. JACKSON and Barbara REESIDE; Wm. REESIDE, Mar. 25, 1887; Barbara RESIDE, May 21, 18(8)7; John (T.) WALL, July 5, 1894; Annie M. WALL, Apr. 20, 1896; Raymond REESIDE, Nov. 16, 1896; Amelia (V.) REESIDE, Nov. 28, 1898; Lillian CAMPBELL, Mar. 28, 1904; Chas. NEWTON, Nov. 11, 191(?); Gordon RESIDE, May 28, 1914; Florence REESIDE, Jan. 14, 1919; Henry G. REESIDE, Dec. 6, 1919; Kate JACKSON, July 13, 1891; Josephine JACKSON, Oct. 5, 1921; Jas. JACKSON (Sr.), Dec. 31, 1935; Jennie JACKSON, Jan. 31, 1940.

LOT 2-D: Elijah BISHOP and Baldwin G. HARRIS; Fannie BISHOP, May 15, 1889; Wm. J. BISHOP, Dec. 14, 1889; (Joanne) BISHOPS, Mar. 25, 1900; Doris E. PORTER, Nov. 20, 1935; Lewis W. PORTER, Feb. 19, 1965; Clara E. PORTER, Aug. 10, 1973, born Feb. 17, 1887, died Aug. 7, 1973. Parents Wm. J. BISHOP and Joanna HAIGHT, funeral home - Witchel-Wiedefeld; Hiram M. HARRIS, Sept. 7, 1885; (Mary J. DUNN), (disinterred is written across this name), Oct. 1, 1890; (B. B. G. HARRIS), Jan. 24, 19(08); Elizabeth HARRIS, Sept. 11, 1902; Chas. L. HARRIS, June 29, 1885; Irene B. HARRISS, Sept. 9, 1957; Mary Frances SCHUMANN, Jan. 13, 1940; Karl SCHUMANN, Jan. 20, 1937.

LOT 3-D: Samuel F. SMITH, E. Beatty GRAFF and HOPKINS; Alexander H. HARRIS, Aug. 26, 1885; Naomi HARRIS, Jan. 24, 1902; Nannie Louise NICHOLSON, June 19, 1958, disinterred Dec. 7, 1936; "old brick grave here"; Naomi E. NICHOLSON, Aug. 6, 1909; Stillborn of T. and F. BARBER, June 4, 1919; Samuel F. SMITH, Apr. 11, 1922; Martha A. SMITH, Dec. 27, 1929; John W. RIGGIN, Mar. 28, 1955, infant; Johns (J. or G. or both) HOPKINS, June 10, 1902; Fannie G. HOPKINS, Feb. 22, 1928; Laurence G. HOPKINS, Feb. 18, 1959 (ashes). Authorization dated June 15, 1958 for the disinterrment of Nannie Louise NICHOLSON, Lot 3-D, owned by Samuel F. SMITH; signed by Martha Alice BROWN, daughter. Authorization dated June 15, 1958, same as above, and signed by Irene L. HAHN and witnessed by J. Allen BROWN.

LOT 4-D: Wm. SMITH and Alfred PRICE, Theodore L. BOIST; Annie C. PRICE, Aug. 20, 1885; Joseph PRICE, Apr. 6, 1886; Alfred L. PRICE, July 6, 1886; W. L. PRICE, Dec. 5, 1887; Sarah A. PRICE, July 23, 1887; Allen P. PRICE, Sept. 28, 1896; Florence A.

PRICE, June 6, 1899; Sadie A. PRICE, Dec. 8, 1889; Annie S. BOIST, Oct. 20, 1884; Caroline WAGNER, Aug. 28, 1888. Last two entries disenterred Apr. 7, 1893.

LOT 5-D: (North half) John B. CLEMENTS and Mary A. M(INTER); Susan V. CLEMENTS, Nov. 27, 1883; Naomi CLEMENTS, Sept. 24, 1890; (Laura) E. CALDWELL, July 29, 1907; Capt. John CLEMENTS, Aug. 17, 1891; Stillborn of (GREEN), Aug. 11, 1900; Wm. M. CALDWELL, Mar. 21, 1922; Lydia GORDON, June 20, 1889; Douglas GORDON, Apr. 5, 1893; Wm. E. GORDON, Mar. 31, 1900; Mary A. MINTER, July 25, 1900 (This name in both cases, the person buried and the lot owner, begins with M, the fourth letter is a t, the rest of the name is not clear); Emily Thomas, Nov. 29, 1906; Stillborn of G. & M. COPIEN, May 5, 1933; Alfred GREEN, Aug. 12, 1939; Naomi Jeanette GREEN, Jan. 25, 1950.

LOT 5-D: (Second part of lot) Margaret M. RINGROSE; Removed from N.B.G., Apr. 23, 1977; Jas. SHAGOGUE, Dec. 13, 1893; Margt. HOBBS, Jan. 7, 1896; Armstaid R. HOBBS, July 5, 1904; Col. John W. RINGROSE, Mar. 3, 1873; Margt. L. RINGROSE, June 30, 1855.

LOT 6-D: (Part I) Caroline V. HEMMICK; J. M. HEMMICK, June 4, 1879; Irene W. HEMMICK, Oct. 23, 1879; John STEWART, Feb. 16, 1880; Margt. E. HEMMICK, May 7, 1894; Stillborn of Thom. HEMMICK, Aug. 28, 1911; Helen (MOXLEY), Sept. 8, 1911; Thos. L. HEMMICK, Feb. 29, 1932; Mary E. HEMMICK, Aug. 29, 1953; Annie M. HEMMICK, Oct. 14, 1967, born Sept. 7, 1874, died Oct. 12, 1967; Thomas HEMMICK, (no date given).

LOT 6-D: (Part II) Thos. VOYCE; Thos. S. VOYCE, Sept. 5, 1892; Thos. VOYCE, May 29, 1914; Bernard F. VOYCE, Feb. 24, 1925; Amanda VOYCE, Aug. 14, 1933; Emma LAYMAN, Dec. 30, 1952; Myrtle M. VOYCE, June 6, 1944.

LOT 7-D: (Part I) Susan R. STEPHENS and John W. DIXON; Edgar STEPHENS, Sept. 11, 1889; Upton C. STEPHENS, Feb. 8, 1893; Sarah R. LANAHAN, Apr. 27, 1896; James W. GALLAHER, Mar. 8, 1906; Ella H. SHIPLEY, Jan. 6, 1908; Issac SHIPLEY, Apr. 12, 1915 (In the same grave space is written the word "Eddie's"); Mable I. DIX, July 9, 1883; Herbert SMITH, July 15, 1891; Florence E. SMITH, June 29, 1897; John W. DIX, Nov. 7, 1910; (Ellerson) H. DIX, Oct. 16, 1924; M. Anna DIX, April 24, 1925, 80 years old; Edith R. BUNDICK, Sept. 30, 1947; P. Ross BUNDICK, Aug. 5, 1955.

LOT 7-D: (Part II) Virginia HUMRICKHOUSE; Removed from N. B. G., Apr. 23, 1877; John R. HUMRICKHOUSE, June 26, 1880; Chas. BURGESE, Jan. 27, 1893; Virginia L. R. HUMRICK-HOUSE, Jan. 12, 1905; James F. HUMRICKHOUSE, Dec. 20, 1906; Thos. J. WARNER, Aug. 16, 1886.

LOT 8-D: (Part I) Wm. RENNIE and Wm. J. BRYAN; Wm. RENNIE, July 18, 1891; John _____ RENNIE, Apr. 4, 1893; Cath. RENNIE, July 25, 1901; Jane G. RENNIE, Jan. 12, 1914; Adam M. RENNIE, July 6, 1929; Albert L. BRYAN, Oct. 7, 1881 (There is an Albert E. BRYAN, possible same person); Henrietta BRYAN, Sept. 16, 1885; Mary MC KELD(O)E, Jan. 3, 1914; Wm. BRYAN, Sept. 27, 1921; Leroy V. BRYAN, May 16, 1932; Agnes RENNIE, June 19, 1939;

Andrew RENNIE, Aug. 2, 1951; "For Miss JAMES nee Ida K. RENNIE;" James G. RENNIE, (no date given); William A. BRYAN, July 1, 1948.

LOT 8-D: (Part II) Charles M. BLOOMFIELD;
Chas. BLOOMFIELD, July 13, 1877; Bessie M. STALLINGS, July 24, 1893; Naoma STALLINGS, July 15, 1897; Carroll STALLINGS, Sept. 29, 1907; Mildred CARTER, Feb. 27, 1908.

LOT 9-D: (Part I) Nancy EPHREN and Elizabeth EPHREN;
Peter EPHREN, Nov. 27, 1866; Nellie V. COOMS, Apr. 27, 1849; Nancy EPHREN, July 2, 1897; Earl COOMS, (no date given), 3 months old; Harry E. BARBER, Nov. 2, 1873; Thos. N. BARBER (3rd), Dec. 22, 1889; Wm. Vernon JAY, Nov. 3, 1903; Al(mira) V. COMES, Sept. 8, 1904 (name also written COOMS and Anne crossed out with new first name above); Stillborn of Lillian and Walter JAY, Dec. 12, 1905; Leroy E. BARBER, June 29, 1906; Ella Blanche HACKNEY, Jan. 22, 1897; Walter M. COOMS, July, ___; Geo. R. HACKNEY, Feb. 11, 1915; Geo. E. COMES, Nov. 21, 1916; Marcelia RINGLEB, Jan. 1, 1920 (The notice "for repairs" notify "Elsie M. HACKNEY" is attached); Harry R. COMES, Oct. 16, 1922; Cath. MITCHELL, June 10, 1878; Matilda MITCHELL, Mar. 19, 1880; Frank W. T(ENNE)MAN, Dec. 20, 1880; Joseph EPHRON, (no date given).

LOT 9-D: (Part II) Wm. H. FIELDS;
Wm. H. FIELDS, Apr. 17, 1916; Mary V. FIELDS, June 12, 1922; Grace E. FIELDS, Apr. 6, 1953.

LOT 10-D: (Part I) Ezeziel SHIPLEY;
Susan GOSNELL, Dec. 24, 1891; Annie V. GOSNELL, Dec. 16, 1893; M. Rebecca GOSNELL, Mar. 25, 1924; Thomas S. GOSNELL, Oct. 4, 1940.

LOT 10-D: (Part II) Harry HALL;
Harry J. F. HALL, Sept. 4, 1876; Sarah Jane HALL, Oct. 20, 1877; Harry L. HALL, Mar. 26, 1892; H. Clifton GALBRAETH, Apr. 26, 1891 (Surname also written - GALBRITH); Francis W. WILLS, Oct. 1, 1897; Rose Stewart HALL, Dec. 5, 1904.

LOT 11-D: (Part I) Thos. SOMERVILLE, Robert HOLLAND and Wm. Louis SCHLEY;
Louis N. SCHLEY, Aug. 8, 1877; Josephine JACKSON, Jan. 4, 1887 (entry crossed out); Wm. L. SCHLEY, May 23, 1912; Cath. SCHLEY, May 20, 1913; Josephine JACKSON, Oct. 5, 1921; Stuart S. SCOTT, Aug. 20, 1925; Mary F. SCOTT, Dec. 14, 1925; Thos. SUMMERVILLE, Sept. 20, 1900; Isabell FLOYD, Dec. 20, 1900; Lydia E. SUMMERVILLE, May 25, 1914; John SUMMERVILLE, June 2, 1915; Elizabeth SUMMERVILLE, Aug. 17, 1917; Hattie BANKERD, June 10, 1952.

LOT 11-D: (Part II) Lewis WESLEY;
George WESLEY, Mar. 23, 1892; Mary BELT, July 27, 1892 (crossed out and error written in); Mary BOWERSOX, Oct., 1908; Lewis WESLEY, Apr. 7, 1897. At another place on the page, not associated with anything is the date Apr. 6, 1897.

LOT 12-D: (Part I) Darzo NIUGARD and James J. CHAL(MERS) (The letters after CHAL on all CHALMERS entries are pure speculation on my part. The writing is just scribble);
Frederick NEUGARD, June 11, 1886; Ella NIUGARD, Sept. 2, 1884; Rebecca NIUGARD, Oct. 7, 1885; Harry H. CHAL(MERS), Dec. 21, 1877; W. S. CHAL(MERS), May 8, 1880; Mary CHAL(MERS), Feb. 17,

1881; Alice CHAL(MERS), July 9, 1881; El(ouis) M. CHAL(MERS), July 11, 1887; Phil(ecor) CHAL(MERS), May 14, 1888; Gertrude E. CHAL(MERS), Oct. 27, 1888; Remains from N. B. G., July 12, 1877; Frank MILLER, June 27, 1880; Geo. SCHAI(FF)ER, May 9, 1880 disinterred; Geo. (I.) (SCHAEFFER), Mar. 18, 18(87), disinterred; Annie M. CHAL(MERS), July 10, 1893; (Philimona) S. CHAL(MERS), Oct. 10, 1899; J. J. CHAL(MERS), July 3, 1902.

LOT 12-D: (Part II) Mary A. NERGHOFF; J. T. and S. H. NERGHOFF, July 17, 1916, disinterred and removed to Louden Park Cemetery.

LOT 13-D: (Part I) Louis FORSYTH and Wm. ELLIOTT; Removed from N. B. G., Feb. 12, 1878; Ellen C. MILES, Apr. 25, 1887, disinterred Oct. 20, 1906 to Western Cemetery (on Edmondson Avenue, Baltimore, Md.); Mildred FORSYTH, Mar. 12, 1895; Louisa FORSYTH, Apr. 16, 1904; James B. FORSYTH, Aug. 20, 1915; Removed from N. B. G., Aug. 9, 1877; Mary BUNTING (and) R. SUMMERVILLE, disinterred May 19, 1884; Thos. FORSYTH, (no date given); James BUCK, (no date given); James FORSYTH, March 17, 1919.

LOT 13-D: (Part II) Lewis N. LIGHT; Mary E. LIGHT, May 26, 1892; Lewis N. LIGHT, Sept. 19, 1892; Stillborn of Mary BATTE, Apr. 9, 1894; John H. BOWEN, Sept. 7, 1905; Elizabeth LIGHT, July 8, 1895; Mary A. LIGHT, May 12, 1916; Isabelle MAN(UEL), Jan. 2, 1918.

LOT 14-D: (Part I) J(a)s. A. RYAN, Sarah A. MORROW, John G. LEONARD and Cath. MORROW; Elizabeth RYAN, Aug. 3, 1889; Jas. A. RYAN, May 5, 1906; Mary Ann MORROW, May 29, 1894; Wm. D. S(ANERLAND), Sept. 14, 1897; Sarah A. MORROW, Jan. 6, 1925; Eliz F. LEONARD, Jan. 23, 1894; John G. LEONARD, Oct. 29, 1900; Wm. P. I(NSBOCH), Apr. 24, 1905; Vernon A. (INS)BACH, Dec. 20, 1912.

LOT 14-D: (Part II) John L. C(RUM)P; John L. C(RUM)P, July 8, 1891 (name appears twice); Wm. H., Martha, John L. CR(UM)P, July 29, 1891, disinterred from 108 A; Geo. NOGULE, Dec. 22, 1894; Eliz R. NOGULE, Aug. 17, 1896; Elizabeth C(RUM)P, Nov. 14, 1914; Sarah A. NOGULE, Aug. 9, 1916; Alice H. NOGULE, Oct. 23, 1916; Still born of NOGULE, Apr. 26, 1917; John H. NOGULE, May 14, 1928.

LOT 15-D: Wm. H. DITMAN, transferred to Chas. R. DITMAN; Removed from N. B. G., Eliza DITMAN, John and Nelson R. DITMAN, Mary CLIFF and Lydia DITMAN, May 30, 1877; Wm. H. DITMAN, Jan. 27, 1879; Lill(ie) Shaffer DITMAN, Feb. 12, 1879; Nelson G. DITMAN, Mar. 15, 1905; Chas. R. DITMAN, Jr., Dec. 28, 1916; Alice DITMAN, Apr. 12, 1927; Sue I. DITMAN, Feb. 6, 1929; Charles R. DITMAN, Aug. 23, 1948; Rachel DITMAN, Jan. 9, 1937.

LOT 16-D: Mary A. GADDESS. There is no record of burials in this lot.

LOT 17-D: Ezekiel SHIPLEY, (Miss) HOLLAND, Wm. H. (GHISSLUR), Eliza L. EARLING; Geo. B. HOLLAND, June 27, 1933; Ezekiel SHIPLEY, Oct. 21, 1936; Infant of (M.) and (E.) (SCHULL), July 17, 18(7)6; Geo. L. EARLING, Aug. 22,1887; Still born of Clara EARLING, Dec. 1, 1904;

Leonard EARLING, Dec. 19, 1906; Howard K. (SN)YDER, Jan. 30, 1913; Clara V. EARLING, Apr. 20, 1921 (There are two instances of this name.); Michael EARLING, July 13, 1936; Parkin Kerr SHIPLEY, April 13, 1956; Laura SHIPLEY, Feb. 20, 1939; Musaoore E. HOLLAND, Feb. 20, 19(69); Catherine ____ EARLING, (no date given). Other names of persons not buried here but associated with this lot are Mrs. Daniel EARLING of Dunkirk, Indiana and Mrs. Chas. WHEELER.

LOT 18-D: Elizabeth POWELL, James E. BATEMAN, Wm. G. YOUNG and Elmer V. YOUNG;
Pamela R. BATEMAN, Aug. 17, 1888; Elizabeth POWELL, Nov. 22, 1882 (In paprenthesis is "(BATEMAN)".); Geo. M. TRAINOR, Apr. 16, 1910; Carrie R. (PRINCE), Mar. 1, 1882; Sarah YOUNG, June 7, 1877; Mary YOUNG, Jan. 7, 1897; Chas. H. YOUNG, Sept. 3, 1901; John R. YOUNG, Sept. 4, 1901; Wm. S. YOUNG, July 6, 1907; Mary W. YOUNG, Aug. 1, 1904; Elmer V. YOUNG, Aug. 29, 1973, born Sept. 24, 1895, died Aug. 26, 1973. Parents William YOUNG and Margaret HARRINGTON, funeral home - Lassahn; Frank C. YOUNG, Aug. 18, 1954. Letter, no date, Frank C. YOUNG is grandson of William G. YOUNG, reserves space in LOT 18-D for himself and his wife Anna YOUNG. Letter dated Oct. 18, 1866, Elmer V. YOUNG state he is last surviving member of the family.

LOT 19-D: Sarah P. CONWAY, Hattie E. CONWAY and Mary E. SPENCE; Jane E. CONWAY, Jan. 15, 1881 (In another place the name is Jane R. CONWAY); "Rev. of Child," NOv. 7, 1881; Marg. E. SPENCE, Feb. 7, 1911; John E. SPENCE, (no date given); Seldon SPENCE, (no date given); Sarah P. CONWAY, Feb. 29, 1924; Edith L. DAVIS, Aug. 8, 1925; John E. SPENCE, Feb. 12, 1901; Annie L. COLE, June 3, 1903; Hattie CONWAY, Mar. 10, 1903; Len. W. BOTZMAN, May 3, 1903 (This first name may be Leon as it seems to be at another entry); Wm. S. SPENCE, Feb. 19, 1907; Hattie CONWAY, Apr. 17, 1914; Charlotte BOZMAN, July 2, 1914; Hattie CARNEY, (no date given); Hattie Carney BRICE, (no date given).

LOT 20-D: Wm. PARKER, Samuel and Mary DECKER; Elizabeth MOFFIT, Mar. 25, 1884; Mary R. PARKER, Jan. 16, 1877; Wm. T. PARKER, Mar. 21, 1893; Alice A. DECKER, June 30, 1887; John Calvin DECKER, Nov. 4, 1884 (There is also a John C. DECKER in another place in the lot.); Ida H. DECKER, Apr. 20, 1887; Thos. DECKER, June 28, 1887; Geo. (T.) DECKER, Aug. 18, 1890; Calvin F. DECKER, Nov. 7, 1894; Margt. A. DECKER, Feb. 18, 1895; Saml. DECKER, Apr. 3, 1897; Saml. W. DECKER, Sept. 30, 1912; Milton E. DECKER, Aug. 23, 1900; Ira B. AYLSWORTH, Feb. 21, 1917; Alice Violetta AYLSWORTH, Jan. 3, 1938; Mollie (no surname given, buried with DECKER), July 20, 1878; Florence (no surname given, buried with DECKER), Aug. 25, 1878.

LOT 133-D: Called "Section D-133" Single Interments (Part I); Henry TINDLE, (no date given); Margaret A. M(OFFITT), Apr. 10, 1936; W. S. (MOFFITT), June 9, 1920; Geo. A. SONDERSTRAM, (no date given); Charles (OLIVER), (no date given); Robert MURRAY, (no date given); Ch(ristian) GA(STRON), (no date given); Thos. WHITE, (no date given).

"Section D-133" Single Interments (Part II);
Miranda GR(illegible), Mar. 15, 1895, age 80 years; Cath(arine) C. ALE(RIUR), Feb. 18, 1929; Mary E. M(ORREIA), Oct. 15, 1927,

disinterred Dec. 6, 1945 to 26-E; Richard H. STEWART, Mar. 9, 1946; L(ura) NOUGLE, July 9, 1925; Flora E. ADAMS, (no date given); Mary MC INTYRE, (no date given); Henrietta K(EOWARTH), July 4, 1925; Julia FA(RMER), Mar 3, 1930; Herman KERWATH, Nov. 28, 1964; H(ester) G. BENTZ, (no date given); Mary A. KA(WCHORD), (no date given).

LOT 21-D: "Not Methodist," "Pickersgill," - "Aged Men and Woman's Home, Calhoun and Lexington St." (The following numbers seem to indicate a relation between this lot and other lots, 545 through 554;
Cremains of Bessie KLINESMITH, died May 25, 1974, age 93 years; Rebecca HAMMILL, May 17, 1886; Charles Hill TODD, Sept. 17, 1946; John HO(U)SLOW, Feb. 27, 1886; Christine K. JOHNSON, Sept. 3, 1947; Mary G(ARDON), Feb. 3, 1886; Samuel M. FRAZIER, Feb. 13, 1948; James PORTER, Dec. 9, 1885; India C. LA COMPTE, Feb. 10, 1948; Conrad LINROTH, Nov. 28, 1885; Ulysses HARRINGTON, April 18, 1949; Charlotte HE(URA), Oct. 14, 1825; Jacob A. BREEDAN, Nov. 10, 1949; Maggie MC INTYRE, July 27, 1885; Edna Blanche GILBIN, July 9, 1951; W. J. DAW, July 22, 1885; George W. TWILLER, Jan. 10, 1952; Ann EAGER, June 2, 1885; Nannie ANDERSON, May 23, 1952; Allie W. BERL, Sept. 20, 1884; Bertha Louise ROBINSON, June 8, 1953; Rebecca FLURRY, June 2, 1884; Mary L. ALLWELL, July 17, 1954; Charlotte AR(EN), Jan. 8, 1884; Wm. E. BOYD, July 7, 1955; Unknown, Aug. 1, 1877; Anna R. LARRIMOFF, July 26, 1955; Eliza Sindoff, Dec. 10, 1877; Chas. H. SCHMIDT, Mar. 21, 1956; Wm. BOLTE, May 16, 1878; Jessie R. CARROLL, May 24, 1956; Rachel BEACHUM, May 16, 1878; Vincent LETVA(ITIS), Jan. 1(2), 1957; James L. WALKER, June 3, 1878; Stella D. CLEVER, Mar. 18, 1957; Mary WA(RE)HAM, June 3, 1879; Georgette DOUGHERTY, Apr. 8, 1951; Marie HENDRY, Oct. 11, 1878; Mary Margaret RUTLEDGE, Feb. 19, (1954); Chas. ALLEN, Jan. 9, 1878; May HAGAN, Jan. 29, 1960 or 1961; Josiah HARRISON, Apr. 16, 1879; (Max DAHM), Mar. 23, 1966; Frederick LEFFLER, Apr. 29, 1879; Peter WIST(HER), Sept. 17, 190(5); Sarah LINTHICUM, May 15, 1879; Elsie (OTTINGER), Dec. 3, _____; Mrs. WAGNER, May 30, 1(8)79; Wm. BOONE, June 27, 1879; Lucy C. VARNER, Oct. 12, 1(?)72; Guy L. WOODALL, Mar. 19, 1(?)73; Margt. MULLER, Aug. 27, 1879; Julia May WEB(?), Mar. 25, 1(?)74; Eliza RIGBY, Sept. 26, 1879; Pauline KING, July 5, 1(?)74; Chas. MOTHERSHEAD, July 4, 1888; Wm. HEMMICK, June 6, 18(8)8; Robert S. MURRAY, May 19, 1888; Richard TAYLOR, Apr. 25, 18(88); Robert ROBERTS, Dec. 3, 1887; Catherine BRIDE, Dec. 3, 1887; Alice Webster, Sept. 9, 1887; Sarah MAC INTYRE, Aug. 12, 18(87); Cecil (LEISKE), Sept. 12, 1880; Caroline (P)OLK, Aug. 2, 1886; Nancy GRAYDON, July 22, 18(9)6; Henry SOHN, Nov. 10, 1879; John F. VAN (W)ERDER, Nov. 17, 1879; Chas. STOLT(Z), June 3, 1880; W. T. DALLY, Jan. 18, 1881; Annie DEER, May 19, 1881; Ann JENKINS, May 22, 18(82); Jacob MC LEAN, May 29, 1882; Martha VALIENT, July 3, 1882; Susan YOUNGER, Feb. 28, 18(8)3; Rebecca KIPPLER, May 5, 188(3); James RAE, Apr. 5, 18(83); Caroline JONES, July 16, 18(83); Eliza CALLAHAN, Nov. 26, 18(83); Edward NATTELE, Dec. 2(9), 18(8)3. The above 80 burials are in 54 spaces. The entries are written very small.

LOT 22-D: Alfred C. BROWN;
Clarence C. BROWN, Apr. 11, 1947; Ella Mae BROWN, Jan. 2, 1940; William I. BROWN, Dec. 10, 1956; Carryl A. BROWN, Nov. 25, 1964; "Reserved for Margaret B. KING"; Annie Florence BROWN, June 18, 1947; Alfred C. BROWN, July 16, 1904; Alfred C. BROWN, Apr. 6,

1886; Annie E. BROWN, July 12, 1919; Alice E. BROWN, June 16, 1876, child.

LOT 23-D: Andrew J. PARLETT;
Isabell TALBERT, Apr. 18, 1881, disinterred; Miron (FARBERST), Aug. 12, 1881; Willie F. PARLETT, Feb. 19, 1885; Emma PARLETT, Sept. 7, 1885 (also Sept. 4, 1886 given); Emma PARLETT, Oct. 8, 1885; Naomi PARLETT, May 19, 1886; Lida A. PARLETT, Sept. 11, 1891; Mollie M. WINN, Aug. 23, 1892; Andrew J. PARLETT, Feb. 31, [sic] 189(4) (also Oct. 28, 1894 given); Sophrono PARLETT, Aug. 28, 1899 or 1897; Siana PARLETT, June 10, 1884; Thos. A. PARLETT, Oct. 19, 1889; Isabella TOLBERT, Nov. 28, 1913, disinterred and moved to Oak Lawn Cemetery; Danl. E. PARLETT, July 10, 1907; Geo. M. MADDOX, Feb. 26, 1915; Margt. E. PARLETT, Sept. 29, 1916; Chas. B. PARLETT, Dec. 22, 1916; Mary A. MILLER, Mar. 8, 1919; Alice E. GERMAN, Mar. 18, 193(9); Webster GERMAN, Jan. 7, 1945; COOKMAN (no other name and (no date given)); Edna GAY, Oct. 5, 1957; Mary (E.) PARLETT, (no date gter GERMAN, Jan. 7, 1945; COOKMAN (no other name and (no date given)); Edna GAY, Oct. 5, 1957; Mary (E.) PARLETT, (no date given).

LOT 24-D: Alex BEAUMONT and Phirgus M. BROOKS;
Daisy BEAUMONT, Oct. 9, 1881; Margt. B. WEEMS, Dec. 19, 1904; Margt. BEAUMONT, July 11, 1913; Alex. H. BEAUMONT, Aug. 17, 1928; Ameria BROOCKS, Mar. 1, 1881; Earnest H. DOBSON, Apr. 17, 1914; Phirgus BROOCKS, July 8, 1915; Wm. C. BROOCKE, Mar. 11, 1918; Lula BROOKE, July 1, 1933; Ma(rie) A. DOBSON, Aug. 15, 1933; Ida B. WEEMS, Jan. 6, 1948; Ernesth DOBSON, Sept. 7, 1957.

LOT 25-D: Louis W. SMITH, Thomas (P.) MORTIMER and Charlotte SENFT;
Florence SMITH, Jan 25, 18(8)3; Mary and Alice SMITH, Jan. 26, 1883; John SMITH, Jan. 27, 1883; Clara A. SMITH, Aug. 14, 1900; Lee M. SMITH, May 3, 1901; Mildred E. WAGNER, June 27, 1911; Enoch HARTLOVE, Apr. (2), 1898; Mary E. SMITH, Nov. 19, 1912; R. SMITH, Sept. 14, 1921; Louis W. SMITH, Feb. 20, 1926; Rosemarie SMITH, (no date given); Minnie L. SMITH, (no date given).

LOT 26-D: David F. SIMMORT and Randolph BECKMAN;
Margt. F. SIMMORT, Nov. 12, 1883; Clarence SIMMORT, Nov. 13, 1882; Wm. T. SIMMORT, Aug. 12, 1885; David T. SIMMORT, June 24, 1886; David F. SIMMORT, Apr. 28, 1891; Chas. I. SIMMORT, Aug. 24, 1892; Mary TAYLOR, Dec. 6, 1897; Chas. H. WHEELER, Nov. 28, 1898; Harry SIMMOIT, Dec. 25, 1898; David SIMMORT, May 6, 1911; Stillborn, July 23, 1883; Stillborn of HOFFMAN, July 27, 1885; Ellinora L. BECKMAN, May 5, 1882; Rudolph BECKMAN, Apr. 3, 1908; Annie BECKMAN, Feb. 19, 1889; John P. BUNGARNER, Aug. 17, 1888; Henry ARNOLD, Nov. 20, 1888; Saml. VODEN, May 27, 1890; Wm. H. ARNOLD, July 26, 1913; J. G. Henry ARNOLD, Dec. 25, 1916; Annie E. ARNOLD, Oct. 7, 1924; Elizabeth C. SIMMOIT, Sept. 8, 1915; Stillborn of KERNS, Oct. 21, 1918; Howard ARNOLD, (no date given); Ashes of Geo. W. ARNOLD, Feb. 14, 1931; Ashes of Mary L. ARNOLD, (no date given); Kate ARNOLD, (no date given); John BRINGST(?), (no date given); Arthur L. SHELTON, (no date given); Philip BECKMAN, Dec. 21, 1929.

LOT 27-D: Samuel P. DIXON and C. F. REATHER;
Geo. W. MC CAFFERTY, Jan. 16, 1882; Margt. H. REATHER, Aug. 16, 1882(or 3); Jeanette REATHER, Apr. 19, 1907; Chas. F. REATHER,

Feb. 12, 1913; Mary K. REATHER, Dec. 18, 1922; Annie E. REATHER, Mar. 17, 1923; John W. REATHER, Feb. 26, 1936; Edward D. DIXON, Apr. 24, 1884; Mary E. DIXON, July 12, 1897; Mary E. DIXON, May 27, 1903; Saml. T. DIXON, Nov. 20, 1931; Chas. Wesley LEDLEY, Nov. 30, 1936; Sophia M. LEDLEY, May 26, 1956; Grace M. DIXON, Oct. 22, 1941; Gertrude REATHER, Oct. 4, 1950.

LOT 28-D: Joseph A. DISNEY and Rev. W. J. GILL;
Louisa DISNEY, May 23, 1884; Joseph A. DISNEY, Maya 5, 1885 (There is a Joseph DISNEY on the right side of the page who may be the same person, Joseph DISNEY, May 1, 1884); Stillborn of A. and G. GLOVER, June 10, 1890; Bernard E. GLOVER, Aug. 27, 1892; Laura K. GOODRICK, Sept. 27, 1908; Julia V. GOODRICK, Feb. 16, 1908; Mertle and W. DUVALL, Nov. 23, 1903; Stillborn of Geo. GLOVER, June 8, 1904; Stillborn of A. E. GLOVER, June 16, 1908; Stillborn of Annie and (Edwd. DUVALL), May 11, 1917; James HILL, Dec. 15, 1881; Dr. Alex. HILL, Jan. 22, 1906; Infant of W. and I. G(U)NDRY, Nov. 15, 1910; Stillborn of Wm. GUNDRY, Sept. 16, 1914; Isabell BELL, May 27, 1915; Wm. J. HILL, June 8, 1933; Ellen Bell HILL, July 31, 193(3 or 5); Joseph DISNEY, Dec. 18, 1917; Lillian R. MC COUBRY, July 1, 1961; Nancy A. HILL, June 27, 1956.

LOT 29-D: Lydia A. CONNOR and Geo. N. SHE(RMAN);
Jas. CONNOR, Mar. 12, 1884; Lydia A. CONNOR, Sept. 2, 1887; Jas. Z. CONNOR, Dec. 23, 1903; Theodore SUMALT, Jan. 22, 1904; Baby MASON, Oct. 31, 1927; Clara Naomi SUMWALT, Nov. 12, 1942; Stillborn of MASON, (no date given); Stillborn of MASON, June 15, 1(9)29; Carrie A. BIRCH, Nov. 14, 1894; Walter W. BIRCH, May 4, 1890; Stillborn of MOORE, Nov. 4, 1894; Mi(nnie) BIRCH, May 24, 1884; Ella G. HANKEY, Nov. 10, 1948; John S. MASON, July 18, 1955; Edna S. MASON, Aug. 8, 1928; George R. BIRCH, Feb. 5, 1937; Jos. BIRCH, May 9, 1915; Mary E. BIRCH, Feb. 3, 1928.

LOT 30-D: Drucilla MC DANIELS and Gustave W. FORD;
Columbus MC DANIELS, Nov. 22, 1886; Drucilla MC DANIELS, Feb. 15, 1889; Mary A. WEAVER, Dec. 17, 1894; Dedrick C. WEAVER, Apr. 17, 1914; Emma J. WEAVER, Feb. 19, 1923; Gustavo W. FORD, Dec. 11, 1906; George P. ARNOLD, Mar. 31, 1969, born Nov. 17, 1897, died Mar. 28, 1969. Letter dated Sept. 21, 1970, Edward C. TOWNSEND, lot owner, declares he is the great-grandson of the original purchaser of lot, Drusilla MC DANIEL. He also states he has a step-daughter named Mrs. Betty R. HARRISON (nee ARNOLD). Lot in question is 30-D.

LOT 31-D: Wm. F. POTEE;
Catherine POTEE, June 8, 1886; Elsie O. POTEE, Aug. 28, 1923; Wm. F. POTEE, Jan. 23, 1929; Mr. John O. BECK, (not yet deceased). In the margin of the page is written "Sept. 24, 1900, disinterred, Nov. 15, 1909 Mildred DICKEL (or DISCKEL or DIXCKEL)".

LOT 32-D: Not Methodist - Aged Men and Women, Calhoun and Lexington Streets;
Sarah PERSINGER, Apr. 23, 1918 (could be RESSINGER or RUSINGER or PUSINGER); James LATCHWOOD, June 3, 1918; Mary E. EVERIT, July 27, 1918; Benj. F. GABLE, Sept. 5, 1918; Wm. C. BLACKBURN, Sept. 14, 1918; Eliza HEWETT, June 5, 1919; Chas. JONES, Oct. 23, 1919; Donald (MC KAY), Dec. 2, 1919; Andrew SIMPSON, Mar. 10, 1900 (entry lined out); Annie R. SCHEOFF, Sept. 10, 1920; Henry D. FAIRCHILD, Feb. 23, 1921; Fannie BROWN, July 13, 1921; Sarah

BEVA(NS), Nov. 7, 1921; M. Eliza BAKER, Oct. 7, 1922; Anna GRAVE, Mar. 7, 1923 (this name may also be GROVE); Chas. H. LEHMAN, Mar. 15, 1923; Delaware (C.) THOMAS, Oct. 8, 1923; Herman K(OENTZER), May 1, 1925; Fran(is) M. CATTLE, Feb. 14, 1924; Jas. STAFFORD, Nov. (12), 1924; Mary L. HA(RWOOD), July (1, 1920).

LOT 33-D: Single Interments.
Stephen and Julia CHORNYET "in #23 and 24 and Barbara WEBER, in #25 (no date given), (a grave apparently reserved for Charlotte F(AULKNER) (no date given) (These two items appear to be for the same grave.); Margaret DAHL, Oct. 5, 1925; George W. DELBROOK, Nov. 18, 1925; William HOCHLER, Dec. 2, 1925; Mary Elizabeth HOCHLER, June 19, 1945; John MRAS, Dec. 16, 1925; Charles HUNT, Jan. 9, 1926; William EVANS, Nov. 18, 1925; Bertha E. JASPER, Dec. 3, 1925; Enright PENTZBORN, Dec. 17, 1925; Grace H. HERTZEL, Jan. 4, 1926; Henry C. SPARROW, Jan. 15, 1926; Gertrude PORTER, Oct. 8, 1927; Mary J. STULTZ, Feb. 20, 1926; John REIN, Mar. 15, 1926; Emma KAUFMAN, Mar. 23, 1926; Karl GUSSEN, May 13, 1926; Charles P. MC CAULEY, May 15, 1926; John MARTINSAN, May 17, 1926; Alice GIBSON, June 7, 1926; Theresa MORRIS, Oct. 8, 1926; Julius CALERA, Jan. 22, 1927; Michael FREDERICK, May 2, 1927; Stephen CHORNYEI, Dec. 31, 1955; Barbara WEBER, May 27, 1927; Julia CHORNYEI, May 23, 1927; "Sold to Flora FREDERICK, May 7, 1927, (marginal note states, "for Galen Frederick or his order"; Flora FREDERICK, July 7, 1941; Carrie Buchner (ELDER), July 13, 1927; William L. FOX, Aug. 24, 1937; Carrie FOX, Dec. 26, 1935; Albert E. ROBERTS, Nov. 14, 1927; Edw. M. RICKER, Dec. 1, 1927; Malcolm SKINNER, Dec. 24, 1927; James W. CAULK, Feb. 25, 1928; Cora SOWERS, Mar. 30, 1928; Mary E. FISHER, Mar. 31, 1928; John SUTCH, Jan. 29, 1929; Kate MORROW, Apr. 9, 1928; Alice G. HARMAN, 55 years, Feb. 3, 1930.

This page reads - "North Baltimore Station Section D Mount Olivet Cemetery." There follows a drawing of lots 33 through 42 and lots 95 through 106. There is a note stating - "1/4 41-D put in P.C." And the name "WODERY." Also below this is "87-(D) put in P.C." and the name "ABBOTT."

LOT 34-D through 35-D: There is no record of these lots in the Lot Book.

LOT 36-D: Baltimore (Station) M.E. Church Lot. Lot owner Wm. P. THOMPSON;
William T. THOMPSON, Dec. 14, 1963; Carrie THOMPSON, Nov. 12, 1974, born Nov. 2, 1891, died Nov. 9, 1974, father Chas. KOELENDER, funeral home was Hahn.

LOT 37-D: Northwest Methodist Church, North Baltimore Station; Lillian Rose EMORY, June 20, 1942; Florence M. THOMAS, Sept. 10, 1949. Letter dated Sept. 9, 1949 from Northwood Methodist Church signed by Frank V. COGGINS, authorized unnamed burial in Lot 37-D.

LOT 38-D: There is no record in the Lot Book for this lot.

LOT 39-D: North Baltimore Station;
Jacqueline BELLAFO(RIE), Oct. 24, 1935; Edwd. SH(AW), Dec. 29, 1936; Flora HOMAK, Jan. 18, 1941; Montez SHAW, Aug. 10, 1956.

LOT 40-D: North Baltimore Station M. E. Church; Edwd. JENKINS, Feb. 18, 1936, (child).

LOT 41-D: This lot sold by North Baltimore Station M.E. Church to James H. WOOLERY; Ella M. WOOLERY, Aug. 18, 1934; James H. WOOLERY, June 11, 1940.

LOTS 42-D through 46-D: There is no record of these lots in the Lot Book.

LOT 47-D: P. H. ROBERTS; Removed from N. B. G., Apr. 17, 1877; Cath. ROBERTS, Nov. 5, 1918; P. H. ROBERTS, May 11, 1926.

LOT 48-D: C. M. YOUNG; Morean T. FRUSH, Dec. 19, 1895 (On right of page name is listed as Moreay F. FURSH); Mary L. YOUNG, May 5, 1919; Chas. M. YOUNG ("in single grave 95 adjoining to north"), (no date given).

LOT 49-D and 49 1/2-D: Susan GUMPMAN (In all instances this name may also be GUMFMAN);
Alfred GUMPMAN, Aug. 12, 1893; Mary GUMPMAN, Jan. 25, 1895; Robert GUMPMAN, Dec. 24, 1896; Viola R. GUMPMAN, Aug. 14, 1899; Carroll GUMPMAN, Jan. 12, 1905; Florence GREEN, Apr. 20, 1912; Susan GUMPMAN, May 1, 1915; Myrtle E. FORD, Jan. 30, 1924.

LOT 50-D - 52-D: William W. MC CAIN;
Mary E. MC CAIN, July 30, 1888, child; Edwin Vernon BURKE, Nov. 2, 1888, child; Sarah A. BALL, Oct. 14, 1895; Carrie L. CLARK, Sept. 7, 1903, child; William W. MC CAIN, May 10, 1938; William BRATLEY, Oct. 16, 1911, child; Charles C. MC CAIN, May 6, 1914; John T. BALL, May 31, 1904; Sarah L. MC CAIN, Dec. 16, 1895; Bertha IRELAND, July 12, 1909; Alice B. MC CAIN, July 20, 1889.

LOT 51-D: John O. MC NEAL;
Mary J. MC NEAL, Dec. 28, 1885; Mary C. (or E.) MC NEAL, May 16, 1905; John O. MC NEAL, July 12, 1933; Albert P. MC NEAL, Aug. 24, 1937; William O. MC NEAL, Aug. 16, 1943.

LOT 52-D: See LOT 51-D.

LOT 53-D: Chas. H. NIEGHOFF;
Ida May NIEGHOFF, July 10, 1888; Edith NIEGHOFF, Sept. 8, 1886; Chas. (A. or S.) NEIGHOFF, July 1, 1930; Isabelle NIEGHOFF, July 6, 1936.

LOT 54-D: (Hendrick) KLAMER;
Infant of KLAMER, July 18, 1875; Gertrude KALMER, July 11, 1887; Henry KLAMER, Aug. 11, 1933; Henrietta KLAMER, Dec. 1, 1934.

LOT 55-D: BUTLUER (This name at every instance in this Lot is written so poorly that BUTLUER is a pure speculation. The name does begin with a B. There is also either a double T or a T and L in the middle.);
Ernest BUTLUER, Oct. 4, 1886; Helen H. BUTLUER, July 19, 1890; Edwd. R. BUTLUER, Nov. 28, 1898; Emma M. COLE, Nov. 21, 1899; Helen H. BUTLUER, Jan. 26, 1903; Geo. W. JEFFERS, Aug. 9, 1906; Emma TREAKEL, Aug. 22, 1936.

LOT 56-D: Saml. DAVIDSON;
Mennie DAVIDSON, July 27, 1885; Edgar T. DAVIDSON, Jan. 30, 1896; Ella May BLANCH, Dec. 3, 1902; Walter L. FISCHER, Aug. 2, 1910; Robert GREEN, Jan. 10, 1912.

LOT 57-D: Wm. H. HICKMAN;
Edgar STEPHENS, Nov. 6, 1883; Elinor MAXWELL, Aug. 24, 1885; Annie B. THOMAS, Oct. 27, 1886; Geo. WALKER, July 7, 1894; (no first name) DONAVAN, Oct. 13, 1896; Geo. CRAMER, Dec. 11, 1894; Blanch MOSES, Nov. 1, 1893; Harry H. HORTON, Mar. 3, 1919; Winter D. HORTON, Mar. 19, 1936; Helen Amelia HORTON, Jan. 27, 1950.

LOT 58-D: Peter SORENSON;
Andrew M. SORENSON, Oct. 24, 1884; Peter SORENSON, Oct. 29, 1910; Augusta AUG(USTENBERGER), May 9, 1913.

LOT 59-D: John W. ROBERTS. No burials recorded in this lot.

LOT 60-D: Lucy A. BROMWELL;
Lucy A. BROMWELL, Aug. 13, 1893; Katherine HARRIS, Aug. 23, 1910; William W. BROMWELL, May 10, 1939; Katherine RICHTER, Mar. 22, 1967, born Dec. 26, 1892, died Mar. 19, 1967.

LOT 61-D through 68-D: No record of these lots can be found in the Lot Book.

LOT 69-D: Mark N. DAVIS;
Mary E. DAVIS, Nov. 29, 1881; Mary R. DAVIS, June 9, 1915; Mark M. DAVIS, Jan. 23, 1919. (This name is probably DAVIS, though it appears as DARIS and in one case DAVES.)

LOT 70-D: Godfrey ORENSHALL;
Annie E. ORENSHALL, Aug. 6, 1877; Godfrey ORENSHALL, Dec. 10, 1884; John E. GRENTZ, Feb. 3, 1900; August ORENSHALL, Apr. 28, 1900; August ORENSHALL, June 23, 1900; Robert V. GRENTZ, July 7, 1902 ("children at bottom"); Margaret A. GRENTZ, Aug. 11, 1906; August VAIN, (no date given).

LOT 71-D: James KIDWELL;
Mary E. KIDWELL, Nov. 28, 1883; John L. HIGDON, Apr. 3, 1890; Catherine BROWN, June 9, 1893; John L. KIDWELL, Sept. 25, 1908 (Disinterred and reinterd in 94-C, Jan. 13, 1955); John KIDWELL, Nov. 15, 1908 (or 1909); Clarence KIDWELL, June 2, 1913; Margt. KIDWELL, July 13, 1914; Geo. KLEINSMITH, Apr. 14, 1915; Geo. KLEINSMITH, June 11, 1915, disinterred and reinterred in LOT 62, Section O); Annie KIDWELL, Oct. 9, 1916; James KIDWELL, Mar. 1, 1923; Edwd. J. KIDWELL, Jan. 24, 1929; Sarah F. KIDWELL, Oct. 7, 1931; Lewisa HIGDON, (no date given).

LOT 72-D: D. E. WHISTLER;
Mary C. WHISTLER, Nov. 10, 1917; David E. WHISTLER, Sr., May 12, 1922. (Both disinterred June 25, 1970 and removed to Lorraine Park Cemetery, Woodlawn, in Baltimore County, Md. Funeral home was Hubbard.)

LOT 73-D: James E. KELLENBERGER;
Mary C. KELLENBERGER, Sept. 8, 1890; Chas. T. KELLENBERGER, Nov. 6, 1891; Walter KELLENBERGER, Jan. 5, 1895; Wm. H. KELLENBERGER, Apr. 11, 1898; Mary E. KELLENBERGER, Aug. 7, 1888; Alice A.

TRUMBO, July 20, 1903; Ella V. MACHER, Nov. 1, 1908; Stillborn of
J. E. KELLENBERGER, June 16, 1913; Kenton K. KELLENBERGER, Jan.
1, 1923.

LOT 74-D: James E. HOPWOOD, over this name is written Fred A.
HOPWOOD;
Carrie G. CROUSE, Sept. 13, 1884; Willie CROUSE, Oct. 24, 1894;
Stella HOPWOOD, Oct. 26, 1885; Myrtle HOPWOOD, Mar. 30, 1887;
Willie H. HOPWOOD, July 16, 1887; Hattie E. HOPWOOD, Dec. 19,
1891; Hannah HOPWOOD, Nov. 24, 1892; Child, Jan. 1, 1897; Russell
L. RIDDLE, Mar. 31, 1898; Jas. HOPWOOD, Jan. 21, 1903; Myrtle
RIDDLE, Aug. 6, 1903; Walter E. ESKELS, Nov. 2, 1910; Frank A.
HOPWOOD, Mar. 30, 1918; Elisha L. RIDDELL, June 28, 1938; Patricia Lee RIDDELL, Jan. 26, 1946, child.

LOT 75-D through LOT 80-D: There is no record of these lots in
the Lot Book.

LOT 81-D: John TOWNSEND;
Annie TOWNSEND, (no date given); Elizabeth DAILEY, (no date
given); James TOWNSEND, (no date given); Harry ROSE, 3 years old,
(no date given). Names of persons controlling burials in this
lot are: Mrs. Mary BELT of Baltimore and Mrs. Gordon R. MATTHEWS
and Miss Mary R. BELT of Hyattsville, Md.

LOTS 82-D through 86-D: No record of these lots appear in the
Lot Book.

LOT 87-D: D. Flor(ence) B. ABBOTT. Transferred from North
Baltimore Station M. E. Church;
Minnie G. ABBOTT, Aug. 2, 1944; Florence B. ABBOTT, Mar. 3, 1955;
Clarence P. ABBOTT, May 31, 1938; Herbert A. GOODING, Jan. 27,
1944.

LOT 88-D: Margaret BLACKBURNE. Transferred from Northwood
Methodist Church;
Mario Elizabeth BLACKBURNE, Nov. 15, 1943; Margaret BLACKBURNE,
Apr. 26, 1951; Frederick BLACKBURNE, Dec. 29, 1943.

LOT 89-D: North Baltimore Station to Sarah A. LONG;
Annie L. WILSON, Jan. 12, 1952; Sarah A. LONG, Oct. 29, 1973,
born Apr. 23, 1897, died Oct. 26, 1973. Parents Edward WILSON
and Annie L. WILSON nee NGE "(also married WILSON)"; funeral home
was Seitz; Charles LONG, Nov. 6, 1939.

LOT 90-D: Charles W. MC CALL;
Mary Hewitt MC CALL, Dec. 31, 1943; Charles N. MC CALL, Oct. 20,
1945; Wendell HUMPHREYS purchased grave from Northwood Methodist
Church.

LOTS 91-D through 96-D: There is no record of these lots in the
Lot Book.

LOT 97-D through 100-D: Quarters 99 and 100 - Harry B. PRICE
transferred from Northwood Church transferred to Shirley MAC
RUSSELL;
"For Mrs. ROUZEE"; Bernard C. ROUZEE, Oct. 5, 1949; Elneta May
RUSSELL, Oct. 9, 1963, stillborn; Arthur ROUZER, Dec. 12, 1970,

born May 9, 1899, died Dec. 13, 1970. Parents George M. ROUZEE and Mary E. FISHER, the funeral home was Heeman.

LOTS 101-D and 102-D: Howard D. ASKEW and Blanche ASKEW, Northwood Methodist Church, formerly transferred from North Baltimore Station;
Emma A. LEVY, Jan. 25, 1971, born May 17, 1881, died Jan. 22, 1971. Parents Carl BOHM and unknown, funeral home - Paul Heemann; Blanche ASKEW, Nov. 2, 1957.

LOT 103-D and 104-D: James H. WILSON (from North Baltimore Station);
Ethel W. BAKER, Oct. 30, 1968, born July 2, 1902, died Oct. 27, 1968; Earl C. BAKER, Feb. 24, 1951; Catherine WILSON, Jan. 4, 1966, (born) Nov. 5, 1875, died Jan. 2, 1966, age 90 years; James H. WILSON, Nov. 7, 1944.

LOTS 105-D through 118-D: THere is no record of these lots in the Lot Book.

LOT 119-D: Elizabeth BENEZE;
Infant, Nov. 2, 1882 (entry crossed out); Elizabeth and Sarah WILLETT, May 10, 1891; Bertha KRAFT, July 26, 1907; Elizabetht BENEZE, Apr. 7, 1908; Danl. M. KRAFT, Aug. 30, 1917; George KRAFT, May 4, 1932; Fredk. BENEZE, Apr. 23, 1877; male infant of MC CANN, Apr. 1, 1948.

LOT 120-D: Allen PRICE;
Allen PRICE, Sept. 5, 1896.

LOT 121-D: R(oemma) MC MULLER;
Removed from N. B. G., Apr. 23, 1877; Removed from N. B. G., May 22, 1877; Annie R. WILLIAMS, Mar. 7, 188(2).

LOT 122-D: Sarah KNOTT;
Remains from N. B. G., Apr. 20, 1877; Wm. (W.) SANDERS, Aug. 31, 1878; Ellen SANDERS, Nov. 13, 1881; Sarah C. KNOTT, May 13, 1887; Annie J. SANDERS, Apr. 7, 18(77 or 97); John Wesley SANDERS, July 20, 1904; Mary E. LIPPEY, J(an.) 26, 1909.

LOT 123-D: Cornelia MC COMAS;
Remains from N. B. G., May 28, 1877; Ida May STUBBS, Nov. 6, 1882; Andrew J. MC COMAS, Jan. 15, 1883; Frances PRICE, Nov. 19, 1883; Wm. G. MC COMAS, June 6, 1884; Caroline F. MC COMAS, May 10, 1889; Minnie E. MC COMAS, Mar. 24, 1894; Delia KLUGENBERG, Mar. 21, 1895; Louisa T. KELLENBERG, Jan. 13, 1914.

LOT 124-D: Ellery C. FOGLER;
Robt. K. FOGLER, Mar. 29, 1880; Geo. P. FOGLER, June 19, 1882; Infant of Ellen C. FOGLER, June 5, 1883; Ellery C. FOGLER, Feb. 14, 1893; Sallie A. FOGLER, June 26, 1894; Ellery C. FOGLER, June 20, 1908; Jennie REED, Oct. 30, 1928.

LOT 125-D through 132-D: There are no records for these lots in the Lot Book.

LOT 133-D: D(r.) H. STARR;
Mary C. BROWN, Sept. 12, 1887 (This name may be BRAUN); John W.

WELCH, May 1, 1891; "Charlotte B. for wife of Abe MORRIS," (no date given); Abe MORRIS, July 9, 1942.

LOT 134-D: Sophia NORRIS;
Remains from N. B. G., July 3, 1877; Sophie NORRIS, July 6, 1886; Marie (S.) NORRIS, Apr. 5, 1894; Chas. F. NORRIS, Apr. 19, 1897.

LOT 135-D: Sarah A. SCHROTE;
Annie SCHROTE, June 9, 1879; Wm. (S.) SCHRATE, July 18, 1881; Sarah SANDERS, Oct. 3, 1890; (Arthur) J. SCHRATE, June 6, 1894; Henry H. SCHRATE, July 16, 1894; Thos. H. SCHRATE, Aug. 24, 1901.

LOT 136-D: Margaret A. COLE;
Remains from N. B. G., Apr. 11, 1878; Cath. E. NEILSON, Sept. 13, 1880; Thos. R. L. COLE, Jan. 15, 1883; Annie (and) W. T. PRICE, Feb. 22, 1884; Elizabeth NIELSON, Feb. 18, 1885; J. L. NIELSON, Feb. 9, 1884; Arthur NIELSON, Apr. 18, 1893.

LOT 137-D: Alex. PRITCHARD;
Mary E. B(RUNN)ER, Feb. 29, 1888; Jos. PRITCHARD, June 17, 1889; Child of PRITCHARD, Aug. 5, 1892; Stillborn of Mc (A.) PRITCHARD, Sept. 12, 1924.

LOT 138-D: John E. CARMAN;
Kate E. WALKER, Mar. 24, 1914; Jas. WALKER, July 29, 1914.

LOT 139-D: Mary E. SMITH;
Julie Ann SMITH, Sept. 28, 1883 (1882); Mary E. SMITH, May 7, 1915.

LOT 140-D: Wm. H. GRIFFITH;
Margt. J. GRIFFITH, Mar. 23, 1884; Wm. H. GRIFFITH, Oct. 3, 1896; (Erim) W. GRIFFITH, June 14, 1906; Wm. H. GRIFFITH, Jr., Apr. 18, 1917; L. Irene HILE, Feb. 24, 1960.

LOT 141-D: Thos. ESSENDER;
Mary E. ESSENDER, Apr. 14, 1893.

LOT 142-D: Wm. G. GEDDESS;
Lillian GEDDESS, Jan. 3, 1887; Stillborn of Wm. GEDDESS, Sept. 27, 1895; Lulu VANCE, Nov. 11, 1895; Infant of Jennie and C. DONELLY, Jan. 23, 1896; Stillborn of Mary and John GEDDESS, Sept. 7, 1896; John REYNOLDS, July 17, 1913; John GEDDESS, Jan. 11, 1902.

LOT 143-D: Margaret GRIFFITH;
Robert H. GRIFFITH, Oct. 8, 1888; Wm. GRIFFITH, Oct. 8, 1895.

LOT 144-D: Elias Geo. MC CONNELL;
Walter B. MC CONNELL, Oct. 26, 1888.

LOT 145-146-D: Eugene H. BANTHAM;
Me(bi)lle BANTHAM, Apr. 15, 1889; Mary E. BANTHAM, June 26, 1897; Mitchell BANTHAM, Apr. 15, 1889 (entry crossed out); Mary E. BANTHAM, Oct. 3, 1900 (There is a Mary C. BANTHAM which may be the same as this entry); Eugene H. BANTHAM, Mar. 23, 1911; Mary E. BANTHAM, Jan. 20, 1916; Eugene H. BANTHAM, June 29, 1916. (In two places the N in BANTHAM is xed out.)

LOT 147-D: (Mrs.) Sarah KIDWELL; Wm. H. FORITZ, May 12, 1923; John E. HESS, Jr., Aug. 18, 1926; Edward ROBERTS, Jan. 16, 1945; James T. KIDWELL, May 8, 1956.

LOT 148-D: Wm. PUTSCHKY to Mary PUTSCHKY; Mary PUTCHSKY, Aug. 16, 1889; Wm. PUTSCHKY, July 10, 1917; Wm. PUTSCHLEY, Apr. 29, 1918; Mary PUTSCHKY, June 8, 1936.

LOT 149-150-D: Frank HARWOOD; Mammie HARWOOD, Aug. 24, 1889; Winter W. POOLE, Jan. 30, 1909; Wm. POOL, Aug. 8, 1932; Frank HARWOOD, Feb. 22, 1910; Cruelia H. HARWOOD, Feb. 2, 1919; Blanche H. HARWOOD, Mar. 31, 1965.

LOT 151-D: August ROUSER; Elizabeth ROUSER, Dec. 5, 1890; Earnest CARROLL, Sept. 4, 1901; Dorbora ROUSER, Dec. 13, 1904; Stillborn of August ROUSER, Dec. 4, 1925; Paul M. ROUSER, Jan. 14, 1911; Gustav ROUSER, Sept. 23, 1920.

LOT 152-D through 154-D: Pleasant PACE and J. W. NOEL; Lillie C. PACE, May 24, 1890; Sarah PACE, July 9, 1891; Laura B. PACE, July 13, 1892; Florence NOEL, Oct. 13, 1893; Annie NOEL, June 16, 1894; Beatrice PACE, Dec. 25, 1899; Helen NOEL, June 18, 1892.

LOT 153-D: Geo. RILEY, at side of Lot Owner line is "was ROBERTS;" "Richard ROBERTS, Jan. 14, 1891 may have been disinterred, do not know;" Elizabeth RILEY, May 22, 1899; Geo. W. RILEY, May 3, 1913 (On the right of the page the date is Apr. 30, 1913); Rebecca RILEY, June 17, 1940.

LOT 154-D: See LOT 152-D above.

LOT 155-D through 157-D: Jos. B. COOK, was Henry KEYNAST; Annie KYNAST, Apr. 14, 1891, disinterred and taken to Western Cemetery, Baltimore, Md.; Stillborn of NIDENHIMER, disinterred, Jan. 3, 1908; Leroy B. (MILLER), Apr. 26, 19(08); (Ossodale) (ORANDE), Dec. 25, 1908; Alice E. MC KNIGHT, Feb. 6, 1908; Stillborn of CR(OGS), Mar. 19, 1909; Mary E. SNEDLEY, June 16, 1913; Wm. HOLDSWORTH, Nov. 18, 1914; Algo R. PARKS, Oct. 15, 1909; Edwd. (or Edwin) PERRIN, May 25, 1915; John MC LARDY, May 1, 1915; Stillborn of Ada and Wm. WILSON, Sept. 27, 1915; Arthur COLEMAN, Aug. 15, 1910; Gus ELISON, Apr. 7, 191(?); Stillborn of (HUTCHINSON), Nov. 2(8), 1912; Geo. M. MARTIN, July 5, 1913; Chas. W. LUMBARD and Anton ANDERSON, Nov. 4, 1914; John WILLIAMS, Dec. 3, 1914; Stillborn of Jacob and Lena GARY, May 2, 1915; Winter S. POOLE, Dec. 6, 1916; Wm. A. (DEISS), Dec. 15, 1914; Estella K(LENLIN), Dec. 29, 1916; Edwd. SEAMAN, July 26, 1917; Jacob WILKENS, (no date given); Jus ELISON, (no date given); John HENDRICKSON, (no date given).

LOT 156-D: Eliz J. COMBES; Elizabeth J. COMBES, Sept. 17, 1891; John R. MC CONKEY, Jan. 24, 1906; Irene G. COMBES, Mar. 24, 1964.

LOT 157-D: See LOT 155-D.

LOT 158-D: Mary E. HOLLAND;
Martha A. BUMPASS, Aug. 14, 1893; Luretta HOLLAND, Oct. 16, 1894; Annie E. HOLLAND, Dec. 28, 1896; Guy O. HOLLAND, Sept. 1, 1897; Estella HOLLAND, July 1, 1895; Hazel M. HOLLAND, Dec. 31, 1899; Bernice L. HOLLAND, Aug. 22, 1905; Mary E. HOLLAND, Jan. 14, 1918; baby HOLLAND, July 30, 1918.

LOT 159-D: Lewis J. SMITH;
Annie A. SMITH, May 20, 1914; Capt. Lewis J. SMITH, July 19, 1923; Annie M. JOHNSON, July 7, 1898; Glady M. JOHNSON, Sept. 12, 1900; Lewis SMITH, Jan. 3, 1910; Mahon SMITH, Jan. 13, 1911.

LOT 160-D: Harry J. SMITH;
Evelyn E. F. SMITH, July 13, 1895; Ellen F. SMITH, July 10, 1902; Ella SMITH, Mar. 17, 1913; Harry J. SMITH, Jan. 6, 1953.

LOT 161-D and 162-D: John W. DISNEY;
John W. DISNEY, Dec. 7, 1938; Florence V. DISNEY, Jan. 6, 1975, born Sept. 23, 1892, died Jan. 2, 1975. Parents John W. DISNEY, Sr. and Mary E. WARWICK, funeral home was Geo. J. Gonce; Clara DISNEY, Oct. 23, 1893; Florence DISNEY, Mar. 25, 1915; John W. DISNEY, Sr., Oct. 3, 1921; Mary E. DISNEY, Apr. 11, 1947.

LOT 161 1/2-D and 162 1/2-D: Henry ARNOLD and Miss Emma ARNOLD of Baltimore, Md.;
Edward ARNOLD, June 1, 1898; Child, Sept. 1, 1899; Christian ARNOLD, Aug. 5, 1905; Harry ARNOLD, Oct. 1,1906; Annie E. ARNOLD, Apr. 11, 19(10); Dora ARNOLD, June 20, 1917; Mary Elizabeth TREADWELL, Mar. 5, 1931; Henry ARNOLD, June 10, 1937 (may be same person as Henry E. ARNOLD which appears on right side of page); "For Emma ARNOLD," (no date given); Cremains of Viola GRASSO, Aug. 3, 1970, age 61 years. Certificate of Cremation, dated July 28, 1970 for Viola M. GRASSO, age 61, who died on July 25, 1970. Issued in Baltimore, Md.

LOT 163-D: Annie WILLIAMS.   No burials are recorded in the Lot Book for this lot.

LOT 164-D: Clara E. MILLS;
Martha B. MILLS, Mar. 30, 1904; Florence I. MILLS, Aug. 4, 1908; Clara E. MILLS, Oct. 9, 1935; Mary E. MILLS, Feb. 10, 1961.

LOT 165-D: Henry MILLER;
Jane E. MILLER, Dec. 23, 1890; Wm. C. MILLER, Aug. 1, 1889; Blanch MILLER, Jan. 16, 1902; Chas. H. MILLER, Dec. 4, 1902; Henry C. MILLER, Oct. 31, 1917; Elizabeth MILLER, Dec. 3, 1920; Mary KIRKNER, July 2, 1956.

LOT 166-D: Wm. HUMMERBOCHER;
Chas. C(RONNER), Dec. 15, 1890; Florence A. HUMMERBOCHER, Oct. 10, 1896.

LOT 167-D and 169-D: Wm. H. MARKEY;
Eliz C. MARKEY, Jan. 1, 1892; Child, Jan. 30, 1897; Myrtle MARKEY, June 7, 1890; Paul E. MARKEY, Jan. 10, 1916; Pearl P. MARKEY, Jan. 29, 1898; Robert H. MARKEY, June 20, 1923; William H. MARKEY, July 8, 1944; Margaret E. MARKEY, Jan. 6, 1951; Mattie MARKEY, Oct. 18, 1950; Joseph C. MARKEY, Jan. 17, 1958.

LOT 168-D: Mary E. DIFFY;
M(inerva) MC KINALEY, Sept. 24, 1890; Mary E. DIFFY, Nov. 14, 1900; Alexandra DIFFY, Dec. 21, 1903; Stillborn of Maggie and Jas. MC KINLEY, July 1, 1904; Mary E. MC KINDLEY, Apr. 22, 1911; Jas. A. MC KINDLY, Jan. 30, 1912; Maggie MC KINDLY, Apr. 6, 1915.

LOT 169-D - See LOT 167-D.

LOT 170-D: Lula DARSEY;
Edith L. DARSEY, Oct. 25, 1889; Julia M. LEEF, Sept. 6, 1900; John G. LEEF, June 24, 1911; Benj. F. MILLER, Aug. 31, 1923.

LOT 171-D and 172-D: Erastus B. TUCKER;
Laura H. TUCKER, Sept. 3, 1887; J. L. TUCKER, Mar. 11, 1893; Wm. L. TUCKER, Sept. 1, 1895; Laura TUCKER, Aug. 28, 1913; Robert S. TUCKER, May 22, 1903; Wm. W. TUCKER, July 25, 1922; E. B. TUCKER, Jan. 8, 1923.

LOT 173-D: John F. FERGUSON;
(Myrele VEAYCE), Aug. 4, 1898 (possible disinterred); Howard W. (VENZIE), Apr. 3, 18(9)9, disinterred; Margt. THOMPSON, June 29, 1900; Margt. THOMPSON, July 23, 1902; Harriet N. EARLE, Nov. 5, 1903; Harriet M. FERGUSON, (Jan., June or Nov.) 5, 1903 (13); Mary E. HILL, Feb. 2, 1914; Georgianna FERGUSON, Apr. 23, 1930; John FERGUSON, Nov. 10, 1930; Sarah LEASE, (no date given).

LOT 17-4D: Mary HARDCASTLE;
Elizabeth HARDCASTLE, July 16, 1887.

LOT 175-D: Sarah LEE;
Anson LEE, Aug. 16, 1887.

LOT 176-D: John H. WATERS;
John H. WATERS, June 1, 1908; Eliza WATERS, Nov. 17, 1917; Margaret VanCatt WATERS, May 6, 1935; Joy (no last name given), 1933 (entry crossed out).

LOT 177-D, 179-D, 181-D:
Prudence GORDON, Sept. 30, 1879 (Lot 177-D); Eliza HOFFMAN, Oct. 28, 1880 (Lot 181-D); Freddie D. SANFORD, May 27, 1885 (Lot 179-D); Henry C. PRATT, Mar. 17, 1887 (Lot 179-D); Daniel A. M(ARNEY), Oct. 22, 1888 (Lot 179-D); Daniel A. SANFORD, May 9, 1889 (Lot 179-D); Emeline HOFFMAN, Feb. 24, 1888 (Lot 177-D); Solomon L. MATTHEWS, Dec. 31, 1891 (Lot 179-D); Infant of Ann CRAWFORD, Aug. 22, 1892 (Lot 177-D); Child of Ann CRAWFORD, May 9, 1901 (possible in 181-D); Mary A. BULL(ER)DICK, May 7, 1895 (lot 179-D); Martha E. HOFFMAN, June 29, 1897 (Lot 181-D); John HOFFMAN, Dec. 10, 1920 (Lot 181-D); Daisy E. CRAWFORD, Sept. 23, 1936 (Lot 177-D); Charles H. CRAWFORD, Feb. 10, 1953 (Lot 177-D); Theodora E. BORTON, Sept. 24, 195(3) (Lot 179-D).

LOT 178-D: Robert H. FOGLER;
Robert H. OLIVER, June 30, 1884; Wm. MORTIMER, June 6, 1894; Clarence E. WINKLER, July 20, 1894; Fannie FOGLER, Mar. 16, 1895; Lloyd H. WINKLER, Nov. 18, 1895; Charles E. MORTIMER, Sept. 9, 1896; Charles ABEY, Jan. 10, 1898; Rayjond E. ABEY, Dec. 8, 1889; James H. LANCASTER, July 19, 1900; Janett MORTIMER, June 24, 1901; Mary E. MORTIMER, Oct. 20, 1903; Chas. MORTIMER, Feb. 6, 1(9)05; Emma M. WINKLER, Jan. 28, 1891; Robert H. OLIVER, May 7,

1883 (name appears twice on right side of page); James H. LANCASTER, (no date given).

LOT 179-D: See LOT 177-D

LOT 180-D: John H. FOSS;
Margt. FOSS, June 1, 1886; Louisa S(CHISTER), Dec. 8, 1886; Sarah L. FOSS, Feb. 5, 1901; Infant of Ann H(ORA), Sept. 23, 1901; John H. FOSS, May 3, 1909; Chas. H. FOSS, Apr. 10, 1906; Wm. H. FOSS, May 3, 1916.

LOT 181-D: See Lot 177-D.

LOT 182-D: Thos. KNIGHT;
Greenbury KNIGHT, May 27, 1883; Wm. T. F. KNIGHT, Mar. 28, 1889; Frances A. KNIGHT, June 10, 1890; Sarah KNIGHT, Mar. 18, 1891; Geo. E. FOSS, Dec. 13, 1884; Sarah KNIGHT, Dec. 8, 1902; Geo. F. KNIGHT, Jan. 6, 1916; John H. BRILL, July 29, 1916; Richard BRILL, Aug. 3, 1916.

LOT 183-D: Jos. L. MARSH;
Gladys V. MARSH, Apr. 24, 1909; Wm. C. ST(ROM), Feb. 16, 1900; Minnie V. MARSH, Aug. 30, 1950; Joseph Franlin MARSH, Jan. 1, 1944.

LOT 184-D: Mary FEFEL;
Stillborn of A. & E. MARKLIN, Aug. 28, 1882; Stillborn (NOLOCK, [sic]), June 11, 1883; Infant of A. & J. M. MARK(HEIMER), Feb. 15, 1886; Infant of MARK(HEIMER), Jan. 21, 1888.

LOT 185-D: James COLE;
Wm. Edwd. COLE, July 6, 1877; Jas. COLE, Mar. 15, 1878; Remains from S. B. G., June 27, 1875; James HITZ(IC)BURGER, Mar. 1, 1886; Mary J. PLUM(MER), May 5, 1925; Chas. W. PLUM(MER), Jan. 29, 1935.

LOT 186-D: Lucy A. DUTTON;
Remains from N. B. G., Mar. 11, 1877; Wm. D. DUTTON, Mar. 6, 1905; Louisa DUTTON, June 29, 1917; Fredk. W. DUTTON, Mar. 14, 1928; Donaldson Leroy DUTTON, Nov. 12, 1929; Mathilda DUTTON, July 1, 1946.

LOT 187-D: Agnes A. HE(AF)LEICK;
Abraham MORRISON, Sept. 8, 1884; N. D. MORRISON, Feb. 18, 1886.

LOT 188-D: Mary Ann NACE, transferred to Mary E. EVANS;
"For the burial of Beatrice Evans TURNER;" Stillborn MITCHELL, July 10, 1924; Frank Andrew EVANS, Mar. 31, 1939; John M. N. NACE, June 30, 1899; Henry BYRNE, Aug. 3, 1912; Remains from Northern Burial Ground, Dec. 12, 1876; Mary E. EVANS, Aug. 23, 1937.

LOT 189-D through 196-D: There is no record of these lots in the Lot Book.

LOT 197-D: Mary J. GOLDEN. There is no record of burials having taken place in this lot.

LOT 198-D: James ROBINTSON; Christian APPLE, Apr. 16, 1877.

LOT 199-D: WELMOT & HA(NLIN); Elizabeth WILMOT, Oct. 5, 1878; Elizabeth MC K(ELDIN), Oct. 3, 1899; Nona R. BRYANT, July 23, 1969, born Oct. 23, 1902, died July 19, 1969; William BRYANT, Dec. 15, 1953.

LOT 200-D: Wm. E. KERBY; Chas. KERBY, Sept. 17, 1877; Frances KERBY, Sept. 17, 1877.

LOT 201-D: Matilda MC KNIGHT; Lorenzo A. WRIGHT, Jan. 16, 1861; John A. SHANNON, June 30, 1883; Ida A. SHANNON, Nov. 6, 1885; Geo. M. SHANNON, Oct. 6, 1893.

LOT 202-D: Sarah R. CORDEY; John MC DERMOT, Oct. 1, 1878; Susie MC DERMOT, Jan. 5, 1888; Cath. E. BOWERS, Jan. 4, 1889; Sarah R. CORDEY, June 9, 1888.

LOT 203-D: A. M. FOSTER; Thos. Y. FOSTER, July 8, 1880; A. N. FOSTER, Mar. 26, 1882; Yale FOSTER, July 7, 1892 (possible child); Hamilton MERRYMAN, Sept. 25, 1920, disinterred July 27, 1942 to LOT 101-E.

LOT 204-D: Samuel WALTZ; Annie WALTZ, May 18, 1882; Samuel E. WALTZ, Nov. 17, 1917; Susan WALTZ, Jan. 17, 1925; Grover C. WALTZ, Mar. 24, 1932.

LOT 205-D: Frank BRASHEARS; Mary E. BRASHEARS, July 3, 1884; Grace L. PRICHARD, July 27, 1887; Sallie PRICHARD, Sept. 16, 1899; Mary J. BRASHEARS, Feb. 5, 1912; Chas. F. JUSTICE, Dec. 12, 1912; Artella R. JUSTICE, June 22, 1920; Frank BRASHEARS, Mar. 10, 1924; Neoma JUSTICE, Aug. 10, 1925.

LOT 206-D: Robert EARECKSON. Remains from Greenmount Cemetery, Sept. 19, 1883.

LOT 207-D: Thos. E. CANBY; Ann V. CANBY, Dec. 11, 1894; Thos. E. CANBY, Jan. 4, 1904; Alice V. WENDLER, July 9, 1936; Harry B. WENDLER, Apr. 10, 1946.

LOT 208-D: Rich. H. JORDAN; Mary L. JORDAN, Oct. 9, 1884; Maud L. JORDAN, Nov. 6, 1893; Tillie BABB, July 11, 1894; Agnes F. FOIL, Dec. 12, 1903; Infant of JORDAN, Oct. 8, 1904; Edwd. E. STEVENS, Aug. 15, 1905; Stillborn of Minnie COBIN, Apr. 20, 1908; Philip R. STEPHENS, July (23), 1908; Jas. COATES, Aug. 1, 1908; Elizabeth JORDAN, July 24, 1914; Stillborn of Rich. and Helen JORDAN, Aug. 24, 1916; Rich. H. JORDEN, April 1, 1919; Minnie R(OZETTA), Apr. 10, 1926; Minnie COBIN, (no date given); Richard T. JORDON, May 21, 1946.

LOT 209-D: Henrietta WHITEFORD; Jas. H. WHITEFORD, July 23, 1888; Wallace J. WHITEFORD, Aug. 1, 1907; Beatrice I. W(AIN), Feb. 26, 1935; Charles E. SULLIVAN, July 21, 1951.

LOT 210-D: Sarah A. LARDUSKEY;
Rachel HARTLEY, June 30, 1887; Stillborn of Albert LARDUSKEY,
Mar. 19, 1907; Sarah A. LARDUSKEY, Feb. 1, 1910.

LOT 211-D: Jacob TRE(ULT)E;
Maggie C. TR(EULT)E, July 18, 1889; Nicholas TRE(UTL)E, Apr. 14,
1891; John T. TEU(LTE), June 19, 1891.

LOT 212-D: Geo. C. F. DRANSOFF;
Laura M. DRANSOFF, Mar. 20, 1888; (Stillborn of) Effie and John
FABOR, Oct. 23, 1897; Effie I. FABOR, Nov. 9, 1897.

LOT 213-D: Jacob KNIGHT;
Otto D. FREEMAN, Feb. 20, 1892; Andrew ROSMAN, Oct. 17, 1898;
Agnes WALTON, Mar. 3, 1909; Ann ROSMAN, Jan. 31, 1910; Margt.
WALKER, Aug. 19, 1912; Emma WALTON, Oct. 5, 1891.

LOT 214-D: Sarah E. THAW;
Samuel THAW, Oct. 1, 1891.

LOT 215-D: George (UHRBROCK);
Kate M. (UKRBROCK), June 23, 1889; Jas. F. (UKRBROCK), June 24,
1889.

LOT 216-D: W. T. RILEY;
Mabel V. RILEY, Apr. 8, 1890; Myrtle B. RILEY, Feb. 12, 1892;
Grace N. RILEY, July 26, 1894; Wm. T. RILEY, July 17, 1915;
Elizabeth RILEY, Dec. 12, 1945.

LOT 217-D: Maria and Louise CROWLEY;
J. B. CROWLEY, Feb. 11, 1891; (W)illie M. SHEARER, Aug. 25, 1914
(first name may also be Millie or Nellie); Maria L. SHEARER,
Sept. 14, 1914; John J. SHEARER, Jan. 1, 1922.

LOT 218-D: Ebenezer RILEY;
Martha Jane RILEY, Sept. 27, 1926; Ebenezer RILEY, Jan. 30, 1929.

LOT 219-D: Annie M. ARMSTRONG;
Theodore ARMSTRONG, Sept. 2, 1903; Wm. H. ARMSTRONG, Aug. 7,
1906; Chas. E. ARMSTRONG, Feb. 4, 1904; Mary A. ARMSTRONG, May
13, 1892; Rich'd ARMSTRONG, Jan. 9, 1933; Louise K. ARMSTRONG,
Mar. 17, 1934.

LOT 220-D: Robt. W. WHALAND;
Mabel H. ZIMMERMAN, July 16, 1909; Robert M. WHALAND, Sept. 23,
1914; Charles H. STOWMAN, Sr., July 9, 1963; Gertrude E. STOWMAN,
born May 28, 1879, died June 7, 1970. Funeral home - Singleton.

LOT 221-D: Samuel APPELBY;
Susan APPELBY, July 23, 1893; Rebecca APPELBY, June 26, 1889;
Saml. F. APPELBY, Aug. 16, 1913; Saml. APPELBY, May 31, 1917;
Charlotte APPELBY, May 18, 1918.

LOT 222-D: Geo. E. HUTTON;
Louis E. HUTTON, May 23, 1893; John G. HUTTON, June 25, 1897;
(Cenelinel) HUTTON, May 13, 1898; Edwin HUTTON, June 11, 1900.

LOT 223-D: Frances (N.) GEORGE;
Maria L. GEORGE, Mar. 14, 1894; Jas. DONOVAN, Feb. 5, 1902; Annie B. GEORGE, Feb. 4, 1902.

LOT 223 1/2-D: Alice FOIL;
Domingo FOIL, Jan. 28, 1907; Alice A. FOIL, Nov. 13, 1915.

LOT 224-D: John T. MUNN, "Feb. 15, 1918 bought 2 feet to north."; Violet B. ROSS, Mar. 13, 1895; Wm. H. ROSS, Jan. 4, 1896; Emma S. MUNN, May 23, 1903; Baby MUNN, Feb. 2, 1914; Danl. H. MUNN, Nov. 10, 1916; Mary MUNN, Jan. 28, 1918; John T. MUNN, Mar. 5, 1924.

LOT 225-D through 234-D: There is no record of these lots in the Lot Book.

LOT 235-D: Nellie CRUM;
Martha A. RUARK, Nov. 20, 1890; Bessie BLACK, July 16, 1901; Helen LOLBEHUSEN, Apr. 5, 1902; Marie SIMONT, Feb. 26, 1913; Wm. ROURKE, Feb. 5, 1917; Jose. STEFFEE, Feb. 31 [sic], 1930; Frederick FARLEY, June 12, 1941.

LOT 236-D: Jessie JACKSON;
Jessie R. JACKSON, June 22, 1888; Florence JACKSON, Aug. 27, 1887; Walter L. JACKSON, Aug. 16, 1899; Child, Sept. 9, 1899; Infant of T. & J. RAWLINGS, July 23, 1900; Wm. J. BROWN, July 22, 1904.

LOT 237-D: Mary L. CROUCH;
Geo. E. WINCHESTER, Nov. 16, 1888, disinterred; Roy WINCHESTER, Jan. 21, 18(97), disinterred; Martha E. MURRY, June 26, 1901; Robert C. RUSSELL, Oct. 1, 1907; (Wm. M.) CROUCH, Jan. 8, 1888; Lilian M. CROUCH, Oct. 15, 1918; Mary L. BULL, Apr. 3, 1926; Mary CROUCH children, (no date, the words Mary and children are lined out).

LOT 238-D: Sarah F. BARTHALOW;
John R. DUDLEY, Mar. 28, 1887; Wm. H. DUDLEY, Aug. 13, 1889; Marion C. DUDLEY, Feb. 11, 1901; Raymond L. BARTHLOW, Dec. 19, 1906; Mary F. MC GREERY, Nov. 29, 1906; Oney L. BARTHLOW, Nov. 29, 1906; Fannie BARTHLOW, Mar. 25, 1918.

LOT 239-D: Louisa DORSEY;
Ch(as.) HIGGINS, Aug. 29, 1887; Ethel HIGGINS, Dec. 11, 1897; Wm. T. DORSEY, Apr. 11, 1898; Wm. T. DORSEY, Oct. 5, 1897; Mary A. JONES, Mar. 18, 1905; Thos. R. DORSEY, Aug. 6, 1886; Louisa DORSEY, Nov. 14, 1912; Mary E. HIGGINS, Dec. 2, 1932.

LOT 240-D: Florence RISTON;
Mary L. RISTON, Mar. 3, 1884; Child of A. & E. LONHARDT, Nov. 11, 1889; Margt. C. LEANEY, Jan. 27, 1888.

LOT 241-D: Mary J. LYONS;
Lizzie LYONS, Jan. 25, 1884; Elanor WILLIAMS, Feb. 5, 1884; Rosanna LUDWIG, June 28, 1898; Estell GRIFFIN, Oct. 2, 1905; Mary J. LYONS, July 1, 1912; Frederick LUDWIG, Dec. 31, 1925.

LOT 242-D: Charles JACOBI and Eliz. JACOBI;
Elizabeth JACOBI, Jan. 22, 1887; Chas. L. JACOBI, May 31, 1895.

LOT 243-D: Theodore L. MARTIN;
Wm. MARTIN, Dec. 23, 1882; Wm. MARTIN, Feb. 14, 1883; James
WILLIAMS, Apr. 18, 1884; Rosa A. MARTIN, May 4, 1905; Florince L.
MARTIN, Mar. 13, 191(0).

LOT 224-D: Sophie DOSS;
Margt. RAYCKHO(S)LI, Aug. 18, 1887; Sophia DOSS, Mar. 11, 1890.

LOT 245-D: Mary A. W(IE)DEFELD;
Removed from N. B. G., Nov. 25, 1878; Thos. W(IE)DEFELD, June 1,
1803; Carrie R. PRIN(C)E, Mar. 1, 1884 (possible spelled PRESUE);
Jas. Y. AMOS, Aug. 11, 1888; Chas. E. AMOS, Jan. 2(3), 1896,
disinterred; Evelyn AMOS, July 15, 1895; Chas. E. AMOS, May 4,
1898; Hannah C. AMOS, Jan. 28, 1898.

LOT 246-D: Sm. H. SMITH;
Wm. H. SMITH, Mar. 23, 1897; Esther SMITH, Dec. 1, 1907; Elizabeth P. SMITH, Aug. 8, 1936; Jennie F. SMITH, Dec. 7, 1943; Harry
P. SMITH, June 4, 1948.

LOT 247-D: John H. FERGUSON;
Margt. A. FERGUSON, Feb. 8, 1882; Jos. HILL, Aug. 27, 1888; Sarah
B. ROBINSON, Dec. 29, 1888; Geo. A. ROBINSON, Feb. 5, 1891; Wm.
F. LEASE, July 5, 1893; Geo. N. W. FERGUSON, Feb. 11, 1888; John
T. FERGUSON, June 6, 1932.

LOT 248-D: William J. POTEE;
Ann Maria FITZGERALD, Oct. 10, 1881; William POTEE, Mar. 9, 1897;
Laura V. RIDGWAY, Feb. 9, 1900; Mammie M. POTEE, Jan. 12, 1901;
Stillborn of John and Mary POTEE, July 31, 1920; Wm. H. (M)ORAN,
Mar. 25, 1903, disinterred; Wm. H. (M)ORAN, Oct. 17, 1910, disinterred and reinterred in LOT-177-B; N. G. POTEE, (no date given);
Rena J. POTEE, (no date given); William J. POTEE, Jan. 27, 1944.

LOT 249-D: Mary C. FANTON;
Susan E. FANTON, Sept. 14, 1896; Ja. H.FANTON, May 8, 1902; Jas.
M. FANTON, Nov. 11, 1912.

LOT 250-D: William HARRIS;
Grace B. HARRIS, Dec. 7, 1878; Edward HARRIS, Mar. 7, 1884;
Barbara E. HARRIS, Mar. 21, 1884; Elizabeth BUSHMILLER, July 27,
1892; Albert B. HARRIS, Feb. 13, 1894; Lee M. HARRIS, Nov. 26,
1899; Stillborn of A. and E. HARRIS, Mar. 13, 1902; Annie M.
HARRIS, Feb. 2,1924; (Wm.) J. HARRIS, Sept. 16, 1925; Nellie A.
HARRIS, Aug. 19, 1929; Gertrude Rose HARRIS, Dec. 2, 1931.

LOT 251-D: Barbara A. MOHLER;
Marion M. MYERS, Mar. 4, 1886.

LOT 252-D: Elwood MATHERS;
Jos. M. MATHERS, Aug. 14, 1877; John WHITE(HURST), May 19, 1883;
Elwood MATHERS, Feb. 13, 1899; Sophie MATHERS, Nov. 9, 1902;
Erasmus E. MATHERS, Jan. 5, 1921; Clarissa G. LUMLEY, Aug. 7,
1936.

LOT 253-D through 260-D: There is no record of these lots in the
Lot Book.

LOT 261-D: Lawrence BLACKMAN, OSSMAN and (?URRICK);
Julius BLACKMAN, Oct. 6, 1879; Dorothea (?URRICK), Nov. 24, 1884;
Elsie I. BLACKMAN, May 23, 1916; Julius BLACKMAN, Oct. 6, 1879;
Chas. BLACKMAN, Oct. 14, 1879; Eliz. OSSMAN, Oct. 11, 1890;
Lawrence BLACKMAN, Nov. 11, 1902; Lawrence BLACKMAN, Oct. 15,
1887; Elizabeth L. BLACKMAN, July 11, 1931. There is also an
entry with no date which appears to be Rose L(illegible)
BLACKMAN.

LOT 262-D: Florence BRADLEY;
Ethel BOSEMAN, Sept. 16, 1898; Florence E. BRADLEY, May 3, 1900;
Melvina BOSEMAN, Dec. 14, 1906; Ida H. ELLIOTT, Mar. 9, 1917.

LOT 263-D: There is no record in the Lot Book for this lot.

LOT 264-D: Joseph LOANE;
Elnor B. S(ER)EENY, Dec. 26, 1877; Chas. MATHEWS, Nov. 28, 1879;
Chas. W. WEBB, Jan. .11, 1881; Edwin C. R(AN)GHT(ER), Sept. 29,
1881; Richard F. CLARK, Aug. 5, 1881; Infant of COUNCIL, Oct. 20,
1881; Infant of Chas. WILSON, Oct. 16, 1882; Lillie WINDLE, Aune
25, 1883; Maggie COUNCIL, July 18, 1883; Stillborn of NOLAN, Apr.
3, 1884; Edna M. LOANE, Nov. 9, 1892.

LOT 265-D: Edward BUNCE;
Remains from N. B. G., June 11, 1898; Geo. Edw. BUNCE, Aug. 13,
1878; Jane BUNCE, Apr. 6, 1895; Edward BUNCE, Jan. 19, 1901;
Hester BUNCE, Dec. 9, 1910; Elizabeth BUNCE, Oct. 10, 1914.

LOT 266-D: Charity A. CU(RR)ILL;
Robt. L. THOMPSON, Dec. 13, 1800; Willie CU(RR)ILL, Jan. 5, 1885;
Sarah J. HITCHCOCK, May 1, 1898; Saml. CU(RR)ILL, Sept. 14, 1906;
Remains from N. B. G., Nov. 9, 1877; Charity A. CU(RR)ILL, Jan.
27, 1898; Robt. CU(RR)ILL, Oct. 10, 1924; Sarah E. CU(RR)ILL,
Dec. 8, 1924.

LOT 267-D: Richard BUNCE;
Frank STAYLOR, Nov. 4, 1886; Richard BUNCE, July 1, 1898; Sarah
BUNCE, May 15, 1889; Margt. STAYLOR, Feb. 7, 1900; Gilson E.
PATTERSON, June 11, 1900; Jas. PATTERSON, July 26, 1911; Wm. G.
PATTERSON, May 31, 1915; Geo. L. BUNCE, Oct. 4, 1918; Annie
BUNCE, Oct. 9, 1918; Olive and Olive C. BUNCE, Oct. 25, 1918;
Emma S. DERTRAM, Apr. 2, 1919; Mary C. MYERS, June 25, 1920;
Chas. W. PATTERSON, May 28, 1921.

LOT 268-D: Joseph ARO (throughout name may also be ARD or ARS);
Remains from N. B. G., May 24, 1877; Jas. H. ARO, Oct. 10, 1877;
Stillborn of Jas. ARO, Oct. 29, 1878; Mary ARO, Jan. 10, 1885;
Joseph ARO, May 14, 1906; Cecelia M. ARO, Jan. 12, 1923.

LOT 269-D: Mary Ann HUGHES;
Remains from N. B. G., Jan. 17, 1879; Mary M. BAYLISS, May 18,
1895; Mary Ann HUGHES, Apr. 30, 1900; Wm. BAYLISS, Jan. 11, 1901;
James REILEY, Mar. 19, 1905; Minnie E. NORTON, Jan. 3, 1946.

LOT 270-D: Joseph BURKHARDT;
Cath. FRANIE, Apr. 25, 1877 (name may also be FRAME); Eliz.
BURKHARDT, Apr. 6, 1907; Joseph BURKHARDT, May 21, 1907; Robert
JOHNSON, Jan. 30, 1910.

LOT 271-D: Margaret LOTZ and Anna M. O'CONNELL;
Nicholas LOTZ, Mar. 8, 1883; John W. WATSON, Aug. 13, 1886; Wm.
O. CONNELL, July 13, 1893; Alfred G. WATSON, Mar. 6, 1894; Thos.
C. WATSON, Jan. 17, 1898; Connal LOTZ, Jan. 14, 1905; Maggie
WATSON, Aug. 4, 1905; Margt. LOTZ, Oct. 24, 1887.

LOT 272-D: Elizabeth MITCHELL;
Remains from N. B. G., Mar. 1, 1877; Stillborn, July 16, 1880;
Rebecca MITCHELL, May 17, 1883; Eliz A. MITCHELL, Sept. 10, 1883;
Jas. H. MITCHELL, Aug. 17, 1897; Margt. I. TAYLOR, Nov. 6, 1908;
Geo. MITCHELL, Nov. 24, 1928; Sophia (CONNOLY), (no date given).

LOT 273-D: Louis R. MEAD;
Louisa MEAD, Dec. 17, 1890; Emma R. MEAD, Oct. 9, 1896; Louis R.
MEAD, June 12, 1902.

LOT 274-D: Sarah SMITH;
Remains from N. B. G., May 3, 1877; Alice V. HARRISS, Apr. 29,
1882; Sarah SMITH, Sept. 22, 1884; Mary J. SMITH, Aug. 15, 1895;
FIZGERALD, (no first name or date given).

LOT 275-D: Chas. L. WISE;
Sarah WISE, Mar. 16, 1882; John L. WISE, May 23, 1885; Chas. L.
WISE, Jan. 1, 1922.

LOT 276-D: Andrew and Rebecca KOONS;
Helen KOONS, Dec. 20, 1880; Henry A. BENNER, Nov. 17, 1903;
Milton O. BUCKINGHAM, July 9, 1904; Alfred A. BUCKINGHAM, July
17, 1913; Andrew KOONS, Aug. 5, 1915; Rebecca E. KOONS, Mar. 14,
1916; Alice E. BUCKINGHAM, Aug. 7, 1917; Wm. L. BUCKINGHAM, Feb.
6, 1919; Alice L. KOONS, Jan. 13, 1949.

LOT 277-D: Ann PERKINS;
Stillborn, June 14, 1879; Sarah GIBSON, Nov. 20, 1891.

LOT 278-D: Rebecca KERHOLTZ "(corrected to KIELHOLTZ)";
Geo. W. KERHOLTZ, May 18, 1889; Rebecca KERHOLTZ, Dec. 31, 1895;
Alice L. KERHOLTZ, May 18, 1896; Geo. C. KIELHOLTZ, Aug. 14,
1953, (the name Chas. V. has been lined out.); Virginia KIEL-
HOLTZ, Mar. 5, 1958.

LOT 279-D through 298-D: There is no record in the Lot Book for
these lots.

LOT 299-D: Christian STAGGE;
Christian STAGGE, July 3, 1904; Wm. J. STAGGE, July 13, 1914;
Louisa STAGGE, Dec. 16, 1916; Christian H. STAGGE, Ap;r. 5, 1924;
Frank W. STAGGE, 1900.

LOT 300-D: A. L. JOHNSON;
Laura JOHNSON, Jan. 4, 1896; A. A. JOHNSON, Nov. 18, 1907; Stillborn of C. JOHNSON, Apr. 16, 1909; Andrew JOHNSON, Mar. 1, 1915;
Infant of JOHNSON, Sept. 23, 1918; Frederick E. REDEL(IUS), Jan.
11, 192(6); Andrew A. JOHNSON, Dec. 29, 1949.

LOT 301-D: Geo. S. WRIGHT;
Georgie E. WRIGHT, Aug. 26, 1885; Geo. S. WRIGHT, June 26, 1893;
Noris WILSON, Mar. 11, 1907; Jas. W. ALLEN, Oct. 7, 1891; Fannie

E. WRIGHT, Aug. 27, 1901; Lula E. GRIPP, Dec. 27, 1948; Louis GRIPP, Dec. 23, 1958.

LOT 302-D: Peter ALLEN;
Emma E. PRICE, Aug. 22, 1885 (entry crossed out); Mamie V. ALLEN, Apr. 21, 1888; Kirk ALLEN, Sept. 30, 1899; Fannie M. ALLEN, Aug. 22,1885; Lawrence ALLEN, July 29, 1918; Mary A. ALLEN, July 2, 1923; Peter ALLEN, June 17, 1932; Robert G. ALLEN, Feb. 5, 1937.

LOT 303-D: Alice HEATH;
Alfred A. HEATH, July 3, 1885; Ethel HEATH, Feb. 13, 1907; Alie HEATH, May 12, 1926; Richard Roy HEATH, Feb. 4, 1948; Margaret E. HEATH, Oct. 16, 1950.

LOT 304-D: Catherine SKINNER, Mrs. Beulah SKINNER of Baltimore, Md.;
Mary SKINNER, May 7, 1898; Thos. W. SKINNER,Nov. 22, 1892; Leonard (O.) SKINNER, July 29, 1913; Leonard O. SKINNER, Nov. 4, 1897; Howard P. SKINNER, Sept. 9, 1944.

LOT 305-D: Abraham MADE;
Mary E. SLADE, Dec. 7, 1872; Willie SLADE, Dec. 14, 1882; John A. SLADE, Dec. 19, 1882.

LOT 306-D: Ellen NICHOLSON;
Thos. NICHOLSON, Nov. 26, 1879; John R. NICHOLSON, Oct. 23, 1922; Ellen NICHOLSON, June 25, 1926; Isabelle MILLER, Jan. 8, 1940.

LOT 307-D: Eli D. HOWARD;
Remains from N. B. G., Nov. 3, 1878.

LOT 308-D: Rev. W. L. MC DOWELL and Anna R.;
Garrison SEWELL, from N. B. G., June 1877; William A. SEWELL, from N. B. G., June 1877; Geo. Washington SEWELL, from N. B. G., June 1877; Garrison SEWELL, 1857; Willhelmna SEWELL, 1835; Geo. W. SEWELL, 1838.

LOT 309-D: Harriett M. KLA(U)K;
Geo. W. KE(M)P, Dec. 12, 1919; (Mrs.) Joshua TOWSON, (no date given).

LOT 310-D: Wesley B. STEVERS;
Willie F. STEVERS, Jan. 1, 1885; Harry D. STEVERS, Dec. 12, 1885; Wesley W. STEVERS, Apr. 2, 1896; Wesley STEVERS, Oct. 22, 1900; Samuel STEVERS, Oct. 22, 1900; Emma C. STEVERS, May 7, 1938.

LOT 311-D: L. E. AIVEY;
Remains of John CO(R)EL and family, Aug. 26, 1877; Howard (V.) WILLEN, May 13, 1896; Louisa E. AIVEY, Oct. 26, 1901; Samuel J. WILLEN, July 7, 1913.

LOT 312-D: Geo. R. (C)LOKER;
Infant of A. M. ALBAUGH, May 14, 1897; Helen E. ALBOUGH, Aug. 1, 1899; Mary A. CLOKER, Mar. 10, 1882; Robert A. HENNING, Feb. 23, 1920.

LOT 313-D: Eliza KEIGLER;
Remains from N. B. G., Oct. 20, 1877; Alice CULLUM, Dec. 27,

1880; Georgana KEIGLER, Apr. 15, 1907; Mary E. LOWERY, July 21, 1911; Wm. K. (LOWERY), Mar. 9, 1929.

LOT 314-D: Margt. A. DOWNS;
John A. DOWNS, Sept. 18, 1905; Eliz. M. DOWNS, July 25, 1906; M. A. MILLER, Feb. 15, 1919; Harry (A.) DOWNS, Oct. 5, 1929; Wm. MC MAINES, G. A. R. (no date given); Carroll DOWNS, Aug. 3, 1903; Hugh ALLEN, Oct. 8, 1801.

LOT 315-D: Thos. CHILDS;
Infant of ROUNEY, June 10, 1891; Annie NEUMAN, (Oct. 28, 1914); Stillborn of CHILDS, Aug. 4, 1893; Eliz NEUMAN, Dec. 17, 1850.

LOT 316-D: Mary E. JAMAR;
Thos. PORTER, May 7, 1878; Cath. A. PORTER, June 23, 1882; Mary Elizabeth JAMER, Dec. 21, 1927.

LOT 317-D through 324-D: There are no records in the Lot Books for these lots.

LOT 325-D: George H. GILL;
George Cooper GILL, 1856; Providence GILL, 1820; John Price GILL, 1825 and children.

LOT 326-D: John T. ROTE;
Jacob K(NI)FE, Dec. 25, 1880; Jos. M. ROTE, Mar. 29, 1886; John T. ROTE, Jan. 11, 1894.

LOT 327-D: Mary Ann GIFFIN;
Removed from N. B. G. (2 bodies) Dec. 12, 1877; Wm. A. BURMAN, Oct. 17, 1884; Elmer BURMAN, Nov. 1, 1884; Nellie C. BURMAN, Feb. 11, 1887; Mary A. GRIFFITH, Apr. 29, 1877; Geo. L. BURMAN, Apr. 14, 1889; Frank GIFFIN, Aug. 23, 1920; Thos. R. GIFFIN, Sept. 1, 1924; G. M. GIFFIN, (no date given).

LOT 328-D: Henry CREICHTON;
Mary D. JACKSON, June 20, 1919; Frances E. COLLISON, Oct. 2, 1937.

LOT 329-D: Oliver T. SMITH;
Albert SMITH, Jan. 10, 1881; Bertie G. SMITH, Sept. 14, 1893; Effie D. ANDERSON, Sept. 6, 1898; Oliver T. SMITH, Oct. 4, 1912; Delia H. SMITH, Dec. 23, 1914; Stillborn of RAYMOND, Mar. 26, 1927; Daniel F. HALL, Sept. 17, 1949; Melva M. HALL, June 8, 1948.

LOT 330-D: Mary J. SMITH;
Eliz L. MARRIOTT, July 1(6), 1883.

LOT 331-D: Rebecca SMITH;
Chas. (W.) JONES, June 13, 1879; Edgar W. JONES, July 16, 1887; Harriet R. JONES, Dec. 29, 1911; Infant of BOYD, May 5, 1928; J. Wesley JONES, Aug. 15, 1898.

LOT 332-D: Mary W. LEWIS:
Kendel M. LEWIS, Dec. 15, 1856; Ann A. LEWIS, Apr. 21, 1860; Amanda LEWIS, Apr. 10, 1895; Elizabeth E. LEWIS, Aug. 9, 1896; Mary W. LEWIS, Jan. 2, 1902.

LOT 333-D: Geo. MATTHEWS;
Helen MATTHEWS, Nov. 11, 1879; Geo. R. MATHEWS, May 29, 1916; Lina B. MATTHEWS, Mar. 26, 1937.

LOT 334-D: Jas. H. MC QUIGG;
Rebecca MC QUIGG, Dec. 30, 1881; Annie MC QUIGG, July 4, 1883; Robt. MC QUIGG, Jan. 4, 1883; Martha A. MC QUIGG, Oct. 26, 1896.

LOT 335-D: Winchester R. BRODWATER;
Joshua BOND, Apr. 7, 1890, disinterred; James E. STRONG, Sept. 13, 1897, disinterred; Joshua BOND, Aug. 3, 1902; James BEAUCHAMP, Sept. 21, 1890 (entry lined out); Raymond BROADWATER, Dec. 1, 1890; Chas. G. BROADWATER, July 2(5), 189(2); Ruth M. BROADWATER, July 22, 1895; Eliza J. BOND, Feb. 27, 1918; Chas. M. BR(AN)T(USTER), Nov. 13, 1918 (in the right of the page the name is BROADWATER).

LOT 336-D: George CASSELL;
Laura L. CASSELL, Mar. 26, 1883; Geo. W. CASSELL, Aug. 10, 1900; Emma E. CASSELL, Mar. 8, 1929.

LOT 337-D: John T. D. MYERS and Chas. W. CRAIGG;
Mary C. MYERS, Apr. 18, 1884; Walter CRAIGG, Sept. 15, 1921; Wm. (R.) GREG(ORY); Oct. 16, 1925.

LOT 338-D: Margt. WHITEHAM;
Laura WHITEHORN, Mar. 18, 1884; Ella L. WHITEHORN, July 12, 1884; Margt. WHITEHORN, Dec. 17, 1884; Emily L. WHITEHORN, Oct. 9, 1889; Revere WHITEHORN, Aug. 12, 1896 disinterred Sept. 14, 1910; Charlotte WHITEHORNE, June 6, 1921.

LOT 339-D: Danl. JAMISON, Jr.;
John JAMMISON, Jan. (14), 1891; Maud MILLER, June 20, 1901; Etta May JAMISON, June 24, 1892; Mary M. MILLER, Aug. 24, 1929.

LOT 340-D: Jacob HAGER;
Mary O. HAGER, Dec. 11, 1887; Eva HAGER, Mar. 8, 1892; Rose HAGER, July 17, 1897; Jacob E. HAGER, Oct. 10, 1872; Jacob HAGER, May 31, 1911; Annie D. HAGER, (no date given); (Carrie) HAGER, (no date given).

LOT 341-D: Geo. LITTLE;
Bessie LITTLE, Oct. 17, 1887; Virginia A. WHEELER, Dec. 8, 1901; Lucy M. LITTLE, Oct. 11, 1913; Wm. H. LITTLE, Apr. 18, 1916; Lydie J. VOLA(N)DT, Dec. 26, 1919.

LOT 342-D: Geo. MYERLY;
Geo. C. MYERLY, Oct. 10, 1887; Geo. P. MYERLY, Jan. 2, 1896; Blanch HULL, Aug. 2, 1899; David HULL, May 27, 1907; Frank J. D(IE)TZ(WAY), Dec. 26, 1933; I(riour) M(ARSLEY), Sept. 24, 1934, disinterred to (Louden Park?) March or May 1 of 12, 1935; Anna Barbara DIETZWAY, Aug. 9, 1941.

LOT 343-D through 352-D: There are no records for these lots in the Lot Book.

LOT 353-D: James MC MULLEN;
Wm. T. MC MULLEN, Oct. 3, 1892; Wm. H. BRAISILL, July 5, 1893;

James MC MULLEN, Sept. 15, 1900; Saml. COLLINS, Jan. 25, 1904; Annie M. COLLINS, May 21, 1904; Rudolph RILEY, May 31, 1908.

LOT 354-D: Mary C. ELKINS;
Wm. H. ELKINS, Apr. 4, 1898; Laura ELKINS, Feb. 4, 1891; Wm. Oliver ELKINS, Jan. 17, 1903; Robt. L. ELKINS, Mar. 11, 1904; Margt. ELKINS, May 16, 1903; Baby GRAHAM, Mar. 6, 1937.

LOT 355-D: Saml. B. DORSEY;
Sarah R. DORSEY, July 27, 1896; Louis C. JONES, Apr. 14, 1908; Kate E. CONNER, Mar. 20, 1908; Infant of Emma COURTNEY, Jan. 25, 1913.

LOT 356-D: Wm. CROSBY;
(A.) CROSBY, Dec. 19, 1891; Sarah E. CROSBY, Mar. 1, 1899; John BARNES, Apr. 10, 1917.

LOT 357-D: August JAEGER;
Aug. JAEGER, Nov. 30, 1896; August JAEGER, Jr., July 23, 1906; Bertha JAEGER, Feb. 5, 1917; Wm. JAEGER, Oct. 23, 1911.

LOT 358-D: Thos. NEWTON;
Thos. NEWTON, Sept. 5, 1892; Mary NEWTON, May 15, 1891 (on the right of the page she is said to have died April 13, 1891.)

LOT 359-D: Daniel W. DORSEY;
Wm. W. DORSEY, May 18, 1887; Danl. W. DORSEY, May 15, 1914; Jane R. DORSEY, Apr. 17, 1919.

LOT 360-D: Martin FURY (FUEHRER);
Florence and Edna FURY, child underneath, Mar. 27, 1886.

LOT 361-D: Belle SMITH;
Edwd. CHAMBERLINE, Oct. 26, 1889; Thos. H. SMITH, Mar. 12, 1908; Isabella C. SMITH, Mar. 13, 1928.

LOT 362-D: Wm. LOVE;
Remains of child from St. Peters (Cemetery), Sept. 12, 1885; Grace May JONES, Feb. 7, 1891; David FREEBERGER, Oct. 9, 1891; Catherine LOVE, Dec. 14, 1892; Mary A. LOVE, Jan. 22, 1893; Wm. A. LOVE, Mar. 25, 1899; Wm. LOVE, Jan. 7, 1902; Mary LOVE, Oct. 12, 1903; Annie V. LOVE, Nov. 8, 1906.

LOT 363-D: Emma SHIVERS;
Wm. A. SHIVERS, Feb. 18, 1893; E. Nillie SHIVERS, Feb. 13, 1905; Nicholes SHIVERS, Sept. 16, 1873.

LOT 364-D: Samuel C. CASSELL;
Remains, July 31, 18(8)3; Martener C. GRIFFITH, Dec. 24, 1891 (This may in fact be Mortemer.); Saml. C. CASSELL, Oct. 8, 1892; Alice GRIFFITH, Nov. 30, 1894; Emory GRIFFITH, May 28, 1910; Mary J. B. GRIFFITH, May 19, 1923.

LOT 365-D: Henry FROCKLING;
Jessie B. FROCKLING, Jan. 10, 1881; Nicholas SHRIVER, Sept. 10, 1883.

LOT 366-D: Joseph DEVLIN;
Jos. DEVLIN, June 7, 1916; Amelia F. DEVLIN, May 24, 1917; Howard Carter DEVLIN, July 19, 1946.

LOT 367-D through 369-D: Randolph EVANS;
Randolph EVANS, Sept. 4, 1882; Laura EVANS, Nov. 26, 1901; Dr. James E. GAULIN, Dec. 6, 1915; Randolph Elmer EVANS, July 19, 1938; Stillborn of BLAMBERG, May 22, 1945 (This burial authorized by Mrs. Thos. DAVIS.); Mary Evans GAULINE, Aapr. 26, 1941; Remains from N. B. G., (no date given).

LOT 368-D: Thos. A. WEEMS;
Geo. E. MATTHEWS, Oct. 28, 1884; C. H. W. WEEMS, Mar. 4, 1890; Stillborn of WEEMS, Mar. 29, 1893; Theopolis N. WEEMS, Aug. 4, 1894; Margt. B. SMITH, Jan. 12, 1915.

LOT 369-D: See LOT 367-D.

LOT 370-D: John P. JACOBS;
Flora JACOBS, Nov. 9, 1877; Annie M. JACOBS, Oct. 10, 1879; John P. JACOBS, Oct. 23, 1890; Geo. W. HOWARD, Oct. 2, 1896; Stillborn of H. C. HOWARD, July 21, 1897; Mary C. JACOBS, Sept. (19), 1898; Stillborn of Ella and Geo. HOWARD, Mar. 16, 1908; Child of Geo. HOWARD, Robert J. HOWARD, Dec. 9, 1903; Saml. A. HOWARD, May 10, 1904; Ellen (E.) HOWARD, Jan. 1, 1916; Stillborn of Geo. HOWARD, Sept. 25, 1902.

LOT 371-D: Louis PASQUAY;
William F. PASQUAY, (no date given).

LOT 372-D: M. V. B. WACHTEL;
Remains from N. B. G., (no date given).

LOT 373-D: Clara HAMILTON;
"Remains from Country," Nov. 22, 1882; Remains of child, Nov. 26, 1891; Sarah ARNOLD, Oct. 1, 1914; Achsah E. TREADWAY, Oct. 23, 1925.

LOT 374-D: Saml. REDGRAVE;
Sadie H. REDGRAVE, Sept. 13, 1892; Doris FABER, Jan. 30, 1913; Saml. B. REDGRAVE, May 17, 1917; Sarah L(OU)REY, Dec. 10, 1917; Jas. A. REDGRAVE, Oct. 26, 1926; Ida V. REDGRAVE, Sept. 8, 1956.

LOT 375-D through 382-D: There are no records in the Lot Book for these lots.

LOT 383-D: Margaret CHILD;
Remains from N. B. G., Mar. 30, 1877.

LOT 384-D: William CARPENTER;
Walter BROWN, June 19, 1890; Infant of MARTIN, Nov. 11, 1893; Norman R. BAKER, Jan. 30, 1900.

LOT 385-D and 389-D: John SHECKLES. No burials recorded in this lot.

LOT 386-D: John and Eliz. WHEAT;
John A. WHEAT, Oct. 7, 1903; Elizabeth D. WHEAT, Mar. 31, 1916; Alice E. WHEAT, Apr. 4, 1925; Clara WHEAT, June 10, 1940.

LOT 387-D: There is no record in the Lot Book for this lot.

LOT 388-D: Sarah MC CAULEY;
Removed from N. B. G. Apr. 24, 1878; Chas. F. MC CAULEY, June 27, 1880; Sarah MC CAULEY, June 20, 1899; Emma MC CAULEY, Oct. 21, 1918.

LOT 389-D: Mr. F. J. BEVAN;
Remains from N. B. G., Juy 18, 1877.

LOT 390-D: Isabel FLYNN;
Remains from N. B. G., Sept. 27, 1877; Isabel FLYNN, Feb. 13, 1888; Elliott D. NOLLEY, June 20, 1942; Leonard B. NOLLEY, Sept. 21, 1943.

LOT 391-D: Catherine HEWETT;
Removed from N. B. G., Sept. 17, 1877; Annie HEWETT, Sept. 18, 1880; Rosetta M. BEACH, Jan. 25, 1884; Cath. HEWETT, Jan. 29, 1884; Thos. BEACH, Aug. 10, 1886.

LOT 392-D: SMITH and TIPPETT;
Remains from N. B. G., Sept. 20, 1877, M. TIPPETT; Rachel TIPPETT, Dec. 12, 1888; Jas. E. HARDESTY, June 17, 1889; Eliz SMITH, Jan. 15, 1898.

LOT 393-D: Greenleaf SAWYER;
Mary Alice SAWYER, July 8, 1901; Greenleaf SAWYER, May 13, 1915; Harry SAWYER, Jan. 29, 1921; Oscar SAWYER, Dec. 1, 1925; Martin Louis SAWYER, Feb. 9, 1927; Clifton A. SAWYER, Dec. 2, 1932; Lillian BOSTWICK, June 15, 1946.

LOT 394-D: Sadie BURKE;
Henry BURKE, Sept. 4, 1882; Blanche E. BURKE, Oct. 27, 1885; Clayton L. BURKE, Oct. 30, 1912; H. C. BURKE, June 27, 1916; Sarah R. BURKE, Feb. 2, 1931 (or 1921); Harry C. BURKE, Sept. 11, 1941; Mary A. BURKE, July 18, 1955.

LOT 395-D: Asa B. FARGO;
Asa B. FARGO, July 12 (or 17), 1889; Frances E. FARGO, Feb. 18, 1877; Edwd. L. FARGO, Nov. 16, 1899; Harriet G. CARNEY, Aug. 21, 1900; Wilson FARGO, Jan. 1, 1899; Hennrietta FARGO, Dec. 11, 1882.

LOT 396-D: Richard ZELA(N)KA;
Minnie A. ZALA(U)KA, Mar. 8, 1886; Hannah E. ZALA(U)KA, Dec. 2, 1889.

LOT 397-D: Conrad HOHL, Frederick and Hilma SPIEGEL (note states "Sold to Mrs. HOHL's daughter.");
Wm. B. HOHL, July 7, 1891; Hilma SPIEGEL, Oct. 4, 1965; Frederick J. SPIEGEL, Feb. 11, 1954. Letter dated Mar. 2, 1936 from C(illegible) C. HOHL transferring LOT 397-D to Frederick and Hilma SPIEGEL.)

LOT 398-D: John W. LAKIN;
Arthur P. LAKIN, May 6, 1891; Child, Mar. 11, 1902; Stillborn, Mar. 1, 1895; Child, Oct. 31, 1896; Geo. B. COOLEY, Apr. 12, 1905; Eliz PILKERTON, Dec. 12, 1910; Louis R. COOLEY, June 13, 1916; Harry W. LAKEN, Oct. 18, 1918; Mahlon SLAYSMAN, Aug. 10,

1932; Margaret SLAYSMAN, June 26, 1922; Anna M. SLAYSMAN, Feb. 13, 1945.

LOT 399-D: Matilda KURTZ;
Mary A. LANGE, Nov. 13, 1891; Henry HAMMOND, June 4, 1894; Infant of HAMMOND, Nov. 18, 1895; Elizabeth HATCH, Oct. 24, 1896; Frances KURTZ, July 31, 1(90)7; Stillborn of Annie KURTZ, Feb. 15, 1914; Stillborn of Robert and Annie NO(LL), Feb. 4, 1918; Alice M. KURTZ, Mar. 19, 1920 (entry crossed out); Ashes of Henry R. SCHMIDT, June 1, 1961, died June 4, 1956; Matilda KURTZ, Sept. 29, 1953.

LOT 400-D: Saml. VOHDEN;
Barbara VOHDEN, Nov. 2, 1891; Remains of Saml. and Maggie VOHDEN, Nov. 12, 1892; Mamie VOHDEN, May 19, 1893; Florence MORGAN, June 8, 1899.

LOT 401-D: Wm. KELLY;
John W. KELLY, Oct. 27, 1892; Wm. J. KELLY, Jan. 21, 1898; Richard KELLY, Aug. 8, 1918; Caroline KELLY, Mar. 13, 1922; Wm. R. KELLY, June 20, 1935.

LOT 402-D: F. REIN; Single Interments;
Wm. E. RYAN, Sept. 28, 1892; Chas. RYAN, Dec. 14, 1918; Fredk. REIN, Oct. 27, 1925; Louis (S.) D(EN)TZ, Mar. 1, 1927; Stillborn of REIN, Mar. 29, 1927; Annie E. REIN, Aug. 22, 1936; Benj. B. REIN, May 1, 1958; Mary E. REIN, May 15, 1886; Wm. PAGE, 45 years, died at (Union) Memorial Hospital, Feb. 14, 1930; John NICHOLIS, Mar. 11, 1930.

LOT 403-D through 406-D: There is no record for these lots in the Lot Book.

LOT 407-D and 408-D: J. LEONARD. There are no burials recorded in these lots.

LOT 409-D: William E. COLE;
Wm. E. COLE, Mr. 1, 1904 (entry crossed out); Henry H. KEIL, Mar. 20, 1925, (On right of page with same name is "Reopened 1934."); Henry H. KEIL, Jan. 19, 1943; Anna M. KEIL, May 25, 1948.

LOT 410-D: Jno. G. LEONARD;
Dr. Benj. F. LEONARD, Apr. 13, 1900; Shearwood M. LINSLEY, Jan. 23, 1911; Ellen L. LINSLEY, Jan. 1, 1919.

LOT 411-D: Mary IRVING;
James D. COLE, Dec. 21, 1895; Henry C. KREBS, May 14, 1903 (entry lined out); Mary E. IRVING, Feb. 23, 1920; Harrey E. KEIL, May 14, 1903; Howard F. IRVING, Aug. 13, 1889.

LOT 412-D: Ferdenhan HURTLE;
Jeanette HURTLE, Feb. 3, 1892; Ferdinand HURTLE, Aug. 20, 1919.

LOT 413-D: Maria BANNISTER;
Rosetta JONES, July 11, 1892; Chas. Lee STONER, June 9, 1893; Amanda LANDENSLAGER, Feb. 14, 1895; Martha T. WARD, Oct. 21, 1903.

LOT 414-D: Henry A. HARIG;
Millard H. HARIG, July 26, 1886; Infant of Lillie HARIG, June 15, 1898; Sadie C. HARIG, Aug. 15, 1914; Henry A. HARIG, Dec. 6, 1915; Milton A. HARIG, Mar. 8, 1918; Virginia HARIG, Aug. 30, 1943.

LOT 415-D: Thos. L. WILCOX;
Octavia C(AV)ELL, Apr. 23, 1900; Maria A. WILCOX, Mar. 14, 1884; Russel PRICE, Apr. 15, 1907; Ida Wilcox BU(RROWS), Apr. 25, 1912.

LOT 416-D: Geo. L. BURMAN and Eugene C. WILLIAMS;
Eva WILLIAMS, Apr. 1, 1885; Olivia WILLIAMS, May 11, 1889; Eugene (H.) WILLIAMS, Nov. 10, 1914; (The last three entries, the bodies were disinterred June 26, 1916 and moved to Druid Ridge Cemetery in Baltimore County); Mary E. BURMAN, Dec. 3, 1920; Geo. L. BURMAN, Feb. 8, 1926.

LOT 417-D: Mamie CRUZER. There are no burials recorded in this lot.

LOT 418-D: Elizabeth WILSON;
Bessie WILSON, July 12, 1894; Elizabeth WILSON, June 9, 1904; Thos. DORSEY, Nov. 26, 1883, disinterred to 109-D; Stillborn of FITZPATRICK, May 18, 1886; Lilly WILSON, disinterred from 366-A, (no date given).

LOT 419-D: Rebecca DAVIS;
Chas. W. DAVIS, Sept. 18, 1882; Margt. DAVIS, Apr. 28, 1884.

LOT 420-D: Geo. DELCHER;
Remains from N. B. G., July 25, 1879; Eva DELCHER, July 17, 1880; Infant, July 20, 1881; Nellie DELCKER, July 26, 1881; Geo. B. DELCKER, Feb. 7, 1887; Frank DELCKER, Mar. 28, 1910; Georgia ALBAUGH, Nov. 5, 1917; George DELCHER, Aug. 19, 1817.

LOT 421-D: David B. BURGESS and HICKMAN;
James HICKMAN, Nov. 13, 1877; Isabell HICKMAN, Aug. 26, 1877; Barney BURGESS, Dec. 7, 1877; John L. BURGESS, Oct. 25, 1879; Josephine BURGESS, Jan. 7, 1882; Mary R. WATTS, Dec. 19, 1916.

LOT 422-D: Dr. H. P. P. YEATES;
Remains from N. B. G., June 14, 1877.

LOT 423-D: Alice JOHNSON;
Henry W. DITTMAN, Oct. 24, 1878; Timothy HERRINGTON, Apr. 1, 1898; Matilda A. HERRINGTON, Apr. 28, 1905.

LOT 424-D: See LOT 462-D.

LOT 425-D: Olivia KAHLEST;
Julius KAHLEST, Mar. 15, 1878; Eliz WILSON, Jan. 25, 1882; Olivia KAHLEST, Sept. 7, 1906.

There is a scrap of paper in the Lot Book which reads - "Blanche - Bouis 424-426-D. Page F. H. (Mr. BLANCHARD) - Theus Leesburg, Fla."

LOT 426-D: (Including LOT 424-D) Rachel BOUIS;
Stephen BOUIS, Mar. 24, 1879; Rachel A. BOUIS, Mar. 29, 1893;

Stephen BOUIS, Feb. 2, 1914; Achsah G. BOUIS, Feb. 1, 1922; Remains from N. B. G., Sept. 22, 1877; Mildred BOUIS, Apr. 8, 1895; Charlotte E. G. BOUIS, Juy 24, 1922.

LOT 427-D: Geo. BUNTING;
Nellie B. BUNTING, Feb. 7, 1880; John W. BUNTING, Jan. 20, 1887; Geo. W. BUNTING, Jan. 19, 1898; Gertrude O. OCHRE, Mar. 22, 1910; Stephenson BUNTING, Feb. 4, 1880.

LOT 428-D: George C. ROSE;
Remains from N. B. G., May 18, 1877; Mary M. ROSE, June 22, 1877 (Middle initial may be W); Cath. A. ROSE, Dec. 10, 1877; Wilson G. SHIPLEY, July 11, 1884; Grace SHIPLEY, Sept. 15, 1887; Geo. C. BROWN, Feb. 8, 1908; Geo. C. ROSE, Aug. 26, 1910; Cath. EVANS, Nov. 2, 1928; Cath. A. Ca(sse) LEGG, Apr. 18, 1928.

LOT 429-D through 436-D: There is no record for these lots in the Lot Book.

LOT 437-D: Helen OHLER;
Remains from N. B. G., Mar. 1, 1877; Sarah WHITE, Jan 20, 1888 (On the right of the page this person's death date is given as July 17, 1880.); Saml. MC VEY, Feb. 16, 1854.

LOT 438-D: Elizabeth WIDERKIND;
Remains from N. B. G., Mar. 1, 1877; Eliza DENON, Sept. 4, 1883.

LOT 439-D: Susan MARSH;
Remains from N. B. G., May 18, 1877; Lydia STRITCH, (no date given); Wm. E. WALTON, June 29, 1854; Ann WALTON, (no date given).

LOT 440-D and 442-D: John D. RILEY;
Rebecca RILEY, June 7, 1890; Marie RILEY, Oct. 25, 1897; Marie T. RILEY, Apr. 2, 1897; John D. RILEY, May 12, 1936; Harry L. RILEY, Oct. 6, 1877; Geo. A. RILEY, Mar. 2, 188(8); Jane E. RILEY, Sept. 14, 1883; Jane E. RILEY, Dec. 21, 1910; John D. RILEY, March 19, 1901; Ida L. RILEY, Dec. 27, 1945; Ma(ur)is RILEY, (no date given).

LOT 441-D: Kate E. KIRK;
Elizabeth HARVEY, Sept. 7, 1887; Lea C. RHEEN, Mar. 16, 1888; Larina WALLACE, Sept. 22, 1890; Phililp ABENTACHAEN, Oct. 6, 1890; Child, Sept. 3, 1894; Stillborn of LANDER, Sept. 21, 1894; Sophino (or Sophono) NICHOLSON, Apr. 23, 1890; Mary RUSSELL, Apr. 6, 1907; James CUMMINGS, May 13, 1912.

LOT 442-D: See LOT 440-D.

LOT 443-D and 445-D: Mary UNDERWOOD;
Remains from N. B. G., June 14, 1877; John J. UNDERWOOD, July 27, 1877; Mary UNDERWOOD, Sept. 21, 1880; Wm. C. TAFFAN, Apr. 8, 1896 (On right of page, probably same person, reads - "Dr. Wm. TAFFAN, Apr. 10, 1895."); Wm. C. CHALMERS, Nov. 28, 1899; Maggie TAFFAN, Mar. 31, 1909; Jos. B. UNDERWOOD, Mar. 22, 1865; Sarah UNDERSOOD, Aug. 5, 1843; Enock UNDERWOOD, Feb. 19, 1864.

LOT 444-D: Thos. A. RUTTER;
Remains from N. B. G., Apr. 22, 1878.

LOT 445-D: See Lot 443-D.

LOT 446-D: Wm. H. COLLISON;
Geo. W. COLLISON, Oct. 19, 1881; Stillborn of W. and H. COLLISON, Mar. 2, 1896; Augustus SCHWARTZ, Oct. 31, 1900; Infant of E. and H. SULLAVIN, Aug. 18, 1903; Georgana GLEMM, Apr. 19, 1904; Geo. O. GLEMM, Apr. 24, 1904; Hazel L. BURKHEAD, June 4, 1906; Wm. H.HOFMEISTER, Aug. 22, 1913; Helen A. COLLISON, Aug. 11, 1924; Wm. H. COLLISON, May 18, 1934 (middle initial may also be A).

LOT 447-D: Mango PURCELL;
Benj. PURCELL, Apr. 3, 1883; Wm. B. PURCELL, Dec. 29, 1883; Ida C. PURCELL, May 17, 1886; Stillborn, Oct. 31, 1888; Mango PURCELL, Dec. 30, 1888.

LOT 448-D: Chas. WORTEN;
Chas. WORTEN, May 21, 1920; Howard D. WORTEN, Aug. 13, 1920.

LOT 449-D: Mary BOOKHOULTZ;
Elmia BOOKHOULTZ, June 21, 1884; Irvin BOOKHOULTZ, Aug. 6, 1885; Child of M. and J. BOOKHOULTZ, Sept. 28, 1892; John BOOKHOULTZ, Apr. 20, 1906; Elmer BOOKHOULTZ, Apr. 4, 1896; Elmira BOOKHOULTZ, June 21, 1881 (entry crossed out); John F. BOOKHOULTZ, Nov. 6, 1909; Mary E. BOOKHOULTZ, Jan. 10, 1921; Geo. E. BOOKHOLTZ, Nov. 27, 193(0 or 1).

LOT 450-D: Mary WROTEN;
Clara V. WOOTEN, Mar. 1, 1883; Stillborn of FITZPATRICK, May 27, 1884; Stillborn of FITZPATRICK, May 20, 1886; Jos. B. FITZPATRICK, Sept. 17, 1888 (may also be Jas.); Wm. H. FITZPATRICK, Jan. 29, 1894; Mary E. FITZPATRICK, Nov. 6, 1901; Infant of J. & E. NEIL, Mar. 23, 1904; Mary C. FITZPATRICK, Apr. 28, 1905; Carrie M. IRELAND, July 22, 1905; Dolly A. KIRLEY, July 30, 1908; Bertha IRELAND, July 12, 1909; Gladis IRELAND, July 26, 1910; Evelyn H. WROTEN, Mar. 9, 1912; E. BODENBENDER, June 21, 1899; Infant of IRELAND, Nov. 6, 1901; Stillborn of J. E. NEAL, Apr. 23, 1912; Laura M. IRELAND, Apr. 6, 1917.

LOT 451-D: Geo. H. STEWART;
Sarah C. STEWART, Feb. 19, 1886; James F. STEWART, Oct. 27, 1887; Kate McC. HURDEL, June 28, 1892; Mable R. STEWART, Mar. 24, 1898; Emma E. STEWART, Jan. 30, 1918; Thos. R. STEWART, Oct. 17, 1931.

LOT 452-D: Louisa SCHNEIDER;
Theodore SCHNEIDER, July 8, 1890; Wm. SCHNEIDER, July 1, 1891; Infant of SCHNEIDER, Oct. 31, 1892; Conrad GRAFLIN, Sept. 16, 1914.

LOT 453-D: Louisa BROWN;
Thos. O. BROWN, Mar. 7, 1892; Augusta KROH, Maya 5, 1908; Louisa BROWN, July 12, 1908; John BROWN, Jan. 15, 1912; Aaron TATTLE, Dec. 6, 1922; Ira FORD, Sept. 26, 1925; Jacob H. BROWN, Dec. 5, 1927; Mary WOLF, Dec. 25, 1927.

LOT 454-D: Mary E. WALLACE;
Sadie O. CAVANAUGH, Mar. 29, 1894; Mary E. WALLACE, Oct. 25, 1904; Geo. W. WALLACE, (no date given); Harry E. WALLACE, May 6, 1918; John O. WALLACE, June 20, 1933.

LOT 455-D: Harriett FORRESTER;
Nicholas FORRESTER, Dec. 31, 1906; Stillborn of C. and L. FRITZ, Mar. 22, 1909; Geo. H. MEREDETH, Jan. 6, 1917; Leonard FORRESTER, Mar. 4, 1950.

LOT 456-D through LOT 458-D: There are no records for these lots in the Lot Book.

LOT 459-D: Rev. Alvin T. PERKINS;
Minnie E. PERKINS, May 5, 1931. Letter dated May 18, 1931. The heirs of Sedney B. TAYLOR, Jr., assign rights in LOT 459-D in Sedney B. TAYLOR, Jr.'s name to Mt. Olivet Cemetery. Signed May 29, 1931 by Mrs. Margaret TAYLOR and witnessed by Mrs. Maud WEIKEL, Mrs. H. GOULDMAN and S. (B.) TAYLOR.

LOT 460-D: Ann R. GITTINGE(S);
Annetta SHRINER, Sept. 31, 1892; Ann R. GITTINGE(S), Nov. 29, 1901.

LOT 461-D: Robert GABLE;
Lydia A. GABLE, Feb. 8, 1888; Jacob F. MILLER, Feb. 27, 1888; Robert GABLE, Dec. 21, 1896; Jas. FORESTER, Oct. 11, 1899; Leonard FORRESTER, Mar. 27, 1905; Harriet Ann FORRESTER, June 5, 1937.

LOT 462-D: Robert HIGDON;
Wm. (SOMMERS), Nov. 25, 1896; Ida REESIDE, Dec. 31, 1901; Annie E. HIGDON, Feb. 11, 1908; Robert HIGDON, Oct. 29, 1908; Wm. T. REESIDE, Oct. 5, 1926.

LOT 463-D: John Q. FIGG;
Mary C. FIGG, July 21, 1885.

LOT 464-D: Philip DE GRIEF;
Sarah A. DE GRIEF, Dec. 19, 1895; Philip A. DE GRIEF, Nov. 24, 1899; Laura BAUMGARTNER, Apr. 29, 1933; August BAUMGARTNER, July 26, 1947.

LOT 465-D: M. (or W.) A. COTTON;
John B. COTTON, Jan. 4, 18(8)5; August M. COTTON, May 1, 1910; M. A. COTTON, Jan. 20, 1913; Lucy B. COTTON, (entry crossed out), (no date given); Wm. E. STIRLING, Jan. 1, 1922; Lucy B. COTTON, Oct. 26, 1929; Louise C. MC ELDOWNEY, Jan. 6, 1959. Authorization from funeral director Stewart Mowen Co. of Baltimore to Mt. Olivet Cemetery for burial of Louise Cotten MC ELDOWNEY on Jan. 6, 1959 in Lot 465-D in name of M. Augustus COTTEN. Date Jan. 6, 1959. The interment is to be over William Edward STIRLING.

LOT 466-D: Margt. GARRETT, transferred to Geo. W. GRAHAM;
Geo. GARRETT, May 15, 1882; Florence B. GARRETT, Nov. 3, 1884; G. C. GRAHAM, May 9, 1924; Geo. W. GRAHAM, Feb. 1, 1926.

LOT 467-D: Elizabeth TOOL (This name may be TOAL. In some instances at appears to be FOAL);
Remains from N. B. G., May 17, 1877; Remains from N. B. G., Sept. 27, 1877; Mary TOOL, Oct. 10, 1882; Elizabeth TOOL, Oct. 13, 1883; Sarah Ann WILCOX, Feb. 25, 19(0)1.

LOT 468-D: Mary Ann EDWARDS;
Remains from N. B. G., May 27, 1877; Annie HIGDON, Apr. 8, 1878.

LOT 469-D and 470-D: Mary MIDDLETON;
Richard Gregory SCHMOLL, May 8, 1943; Blanche R. SCHMOLL, Oct. 28, 1961; Donald F. SCHMOLL, Oct. 12, 1927; Adeline KENNEDY, Apr. 20, 1881. (A stone with "CLENN ?" apparently on lot.)

LOT 471-D: CHANEY and SMITH;
Remains from N. B. G., Sept. 21, 1877; Sarah A. SMITH, Nov. 14, 1895.

LOT 472-D: Mary A. FERGUSON;
Nehimiah FERGUSON, Mar. 15, 1880; Fredk. FERGUSON, Apr. 1, 1880; July A. FERGUSON, July 26, 1880; A. E. FERGUSON, Aug. 10, 1882; Mary A. FERGUSON, Oct. 9, 1889; Chas. E. LETCHFIELD, Sept. 27, 1890.

LOT 473-D: Mary A. COSTER;
Joseph COSTER, (no date given).

LOT 474-D: Richard LAWTON;
Mary Louise LAWTON, May 6, 1924; Richard LAWTON, Dec. 20, 1926.

LOT 475-D: Wm. L. RILEY (The middle initial -M- has been crossed out and -L- written in.);
Child of RILEY, Aug. 16, 1877; Ella May RILEY, Nov. 19, 1877; Chas. H. RILEY, Dec. 7, 1877; Frances E. RILEY, Nov. 4, 1878; Stillborn of RILEY, Oct. 28, 1879; Howard RILEY, Sept. 7, 1883; Mary E. R. BECK, Apr. 24, 1916; Howard Fred. BECK, Jan. 4, 1955. Authorization dated Apr. 30, 1949 for Mt. Olivet to bury Howard Frederick BECK next to Mary E. BECK and move grave of Mary B. RITTER, Lot 475-D in name of Wm. L. RILEY. The authorization was signed by Edith B. GARRETTSON, the granddaughter of original lot owner. Witness is E. L. MESSERSMITH.

LOT 476-D: Jas. W. CLARKSON;
Edw. O. CLARKSON, Feb. 26, 1877; Annie A. CLARKSON, Sept. 27, 1882; Stillborn, Aug. 25, 1887; Emma E. CLARKSON, Apr. 7, 1892.

LOT 477-D through 484-D: No record of these lots can be found in the Lot Book.

LOT 485-D: Ann E. TAYLOR. No burials recorded in this lot.

LOT 486-D: Sarah J. MAYES;
Mary J. STEWART, Nov. 19, 1878; John R. MAYES, Apr. 4, 1890; Sarah E. MAYES, June 28, 1894.

LOT 487-D: Mary and Kate ARMONS;
Remains from N. B. G., Apr. 13, 1877; Mary ASKEW, Apr. 13, 1877; Geo. H. BAYLIES, Jan. 31, 1907; Susan R. BAYLIES, Oct. 27, 1903; Annie A. BAYLIES, Mar. 5, 1935; Harry T. BAYLIES, Feb. 4, 1938.

LOT 488-D: Wm. H. RILEY and Mrs. W. SHAFFER;
Wm. L. BECK, July 1, 1891; Wm. H. RILEY, May 1, 1903; Emma I. RILEY, Apr. 2, 1902.

LOT 489-D and 490-D: William (L.) VICK and James C. VICK; James L. VICK, Apr. 25, 1877; Carrie V. VICK, June 23, 1877; Frank T. VICK, June 26, 1877; James L. VICK, July 3, 1886; Eliza VICK, May 2, 1888; Harriet C. VICK, May 2, 1889; John W. VICK, Mar. 5, 1909; M. V. RODELOFF, Sept. 27, 1912; Harry Penn VICK, Feb. 10, 1938; James CROSBY, Apr. 13, 1898; Eliza T. CROSBY, (no date given); W. P. VICK, July 16, 1926; Mary L. VICK, Dec. 18, 1934; Remains from N. B. G., Mar. 12, 1877.

LOT 491-D: Martha HAYMAN (This family name may be HYMAN, the A is crossed out in some names.); Remains from N. B. G., Apr. 20, 1877; James LEWIS, Apr. 20, 1877; Geo. W. HAYMAN, Feb. 1, 1885; Geo. HAYMAN, Aug. 25, 1887; Bertha E. LAFRTY, Mar. 29, 1894; Edwd. L. LAFFERTY, Jan. 3, 1900; Stillborn of E. and R. LAFERTY, Jan. 17, 1900; Stillborn, Apr. 14, 1921; Abby C. HYMAN, Dec. 27, 1926.

LOT 492-D: Wm. H. CROZIER; Remains from N. B. G., Apr. 4, 1877; Horace CROZIER, July 23, 1877.

LOT 493-D: Eliz A. FOY; Remains from N. B. G., June 14, 1877; Robert T. WELLS, Sept. 29, 1881; Nita BAWLING, Feb. 6, 1882; Julia A. FOY, July 28, 1883; John WELLS, Apr. 27, 1888.

LOT 494-D: Emily PERRY. No burials recorded in this lot.

LOT 495-D: Thos. C. GITTINGE(S); Thos. GITTINGE(S), Nov. 2, 1891; L. V. GITTINGE(S), (no date given); Roland GITTINGE(S), Jan. 7, 1916; Gertrude G. RYAN, May 3, 1965.

LOT 496-D: Virginia FOLIN. No burials are recorded in this lot.

LOT 497-D: Wm. P. HOOD; Remains from Baltimore Cemetery, Sept. 4, 1883; Ida P. HOOD, Apr. 12, 1897; Estella A. (WENTWORTH), Dec. 26, 1897; Mary (S.) HOOD, Jan. 20, 1913; Chas. WAGNER, July 9, 1913; Etta L. WAGNER, Feb. 11,1927.

LOT 498-D: John J. KREBS; Bernard KREBS, Aug. 28, 1886; John B. KREBS, Jan. 28, 1886; John J. KREBS, July 15, 1916; Maggie KREBS, Oct. 26, 1918; John P. KREBS, Jan. 14, 1896.

LOT 499-D and 500-D: Louisa THON; Wm. THORN, Feb. 13, 1892; Geo. FEELER, May 14, 1900; Wilbur WELLER, Mar. 1, 1901; Pauline WELLER, Jan. 4, 1902; Paul L. WELLER, Mar. 14, 1902; John MESSICK, Apr. 8, 1907; August THORN, Feb. 8, 1911; Louisa THON, Dec. 26, 1925; Christian THON, Oct. 28, 1944; Mary THON, Feb. 16, 1948.

LOT 501-D and 502-D: There is no record of these lots in the Lot Book.

LOT 503-D: L. P. FOWLER; John P. W. FOWLER, Mar. 12, 1893.

LOT 504-D: There is no record in the Lot Book for this lot.
LOT 505-D: Annie C. GARDNER;
Anthony B. GARDNER, 1892; Annie C. GARDNER, Jan. 3, 1920.
LOT 506-D: Eliza HIGDON;
Nancy BAZIET, Feb. 10, 1894; Eliza HIGDON, Feb. 26, 1914; Chas.
E. BRIGHT, Jan. 22, 1917; Stillborn, May 5, 1921; Sarah A. R.
JORY, May 17, 1921; Rich'd. T. IRELAND, Aug. 3, 1931.

LOT 507-D: M. S. MARINER;
Thos. MARINER and Geo. DAVIS (child), Feb. 6, 1883; Infant, Nov.
23, 1881; Bertha L(IN)K, Oct. 1, 1901 (This name may also be LUCK
or LUIK.); Indianna GOO(L)ACK, July 6, 1903; Sarah MARINER, June
18, 1903; Elsie M. LINK, Nov. 18, 1907 (This name may also be
LUCK or LUIK.); Jas. T. RYAN, Aug. 14, 1908; Thos. MARINER, Apr.
14, 1922.

LOT 508-D: E. F. LUPTON;
Grace LUPTON, Oct. 22, 1892; Mary LUPTON, Nov. 17, 1893; Wilbur
LUPTON, Mar. 2(8), 1892; Ephron LUPTON, (no date given); Ephron
Filmore LUPTON, Mar. 31, 1944.

LOT 509-D: See LOT 511-D.

LOT 510-D: John F. CLARKE;
Mary E. CLARKE, May 22, 1888; Chas. G. CLARKE, Mar. 21, 1889;
Arthur GARFIELD, Dec. 23, 1881; John F. CLARKE, Jan. 28, 1936.

LOT 509-D through 511-D: Robert E. ENOS;
Harriet (I.) SMALL, Dec. 14, 1887; Marion B. LITTLE, July 11,
1902; Alice V. ENOS, July 5, 1933; Sarah ENOS, Sept. 17, 1878;
Child of Newton ENOS, Sept. 17, 1878; Robert E. ENOS, May 18,
1897; Mary D. ENOS, Apr. 9, 1900; Mary J. ENOS, Jan. 24, 1918;
"for Thos. C. DORAN."

LOT 512-D: Mary A. FLYNN;
Herbert FLYNN, Nov. 1, 1881; Arthur G. CLARK, Dec. 23, 1881; John
A. FLYNN, Oct. 10, 1881 (Date Sept. 19, 1881 also given.); Mary
C. CLARK, Apr. 22, 1886; Mary A. FLYNN, Nov. 19, 1913; Ella
FLYNN, Oct. 27, 1934; "Children in north side, Henrietta FLYNN,
Arthur and Mary CLARK." (no date given).

LOT 513-D: Sarah CROCKETT;
Remains of child, Apr. 4, 1878; Sarah CROCKETT, Jan. 22, 1879;
Anna B. CROCKETT, Nov. 15, 1881; Theo. S. CROCKETT, May 27, 1903;
Mary Frances CROCKETT, Jan. 17, 1927; Wm. CROCKETT, Jan. 29,
1851.

LOT 514-D: Wm. E. HOLLAND;
Grace E. YOUNG, Dec. 4, 1893; Wm. E. HOLLAND, Dec. 28, 1899;
Margt. TRICKLE, June 15, 1906; Sarah E. CARMINE, May 10, 1921.
(On the right of the page the middle initial is H.)

LOT 515-D: George H. HARTMAN;
Joseph HARTMAN, Mar. 19, 1881; Robert HARTMAN, Sept. 14, 1835;
Infant, Dec. 8, 1884; Geo. HARTMAN, June 1, 1892; Lydia HARTMAN,
Oct. 1, 1895; Mary E. HEIN, Aug. 22, 1896; Geo. HEIN, July 2,

1897; Stillborn, Dec. 28, 192(3); Mary BUSHNELL, Nov. 10, 1928; Patricia BLANKENSHIP, (child), July 3, 1948.

LOT 516-D: John COATH (Note says "See 518-D."); L(olleac) M. COATH, Dec. 2, 1930; Clarence J. COATH, May 22, 1952.

LOT 517-D: Susan MEREDITH; Wm. H. MEREDITH, May 20, 1881; Howard M. GARRETT, May 5, 1893; Nannie M. WILLIAMS, Apr. 27, 1902; Martha F. SMITH, July 16, 1903; Edwd. J. MEREDITH, Oct. 29, 1907.

LOT 518-D: Marie COATH; Remains from N. B. G., Mar. 21, 1877; Remains from N. B. G., July 3, 1877; Rose E. COATH, July 15, 1882; Wm. COATH, Apr. 8, 1909; Henry WALTON, June 5, 1913.

LOT 519-D: Hezekiah KANLY (also spelled KANELY); Remains of John KANLEY and family, Aug. 16, 1877; Jessie T. HAMPTON, Sept. 11, 1879; Henry W. HAMPTON, Sept. 21, 1881 (Also called Harry.); James KANLEY, Sept. 28, 1914; K. KANLEY, Mar. 13, 1879; Annie M. KANLEY, Oct. 4, 1921; John G. KANLEY, Nov. 24, 1928; Minnie Lee KANLEY, Apr. 15, 1936; Eugene KANLEY, Feb. 11, 1937.

LOT 520-D: Wm. GALLOWAY; Remains of Wm. GALLOWAY and wife, Aug. 16, 1877; Aquilla HENRY, July 13, 1908; (Margt.) HENRY, May 23, 1909 (There is a hole through this entry making it only part legible.); Wm. E. TROUGHT, June 16, 1916.

LOT 521-D: Dixon FITCHETT; Sarah A. FITCHETT, (March or May) 13, 1878; Dixon FITCHETT, June 24, 1889; Eliza GILL, May 11, 1912; Sarah SHELTON, Oct. 1, 1925; John Dixon FITCHELL, Sept. 7, 1929; Alke E. FITCHETT, July 5, 1961.

LOT 522-D: John T. ROBERTS; John P. ROBERTS, Mar. 2, 1978; John A. ROBERTS, Nov. 6, 1886; Helen E. ROBERTS, Mar. 16, 1891; Mildred A. ROBERTS, Nov. 10, 1898; Walter F. ROBERTS, Dec. 2, 1901; Maud E. POLTON, Jan. 9, 1902; John T. ROBERTS, June 21, 1902; Rebecca E. ROBERTS, Oct. 11, 1902; John T. ROBERTS, June 26, 1922.

LOT 523-D: Margaret PA(M)PHILON; Clarence PA(M)PHILON, Mar. 5, 1883; Annie E. PA(M)PHILON, Dec. 10, 1886; Stillborn of (ZEMIER), Sept. 3, 1898; PA(M)PHELON, (Sept.) 1, 1899; Chas. W. PA(M)PHILON, Sept. 23, 1878.

LOT 524-D: Charles A. JACOBI; Catherinee JACOBI; Jan. 29, 1901; Henry G. JACOBI, Jan. 22, 1924; Chas. A. JACOBI, Apr. 5, 1932; Catherine JACOBI, May 10, 1957.

LOT 525-D: Oliver REESIDE; Remains of Eliz GILL and family from N. B. G., June 8, 1877; Mary E. REESIDE, Oct. 10, 1881; Infant of M. and W. F. REESIDE, Nov. 1, 1886; Kinzie M. REESIDE, May 9, 1891; Jas. W. REESIDE, June 18, 1897; Edwd. C. MC MENAMEN, Feb. 28, 1912; Wm. MC MENAMEN, Apr. 15, 1910 (U.S. Army Stone); Stillborn of Mr. & Mrs. John

PRILL, Aug. 24, 1916; Jas. MC MENAMEN, Feb. 25, 1919; Sarah MC MENAMEN, May 20, 1931; Stillborn, 1897; Sarah A. MOORE, Sept. 3, 1960; John W. MOORE, May 6, 1968; Joseph MC MENAMEN, Oct. 19, 1956; Donald W. DILL, July 24, 1922.

LOT 526-D: Laura WILSON;
Benj. RAY, Jan. 5, 1895; John MC CLENNON, Apr. 15, 1910 (entry crossed out); (On the right of this page under the deleted name is written KROZIER, Dec. 17, 1881.); Mary E. WILSON, Nov. 19, 1919, 37 years, 5 months, 12 days.

LOT 527-D: No record appears in the Lot Book for this lot.

LOT 528-D: Jas. M. DULANEY;
Mary E. DULANEY, Nov. 22, 1882; Lavinia ATKINSON, July 27, 1892; James M. DULANEY, Jan. 30, 1909.

LOT 529-D: Mary E. FARRELL;
Wm. FARRELL, Dec. 5, 1882; Wm. FARRELL, Jan. 9, 1883; Stillborn of Sarah MUSGRAVE, Jan. 5, 1895; Child of E. A. MUSGRAVE, Aug. 12, 1898; Stillborn of Clara SOLAN, June 3, 1899; Mary C. WALL, May 1, 1905; Geo. J. MUSGRAVE, May 7, 1894.

LOT 530-D: See LOT 532-D.

LOT 531-D: Matilda WEEKES;
"Inscription Blanche E. WEEKES, Feb. 28, 1950 - Miss Blanche WEEKS, Santa Monica, Calif. . . " (no other date given); Cremated remains of Blanche E. WEEKES, Apr. 20, 1950; Charles C. WEEKES, Nov. 5, 1923; Cremated remains of Maud S. WEEKES, July 27, 1948; George W. FERRIER, Jan. 5, 1924; John Y. WEEKES, July 24, 1940; Sealy WEEKES, Jan. 12, 1894; Matilda WEEKES, Dec. 6, 1930; Agnes WEEKES, Jan. 4, 1936. Authorization for burial dated May 24, 1949 for burial of Blanche E. WEEKES in Lot 531-D held by Matilda WEEKES. Signed by Blanche E. WEEKES of Santa Monica, Calif. A note found in the Lot Book reads: "For MERKEL - Blanche E. WEEKS - died (2-19-50) - 2-28-50."

LOT 530-D and 532-D: Thos. W. SNYDER;
Mary V. SNYDER, Sept. 15, 1892; Lydia A. SNYDER, Sept. 5, 1898; Henrietta S. SNYDER, June 15, 1905; Isaac W. SNYDER, May 19, 1891; Lydia REESIDE, Jan. 15, 1901; Thos. W. SNYDER, Apr. 13, 1925; Henrietta Carroll SNYDER, Feb. 20, 1933; John David LOVE, Jan. 8, 1964; Joaob C. MC LAUGHLIN, July 18, 1974, born Sept. 25, 1911, died July 14, 1974. Funeral home was - Schimunek.

LOT 533-D: John H. IRELAND;
Geo. Washington R(ECKER), Mar. 1, 1893. (Might also be RIEKES or RIEKER).

LOT 534-D: Edna C. CLARKE. There are no burials recorded in this lot.

LOT 535-D: Julia A. COOK;
Chas. COOK, Apr. 10, 18(8)3; Annie E. CARNEY, July 25, 1883; Chas. CARNEY, July 16, 1884; Chas. H. COOK, Oct. 21, 18(8)5; Chas. D. COOK, Jan. 2, 1889; Stillborn of CARNEY, Oct. 17, 1890; Mary COOK, Apr. 4, 1892; Frances E. CARNEY, Jan. 13, 1893 (Middle initial also given as S. on right page.); Julia A. COOK, Oct. 9,

1907; Agnes C. CLARK, June 27, 1910; Bertha M. COOK, Sept. 3, 1921; Jesse L. COOK, Apr. 12, 1940.

LOT 536-D: Josephus STIER;
Mrs. L. STIER, Apr. 5, 1882; Josephus STIER, Oct. 4, 1901; Peter BLANK, Dec. 5, 1934; Jennie HACKETT, Oct. 25, 1968, born Nov. 9, 1877, died Oct. 22, 1968. William STIER sells Richard W. MEYER two spaces in 536-D. STIER is resident of Baltimore, Md. Authorization dated Oct. 23, 1968 to inter remains of Jennie HACKETT in 536-D. Signed by Mrs. Florence RICHARDSON and witnessed by John A. MOLAN.

LOT 537-D: James HANLON;
James P. HANLON, July 21, 1881; Margt. HANLON, Mar. 25, 1913; James HANLON, July 24, 1922.

LOT 538-D: August BENNETT;
August BENNETT, May 13, 1902; Henrietta BENNETT, Apr. 9, 1914; Mrs. PH(AI)FER, (no date given).

LOT 539-D and 540-D: Mary LAURY;
Remains from N. B. G., Nov. 12, 1878; Mary LAURY, Dec. 4, 1885; Mary A. LAURY, May 8, 1889; Howard B. LOURY, Nov. 16, 1907; Florence WHITNEY, Aug. 4, 1910; Annie E. WHITNEY, Feb. 15, 1915; Chas. H. LOURY, Dec. 19, 1917.

LOT 541-D and 542-D: S. W. FORRESTER;
Elmer W. FORRESTER, Apr. 27, 1878; Saml. W. FORRESTER, Feb. 24, 1903; Susanna FORRESTER, Feb. 2, 1917; Elizabeth MADDOX, Jan. 12, 1894; Margt. MADDOX, Feb. 10, 1894.

LOT 543-D: David W. RONSAVILLE;
Remains from N. B. G., May 10, 1878; Christ(ema) RONSAVILLE, Sept. 17, 1880. (On right of page the first name is lined out and CLINTON is entered.)

LOT 544-D: Beverly W. DOUGHERTY;
Helen DOUGHERTY, May 1, 1877; Rev. B. W. DOUGHERTY, July 28, 1895.

LOT 555-D and 555 1/2-D: Jennie BROWN;
Joseph E. BROWN, June 4, 1902; Sadie BROWN, Oct. 11, 1918; Maria L. BELT, Mar. 17, 1884; Alonza E. BROWN, Nov. 14, 1893; Randolph R. BROWN, Dec. 2, 1910; Kate BROWN, May 28, 1932; Homer W. GAULD, July 4, 1934; Sophia GOULD, July 1, 1939.

LOT 556-D: Saml. MARSHALL;
Saml. MARSHALL, Nov. 20, 1893, disinterred July 21, 1921.

LOT 557-D: Rev. L. E. HERRON;
Annie D. HERON, July 22, 1888; Rev. R. G. HERRON, Apr. 5, 1897.

LOT 558-D: Robert and Eliz. INNERST;
Margt. A. INNERST, Apr. 23, 1884, disinterred; Alonza E. INNERST, Apr. 23, 1884, disinterred; Margt. A. INNERST, Sept. 7, 1897; Wm. INNERST, Oct. 26, 1898; Ethel INNERST, Oct. 29, 1900; Annie DISNEY, July 22, 1905; Baby SCHMIDT, Apr. 20, 1920; Baby INNERST, Mar. (18), 1922.

LOT 559-D: Susan E. MOORE;
Wm. T. MOORE, Feb. 2, 1880; Susan E. MOORE, May 24, 1904.

LOT 560-D: Samuel JENKINS;
Blanch T. JENKINS, Mar. 29, 1880; Martha (I.) JENKINS, Dec. 11, 1889; H. JENKINS, Apr. 7, 1900; Annie C. JENKINS, May 19, 1893; Stillborn of Wm. and Ada BYRD, Oct. 26, 1917. Letter dated Nov. 2, 1960 states that Ada Hicks JONES is next of kin to Samuel JENKINS and last of her generation.

LOT 561-D: Chas. LITCHFIELD;
Saml. H. LITCHFIELD, Oct. 28, 1902 (The date Oct. 17, 1887 given on right of page.); Miranda LITCHFIELD, Mar. 16, 1900 (The dte Feb. 10, 1900 given on right of page); Charles R. LITCHFIELD, Feb. 10, 1882.

LOT 562-D: John MC GREGOR (The tombstone reads: MC GROEGER);
Ida MC GREGOR, July 25, 1882; Howard BURKHARDT, Jan. 6, 1895 (Entry directly below this states disinterred & put in 11-F); Capt. Joseph MC GREGOR, Dec. 5, 1900; Emma MC GREGOR, Feb. 6, 1929; Florence MC GREGOR, Nov. 25, 19(30).

LOT 563-D: Mary J. MC GREGOR transferred to Annie E. CORLETTE;
Remains from N. B. G., Nov. 12, 1878; Mary J. MC GREGOR, Aug. 30, 1909; Ann CURLETT, Feb. 7, 1931, removed from Hiss M. E. Cemetery, died Jan 19, 1899; Geo. MC GREGOR, Dec. 1, 1857.

LOT 564-D: Thos. KEERL;
Adolph SANDOR, May 7, 1879 (On right of page is entered Feb. 7, 1879.); Stephanie SANDOR, Jan. 6, 1895; Cecil R. SANDOR, June 11, 1895.

LOT 565-D through 574-D: There is no record of these lots in the Lot Book.

LOT 575-D: Susan E. HARTLEY;
Geo. W. HARTLEY, Apr. 5, 1880.

LOT 576-D: Ann HOLSTON;
Margt. A. ROBINS, July 19, 1881; Louis A. HOLSTON, Mar. 4, 1902; Ann HOLSTON, Dec. 15, 1919.

LOT 577-D: Milton B. DECKER;
Daisy M. DECKER, Sept. 30, 1879; Stillborn, Mar. 11, 1882; David HENNINGER, Apr. 9, 1894; Mabel DECKER, Jan. 2, 1901; Georgana DECKER, June 15, 1908; Milton B. DECKER, Jan. 1, 1916; Stillborn Jan. 1(8), 1921; Morris DACKER, Oct. 30, 1922; Arthur G. DECKER, Feb. 3, 1948; "for Mary HENKEL"; Bertrame HENKEL, Feb. 3, 1971, born Sept. 5, 1913, died Jan. 31, 1971. Parents George HENKEL and Mary E. DECKER. Funeral Home - Witzke.

LOT 578-D: Catherine WARE;
Annie C. CLARK, Mar. 23, 1893, disinterred; Joseph WARE, Apr. 7, 1880; James WARE, Oct. 4, 1907; Fredk. GENT, Aug. 28, 1911 (also date of Sept. 13, 1911); Catherine GENT, May 22, 1923.

LOT 579-D: Fredk. KIRBY;
Remains from N. B. G., Jan. 23, 1881; Edith KIRBY, May 28, 1900,

disinterred; Mary E. LAWDER, Feb. 22, 1919; Alex H. ROBINSON, Jan. 2, 1931; Mary Emily LAWDER, Mar. 21, 1938.

LOT 580-D: Susan J. TUCKEY;
Susan J. TUCKEY, Oct. 15, 1893; Elisha TUCKEY, July 12, 1881; Sarah PRICHARD, Aug. 4, 1890.

LOT 581-D: Henry P. EAST;
Jas. M. EAST, Aug. 21, 1882 (Entered at right of page as John M. EAST.); Stillborn, Sept. 6, 1884; Robert P. EAST, Jan. 20, 1892; Henry P. EAST, Sept. 3, 1896; Emily E. EAST, Feb. 23, 1914; Arletta M. EAST, Apr. 7, 1924.

LOT 581 1/2-D: David PERKINS;
Martha B. PERKINS, Feb. 20, 1894; David R. PERKINS, Jan. 18, 1933; Florence B. PERKINS, May 1, 1945.

LOT 582-D: Mary COSDEN;
Wm. W. COSDEN, Dec. 4, 1894; Wm. A. THOMAS, Nov. 4, 1915; Mary E. COSDEN, Mar. 2, 1926; Johanna C. THOMAS, July 25, 1938.

LOT 583-D: Marion ADAMS;
W. J. F. ADAMS, Mar. 23, 1894; Infant ADAMS, Nov. 26, 1896.

LOT 583-D and 584-D: Chas. E. DINNIS of Philadelphia and Edna DENNIS;
Edw. DENNIS, Apr. 10, 1899; Samuel DINNIS, Jan. 23, 1922; WM. E. DINNIS, Sept. 6, 1881; Infant of M. E. and John TREAS., Nov. 27, 1888; Lillian M. DENNIS, Oct. 24, 1881; Wm. J. DENNIS, Nov. 14, 1899; Benj. H. DINNIS, July 26, 1890; Wm. D. TRESS, Aug. 18, 1890; Stillborn of P. and E. DINNIS, May 21, 1893; Stillborn of P. W. and E. DENNIS, Sept. 9, 1895; Stillborn of P. and E. DINNIS, Aug. 7, 1897; Louie Grace DINNIS, Aug. 1, 1963; Emma Retta DINNIS, May 30, 1940.

LOT 585-D: Alex. JESSUP;
Edwd. JESSUP, Dec. 24, 1888; John JESSUP, June 7, 1899; Edwd. JESSUP, Oct. 1, 1879.

LOT 586-D: Dennis H. HICKEY;
Ellen Louise HICKEY, July 8, 18(8)1; Virginia HICKEY, Oct. 7, 1881; Denn(ies) H. HICKEY, Jan. 20, 1894.

LOT 587-D: Chas. R. BRIDGES;
Fannie E. BRIDGES, Sept. 23, 1879; Elizabeth W. BROWN, Oct. 15, 1882; John CASSADY, Sept. 22, 1902.

LOT 588-D: Alonza G. CAULK;
Sarah CAULK, May 31, 1880.

LOT 589-D: Oneida HULL;
Harvey L. HALL, Aug. 2, 1893; Oneida HULL, July 13, 1903.

LOT 590-D: Kate VANDIFORD;
Abraham VANDIFORD, May 9, 1881; Viola VANDIFORD, July 11, 1881; Infant of Kate COOPER, Nov. 1, 1895; Catherine W. COOPER, Apr. 2, 1928; Thos. F. COOPER, Aug. 30, 1932.

LOT 591-D: Hugh QUINN;
Ellen (or Ella) M. QUINN, Oct. 14, 1879; Edwd. QUINN, June 18, 1883; Hugh QUINN, child, Oct. 16, 1884; Louisa M. QUINN, July 29, 1887; Virginia A. QUINN, Mar. 4, 1901; Hugh QUINN, Apr. 13, 1903; Geo. H. QUINN, Mar. 15, 1907; Lawrence N. QUINN, July 25, 1907 (or 1917); Maria QUINN, Apr. 29, 1912; Catherine SMITH, Nov. 3, 19(3)3; Bernard QUINN, June 4, 1953.

LOT 593-D: Mary AHREND;
Herman AHREND, Aug. 5, 1881; Mary AHREND, Mar. 30, 1909.

LOT 593-D: Emma ROLOSON;
Edwd. ROLOSON, Apr. 5, 1892; Emma WILLIAMS, Jan. 21, 1898.

LOT 594-D: Cordelia K. PERKINS;
Jas. A. PERKINS, May 9, 1894; Cordelia K. PERKINS, Sept. 20, 1927.

LOT 595-D: Rev. David (S.) MONROE;
Remains from H(OO)PERs lot . . . June 10, 1881; Carroll MONROE, Feb. 15, 1892; Caroline M. MONROE, Oct. 18, 1899; Rev. David (S.) MONROE, Nov. 17, 1910. There are two graves on the right of the page with the following: in one is C. E. M. in the second, J. H. M. and under it John Harrison MONROE.

LOT 596-D: Alice W(EIR)TLING (Name may be W(EIS)TLING also.); David B. W(EIR)TLING, Dec. 1, 1896; Alice W(EIR)TLING, Aug. 30, 1900. There is a note - "Benj. R. DITRICKS" Washington, D.C. for this lot."

LOT 596 1/2-D: John M. FLYNN;
Geo. A. FLYNN, Jan. 6, 1908, disinterred May 31, 1912 and taken to Louden Park Cemetery; Jno. M. FLYNN, Nov. 1, 1916; Mary H. FLYNN, June 24, 1924. There is the word Ivy or Joy and the date 1933 written in the grave space.

LOT 597-D: Michael WOODS;
Matilda WOODS, Oct. 7, 1879; Mary WOODS, Mar. 5, 1906; Mary WOODS, Aug. 22, 1916.

LOT 598-D: T. H. WILSON;
Edith WILSON, July 6, 1881; Martha WILSON, Mar. 18, 1895.

LOT 599-D: George LOOKINGLAND and Mrs. Geo. R. LOOKINGLAND; Aloesta LOOKINGLAND, Oct. 1, 1880; Geo. R. LOOKINGLAND, May 25, 1881; Mary LOOKINGLAND, Nov. 1, 1888; Geo. LOOKINGLAND, Jan. 26, 1904; Lydia M. LOOKINGLAND, June 20, 1907; Geo. R. LOOKINGLAND, Mar. 29, 1911; Albert W. CHILDS, Aug. 4, 1919; Jos. (I.) CHILDS, Jan. 9, 1935.

LOT 599 1/2-D: Lena MARSHALL;
Wm. MARSHALL, Jan. 29, 1890; Lena MARSHALL, May 30, 1906.

LOT 600-D: Helen CROOK;
Alex. A. CROOK, May 15, 1890; Helen M. PRIDE, Jan. 2, 1926. Letter from Willmer Grove, Va., dated Jan. 25, 1947 from Mrs. Anna (DANSON) KRENSON to Mt. Oliver Cemetery. Would like to have her niece and niece's husabnd, Mr. and Mrs. John NEALEN of Ebensburg, Penn. buried in Lot 600-D. This lot is in Mrs. KRENSON's

mother's name, which is Helen Myra CROOK. Authorization dated Apr. 5, 1951 for burial of Mrs. Viola G. NEALEN and her husband John NEALEN of Ebensburg, Pa. in 600-D.

LOT 600 1/2-D: HANAWAY and GREENWOOD;
John F. REILLY, Apr. 4, 1939; "For Mrs. REILLY"; Charles H. HEALEY, Sept. 24, 1902. There is also written in this space the date May 5, 1894.

LOT 601-D: Chas. A. POLTON;
Mary F. POLTON, Aug. 6, 1880; Chas. E. POLTON, Oct. 5, 1917 removed from Druid Ridge Cemetery; Alice V. POLTON, Sept. 23, 1943.

LOT 602-D: Single Interments;
Norwood MC ALLISTER, June 24, 1894; John FERGUSON, June 23, 1930; Annie E. WILSON, Aug. 5, 1930, disinterred to 9(2)-E.; Katherine (L.) HUMPHREYS, Nov. 25, 1930, disinterred to 104-E; Warner McC. RANIER, May 21,1929; Anna Viola WILSON, (grave paid for Nov. 16, 1951, no other date given).

LOT 603-D and 604-D: Single graves.
Clara HARDING, May 18, 1899; Sarah RICHARDSON, May 18, 1899; Chas. B. HARDING, Mra. 8, 1920; Ada(delkehead) IGLEHART, Sept. 23, 1929. The first 3 graves are by authority of Mrs. Harry F. BAUGHMAN of Baltimore, Md.

LOT 605-D through 608-D: There is no record of these lots in the Lot Book. However, a note in 603-D Lot pages states Lots 605-608-D are Single Interments.

LOT 607-D: Elizabeth J. NICHOLS;
Elizabeth NICHOLS, Jan 12, 1894 and Feb. 24, 1894.

INDEX

AARON, D., 51-B
  Doractry, 51-B
  J. T., 51-B
  Marscellus, 51-B
ABBOTT, Clarence P., 87-D
  D. Florence B., 87-D
  Elizabeth J., 165-B
  Florence B., 87-D
  Gertrude W., 165-B
  John F., 165-B
  Jos. W., 165-B
  Lillian B., 165-B
  Minnie G., 87-D
  Noal (Noah), 165-B
  Walter W., 165-B
ABELL, Samuel, 493-A
  Sarah, 493-A
  Sarah E., 493-A
  Thos. J., 493-A
  Wm. E., 493-A
ABENTACHAEN, Phililp, 441-D
ABEY, Charles, 178-D
  Michael, 56-A
  Rayjond E., 178-D
ACTON, A. L., 81-B
  Camella, 228-A
  Mary E., 228-A
ADAMS, Charles, 103-A
  Charlotte, 223-A
  Flora E., 133-D
  George, 30-A
  Jas. Edw., 223-A
  Jno. G. R., 223-A
  John, 103-A
  Jos. C., 223-A
  Marion, 583-D
  Martha G., 223-A
  Prescilla, 380-A
  Sebastian A., 126-A
  Stella M., 223-A
  W. J. F., 583-D
  Wm. G. W., 224-A
ADDISON, Edw. P., 181-B
  George W., 56-B
  John, 181-B
  John W., 181-B
  Katherine W., 56-B
  Laura V., 28-B
  Mary A., 56-B
  Nancy, 181-B
  Saml. S., 28-B
  Sarah D., 181-B
  Susan, 28-B
  Taylor, 56-B
  Virginia, 181-B
  W. W., 28-B
  Walter A., 28-B

ADDISON, Wm., 56-B
  Wm. W., 28-B
ADERDIRE, Jos., 200-A
AGNES, Barbara, 425-A
AHLSEGER, Ann R., 257-A
AHLSLEGER, Emma, 257-A
  William S., 257-A
AHREND, Herman, 592-D
  Mary, 592-D
AIST, Annie May, 75-C
  Arthur E., 75-C
  Arthur L., 75-C
  Betty Lou, 75-C
  Carlton W., 75-C
  Ella (JONES), 75-C
  Ella Rebecca, 75-C
  George Roy, 75-C
  Isabel, 75-C
AIVEY, L. E., 311-D
  Louisa E., 311-D
ALBAUGH, A. M., 312-D
  Georgia, 420-D
ALBOUGH, Helen E., 312-D
ALDERDICE, Jennie H., 200-A
  Sarah J., 200-A
  William E., 200-A
ALDERDIS, John, 200-A
ALDERDISE, John, 200-A
ALDRIDGE, John A., 92-B
ALERIUR, Catharine C., 133-D
ALEXANDER, Emma P., 146-B
  Grace, 34-C
  Grace (BE(?)CROFT/DE(?)CRAFT), 34-C
  Grace A., 34-C
  Harry E., 146-B
  Howard R., 41-C
  James, 194-A
  Jas. W., 231-A
  Mary, 89-B, 133-A
  Mary E., 133-A, 146-B
  Nathan, 146-B
  Nathan E., 146-B
  Nathan L., 231-A
  Nathan Leroy, 146-B
  Robert E., 41-C
  Samuel I., 34-C
ALFORD, James E., 127-B
  Mary M., 127-B
ALLDERDICE, Lucelle, 200-A
  Lucille F., 200-A
ALLEN, (?), 110-A
  Alice A., 140-A
  Alice V., 140-A
  Bryon, 38-B
  C. J., 162-B
  Chas., 21-D

ALLEN, Clara, 194-A
 Dora, 140-A
 E., 162-B
 Edna Marie, 162-B
 Edw. T., 38-B
 Eliel, 162-B
 Elizabeth, 153-A, 162-B, 214-A
 Emily, 140-A
 Fannie M., 302-D
 Hugh, 314-D
 James M., 162-B
 James W., 162-B
 Jane, 162-B
 Jas., 140-A
 Jas. H., 218-A
 Jas. W., 301-D
 John L., 38-B
 John W., 153-A
 Joseph, 140-A
 Joseph E., 140-A
 Kirk, 302-D
 L., 162-B
 Laura, 38-B
 Lawrence, 302-D
 Lawrence W. S., 162-B
 Leona L., 38-B
 Mamie V., 302-D
 Margt., 473-A
 Mary, 38-B
 Mary A., 302-D
 Matilda, 218-A
 Permelia, 162-B
 Peter, 140-A, 302-D
 Peter R., 140-A
 R. A., 140-A
 Robert G., 302-D
 Sarah, 38-B
 Thos. S., 214-A
 Wm., 361-A
 Zachariah, 214-A
ALLENDER, Max, 112-C
ALLEWALT, Margaret T., 278-A
ALLISON, Elizabeth, 466-A
ALLSWORTH, Eliz., 76-B
ALLWELL, Mary L., 21-D
ALRAMS, John, 103-A
ALRICH, B. Don Benjamin, 15-C
 Benj. P., 15-C
 Benjamin P., 15-C
 Julia (BROWN), 15-C
 Julia B., 15-C
ALSEGER, Mary R., 257-A
ALT, Grace R., 126-A
ALTDERDISS, Charles E., 200-A
ALTER, Elizabeth M., 20-B
 George W., 20-B
 Marg. L., 20-B
 Walter A., 20-B
AMETT, Chas., 140-A

AMEY, Adele, 73-A
 Alonzo, 73-A
 Florence A., 73-A
 Joseph, 73-A
 Levy, 73-A
 Margt. E., 73-A
 Rose A., 73-A
 Wm., 73-A
AMOS, Chas. E., 245-D
 E. M., Rev., 17-C
 Evelyn, 245-D
 Hannah C., 245-D
 Jas. Y., 245-D
 Jos., 117-B
 M., 117-B
AMS, Barton, 89-A
ANDEKIN, Lum, 371-A
ANDERSON, Ambrose, 46-B
 Anton, 155-D
 Arthur A., Jr., 6-C
 David, 44-B
 Edna May, 98-B
 Effie D., 329-D
 Eliza, 44-B
 Geo., 182-B
 George M., 44-B
 James, 44-B
 James K., 44-B
 John, 88-B
 Kate R., 44-B
 Margt., 44-B
 Nannie, 21-D
 Rose, 46-B
 Williams, 46-B
ANDREWS, (?), 425-A
 Eliza, 163-B
 James, 163-B
 Mary A., 163-B
ANGELL, Kate M., 189-B
ANIGEN, Wm. E., 93-B
ANSTINE, Amanda A., 193-B
 Chester C., 193-B
 Henry E., 193-B
 Ida B., 193-B
 Wm. H., 193-B
 Wm. Henry, 193-B
ANTHONY, Earl, 34-B
 Fitzhorn L., 34-B
 Imines, 34-B
APPELBY, Charlotte, 221-D
 Rebecca, 221-D
 Saml., 221-D
 Saml. F., 221-D
 Susan, 221-D
APPLE, Christian, 198-D
APPLEGISTH, Gennethe, 344-A
ARARK, Mary Ann, 169-B
ARCHOR, Geo., 44-A
ARDY, William M. H., 240-A

AREN, Charlotte, 21-D
ARENDT, Bell, 136-A
  Eliza, 136-A
  Emma C., 136-A
  Frank, 136-A
  George, 136-A
  Kate, 136-A
ARGO, Cath., 98-A
  Leuis, 98-A
ARMACOST, Thomas, 193-A
ARMAGER, A. Margaret, 211-B
  J. Reese, 211-B
  Jessie, 211-B
  Jessie S., 211-B
  Julia A., 211-B
  Lore, 211-B
ARMIGER, (?), 32-A
  James, 32-A
  Jessie S., 173-B
ARMONS, Kate, 487-D
  Mary, 487-D
ARMOR, John, 159-A
  William A., 159-A
  Wm., 159-A
ARMORIS, Maynard, 159-A
ARMSTRONG, (?), 325-A
  Ann, 110-A
  Annie M., 219-D
  Caroline V., 110-A
  Cath., 110-A
  Cath. E., 110-A
  Chas. E., 219-D
  Clara L., 110-A
  Clara V., 110-A
  Clarence M., 105-B
  Danl., 110-A
  George W., 400-A
  Hannah A., 110-A
  Jno. M., 110-A
  John M., 110-A
  Josephine L., 488-A
  Julia L., 110-A
  Louise K., 219-D
  Mary A., 219-D
  Mollie A., 110-A
  Morris, 110-A
  Peter, 56-B
  Rich'd, 219-D
  Robt. G., 178-A
  Saml., 110-A
  Theodore, 219-D
  Wm., 110-A, 137-B
  Wm. H., 219-D
ARNOLD, Annie E., 26-D, 161 1/2-D
  Antonia M., 205-B
  Christian, 161 1/2-D
  Dora, 161 1/2-D
  Edward, 161 1/2-D

ARNOLD, Elizabeth, 406-A
  Emma, 161 1/2-D
  Geo. W., 26-D
  George P., 30-D
  Harry, 161 1/2-D
  Henry, 26-D, 161 1/2-D, 205-B
  Henry E., 161 1/2-D
  Henry P., 205-B
  Howard, 26-D
  J. G. Henry, 26-D
  J. R., 205-B
  James R., 205-B
  John T., 406-A
  Kate, 26-D
  Lewis, 406-A
  Lula May, 73-C
  Martha E., 205-B
  Mary, 205-B
  Mary A., 205-B
  Mary L., 26-D
  Sarah, 373-D
  Sarah A., 205-B
  Wm., 205-B
  Wm. H., 26-D, 205-B
ARO, Cecelia M., 268-D
  Jas., 268-D
  Jas. H., 268-D
  Joseph, 268-D
  Mary, 268-D
ASBURY, Francis Bishop, 67
ASHCROFT, Wells A., 363-A
ASHLEY, Henrietta, 312-A
  Millicent, 312-A
  Wm. E., 322-A
ASHTON, Chas. E. (or A.), 33-A
  Elizabeth, 33-A
  John M., 33-A
  Myrtle, 448-A
  Thos., 33-A
  Thos. H., 33-A
ASHVILLE, Mary, 202-A
ASKEW, Blanche, 101-D
  Eliza, 96-B
  Howard D., 101-D
  Isabella, 22-B
  Mary, 487-D
  Wm. N., 22-B
ATKINSON, Elizabeth P., 32-A
  John P., 32-A
  Lavinia, 528-D
AUGUSTENBERGER, Augusta, 58-D
AULD, A. J., 249-A
  Albert A., 249-A
  Danson, 249-A
  Edwd. C., 249-A
  Edwd. M., 249-A
  Emma V., 244-A, 249-A
  Harry E., 249-A
  Jos. H., 244-A, 249-A

AULD, Joseph K., 249-A
Margt., 249-A
Margt. A., 244-A
Mary E., 249-A
Philip, 249-A
Philip F., 249-A
Philip, Jr., 249-A
AULL, Jno. W., 469-A
AUSTIN, John, 146-A
Sarah, 146-A
Sarah A., 146-A
AVARD, Charles L., 68
AWAS, Jos., 117-B
M., 117-B
AYLESWORTH, Hay C. (or Nay E.), 34-A
AYLSLWORTH, Mary I., 34-A
Alice Violetta, 20-D
Annie R., 34-A
Bowen McG., 34-A
Chas. B., 34-A
Helen M. I., 34-A
Ira B., 20-D
Mary E., 34-A
BAAS, Fredk., 150-B
Mary, 150-B
BABB, Tillie, 208-D
BABBITT, Sarah M., 99-A
BADGER, Margt. I., 269-A
BAGER, Margaret I., 269-A
BAGGS, John F., 68
BAGLY, Frances A., 54-A
BAILEY, Ann, 53-A
Clinton D., 147-B
Elijah, 53-A
Frances, 312-A
Grace A., 79-A
James, 53-A, 312-A
Jonah, 53-A
Josiah, 53-A
Mary, 96-B
Rose, 84-B
Sarah E., 147-B
Susan, 53-A
Virginia Marion, 147-B
W. L., 147-B
Willie, 147-B
Wm. B., 147-B
Wm. F., 12-A
Wm. G., 147-B
BAKER, Angelia Mary, 491-A
Ann Rebecca, 83-B
Arabella E., 90-A
Barbury A., 442-A
Charlotta, 83-B
Earl C., 103-D
Elizabeth, 22-A
Elmer E., 472-A
Emily, 83-B

BAKER, Emma M., 90-A, 91-A
Ethel W., 103-D
Fannie May, 81-C
Franklin, 443-A
George A., 472-A
Grace, 90-A
Howard B., 81-C
Isaac, 83-B
John R., 35-A
M. Eliza, 32-D
Margaret, 96-B
Mary Ann, 184-B
Mary E., 472-A
Matilda A., 22-C
Norman R., 384-D
Robert B., Sr., 442-A
Theodore, 442-A
W. D., 90-A
Wilhelmina D., 90-A
Wm., 90-A
Wm. E., 83-B
BALDERSON, Clara V., 45-B
Thos., 45-B
BALDWIN, Fannie M., 206-B
Francis, 206-B
Frederick, 112-A
Geo. S., 206-B
Jno. F., 392-A
Maggie, 112-A
Margaret R., 112-A
Margaret Retta, 112-A
R. M., 206-B
Rachel M., 206-B
Robert D., 206-B
Thos. M., 206-B
Thos. P., 206-B
Wm. H., 112-A
BALL, Aleaista V., 87-B
Carrie, 87-B
Chas. C., 13-B
Dabney, 67
Dabney W., 13-B
Dabney, Rev., 13-B
David, 87-B
David E., 87-B
Ella, 161-B
Ellen R., 161-B
Geo. C., 87-B
H. Clay, 87-B
Henry, 67
Herbert, 161-B
John S., 87-B
John T., 50-D
Lillian N., 13-B
Lloyd O., 161-B
Mary, 161-B
Mary D., 13-B
Sarah, 87-B
Sarah A., 50-D

BALL, Virginia W., 13-B
Walter, 161-B
Walter, 87-B, 161-B
Walter R., 161-B
Walter Randall, 161-B
BANGS, Frances M., Jr., 374-A
BANKER, Va., 72-B
BANKERD, Hattie, 11-D
BANNISTER, Maria, 413-D
BANSET, Mildred L., 99-A
BANTHAM, Eugene H., 145-D
Mary E., 145-D
Mebille, 145-D
Mitchell, 145-D
BARBER, F., 3-D
Harriet J., 119-B
Harry E., 9-D
Leroy E., 9-D
T., 3-D
Thos. N. III, 9-D
BARGE, Wm. E., 136-B
BARGER, Margt. I., 269-A
BARKER, Annie M., 31-A
Jos. W., 285-A
Leah, 31-A
Leonard, 31-A
Milton L., 31-A
Patence, 31-A
Sidney, 31-A
Sophia A., 285-A
William, 31-A
William L., 31-A
BARKMAN, George, 430-A
Louisa M., 43-A
BARLING, Sarah, 44-A
BARLOW, Frank, 46-B
Frank Jas., 46-B
Frank W., 46-B
Gladys, 46-B
Joseph, 46-B
Louis A., 46-B
Mary C., 46-B
BARNES, Annie M. (FISHER), 107-B
Chas. M., 152-A
Ellen R., 306-A
Ethel A., 72-C
Jno. H., 152-A
John, 356-D
Maurice Granger, 106-A
Salina, 153-A
Saline, 153-A
Saml., 306-A
Saml. F., 306-A
BARNETT, Chas., 140-A
Georgia, 88-B
Harriett, 115-B
Wm., 110-A
BARNEWELL, Rose E., 202-A

BARNEWELL, Sarah Eugenia, 202-A
BARNEY, (?), 196-B
BARNUM, (?), 195-A
Caroline, 195-A
Eliza, 195-A
Richard, 195-A
BARRETT, Ella A., 425-A
BARRON, Cath., 107-A
Chas. E., 107-A
G. W., 107-A
J. W. S., 107-A
Jno. C., 107-A
John C., 107-A
Thos., 107-A
Wm. C., Jr., 107-A
BARTHALOW, Sarah F., 238-D
BARTHLOW, Fannie, 238-D
Oney L., 238-D
Raymond L., 238-D
BARTHOMLEW, Ethel, 339-A
BARTLETT, Budie, 139-A
Chas W., 246-A
Margaret, 246-A
Mary E., 155-C
BARTON, Cora (FITTECH), 154-A
Edurn., 237-A
Jennings, 237-A
Walter J., 154-A
BASS, Fredk., 152-B
BASSFORD, Albert E., 132-B
Thomas, 67, 132-B
Thomas B., 132-B
BAST, Frank E., 59-C
Franke Augusta, 59-C
BATEMAN, Alice, 89-A
Bridget, 89-A
Elizabeth A., 89-A
James E., 18-D
Lillie, 89-A
Pamela R., 18-D
BATERMAN, Joseph, 30-A
BATHGATE, Genevieve, 95-B
Sarah E., 95-B
BATTE, Mary, 13-D
BATTEE, Dennis H., 68
BAUER, Ann, 488-A
BAUGHMAN, (?), 210-B
Annie V., 210-B
Chas. A., 210-B
Christian, 210-B
Elizabeth A., 210-B
Frances M., 97-A
Harry F., Mrs., 603-D
Maggie, 210-B
Mary Ellen, 97-A
Robert J., 210-B
Saml. W., 210-B
BAUMGARDNER, Amos, 107-B
Charles W., 107-B

169

BAUMGARDNER, Daisey (SPILLMAN), 107-B
BAUMGARTNER, August, 464-D
  Charles W., 107-B
  Laura, 464-D
BAUSMITH, Chas., 226-B
  Clarence, 226-B
  Ella F., 226-B
  Estelle, 226-B
  Geo. W., 226-B
  Julia A., 226-B
  Nora, 226-B
  Walter, 226-B
BAVE, Irene, 183-C
  L. C., 183-C
BAVER, Carl B. J., 183-C
  Irene, 183-C
  Robert C., 183-C
BAWLING, Nita, 493-D
BAYLEY, Susan, 207-B
BAYLIES, Annie A., 487-D
  Geo. H., 487-D
  Harry T., 487-D
  Susan R., 487-D
BAYLISS, Mary M., 269-D
  Wm., 269-D
BAZIET, Nancy, 506-D
BE(?)CROFT, Grace, 34-C
BEACH, Rosetta M., 391-D
  Thos., 391-D
BEACHER, Nathan, 30-A
BEACHUM, Rachel, 21-D
BEALE, Mary E., 85-A
  Oliver, 67
BEALL, Eugene E., 147-B
  Horatio, 80-B
  Horatio, Jr., 80-B
  Pauline, 147-B
  Sallie A., 147-B
BEAN, Rose, 301-A
BEASON, Thomas, 147-A
  Thomas M., 147-A
BEAUCHAMP, Caroline, 349-A
  Chas., 349-A
  George A., 349-A
  James, 335-D
BEAUMONT, Alex, 24-D
  Alex. H., 24-D
  Daisy, 24-D
  Margt., 24-D
BEAVER, Mary E., 134-A
BECK, Emma V., 389-A
  Howard Fred., 475-D
  John E., 389-A
  John H., 170-A
  John O., 31-D
  Maria E., 170-A
  Mary E., 389-A, 475-D
  Mary E. R., 475-D

BECK, Perry, 389-A
  Wm. L., 488-D
BECKER, Agatha (MILLER), 72-C
  Carl, 72-C
  Emma V., 37-C
  George Miller, Jr., 72-C
BECKMAN, Ann, 278-A
  Annie, 26-D
  Ellinora L., 26-D
  J. H., 278-A
  Philip, 26-D
  Randolph, 26-D
  Rudolph, 26-D
BECREAFT, (?) (WINKS), 34-C
  Perry, 34-C
BEEBE, Frank C., 373-A
  Laura May, 373-A
BEEBEE, Frank, 373-A
  Harry W., 373-A
BEESEY, Sarah, 156-B
BELL, Benjamin E., 114-C
  Bertha E., 87-A
  Bessie E., 87-A
  Charles F., 87-A
  Chas. A., 404-A
  Clara A., 404-A
  Earnest, 112-B
  Elizabeth, 404-A
  Elsie May, 114-C
  George, 369-A, 404-A
  Harry, 87-A
  Henry, 42-B
  Isabell, 28-D
  Jane, 42-B
  John, 404-A
  Jos., 87-A
  Jos. W., 385-A
  Joseph T., 87-A
  Laura (REYNOLDS), 87-A
  Laura V., 87-A
  Mary, 81-B
  Mary Ellen, 385-A
  Mary L., 87-A
  Roy F., 87-A
  Sarah, 404-A
  Thomas R., 87-A
  Wain, 112-B
  William C., 233-A
  William H., 385-A
BELLAFORIE, Jacqueline, 39-D
BELSCHNER, John, 407-A
BELT, Maria L., 555-D
  Mary, 11-D, 81-D
  Mary Ann (ROSE), 147-C
  Mary R., 81-D, 147-C
  Mary Roberta, 147-C
  Samuel H., 147-C
BENDER, Thomas, 264-A
BENETT, Ella May, 129-A

BENEZE, Elizabeth, 119-D
  Fredk., 119-D
BENNER, Henry A., 276-D
BENNETT, Allen, 18-A
  August, 538-D
  Benj. F., 18-A
  Elenora A., 18-A
  Eliza, 163-B
  Elizabeth H., 18-A
  Henrietta, 538-D
  Jas. A., 358-A
  John H., 358-A
  Kate H., 18-A
  L. S., 163-B
  Sallie, 18-A
  Wm., 228-A
BENNING, Madeline, 96-B
BENSON, Anna Louise, 35-A
  Elizabeth, 25-A
  John W., 144-A
  Nora P., 186-B
BENTON, Roland Edward, 102-C
  William H., 4-C
BENTZ, Hester G., 133-D
BERL, Allie W., 21-D
BERLINER, Hannah, 171-C
BERNHARDT, Virginia, 193-A
BEROTT, Thos. M., 126-A
BERRY, Alice L., 331-A
  Annie R., 83-B
  B. D., 331-A
  Benj., 331-A
  Benj. D., 331-A
  Charlotte, 83-B
  Daniel D., 102-B
  Dorsey, 331 A
  E. D., 331-A
  Edwd. D., 331-A
  Edwd. Daisy, 331-A
  Elizabeth E., 331-A
  Elizabeth J., 462-A
  Ellen, 331-A
  Frank B., 83-B
  Jno. W., 102-B
  Mary E., 331-A
  Olivia, 102-B
  Sidney E., 331-A
  Wm., 83-B
  Wm. R., 83-B
BESSLING, Albert W., 27-C
  John M., 27-C
  Mary L., 27-C
BEST, Mary Elliott, 26-C
  W. Elliott, 17-C
  Wm. H., 26-C
BEUZLEY, Dollis, 460-A
  William F., 460-A
BEVAN, F. J., 389-D
BEVANS, Sarah, 32-D

BIBB, Amanda M., 160-B
  Bently C., 160-B
  Bently S., 160-B
  Carmen A., 160-B
  Louesa M., 160-B
BIBER, Albert, 251-A
BICHE, (?), 47-C
BICKLURARN, Barbara, 80-A
BIDD, Carmen A., 100-B
BIEMAN, Brian W., Sr., 139-B
  Charlotte (EADER), 139-B
  Geo. Wm., 139-B
BIERAU, Clara M., 193-A
  Ludwig, 193-A
BILLAFES, Chas. H., 88-B
BILLEGHS, Chas. H., 88-B
BILLINGER, Edud. N., 199-A
  Nora, 199-A
  Sallie, 199-A
BILLINGS, Edward C., 199-A
  Laura V., 199-A
  Lillian G., 199-A
BIRCH, Carrie A., 29-D
  David F., 98-A
  George R., 29-D
  Henry B., 205-A
  Jos., 29-D
  Margaret Davy, 205-A
  Mary A., 98-A
  Mary E., 29-D
  Minnie, 29-D
  Temperance, 205-A
  Walter W., 29-D
BIRCK, Chas., 205-A
BISHOP, Elijah, 2-D
  Elijah, 204-A
  Fannie, 2-D
  George W., 204-A
  Joanna (HAIGHT), 2-D
  Joanne, 2-D
  Saml., 204-A
  Wm. J., 2-D
BIXLER, Benj. M., 38-B
  Daniel, 38-B
  Danl., Jr., 38-B
  David, 38-B
  Grace, 71-B
  H. Elizabeth, 71-B
  Harriet, 38-B
  John, 71-B
  Julia G., 71-B
  Louis A., 38-B
  Marie Louise, 38-B
  William H. H., Jr., Dr., 71-B
  Wm. H., 38-B, 71-B
  Wm. H. H., 71-B
  Wm. H. H., Sr., 71-B
BLACK, Bessie, 235-D
  Eleanor, 47-B

BLACK, John, 47-B
  Saml. S., 163-A
  Sarah J., 100-B
BLACKBURN, Elizabeth J., 105-B
  Henry F., 105-B
  Wm. C., 32-D
BLACKBURNE, Frederick, 88-D
  Margaret, 88-D
  Marie Elizabeth, 88-D
BLACKMAN, Chas., 261-D
  Elizabeth L., 261-D
  Elsie I., 261-D
  Julius, 261-D
  Lawrence, 261-D
  Rose L(illegible), 261-D
BLADE, Mary C., 85-A
BLAIR, Molly, 92-B
BLAKE, Elizabeth, 366-A
  Jno. W., 148-A
  John R., 100-B
  Sarah, 148-A
  Sarah A., 148-A
  Sarah J., 100-B
BLAMBERG, (?), 367-D
BLANCH, Annie E., 189-A
  Ella May, 56-D
BLANDY, Albert B., 72-B
  Alfred H., 72-B
  Lucy H., 72-B
BLANK, Peter, 536-D
BLANKENSHIP, Patricia, 515-D
BLASINI, Gertrude E., 15-C
BLEDSOE, Alice K., 7-C
  Beulah E., 21-A
  Filice K., 7-C
  Harry C., 7-C
  Katherine V., 238-A
  Margaret Jane, 238-A
  Robert, 238-A
  Robert H. (or M.), 238-A
  Robert H., Jr., 238-A
  Robert Lee, 238-A
  Robt. Lee, 21-A
BLEDSOR, Robert Lee, 21-A
BLOOMFIELD, Charles M., 8-D
  Chas., 8-D
BLOUNT, E. E., 68
BLUMENAUER, Sophia, 37-B
BLUMENAUR, Louis A., 37-B
BLUNT, Laura, 46-C
  Nancy, 207-B
BLYON, (?), 78-A
BLYZARD, Ann, 183-A
BODENBENDER, E., 450-D
BODENICK, George, 136-B
BODENSICK, Auguste M., 136-B
  Fred., 53-B
  Fredk., 136-B
  Geo., 136-B

BODINE, John W., 12-A
BOGART, H. A., 29-B
BOHAUMON, Isabella, 107-A
BOHM, Carl, 101-D
BOIES, Norma F., 142-C
BOIST, Albert V., 24-B
  Annie S., 4-D
  Theodore L., 4-D
BOLAND, Margt., 219-B
  Margt. A., 219-B
BOLSTER, Thos., 66
BOLTE, Wm., 21-D
BOLTON, Bessie, 26-B
  Harry M., 26-B
BOND, Eliza J., 335-D
  George E., Jr., 114-C
  Joshua, 335-D
BONSELL, Robert, 298-A
  Robert F., 298-A
BONWELL, Margt. A., 226-B
BOOKER, Samuel, 43-B
BOOKHOLTS, George, 164-A
  Sarah R., 164-A
BOOKHOLTZ, Carroll, 164-A
  Geo. E., 449-D
  Sarah G., 164-A
  Wm. H., 164-A
BOOKHOULTZ, Elmer, 449-D
  Elmia, 449-D
  Elmira, 449-D
  Irvin, 449-D
  J., 449-D
  John, 449-D
  John F., 449-D
  M., 449-D
  Mary, 449-D
  Mary E., 449-D
BOOKS, Margt., 54-B
BOON, G. B., 179-B
  Margt. E., 179-B
BOONE, Benj., 179-B
  Wm., 21-D
BOOZE, Ida, 67
BORAT, Albert V., 24-B
BORDLEY, H., 67
BORIS, Joseph, 425-A
BORKE, Tobias, 32-B
BORKKENS, Ida E., 112-A
BORNELL, Mary, 39-A
BORRINCER, Atunnonn, 74-C
BORTON, Theodora E., 177-D
BOSEMAN, Ethel, 262-D
  Melvina, 262-D
BOSNELL, Mary C., 25-A
  Saml. G., 298-A
BOSS, Chas. O., 225-B
BOSTON, J. A., 51-B
  L. E., 51-B
  M. F., 51-B

BOSTON, Mary, 51-B
BOSTWICK, Lillian, 393-D
BOSWELL, Margt. A., 282-A
  Susan, 239-A
BOTZMAN, Len. W., 19-D
  Leon W., 19-D
BOUGHMAN, Charles S., 195-B
BOUIS, Achsah G., 426-D
  Charlotte E. G., 426-D
  Mildred, 426-D
  Rachel, 426-D
  Rachel A., 426-D
  Stephen, 426-D
BOUNDS, Harvey, 108-B
BOUNEY, Mary E., 425-A
BOURKE, Ann E., 32-B
  Mary, 32-B
  Phetillah, 32-B
  William F., 32-B
  Wm. H., 32-B
  Wm. T., 32-B
BOWEN, E. J., 325-A
  James, 100-A
  John H., 13-D
  John J., 232-A
  Sarah A., 100-A
BOWER, Barbara, 82-A
  Barbara, 82-A
  George W., 82-A
  Gloxia Bell, 82-A
  Isabell, 82-A
  Kate P., 82-A
  Mary Ann, 82-A
  Susan A., 93-B
BOWERMAN, Emma J., 146-B
BOWERS, Benj. P., 35-B
  Cath. E., 202-D
  James, 100-A
  Sarah A., 100-A
BOWERSOX, John, 26-A
  Mary, 11-D
BOYD, (?), 331-D
  Annie Belle, 126-B
  Cornelius, 275-A
  Daisy, 126-B
  James, 428-A
  Louis, 4-C
  Louis L., 4-C
  Mary A., 4-C
  Wm. D., 52-A
  Wm. E., 21-D
  Wm. F., 52-A
BOYER, Carrie, 71-B
  George, 270-A
  John T., 71-B
BOYL, Rich. B., 54-A
BOYLE, Elizabeth J., 54-A
  George H., 54-A
  John S., 54-A

BOYLE, Luttle L., 54-A
  Rebecca C., 54-A
  Wm. K., 54-A
BOZMAN, Charlotte, 19-D
BRADFORD, Ethel C., 87-A
  Lelia M., 163-A
BRADLEY, Florence, 262-D
  Florence E., 262-D
  Jas., 288-A
BRADS, James, 68
BRADY, Edwin, 150-A
  Elisha, 108-A
  Greenbury, 215-B
  John H., 215-B
  Martha L., 215-B
  Mary, 215-B
  Ward, 37-A
BRAIN, Ann C., 187-A
BRAISILL, Wm. H., 353-D
BRALEY, Kate, 37-A
  Katherine, 37-A
  W. H., 37-A
BRALFORD, Wm. L., 163-A
BRAMLEY, Wm. T., 266-A
BRAN, Ann C., 187-A
BRANAGAN, Chas. F., 25-A
  Lillian N., 25-A
BRANNAN, C. A., 179-B
  Chas. H. L., 163-B
  D., 179-B
  Dremorl, 179-B
  Margt. M., 163-B
  Martin C., 163-B
  Sarah D., 179-B
BRANNON, Clarisa, 172-B
  George A., 172-B
  Sarah, 172-B, 179-B
  Sarah W., 179-B
BRANT, Isabella C., 73-B
  John, 73-B
BRANTUSTER, Chas. M., 335-D
BRASHEARS, (?), Mrs., 44-A
  Frank, 205-D
  Mary E., 205-D
  Mary J., 205-D
BRASS, Andrew J., 228-B
  Annie M., 206-A
  Cara, 228-B
  James H., 228-B
  James T., 228-B
  John W., 206-A
  Louisa M., 228-B
  Lucy, 228-B
  Minnie, 228-B
BRATLEY, William, 50-D
BRATT, Gertrude, 7-C, 42-B
  Sarah, 407-A
BRAUDE, Maria, 152-B
BRECKENRIDGE, John P., 76-A

BRECKENRIDGE, Vavina H., 76-A
BRECKHAUSER, Albert, 487-A
BREEDAN, Jacob A., 21-D
BREWER, Alfred T., 101-C
  Frank Y., 134-A
  Verdie M., 101-C
BRIAN, Laura E., 163-A
BRICE, Hattie Carney, 19-D
  Hellen E., 25-A
BRICK, (?), 414-D
  Benjamin C., 173-B
  Chas. C., 173-B
  Sarah Jacob, 100-B
BRICKHEAD, Casandra, 52-A
BRIDE, Catherine, 21-D
  Eliz, 120-B
  Eliza, 119-B
  Gustavus A., 119-B
  John H., 120-B
BRIDGE, Amanda J., 55-A
  Everet L., 55-A
  Everett L., 55-A
  Maggie S., 55-A
  Mollie, 55-A
BRIDGES, Chas. R., 587-D
  Fannie E., 587-D
BRIDING, Annie M., 210-A
  E. W., 210-A
  Earnest W., 210-A
  Emily, 201-A, 210-A
  Ernest W., 210-A
  Martha H., 210-A
BRIGGEMAN, Kate, 21-A
  Kate F., 92-A
  Lewis, 21-A
  Lewis E., 92-A
  Nellie, 21-A
  Nellie B., 92-A
  R., 21-A
  Raymond L., 92-A
BRIGGERMAN, Lewis E., 21-A
BRIGHT, Chas. E., 506-D
  Leona W., 80-B
  Susan, 21-A
BRILL, John H., 182-D
  Lula Virginia, 69-C
  Luther M., 69-C
  Mary, 69-C
  Richard, 182-D
BRINGST(?), John, 26-D
BRINKMAN, Mae Fee, 37-C
BRISON, Mary M., 58-B
  Samuel, Rev., 58-B
BRISTON, Samuel, 67
BRITT, Gainor, 38-A
  Robert L., 38-A
  Seven, 38-A
  Severn, 38-A
BROADWATER, Chas. G., 335-D

BROADWATER, Raymond, 335-D
  Ruth M., 335-D
BROBST, Elizabeth, 138-A
BRODWATER, Winchester R., 335-D
BROMLEY, Jessie, 367-A
  Jos., 367-A
  Wm. T., 367-A
BROMWELL, Berton A., 68
  Dwight L., 68
  Fannie, 226-B
  Francis, 226-B
  Georgia, 226-B
  Joseph D., 226-B
  Lucy A., 60-D
  William W., 60-D
BRONWELL, John T., 226-B
  Wm., 226-B
  Wm. R., 226-B
BROOCKE, Wm. C., 24-D
BROOCKS, Ameria, 24-D
  Phirgus, 24-D
BROOK, George E., 391-A
BROOKE, Lula, 24-D
BROOKS, (?), Mrs., 178-A
  Amanda R., 174-A
  Anna H., 391-A
  Annie H., 204-A
  Annie O., 191-A
  Blanch B. G., 30-A
  Charles H., 191-A
  Chas., 391-A
  Chas. H., 191-A
  Christopher, 68
  Edw., 191-A
  Edwin, 191-A
  Florence U., 191-A
  Geo. W., 112-B
  Harriett, 112-B
  Harris C., 191-A
  Henrietta, 112-B
  J. Emory, 54-B
  Jerimiah, 54-B
  John, 54-B
  John J., 191-A
  John T., 191-A
  John Thomas, 191-A
  Katherine R., 228-B
  Littie M., 174-A
  Mary, 191-A
  Mary C., 54-B
  Mary G., 191-A
  Mary J., 204-A
  Mary V., 204-A
  Mollie E., 191-A
  Oliver, 191-A
  Peter B., 204-A
  Phirgus M., 24-D
  Robt., 112-B
  Sara A., 112-B

BROOKS, Thos., 191-A
Wm., 54-B, 112-B
Wm. M., 174-A
BROOME, Henry, 202-A
Sallie A., 202-A
BROOMFIELD, Chas., 110-B
BROONE, Fannie T., 202-A
Franzina, 202-A
Henry, 202-A
John N., 202-A
Mary A., 202-A
BROSON, Mary O'Keefe, 126-A
BROTT, C. Melvin, 253-A
Charles W., 253-A
Florence Jones, 253-A
BROWN, (?), 288-A
Ada, 136-B
Alex, 133-A, 194-B
Alex P., 393-A
Alex W., 194-B
Alex W., Mrs., 194-B
Alfred C., 22-D
Alice, 49-A
Alice E., 22-D
Alonza E., 555-D
Ann, 49-A
Ann Louisa, 27-C
Annie E., 22-D
Annie Florence, 22-D
Aviedo, 78-A
Benj. C., 104-A
Benj. D., 133-A
Benjamin, 133-A
Bessie C., 194-B
C. H., 185-A
Carryl A., 22-D
Catherine, 71-D
Charles P., 104-A
Charles Philip, 104-A
Chas. B., 185-A
Chas. H., 91-B, 185-A
Chas. L., 191-B
Chas. P., 17-A, 104-A
Clarence C., 22-D
Cornelius A., 136-B
Cornelius E., 136-B
Delia A., 194-B
Eddie, 174-A
Edward, 104-A
Elenor, 211-A
Eliza, 49-A
Eliza Ann, 133-A
Eliza S., 136-B
Elizabeth, 25-A, 262-A
Elizabeth C., 197-B
Elizabeth W., 587-D
Ella Mae, 22-D
Emma, 49-A
Emma B., 194-B
BROWN, Emma R., 115-C
Esther A., 185-A
Fannie, 32-D
Geo. C., 428-D
Geo. Ewing, 194-B
Geo. M., 258-A
George C., 49-A
George Ewing, Mrs., 194-B
George W., 133-A
Hamilton F., 69-B
Hannah M., 133-A
Harriet M., 428-A
Harry, 133-A
Henrietta, 104-A
Henrietta Rhode (MC CUILY), 104-A
Hester, 185-A
Hester A., 91-B
Hester Ann, 91-B
Ida E., 194-B
Isabella Gregory Hough, 69-B
J. Allen, 3-D
Jacob H., 453-D
James H., 48-C
Jane V., 258-A
Jas., 258-A
Jas. A., 258-A
Jas. O., 136-B
Jas. R., 185-A, 211-A
Jas. V., 258-A
Jennie, 555-D
Jno., 133-A
Jno. W., 133-A
John, 25-A, 133-A, 258-A, 453-D
John B., 258-A
John C., 258-A
John J., 91-B
John M., 133-A
Jos. W., 91-B
Joseph, 67
Joseph E., 555-D
Julia, 15-C, 133-A
Kate, 555-D
Laura H., 49-A
Laura V., 258-A
Lewis P., 428-A
Louis P., 428-A
Louisa, 453-D
Luella, 134-B
Lulu A., 258-A
M. G., 185-A
Margaret, 104-A
Margaret Virginia, 104-A
Margt., 136-B, 258-A
Margt. B., 258-A
Marion M., 191-B
Martha Alice, 3-D
Mary, 258-A

BROWN, Mary C., 133-D
Mary E., 191-B
Mary I., 166-A
Mary L., 194-B
Mary Lavinia, 194-B
May Belle, 48-C
Nicholas S., 393-A
Oscar H., 104-A
Penbrook, 133-A
Rachel, 393-A
Ralph, 120-B
Randolph R., 555-D
Rebecca, 475-A
Richard, 68, 136-B
Sadie, 555-D
Saml., 136-B
Saml. C., 191-B
Sarah, 49-A, 258-A
Sarah E., 258-A
Sarah J., 49-A
Sophia C., 133-A
Susan W., 120-B
Thos., 28-A
Thos. O., 453-D
Walter, 384-D
Walter L., 134-B
Wilbur J., 191-B
Wilhelmina, 136-B
William, 211-A, 365-A
William F., 133-A
William H. L., 104-A
William I., 22-D
William O., 104-A
Wm., 120-B
Wm. E., 136-B, 258-A
Wm. Geo., 185-A
Wm. H., 258-A
Wm. J., 236-D
Wm. K., 258-A
Wm. S., 133-A
Wm. T., 136-B
BROWNE, Frances, 28-A
Thomas, 28-A
W. S., 28-A
Wm. T., 28-A
BROWNING, Evelin, 14-A
J., 93-B
John W., 14-A
Louisa K., 14-A
Mary A., 14-A
Mary J., 14-A
P. G., 280-A
Ritzen, 14-A
Susan, 14-A
Virginia, 14-A
Wm. R., 93-B
BRUCHEY, Lucy, 223-A
BRUFF, Annie M., 153-B
Beulah M., 153-B

BRUFF, Harold, 153-B
Jos. C., 153-B
Jos. D., 153-B
Martha, 153-B
Saml. G., 153-B
BRUNCHEY, Ella, 223-A
Jas. W., 223-A
Jos., 223-A
Lucy, 223-A
BRUNCK, Carl F., 37-A
Oscar, 37-A
BRUNDIGE, Flora Belle, 188-B
Rebecca, 188-B
Sallie, 188-B
Samuel B., 188-B
Sarah, 188-B
William, 188-B
BRUNICK, Julius, 37-A
BRUNNER, Mary E., 137-D
BRUSHMILLER, Chas., 224-A
Sarah, 224-A
BRYAN, (?), 440-A
Albert L., 8-D
Henrietta, 8-D
Leroy V., 8-D
Lucretia, 55-A
Vermillion, 11-A
W. H., 440-A
William A., 8-D
Wm., 8-D
Wm. H., 11-A
Wm. J., 8-D
BRYANT, Nona R., 199-D
William, 199-D
BRYEN, Sarah, 2-B
BRYNE, Eliza J., 179-B
BUCH, Mary C., 10-B
BUCK, Benj. G., 173-B
Benj. J., 173-B
Bertha, 28-B
Edward, 179-C
Emily A., 173-B
J. J., 204-A
Jacob, 204-A
James, 13-D
Lambden S., 266-A
Sarah E. (EMERSON), 179-C
BUCKINGHAM, Alfred A., 276-D
Alice, 30-A
Alice E., 276-D
Cath., 31-A
Chas. W., 45-B
Elizabeth, 31-A
Henry C., 33-A
John E., 33-A
Levi, 31-A
Lydia E., 33-A
Margt., 33-A
Mary E. Woods, 448-A

BUCKINGHAM, Mary P., 45-B
　Milton O., 276-D
　Wm. L., 276-D
BUCKLEY, Arthur, 85-A
　Danl., 85-A
　Danl. L., 85-A
　Danl. Z., 85-A
　David, 85-A
　David Z., 85-A
　Harriet P., 85-A
　May, 85-A
　Pauline, 85-A
　Thos., 85-A
　Thos. G., 85-A
BUFTER, Josephine, 337-A
BUJAC, M. Ellen, 25-C
　William J., 25-C
BUK, Wm., 126-B
BULL, Charles, 115-C
　Francis Wm., 99-A
　Mary L., 237-D
BULLERDICK, Mary A., 177-D
BUMPASS, Martha A., 158-D
BUNCE, Annie, 267-D
　Edward, 265-D
　Elizabeth, 265-D
　Geo. Edw., 265-D
　Geo. L., 267-D
　Hester, 265-D
　Jane, 265-D
　Olive, 267-D
　Olive C., 267-D
　Richard, 267-D
　Sarah, 267-D
BUNDICK, Edith R., 7-D
　P. Ross, 7-D
BUNGARNER, John P., 26-D
BUNTING, Geo., 427-D
　Geo. W., 427-D
　John W., 427-D
　Mary, 13-D
　Nellie B., 427-D
　Stephenson, 427-D
BUONHAM, Pumphrey W., 207-B
BURCH, Margt., 205-A
　Maria, 205-A
　Mary, 205-A
BURDS, Clarence P., 210-B
BURGESE, Chas., 7-D
BURGESS, Ann, 184-A
　Ann D., 399-A
　Anna A., 46-B
　Annette Smith, 44-A
　Barney, 421-D
　Basel, 184-A
　Basiel, 184-A
　Basil, 184-A
　C., 184-A
　David B., 421-D

BURGESS, E., 184-A
　Ella, 399-A
　F., 184-A
　Harry L., 184-A
　Harvey, 46-B
　Herbert, 184-A
　Jno. M., 184-A
　John L., 421-D
　Josephine, 146-B, 421-D
　Kanelia, 184-A
　Milton, 184-A
　O., 184-A
　Owan D., 395-A
　Owen, 184-A
BURGMAN, Edna, 75-A
　George, 75-A
　Wm., 75-A
BURHAM, Hazel L., 207-B
　Pumphrey W., 207-B
BURKE, Blanche E., 394-D
　Clayton L., 394-D
　Edwin Vernon, 50-D
　H. C., 394-D
　Harry C., 394-D
　Henry, 394-D
　Mary A., 394-D
　Sadie, 394-D
　Sarah R., 394-D
BURKHARDT, Eliz., 270-D
　Howard, 562-D
　Joseph, 270-D
BURKHART, Kate, 22-A
BURKHEAD, Hazel L., 446-D
BURKMAN, Frederick W., 75-A
　Lena D., 75-A
BURLEW, (?) (CHENNGE), 41-C
　Carolyn H., 41-C
　John, 41-C
BURMAN, Elmer, 327-D
　Geo. L., 327-D, 416-D
　Margaret E., 49-C
　Mary E., 416-D
　Nellie C., 327-D
　Wm. A., 327-D
BURMINGHAM, Wm., 476-A
BURNAP, Alice L., 446-A
BURNETT, Eddie, 250-A
　Edgar, 250-A
　Geo. R., 250-A
　Saml., 42-A, 250-A
　Saml., Jr., 250-A
　Sarah, 250-A
　W. F., 250-A
　Wm. T., 250-A
BURNHAM, Mary E., 207-B
　William E., 233-A
BURNS, Grace Irene, 210-B
　Rachel, 392-A
BURON, Jas. H., 163-A

BURREGHT, Wads, 35-A
BURROWS, Florence V., 163-A
  Florence Virginia, 184-A
  Ida Wilcox, 415-D
BURST, Frank M., 87-B
  Harriett L., 87-B
BURT, Carroll, 194-B
  Leonard, 194-B
  Nellie L., 194-B
  Oscar E., 194-B
BURTON, Annie Elizabeth, 156-C
  Arthur, 156-C
  Francis E., 157-C
  Helen Lee, 157-C
  Isabella K., 156-C
  John W., 196-A
  Mary, 196-A
  Mary A., 313-A
  Mary V., 122-B
  Munay, 196-A
  Richard, 12-A
  Robert, 157-C
  Robert E., 157-C
  Robert J., 156-C
  Robert R., 157-C
  Sue, 157-C
  Susan R., 157-C
  Wm., 12-A
  Wm., 122-B
BURY, Irene L., 7-C
  Thomas J., 7-C
BUSCH, Elizabeth, 10-B
  Flossie, 10-B
  George, 10-B
  Henry, 10-B
  Mary C., 10-B
BUSEY, Chas., 159-B
  Emma, 159-B
  Lethe R., 159-B
  Nellie, 159-B
  Sarah N., 159-B
  Thos., Rev., 159-B
  Willie A., 159-B
BUSH, Carroll A., 179-B
  Grover C., 179-B
  Sarah C., 19-B
  W. J. E., 179-B
BUSHEY, Susanna A., 228-B
BUSHMILLER, Elizabeth, 250-D
BUSHNELL, Mary, 515-D
BUSSEY, Thomas S., 67
BUTLUER, Edwd. R., 55-D
  Ernest, 55-D
  Helen H., 55-D
BUTTS, Elizabeth M., 35-A
BYRD, Ada, 560-D
  Annie C., 490-A
  Harry (or Henry), 490-A
  Jas. M., 490-A

BYRD, Wm., 560-D
BYRNE, Annie, 179-B
  Henry, 188-D
  Matthew, 179-B
BYROM, Chas. H., 440-A
CADDELL, Eliza A., 177-B
  Mary B., 177-B
  Raymond, 177-B
CADE, Wilford, 121-B
CADELE, James H., 117-B
CADELL, Mary, 177-B
CALBAUGH, (?), 13-A
CALDWELL, Laura E., 5-D
  Wm. M., 5-D
CALERA, Julius, 33-D
CALLAHAN, Eliza, 21-D
CALLOW, (?), 187-A
CALTON, Jean, 10-A
  John, 187-A
CALVERT, Amy, 92-B
  Chas. J., 92-B
  Ebert, 92-B
  Edward B., 92-B
  Elizabeth V., 92-B
  Florence V., 92-B
  Jas. B., 92-B
  Jno. A., 92-B
  John, 92-B
  John B., 92-B
  John G., 92-B
  Jos. B., 92-B
  Kate C., 92-B
  Mary, 92-B
  Mary A., 92-B
  Mary E., 92-B
  Mary L., 92-B
  Molly (BLAIR), 92-B
  Sarah, 92-B
  Vitue H., 92-B
CALWELL, Laura, 467-A
CAMPBELL, Elvina, 80-B
  Isabella, 80-B
  Jas. J., 176-B
  Lillian, 1-D
  Lula W., 176-B
  Martha A., 176-B
  Minnie A., 176-B
CANBY, Ann V., 207-D
  Thos. E., 207-D
CANECK, Nellie, 32-B
CANFIELD, Ira C., 168-B
  Isabel, 168-B
  Isabell H. F., 168-B
  Walter Bliss, 168-B
CANNOX, Geo. D., 38-A
  Jos., 38-A
  Lydia, 38-A
CARANTHEW, G. C., 32-A
CARAOTHERS, Magdelene, 187-B

CARE, Patricia Ann, 82-C
CARMAN, John E., 138-D
CARMINE, Carroll, 16-A
　Elizabeth D., 16-A
　J. L., 16-A
　James L., 16-A
　John Francis, 16-A
　Sarah E., 514-D
CARNEY, Annie E., 535-D
　Chas., 535-D
　Frances E., 535-D
　George, 133-A
　Harriet G., 395-D
　Hattie, 19-D
　James E., 278-A
　Jas., 278-A
　John A., 133-A
　Louisa, 133-A
　Mary A., 278-A
　Mary M., 278-A
　Thomas, 133-A
　Wm. H., 133-A
CARNOX, Joseph, 38-A
CAROLAN, John, 460-A
CARPENTER, Fayette D., 34-B
　William, 384-D
CARR, Elizabeth, 376-A
　Emma R., 376-A
　Greenbury, 376-A
　Mary J., 490-A
CARRIE, Alex M., 88-A
　Cath., 88-A
　Daniel B., 88-A
　Geo. D., 88-A
　James, 88-A
　Peter, 88-A
　Wm., 109-B
CARROLL, Earnest, 151-D
　Jessie R., 21-D
　Mary Eliza, 473-A
CARSON, David, 168-A
　Eliza, 42-B
　Emory, 163-B
　George, 42-B
　John E., 163-B
　Mary E., 163-B
CARTER, Ada V., 104-B
　Alex, 194-A
　Catharine, 21-B
　Catherine R., 21-B
　Evalious J., 21-B
　Henry, 104-B
　Ida, 138-A
　Isaac W., 68
　John, 104-B
　Laban W., 138-A
　Matilda, 138-A
　Matilda W., 138-A
　Mildred, 8-D

CARTER, Mollie B., 104-B
　Ruth, 138-A
　Sarah, 138-A
　Susan J., 104-B
　Wm. T. (or F.), 138-A
CARTHERS, Magdelene, 187-B
CARVER, David J., Dr., 11-C
　Hally M., 11-C
　Sarah A. E., 43-A
CASDORF, (?) Philis, 66
CASE, Watson, 68
CASEY, Mary A., 35-C
　Pauline, 166-A
CASH, Geo. W., 222-B
CASSADY, John, 587-D
CASSEL, Rebecca, 186-B
CASSELL, Abel, 186-B
　Abraham, 186-B
　Ann E., 185-B
　Edwin, 185-B
　Eliz, 185-B
　Emily V., 185-B
　Emma E., 336-D
　Frank, 185-B
　Fredk., 185-B
　Geo. R., 185-B
　Geo. W., 336-D
　George, 336-D
　John D., 185-B
　Joseph, 185-B
　Josephine Amanda, 134-A
　Laura L., 336-D
　Lena, 252-A
　Leonard, 67, 185-B
　Margery, 149-B
　Marqt. E., 185-B
　Mary J. Dear, 185-B
　Morris Douglas, 149-B
　Rebecca, 185-B, 186-B
　Saml. C., 364-D
　Susan A., 149-B
　Wm. E., 134-A
　Wm. G., 149-B
CASSETL, W. E., 134-A
CASTLEMAN, Rose, 371-A
CATTLE, Franis M., 32-D
CAUDILL, Ethel L., 26-C
　William S., 26-C
CAULK, Alonza G., 588-D
　Elizabeth, 183-A
　Fillmor, 183-A
　George T., 183-A
　Harry, 183-A
　Henry T., 183-A
　James, 183-A
　James T., 183-A
　James W., 33-D
　John R., 183-A
　Margt., 183-A

CAULK, Mary C., 183-A
　Mary S., 183-A
　Sarah, 588-D
　Wm., 21-A
　Wm. H., 183-A
CAULTER, Sarah, 100-B
CAVANAUGH, Sadie O., 454-D
CAVELL, Octavia, 415-D
CAYER, Maggie, 327-A
CHALMERS, Alice, 12-D
　Annie M., 12-D
　Arthur, 192-B
　Charles J., 192-B
　Elouis M., 12-D
　Evelyn, 192-B
　Gertrude E., 12-D
　Harry, 192-B
　Harry H., 12-D
　J. J., 12-D
　James J., 12-D
　Mary, 12-D
　Philecor, 12-D
　Philimona S., 12-D
　Rawlins, 192-B
　W. S., 12-D
　Wm. C., 443-D
CHAMBERLAIN, Hettie, 160-A
　Hettie R., 160-A
　John, 160-A
　John C. R. B., 160-A
　Rebecca, 160-A
　Rebecca A., 160-A
　Wm. F., 160-A
CHAMBERLINE, Edwd., 361-D
CHAMBERS, Caroline, 53-A
　Elizabeth, 183-A
　James, 183-A
　Laura, 192-B
　Mary M., 183-A
　Robert J. A., 183-A
　Sarah R., 179-B
CHANCE, Emma R. (BROWN), 115-C
　John Tillman, 115-C
CHANDLER, (?), 128-C
　Amelia, 98-A
　Benjamin A., 241-A
　Charlotte, 241-A
　Daniel, 241-A
　Estell D., 241-A
　Ethel D., 241-A
　Frank H., 241-A
　George, 241-A
　George S., 241-A
　George W., 241-A, 450-A
　Harriott J., 308-A
　Hugh, 241-A
　Hugh E., 241-A
　John H., 89-B
　Margt., 241-A

CHANDLER, Mark W., 241-A
　Myrtle, 127-C
　N. A., 241-A
　Nancy A., 241-A
　Paul, 241-A
　Peter T., 241-A
　Robert H., 127-C
　Saml., 308-A
　Sarah L., 241-A
　Sarah S., 241-A
　Susan, 89-B
　William A., 241-A
　William E., 241-A
CHANEY, (?), 471-D
　Benjamin, 244-A
　Christian, 244-A
　Harry M., 476-A
　Susan, 244-A
　Wm., 244-A, 394-A
CHANON, Edward J., Jr., 156-C
CHAPMAN, William H., 68
CHAPPELL, Annie P., 45-B
　C/Philap/Edmond, 45-B
　Grace M., 45-B
　John C., 45-B
　John G., 45-B
　M. T., 45-B
　Philip, 45-B
　Priscilla E., 45-B
　Rachel M., 45-B
　Rebecca, 45-B
　Rebecca I. M. A., 45-B
CHARD, Hattie B., 72-C
　John, 72-C
　John Crane, 72-C
　Lawrence, 72-C
　Samuel, 72-C
　Victoria (CRANE), 72-C
CHARLTON, Clara R., 10-C
　Wilbur L., 10-C
CHEN, Chao Ming, 15-C
CHENNGE, (?), 41-C
CHENOWETH, A. V., 140-B
CHESTER, Ella M., 191-B
　Grace C., 191-B
CHETELAT, Frank, 37-B
CHILD, (?), 184-A
　Afton, 106-A
　Margaret, 383-D
　Willa, 203-A
CHILDS, (?), 315-D, 414-A
　Albert W., 599-D
　Helen J., 36-C
　Jos. I., 599-D
　Thos., 315-D
　William D., 36-C
CHIN, Tsang Ian, 464-A
CHORNYEI, Julia, 33-D
　Stephen, 33-D

CHORNYET, Julia, 33-D
　Stephen, 33-D
CHRINGTON, Eunice, 84-B
CHRISTA, Alexander, 36-A
CHRISTEIN, Clara M., 46-B
CHRISTHIFF, Frances Adell, 148-B
　Frances E., 148-B
　Geo. A., 148-B
　Geo. S., 148-B
　Henry B., 148-B
　Laura O'Dell, 148-B
CHRISTIE, E. O., 251-A
　Edud. G., 251-A
　Elizabeth, 251-A
CHRISTLIFF, (?), (Mrs.), 78-B
　Adele F., 78-B
　Frances, 78-B
　George Henry, 78-B
　Henry, 78-B
　Lom., 78-B
　Margt. A., 78-B
　Sarah, 78-B
　Susan F., 78-B
CHRISTNER, Harry, 451-A
CHWERCEL, Hopewell, 258-A
CLAGG, George, 168-A
CLARK, (?) M., 103-B
　Agnes C., 535-D
　Ann, 103-B
　Annie C., 578-D
　Arthur, 512-D
　Arthur G., 512-D
　Carrie L., 50-D
　D. W., 103-B
　D. W., Mrs., 103-B
　Daniel, 103-B
　Gresa, 100-A
　James P., 31-A
　Mable, 103-B
　Mary, 512-D
　Mary C., 31-A, 512-D
　Mary E., 254-A
　Richard F., 264-D
　Risenard, 395-A
CLARKE, Chas. E., 96-B
　Chas. G., 510-D
　Edna C., 534-D
　Helen A., 96-B
　John F., 510-D
　Mary E., 510-D
CLARKSON, Annie A., 476-D
　Edw. O., 476-D
　Emma E., 476-D
　Jas. W., 476-D
CLARY, Alvin, 423-A
CLATCHEY, Chas. S., 480-A
　Hannah M., 480-A
　Jacob, 480-A

CLATCHEY, James M., 480-A
　Rich. H., 480-A
　Sarah P., 480-A
　Thos. L., 480-A
　Thos. T., 480-A
　Wm. S., 480-A
CLAY, John H., 49-C
　John W., 49-C
　Margaret Eva, 49-C
　Mary M., 49-C
CLAYTON, Ann, 24-A
　Carrie, 141-B
　Joseph S., 141-B
　Lelia A., 24-A
　Saml., 24-A
CLAZZ, John W., 313-A
CLEMENTS, John B., 5-D
　John L., 157-A
　John, Capt., 5-D
　Naomi, 5-D
　Norman S., 95-A
　Rubie, 95-A
　Sallie, 95-A
　Saml. W., 95-A
　Susan V., 5-D
CLEMM, John R., 137-A
　Rebecca R., 137-A
　William E., 137-A
　William T. D., 68
CLEMONS, Sarah E., 96-B
CLEMUS, Sarah E., 96-B
CLEVER, Stella D., 21-D
CLIFF, Mary, 15-D
CLIFT, Annie E., 314-A
　George R., 60-C
　George R. J., 60-C
　George K., 3r., 314-A
　Mary Edith, 60-C
　Thomas H., 101-C
CLINE, Lydia, 430-A
CLINTON, (?), 543-D
CLOGETT, (?), 44-A
CLOKER, Geo. R., 312-D
　Mary A., 312-D
CLOSE, Barbara, 82-B
　Christian, 82-B
　Susannah, 82-B
CLOUGH, Ellen Fleuheart, 144-A
COALMAN, Mary C., 408-A
COATES, Elizabeth, 183-A
　Jas., 208-D
COATH, Clarence J., 516-D
　John, 516-D
　Lolleac M., 516-D
　Marie, 518-D
　Rose E., 518-D
　Wm., 518-D
COBIN, Minnie, 208-D
COCHRAN, Elizabeth, 31-B

COCHRAN, Mary, 31-B
　Richard, 31-B
COCKEY, Emma, 198-B
　Evelyn, 198-B
　Ida K., 198-B
　William H., 198-B
　Wm. H., 198-B
COE, Laura B., 50-C
　Samuel W., 68
　Samuel W., Rev., 50-C
COGGINS, Ann May, 457-A
　Clara B., 457-A
　Ensous Howe, 26-B
　Frank V., 37-D
　George E., 26-B
　John, 26-B, 67
　Marea, 26-B
　Mary A., 457-A
　Richard, 26-B
　Robert, 457-A
COHA, Annie M., 372-A
COLE, Ann, 31-A
　Annie L., 19-D
　Carrie D., 3-B
　Emma M., 55-D
　James D., 411-D
　Jas., 185-D
　Joshua, 31-A
　Margaret A., 136-D
　Mary A., 3-B
　Rachel, 137-A
　Ruth A., 162-B
　Sarah, 31-A
　Thomas J., 3-B
　Thos. R. L., 136-D
　William A., 3-B
　Wm. E., 409-D
　Wm. Edwd., 185-D
COLEMAN, Ada R., 185-B
　Alex, 146-B
　Arthur, 155-D
　Elmer E., 185-B
　Hennrieta, 67
　James A., 146-B
　Jas. A., 243-A
　Margaret A., 146-B
　Mollie, 66-C
　Saml., 408-A
　Virginia F., 192-A
　Warren G., 146-B
COLING, Susan, 181-B
COLLENBY, Henry T., 152-A
　Mary I., 152-A
COLLIER, (?), 181-A
　Henry, 372-A
COLLINGTON, Emma C., 22-B
COLLINS, Annie M., 353-D
　Cath., 45-A, 98-A
　Chas. V., 220-B

COLLINS, Danl., 98-A
　David, 88-B
　Ellen F., 98-A
　Eugene A., 98-A
　Frances T., 98-A
　Geo., 98-A
　Isaac, 67
　Jas. L., 66
　John A., 67
　Saml., 353-D
　Theresa, 84-B
COLLISON, Frances E., 328-D
　Geo. W., 446-D
　H., 446-D
　Helen A., 446-D
　Milton C., 147-A
　W., 446-D
　Wm. H., 446-D
　Wm. W., 147-A
COLLMAN, Lillian V., 184-A
COMBES, Elizabeth J., 156-D
　Irene G., 156-D
COMES, Almira V., 9-D
　Geo. E., 9-D
　Harry R., 9-D
COMSTARET, Elizabeth, 81 1/2-B
CONDEN, Edward, 103-A
　Isabella, 103-A
CONDON, Edward, 103-A
　J. H., 103-A
　Wm. H., 103-A
CONNALLY, Edwd. A., 85-A
　Frances O., 85-A
　James P., 85-A
CONNELL, Wm. O., 271-D
CONNELLY, James E., 36-C
　John E., 85-A
　Malinda, 36-C
　Malinda A., 36-C
　Mary (GOVIOR), 85-A
　Michael, 36-C
　Wm., 52-A
CONNER, Ann C., 467-A
　Jonathan J. E., 467-A
　Kate E., 355-D
　Maranda E., 175-B
CONNOLY, Sophia, 272-D
CONNOR, Eliz, 175-B
　Eliz., 138-B
　Elizabeth M., 175-B
　J. J. H., 175-B
　Jas., 29-D
　Jas. Z., 29-D
　Lydia A., 29-D
CONRADE, Ellen R., 190-B
CONWAY, (?), 149-B
　Ada, 149-B
　Alfred, 72-A
　Celestine, 72-A

CONWAY, Elizabeth, 56-A, 72-A
  Elsie, 25-C
  Hattie, 19-D
  Hattie E., 19-D
  Ida, 72-A
  James, 56-A
  Jane E., 19-D
  John, 72-A
  Joseph Edward, Sr., 154-B
  Lawrence H., 154-B
  Lillie W., 149-B
  Louisa, 217-B
  Margaret, 154-B
  Martha, 25-A
  Mary R., 72-A
  Rachael, 72-A
  Sarah P., 19-D
  W., 149-B
  Wm. H., 128-B
COOK, Ann M., 282-A
  Bertha M., 535-D
  Cath., 160-B
  Charles E. F., 187-B
  Chas., 535-D
  Chas. D., 535-D
  Chas. H., 535-D
  Chas. W. S., 187-B
  Edmond, 187-B
  Eliza, 79-B
  Hatck, 460-A
  Isaac P., 100-B
  Jane Margery, 8-B
  Jesse L., 535-D
  Jos. B., 155-D
  Jos. R., 109-A
  Julia A., 535-D
  Lucy, 109-A
  M., 282-A
  Mary, 100-B, 160-B, 535-D
  Robert, 160-B
  Sarah E., 109-A
COOKE, Blanche K., 15-C
  Caleb, 79-B
  James C., Jr., 15-C
  James Clinton, 13-C
  Mary, 160-B
  Matilda E., 13-C
COOKMAN, (?), 23-D
COOLEY, Geo. B., 398-D
  Louis R., 398-D
COOMS, Earl, 9-D
  Nellie V., 9-D
  Walter M., 9-D
COOPER, Catherine W., 590-D
  Chas., 12-A
  Frank, 99-A
  George, 74-B
  George H., 12-A
  George W., 12-A, 68

COOPER, Joseph N., 96-C
  Kate, 590-D
  Laura F., 13-C
  Laura V., 12-A
  Margt., 12-A
  Maude A., 96-C
  Maude Amelia, 96-C
  Susan H., 184-A
  Susie, 148-B
  Thos. F., 590-D
  Walter, 82-A
  Wells (or Wilk), 184-A
  Wilk (or Wells), 184-A
  William A., 13-C
  Wm., 12-A
  Wm. A., Mrs., 13-C
COPENHAGEN, Sallie, 188-A
COPERY, Susan, 96-B
COPIEN, G., 5-D
  M., 5-D
COPING, Susan, 96-B
CORAN, Chas., 187-A
  Hester, 187-A
  J., 187-A
CORBY, Lucy E., 144-A
CORDEY, Sarah R., 202-D
COREL, John, 311-D
CORK, Margt., 21-A
CORLETTE, Annie E., 563-D
CORMAN, Ellen, 336-A
CORNELIUS, Priscilla, 145-B
  Samuel, 68
CORNISH, Lilly L., 92-B
CORRELL, Cora, 105-A
  J. M., 105-A
  Jas. M., 105-A
  Olivia Jane, 105-A
COSBY, L(?) E., 144-A
COSDEN, Mary, 582-D
  Mary E., 582-D
  Wm. W., 582-D
COSLEY, (?), 301-A
COSTER, Etta V., 384-A
  Frank E., 384-A
  George E., 384-A
  Joseph, 384-A, 473-D
  Joseph L., 384-A
  L. F., 384-A
  Maggie E., 384-A
  Mary A., 473-D
  Mary E., 384-A
  Nora L., 384-A
  P. R., 384-A
  Wilber H., 384-A
  Wm. Elijah, 384-A
COTTEN, M. Augustus, 465-D
COTTON, August M., 465-D
  J. L., 141-A
  John B., 465-D

COTTON, Lucy B., 465-D
M. A., 465-D
COTTRELL, Chas., 41-A
Henry W., 41-A
Mary E., 41-A
COU, Ann, 150-A
COUAY, Chas. L., 56-A
COULTE, Mary V., 150-A
COULTER, (?), Mrs., 215-A
  Annie, 150-A
  Burley, 173-A
  Ellen L., 150-A
  Eva P., 178-B
  George, 94-A
  Hannah A., 178-B
  Jane, 178-B
  John, 150-A, 375-A
  Levindas, 173-A
  Lydia A., 173-A
  Mary, 150-A, 375-A
  Robert, 150-A
  Robert A., 150-A
  Samuel, 178-B
COUNCIL, Maggie, 264-D
COUNCILL, Margaret (MORAN), 11-C
  V. H., Rev., 11-C
COURTNAY, A. M., Rev., 27-B
COURTNEY, Chas., 27-B
  Ellen W., 27-B
  Emma, 355-D
  Mary F., 27-B
  Mildred W., 27-B
  Reginald, 27-B
  Thos. E., 27-B
COWARD, Elizabeth, 67
COX, Ann, 189-B
  Annie E., 189-B
  Annie M., 189-B
  Emily S., 456-A
  Eugene, 189-B
  Harry C., 189-B
  Isaac, 189-B
  Mary J., 189-B
  W., 189-B
  Walter, 189-B, 199-B
  William F., 457-A
  Wm. H., 189-B
CRAGG, Annie R., 10-B
  Cath. R., 10-B
  Emma, 10-B
  Jas., 10-B
  Jos., 10-B
  Katherine, 10-B
  Margaret E., 10-B
  Saml. W., 10-B
CRAIG, Eva B., 420-A
  Lenn, 420-A
  Mary, 420-A

CRAIGG, Chas. W., 337-D
  Walter, 337-D
CRAMBLETT, Catharine, 122-B
  Emma, 122-B
  Geo. W., 122-B
  Thos. A., 122-B
  Wm., 122-B
CRAMER, Geo., 57-D
  Luara A., 285-A
CRANE, Victoria, 72-C
CRANGLA, Ren, 102-A
CRANGLE, Taylor, Dr., 102-A
CRAWFORD, Ann, 177-D
  Ann, 96-B
  Charles H., 177-D
  Daisy E., 177-D
  Dorothy, 26-B
  Harry E., 164-B
  Ida A., 129-A
  N. W., 37-A
CREIGHTON, Henry, 328-D
  Ida V., 394-A
  Robert, 394-A
CREMEN, Florence B., 131-C
  William R., 131-C
CREMM, Charlie, 137-A
  Willie, 137-A
CRESMIER, Harry E., 451-A
CRISP, Edna, 141-B
  I. F., 141-B
CRISPEN, Annie O., 93-B
CRISWELL, John F., 226-A
  Mary B., 226-A
  Thomas, 226-A
CROCKETT, Anna B., 513-D
  Mary Frances, 513-D
  Sarah, 513-D
  Theo. S., 513-D
  Wm., 513-D
CROFFER, Mary A., 210-B
CROGS, (?), 155-D
CRON, Sarah, 111-A
CRONAN, C. C., 68
CRONBLY, H., 55-A
CRONE, Esther Brown, 37-C
CRONMILLER, Isabel, 30-A
  Thos., 30-A
CRONNER, Chas., 166-D
CROOK, Alex. A., 600-D
  George R., 67
  Helen, 600-D
  Helen Myra, 600-D
CROOKS, (?), Rev., 70-B
  George R., Rev., 70-B
  Katherine M., 70-B
  Nellie, 70-B
  S. Frances Emory, 70-B
CROPPER, Mary A., 210-B
CROSBY, A., 356-D

CROSBY, Bessie May, 81-C
 Eliza T., 489-D
 James, 489-D
 Lillian, 129-C
 Lois, 81-C
 Sarah E., 356-D
 Wm., 356-D
CROSLY, Thos. S., 411-A
CROSS, Carrie S., 138-B
 Geo. W., 138-B
 J. R., 138-B
 Lillian M., 245-A
 Mary, 96-B, 149-B
 S. R., 138-B
 Saml. B., 138-B
 Sophia, 138-B
 Wm. H., 138-B
CROTHERS, Illinois, 433-A
 Missoun, 433-A
 Virginia, 433-A
CROUCH, John, 420-A
 Lilian M., 237-D
 Mary, 237-D
 Mary H., 180-A
 Mary L., 237-D
 Wm., 368-A
 Wm. M., 237-D
CROUSE, Carrie G., 74-D
 Elmer E., 348-A
 Willie, 74-D
CROW, (?), 312-A
 Elsie, 470-A
 Jane, 370-A
CROWLEY, J. B., 217-D
 Louise, 217 D
 Maria, 217-D
CROWN, Estelle, 23-C
 Marion A., 23-C
CROWSON, Rachell (GEALORD), 95-B
 Robert, 95-B
CROZIER, Horace, 492-D
 Wm. H., 492-D
CRUM, Edith, 2-C
 Harry, 2-C
 Nellie, 235-D
CRUMP, Elizabeth, 14-D
 John L., 14-D
 Martha, 14-D
 Wm. H., 14-D
CRUTCHLEY, Lillian (CROSBY), 129-C
 Wm., 129-C
CRUZER, Mamie, 417-D
CULEMBER, Rebecca, 264-A
CULLEY, Albert W., 146-A
 Armistead, 146-A
 George L., 146-A
 Langley B., 146-A

CULLEY, Mary, 146-A
 Mary A., 146-A
 Mary Jane, 146-A
 Wm. R., 146-A
CULLUM, Alice, 313-D
CULLY, George, 146-A
 Langly B., 146-A
 Longly B., 102-A
 Wesley, 146-A
CULVERELL, Rachel, 434-A
 Stephen, 434-A
CUMMINGS, James, 441-D
 Samuel H., 68
CURLETT, Ann, 563-D
 Ann Rebecca, 14-B
CURN, Emma J., 143-A
CURRAN, Patrick, 143-A
CURRILL, Charity A., 266-D
 Robt., 266-D
 Saml., 266-D
 Sarah E., 266-D
 Willie, 266-D
CURRY, John, 80-B
 Lydia, 80-B
CUTTLER, (?), 152-A
DACKER, Morris, 577-D
DAHL, Margaret, 33-D
DAHM, Max, 21-D
DAHNS, Florence, 195-A
DAILEY, Elizabeth, 81-D
DALE, Reva E., 129-A
DALLION, Peter D., 229-A
DALLY, W. T., 21-D
DALRYMPLE, C. F., 177-A
 C. W., 68
 C. W., Rev., 177-A
 Chas., 177-A
 Elizabeth, 177-A
 J. W., Rev., 177-A
DAMAR, (?), 370-A
DAMMER, Wm. M., 67
DANAKER, (?) H., 259-A
 Charlotte H., 259-A
 Daisey, 259-A
 Florence E., 259-A
 George D., 423-A
 George H., 423-A
 Harry S., 259-A
 Jas. D., 259-A
 John, 259-A
 John C., 259-A
 Jos. D., 259-A
 Maria M., 260-A
 Mary E., 259-A
 Orman, 260-A
 Osman A., 259-A
 Wm. H., 259-A
DANGERFIELD, Clara, 84-B
DANIELS, Alice, 108-B

DANIELS, Margaret, 108-B
DANVILLE, (?), 326-A
DARLING, Mary, 37-B
DARLY, Wm., 133-A
DARR, Wm., 84-B
DARRS, Keith, 140-A
DARSEY, Edith L., 170-D
  Lula, 170-D
DARYMPLE, Chas., 177-A
  J. A., 177-A
DAUGHERTY, Beverly, 68
DAVAM, Joseph, 249-A
DAVIDSON, Chas. M., 211-A
  Chas. N., 211-A
  Edgar T., 56-D
  John E., 234-A
  Mary, 96-B
  Mennie, 56-D
  Saml., 56-D
DAVIS, (?), 154-B, 259-A
  Alice L., 359-A
  Amelia, 81-A
  Amelia R., 81-A
  Amos M., 438-A
  Annie E., 296-A
  Arthur H., 143-A
  Benj., 347-A
  C. H., 259-A
  Catherine H., 140-A
  Charles A., 143-A
  Chas. W., 143-A, 419-D
  Edith L., 19-D
  Eliza J., 143-A
  Elizabeth, 143-A
  Elizabeth B., 399-A
  Elizabeth V., 438-A
  Emelia, 81-A
  Emily, 143-A
  Emma, 296-A
  Esther, 190-B
  Frank E., 179-C
  Franklin P., 143-A
  G. N., 359-A
  Geo., 507-D
  George W., 143-A
  Hester, 366-A
  Irene, 359-A
  Isabelle, 438-A
  James, 143-A
  James F., 399-A
  Jno. W., 143-A, 172-A
  John, 178-A, 306-A
  John W., 143-A
  Lillie M., 144-A
  Margt., 419-D
  Margt. A., 121-B
  Mark M., 69-D
  Mark N., 69-D
  Mary, 438-A

DAVIS, Mary E., 69-D
  Mary R., 69-D
  Min, 101-A
  Nannie B., 190-B
  Nellie V., 179-C
  Percy M., 190-B
  Rebecca, 419-D
  Rich, 306-A
  Ruth E., 101-A
  Saml. L., 81-A
  Sarah, 179-C
  Susan R., 296-A
  Susan S., 296-A
  Thomas, 101-A
  Thos., Mrs., 367-D
  W. R., 296-A
  Wm., 296-A
  Wm. B., 81-A
  Wm. T., 101-A, 190-B
DAW, W. J., 21-D
DAWSON, Fredk., 244-A
  Mary W., 139-B
  Wm. A., 139-B
DAY, Walter, 126-A
DAYTON, Chas., 230-A
  Hester A., 262-A
  Mary E., 352-A
DE CORSE, Barney, 88-B
DE FOREST, Margaret, 96-B
DE GRIEF, Philip, 464-D
  Philip A., 464-D
  Sarah A., 464-D
DE KUBLER, Susanna, 277-A
DE LANNEY, (?), 288-A
DE MONT, Julius, 130-A
DE SHIELS, Margaret (JONES),
  74-C
  Wm., 74-C
DE(?)CRAFT, Grace, 34-C
DEAVER, Elizabeth, 75-B
  Elizabeth Ann, 75-B
  Emmanuel Kent, 75-B
  John Lucas, 75-B
  John Talbott, 75-B
DECK, Charles, 113-C
  Mary E., 113-C
DECKER, Alice A., 20-D
  Arthur G., 577-D
  Calvin F., 20-D
  Daisy M., 577-D
  Geo. T., 20-D
  Georgana, 577-D
  Grace Estella, 207-A
  Grace Miles, 207-A
  Ida H., 20-D
  John C., 20-D
  John Calvin, 20-D
  Mabel, 577-D
  Margt. A., 20-D

DECKER, Mary, 20-D
  Mary E., 577-D
  Milton B., 577-D
  Milton E., 20-D
  Saml., 20-D
  Saml. W., 20-D
  Samuel, 20-D
  Thos., 20-D
DECUS, James, 174-B
  John, 174-B
  Mary E., 174-B
DEEMS, George W., 68
DEEN, Sarah, 76-B
DEER, Annie, 21-D
DEHN, Elizabeth, 402-A
DEISS, Wm. A., 155-D
DELBROOK, George W., 33-D
DELCHER, Eva, 420-D
  George, 420-D
DELCKER, Frank, 420-D
  Geo. B., 420-D
  Nellie, 420-D
DELEHAY, Cath., 103-A
DELEVIE, Livingston L., 74-C
DELIVIE, Alma Estella, 74-C
DEMPSTER, Ann, 386-A
  Geo. E., 196-B
  George, 196-B
  Grace A., 196-B
  Hattie M., 196-B
  John, 196-B
  Maria, 142-A
  Mary A., 196-B
  Mary M., 196-B
  Thos., 196-B
DENBER, Mary A., 417-A
DENBOER, Abraham, 417-A
DENBORE, Julia A., 417-A
DENBOREN, Mary A., 417-A
DENNIS, E., 583-D
  Edna, 583-D
  Edw., 583-D
  Lillian M., 583-D
  P. W., 583-D
  Wm. J., 583-D
DENNY, Chas., 185-A
  Clinton, 185-A
  Mary, 408-A
  Thos., 185-A
DENON, Eliza, 438-D
DENTZ, Louis S., 402-D
DEPELL, Martin, 340-A
DERICKSON, Elizabeth, 112-A
DERTRAM, Emma S., 267-D
DETTUS, (?), 175-B
DEULIN, Lilly, 467-A
  Rebecca, 467-A
DEVERE, G., 15-A
  Lucy, 15-A

DEVLIN, Amelia F., 366-D
  Howard Carter, 366-D
  Jos., 366-D
DICKEL, Mildred, 31-D
  William P., 290-A
DICKENS, George, 152-A
  Mary A., 152-A
DICKENSON, Elisha, 386-A
  Mary, 240-A
DICKERSON, Elisha, 386-A
  Mary Ann, 386-A
DICKINS, Josiah, 96-B
DICKSON, James, 210-B
  Martha, 210-B
DIDEDHOVER, Chas. B., 404-A
DIDENHOVER, Harry R., 404-A
  Henry W., 404-A
  Ida Clara, 404-A
DIETER, (?) (BICHE), 47-C
  John, 47-C
  Leola C., 85-C
DIETZ, Chas. F., 233-A
DIETZWAY, Anna Barbara, 342-D
  Frank J., 342-D
DIFFORY, A., 232-A
DIFFY, Alexandra, 168-D
  Mary E., 168-D
DILL, Donald W., 525-D
  Ellen, 281-A
  Harry, 81-A
DILLA, Wm., 229-A
DILLAHUNT, Wm. L., 278-A
DILLEHANEY, Mary, 49-A
DILLEHEY, John, 149-A
DILLEHUNT, Jno., 278-A
DILLION, Frank, 81-A
DILLON, Harry, 81-A
DINBROW, John C., 205-A
DINNIS, Benj. H., 583-D
  Chas. E., 583-D
  E., 583-D
  Emma Retta, 583-D
  Louie Grace, 583-D
  P., 583-D
  Samuel, 583-D
  Wm. E., 583-D
DISCKEL, Mildred, 31-D
DISNEY, Annie, 558-D
  Clara, 161-D
  Florence, 161-D
  Florence V., 161-D
  Isabell J., 153-A
  J., 14-A
  Jas., 194-A
  Jas. M., 153-A
  John W., 161-D
  John W., Sr., 161-D
  Joseph, 28-D
  Joseph A., 28-D

DISNEY, Louisa, 28-D
Margt. A., 194-A
Mary, 153-A
Mary B., 14-A
Mary E., 161-D
Mary E. (WARWICK), 161-D
Ruth B., 6-C
Thomas H., 14-A
Wesley, 14-A, 194-A
Wm., 153-A
DISTES, (?), 154-B
DITMAN, Alice, 15-D
Chas. R., Jr., 15-D
Eliza, 15-D
John, 15-D
Lillie Shaffer, 15-D
Lydia, 15-D
Nelson G., 15-D
Nelson R., 15-D
Rachel, 15-D
Sue I., 15-D
Wm. H., 15-D
DITMAR, Frederick, 246 1/2-A
DITRICKS, Benj. R., 596-D
DITTMAN, Henry W., 423-D
DITTUS, Hester L., 175-B
DIX, Ellerson H., 7-D
John W., 7-D
M. Anna, 7-D
Mable I., 7-D
DIXCKEL, Mildred, 31-D
DIXON, Edith, 51-A
Edward D., 27-D
Grace M., 27-D
John W., 7-D
Mary E., 27-D
Saml. T., 27-D
Samuel P., 27-D
DOANE, Fannie E., 428-A
DOBBS, Ann, 44-B
DOBSON, Earnest H., 24-D
Ernesth, 24-D
Marie A., 24-D
DODD, Daniel, 126-B
Ella V., 105-B
Ellen, 126-B
Emma L., 105-B
Helen, 126-B
Jane, 105-B
John, 105-B, 126-B
Martha, 126-B
Robert, 126-B
Robt., 126-B
Sallie R., 105-B
Saml., 126-B
Thos., 126-B
DOGGE, (?), 68-C
DOLL, Mary C., 98-A
Michal, 98-A

DOLSON, Alice J., 85-A
DONALD, Ellen M., 49-A
DONALDSON, George W., 68-C
Lily Mae, 68-C
S., 239-A
DONAVAN, (?), 57-D
Alfred M., 130-A
Claressa, 130-A
Clarissa, 130-A
Conelia, 130-A
Isabella, 130-A
Richard I., 130-A
DONELLY, C., 142-D
Jennie, 142-D
DONOVAN, James, 24-B
Jas., 223-D
DORAN, Thos. C., 509-D
DORRETT, LaRue V., 51-B
DORSEY, Daniel W., 359-D
Durbrow, 205-A
Edwin, 68
Elizabeth, 141-A
Hannah, 149-A
Jane R., 359-D
Jas. B., 402-A
John H., 136-A
John M., 136-A
John W., 141-A
Louisa, 239-D
Mary A., 141-A
Mary E., 141-A
Rebecca, 477-A
Rebecca A., 478-A
Saml. B., 355-D
Sarah R., 355-D
Thomas, 141-A
Thos., 418-D
Thos. R., 239-D
Wm. T., 141-A, 239-D
Wm. W., 359-D
DOSH, John H. C., 68
DOSS, Sophia, 244-D
Sophie, 244-D
DOUGHERTY, (?), 79-B
B. W., Rev., 544-D
Beverly W., 544-D
Georgette, 21-D
Georgianna, 79-B
Helen, 544-D
Jeanette L., 79-B
Sarah A., 263-A
Warren, 79-B
DOUGLAS, Elizabeth A., 56-B
DOUNEY, Thomas, 264-A
DOVE, Clarence, 56-A
Grace O., 37-C
DOWDEN, Esther, 192-B
DOWNS, Carroll, 314-D
Charlotte, 149-A

DOWNS, Eliz. M., 314-D
Elizabeth, 149-A
Ethel B., 147-B
Geo. W., 39-A
Gilbert, 132-A
Harry A., 314-D
Henry O., 147-B
J. Randolph, 132-A
John A., 314-D
John J., 149-A
Joseph, 149-A
Laura A., 39-A
Maggie, 149-A
Margt. A., 314-D
Sarah, 147-B
Willard W., 147-B
William, 39-A
Wm. F., 147-B
DOXON, Wm. H., 167-A
DOXYON, Wm. H., 167-A
DRANSOFF, Geo. C. F., 212-D
Laura M., 212-D
DRESDLET, Laura M., 175-B
DREXEL, Grace V., 128-C
John M., 128-C
John McMahon, 128-C
Mary (O'RILEY), 128-C
Richard, 128-C
DRIVER, Margaret M., 86-A
R. E. L., 86-A
DU MONT, Eliza A., 130-A
DUBLIN, Rebecca, 467-A
DUCKETT, Annie, 144-A
DUDLEY, Carrie N., 244-A
John R., 238-D
Marion C., 238-D
Mary J., 73-A
Merins L., 73-A
Rebecca, 73-A
Wm. H., 238-D
DUKE, Chas. C. III, 137-B
Marie V., 137-B
DULANEY, James M., 528-D
Mary E., 528-D
DULEY, Bessie, 318-A
Georgana, 318-A
DULL, Harry, 98-A
Ida, 98-A
DUN, Alverdd, 185-A
DUNGER, Maria L., 121-B
DUNLAP, Samuel B., 67
DUNLOP, Laura, 88-A
Margt. A., 88-A
DUNN, Mary J., 2-D
Susan H., 79-B
DUNNING, Ledie Waugh, 194-A
DURAN, Mary J., 55-A
DURAND, Annie, 96-B
John A., 55-A
DURAND, John B., 96-B
John H., 55-A
Wm. T., 55-A
DURFFIELD, Jane, 7-C
DURHAM, (?), 358-A
Cath., 91-A
George N., 5-C
Jeremiah D., 91-A
John, 91-A
Katie E., 5-C
Lillian C., 5-C
Martha, 91-A
Mary, 353-A
Mary A., 91-A
Wm., 29-B
Zachues, 353-A
DURICKSON, Eliz., 112-A
DURLROW, Elizabeth W., 205-A
DURR, Boran W., 292-A
DURY, Thomas H., 31-B
DUTTON, Donaldson Leroy, 186-D
Fredk. W., 186-D
Louisa, 186-D
Lucy A., 186-D
Mathilda, 186-D
Wm. B., 186-D
DUVAL, Chas. C., 339-A
DUVALL, Annie, 28-D
Edna Rowe, 250-A
Edwd., 28-D
I. M., Miss, 205-B
Mertle, 28-D
W., 28-D
DUYER, Frank P., 137-B
Maria, 137-B
DWYER, Daniel C., 137-B
DYER, Eliz., 260-A
DYKES, George, 307-A
DYSART, Ann, 315-A
Catherine, 21-B
EADER, Ada, 98-B
Charlotte, 139-B
Mary V., 98-B
EAGER, Ann, 21-D
EARECKSON, Federal, 3-B
Hennrietta, 3-B
Julia A., 3-B
Mary, 3-B
Riza, 3-B
Robert, 206-D
EARL, Mary, 372-A
EARLE, Harriet N., 173-D
EARLING, Catherine (?), 17-D
Clara, 17-D
Clara V., 17-D
Daniel, Mrs., 17-D
Eliza L., 17-D
Geo. L., 17-D
Leonard, 17-D

EARLING, Michael, 17-D
EARNEST, Cath., 215-A
  Elizabeth, 215-A
EARP, Estelle, 208-B
EAST, (?), 127-B
  Abigal, 127-B
  Arletta M., 581-D
  Emily E., 581-D
  Fredk. C., 127-B
  Harry, 127-B
  Henry, 127-B
  Henry P., 581-D
  Jas. M., 581-D
  John M., 581-D
  Robert P., 581-D
  Thos. A. B., 127-B
EBAUGH, Belle Mercer, 201-B
  Beverly H., 201-B
  Herbert S., Sr., 201-B
EBER, Earl Vernon, 20-C
  Eliz. Mildred, 20-C
EBORALL, John, 299-A
ECKMAN, Howard A., 99-C
  Howard Arthur, 99-C
  Thelma Mae, 99-C
EDDY, Geo. W., 261-A
  Gordan W., 261-A
  Lurinda W., 261-A
EDGAR, Florence E. (TUCKEY), 94-B
  Florence Evelyn, 94-B
  Geo., 94-B
  Harold, 94-B
  James W., 94-B
  Lydia M., 13-C
  Mary, 101-A
  Susan, 94-B
  Susan Jeanett, 94-B
  T., 94-B
  Thos., 94-B, 101-A
EDGER, Anna Hall, 101-A
  Geo. W., 101-A
EDMONDSON, Moses L., 101-B
  Susan K., 135-B
  Susanna, 127-B
EDMONSON, (?), Mrs., 127-B
  (?), Mrs., 135-B
EDWARDS, Eliza, 134-B
  Hannah, 116-B
  Louisa, 315-A
  Mary Ann, 468-D
  Melaire R., 39-A
  Robert, 116-B
  Thomas, 84-B
EGERTEN, Virginia A., 220-B
EGERTON, James C., 220-B
  Walter C., 220-B
EGGELSTON, Ecelia, 142-B
EGGERTON, Maud, 220-B

EICHELLEGER, John W., 96-A
EICK, Nellie F., 126-A
EIGELBERGER, Malcolin, 96-A
EIGELBERNER, Anna Mary, 140-B
  C. V., 140-B
  Catherine V., 140-B
  Ellenor V., 140-B
  Mabel, 140-B
  Thomas A., 140-B
EINWICH, Francis V., 85-C
  Leola, 85-C
  Leola C. (DIETER), 85-C
EIPMAN, Sallie E., 168-B
EISHELLUGER, Malcolin, 96-A
ELAPANB, An K., 81-B
ELDER, Carrie Buchner, 33-D
ELDERDIRE, Mary, 235-A
ELISON, Gus, 155-D
  Jus, 155-D
ELKINS, Annie L., 200-B
  Chas. E., 200-B
  Laura, 354-D
  Margt., 354-D
  Mary C., 354-D
  Nannie C., 200-B
  Robt. L., 354-D
  Sarah C., 200-B
  Wm. H., 354-D
  Wm. Oliver, 354-D
ELLICOTT, Annie R., 188-B
ELLIOTT, Allie F., 414-A
  Edward G., 414-A
  Frances A., 482-A
  Geo. T., 217-B
  Gideon, 414-A
  Gideon A., 482-A
  Gilbert R., 59-C
  Gorden B., 414-A
  Ida H., 262-D
  James, 482-A
  Jos., 482-A
  Lillian J., 414-A
  Saml. A., 414-A
  Sarah, 414-A
  Sarah E., 414-A
  Wm., 13-D
  Wm. T., 482-A
ELLIS, Della Plummer, 87-C
  Ruben, 67
ELLISON, Clara S., 440-A
  Florence C., 469-A
  George H., 440-A
  Ida V., 469-A
  Jennie, 469-A
ELY, Ann, 131-A
EMERICK, Ang C., 54-A
EMERSON, Sarah E., 179-C
EMINIZER, Bessie M., 157-C
  Roscoe, 157-C

EMMART, David G., 121-B
Emma Pearce, 121-B
EMMERICK, Aug, 54-A
EMMERLICK, Anna G., 54-A
EMMERSON, Rebecca, 73-A
EMMICK, Albert, 157-B
Eliz., 157-B
John T., 157-B
John V., 157-B
Nicholas, 157-B
EMORY, (?), 301-A
Ann L., 158-B
Frances, 158-B
John, 67
John, Rev., 70-B
Katherine, 70-B
Lillian Rose, 37-D
Margt., 158-B
Maria, 158-B
Reober, 70-B
Robert, 67
Robt. T., 111-B
Sue, 158-B
ENGLISH, M., Mrs., 41-B
ENNIS, Margaret, 204-A
ENOS, Alice V., 509-D
Mary D., 509-D
Mary J., 509-D
Newton, 509-D
Robert E., 509-D
Sarah, 509-D
ENSOR, Daniel, 376-A
William F., 46-B
ENTZ, Andrew, 207-A
Harriett, 207-A
Henrietta, 207-A
EPHREN, Elizabeth, 9-D
Nancy, 9-D
Peter, 9-D
EPHRON, Joseph, 9-D
ERB, Norman, 217-A
ERCKSON, Axel, 96-B
ERDMAN, Annie T., 161-A
Mildred F., 161-A
Millard, 161-A
Millard F., 161-A
Sallie E., 161-A
EREDMAN, John F., 161-A
ERICKSON, Abel, 224-A
ERIKSON, Maria, 96-B
ERNST, Simon, 193-A
ESHAM, Fannie, 179-B
Herman L., 179-B
ESIKSAM, Abel, 224-A
ESKELS, Walter E., 74-D
ESPEY, Hannah E., 183-C
ESRICK, Mary E., 288-A
ESSENDER, Cath., 74-A
Edward, 74-A

ESSENDER, Jas., 74-A
John, 74-A
John R., 74-A
Louis, 74-A
Mary, 74-A
Mary E., 141-D
Thos., 141-D
Wilber, 74-A
William, 74-A
EVANS, Annie E., 224-B
Cath., 428-D
Frank Andrew, 188-D
George W., 68
Laura, 367-D
Mary E., 188-D
Randolph, 367-D
Randolph Elmer, 367-D
William, 33-D, 68
EVERIT, Mary E., 32-D
EVLON, Philip, 4-B
EWARD, John R., 39-A
EWELL, Thos., 204-A
EWING, Mary, 106-A
EYLEREY, Mary E., 25-A
EZELL, (?), 112-C
FABER, Doris, 374-D
FABIAN, Caroline, 164-C
Elizabeth W., 164-C
Jas., 164-C
John E., Sr., 164-C
FABOR, Effie, 212-D
Effie I., 212-D
John, 212-D
FAGER, Emma, 142-B
FAIDLEY, Edward J., 86-C
Flossie May, 86-C
John W., 86-C
Robert S., 86-C
FAIRBANK, Emma, 145-B
James Mercer, 145-B
FAIRCHILD, Henry D., 32-D
FAIRMAN, Elizabeth Jane, 112-C
Elizabeth W., 112-C
Frank W., 112-C
Frank Willard, 112-C
Robert W., 112-C
Virgie May, 112-C
FAITH, Mary, 96-B
FALK, Anne F., 88-C
FALKNER, Elizabeth, 67
FALL, Rhods, 140-A
FANTON, Ja. H., 249-D
Jas. M., 249-D
Mary C., 249-D
Mary R., 34-B
Susan E., 249-D
FARBERST, Miron, 23-D
FARGO, Asa B., 212-B
Asa B., 395-D

FARGO, Edwd. L., 395-D
  Frances E., 395-D
  Hennrietta, 395-D
  Mary V., 212-B
  Wilson, 395-D
FARINHOLT, Frank Walter, 85-C
  Paul Berry, 85-C
FARLEY, Frederick, 235-D
FARMER, Julia, 133-D
FARRELL, Mary E., 529-D
  Wm., 529-D
FARRING, Elizabeth, 127-B
  Ely, 127-B
  Henry, 67
  Henry, Rev., 127-B
FARSLEY, John, 126-B
FARSON, Clara E., 37-C
  Jennie, 48-C
  Percy L., 48-C
FATHAMS, Elizabeth, 48-A
FAULKNER, Charlotte, 33-D
FAWBANTA, Geo., 134-B
FEAZARE, John, 96-B
FEE, Bertie, 131-C
  Bertie V., 131-C
  Herbert M., 131-C
  John R., 131-C
  John Russell, 131-C
  Lawrence A., 131-C
  Milton, 131-C
FEELEMEYER, Annie, 182-B
  Ch., 182-B
  David, 67, 182-B
  Emma, 182-B
  Geo. W., 182-B
  George W., 67
  Mary, 182-B
  Wm. M., 182-B
FEELER, Geo., 499-D
FEFEL, Mary, 184-D
FELLER, Geo., 26-C
  Geo. V., 26-C
  Lula M., 26-C
  Methilda (THON), 26-C
FENDLEY, Sarah E., 174-A
FERGERSON, Mary, 382-A
  Wm., 382-A
FERGUSON, A. E., 472-D
  Clara L., 4-C
  Fredk., 472-D
  Geo. N. W., 247-D
  Georgianna, 173-D
  Harriet M., 173-D
  John, 173-D, 602-D
  John F., 173-D
  John H., 4-C, 247-D
  John T., 247-D
  July A., 472-D
  Margt. A., 247-D

FERGUSON, Mary A., 472-D
  Nehimiah, 472-D
FERRIER, George W., 531-D
FESTER, Annie C., 149-A
  Philip, 149-A
FETHERS, Leroy, 81-B
  Walter L., 81-B
FIELDS, Elizabeth, 67
  Grace E., 9-D
  Mary V., 9-D
  Saml. A., 66
  Wm., 67
  Wm. H., 9-D
FIGG, John Q., 463-D
  Mary C., 463-D
FINK, Charles W., 102-C
  Margaret H., 102-C
  William L., 102-C
FINN, Edwin A., 449-A
  Ella, 449-A
  John A. S., 449-A
FINSH, Cassinda, 98-B
FISCHBECK, Agnes S., 71-C
  John A., 59-C, 71-C
  Scott J., 71-C
FISCHER, Margt. J., 147-B
  Walter L., 56-D
  Wm. A., 147-B
FISCKER, Geo. A., 147-B
FISHBURN, M., 383-A
  S., 383-A
FISHER, Abraham, 167-A
  Albert M., 167-A
  Amanda, 167-A
  Annie M., 107-B
  Carroll, 84-B
  George F., 167-A
  Jas., 200-A
  M. L. H., 181-B
  Mary E., 33-D, 97-D
  Rebecca, 107-B
  Robert, 107-B
  Sarah, 200-A
  Sarah A., 200-A
  Wm. W., 107-B
FISSEL, Rachel, 123-B
FITCHELL, John Dixon, 521-D
FITCHETT, Alke E., 521-D
  Dixon, 521-D
  Sarah A., 521-D
FITTECH, Cora, 154-A
FITZ, John, 98-B
  Sarah, 98-B
FITZGERALD, Ann Maria, 248-D
  Clara V., 10-A
  Eliza Jane, 240-A
  Frank H., 10-A
  George, 16-A
  James, 10-A

FITZGERALD, Louis W., 10-A
Mary M., 16-A
Michael J., 345-A
FITZMORRIS, Mary, 140-A
Mary E., 140-A
FITZPATRICK, (?), 418-D
Elizabeth, 73-A
Ella, 205-B
Geo. H., 73-A
Jos. B., 450-D
Mary C., 450-D
Mary E., 450-D
Wm. H., 450-D
FIZGERALD, (?), 274-D
FLAHERTY, Thomas I., 34-C
FLAXCOUCH, Harry, 1-B
Mary, 1-B
William, 1-B
FLEAGLE, G. (TROMAN), 200-A
Ira, 200-A
FLEMING, James P., 447-A
FLETCHER, Elizabeth, 312-A
FLINT, Dorothy Jean, 130-C
FLOOD, Elizabeth, 381-A
Thomas A., 381-A
Thomas G., 381-A
FLOYD, (?), 332-A
Isabell, 11-D
Philener, 328-A
Robt. McClary, 228-A
William J., 68
Wm. J., 228-A
FLURRY, Rebecca, 21-D
FLYNN, Ann C., 469-A
Ella, 512-D
Geo. A., 596 1/2-D
George F., 469-A
Henrietta, 512-D
Herbert, 512-D
Isabel, 390-D
Jno. M., 596 1/2-D
John A., 512-D
Mary A., 512-D
Mary H., 596 1/2-D
FOGELMAN, Chas., 154-B
FOGLER, Ann, 298-A
Ellen C., 124-D
Ellery C., 124-D
Fannie, 178-D
Geo. P., 124-D
Ida M., 298-A
John, 298-A
John S., 298-A
Martha A., 298-A
Martha E., 298-A
Robert H., 178-D
Robt. K., 124-D
Sallie A., 124-D
FOIL, Agnes F., 208-D

FOIL, Alice, 223 1/2-D
Alice A., 223 1/2-D
Domingo, 223 1/2-D
FOLIN, Virginia, 496-D
FOLK, Blanche Baker, 90-A
FOOKE, Ella, 96-B
FORBES, M. L., 68
FORD, Allen, 25-A
Anna E., 81-B
Annie, 187-B
Edward P., 15-C
Franklin, 187-B
Franklin C., 81-B
Grace, 191-B
Gustave W., 30-D
Ira, 453-D
Myrtle E., 49-D
FOREMAN, Crissie D., 73-C
Hannah, 149-A
Henrietta, 149-A
Mary A., 149-A
Sarah E., 139-A
FORESTER, Ann E., 394-A
Ida C., 394-A
Jas., 461-D
FORITZ, Wm. H., 147-D
FORMAN, Mary A., 149-A
FORNEY, Charles M., 156-B
Chas. Meredith, 156-B
Hilda K., 156-B
Mason Edwin, 156-B
FORRESTER, Elmer W., 541-D
Harriet Ann, 461-D
Harriett, 455-D
Leonard, 455-D, 461-D
Nicholas, 394-A, 455-D
S. W., 541 D
Saml. W., 541-D
Susanna, 541-D
FORRISTON, Winfield, 146-B
FORSYTH, Annie, 218-B
David, 218-B
David J., 218-B
James, 13-D
James B., 13-D
Josephine, 218-B
Lillie M., 218-B
Louis, 13-D
Louisa, 13-D
Mildred, 13-D
Susanne A., 218-B
Thos., 13-D
FORSYTHE, Joseph P., 30-A
FOSBENNER, Ann, 22-A
Daniel J., 22-A
Danl. F., 22-A
Elizabeth, 22-A
S. W., 22-A
Susannah, 22-A

FOSBENNER, W. G., 22-A
Wm. G., 22-A
FOSS, Chas. H., 180-D
Elizabeth, 78-A, 368-A
Geo. E., 182-D
George, 78-A
Jacob, 368-A
Jno. H., 368-A
John A., 368-A
John H., 180-D
Margt., 180-D
Mary, 78-A
Sarah L., 180-D
Wm. H., 180-D
FOSTER, A. M., 203-D
A. N., 203-D
Adele M., 164-B
Anna C., 149-A
Bertha A., 164-B
David B., 164-B
Eliza P., 164-B
Elizabeth, 113-C, 305-A
Elizabeth A., 305-A
Harry E., 164-B
Ida L., 164-B
James, 164-B
Mary, 164-B
Mary A., 305-A
Mary M., 164-B
Philip, 149-A
Philip W., 149-A
Robert G., 394-A
Saml., 305-A
Thos. Y., 203-D
Yale, 203-D
FOUNCE, John, 437-A
Mary, 437-A
Robert, 437-A
Sarah J., 361-A
FOWBLE, Lilia, 62-C
Wilbert A., 62-C
FOWLER, Ann C., 209-A
J. W. H., 304-A
John P. W., 503-D
L. P., 503-D
Maggie, 209-A
Margt., 261-A, 477-A
Mary E., 134-A
Susanna, 304-A
William, 304-A
FOX, Annie E., 206-A
Carrie, 33-D
Conrad, 206-A
Susan, 54-B
William L., 33-D
FOXWELL, (?), 225-B
(?), 229-A
Annie E., 225-B
Catherine, 460-A

FOY, Eliz A., 493-D
Julia A., 493-D
FRANCE, H. S., 68
Joseph, 68
FRANIE, Cath., 270-D
FRANK, Alice, 343-A
Alverda, 343-A
Margt. A., 243-A
Mary A., 343-A
Wm. B., 343-A
FRANKLIN, Ann M., 101-A
Enos W., 126-A
Isiah, 101-A
Leroy, 45-A
FRAZIER, Adeline, 150-B
Alverda E., 150-B
H. A., 150-B
Harriett A., 150-B
Harry F., 150-B
John, 150-B
Lillian Estell, 150-B
Mary E., 150-B
Mary Helen, 150-B
Rich, 150-B
Rich H., 150-B
Rich M., 150-B
Samuel M., 21-D
FREDERICK, Chas., 101-A
Flora, 33-D
Galen, 33-D
Michael, 33-D
FREEBERGER, David, 362-D
FREEDENBERGER, Virginia, 192-B
FREELAND, Annie E., 103-B
Edith E., 103-B
Edwd., 272-A
Eluona, 39-B
George D., 103-B
John, 103-B
T., 39-B
Thomas H., 39-B
Wilbur K., 103-B
FREEMAN, A. G., 192-B
Charles S., 192-B
F. James Edw., 45-C
Gordon H., 46-C
Grace, 192-B
Herbert B., Jr., 192-B
James, 192-B
James Edward, 46-C
Leona, 45-C
Levin, 330-A
Mary A., 192-B
Nellie G., 46-C
Otto D., 213-D
Sarah I., 330-A
Stanley P., 45-C
Walter R., 192-B
FREENEY, Benj., 176-A

FRENCH, Cornelius, 468-A
Francis M., 199-B
FRESHOUR, Catherine, 103-B
Elizabeth, 103-B
Greenberry, 103-B
Wm. H., 103-B
FRIDAY, Eliza M., 131-B
FRITZ, C., 455-D
Carrie (KRIETZ), 127-C
Charles, 127-C
L., 455-D
FRIZZELL, Rebecca, 51-B
FRNSH, Cassinda, 98-B
FROCKLING, Henry, 365-D
Jessie B., 365-D
FROST, Annie B., 164-A
C. Walter, 164-A
Elias W., 164-A
FRUEHSORGER, Frank, 36-C
Marie, 36-C
FRUSH, Cassinda, 98-B
Morean T., 48-D
FRY, Eliz. J., 110-A
FUEHRER, Martin, 360-D
FUGLER, Alice, 481-A
FUNBAUGH, Stewart N., 149-A
FURGERSON, Mary, 382-A
FURL, Ruby, 38-C
Ruby (MC DANIEL), 38-C
FURLONG, Eliza, 374-A
Elizabeth, 374-A
Henry, 68
Henry B., 67
Thos., 374-A
Wm. L., 56-A
FURSH, Moreay F., 48-D
FURY, Edna, 360-D
Florence, 360-D
Martin, 360-D
GABLE, Benj. F., 32-D
Lydia A., 461-D
Robert, 394-A, 461-D
GADDESS, John, 283-A
Mary A., 16-D
GAFFARD, Margt., 96-B
GAITHER, Cath., 240-A
Greenbury, 240-A
Harry C., 208-B
Hettie, 240-A
Saml., 240-A
Vergie E., 208-B
William T., 240-A
GALBE, Wm. H., 394-A
GALBRAETH, H. Clifton, 10-D
GALBRITH, H. Clifton, 10-D
GALLAGHER, Margt., 427-C
GALLAHER, James W., 7-D
GALLAWAY, George Lee, 156-A
George W., 156-A

GALLEON, Estella E., 80-A
GALLGHER, Margt., 410-A
GALLION, Esstella E., 60-C
John D., 60-C
Mary, 60-C
Oliver, 60-C
Wm. E., 60-C
GALLOWAY, Wm., 520-D
GARDNER, Annie C., 505-D
Anthony B., 505-D
Arthur B., 111-C
Clara A. H., 208-B
Everet, 208-B
Jas., 73-A
Jos., 38-A
Katherine, 111-C
Rosa V., 73-A
GARDON, Mary, 21-D
GARFIELD, Arthur, 510-D
GARLAND, (?), 78-A
Laura V., 88-B
GARMAN, Joseph B., 131-B
GARRETT, Elizabeth, 310-A
Florence B., 466-D
Geo., 466-D
Howard M., 517-D
Jas. C., 1-B
Julian H., 310-A
Margt., 466-D
Mary, 310-A
R. F., 310-A
Robert, 310-A
Robert W., 310-A
Wm. A., 310-A
GARRETTSON, Edith B., 475-D
GARRISON, Howard, 377-A
GARVER, Pearl F., 129-A
Pearl Zepp, 129-A
GARY, Jacob, 155-D
Jeremiah, 131-A
Lena, 155-D
GASTRON, Christian, 133-D
GATCH, Chas. H., 236-A
Condua, 236-A
Edwd. L., 236-A
Jane W. N., 236-A
Jane White, 236-A
Jas. E., 236-A
Lillian E., 236-A
Margt. A., 236-A
Martha J., 236-A
Mary, 236-A
GATTEN, Thomas E., 14-C
GAULD, Homer W., 555-D
GAULIN, James E., 367-D
GAULINE, Mary Evans, 367-D
GAWTHROP, Alice M., 209-B
GAY, Edna, 23-D
GEALORD, Rachell, 95-B

GEDDES, George W., 268-A
  John C., 268-A
  Kate, 268-A
GEDDESS, George, 268-A
  Jane, 268-A
  Jas. P., 268-A
  John, 142-D
  John C., 268-A
  Lillian, 142-D
  Mary, 142-D, 268-A
  Wm., 142-D
  Wm. G., 142-D
GEESE, Frank, 310-A
GEGLUIE, (?), 153-B
GEISLER, Mary, 113-C
GELBEE, Elizabeth M., 430-A
GENT, Catherine, 578-D
  Fredk., 578-D
GENTRY, George W., 38-C
  Mildred M., 38-C
GEORGE, Annie B., 223-D
  Enoch Bishop, 67
  Frances N., 223-D
  John W., 24-B
  Maria L., 223-D
  Matilda, 128-B
  Nellie, 24-B
  Pearl E., 24-B
GEORGUS, Walter W., 84-B
GERE, John A., 67
  John A., Rev., 129-B
  Sarah, 129-B
GERICK, Clara L., 398-A
GERMAN, Alice E., 23-D
  Mary Elizabeth, 96-C
  Webster, 23-D
GETTIER, Ella Virginia, 110-B
  Jacob, 110-B
  Margt., 110-B
  Mary, 110-B
  Wm. P., 110-B
GHISSLUR, Wm. H., 17-D
GIBBS, Elizabeth, 196-A
  John, 196-A
  Sarah J., 42-B
GIBSON, (?), 154-B
  Alice, 33-A
  Ella M., 155-A
  Jean M., 155-A
  John J., 24-C
  Mabel F., 24-C
  Mary A., 132-A
  Sarah, 277-D
  Virginia Way, 155-A
  William L., 155-A
  William Seebert, Dr., 155-A
GIFFIN, Frank, 327-D
  G. M., 327-D
  Mary Ann, 327-D

GIFFIN, Thos. R., 327-D
GILBEE, Cath., 430-A
  Catharine, 430-A
  Sophia, 430-A
GILBERT, Isabel H., 430-A
  M. V., 442-A
GILBIN, Edna Blanche, 21-D
GILBLELRT, Thos., 218-B
GILDEN, Joan C. B., 85-C
GILES, Ellen, 196-A
  Emma, 196-A
  Henry G., 109-A
  John, 196-A
  Jos., 179-A
  Jos. D., 179-A
  Joseph, 179-A
  M. F., 179-A
  Maggie E., 179-A
  Margt. A., 109-A
GILL, A., 425-A
  A. J., 425-A
  Anna H., 143-B
  E. M., 143-B
  Eliz, 525-D
  Eliza, 521-D
  Estella M., 143-B
  George Cooper, 325-D
  George H., 325-D
  Helen W., 220-B
  John, 425-A
  John Price, 325-D
  Mary Elizabeth, 23-B
  Providence, 325-D
  Saml. H., Dr., 220-B
  T., 425-A
  Terese J., 220-B
  Theofilus P., 23-B
  Theopolius, 23-B
  W. J., Rev., 28-D
  William J., 143-B
  William M., 143-B
GILLBEE, Sophia, 430-A
GILMORE, Lois Anna Holley, 155-A
GILSON, Agnes, 208-A
  Ann E., 354-A
  Harriott, 354-A
  M. E., 208-A
  Mary, 208-A
  William F., 208-A
GIRDWOOD, Augusta, 227-B
  Christine O., 227-B
  Jas., 227-B
  Jessie B., 227-B
  Josephine, 227-B
  Margt. C., 227-B
GISRIEL, Martha W., 145-B
  Mary Beulah, 145-B
  William, 145-B

GITTINGES, Ann R., 460-D
  L. V., 495-D
  Roland, 495-D
  Thos., 495-D
  Thos. C., 495-D
GLALDING, Saml., 97-A
GLANVILLE, Harriet, 439-A
  Mary, 439-A
GLAPSCOCK, Mary A., 156-B
GLASSCOCK, Mary A., 156-B
GLEMM, Geo. O., 446-D
  Georgana, 446-D
GLENDENNING, Dora, 168-A
  John, 168-A
GLENDING, Clara E., 168-A
GLENN, Lewis, 486-A
  Louisa, 486-A
GLOCKER, Elizabeth E., 207-A
GLOVER, A., 28-D
  A. E., 28-D
  Bernard E., 28-D
  G., 28-D
  Geo., 28-D
  Julia Ware Reinhard, 251-A
  Saml. W., 85-A
GODFREY, George, 154-A
  Lenna, 154-A
  Lottie, 154-A
  Martha E., 154-A
  Mary A., 154-A
GODMAN, Ann M., 212-A
  Arminta, 53-A
  Cath., 212-A
  Edward C., 212-A
  Eliza, 53-A
  I., 212-A
  Jno., 212-A
  John, 212-A
  Katherene, 212-A
  Marion, 212-A
  Mary A., 212-A
  Mary L., 212-A
GODRICH, Levi, 45-A
GOEE, Peggy, 66
GOFF, James, 206-A
  James P. R., 206-A
  James R. P., 206-A
GOLDEN, E. W., 192-A
  Mary J., 197-D
GOODHAND, Alice J., 23-A
  Elizabeth, 23-A
  J., 23-A
  J. Frank, 23-A
  James B., 23-A
  Jas. B. (or E.), 23-A
  John P., 23-A
  Jos. B., 23-A
  M., 23-A
  Martha G., 23-A

GOODHAND, Thos. B., 23-A
GOODING, Herbert A., 87-D
GOODRICK, Julia V., 28-D
  Laura K., 28-D
GOODWIN, Ruth, 96-B
GOOLACK, Indianna, 507-D
GORDON, Douglas, 5-D
  Lydia, 5-D
  Prudence, 177-D
  Wm. E., 5-D
GORE, Albert P., Dr., 75-B
  Clarence S., Dr., 75-B
  Fannie S., 75-B
GORSUCH, Emma L., 401-A
  Jas. S., 47-B
  Jophianna, 47-B
  Robert, 47-B
  Thos. H. S., 47-B
GOSNELL, Annie V., 10-D
  M. Rebecca, 10-D
  Susan, 10-D
  Thomas S., 10-D
  Wm. F., 186-A
  Wm. T., 186-A
GOTE, Pe(?), 66
GOULD, Adda, 439-A
  Amelia, 258-A
  Annie A., 439-A
  Sophia, 555-D
GOULDMAN, H., Mrs., 459-D
GOVIOR, Mary, 85-A
GRABE, Robert, 395-A
GRAFF, E. Beatty, 3-D
GRAFFLER, Mary, 4-B
GRAFLIN, Conrad, 452-D
GRAHAM, (?), 354-D
  Edw., 269-A
  Edwd., 269-A
  G. C., 466-D
  Geo. W., 466-D
  Imogene, 14-B
  Jennie, 47-C
  John, 269-A
  Mary J., 269-A
GRANBERRY, Albert B., 88-B
GRANBURY, Albert B., 88-B
GRANGER, (?), 328-A
  Albert, 106-A
  Emma, 106-A
  Harriet Purdy, 106-A
  Harriett, 106-A
  Henry K., 106-A
  Howard, 106-A
  Jas., 106-A
  John, 106-A
  John W., 106-A
  Maggie, 106-A
  Mary, 106-A
  Sarah A., 106-A

GRANGER, William H., 106-A
  Wm., 106-A
  Wm. H., 106-A
  Wm. H., 106-A
GRASSO, Viola, 161 1/2-D
GRAUEY, Dorothy, 288-A
GRAVE, Anna, 32-D
  David, 139-B
  Rachel B., 139-B
GRAVES, Cath. D., 134-B
  Harriet, 233-A
  Jno., 91-B
GRAY, Bertha, 106-B
  Chas., 106-B
  Frank G., 156-A
  Ida V., 106-B
  John B., 465-A
  Lewis, 473-A
  Margt., 473-A
  Robert W., 214-A
  Samuel, 88-B
GRAYDON, Nancy, 21-D
GREEN, (?), 5-D
  Alfred, 5-D
  Arthur D., 210-B
  Edward, 177-B
  Elizabeth, 217-B
  Florence, 49-D
  Henry, 182-A
  Ida A., 210-B
  John, 210-B
  John J., 68
  Mary, 157-A, 177-B
  Mary T., 184-B
  Naomi Jeanette, 5-D
  Robert, 56-D
GREENFIELD, Chas. R., 166-B
  Clara B., 166-B
  Wm. E., 166-B
GREENTREE, Eliz, 91-B
  Ester A., 91-B
  Florence D., 91-B
  Florence W., 91-B
  Harriett, 91-B
  Harriett R., 91-B
  Howard, 91-B
  M. Z., 91-B
  Rebecca S. (or A.), 91-B
  Wm. H., 91-B
GREENWALT, Thos. S., Jr., 148-B
GREENWOOD, (?), 600 1/2-D
  Thos., 110-A
GREGORY, George W., 53-A
  Jas. E., 53-A
  Mary J., 53-A
  Wm. R., 337-D
GRENTZ, John E., 70-D
  Margaret A., 70-D
  Robert V., 70-D

GRENZ, Maude Alma, 70-C
  Walter A., 70-C
GRIENER, Louisa E., 29-B
GRIEVER, Eliza, 29-B
GRIFFIN, Estell, 241-D
  Jennie (Virginia) L., 26-C
  Mandekla, 290-A
  Virginia L. (Jennie), 26-C
  William R., 26-C
GRIFFITH, Alice, 364-D
  David L., 290-A
  Ellenor L., 223-A
  Emory, 364-D
  Erim W., 140-D
  Joseph B., 204-A
  Margaret, 143-D
  Margt. J., 140-D
  Martener C., 364-D
  Mary A., 327-D
  Mary J. B., 364-D
  Robert H., 143-D
  Rose D., 204-A
  Wm., 143-D
  Wm. A., 26-C
  Wm. H., 140-D
GRILLETT, Saml., 445-A
GRIPP, Louis, 301-D
  Lula E., 301-D
GRONEWELL, Alice E., 183-C
GROSLAND, Henry, 277-A
GROVES, C. D., 134-B
  Sarah, 134-B
GRUBB, Elizabeth, 207-A
  Saloni, 207-A
GUEST, Emma, 209-B
  Harry, 209-B
  Henry, 209-B
  M. C., 135-B
  Madola Christian, 152-B
  Mary Ann, 209-B
  Mary L., 135-B
  Rebecca, 135-B
  Rich. G., 135-B
  Sallie, 135-B
  Samuel, 135-B
  Sarah C., 135-B
  Susan, 135-B
GUMPMAN, Alfred, 49-D
  Carroll, 49-D
  Mary, 49-D
  Robert, 49-D
  Susan, 49-D
  Viola R., 49-D
GUNDRY, I., 28-D
  Isabella H., 99-C
  W., 28-D
  William Pressman, 99-C
  Wm., 28-D
GUNDY, Isabella H., 99-C

GUNTHER, Raymond, 41-C
  Viola Stanley, 41-C
  Walter S., 41-C
GURNEY, Bradley, 199-A
GUSSEN, Karl, 33-D
GUTMAN, Allen, 66
GUYER, Albert, 101-A
  Eliz., 101-A
  John, 101-A
GWYNN, W. R., 68
HABERKAM, Bessie E., 49-C
HABERKOM, William, 49-C
HACKETT, Jennie, 536-D
HACKNEY, Ella Blanche, 9-D
  Elsie M., 9-D
  Geo. R., 9-D
HADAWAY, Edwd., 56-A
  Jas. E., 56-A
  Wm. H., 56-A
HADNER, Fredk. J., 453-A
HAEFFNER, Marie J., 329-A
HAGAN, May, 21-D
HAGER, Annie D., 340-D
  Carrie, 340-D
  Eva, 340-D
  Jacob, 340-D
  Jacob E., 340-D
  Mary O., 340-D
  Rose, 340-D
HAGERTY, John, 67
HAGGAIT, Mary, 205-A
HAGNER, Adam, 422-A, 453-A
  Earl F., 160-C
  Frank R., 422-A
  Fred., 422-A
  H. W., 453-A
  John T., 160-C
  Kimberly O., 160-C
  Maggie, 453-A
  Mary, 422-A
  Sophie, 160-C
  Susan, 453-A
  Susannah, 422-A
  William T., 453-A
HAHN, Chas. E., 111-B
  Irene L., 3-D
HAIGHT, Joanna, 2-D
HAILEY, T. N., 92-B
HAINES, Clara, 166-B
HALBEY, Sadie C., 92-B
HALE, Anna G., 224-B
  Charles W., 224-B
  Frances M., 224-B
  Helena S., 224-B
  John E., 224-B
HALL, (?), Mrs., 221-A
  Adah, 87-C
  Adah S., 87-C
  Ann, 301-A

HALL, Annie, 363-A
  Charles A., 87-C
  Daniel F., 329-D
  E., Rev., 208-B
  Estelle (EARP), 208-B
  Everet, 208-B
  George R., 132-A
  Harry, 10-D
  Harry J. F., 10-D
  Harry L., 10-D
  Harvey L., 589-D
  Heias (or Aelas) R., 185-B
  Hester, 443-A
  Jennie, 301-A
  John H., 208-B
  John R., 132-A
  Levin, 443-A
  Lula, 107-A
  Maria J., 266-A
  Mark J., 436-A
  Mary, 363-A
  Melva M., 329-D
  Milton, 208-B
  Missouri, 140-C
  Randolph, 132-A
  Re(?) P., 208-B
  Rose Stewart, 10-D
  Saml. P., 132-A
  Sarah Jane, 10-D
  Sophia, 363-A
  Susan A., 132-A
  Walter Lee, 436-A
HALLEY, Edith C., 92-B
  Franklin T., 92-B
  Kate C., 92-B
  Leonard T., 92-B
  Mary M., 92 B
HALLIDAY, William H., 67
HALLWIG, Edw. O., 194-B
  Ellen, 194-B
  Oscar, 194-B
  Wm., 194-B
HALTZMAN, Anna, 76-B
  George, 76-B
  Kate, 76-B
  M. C., 76-B
  Margt., 76-B
HALWIG, Mary, 194-B
HAMBLETON, Alexander, 192-B
HAMILTON, Alexander, 94-A
  Clara, 373-D
  Clara, 49-C
  Sarah R., 186-B
HAMMEL, Mary, 143-A
HAMMELL, Mary C., 14-B
HAMMILL, Rebecca, 21-D
HAMMOND, Ann, 205-A
  Henry, 399-D
HAMPT, C. M., 134-A

HAMPTON, Henry W., 519-D
  Jessie T., 519-D
HANAWAY, (?), 600 1/2-D
HANBACK, Chas. A., 34-B
HANCOCK, Eliz., 138-B
  Lottie, 84-B
HAND, Emily, 203-B
HANDY, John, 86-A
HANER, James, 23-A
HANEY, Chas. A., 476-A
HANKEY, Ella G., 29-D
HANLIN, (?), 199-D
HANLON, James, 537-D
  James P., 537-D
  Margt., 537-D
HANNA, Ann, 110-A
  Cowin Colson, Jr., 76-A
  Edwin F., 76-A
  J. Herbert, 76-A
  Laura, 76-A
  Mabel Hardy, 76-A
  R. F., Jr., 76-A
  Vavina D. H., 76-A
  Verine (HERBERT), 76-A
HANNAH, Ann, 110-A
HANNING, Cath., 444-A
HANORD, John J., 413-A
HARBOUR, Jessie S., 202-A
HARDCASTLE, Elizabeth, 174-D
  Mary, 174-D
HARDESTY, Chas. R., 362-A
  Edwd., 91-A
  Elinor, 39-C
  James T., 30-A, 39-C
  Jas. E., 392-D
  M., 91-A
  Martha, 91-A
  William, 240-A
HARDING, Annie, 96-B
  Chas. B., 603-D
  Clara, 603-D
HARDY, Lilitia A., 348-A
HARE, Ruth, 21-B
HARGETT, Charles R., 99-C
  Rachel S., 99-C
HARIG, Henry A., 414-D
  Lillie, 414-D
  Millard H., 414-D
  Milton A., 414-D
  Sadie C., 414-D
  Virginia, 414-D
HARLOW, Isaac, 350-A
HARMAN, Alice G., 33-D
  Earl E., 27-C
  William H., 109-A
  Wm., 109-A
HARN, Anna, 129-C
  Dalton L., 129-C
HARRINGTON, Margaret, 18-D

HARRINGTON, Ulysses, 21-D
HARRIS, A., 250-D
  Albert B., 250-D
  Alexander H., 3-D
  Annie M., 250-D
  B. B. G., 2-D
  Baldwin G., 2-D
  Barbara E., 250-D
  Chapin A., 72-B
  Chapin B., 72-B
  Chas. L., 2-D
  Darwin B., 72-B
  E., 250-D
  Edward, 250-D
  Elizabeth, 2-D, 72-B
  Gertrude Rose, 250-D
  Grace B., 250-D
  Hiram M., 2-D
  Irwin L., 72-B
  James, 72-B
  Katherine, 60-D
  Lee M., 250-D
  Libbie, 72-B
  M. Mary, 45-C
  Mary C., 72-B
  Naomi, 3-D
  Nellie A., 250-D
  Sarah J., 189-A
  Thos. J., 302-A
  William, 250-D
  Wm. J., 250-D
HARRISON, Annie E., 275-A, 351-A
  Barbara, 140-C
  Betty R. (ARNOLD), 30-D
  Fannie, 14-A
  John L., 38-B
  Josiah, 21-D
  Tobetha, 275-A
  Vertie, 251-A
  William O., 140-C
HARRISS, Alice V., 274-D
  Irene B., 2-D
  James, 302-A
  Martha, 438-A
  Mary A., 251-A
  Samuel, 251-A
  Sarah E., 251-A
  Thomas, 302-A
  Thos. G., 251-A
  William T., 438-A
HARRORD, John J., 413-A
HARRSON, Elizabeth A., 140-A
HARTLEY, Geo. W., 575-D
  Rachel, 210-D
  Susan E., 575-D
HARTLOVE, Ada M., 17-A
  Alice, 17-A
  Alice S., 17-A

HARTLOVE, Annie E., 17-A
  Chas. F., 17-A
  Chas. H., 17-A
  Eliza A., 17-A
  Elizabeth, 17-A, 39-A
  Enoch, 25-D
  Estell, 39-A
  Harry S., 39-A
  James, 39-A
  John, 39-A
  Joseph, 39-A
  Joshua, 39-A
  Marg. E., 39-A
  Mary E., 39-A
  Mary F., 39-A
  Saml. E., 39-A
  Walter, 39-A
  Wesley, 39-A
  Wm., 39-A, 484-A
HARTMAN, (?), 56-A
  Christian, 80-A
  Danl., 104-A
  Eliz. J., 109-A
  Ernest, 80-A
  Frank, 80-A
  Frederick, 80-A
  Fredk., 80-A
  Geo., 515-D
  George H., 515-D
  Harry, 80-A
  Isabell, 109-A
  John, 80-A, 104-A
  Joseph, 515-D
  Julia, 104-A
  Lydia, 515-D
  M. E., 80-A, 104-A
  Margt., 104-A
  Mary A., 80-A
  Philip, 80-A
  Robert, 515-D
  Tredena, 80-A
  William, 104-A
  Wm. H., 109-A
  Wm. H., Jr., 109-A
HARTY, Mynette A. (or F.), 185-B
HARVEY, (?), 33-A
  A. Edgar, 108-B
  Andrew, 108-B
  Ann Jane, 89-B
  Chas. A., 476-A
  Chas. M., 476-A
  Elizabeth, 441-D
  Fielding M., 476-A
  Frank, 476-A
  Lydia F., 108-B
  Mary A., 476-A
  Mary C., 108-B
HARWOOD, Blanche H., 149-D

HARWOOD, Cruelia H., 149-D
  Frank, 149-D
  Mammie, 149-D
  Mary L., 32-D
HASEY, Elinna G. H., 309-A
HASHIP, Cath., 107-A
  John, 107-A
HASLAN, Alice, 436-A
  Anna, 34-B
  Emily J., 34-B
  Rebecca, 34-B
  Saml., 34-B
HASLUP, R. C., 67
HASSON, Ceal C., 111-A
  Mary E., 111-A
HASTY, Chas. B., 185-B
HATCH, Elizabeth, 399-D
HATFIELD, Herbert Daniel, 115-C
  Herbert R., 115-C
  Mary A., 115-C
HATHING, Annie, 96-B
HAUBACK, Charles, 34-B
  Chas. A., 34-B
  J. S., 34-B
  John, 34-B
  Nellie, 34-B
HAUS, Eileen deChantel, 172-C
  John, 172-C
  Kenneth Lee, 172-C
  Leida, 172-C
  Leida F., 172-C
HAUSE, Elizabeth, 162-A
HAVILAND, Evelyn T., 152-B
HAWKINS, Estella May, 348-A
  Florence I., 205-B
  George P., 19-B
  Joooph M., 348-A
  Samuel, 19-B
  Sarah, 19-B
HAWKS, Madline, 78-A
HAWLEY, I. M., 68
HAWTHORN, (?), Rev., 254-A
HAYES, Charity, 154-B
  Ida, 154-B
  James, 154-B
  Jos. L., 154-B
  Marion, 176-B
  Susan, 200-A
HAYMAN, Geo., 491-D
  Geo. W., 491-D
  Martha, 491-D
HAYS, Chas. A., 341-A
  David, 341-A
  Emily, 341-A
  Frances V., 341-A
  George W., 233-A
  Jno. W., 233-A
  Walter E., 341-A
HEAD, Sarah A., 47-B

HEAFLEICK, Agnes A., 187-D
HEALEY, Charles H., 600 1/2-D
HEARD, Sarah A., 47-B
HEART, George, 178-B
HEATH, Alfred A., 303-D
  Alie, 303-D
  Ethel, 303-D
  Margaret E., 303-D
  Richard Roy, 303-D
HEATON, Harriett, 102-A
  Harriett A., 102-A
  Jessie, 102-A
HEDGES, J. W., 68
HEDRICK, Bernice P., 45-C
  Frank B., Sr., 45-C
HEGSELL, (?), 66
HEIDERMAN, Emma J., 157-A
HEIMILLER, Edward, 246 1/2-A
HEIN, Geo., 515-D
  Mary E., 515-D
HEIRING, Susannah, 189-A
HEISER, Danl. E., 223-A
HELLBACK, Emilie (SCHWANEBACK), 33-C
  Henry, 33-C
HELLER, Allen B., 38-C
  Fred B., 30-B
  Mary Alice, 38-C
HELLMAN, Francis J., 392-A
HELLMANN, C. Joseph, 392-A
  Edythe Ray, 392-A
HELMING, Susan E., 162-A
HELMLING, Annie, 162-A
  Cardelia, 162-A
  Chas. J., 306-A
  George R., 162-A
  Gertrude, 162-A
  Henry, 162-A
  Jas. E., 162-A
  Jno., 162-A
  John, 162-A
  Wm., 162-A
  Wm. H., 162-A
HELWIG, Oscar, 194-B
HEMMICK, Annie M., 6-D
  Caroline V., 6-D
  Irene W., 6-D
  J. M., 6-D
  Margt. E., 6-D
  Mary E., 6-D
  Thom., 6-D
  Thos. L., 6-D
  Wm., 21-D
HEMMUK, Chas. R., 429-A
  George, 429-A
  John C., 429-A
HENDRICKSON, John, 155-D
HENDRY, Marie, 21-D
HENKEL, Bertrame, 577-D

HENKEL, George, 577-D
  Jacob, 53-B
  Mary, 577-D
  Mary E. (DECKER), 577-D
HENNABURG, Rachel, 184-B
HENNING, Jeremiah, 198-B
  Mary E., 198-B
  Robert A., 312-D
HENNINGER, David, 577-D
HENRY, Aquilla, 520-D
  Margt., 520-D
HENTHORN, James, 141-B, 156-A
  James H., 141-B
  Jos. H., 156-A
  Mary E., 141-B
  Robert E., 141-B, 156-A
  Sarah E., 141-B
  Thomas, 156-A
HENTHORNE, Mary, 156-A
  Robert T., 156-A
  William J., 156-A
HENTZE, Wm., 380-A
HEPBURN, Aluera (or Alueta), 155-B
  Alueta (or Aluera), 155-B
  Arthur B., 208-B
  Clara V., 208-B
  David, 208-B
  David H., 155-B
  Harry, 208-B
  Jas., 208-B
  Louis, 155-B
HERBERT, Alex. J., 36-A
  Catherine F., 76-A
  Felix McCurley, 36-A
  Francis, 76-A
  Harlan, 76-A
  John H., 76-A
  Joseph A., 36-A
  Laura, 76-A
  Margaret B., 76-A
  Mary A., 36-A
  Mary Sawyer, 76-A
  Milchor, 36-A
  Rebecca, 36-A
  Richard, 36-A
  Sarah A., 76-A
  Sarah Ann, 76-A
  Thos., 36-A
  Verine, 76-A
  W. F., 76-A
  William Frank, 76-A
HERN, Maria, 66
HERON, Annie D., 557-D
HERPEL, Margaret, 47-C
  Michael O., Sr., 47-C
HERRINGTON, Matilda A., 423-D
  Timothy, 423-D
HERRON, Jas., 184-B

HERRON, L. E., Rev., 557-D
  Lewis, 184-B
  Lewis D., 68
  R. G., Rev., 557-D
HERTZEL, Grace H., 33-D
HESBBARD, (?), 305-A
HESS, John E., Jr., 147-D
HESSEY, Caroline, 462-A
  Jennie, 309-A
  Mary, 462-A
  Saml. A., 462-A
HEURA, Charlotte, 21-D
HEVALY, Mary, 139-A
HEWETT, Annie, 391-D
  Cath., 391-D
  Eliza, 32-D
HEYDE, Carrie R., 137-A
HICHEL, M. G. Adolph, 210-A
HICKEY, Dennies H., 586-D
  Dennis H., 586-D
  Ellen Louise, 586-D
  Virginia, 586-D
HICKMAN, Isabell, 421-D
  James, 421-D
  Wm. H., 57-D
HICKS, Isabel Disney, 82-A
HIEHLE, Emily M., 210-A
HIEKEL, G. A., 210-A
HIGDON, Alexander, 466-A
  Annie, 468-D
  Annie E., 462-D
  Baptist, 466-A
  Eliza, 506-D
  Elizabeth, 446-A
  Ernestine, 34-B
  George, 466-A
  George W., 378-A
  Harriet, 379-A
  Harriot, 379-A
  J. B., 466-A
  James, 34-B
  John L., 71-D
  Jos., 379-A
  Lawrence, 34-B
  Lewisa, 71-D
  Lydia A., 365-A
  M. C., 379-A
  Maggie, 365-A
  Mary, 379-A
  Mary J., 365-A
  Ralph, 379-A
  Robert, 379-A, 462-D
  Thomas, 378-A
  Willie, 378-A
  Wm., 34-B
  Wm. F., 378-A
  Wm. H., 365-A
  Wm. T., 379-A
  Zenobia, 365-A
HIGGINS, Chas., 239-D
  Ethel, 239-D
  Margt., 12-A
  Mary E., 239-D
HIGH, Benj. F., 257-A
  Chas. S., 257-A
  Elizabeth, 257-A
  George, 321-A
  Hannah, 237-A
  Henry, 321-A
  Ida E., 257-A
  Jas., 237-A
  Joseph, 257-A
  Mary E., 257-A
  Rachel, 139-B
  S., 321-A
  Sarah, 139-B, 321-A
  Susan, 257-A
  Wm., 139-B, 257-A
  Wm. F., 257-A
  Wm. T., 257-A
  Wm. Thos., 257-A
HIGNET, Elizabeth, 446-A
HILDITCK, Mary Ann, 170-A
  Peter R., 170-A
HILE, L. Irene, 140-D
HILGARTNER, Katherine, 200-B
HILL, (?), 229-A
  Agnes A., 436-A
  Alex., Dr., 28-D
  Annie H., 111-C
  Eliza, 436-A
  Elizabeth, 337-A, 436-A
  Ellen, 436-A
  Ellen Bell, 28-D
  Florence S., 72-C
  James, 28-D
  James B., 111-C
  Jos., 247-D, 337-A
  Joseph S., 72-C
  Mark, 436-A
  Mary, 337-A
  Mary E., 173-D
  Nancy A., 28-D
  William, 337-A
  William H., 337-A
  William H. H., 337-A
  William, Jr., 337-A
  Wm. J., 28-D
HILLEDGE, Eliza, 96-B
HILLYARD, Benj., 158-A
  Harriet, 158-A
  Martha E., 158-A
HILMILLER, Catherine, 84-C
HILTNER, Hasson, 69-C
  Hasson E., 69-C
  John, 69-C
  Margaret, 69-C
HILTON, John J., 152-B

HINDES, Benjamine F., 48-B
　Fanhine (or Jahine) B., 48-B
　Jacob H., 48-B
　John, 48-B
　John B., 48-B
　John J., 48-B
　Mary A., 48-B
　Moses G., 48-B
　Rebekah, 48-B
　Theodore, 48-B
　William, 32-A, 48-B
　William T., 48-B
HINDMAN, Blanch, 179-B
　Chas. R., 179-B
　Emily, 179-B
　Kate, 179-B
　Peter, 179-B
　Peter M., 179-B
　Susan, 163-B
　W. J., 179-B
HINDS, George, 32-A
HINES, Geo., 32-A
　John, 32-A
　Wm., 32-A
HINKEL, Minnie, 48-C
HIPBURN, David, 155-B
HIRCORNE, Mary E., 96-B
HIRSHFIELD, John, 144-A
HIRST, William, 67
HISSEY, Ann E., 133-A
　Ann M., 182-A
　Annie E., 309-A
　B. M., 182-A
　Chas. B., 182-A
　Chas. H., 182-A
　Frank E., 182-A
　Hannah, 133-A
　Ida Wall, 182-A
　John A., 309-A
　John A., 331-A
　William, 133-A, 462-A
HISSY, Franklin, 133-A
HITCHCOCK, Jishella, 159-A
　Joabelle, 157-A
　Sallie, 159-A
　Sarah J., 266-D
HITZELBERGER, Hannah, 313-A
　John A. B., 313-A
HITZIBURGER, Jno., 313-A
HITZICBURGER, James, 185-B
HOBBS, Anne Rebecca, 70-C
　Armstaid R., 5-D
　B. B., 79-B
　B. Ormon, 70-C
　Edw., 484-A
　Emma E., 79-B
　M. L., 484-A
　Mamie H., 79-B
　Margt., 5-D

HOBBS, Margt. A., 484-A
　Virgel G., Mrs., 49-C
　Virgil, 49-C
　Washington H., 484-A
HOBLITZELL, M. Nettie, 199-A
HOCHLER, Mary Elizabeth, 33-D
　William, 33-D
HODGES, (?), 170-A
　Milcah, 73-C
　Milcah M., 73-C
　Wm. R., 73-C
HOFFACKER, Annie W., 140-C
　Charles F., 140-C
HOFFMAN, (?), 26-D
　Eliza, 177-D
　Emeline, 177-D
　Harry, 163-B
　John, 177-D
　Martha E., 177-D
　Martha Louisa, 73-C
　Mary, 163-B
　Samuel W., 66
HOFFNAGLE, Jos. R., 395-A
HOFMEISTER, Wm. H., 446-D
HOGAN, Mary V., 164-A
　Nicholas, 80-B
HOGG, Alexander S., 195-B
　E. A., 49-A
　Eliza A., 49-A
　Elizabeth, 49-A
　Elizabeth A., 49-A
　H., Mrs., 49-A
　Joseph, 49-A
　Margt., 49-A
　Martha A., 49-A
　Mary E., 49-A
　Rachel, 49-A
　Sarah, 49-A
　Virginia M., 195-B
　Wm. H., 49-A
HOHL, Conrad, 397-D
　Wm. B., 397-D
HOHLSYD, Walter W., 30-A
HOHN, Evelyn E., 198-B
　Florence E., 198-B
　Thomas W., 198-B
HOKHUACHEN, (?), Miss, 15-C
HOLBITGELL, Frank H., 199-A
HOLDSWORTH, Wm., 155-D
HOLLAND, Ama, 183-B
　Amanda, 183-B
　Annie E., 158-D
　Bernice L., 158-D
　Carroll H., 127-C
　Chas., 183-B
　Edward H., 126-C
　Estella, 158-D
　Geo. B., 17-D
　Gertrude H., 219-B

HOLLAND, Guy O., 158-D
  Hazel M., 158-D
  Helen Mary, 113-C
  Horace S., 67
  Horas, Rev., 183-B
  John Alvin, 113-C
  Luretta, 158-D
  Maggie, 415-A
  Mary E., 158-D
  Musaoore E., 17-D
  Nannie G., 126-C
  Nelson O., 126-C
  Percy S., 142-B
  R. H., 67
  Richard H., 183-B
  Robert, 11-D
  Saml., 305-A
  Wm. E., 514-D
HOLLANS, (?), 62-C
HOLLEY, Lois M., 155-A
HOLLINGSHEAD, Amelia R., 199-A
  Frances, 199-A
  Frances, Capt., 199-A
  Frank, 199-A
  Frank, Capt., 199-A
  George, 199-A
  George F., 199-A
  James, 199-A
  John B., 199-A
  Saml. O., 199-A
  Sarah, 477-A, 478-A
HOLLY, Lois M., 155-A
HOLMES, Annie, 214-B
  Cora G., 145-B
  George, 154-A
  Isabol, 214-B
  John, 214-B
  Mary A., 154-A
  Newman C., 145-B
  Robt., 214-B
  Sarah J., 214-B
  Thos., 214-B
  Wm., 214-B
  Wm. R. Lloyd, 214-B
HOLSTEIN, Wm. H., 137-A
HOLSTINE, Lydia, 137-A
  William H., 137-A
HOLSTON, Ann, 576-D
  Louis A., 576-D
HOLTGELL, Mary E., 199-A
HOLTYN, (?), 347-A
HOLTZ, Olivia R., 55-A
  Sadie M., 55-A
HOLTZER, Jno., 422-A
HOLTZMAN, A. J., 345-A
  Sarah Ann, 76-B
HOLYROOD, Frank W., 30-A
HOMAK, Flora, 39-D
HOMER, John E., 88-B

HONEYWELL, Albert W., 79-B
  Charles B., 79-B
  James B., 79-B
  Kate, 79-B
  Malina, 79-B
  O. J., 79-B
HOOD, Ida P., 497-D
  Mary S., 497-D
  Wm. P., 497-D
HOOFNAGLE, William, 395-A
HOOK, Margaret, 87-C
  Samuel J., 87-C
HOOPER, (?), 595-D
  Florence Simerine, 33-B
  John P., 390-A
  William, 239-A
  William H., 235-A
  Wm. D., 33-B
  Wm. K., 33-B
HOOVER, Peter, 42-A, 373-A, 375-A
  Sarah, 42-A
HOPKINS, (?), 3-D, 345-A
  Clara, 62-C
  F. Stewart, 86-A
  Fannie G., 3-D
  Hettie M., 86-A
  James H., 86-A
  Joan M., 71-B
  John C., 19-B
  Johns J. (or G. or both), 3-D
  Laurence G., 3-D
  Martha A., 217-B
  Mary E., 86-A
  Sallie, 88-B
  Sarah J., 440-A
  Stewart F., 86-A
  Wm. T. B., 53-B
HOPWOOD, Elmer E., 32-C
  Frank A., 74-D
  Fred A., 74-D
  Hannah, 74-D
  Hattie E., 74-D
  James E., 74-D
  Jas., 74-D
  Myrtle, 74-D
  Stella, 74-D
  Willie H., 74-D
HORA, Ann, 180-D
HORN, Almira, 491-A
  David, 198-B
  Hannah, 199-B, 491-A
  Henry, 491-A
  John T., 198-B
  Kate, 198-B
  Margt., 198-B
  Willie, 198-B
HORNER, John C., 88-B
  Laura V., 88-B

HORSEMAN, C. R., 85-A
Mary E., 85-A
Sarah, 85-A
HORTON, Harry H., 57-D
Helen Amelia, 57-D
Winter D., 57-D
HORWITZ, Ella M., 30-A
HOUGH, Edw. S., 69-B
Edward Hamilton, 69-B
Harrie, 69-B
Nannie Whiting Hamilton, 69-B
Susan A., 69-B
HOUSE, (?), 204-B
Jas. H., 79-A
HOUSLOW, John, 21-D
HOVADER, Florence, 71-C
Gary, 71-C
HOWARD, Ann, 121-B
Beal, 121-B
Charles, 99-A
Christopher, 121-B
Debora, 121-B
Eli D., 307-D
Ella, 370-D
Ellen, 436-A
Ellen E., 370-D
Geo., 370-D
Geo. W., 370-D
Glemia R., 78-A
H. C., 370-D
Henry, 121-B
Joseph W., 69-C
Kate C., 436-A
Lucy A., 273-A
Mary, 121-B
Mary C., 440-A
Mary R., 69-C
Robert J., 370-D
Saml. A., 370-D
W. G. N., 436-A
Wallace E. B., 233-A
HOWE, Mary E., 26-B
HOWELL, Mary, 83-A
HUBBA(?)RD, Mary F., 66
HUBBARD, Roy, 106-A
HUBBELL, Edward, 67
HUBER, Fred. P., 47-C
Gladys I., 47-C
John, 96-C
Mary Elizabeth (GERMAN), 96-C
HUCK, Thos., 96-A
HUDSON, Kalura, 96-A
HUGHES, George G., 97-C
Gertrude F., 15-C
Mamie O., 97-C
Mary Ann, 269-D
Mary E., 29-B
Robert, 29-B
Sarah, 29-B

HUKE, Wm. Elmer, 380-A
HULL, Ann, 66
Blanch, 342-D
David, 342-D
Fannie B., 20-A
Julia, 66
Oneida, 589-D
HULSANT, Edward, 99-A
HUMMERBOCHER, Florence A., 166-D
Wm., 166-D
HUMPHREYS, Katherine L., 602-D
Wendell, 90-D
HUMRICKHOUSE, James F., 7-D
John R., 7-D
Virginia, 7-D
Virginia L. R., 7-D
HUNT, Annie G., 30-A
Charles, 33-D
HUNTER, Elizabeth, 43-B, 91-A
Ella, 95-A
Godfrey, 95-A
Ida, 45-A
HURCORNE, Mary E., 96-B
HURD, Margaret P., 74-C
HURDEL, Kate McC., 451-D
HURLEY, Alice M., 322-A
Andrew, 322-A
Anna E., 217-B
HURLOCK, A., 162-B
C., 162-B
HURST, Rebeccs (or Rehus), 195-A
HURTLE, Ferdenhan, 412-D
Ferdinand, 412-D
Jeanette, 412-D
HUSH, Saml. C., 101-A
HUSTON, Michael, 409-A
HUTCHINS, Amanda A., 166-A
Ann, 166-A
Elizabeth J., 35-C
Elizabeth Jane, 35-C
Richard, 166-A
HUTCHINSON, (?), 155-D
Eliza D., 156-B
Elizabeth, 156-B
Florence H., 156-B
Gaither, 156-B
Grace, 156-B
Helen A., 34-C
I. L., 174-A
J. H., 156-B
John Franklin, 34-C
John W., 174-A
Margt., 174-A
Mary A., 174-A
Robt., 174-A
Susan, 156-B
Thomas K., 156-B

HUTCHINSON, Thomas R., 156-B
  Wm., 174-A
  Wm. A., 174-A
  Wm. C., 174-A
  Wm. H., 174-A
HUTTON, Cenelinel, 222-D
  Edwin, 222-D
  Geo. E., 222-D
  John G., 222-D
  Louis E., 222-D
HUTZER, Wm., 143-A
HYDE, Edw., Capt., 137-A
  H. C., Dr., 131-C
  Harry C., Dr., 131-C
  Mary Kate, 131-C
  Sarah, 465-A
HYLLARD, Benj. R., 158-A
HYMAN, Abby C., 491-D
HYNSON, Geo. H., 104-B
  George H., 104-B
  J. R., 104-B
HYSON, J. W., 214-A
IGLEHART, Adadelkehead, 603-D
IHRIE, Edith J., 75-C
  William P., 75-C
INGHAM, Elizabeth D., 261-A
  George, 261-A
  M. Sophia, 261-A
  Rachel, 261-A
  Susannah Virginia, 261-A
  William T., 261-A
  Wm., 261-A
INGLIS, Margaret I., 269-A
  Margt., 269-A
INNERST, Alonza E., 558-D
  Eliz., 558-D
  Ethel, 558-D
  Margt. A., 558-D
  Robert, 558-D
  Wm., 558-D
INSBACH, Vernon A., 14-D
INSBOCH, Wm. P., 14-D
IRELAND, Bertha, 50-D, 450-D
  Carrie M., 450-D
  Dan D., 39-B
  Gladis, 450-D
  Hugh E., 24-B
  John H., 533-D
  Laura M., 450-D
  Lawrence E., 81-C
  Rich'd. T., 506-D
IRLAND, Isaac M., 24-B
  Martha A., 183-B
IRONS, C. (or E.) P., Dr., 32-A
IRVING, Howard F., 411-D
  Mary, 411-D
  Mary E., 411-D
IRWIN, Chas. M., 21-B
  Emma V., 21-B

IRWIN, Florence I., 186-B
  Harry C., 21-B
  John H., 21-B
  Mary Elizabeth, 21-B
ISAAC, Charles O., 68
ISAACS, Mary A., 175-B
IVAS, Margt., 40-A
IVES, Elizabeth, 40-A
  James, 40-A
  Jas., 40-A
  Mary J., 40-A
JACKSON, Catherine, 277-A
  Emma, 25-A
  Florence, 236-D
  George M., 277-A
  George W., 277-A
  J. M., 55-A
  Jas., 1-D
  Jas. A., 1-D
  Jennie, 1-D
  Jessie, 236-D
  Jessie R., 236-D
  Josephine, 1-D, 11-D
  Kate, 1-D
  Lilie M., 55-A
  Luke, 55-A
  M. A., 317-A
  Mary D., 328-D
  Sarah E., 134-B
  Walter L., 236-D
JACOB, Edna M., 6-C
  Frederick W., 6-C
JACOBI, Catherine, 524-D
  Charles, 242-D
  Chas. A., 524-D
  Chas. L., 242-D
  Elizabeth, 242-D
  Henry G., 524-D
JACOBS, Annie M., 370-D
  Edna Marie, 49-C
  Flora, 370-D
  Fred. J., 49-C
  John P., 370-D
  Mary C., 370-D
JACOBSON, William, 35-A
JAEGER, Aug., 357-D
  August, Jr., 357-D
  Bertha, 357-D
  Wm., 357-D
JAMAR, Mary E., 316-D
  Mary Elizabeth, 316-D
JAMES, Eliz., 136-B
  Lillian M., 72-B
  Mary, 488-A
  Rich. H., 72-B
  Robert, 488-A
JAMISON, Danl., Jr., 339-D
  Etta May, 339-D
JAMMISON, John, 339-D

JANES, Wm., 10-B
JANVIER, Florence Baker, 90-A
  Meridith, 90-A
JARRETT, Aaron M., 213-A
  Anna Maire, 213-A
  Christopher, 213-A
  Clarense, 213-A
  Edud. I., 213-A
  Ellen, 213-A
  Francie, 213-A
  Fredk., 213-A
  Girdeon A., 202-B
  John, 213-A
  Mary, 213-A
  Sarah, 160-B, 213-A
  Sarah H., 213-A
  Sarah J., 202-B
  Thos., 213-A
JASPER, Bertha E., 33-D
JAY, Elizabeth, 37-A
  John W., 37-A
  Lillian, 9-D
  M. Joseph, 37-A
  Thos. W., 37-A
  Walter, 9-D
  Wm. H., 37-A
  Wm. Vernon, 9-D
JEFERIES, Virginia Lee, 138-A
JEFFERIES, John, 139-A
JEFFERIS, Ann, 15-B
  Sarah, 15-B
JEFFERS, Geo. W., 55-D
JEFFERSON, Hamilton, 67
JEFFRIES, Harry C., 159-A
  Jas. E., 138-A
JENKINS, Ann, 21-D
  Annie C., 560-D
  Annie L., 12-A
  Blanch T., 560-D
  Chas. D., 12-A
  Edwd., 40-D
  H., 560-D
  Henry, 224-A
  James, 12-A
  John, 12-A
  Mark, 12-A
  Martha I., 560-D
  Mary K., 12-A
  Saml. T., 12-A
  Samuel, 560-D
JENNINGS, Eliza Ann, 491-A
  George, 81-B
  Mary, 81-B
  Nellie M., 81-B
  Saml. K., 491-A
JESSOP, Annie C., 202-B
  Chas. L., 202-B
  Ella M., 202-B
  Emma, 202-B

JESSOP, Geo. H., 202-B
  Girdeon A., 202-B
  James M., 202-B
JESSUP, Alex., 585-D
  Edwd., 585-D
  John, 585-D
JOHNSON, (?), 261-A
  A. A., 300-D
  A. L., 300-D
  Alice, 423-D
  Andrew, 300-D
  Andrew A., 300-D
  Annie M., 159-D
  C., 300-D
  Carrie W., 420-A
  Cath., 246-A
  Charlotte, 203-B, 246-A
  Christine K., 21-D
  Edna M., 32-C
  Elijah R., 203-B
  Emma, 227-A
  George Bil., Rev., 251-A
  George W., 241-A
  Glady M., 159-D
  Grace T., 289-A
  Helen, 245-A
  Helen L., 245-A
  Henry F., 55-A
  John H., 203-B, 241-A
  Joseph, 205-A
  Jowet, 81 1/2-B
  Julia, 227-A, 272-A
  Laura, 300-D
  Loran, 464-A
  M. C., 205-A
  M. Helen, 251-A
  Mary, 214-B
  Minnie E., 207-B
  Oliver, 246-A
  Redman, 203-B
  Rich., 227-A
  Robert, 270-D
  Robt., 203-B
  Samuel P., 68
  Stewart M., 107-A
  Thomas P., 32-C
  W. L., 38-A
  Willis, 84-B
  Wm., 227-A
JONES, (?), Serg(n)t, 81-B
  Ada Hicks, 560-D
  Addie I., 329-A
  Alice M., 206-B
  Ann, 31-A, 187-B
  Annie, 217-B
  Annie E., 100-A
  Arthur, 329-A
  Caroline, 21-D
  Catherine, 81-B

JONES, Charles A., 68
Chas., 32-D
Chas. H., Jr., 328-A
Chas. M. J., 359-A
Chas. W., 331-D
E. Newton, 100-A
E. Stanley, 83-C
Edgar W., 331-D
Edwd. T., 359-A
Elizabeth, 39-C, 85-A
Ella, 75-C
Ellen, 351-A
Ellen A., 351-A
Eunice, 83-C
Fleoance, 217-B
Florence, 100-A
Geo. B., 100-A
Grace May, 362-D
Hannah, 458-A
Harriet R., 331-D
Henrietta G., 100-A
Isaac, 81-B
Isaac W., 81-B
J. Wesley, 331-D
James, 100-A
James T., 351-A
John, 31-A, 359-A
John H., 359-A
John M., 67, 359-A
John R., 450-A
Jos. H., 187-B
Joshua, 458-A
Julia A., 175-B
LaRue H., 87-C
Laura V., 75-C
Levin, 100-A
Levin P., 100-A
Levin T. (or F.), 100-A
Louis C., 355-D
Louis R., 68
Lucy, 84-B
Luke K., 181-B
Mar. H. P., 100-A
Margaret, 74-C
Mary, 359-A
Mary A., 220-B, 239-D
Mary E., 100-A, 187-B
O. O., 193-A
Philip R., 187-B
Rebecca, 35-B
Rosetta, 413-D
Royston L., Sr., 87-C
Royston Paul, 87-C
Saml., 152-A, 458-A
Sarah, 31-A, 447-A
Sarah E., 156-A
Therane, 120-B
Thomas L., 253-A
Thos. L., 252-A

JONES, Uriah, 187-B
Walter, Dr., 100-A
Willie, 81-B
Zanetta, 100-A
JORDAN, (?), 208-D
Elizabeth, 208-D
Helen, 208-D
Martha, 435-A
Mary L., 208-D
Maud L., 208-D
Rich. H., 208-D
Wm., 435-A
JORDEN, Rich. H., 208-D
JORDON, Richard T., 208-D
JORY, Bernice E., 157-C
Caroline, 96-A
Elija, 96-A
Gladys M., 25-C
M. Vernon, 25-C
Mary Ann, 96-A
Morris G., 157-C
Sarah A. R., 506-D
Stephen, 96-A
Wm., 96-A
JOYCE, Robert H., 232-A
Sarah E., 232-A
JUENER, Howard A., 229-B
Margaret, 229-B
Mary, 229-B
JUMP, Alice L., 66-C
JUSTICE, Artella R., 205-D
Chas. F., 205-D
Neoma, 205-D
JUSTSICE, Benj. J., 167-B
KAHLEST, Julius, 425-D
Olivia, 425-D
KAHN, Allen, 476-A
Annie R., 155-A
Gustave, 155-A
KALKMAN, Harry H., 36-A
KALLER, Rachel, 96-B
KALMER, Gertrude, 54-D
KANE, G. K., 67
G., Rev., 131-B
Goellive K., 131-B
Margt., 131-B
KANELY, Eugene, 519-D
Minnie Lee, 519-D
KANLEY, Annie M., 519-D
James, 519-D
John, 519-D
John G., 519-D
K., 519-D
KAPFER, Anita, 172-C
KAUFMAN, Emma, 33-D
KAULKMAN, (?), 36-A
KAVDRASSLE, John, 172-B
KAWCHORD, Mary A., 133-D
KEARUS, Frank, 126-A

KEASLER, Margaret, 102-A
KEATCH, C. W., 240-A
KEELSEY, Sarah, 96-B
KEENER, Gertrude, 199-B
  John H., 199-B
  Martha J., 199-B
KEERL, Thos., 564-D
KEEUN, J., 199-B
KEFFLER, Martha, 435-A
KEHL, A. C., 216-B
  Christopher, 216-B
  Wm., 216-B
KEHLE, Christopher, 216-B
  Katherine E., 216-B
KEIGLER, Eliza, 313-D
  Georgana, 313-D
KEIL, Anna M., 409-D
  Harrey E., 411-D
  Henry H., 409-D
KELLAN, Kate, 88-B
KELLENBERG, Louisa T., 123-D
KELLENBERGER, Chas. T., 73-D
  J. E., 73-D
  James E., 73-D
  Kenton K., 73-D
  Mary C., 73-D
  Mary E., 73-D
  Walter, 73-D
  Wm. H., 73-D
KELLER, Angelina, 55-A
  Goldie G., 175-B
  Harriet, 175-B
  Hester, 175-B
  John, 175-B
  John T., 175-B
  Pauline E., 175-B
  Thos. P., 175-B
KELLEY, Annie, 187-A
KELLINGER, Elizabeth R., 8-B
  William J., 8-B
KELLNER, Elsie, 82-C
  Julius W., 82-C
  N. J., 95-C
KELLOGG, Thomas, 4-C
KELLY, Annie, 109-A, 365-A
  Caroline, 401-D
  Carrie, 35-A
  D. R., Mrs., 198-A
  Eva, 420-A
  Helen M., 107-A
  Jas. C., 107-A
  John W., 401-D
  Laura A. Stewart, 107-A
  Lula, 107-A
  Richard, 401-D
  Wm., 365-A, 401-D
  Wm. J., 401-D
  Wm. R., 401-D
KEMBLE, M. O., 218-A

KEMP, Geo. W., 309-D
KENDALL, Ann E., 156-B
  Harry L., Jr., 156-B
  Mary, 156-B
KENEAM, Anna J., 94-B
  John R., 94-B
KENEAN, Laura V., 94-B
  Saml. D., 94-B
KENLEY, Susan, 215-A
KENNARD, Ada A., 29-B
  Amelia, 189-B
  Florence E., 29-B
  Louisa S., 29-B
  Wm. H., 29-B
KENNEALLY, Mary, 276-A
KENNEDY, Adeline, 469-D
  Catherine Alberta, 131-A
  Chas. A., 131-A
  Ethel May, 131-A
  Frank M., 131-A
  Fredk., 131-A
  Jas. H., 131-A
  Lizzie, 131-A
  Margaret, 131-A
  Margaret G., 131-A
  Nettie Margaret, 131-A
  Robert A., 131-A
  Wm. H., 131-A
KENNELEY, George R., 287-A
KENNELLY, Emily G., 287-A
  George, 287-A
  Mary, 276-A
  Mary A., 287-A
KENNELY, Eliza, 287-A
KENNY, (?), 78-A
  Sarah, 278-A
  Wm., 278-A
KEOWARTH, Henrietta, 133-D
KER, Herbert, Jr., 13-B
  Isabel Stewart, 13-B
KERBY, Chas., 200-D
  Frances, 200-D
  Wm. E., 200-D
KERHOLTZ, Alice L., 278-D
  Geo. W., 278-D
  Rebecca, 278-D
KERNS, (?), 26-D
KERR, John E., 142-B
  John M., 142-B
  Rose A., 142-B
KERWATH, Herman, 133-D
KESSLER, Mary M., 102-A
KEYNAST, Henry, 155-D
KEYS, Richard W., 12-A
KEYSER, John, 102-A
KEYWORTH, Annie E., 254-A
  Charles B., 68, 254-A
  Chas. B., 254-A
  Danl. T., 254-A

KEYWORTH, Elizabeth, 254-A
KIDIA, Eliz., 66-B
KIDWELL, Annie, 71-D
 Clarence, 71-D
 Edwd. J., 71-D
 James, 71-D
 James T., 147-D
 John, 71-D
 John L., 71-D, 94-C
 Lillie May, 94-C
 Margt., 71-D
 Mary E., 71-D
 Sarah, 147-D
 Sarah F., 71-D
KIEHLMAN, Annie M., 229-B
KIELHOLTZ, Geo. C., 278-D
 Virginia, 278-D
KIERRIAN, Elizabeth, 95-A
KILDOSS, Margaret M., 299-A
KINCAID, Caroliner, 198-A
KING, Adam, 127-B
 Caroline, 157-A
 Eliza J., 150-A
 Elizabeth, 157-A
 Eva, 45-A
 George W., 103-B
 Hester, 194-A
 Jacob, 68
 Jacob, Rev., 194-A
 Joseph, 150-A
 Lavora, 150-A
 Margaret B., 22-D
 Mary, 150-A, 161-B
 Mary E., 450-A
 Pauline, 21-D
 R. E., 450-A
 Sarah, 103-B
KINSELLA, Hannah, 402-A
KIPPLER, Rebecca, 21-D
KIRBY, Amah J., 113-B
 C. M., 113-B
 Catherine, 13-B
 Clarence A., 113-B
 E., 113-B
 Edith, 579-D
 Edwd. C., Dr., 113-B
 Elizabeth A., 243-A
 Fredk., 579-D
 John E., 113-B
 Joseph, 171-A
KIRK, Gertrude, 42-B
 Gertrude (BRATT), 7-C
 J. W., 7-C
 Joseph W., Rev., 42-B
 Kate E., 441-D
 Martha H., 42-B
 Mary (?), 42-B
KIRKNER, Mary, 165-D
KIRKWOOD, Cath., 98-A

KIRKWOOD, Ella M., 314-A
 Jno. J., 314-A
 John, 314-A
 Julia A., 314-A
 William J., 314-A
KIRLEY, Dolly A., 450-D
KIRLY, Elizabeth A., 243-A
KLAMER, Hendrick, 54-D
 Henrietta, 54-D
 Henry, 54-D
KLAUK, Harriett M., 309-D
KLECH, Zelda (or Zelola), 118-B
KLEINSMITH, Geo., 71-D
KLENLIN, Estella, 155-D
KLERLEIN, Blanche V., 69-C
 John H., 69-C
KLINESMITH, Bessie, 21-D
KLUGENBERG, Delia, 123-D
KNAPP, Burton E., 147-A
 H. G., 147-A
 Henry, 147-A
 Jos. D., 147-A
 Sophia, 147-A
KNIFE, Jacob, 326-D
KNIGHT, Ann M., 112-A
 Annie, 106-A
 Chas., 106-A
 Elizabeth, 106-A, 143-A
 Frances A., 182-D
 Geo., 106-A
 Geo. F., 182-D
 Geo. T., 106-A, 368-A
 George T., 273-A
 Greenbury, 182-D
 Henry N., 112-A
 Jacob, 213-D
 Jas. E., 368-A
 Mary C., 112-A
 Mary E., 112-A
 Peter, 52-B
 Sarah, 182-D
 Sarah C., 154-B
 Thos., 106-A, 182-D
 William T., 368-A
 Wm. T. F., 182-D
KNOTT, Sarah, 122-D
 Sarah C., 122-D
KNOX, John D., 67
KOCHLER, Sarah, 233-A
KOEHLER, Chas W., 203-A
KOELENDER, Chas., 36-D
KOENIG, Anna, 72-C
 Charles W., 72-C
KOENTZER, Herman, 32-D
KOETHER, Emil A., Sr., 171-C
 Myra, 171-C
 Myrab Bette, 171-C
KOHILFHOFF, Emiel R., 229-A
KOHLHOFF, Richard F., 229-A

KOHLHOFF, Zeta, 229-A
KOONS, Alice L., 276-D
  Andrew, 276-D
  Helen, 276-D
  Rebecca E., 276-D
KOSTER, John H., 398-A
KRAFT, Bertha, 119-D
  Danl. M., 119-D
  Edwin, 20-B
  George, 119-D
  Mauida, 20-B
KRAMER, Samuel, 68
KRANZ, (?), 88-C
  George A., 88-C
KRAUSE, (?), 204-B
KRAUSS, Anna M., 235-A
  Chas. T., 235-A
  Chas. Thos., 235-A
KREAMER, Mary E., 101-A
KREBS, Bernard, 498-D
  Elenora M., 334-A
  Elizabeth, 297-A
  George, 297-A
  George M., 297-A
  Henry C., 411-D
  John B., 498-D
  John J., 498-D
  John P., 498-D
  Maggie, 498-D
  Mary J., 297-A
  William, 68
KRENSON, Anna (DANSON), 600-D
KRETZER, Ann, 143-A
  Elizabeth, 143-A
  Hannah, 143-A
  Jacob B., 143-A
  John B., 143-A
  Wm., 143-A
KRIDER, John Lee, 86-B
KRIETZ, Carrie, 127-C
KROEGER, Anna Bell, 116-C
  Audrey, 116-C
  Conrad, 116-C
KROH, Augusta, 453-D
KROUSE, (?), 143-A
KROZIER, (?), 526-D
KUHLMAN, Henry, 229-B
KUHN, Algie L., Dr., 219-B
  Annie, 219-B
  Chas. E., 219-B
  D., 219-B
  Eberhart, 219-B
  Elica, 37-B
  Eliza, 219-B
  Elmer, 37-B
  Everhard, 219-B
  Frances, 219-B
  Frank B., 219-B
  Geo. J., 37-B

KUHN, John, 219-B
  Kara K., 37-B
  Leibrecht, 219-B
KUMMILL, Annie O., 307-A
KURTZ, Alice M., 399-D
  Annie, 399-D
  Catherine (WARD), 140-A
  Frances, 399-D
  John L., 140-A
  Matilda, 399-D
KYNAST, Annie, 155-D
L(?)ERSSON, (?), 35-A
LA BARRE, Elsie (CONWAY), 25-C
  John, 25-C
LA COMPTE, India C., 21-D
LA CROIX, Agnes, 200-B
LA CROSS, Celestor (or
  Calester), 189-B
LACH, Wm., 81-A
LADS, Frank, 30-A
LAFERTY, Bertha E., 491-D
  E., 491-D
  R., 491-D
LAFFERTY, Edwd. L., 491-D
LAKE, Reuben H., 480-A
LAKEN, Harry W., 398-D
LAKIN, Arthur P., 398-D
  John W., 398-D
LAMBDEN, Thos., 74-A
LAMBETEN, Thos., 74-A
LAMBIN, (?), 223-B
LAMEY, Edna M., 154-B
LANAHAN, Sarah R., 7-D
LANCASTER, Chas. F., 101-A
  Eva, 134-B
  Geo. W. T., 225-A
  Hannah, 101-A
  James H., 178-D
  Joseph, 101-A
  Sarah, 225-A
  Wm., 225-A
LANDENSLAGER, Amanda, 413-D
LANDER, (?), 441-D
LANDON, Geo., 209-B
  Josiah, 209-B
  Margaret E., 209-B
  Minnie, 209-B
  Minnie E., 209-B
LANG, Alice, 221-A
  Edward W., 221-A
  Emma Virginia, 68-C
  Henry C., 68-C
  Maba, 221-A
  Mabel, 221-A
  Robert D., 39-A
  Ruth M., 221-A
LANGE, Mary A., 399-D
LANGFORD, Earl, 56-A
  Earl O., 56-A

LANGFORD, Eva, 131-A
Mary L., 56-A
LANGHELD, G. Frederick, 184-A
Mary C., 184-A
LANGLEY, Mary, 85-A
Wm. H., 139-A
LANGRILLE, Ann E., 139-A
Anne G., 139-A
Chas. R., 139-A
Elizabeth, 139-A
Jefferson, 139-A
John T., 139-A
Mary E., 139-A
Wm. H., 139-A
LANGSTON, Edna M., 206-B
John R., 206-B
LANGVILLE, George C., 23-C
Madelon, 23-C
LANTRAM, (?), 227-A
LARDUSKEY, Albert, 210-D
Sarah A., 210-D
LARKINS, Jacob, 68
LARRABEE, Edith, 149-B
LARRIMOFF, Anna R., 21-D
LASH, (?), 207-A
Maria S., 207-A
LATCHFORD, Alice, 108-B
George, 108-B
Wm., 217-A
LATCHWOOD, James, 32-D
LATHAM, John, 48-A
Laura, 48-A
LATHE, Elizabeth, 365-A
LATTA, Frank, 30-A
LAUCK, Jane, 74-B
LAUGHLIN, A. H., 188-A
A. M., 188-A
Lavinia, 188-A
Tho. H., 188-A
Thomas Henry, 188-A
Thos., 188-A
LAUGHTON, (?), 66
LAUMAN, Maniella, 157-B
Martha B., 154-B
Wm., 157-B
LAUPE, Olie, 154-B
LAURENSON, Jas. Summerfield, 105-A
Margt., 105-A
LAURY, Mary, 539-D
Mary A., 539-D
LAVILLE, Mary R., 477-A
LAWDER, Mary E., 579-D
Mary Emily, 579-D
LAWRENCE, Caleb Van Buren, 36-B
Edw. D., 36-B
Fannie L., 58-B
Francis, 36-B
Geo. E., 58-B

LAWRENCE, Geo. W., 36-B
Hammond D., 36-B
L. King, 36-B
Larkin H., 36-B
Louis A., 36-B
Louisa L., 36-B
Lubries H., 36-B
Margt. A., 58-B
LAWSON, Emma Virginia, 93-B
Florence V., 93-B
J. Frank, 93-B
John T., 93-B
Leanord V., 93-B
Wm. L., 93-B
Wm. L., Mrs., 93-B
LAWTOM, (?), 137-B
LAWTON, Anne M., 12-A
Cathrin, 325-A
Chas. H., 325-A
Marion, 12-A
Mary E., 325-A
Mary Louise, 474-D
Richard, 474-D
Wm., 229-A
LAYMAN, Emma, 6-D
LE COMPT, George, 290-A
Lloyd, 290-A
LE COMPTE, Emily, 290-A
LEACH, Albert, 24-B
Arthur M., 39-A
Caroline M., 39-A
Edith, 39-A
Edwd. S., 39-A
Geo. E., 88-B
Geo. M., 39-A
James E., 39-A
LEADLEY, Ann M., 194-A
LEANEY, Margt. C., 240-D
LEARY, Jennie, 86-B
LEASE, Clara B., 62-C
Sarah, 173-D
Wm. F., 247-D
Wm. M., Sr., 62-C
LECOMPT, Caston, 390-A
Cynthia, 51-B
George, 290-A
Hooper, 51-B
Jos. L., 290-A
Mary J., 51-B
Walter J., 290-A
LECOMPTE, Thos. F., 51-B
LEDDON, Benj. III, 189-A
Benjamin, 189-A
Helen C., 189-A
Irving B., Jr., 189-A
Irving Benjamin, 189-A
LEDLEY, Alex., 194-A
Chas. Wesley, 27-D
Jacob, 194-A

LEDLEY, Margt., 194-A
Sophia M., 27-D
William A., 194-A
LEE, Almarilla, 404-A
Anson, 175-D
C. W., 145-A
Dorothy Mae, 208-B
E. (?), 150-A
Eliza, 145-A
Elizabeth, 10-A, 145-A
James R., 10-A
Jas. A., 10-A
Jessie, 67
John R., 145-A
John S., 145-A
John T., 10-A
Kate, 150-A
Martha, 10-A
Martha A., 10-A
Mary, 145-A
Mary A., 10-A
Sarah, 175-D
Wilson, 67
LEEF, John G., 170-D
Julia M., 170-D
LEESON, Elizabeth J., 172-A
John, 172-A
LEFFLER, Albert, 220-B
Andrew J., 10-B
Ann, 220-B
Ann L., 220-B
Annie, 10-B
Chas., 220-B
Frederick, 21-D
Geo., 220-B
Geo. R., 220-B
George D., 10-B
Georgeanna, 220-B
Hester A., 10-B
John, 10-B
Robert S., 220-B
LEGG, Cath. A. Casse, 428-D
LEHMAN, Chas. H., 32-D
LEHNERT, Gladys A., 7-C
Robert A., 7-C
LEINBACK, Ruth Josephine, 54-A
LEINTLAND, Julia, 133-A
Julia A. (or O.), 133-A
LEISKE, Cecil, 21-D
LEMON, Jas. H. M., 174-B
Maggie, 174-B
LEMOUR, Elizabeth, 254-A
LEMUEL, Dallas, 224-A
LENCLL, George W., 83-B
LENNAN, (?), 440-A
LENNON, Bridget, 107-A
LEOCHLER, Chas. W., 203-A
LEONARD, Benj. F., Dr., 410-D
Eliz F., 14-D

LEONARD, J., 407-D
Jno. G., 410-D
John G., 14-D
Katherine D., 47-C
Paul Benson, 47-C
LEORY, Margt. A., 473-A
LEREAMOR, Horatio, 233-A
LERRY, J. R., 198 1/2-A
LESSON, John, 172-A
LESTER, Shipley, 320-A
LETCHER, Harriett E., 71-C
Harriette E., 71-C
Henry L., 71-C
LETCHFIELD, Chas. E., 472-D
LETTING, Nellie J., 90-B
LETVAITIS, Vincent, 21-D
LEVEE, Gertrude L., 209-B
LEVY, Edna M., 84-B
Emma A., 101-D
LEWIS, (?), 309-A, 483-A
Amanda, 332-D
Ann A., 332-D
Anna M., 178-C
Chas. B., 28-A
Chas. R., 28-A
Edwd., 28-A
Elizabeth, 28-A
Elizabeth E., 332-D
Frances Brown, 28-A
Geo., 66
Gordon L., 179-C
Hennrietta, 209-B
James, 491-D
Jno. T., 28-A
John N., Jr., 28-A
Jos. N., 28-A
Joseph, 28-A
Joseph E., 28-A
Kendel M., 332-D
Laura V., 130-B
Margt., 130-B
Mary E., 28-A
Mary W., 332-D
Nellie, 129-A
Pricilla G., 28-A
Prisulla, 28-A
Robert P., 28-A
Thos. B., 28-A
LIENTLAND, Julia C., 133-A
LIESTER, Josephine, 51-B
LIGHT, Elizabeth, 13-D
Lewis N., 13-D
Mary A., 13-D
Mary E., 13-D
LILLY, Ada F., 149-A
Charlotte, 84-B
Eugene, 149-A
LINDER, Chas. E., 66
LINDSAY, Mary A., 223-B

LINDSAY, Mary E., 223-B
LINDSEY, Archibold, 425-A
  Rich, 412-A
  Rich. A., 425-A
  Sarah A., 293-A
  Sarah M., 293-A
LINGEY, Margt. A., 134-A
LINK, Annie, 56-A
  Bertha, 507-D
  Elsie M., 507-D
LINROTH, Conrad, 21-D
LINSLEY, Ella McKay, 51-C
  Ellen L., 410-D
  Shearwood M., 410-D
LINTHICUM, Annie E., 200-B
  Carrie M., 200-B
  Chas. E., 200-B
  Chas. H., 322-A
  Clara, 261-A
  Edwd. E., 322-A
  Elya, 28-A
  Henry, 28-A
  Lillie S., 322-A
  Margaret, 261-A
  Mary L., 200-B
  Mathias, 200-B
  Matthias, 200-B
  Samuel, 322-A
  Sarah, 21-D
  Thos., 200-B
LINZEY, John R., 293-A
LIPINSKY, Ruby R., 185-B
LIPPEY, Mary E., 122-D
LIPSCOMB, Bettie, 109-B
  Chas. A., 179-B
  Elizabeth, 109-B
  Marie, 109-B
  Philip, 67, 109-B
  Philip D., 109-B
LISH, A. R. J., Dr., 113-B
  Bailey, 113-B
  Eliz M., 113-B
  L. F. V., 113-B
  Lititia F., 113-B
  Marie L., 113-B
  Wm. B., 113-B
  Wm. Bruce, 113-B
  Wm., Dr., 113-B
LITCHFIELD, Charles R., 561-D
  Chas., 561-D
  Miranda, 561-D
  Saml. H., 561-D
LITTING, Mary L., 90-B
LITTLE, Bessie, 341-D
  Chas., 434-A
  Edw. C., 451-A
  Geo., 341-D
  Lucy M., 341-D
  Marion B., 509-D

LITTLE, Orlana R., 434-A
  Thos., 434-A
  Wm. H., 341-D
LITTLEFIELD, Anne M., 103-B
  John H. (or W.), 165-B
  Mary B., 165-B
  Sallie Byrd, 165-B
LIVINGSTON, (?), 149-B
  Amelia, 149-B
  E., 149-B
  John Wesley, 149-B
  Maiue, 149-B
  Martha, 149-B
LLOYD, Annie E., 256-A
  Robt. G., 256-A
  Robt. R., 256-A
  Wm. M., 256-A
LOANE, Edna M., 264-D
  Joseph, 264-D
  Marie, 417-A
LOBER, Martha C., 451-A
LOETZ, Emil J., 156-C
  Rose E., 156-C
LOFLIN, Jos. B., 76-A
  Virginia L. H., 76-A
LOLBEHUSEN, Helen, 235-D
LONG, Charles, 89-D
  Daniel, 139-A
  Eliza A., 218-A
  Elizabeth, 218-A
  Emma V., 39-A
  Hannah, 445-A
  Hannah A., 445-A
  J. T., 445-A
  Jemima, 139-A
  John, 445-A
  John F., 445-A
  John F., Jr., 445-A
  L. R., 445-A
  Laura Coulter, 178-B
  Louis P., 178-B
  Margt A., 404-A
  Margt., 404-A
  Mary, 253-A
  Mary A., 218-A
  Mary L., 35-A
  Robert D., 39-A
  Sarah A., 89-D
  Susie T., 445-A
  W. A., Rev., 93-B
  William A., 67
  Wm., 139-A
LONGLEY, (?), 139-A
  Amanda, 190-A
  Elenora, 190-A
  Elonora, 190-A
  John, 190-A
  Mary E., 139-A
LONHARDT, A., 240-D

LONHARDT, E., 240-D
LOOKINGLAND, Aloesta, 599-D
  Geo., 599-D
  Geo. R., 599-D
  Lydia M., 599-D
  Mary, 599-D
LOTZ, Caroline, 141-A
  Caroline S., 141-A
  Connal, 271-D
  John, 141-A
  John M., 141-A
  Julius, 141-A
  Margt., 271-D
  Nicholas, 271-D
LOUREY, Sarah, 374-D
LOURY, Chas. H., 539-D
  Howard B., 539-D
LOVE, Alice Cordelia, 249-A
  Annie V., 362-D
  Catherine, 362-D
  Chas., 249-A
  Jacob, 249-A
  Jas. K., 249-A
  John David, 530-D
  Jos. K., Jr., 249-A
  Joseph, 249-A
  Joseph Damson, 249-A
  Mary, 362-D
  Mary A., 249-A, 362-D
  Mary Ann, 249-A
  Mary E., 249-A
  Sarah, 249-A
  Senena, 249-A
  Serine A., 249-A
  Wm., 362-D
  Wm. A., 362-D
LOWERY, Edith M., 243-A
  Margt. S., 243-A
  Mary E., 313-D
  Wm. K., 313-D
LOWMAN, Annie L., 127-B
  William E., 127-B
LOYETT, Samuel J. III, 98-C
LUCAS, Anne E., 242-A
  Margt. C., 446-A
  Mary A., 446-A
  Mary R., 152-A
LUDWIG, Frederick, 241-D
  Rosanna, 241-D
LUMBARD, Chas. W., 155-D
LUMLEY, Clarissa G., 252-D
LUPTON, Alfred H., 80-A
  E. F., 508-D
  Ephron, 508-D
  Ephron Filmore, 508-D
  Grace, 508-D
  Mary, 508-D
  Wilbur, 508-D
LUSBY, Della, 162-B

LUTZ, Margaret E., 6-C
  Margt., 24-B
  Margt. E., 24-B
  Mary Ellen, 6-C
  Peter A., 6-C
  William L., 6-C
  William T., 6-C
LUZEY, Lee G., 134-A
LYHANT, Joseph, 303-A
  Julia, 303-A
  Julia A., 303-A
  Mary, 303-A
LYNCH, C., Rev., 209-B
  Catherine, 4-B
  George R., 4-B
  Howard M., 427-A
  John, 4-B
  John H., 155-A
  John T., 427-A
  Mary, 4-B
  Naomi, 4-B
  Sarah E., 427-A
  Sidney, 4-B
  Tramsall, 155-A
  Walter E., 153-B
  William C., 4-B
LYON, Wm. B., 224-B
LYONS, Lizzie, 241-D
  Mary J., 241-D
  Nancy, 342-A
LYTLE, Saray, 185-B
MAC INTYRE, Sarah, 21-D
MAC RUSSELL, Shirley, 97-D
MACARTNEY, Kate, 160-B
  Kate V., 160-B
  Malvina, 160-B
  Mary, 160-B
  Robert H., 215-B
  Robt., 215-B
  Robt. R., 215-B
MACCARTNEY, Mary M., 160-B
MACHER, (?), 235-A
  Anna E., 111-B
  Benjamin, 111-B, 235-A
  Elbert, 111-B
  Elizabeth, 235-A
  Ella V., 73-D
  Emma Augusta, 235-A
  Frances E., 111-B
  Jas. P., 111-B
  John S., 111-B, 235-A
  Kate E., 111-B
  Mary E., 111-B
MACKER, A. C. Ridgeway, 111-B
MACKER, Margaret J., 111-B
MACKINSON, Robert E., 398-A
MADDEN, Ann E., 195-A
  John, 195-A
  John F., 195-A

MADDEN, Louise E., 195-A
MADDOX, Edward, 14-B
  Edwd. J., 14-B
  Elizabeth, 541-D
  Emma, 173-C
  Geo., 165-B
  Geo. M., 23-D
  Jas. F., 14-B
  M. Rebecca, 14-B
  Margt., 541-D
  Mary (or Margt.) Ann, 165-B
  Rachel, 14-B
MADE, Abraham, 305-D
MADERY, Alex. R., 319-A
  Alexandra, 319-A
MADGRICK, Emily, 325-A
MADILL, Margaret J., 23-C
MAEWER, J., 66
MAGARLEY, John, 160-B
MAGARTNEY, Cath. C., 160-B
  Eliz., 215-B
  Frances, Rev., 160-B
MAGE, Jane, 258-A
MAGNESS, A., 152-B
  Mary, 139-B
  Moses N., 244-A
  Susan B., 139-B
  Thos., 139-B
  Wesley, 152-B
  Zachariah, 152-B
MAGUIRE, Jas. R., 225-B
  Mary R., 225-B
  Mildred, 225-B
MAGURE, Louis C., 225-B
MAGURIE, J. R., 225-B
MAHR, Edith M., 6-C
MAILHOT, Joseph O., 299-A
MAKOLING, Jos. N., 93-B
MALCOM, Julia, 66
MALE, Elizabeth, 415-A
  Jos., 415-A
  Mary E., 415-A
  Wm. H., 415-A
MALLAN, (?), 201-A
MALLONEE, Ida May, 136-A
MALLOW, Ann, 123-B
  Benj., 123-B
MALONE, Julia, 229-B
MANANOWSKI, Raymond J., 45-C
MANLEY, John, 199-B
  Martha J., 199-B
  Naomi, 199-B
MANN, Cecil S., 173-C
  Edna V. M., 173-C
  Eliza E., 475-A
  Ida Kate, 475-A
  Kenneth L., 173-C
MANSTER, Edith I., 339-A
MANUEL, Isabelle, 13-D

MANUS, Jas., 475-A
MAPP, A. Upshur, 195-B
  Douglas W., 195-B
  Florida Wellbourne, 195-B
  Upshur W., 195-B
MARBURGER, Wm., 181-B
MARCH, Elizabeth, 25-A
  Ellen L., 487-A
  Jacob, 487-A
  Margt. L., 25-A
  Martha A., 487-A
  Martin, 25-A
  Philip, 487-A
  Willie, 487-A
  Wilmer, 67
MARINER, Chas., 89-A
  M. S., 507-D
  Sarah, 507-D
  Thos., 507-D
MARKEY, Eliz C., 167-D
  Joseph C., 167-D
  Margaret E., 167-D
  Mattie, 167-D
  Myrtle, 167-D
  Paul E., 167-D
  Pearl P., 167-D
  Robert H., 167-D
  William H., 167-D
MARKHEIMER, A., 184-D
  J. M., 184-D
MARKLIN, A., 184-D
  E., 184-D
MARKS, John H., 68
MARLEY, Elsie M., 143-B
  Geo. W., 143-B
  George W., 143-B
  Herman M., 143-B
  James, 143-B
  Sarah J., 143-B
MARNEY, Daniel A., 177-D
MARPHLE, Ephram, 176-A
MARPOE, Francis, 54-B
  Joseph, 54-B
  Louis C., 54-B
  Marg. A., 54-B
  Mary E., 54-B
MARR, Chas., 279-A
  Wm. G., 52-A
MARRAGOR, Anna, 147-B
MARRINGLY, John, 131-B
MARRIOTT, Eliz L., 330-D
MARRON, Isabella, 42-B
MARROW, John, 68
MARS, Chas., 279-A
MARSH, (?), 332-A
  Eliza, 66
  Elizabeth, 25-A
  George, 332-A
  Gladys V., 183-D

MARSH, Hester, 67
  Jos. L., 183-D
  Joseph Franlin, 183-D
  Margt. L., 25-A
  Minnie V., 183-D
  Susan, 439-D
MARSHAL, Annie, 84-B
MARSHALL, Alexander, 149-B
  John W., 434-A
  Lena, 599 1/2-D
  Saml., 556-D
  Sarah J., 97-A
  Wm., 599 1/2-D
MARSLEY, Iriour, 342-D
MARTIN, (?), 384-D
  A., 279-A
  Ann E., 394-A
  Clara V., 279-A
  Elizabeth, 349-A, 363-A
  Florince L., 243-D
  Frances, 192-A
  Francis, 192-A
  Geo. M., 155-D
  George S., 349-A
  Herman J., 363-A
  I., 279-A
  Maria, 349-A
  Martha V., 456-A
  Mary, 349-A
  Resvell, 88-B
  Rosa A., 243-D
  Saml., 369-A
  Saml. B., 279-A
  Sarah E., 437-A
  Theodore L., 243-D
  Wm., 243-D
MARTINSAN, John, 33-D
MARTOIST, O. C., 168-B
MARVEL, Charles Edward, Sr., 98-C
  Hattie, 98-C
  Hattie Lee, 98-C
  Jane Ann, 98-C
  William Robert, 98-C
MASELL, Chas. W., 176-A
MASINGO, Mary A., 174-A
MASK, Chas. W., 291-A
  Franklin, 291-A
  George R., 291-A
  John, 291-A
  Joseph, 291-A
  Josephine, 291-A
  Patiance, 291-A
  Saml. E., 291-A
  Wm., 291-A
MASON, (?), 29-D
  Almira, 53-B
  Edna S., 29-D
  Eliza, 53-B

MASON, Elizabeth, 310-A
  George, 24-B
  George T., 24-B
  John S., 29-D
  John T., 307-A
  John W., 53-B
  Maria, 53-B
  Maria A. E., 53-B
  Mos, 53-B
  Philip H., 91-B
  Robert, 53-B
  Sarina, 53-B
  Wesley, 53-B
MASSEY, Caroline, 424-A
  James A., Rev., 424-A
MATCHETT, Mary J., 220-A
MATCHSET, James, 220-A
MATHERS, Elwood, 252-D
  Erasmus E., 252-D
  Jos. M., 252-D
  Sophie, 252-D
MATHEWS, Chas., 264-D
  Eunice J., 83-C
  Geo. R., 333-D
  Helen, 333-D
  James Scott, 169-B
  Lydia, 329-A
  Wilbur F., 169-B
MATTAX, Ann M., 96-B
  Chas. A., 96-B
MATTESON, Esther, 473-A
MATTHEWS, C. Starr, 23-B
  Edward, 67
  Eliza B., 169-B
  Elizabeth, 54-A
  Ethel, 23-B
  Geo., 23-B, 333-D
  Geo. E., 368-D
  Georganna, 23-B
  Gordon R., Mrs., 81-D
  Grace, 23-B
  Henry R., 75-A
  John, 194-A
  Lina B., 333-D
  Mary Ellen, 169-B
  Mary J., 169-B
  Ruth B., 147-C
  Solomon L., 177-D
  T. L., 23-B
  Thos. L., 23-B
  Virginia R., 194-A
  Wilbur L., 169-B
  Wilbur T., 169-B
MATTINGLY, Cath., 131-B
  John T., 131-B
MATTOX, Alonzo D., 163-B
  Edith M., 163-B
  Maggie D., 163-B
MAULL, Edward A., 151-A

MAULL, Elizabeth A., 151-A
Marg. B., 151-A
Mary B., 151-A
MAXWELL, Cath., 139-A
Elinor, 57-D
MAY, Margt., 204-A
MAYDWELL, John. C., 99-A
Sarah, 99-A
Sarah M., 99-A
MAYER, Pauline, 194-B
Wm. H., 45-A
MAYES, John R., 486-D
Sarah E., 486-D
Sarah J., 486-D
MAYNARD, Elizabeth, 17-A
James A., 17-A
Mary N., 17-A
Nancy, 17-A
MAYS, Thomas J., 400-A
Wala F., 400-A
MAZANOWSKI, Myrtle M., 45-C
MC ALLISTER, Eliz, 105-B
Norwood, 602-D
MC CAFFERTY, Geo. W., 27-D
MC CAFFERY, Jas., 159-A
MC CAIN, Alice B., 50-D
Charles C., 50-D
Mary E., 50-D
Sarah L., 50-D
William W., 50-D
MC CALL, Charles N., 90-D
Charles W., 90-D
Mary Hewitt, 90-D
MC CANN, (?), 119-D
Clara M., 155-A
MC CARTING, Emily, 181-B
MC CARTNEY, Francis A., 67
MC CAULEY, Charles P., 33-D
Chas. F., 388-D
Elizabeth Ann, 98-B
Emma, 388-D
Harrie E., 123-B
Harriet E., 123-B
James, 123-B
John W., 123-B
Marrie E., 123-B
Mary L., 123-B
Mary M., 123-B
Samuel S., 98-B
Sarah, 388-D
Sarah May, 123-B
MC CAUSLAND, Elizabeth (JONES), 39-C
Thomas, 39-C
Thomas E., 39-C
Thomas E., Jr., 39-C
MC CLANDISH, Phylis G., 121-B
MC CLEARY, Geo. B., 228-A
Holland, 183-B

MC CLEARY, Julia A., 228-A
Mary E. Holland, 183-B
MC CLENDISH, P. G., 121-B
MC CLENNON, John, 526-D
MC CLINTOCK, Anna H., 38-A
Annie H., 38-A
Elmer E., 38-A
MC CLURE, Richard, 53-B
Richard M., 53-B
Virce, 53-B
MC CLUSE, Sarah, 327-A
MC COLGAN, Andrew J., 198-B
Eddie, 198-B
Josephine, 198-B
MC COMAS, Andrew J., 123-D
Caroline F., 123-D
Cornelia, 123-D
Minnie E., 123-D
Wm. G., 123-D
MC CONKEY, John R., 156-D
MC CONN, Chas. B., 155-B
Wm. F., 155-B
MC CONNELL, Elias Geo., 144-D
Walter B., 144-D
MC CORD, Chas. R., 476-A
John A., 476-A
Lilly M., 476-A
MC CORMECK, Nellie, 94-A
MC CORMICK, Thomas, 68
MC CORNISH, Lilly L., 92-B
MC COUBRY, Lillian R., 28-D
MC COY, Margaret, 253-A
MC CRA, Sarah, 474-A
MC CRACKEN, Jas., 394-A
MC CRAY, John, 474-A
MC CUBBIN, Davidge, 312-A
MC CUILY, Henrietta Rhode, 104-A
MC CULLOUGH, (?), 266-A
MC CURDY, Amanda J., 181-A
Elizabeth, 56-A
James, 181-A
Jas., 181-A
Walter S., 181-A
MC CURLEY, Ann R., 40-B
Felix, 40-B
MC DANIEL, Alethea, 45-A
Ella May, 38-C
Frances, 149-B
George E., 38-C
George L., 38-C
Maria B., 89-A
Marion F., 89-A
Wm. F., 89-A
MC DANIELS, Columbus, 30-D
Cora, 166-B
Drucilla, 30-D
Geo., 166-B
Geo. W., 166-B

MC DANIELS, Leona M., 166-B
  Mary, 166-B
MC DERMOT, John, 202-D
  Susie, 202-D
MC DERMOTT, John G., 131-C
  Luetta C., 131-C
  William, 131-C
MC DONALD, William A., 68
MC DOWALL, Elizabeth, 15-A
MC DOWELL, Anna R., 308-D
  Chas., 15-A
  Lectie Helmling, 162-A
  Thomas A., 103-A
  W. L., Rev., 308-D
  William P., 67
MC ELDOWNEY, Louise C., 465-D
  Louise Cotten, 465-D
MC ELHANEY, A., 431-A
  Alexandra, 431-A
  Ann, 431-A
  Cath., 431-A
  John, 431-A
  Saml., 431-A
  Sarah, 431-A
MC ELLANEY, Sarah, 287-A
MC FARLAND, Annie E., 59-B
  Annie M., 59-B
  Fanny, 59-B
  Franc(?)s, 59-B
  Harry, 59-B
  James H., 59-B
  John, 59-B
  Kava A., 59-B
  Mable A., 59-B
  Mary, 59-B
  Sarah J., 59-B
  Wm., 59-B
MC G(?)GAR, Mary, 198-B
MC GADEY, (?), 187-B
MC GEOY, Charles J., 37-C
  Mattie R., 37-C
MC GILL, Catherine, 137-B
  Eliza, 137-B
  Elizabeth, 137-B
  Geo. T., 137-B
MC GLUE, Caroline B., 38-A
MC GOWAN, Heigh, 446-A
MC GRADEY, E. E., 187-B
  Jennie G., 187-B
MC GRATH, Mary J., 79-A
MC GREERY, Mary F., 238-D
MC GREEVY, George, 451-A
MC GREGOR, Emma, 562-D
  Florence, 562-D
  Geo., 563-D
  Ida, 562-D
  John, 562-D
  Joseph, Capt., 562-D
  Mary J., 563-D

MC GROEGER, John, 562-D
MC HEAN, A., 24-A
MC ILHENNY, Clara Belle, 20-A
  Marshall, 20-A
MC INTYRE, Maggie, 21-D
  Mary, 133-D
  Robert, Lt., 47-B
MC KAY, Donald, 32-D
MC KEE, Mary T., 475-A
  Patrick, 315-A
MC KEEVER, Sarah A., 265-A
MC KELDIN, Elizabeth, 199-D
  Sophia, 198-A
MC KELDOE, Mary, 8-D
MC KELDRY, Rebecca, 471-A
MC KENLY, Nancy, 320-A
MC KENZIE, Belle, 88-B
  Chas., 183-B
  Deborah, 183-B
  Geo. W., 183-B
MC KINALEY, Minerva, 168-D
MC KINDLEY, Mary E., 168-D
MC KINDLY, Jas. A., 168-D
MC KINLEY, Jas., 168-D
  Maggie, 168-D
MC KNIGHT, Alice E., 155-D
  Matilda, 201-D
MC LAIN, Bessie, 30-B
  Bessie M., 30-B
MC LANAHAN, Martha J., 117-B
  Robert C., 117-B
  Wm. A., 117-B
MC LANHAN, Martha Johnstone, 117-B
MC LARDY, John, 155-D
MC LAUGHLIN, (?), 114-B
  George R., 51-A
  Joaob C., 530-D
  Mary S., 51-A
  Vida B., 51-A
  Wm. E., 51-A
MC LAURIN, A., 66
MC LEAD, Alex W., 73-B
  George, 73-B
  George H., 73-B
  Geosett, 73-B
MC LEAN, Jacob, 21-D
MC LEOD, Alexander W., 67
  Georgiana Hulse, 73-B
  Sarah Truman, 73-B
MC MAHON, Andrew, 274-A
MC MAINES, Wm., 314-D
MC MENAMEN, Edwd. C., 525-D
  Jas., 525-D
  Joseph, 525-D
  Sarah, 525-D
  Wm., 525-D
MC MINN, Florence A., 246 1/2-A
  William J., Dr., 246 1/2-A

MC MULLEN, Harriet A., 146-A
James, 353-D
M. S., 146-A
Margt. E., 146-A
S., Rev., 146-A
Solomon, 68
Wm., 110-A
Wm. T., 353-D
MC MULLER, Roemma, 121-D
MC NEAL, Albert P., 51-D
John O., 51-D
Mary C. (or E.), 51-D
Mary J., 51-D
William O., 51-D
MC NEIR, John, Sr., 158-A
Mary, 158-A
MC NIER, Mary, 158-A
MC PHERSON, Samuel, 67
MC QUIGG, Annie, 334-D
Jas. H., 334-D
Martha A., 334-D
Rebecca, 334-D
Robt., 334-D
MC VEY, Eliza A., 140-B
James, 140-B
James M., 140-B
Saml., 437-D
MEAD, Ann M., 225-B
Emma R., 273-D
Geo., 225-B
Louis R., 273-D
Louisa, 273-D
Wm. H., 225-B
MEARS, John B., 97-A
Sarah J., 97-A
MEDAIRY, Cyrus, 240-A
Norman, 196-A
Rich., 196-A
MEDARY, Cyrus, 319-A
Jacob, 196-A
Jacob H., 196-A
John, 196-A
Kate, 319-A
Lavenia, 319-A
Rachel, 196-A
S., 196-A
Wm. H., 319-A
MEDENING, J. Harry, 189-B
J. Henry, 189-B
MEDINGER, Charles H., 46-C
Fredk., 203-A
Herbert S., 203-A
Jno. G., 203-A
John C. (or G.), 203-A
Louisa, 203-A
Margt., 203-A
William H., 203-A
MEEHAN, Grace Lorraine, 34-C
MEEK, Elizabeth, 126-A

MEEKIN, Caroline, 157-A
Jacob, 157-A
MEEKINS, Mary, 103-A
Nathaniel, 86-B
MEEKS, Eliza, 56-A
George A., 172-B
Louisa, 56-A
W. H., 56-A
Wm., 56-A
Wm. W., 56-A
MEETH, Elmer, 23-C
Margaret J., 23-C
MELLOR, Ann, 123-B
Robert H., 123-B
MELNS, Mary W., 139-B
MENDEL, Charles G., 58-C
MENDELL, Elmer, 75-A
MENEFEE, (?), 258-A
MERCER, Basiel B., 184-A
Charles H., 201-B
Harriet A., 201-B
Isah, 97-A
Isiah, 201-B
Margaret A., 201-B
Mary E., 201-B
Mary Emma, 201-B
Virgil T., 201-B
MEREDETH, Geo. H., 455-D
MEREDITH, Edwd. J., 517-D
Susan, 517-D
Wm. H., 517-D
MERKEL, (?), 531-D
MERRILL, Harry M., 208-A
Henry M., 208-A
Mary, 208-A
MERRITT, Ann E., 232-A
Fredk., 372-A
MERRYMAN, A., 184-A
Hamilton, 203-D
MESKEL, George M., 157-A
MESSERSMITH, E. L., 475-D
Ellen L., 51-C
Ellen M., 51-C
MESSICK, John, 499-D
METZDORF, Eliz. A., 81-A
METZEL, Charles A., 124-B
Kate Murray, 124-B
MEUSHAW, Caroline, 10-A
MEYER, Adolph, 345-A
Richard W., 536-D
MEYERS, (?), 128-C
Amelia, 186-A
Chas., 186-A
Chas. A., 186-A
Chas. L., 22-A
Crissie D., 73-C
Crissie D. (FOREMAN), 73-C
Ellen Amanda, 186-A
Eva E., 186-A

MEYERS, Fredk., 214-A
Fredk. F. J., 214-A
Fredk. P., 214-A
Gordon H., 99-A
Harry F., 155-C
Hester A., 22-A
Homer E., 186-A
Ida K., 127-C
J. E., 127-C
Jacob E., 127-C
Jacob W., 186-A
Jas., 233-A
Jessie H. (or A.), 186-A
Joseph G., 73-C
Lelia H., 155-C
Margt. D., 186-A
Mary, 221-B
Mildred Grace, 73-C
Myrtle L., 155-C
Rachel A., 186-A
Sallie Ann, 186-A
William C., Sr., 73-C
Wm. C., 73-C
MICHAEL, Elizabeth A., 214-A
Francis, 214-A
MICHAEN, Almieda, 348-A
Cath., 348-A
George, 348-A
Thos. J., Dr., 348-A
MICHION, Alminda, 348-A
MIDDLETON, Mary, 469-D
MILBURIN, Jas. J., 214-A
MILBURN, Robert Lee, 86-B
MILES, Annie, 134-A
Cath., 134-A
Elizabeth, 78-A
Ellen C., 13-D
Emma, 134-A
Flora B., 85-A
George, 34-A
George C., 468-A
George R., 134-A
John, 134-A
John W., 134-A
Joseph H., 98-B
Lydia, 134-A
Mary A., 416-A
Mary P., 98-B
Robert, 134-A
Robert C., 416-A
Thos., 134-A
Wm., 134-A
Wm. R. L., 134-A
MILK, (?), 347-A
MILL, Mary, 126-A
MILLER, Adeline, 73-B
Adolph, 42-A
Agatha, 72-C
Benj. F., 170-D

MILLER, Blanch, 165-D
Buck M., 16-B
Chas. H., 165-D
Chas. V., 218-B
Danl., 201-A
Eliza, 201-A
Elizabeth, 165-D
Ella M., 314-A
Ellen, 39-B, 59-B
Ellen A., 201-A
Emma J., 215-B
Frances O., 209-B
Frank, 12-D
Geo., 66
Henry, 165-D
Henry C., 165-D
Isabelle, 306-D
Jacob F., 461-D
Jacob L., 97-C
Jane E., 165-D
Jno. H., 201-A
John, 68
John A., 73-B
John H., 73-B, 201-A
John T., 73-B, 201-A
John W., 377-A
Julius, 229-B
Laura A., 42-A
Leroy B., 155-D
Leroy J., 179-C
M. A., 314-D
Maggie, 73-B
Margt. S., 105-A
Mary A., 23-D
Mary E., 201-A
Mary M., 339-D
Maud, 339-D
Rebecca, 333-A
Ruth, 73-B
Sarah, 179-C
Sarah J., 73-B
Valentine A., 201-A
W. E., 229-B
William C., 201-A
Willie A., 215-B
Wm. A., 215-B
Wm. C., 165-D
MILLS, Ann, 194-A
Annie, 194-A
Clara E., 164-D
Elizabeth, 194-A
Florence I., 164-D
Martha B., 164-D
Mary, 194-A
Mary E., 164-D
Willemina T., 207-A
MINNER, Edward C., 68
MINNICK, Chas. E., 29-B
Clarence G., 29-B

MINNICK, Conrad A., 87-A
  Louisa, 87-A
  Maria A., 29-B
  Wm. H., 29-B
  Wm. T., 29-B
MINOR, Alice L., 34-A
  Carroll D., 34-A
  Harry, 34-A
  Oleie, 34-A
  Samuel H., 38-C
MINTER, Mary A., 5-D
MINTON, Robert Leon, 168-C
  Wm. J., 168-C
MISSELMAN, John H., 219-B
  M. Cassander, 219-B
MISTER, Elizabeth, 51-A
  Levin, 51-A
MITCHELL, (?), 188-D
  Abevilla, 34-B
  Annie, 205-B
  Annie K., 144-A
  Bessie T., 142-A
  Calvin K., 420-A
  Cath., 9-D
  Charles R., 142-A
  Danl. C., 13-A
  David, 13-A
  Eliz A., 272-D
  Elizabeth, 71-B, 198-A, 272-D, 276-A
  Ella May, 205-B
  Eloise K., 198-A
  Emma, 139-A
  Frances, 407-A
  Geo., 272-D
  Geo. W., 205-B
  George R., 407-A
  George W., 13-A, 139-A
  Henrieta M., 475-A
  Henry M., 193-B
  Herbert F., 66-B
  Isaac, 71-B
  James B., 475-A
  Jane, 13-A
  Jas. H., 272-D
  Jno., 407-A
  John, 407-A
  John R., 407-A
  John T., 407-A
  Jos. B., 198-A
  Lillie C., 205-B
  Margt., 142-A, 407-A
  Mary A., 198-A
  Mary E., 139-A
  Mary L., 198-A
  Mary P., 66-B
  Matilda, 9-D
  Micajah G., 34-B
  Monroe, 142-A
MITCHELL, Octavia M., 193-B
  Rebecca, 272-D
  Robert G., 274-A, 276-A
  Sadie T., 142-A
  Saml., 205-B, 407-A
  Sarah A., 407-A
  Susie Rose, 142-A
  T. B., 475-A
  Walter E., 205-B
  Walter Z., 193-B
  Wm., 407-A
  Wm. H., 13-A
MOCHLER, W., 203-A
MOFFIT, Elizabeth, 20-D
  Rebecca, 402-A
MOFFITT, Anna, 132-B
  John, 167-B
  John F., 132-B
  John T., 167-B
  Jos., 402-A
  Margaret A., 133-D
  Mary C. R., 132-B
  Rachel, 167-B
  Rebecca, 402-A
  Richd., 132-B
  Richd. F., 132-B
  Sophia, 167-B
  W. S., 133-D
  William E., 201-A
  Wm. H., 167-B
  Wm. R., 167-B
MOGNESS, Moses N., 244-A
MOHLER, Barbara A., 251-D
MOLAN, John A., 536-D
MOLEY, Sarah L., 56-A
MOLLOHIN, Edud., 201-A
MOMBERGER, Cladys M. (JORY), 25-C
MONROE, A. Warfield, 130-B
  Caroline M., 595-D
  Carroll, 595-D
  David S., 68
  David S., Rev., 595-D
  Emma L., 130-B
  John Harrison, 595-D
  Mary V., 130-B
  Sarah A., 130-B
  T. H. W., 67
  T. H. W., Rev., 130-B
  Virginia, 130-B
  Warfield, 130-B
MONTAGUE, Josephine, 218-B
  Wm. H., 218-B
  Wm. W., 218-B
MOON, Blanch, 198-B
MOOR, Blanch, 198-B
MOORE, (?), 29-D
  Charlotte K., 83-A
  Chas., 144-A

MOORE, Chas. C., 199-B
David, 83-A
Ellen Jane, 117-B
George M., 6-C
Harry W., 12-C
Harry Wilson, 12-C
Henry W., 117-B
James, 114-B
James J., 117-B
John, 470-A
John W., 525-D
Louisa K., 6-C
Luly, 46-A
Margaret, 83-A
Margt., 470-A
Martha J., 117-B
Mary, 144-A
Nancy Phillips, 119-B
Pamela, 169-A
Pamelia, 169-A
Saml. H., 83-A
Sarah A., 525-D
Susan E., 559-D
Verda, 46-A
Wm. T., 559-D
MORAN, (?), 177-B
Chas. H., 245-A
Frank, 245-A
Margaret, 11-C
Maria, 245-A
Mary, 245-A
Mary E., 177-B
Viola M., 177-B
Wm. G., 245-A
Wm. H., 177-B, 248-D
Wm. J. E., 245-A
MORGAN, Ann W., 57-B
Caroline D., 57-B
Cath. A., 57-B
Elizabeth, 57-B
Elizabeth A., 20-B
Florence, 400-D
Frances C., 57-B
Frances R., 57-B
G. C., Rev., 5-B
G. W., 67
Gerard, 67
Gertrude, 92-B
Howard, 20-B
J. A., 57-B
Joshua, 30-A
Lyttelton B., 57-B
Lyttleton A., 67
Mary E., 5-B
N. J. B., 67
N. P., 57-B
Randolph, 20-B
Rosana H., 5-B
Rose (ALLEN), 20-B
MORGAN, Susan A., 57-B
Susan J., 57-B
Susie, 57-B
T. A., Rev., 57-B
Tillison A., 67
Tillison M., 57-B
U. J. B., Rev., 5-B
Virginia, 5-B
Wilber P., Rev., 5-B
Wilbur D., 5-B
MORIE, Jas., 42-A
MORREIA, Mary E., 133-D
MORRIS, Abe, 133-D
Carrie, 66
Joseph L., 67
Martha E., 316-A
Rebecca Ann, 98-C
Tallie E., 98-C
Tallis E., 98-C
Theresa, 33-D
MORRISON, Abraham, 187-D
Elizabeth W., 234-A
Elwood, 234-A
Hannah, 234-A
I. Elwood, 234-A
J. Elwood, 234-A
John Elwood, 234-A
Lockwood, 234-A
M. M., 234-A
Mary, 234-A
N. D., 187-D
Susan, 234-A
Sylvester W., 234-A
Virginia L., 234-A
William, 234-A
MORROW, Carrie, 30-B
Cath., 14-D
Glanville, 154-B
Hugh L., 154-B
Ida Louise, 30-B
James S., 154-B
Jane, 30-B
John, 67, 68
John R., 30-B
Kate, 33-D
Mary Ann, 14-D
Partick, 30-B
Sarah A., 14-D
Wm., 30-B
MORSE, Mary, 199-B
Sarah A., 199-B
Wm. L., 199-B
MORSEL, Josephine, 85-A
Mollie, 85-A
MORSELL, Chas. H., 108-A
Elizabeth J., 176-A
Freddy, 108-A
Mary E., 108-A
Mary F. A., 108-A

MORSELL, Sallie, 165-A
  Sarah R., 108-A
  Wm., 108-A
  Wm. H., 108-A
MORTIMER, A. Maria, 207-A
  Amelia G., 145-A
  Armeda (or Almeda), 145-A
  Charles E., 178-D
  Chas., 178-D
  Ella T., 145-A
  Harry, 88-B, 207-A
  Henry, 22-A
  Henry H., 207-A
  Janett, 178-D
  Jessie, 207-A
  Jno. W., 206-A
  John H., 145-A
  Maria A., 207-A
  Mary E., 178-D
  Saml. B., 145-A
  Saml. C., 443-A
  Thomas, 145-A
  Thomas P., 25-D
  Thos., 145-A
  Willie, 207-A
  Wm., 178-D
MOSES, Blanch, 57-D
MOTHERSHEAD, Chas., 21-D
MOXLEY, Helen, 6-D
MRAS, John, 33-D
MUELLER, Herman Ernest, 101-C
  Wilhelmina K., 101-C
MULES, Florence I., 98-B
MULLEN, L. G. M., 146-A
  Solomon, Rev., 146-A
MULLER, Jennie, 14-C
  Margt., 21-D
  Warren, 14-C
MULLIKIN, Robert B., 303-A
  Robert J., 303-A
MUNN, Danl. H., 224-D
  Emma S., 224-D
  John T., 224-D
  Mary, 224-D
MURPHEY, Anna, 243-A
  James, 243-A
MURPHY, Edith B., 12-C
  Louis C., 12-C
MURRAY, Annie Barbara, 124-B
  Cath. B., 105-B
  Charlotte C., 225-B
  F. Gracey, Mrs., 225-B
  Howard L., 124-B
  John P., 105-B
  Mary E., 105-B
  Robert, 133-D
  Robert S., 21-D
  Thomas O., 105-B
  Thos. C., 105-B

MURRAY, Wm. Emory, 124-B
  Wm. R., 124-B
MURRY, Amelia M., 74-A
  Ann R., 124-B
  J. P., 124-B
  Martha E., 237-D
  Mary, 74-A
  W. Emory, 124-B
MUSGRAVE, E. A., 529-D
  Geo. J., 529-D
  Sarah, 529-D
MUSHAW, Annie E., 10-A
  Cath. E., 10-A
  Fannie H., 10-A
  George, 10-A
  Lewis H., 10-A
  Mary, 10-A
  Wm. A., 10-A
MUSSELMAN, Annie C., 162-A
  Fannie, 162-A
  Florence, 162-A
  George R., 162-A
  Harriet, 162-A
  Hiram D., 162-A
  John, 162-A
  Mary M., 162-A
MUTH, Chas., 461-A
  Chas. E., 461-A
  George W., 334-A
  Hortence E., 334-A
  Urnie Belle, 461-A
  Wm. S., 334-A
MYER, Geo. W., 225-B
  Mary J., 225-B
MYERLY, Geo., 342-D
  Geo. C., 342-D
  Geo. P., 342-D
MYERS, Chas. E., 221-B
  Chas. R., 221-B
  Conrad R., 221-B
  D. W., 225-B
  Elizabeth E., 214-A
  Emma C., 225-B
  Franklin P., 214-A
  Fredk., 214-A
  Geo. W., 221-B
  Hannah, 233-A
  John E., 221-B
  John T. D., 337-D
  Margt. D., 214-A
  Marion M., 251-D
  Mary C., 267-D, 337-D
  Mary J., 221-B, 225-B
  R. J., 214-A
  R. Minerva, 186-A
  Rebecca, 221-B
  Robert, 416-A
  Stephen, 233-A
  Wm. F., Jr., 221-B

NACE, Carrie M., 85-C
John M. N., 188-D
John W., 85-C
Mary Ann, 188-D
NAGEL, John, 48-C
Minnie (HINKEL), 48-C
NAGLE, Emma, 152-B
John H., 152-B
Martha A., 235-A
NAIRN, Francis T., 50-B
John C., 50-B
NASH, Annie E., 157-A
Benella, 157-A
Chas., 157-A
Elizabeth, 12-A
Elizabeth C., 12-A
Ephram, 157-A
George A., 157-A
James, 157-A
Louisa, 157-A
Wm., 12-A
Wm. A., 157-A
NATTELE, Edward, 21-D
NEAL, Abner, 67
Abner, Rev., 129-B
Barbara, 129-B
J. E., 450-D
Joseph, 129-B
Sarah, 129-B
NEALEN, John, 600-D
Viola G., 600-D
NEARY, Harry S., 164-A
John G., 164-A
John T., 164-A
Sarah E., 164-A
NEAVY, Addie C., 425-A
Michael E., 425-A
NECOLAI, Ludwig, 13-B
NEIGHOFF, Chas. A. (or S.), 53-D
Isabelle, 53-D
NEIL, E., 450-D
J., 450-D
NEILSON, Cath. E., 136-D
NELSON, (?), 34-C
NERGHOFF, J. T., 12-D
Mary A., 12-D
S. H., 12-D
NETTLESHIF, Ann, 45-A
NEUGARD, Frederick, 12-D
NEUMAN, Annie, 315-D
Eliz, 315-D
NEWELL, Cecelia, 332-A
Jas., 332-A
Martha E., 332-A
Mary E., 332-A
Matilda C., 332-A
NEWHOUSE, Carson, 432-A
Frank, 45-A

NEWHOUSE, Fredk., 45-A
John, 241-A
NEWMAN, Florence, 159-A
NEWTON, A., 270-A
Alfred C., 42-A
Carrie, 42-A
Chas., 1-D
Chas. E., 270-A, 373-A
Edward D., 42-A
John W., 42-A
Mary, 358-D
Mary A., 42-A
Nathaniel, 270-A
Sarah, 151-B
Sarah E., 270-A
Sophia, 42-A
Susanna, 42-A
Thos., 42-A, 358-D
Willie E., 42-A
NICE, Henry, 68
NICHOLIS, John, 402-D
NICHOLS, Elizabeth, 607-D
Elizabeth J., 607-D
George A., 25-A
NICHOLSON, Ellen, 306-D
John R., 306-D
Nannie Louise, 3-D
Naomi E., 3-D
Robert, 141-A
Sophino (or Sophono), 441-D
Thos., 306-D
NICOLL, Adam A., 223-B
Adams A., 223-B
Catherine, 223-B
Louisa W., 223-B
NIDENHIMER, (?), 155-D
NIEGHOFF, Chas. H., 53-D
Edith, 53-D
Ida May, 53-D
NIELSON, Arthur, 136-D
Elizabeth, 136-D
J. L., 136-D
NINER, Alice A., 230-A
John, 230-A
NISE, Jos., 66
NIUGARD, Darzo, 12-D
Ella, 12-D
Rebecca, 12-D
NOEL, Annie, 152-D
Edw. G., 216-B
Ella S., 216-B
Florence, 152-D
Frank M., 216-B
Geo. M., 216-B
Grace R., 216-B
Helen, 152-D
J. W., 152-D
Sadie, 216-B
Sarah E., 216-B

NOEL, Wm. A., 216-B
NOFSINGER, Ruth S., 113-C
　Warren H., 113-C
NOGULE, Alice H., 14-D
　Eliz R., 14-D
　Geo., 14-D
　John H., 14-D
　Sarah A., 14-D
NOLAN, (?), 264-D
NOLAND, Mary M., 178-A
NOLEN, Elizabeth R., 243-A
NOLL, Annie, 399-D
　Robert, 399-D
NOLLEY, Elliott D., 390-D
　Leonard B., 390-D
NOLOCK, (?), 184-D
NORBURY, Emma, 16-C
　Walter, Sr., 16-C
NORIS, John D., 46-A
　Margt., 46-A
NORMAN, Ella, 96-B
NORMON, Columbus, 301-A
NORRIS, Chas. F., 134-D
　George W., 426-A
　Marie S., 134-D
　Sidney, 4-B
　Sophia, 134-D
　Sophie, 134-D
NORTH, Elizabeth, 74-B
　George, 323-A
　Wm. J., 165-B
NORTON, Minnie E., 269-D
NORWOOD, Phoebe A., 301-A
NOUGLE, Lura, 133-D
O'BRIEN, John, 185-B
O'CONNELL, Anna M., 271-D
O'LARY, Fanny, 274-A
　Mary, 274-A
O'RILEY, Elizabeth M., 469-A
　Mary, 128-C
O'SHEA, Jos. F., 198-A
OADES, Harry, 86-B
OCHRE, Gertrude O., 427-D
OFFUTT, Elizabeth Evaline, 80-B
　Levina Beall, 80-B
OHLEADORF, Cara, 122-B
　J. W., 122-B
OHLENDORF, Cora A., 122-B
　John W., 122-B
OHLER, Helen, 437-D
OLDHAM, John, 98-A
　Jos., 43-B
　Jos. D., 43-B
　Josephine, 43-B
　Mary, 98-A
　Namia, 55-A
　Samuel, 43-B
　Susannah L., 43-B
　Wm. M., 43-B

OLDSON, Clarence H., 16-B
　Ella S., 16-B
　Ellen S., 16-B
　H. G., 16-B
　Homer H., 16-B
　John B. W., 16-B
OLER, Harry T., 229-B
OLIVER, Charles, 133-D
　John, 24-B
　Joseph, 101-A
　Margt., 24-B
　Robert H., 178-D
OLLINGER, (?), 101-A
ORAM, William S., 468-A
ORANDE, Ossodale, 155-D
OREM, Biddy J., 19-B
　Chas. W., 19-B
　Edward, 67
　Eliza A., 19-B
　Elizabeth (FOSTER), 113-C
　John, 43-A, 113-C
　John E., 19-B
　John H., 43-A
　Keziah, 468-A
　Wm., 468-A
ORENSHALL, Annie E., 70-D
　August, 70-D
　Godfrey, 70-D
ORR, Edith, 340-A
　James C., 340-A
OSBORN, Adella, 151-B
OSBORNE, W. M., 68
OSBURN, Oram, 259-A
OSSMAN, (?), 261-D
　Eliz., 261-D
OSTOVIT, Gordon J., 16-C
　Grace M., 16-C
　William E., 16-C
OTTINGER, Elsie, 21-D
OULD, Lancaster, 213-B
OULER, Sarah A., 201-A
OULTAN, Elizabeth, 201-A
OUSLER, Anna E., 418-A
　Curtis, 418-A
　Wm. W., 418-A
OWENS, Grace W., 186-B
　Saml. G., 366-A
　Samuel, 199-A
　William W., 186-B
OWINGS, Catherine E., 82-C
　Howard M., 82-C
PACE, Beatrice, 152-D
　Laura B., 152-D
　Lillie C., 152-D
　Pleasant, 152-D
　Sarah, 152-D
PADDY, Wm. Lee, 216-B
PADGETT, James E., Jr., 100-C
　James E., Sr., 100-C

PADGETT, Molley B., 100-C
PAGE, Wm., 402-D
PALMER, Edward T., 95-B
  William, 95-B
  William P., 95-B
PAMPHELON, (?), 523-D
PAMPHILON, Annie E., 523-D
  Chas. W., 523-D
  Clarence, 523-D
  Florence, 188-A
  Ida, 188-A
  Margaret, 523-D
  Margt., 188-A
  Nicholas, 188-A
PANCOAST, Alice, 72-A
PANCOS, Helen, 99-A
PANCOST, Lillian, 72-A
PARDO, Jennie, 152-A
PARKER, Delphine C., 143-C
  Mary J., 490-A
  Mary R., 20-D
  Robert, 490-A
  Sarah, 79-B
  William A., Sr., 143-C
  Wm., 20-D
  Wm. T., 20-D
PARKS, Algo R., 155-D
  Anne E. (LUCAS), 242-A
  Charles A., 190-A
  E. Florence, 190-A
  Ellan N., 242-A
  Emma Jane, 190-A
  Geo. C., 242-A
  J. W., 68
  Jno. W., 219-A
  John A., 190-A
  John E., Sr., 242-A
  John Edger, Jr., 242-A
  Lydia, 190-A, 219-A
  Marion, 190-A
  Mary C., 190-A
  Mary E., 190-A
  Sarah H., 190-A
  Thos. A., 99-A
PARLETT, Andrew J., 23-D
  Ann Louisa (BROWN), 27-C
  Anna L., 27-C
  Benj. F., 167-B
  Benj. J., 167-B
  Benjamin, 27-C
  Chas. B., 23-D
  Danl. E., 23-D
  Edward Gardner, 27-C
  Eliza E., 167-B
  Emma, 23-D
  Henry C., 162-B
  Lida A., 23-D
  Margt. E., 23-D
  Mary E., 23-D, 27-C

PARLETT, Matilda G., 167-B
  May Estelle, 27-C
  Minnie F., 167-B
  Naomi, 23-D
  Nellie S., 27-C
  Rachel, 167-B
  Rebecca, 167-B
  Siana, 23-D
  Sophrono, 23-D
  Thos. A., 23-D
  Walter S., 167-B
  Willie F., 23-D
PARRISH, Edud. S., 209-A
  Eliza, 209-A
  Jacob J., 209-A
  Laura Z., 209-A
  Marie L., 127-B
  William H., 209-A
PARROTT, Ann, 99-A
  Jas. F., 99-A
  Jas. W., 99-A
  Jea, 99-A
  Jno. W., 99-A
  Julia A., 99-A
  Margt., 99-A
  Mary, 99-A
  Nancy, 99-A
PARSON, Chas., 158-A
  Elizabeth, 261-A
  Ellen, 397-A
  Elmer, 397-A
  Emma E., 158-A
  George H., 136-A
  Jonathan, 158-A
  Jos., Jr., 427-A
  Mary A., 158-A
  Mary B., 158-A
  Thos., 185-B, 261-A
PARSONS, Catherine, 44-B
  Elenor, 397-A
  Gussie, 44-B
  Janie A., 44-B
  John, 397-A
  John C., 427-A
  Jonatha, 158-A
  Jos., 427-A
  Joseph, 427-A
  Joseph M., 397-A
  Margt., 427-A
  Priscilla, 427-A
  Rose, 44-B
  Theo., 44-B
  Thos., 261-A
  Wesley W., 44-B
  William Webster, 44-B
  Wm., 397-A
PASAPIE, Jos., 126-B
PASCAL, Frances W., 165-A
PASQUAY, Louis, 371-D

PASQUAY, William F., 371-D
PASSAPAE, Cecelis Boisseau, 458-A
  Cecellie, 458-A
  Hannah, 458-A
  Monroe, 458-A
PATRICK, Marie H., 470-A
PATTERSON, (?), 143-C
  A. F., 52-A
  Ann, 84-A
  Chas. W., 267-D
  Gilson E., 267-D
  Jas., 267-D
  Martha A., 451-A
  Mary, 22-A, 134-B
  Mary M., 38-B
  Susan H., 84-A
  William, 84-A
  Wm. G., 267-D
  Wm. R., 143-C
  Wm., Capt., 84-A
PATTON, Eliz, 74-B
  Mildred Leo, 21-C
  Roland A., 21-C
PAUL, James, 421-A
  Mary T., 421-A
PAYNE, Jane E., 96-B
PEACH, Rae, 286-A
PEACOCK, Ann, 237-A
PEANINGTON, Mary C., 96-B
PEAR, John W. H., 30-A
PEARCE, Chas., 121-B
  Edna Mae, 121-B
  Emma (SCHULTE), 121-B
  Jas. G., 121-B
  John A. W., 121-B
  John W., 121-B
  Ruth A., 121-B
  Wilbur, 121-B
  Wilbur T., 121-B
PECK, Catharine, 82-A
  Clara M., 234-A
  David V. J., 82-A
  Elizabeth, 82-A
  Ella L., 82-A
  Harriet, 82-A
  Stephen, 82-A
PEDDICORD, John, 34-B
PEDRICK, Franklin, 178-B
  Martha, 178-B
PEFFER, Charles C., 1-C
  Mercy B., 1-C
PENN, Ann, 241-A
  Elijah, 241-A
  Elizabeth, 96-B, 241-A
  Emma, 241-A
  Emma C., 241-A
  Emma V., 241-A
  Harry N., 241-A

PENN, Henry, 241-A
  Jacob, 241-A
  Jacob, Jr., 241-A
  Walter F., 241-A
  William, 241-A
PENTZ, Jos. A. P., 104-B
PENTZBORN, Enright, 33-D
PEREGOY, (?), 78-A
  Althea, 163-A
  Ann, 165-A
  Archey, 163-A
  Chas., 165-A
  Edwd. N., 165-A
  Ernest, 177-B
  Geo., 177-B
  Hannah, 165-A
  Hannah N., 163-A
  Jennie, 177-B
  John, 163-A
  Jos., 163-A
  Joshua, 163-A
  Josua, 163-A
  Laura V., 177-B
  Margaret J., 177-B
  Nicholas, 165-A
  Sallie, 207-B
  Virginia, 177-B
  Walter T., 165-A
  Wm. P., 165-A
PERKINS, Alvin T., Rev., 459-D
  Ann, 277-D
  Anna B., 102-B
  Cordelia K., 594-D
  David, 581 1/2-D
  David R., 581 1/2-D
  Edith R., 102-B
  Florence B., 581 1/2-D
  Henry M., 102-B
  Jas. A., 594-D
  Jeannette Vinton, 102-B
  John H., 427-A
  Marianna, 102-B
  Martha B., 581 1/2-D
  Mary, 427-A
  Millard L., 102-B
  Minnie E., 459-D
  Robert S. V., 102-B
  Wm. H., 427-A
PERRICIE, Ann, 87-B
PERRIGO, Fannie, 79-A
PERRIN, Edwd. (or Edwin), 155-D
PERRY, Ann E., 81-A
  Emily, 494-D
  George, 474-A
  Isabell, 81-A
  Mary C., 81-A
  R., 81-A
  Rachel A., 81-A
PERSINGER, Sarah, 32-D

PESINA, John, 164-A
PETERS, Bertha C., 123-B
PETERSON, John, 225-B
PETTYMAN, Eliza B., 271-A
　Emma, 271-A
PFAFF, Catherine (HILMILLER), 84-C
　Edwin W., 84-C
　Henry, 84-C
　Margaret Tompkins, 84-C
PHAIFER, (?), Mrs., 538-D
PHELPS, Chas. M. H., 66-B
　E. Cordelia R., 66-B
　E. P., 66-B
　Elisha P., 66-B
　Mary J., 66-B
　Mary W., 66-B
　Rachal, 5-B
　Thomas W. S., 66-B
PHILIPS, Felexana, 40-B
　Sarah, 480-A
PHILLIP, Geo., 106-A
　M. E., 106-A
PHILLIPS, Adeline, 96-A
　Alexander Crawford, 119-B
　Birtie, 96-A
　Caroline, 120-B
　Elisha, 67
　Fredk., 96-A
　Harry D., 120-B
　Jane H., 120-B
　John A., 425-A
　John R., 119-B, 120-B
　John Robert, Jr., 119-B
　John, Rev., 425-A
　Mary E. Dalrymple, 119-B
　Molly D., 120-B
　Molly Dalrymple, 119-B
　William B., 119-B
　William Benjamin, 119-B
　Williams B., 119-B
　Wm. B., 120-B
PHOEBUS, Mary P., 424-A
PICHTER, John G., 227-B
PICKETT, Daisy W., 61-C
PIEPGRAS, Carl, 88-B
PIERPOINT, Mary Ann, 459-A
　Thomas H., 411-A
　Thomas S., 411-A
PILKERTON, Eliz, 398-D
PILSON, Robert, 41-B
　Saml., 41-B
PINDIN, Mary, 98-B
PINE, Jennie E., 472-A
PIPER, Elizabeth, 211-A
　Kate, 211-A
　Mary, 211-A
　Mary A., 211-A
　Mary J., 185-B

PIPER, Philip, 211-A
　Sarah, 211-A
PITCHER, William H., 68
PLEASANT, S. S., 234-A
PLOTNER, Joseph, 67
PLUMMER, Chas. W., 185-D
　Margaret D., 74-C, 87-C
　Margaret Ellen, 74-C
　Margaret L., 87-C
　Mary J., 185-D
　Maude M., 87-C
　Ralph G., 87-C
　Ralph G., Jr., 74-C
　Ralph G., Sr., 74-C
　Saml., 132-A
POE, Charles Rigley, 207-B
　Matilda R., 207-B
POETZOLD, (?), 59-C
　Ernest R., 59-C
　Grace A., 59-C
POISAL, John, 68
POLECK, Nathan, 66
POLK, Caroline, 21-D
POLTON, Alice V., 601-D
　Chas. A., 601-D
　Chas. E., 601-D
　Mary F., 601-D
　Maud E., 522-D
POOL, Wm., 149-D
POOLE, Charlotte, 440-A
　Charlotte E., 62-C
　Winter S., 155-D
　Winter W., 149-D
POPP, Emma G., 52-A
PORCELLA, Mary M., 179-C
PORTER, Cath. A., 316-D
　Chas. H., 197-B
　Clara E., 2-D
　Doris E., 2-D
　Gertrude, 33-D
　James, 21-D
　Lewis W., 2-D
　Lillie E., 197-B
　Thos., 316-D
POSTE, Kate F., 302-A
POTEE, Catherine, 31-D
　Elsie O., 31-D
　Isaac, 138-A
　John, 248-D
　Lena T., 56-A
　Mammie M., 248-D
　Mary, 248-D
　Mary C., 138-A
　Mary E., 56-A, 138-A
　N. G., 248-D
　Rena J., 248-D
　William, 248-D
　William H., 138-A
　William J., 248-D

POTEE, Wm. F., 31-D
POTEET, Mary, 101-A
Thos., 101-A
William George, 101-A
POTTE, John. F., 56-A
POTTEE, George A., 56-A
POTTER, Elijah, 403-A
Elizabeth, 403-A
POWELL, Dora, 7-C
Elizabeth, 18-D
Keith M., 115-C
Mary, 104-A
Mary M., 115-C
Mary Margaret, 115-C
Milton, 7-C
PRATT, Henry C., 177-D
PRESTON, Caroline, 248-A
Cath., 208-A
Elizabeth, 248-A
Ella, 248-A
Harry Merrill, 208-A
Henry, 208-A
John, 208-A, 248-A
John T., 248-A
Laura, 208-A
William, 208-A
Wm., 248-A
Wm. H., 248-A
PRETTYMAN, Eliza B., 271-A
Emma A., 271-A
Penelope, 271-A
Wesley, Rev., 271-A
William, 68
Wm., 271-A
Wm., Rev., 271-A
PRICE, Ada A., 203-B
Alfred, 4-D
Alfred L., 4-D
Allen, 120-D
Allen P., 4-D
Amelia M., 188-A
Annie, 136-D
Annie C., 4-D
Clarence, 203-B
Courtney L., 26-C
E. J., Mrs., 227-B
Eliza, 203-B
Emma E., 302-D
Florence A., 4-D
Frances, 123-D
Francis S., 48-B
Geo. D., 203-B
Geo. T., 203-B
Harry B., 97-D
John H., 188-A
Joseph, 4-D
Lulabelle, 299-A
Odna, 26-C
Robert Lee, 203-B
PRICE, Russel, 415-D
Sadie A., 4-D
Sarah A., 4-D
Sarah B., 203-B
W. L., 4-D
W. T., 136-D
Wm. T., 203-B
PRICHARD, Grace L., 205-D
Sallie, 205-D
Sarah, 580-D
PRIDE, Helen M., 600-D
PRILL, John, 525-D
PRINCE, Carrie R., 18-D, 245-D
PRITCHARD, (?), 137-D
Alex., 137-D
Jos., 137-D
Mc A., 137-D
PROBST, Dorothy L. (ROSS), 34-C
PROPST, John, 34-C
William Dewey, 34-C
PRUIGTON, Dorothy, 121-B
PUE, Chas. R., 207-B
Frank R., 207-B
John, 67
Matilda R., 207-B
PULTERSON, Hester, 91-A
PUMPHERY, Ebenezer, 81-A
Ebinezer, 81-A
Susie, 81-A
PUMPHREY, Alice V., 81-A
B., 47-A
Geo. E., 47-A
Geo. S., 47-A
Lillie J., 47-A
Lloyd P., 47-A
Lloydia, 47-A
Mary A., 47-A, 81-A
Mary V., 47-A
Rachel, 47-A
Rebecca B., 47-A
Ruth V., 47-A
Theodore, 81-A
PURCELL, Benj., 447-D
Ida C., 447-D
Maggie, 447-A
Mango, 447-D
Wm. B., 447-D
PURDEN, Mary, 98-B
Mary A., 98-B
PURNELL, Daisy A., 95-B
James, 88-B
Mary M., 95-B
PURPER, Ann B., 187-A
Chas., 187-A
Christian, 187-A
PURRIS, Hester, 312-A
PUTCHSKY, Mary, 148-D
Wm., 148-D
PUTSCHLEY, Wm., 148-D

QUAIL, John, 322-A
QUAY, Chas. H., 189-B
  John C., 189-B
  Mary A., 189-B
QUIGLEY, Ann C., 202-B
  Elizabeth, 202-B
  Fannie E., 202-B
  John, 202-B
  Martha W., 202-B
  Wm., 202-B
  Wm. S., 202-B
QUINN, Bernard, 591-D
  Edwd., 591-D
  Ellen (or Ella) M., 591-D
  Geo. H., 591-D
  Hugh, 591-D
  Jane, 187-A
  Lawrence N., 591-D
  Louisa M., 591-D
  Maria, 591-D
  Ruthanna, 243-A
  T. H., 243-A
  Virginia A., 591-D
RAE, James, 21-D
RAENER, (?), Mrs., 222-B
RALEIGH, Carno, 228-B
  Tabitha W., 228-B
  Walter, 228-B
  Walter A., 228-B
  Wm. E., 228-B
RANDOLPH, Lillie A., 235-A
RANGHTER, Edwin C., 264-D
RANIER, Warner McC., 602-D
RAPPOLD, Elizabeth (RODGERS), 173-C
  Grace M., 173-C
  Grace Margaret, 173-C
  Howard F., 173-C
  Howard Franklin, 173-C
  John Henry, 173-C
RATLIFF, Mary, 134-A
RAUSCHENBERG, Anna, 96-B
  Annie, 96-B
  Carl H., 96-B
RAWLINGS, J., 236-D
  T., 236-D
RAY, (?), 110-B
  Benj., 526-D
  Emily, 112-B
  John, 112-B
RAYCKHOSLI, Margt., 244-D
RAYMOND, (?), 329-D
  Annie E., 338-A
  Benj., 338-A
  Elarkin, 338-A
  Lizzie, 338-A
REANEY, Chas., 402-A
  Evelyn, 402-A
  Harvey E., 94-C, 95-C

REANEY, Mary, 402-A
  Susan Carol, 95-C
REASON, Jos., 11-A
REATHER, Annie E., 27-D
  C. F., 27-D
  Chas. F., 27-D
  Gertrude, 27-D
  Jeanette, 27-D
  John W., 27-D
  Margt. H., 27-D
  Mary K., 27-D
RECKER, Geo. Washington, 533-D
RECKERT, Chas. A., 197-B
  Florence, 197-B
  Florence M., 197-B
  Geo., 197-B
  H. E., 197-B
  Hester A., 197-B
  John, 197-B
  Mary (or May) E., 197-B
  Mary A. (or H.), 197-B
  Matilda, 197-B
REDDER, Lelia Noel, 216-B
REDELIUS, Frederick E., 300-D
REDFORD, Anna Hart, 62-C
  Clara (HOPKINS), 62-C
  Louis Albert, 62-C
  Thomas, 62-C
REDGRAVE, Ida V., 374-D
  Jas. A., 374-D
  Sadie H., 374-D
  Saml., 374-D
  Saml. B., 374-D
REDLFIELD, Vernon A., 400-A
REDMAN, Ann, 156-A
  Ann Rebecca, 156-A
  Saml., 156-A
REDMOND, Elizabeth, 156-A
  Samuel, 156-A
REED, Carolina A. G., 21-A
  Cath., 158-A
  Harry J., 6-C
  Harry John, 5-C
  Jennie, 124-D
  Margt., 37-A
  Mary, 37-A
  Mary M., 5-C, 6-C
  Matilda R., 207-B
  Roger, 309-A
REEOL, John S., 21-A
REESE, Ann, 106-B
  Aquila, 68
  Bessie, 84-A
  D. E., 68, 137-A
  Daniel M., 67, 84-A
  Daniel M., Rev., 106-B
  E. I., 106-B
  Fannie E., 106-B
  Frances B., 184-B

REESE, John L., 68
Mary Ann, 18-A
Mary E., 21-A
Mary V., 84-A
Rebecca K., 215-B
Robt. P., 215-B
Ruth, 137-A
Sarah G., 38-A
Thomas M., 68
Walter M., 84-A
William, 340-A
Wm. D., 242-A
REESIDE, Amelia V., 1-D
Barbara, 1-D
Elizabeth, 81-A
Florence, 1-D
Henry G., 1-D
Ida, 462-D
Jas. W., 525-D
Kinzie M., 525-D
Lydia, 530-D
M., 525-D
Mary E., 525-D
Oliver, 525-D
Raymond, 1-D
W. F., 525-D
Wm., 1-D
Wm. T., 462-D
REGESTER, Ada G., 58-B
Annie E., 58-B
Saml., Rev., 58-B
REGISTER, Annie E., 58-B
Fannie Gray, 58-B
Paul, 58-B
Samuel, 67
REID, Alice E., 130-C
B. G. W., 68
Lillian, 129-C
Mary J., 88-B
Robert E., 129-C
REIGN, Walter, 185-B
REILEY, James, 269-D
REILLY, John F., 600 1/2-D
REIN, Annie E., 402-D
Benj. B., 402-D
F., 402-D
Fredk., 402-D
John, 33-D
Mary E., 402-D
REINHARD, Harold Ware, 251-A
REIP, Annie L., 30-B
Daisy M., 30-B
Jos. L., 30-B
Mary G., 30-B
Thos. H., 30-B
William P., 30-B
REISINGER, Marion V., 90-B
Mary A., 90-B
Wm., 90-B

REISS, T. Henry, 30-B
REITER, A. I., 206-A
Abraham, 206-A
Annie D., 206-A
Dorothy, 206-A
Emily, 206-A
Jessie B., 206-A
Mary J., 206-A
Peter, 206-A
Willie G., 206-A
RENBLE, Ann, 361-A
RENNIE, Adam M., 8-D
Agnes, 8-D
Andrew, 8-D
Cath., 8-D
Ida K., 8-D
James G., 8-D
Jane G., 8-D
John (?), 8-D
Wm., 8-D
RENTT, Elizabeth, 163-A
RESIDE, Barbara, 1-D
Gordon, 1-D
RESTON, George, 35-A
REVERE, Annie R., 160-A
REVIS, Della C., 167-C
Evelyn Mae, 167-C
James H., 167-C
REVORE, Annie R., 74-A
REYNOLDS, (?), 88-A, 107-A
Carrie, 141-B
Chas. E., 141-B
Edw., 87-A
Edw. C., 141-B
Eliz., 87-A
Eneas W., 87-A
Ethel, 141-B
George W., 87-A
Harry C., 87-A
James C., 87-A
Jane, 120-B
John, 142-D
Kate, 25-A
Laura, 87-A
Louise C., 87-A
Margaret, 141-B
Raymond W., 87-A
Sadie, 164-C
Sarah A., 164-C
Thomas, 87-A
Walter J., 10-B, 120-B
Wm. S., 164-C
RHEEN, Lea C., 441-D
RHODES, Jemimah, 139-A
RHOLEDER, Lollie, 30-B
RIBBON, Laura, 13-C
RICE, Ada M., 55-B
Eliza, 55-B
John, 67

RICE, John T., 55-B
John T., Jr., 55-B
John Thomas, 55-B
John, Rev., 55-B
Jos. J., Jr., 99-A
M. B. J., 68
Maria, 154-B
Sarah, 55-B
Sarah S., 55-B
RICHARDS, Annie L., 54-B
Ephran H., 98-A
Susan, 54-B
T. T. S., 67
RICHARDSON, (?), 215-A
Bertha J., 90-B
Calvin J., 344-A
Caris W., 90-B
Carrie C., 124-B
Dave (or Dora), 344-A
Dora (or Dave), 344-A
Edith V., 124-B
Elizabeth, 89-A, 124-B, 282-A
Elizabeth A., 89-A
Emma Jane, 405-A
Ethel, 89-A
Florence, 536-D
Frances, 344-A
George, 22-A
George C., 19-B
Hattie (ZELL), 90-B
Jno. F., 256-A
Jno. T., 485-A
John C., 344-A
John L., 89-A
John S., 90-B
John V., 89-A
John W., 67, 282-A
Jos. B., 344-A
Jos. C., 344-A
Joseph, 124-B
Joseph Vincent, 344-A
Julia A., 405-A
Margt. A., 282-A
Mary, 24-A
Mary E., 124-B
Maude B., 19-B
Minnie, 89-A
Nathan, 67
Nathan, Rev., 125-B
Nora C., 71-C
Philip E., 89-A
Raba, 89-A
Rich. M., 89-A
Robert, 89-A
Robert M., 89-A
Robt., 89-A
Samuel A., 71-C
Sarah, 603-D
Sarah J., 89-A
RICHARDSON, Sophia, 124-B
Thos., 89-A, 344-A
Va., 179-B
Virginia A., 124-B
Wm. J., 89-A
Wm. L., 124-B, 405-A
Wm. V., 405-A
RICHE, Richard E., 99-A
RICHLER, Frederick, 232-A
Thos., 232-A
RICHTER, (?), 332-A
Katherine, 60-D
Mary M., 232-A
Susan A.H., 184-A
RICKER, Edw. M., 33-D
RICKETTS, Blanch, 16-A
Cora D., 16-A
David, 16-A
Emily, 16-A
Fannie, 16-A
John, 16-A
Louise, 16-A
Margt. M., 16-A
Mary, 16-A
Mary D., 16-A
RICKEY, A. Maud, 206-B
Albert, 206-B
Alice M., 206-B
Alice M. (JONES), 206-B
Chas. T., 206-B
RIDDELL, Elisha L., 74-D
Patricia Lee, 74-D
RIDDLE, Myrtle, 74-D
Russell L., 74-D
RIDGELL, Charles, 140-C
John W., 140-C
Missouri (HALL), 140-C
Viola N., 140-C
RIDGELY, Ida, 251-A
Nicholas, 335-A
RIDGEWAY, Dora L., 96-B
John B., 68-C
RIDGLEY, (?), Mrs., 180-B
Ann, 335-A
Chas., 334-A
Jas., 66
Mary L., 161-B
Nicholas, 335-A
RIDGWAY, Laura V., 248-D
RIGBY, Eliza, 21-D
Jerry L., 24-B
RIGG, Charlisannia, 102-A
Howard A., 102-A
Isabel, 102-A
Jessie A., 102-A
Margt., 102-A
RIGGIN, Emily, 260-A
I., 260-A
Israel, 260-A

RIGGIN, Isriel, 260-A
  John W., 3-D
  Maggie S., 260-A
  Sadie M., 260-A
  Wm. I., 260-A
RIGGS, Howard A., 102-A
RIGLY, Jos. J., 415-A
RILEY, Chas. H., 475-D
  Ebenezer, 218-D
  Edwd., 475-A
  Elizabeth, 153-D, 216-D
  Ella May, 475-D
  Emma I., 488-D
  Frances E., 475-D
  Geo., 153-D
  Geo. A., 440-D
  Geo. W., 153-D
  Grace N., 216-D
  Harry L., 440-D
  Howard, 475-D
  Ida L., 440-D
  Jane E., 440-D
  John D., 440-D
  Mabel V., 216-D
  Marie, 440-D
  Marie T., 440-D
  Martha Jane, 218-D
  Mauris, 440-D
  Myrtle B., 216-D
  Rebecca, 153-D, 440-D
  Rudolph, 353-D
  W. T., 216-D
  Wm. H., 488-D
  Wm. L., 475-D
  Wm. T., 216-D
RINGLAND, Mary, 335 A
RINGLEB, Marcelia, 9-D
RINGOLD, Susan H., 79-B
RINGROSE, John W., Col., 5-D
  Margaret M., 5-D
  Margt. L., 5-D
RIRTGEWAY, Dora L., 96-B
RISTON, Florence, 240-D
  Mary L., 240-D
RITCHIE, Ella M., 420-A
RITER, Clifton W., 127-B
RITTER, Emma R., 127-B
  Mary B., 475-D
ROATAN, Sarah J., 175-B
ROBB, Acksah, 180-B
  John, 67, 180-B
ROBBINS, Harre, 69-B
  Nannie L., 69-B
ROBERTS, Albert E., 33-D
  Alonza, 134-B
  Amelia, 68-B
  Bertamin, 420-A
  Brantley E., 114-C
  Cadelia, 74-A

ROBERTS, Cath., 47-D
  Chas. E., 67-B
  Clarence E., 24-C
  Clarence Elmer, 24-C
  Cordelia M., 74-A
  David, 72-A
  Edward, 147-D
  Elizabeth, 68-B, 72-A
  George, 73-B, 420-A
  George C. M., 67, 68-B
  George M., 483-A
  George W., 68-B
  Helen E., 522-D
  Ida M., 24-C
  Isac G., 74-A
  John A., 522-D
  John P., 522-D
  John T., 522-D
  John W., 59-D
  Josphene, 72-A
  Lillian, 72-A
  Mary E., 114-C
  Mary Elizabeth, 24-C
  Mildred A., 522-D
  P. H., 47-D
  Ray E., 143-C
  Raymond E., 143-C
  Rebecca E., 522-D
  Richard, 153-D
  Robert, 21-D
  Sallie M., 143-C
  Susan M., 67-B
  Susanna, 68-B
  Susannah M., 67-B
  Walter F., 522-D
ROBEY, Anna, 323-A
  Annie E., 323-A
  James F., 323-A
  James W., 323-A
ROBINS, Margt. A., 576-D
ROBINSON, Alex H., 579-D
  Bertha Louise, 21-D
  Chancy M., 427-A
  Elizabeth M., 71-B
  Geo. A., 247-D
  George, 469-A
  James E., 71-B
  Jos., 46-C
  Laura (BLUNT), 46-C
  Sarah B., 247-D
  Sarah E., 420-A
ROBINTSON, James, 198-D
ROCKFORD, Joseph M., 363-A
  M. M., 363-A
RODELOFF, M. V., 489-D
RODGERS, Elizabeth, 173-C
  John, 156-A
  John W., 156-A
ROGERS, Caroline, 8-B

235

ROGERS, Carrie, 8-B
Charles R., 8-B
Elizabeth, 156-A
Emma May, 8-B
Florence G., 8-B
George, 8-B
George H., 8-B
George Poe, 8-B
Glades, 156-A
Gladys, 156-A
James E., 156-A
John J., 8-B
Joseph, 156-A
Louisa, 72-A
Mary, 492-A
Mary A., 492-A
Mary E., 8-B
Rosalie, 8-B
Rowland, 492-A
Saml., 156-A
Sarah T., 492-A
ROHR, (?), 78-A
Thelma, 78-A
ROHSIEPE, Caroline, 128-C
ROLOSON, Edwd., 593-D
Emma, 593-D
ROMNEY, Ann Rel, 188-A
Jane, 188-A
RONNENBERG, Cora E., 111-C
Henry L., 111-C
RONSARILLE, David C., 111-A
David G., 111-A
Dayton, 111-A
Frank E., 111-A
Mary, 111-A
Sarah D., 111-A
Sarah T., 111-A
William, 111-A
Wm. F., 111-A
RONSAVILLE, Christema, 543-D
David W., 543-D
RONSRILLE, David, 111-A
ROOKER, Mary A., 43-B
Samuel, 43-B
ROSA, Wm., 222-B
ROSE, Cath. A., 428-D
Geo. C., 428-D
Georgia A., 142-A
Harry, 81-D
Mary Ann, 147-C
Mary M., 428-D
Paul, 163-A
Wm., 163-A
ROSELLA, Ida, 159-B
ROSENBROCK, Adeline, 13-B
ROSHER, Jos., 121-B
Nelson, 121-B
ROSMAN, Andrew, 213-D
Ann, 213-D

ROSS, Ann C., 81-A
Annie E., 81-A
Brooke F., 34-C
Charlotte, 385-A
Daniel, 165-A
Elizabeth, 165-A
Frank, 358-A
George W., 81-A
Leory C., 385-A
Mary, 165-A
Mary (or May), 142-A
Mary E., 142-A
Rich S., 142-A
Robert R., 142-A
Robert W., 142-A
Sarah, 222-B
Sarah E., 142-A
Violet B., 224-D
William, 358-A
William G., 358-A
Willie M., 142-A
Wm. H., 224-D
ROSSBERG, Burkhore N., 463-A
Carl W., 463-A
Clara B., 463-A
Herman, 463-A
ROSSEAN, Rachel, 272-A
Rhena, 215-A
ROSTMAN, Carmelia, 361-A
Kate, 361-A
Philip, 361-A
ROSWELL, (?), 293-A
ROTE, John T., 326-D
Jos. M., 326-D
ROUNEY, (?), 315-D
ROURKE, Wm., 235-D
ROUSER, August, 151-D
Dorbora, 151-D
Elizabeth, 151-D
Gustav, 151-D
Paul M., 151-D
ROUSSELL, Augusta R., 179-B
Frank A., 179-B
ROUZEE, (?), Mrs., 97-D
Bernard C., 97-D
George M., 97-D
Mary E. (FISHER), 97-D
ROUZER, Arthur, 97-D
ROWE, Alice E., 209-B
Glina A., 187-B
Joseph, 187-B
Wm. E., 244-A
Wm. W., 244-A
ROZE, Georgia A., 142-A
ROZETTA, Minnie, 208-D
RUARK, Elizabeth, 313-A
Maria H., 72-A
Martha A., 235-D
RUCKLE, Elizabeth A., 485-A

RUCKLE, Rosa M., 485-A
Thos., 485-A
Thos. C., 485-A
RUHLAND, Conrad C., 56-A
Frederick M., 56-A
Viola A., 56-A
RUMNEY, Edwd. A., 112-B
Elizabeth, 112-B
Frances, 112-B
Howard D., 112-B
Ida May, 188-A
Jane, 188-A
John W., 112-B
M. F., 112-B
Millard F., 112-B
RUNDLE, Chas., 109-A
Elizabeth, 109-A
Eloner, 109-A
Geo. L., 109-A
John P., 109-A
John S., 109-A
Jos., 109-A
Joseph, 109-A
Sarah, 109-A
RUPPERT, Lloyd, 88-B
RUSHWORTH, Esther W., 68-C
John J., 69-C
Jos. P., 68-C
Mary, 69-C
Mary (WALKER), 68-C
Maurice, 69-C
Ralph W., 68-C
Ralph Walker, 68-C
RUSSELL, Annie A., 25-A
Elneta May, 97-D
Geo. G., 25-A
Hardy, 25-A
Hester, 25-A
Hester M., 298-A
Jas. H., 298-A
John, 214-A
Mary, 441-D
Minnie J., 298-A
Robert C., 237-D
Robert H., 298-A
Thos., 437-A
RUST, Cath., 231-A
Lucy, 231-A
Patience, 231-A
Paul, 231-A
RUTLEDGE, Mary Margaret, 21-D
RUTTER, Thos. A., 444-D
RYAN, Chas., 402-D
Eliza, 96-B
Elizabeth, 14-D
Gertrude G., 495-D
Jas. A., 14-D
Jas. T., 507-D
Wm. E., 402-D

RYLAND, Mary, 85-A
SADILLE, Frank, 94-A
SADLER, Sallie S., 176-B
Sallie Sluting, 176-B
Wm. H., 66
SAFNER, A. Leslie, 98-B
SALILDIENE, Michael, 137-A
Sarah B., 137-A
SALISBURY, Sallie S., 339-A
SALMON, Florence M., 124-B
SALTMARSH, A., Mrs., 30-B
SANDERS, (?), 210-B
Annie J., 122-D
Ellen, 122-D
Emma, 25-A
John Wesley, 122-D
Sarah, 135-D
Wm. W., 122-D
SANDOR, Adolph, 564-D
Cecil R., 564-D
Stephanie, 564-D
SANERLAND, Wm. D., 14-D
SANFORD, Daniel A., 177-D
Fannie M., 155-C
Freddie D., 177-D
George W., 155-C
Rachel Ann, 14-B
SANKS, Anne T., 73-B
Annie, 164-A
Elijah, 164-A
Ruth A., 73-B
William, 73-B
SANTMYER, Elizabeth, 234-A
SANTRIGER, E. M., 234-A
SARBACHER, Elmer Webster, 140-B
Georgiana D., 140-B
Joseph C., 140-B
SARBAUGH, Amanda, 391-A
SARBOUGH, Amanda, 391-A
SARILLE, Chas. A., 94-A
Mary C., 94-A
Saml. W., 94-A
Wm. W., 94-A
SASCHARD, Elizabeth, 88-B
SATTERFIELD, Hannah, 96-B
SAUBAUGH, J., 391-A
SAULSBURY, Edw., 451-A
Edw. H., 451-A
Elizabeth, 451-A
Maggie L., 451-A
SAUMEIG, Jacob, 238-A
SAUMENIG, Edward, 238-A
SAUSIN, Rich'd., 135-B
SAUTZER, George, 442-A
Henrietta, 442-A
SAVAGE, H. R., 68
SAVILLE, Chas. A., 94-A
Frank, 94-A
Mary C., 94-A

SAVILLE, Saml. W., 94-A
Wm. W., 94-A
SAVIN, Augustus, 135-A
Eliza M., 135-A
Elizabeth, 135-A
F. W., 135-A
Marcus D., 135-A
Thos. L., 135-A
Wm. T., 135-A
SAWERS, Wm., 103-A
SAWYER, Clifton A., 393-D
Greenleaf, 393-D
Harry, 393-D
Martin Louis, 393-D
Mary Alice, 393-D
Oscar, 393-D
SCARBOROUGH, Theo. T., Mrs., 45-C
Theodore, 45-C
SCHAEFFER, Geo. I., 12-D
SCHAFFER, Edward, 46-B
SCHAFFNER, Arthur, 85-A
Mary E., 85-A
William E. (or C.), 85-A
Wm. H., 85-A
SCHAIFFER, Geo., 12-D
SCHAMM, Violet, 345-A
SCHAUM, Benj. O., 17-A
Bessie, 17-A
SCHELHAUS, Arthur H., 229-B
John C., 113-C
Mary E., 113-C
SCHEOFF, Annie R., 32-D
SCHERER, Caroline, 16-A
Clarence H., 16-A
SCHISTER, Louisa, 180-D
SCHLEY, Cath., 11-D
Louis N., 11-D
Wm. L., 11-D
Wm. Louis, 11-D
SCHLOTT, Catherine, 95-A
Conrad, 95-A
SCHMIDT, (?), 558-D
Chas. H., 21-D
Henry, 97-C
Henry R., 399-D
Nellie Ida, 97-C
SCHMOLL, Blanche R., 469-D
Donald F., 469-D
Richard Gregory, 469-D
SCHNAILL, Frances, 420-A
SCHNEIDER, Louisa, 452-D
Theodore, 452-D
Wm., 452-D
SCHNEPF, Carrie, 49-C
George M., 49-C
SCHOENBORN, Susan, 96-B
SCHOFIELD, Ann, 193-B
Ann A., 201-B

SCHOLMAN, William D., 93-B
SCHOPPERT, Elmer C., 88-B
SCHORCKEY, Antionaitte, 213-A
SCHOTTA, August, 123-B
Augustus R., 123-B
Sallie A., 123-B
Sarah S. (or H.), 123-B
SCHRATE, Arthur J., 135-D
Henry H., 135-D
Thos. H., 135-D
Wm. S., 135-D
SCHROTE, Ann E., 232-A
Annie, 135-D
Edwin J., 232-A
John, 232-A
Sarah A., 135-D, 232-A
SCHROTH, Amelia J., 85-C
Charles G., 85-C
George J., 85-C
Irene, 85-C
Mary, 85-C
SCHUELER, Ida E., 13-C
J. Edmund, 13-C
SCHULL, E., 17-D
M., 17-D
SCHULTE, Emma, 121-B
SCHUMANN, Karl, 2-D
Mary Frances, 2-D
SCHWANEBACK, Emilie, 33-C
SCHWARTZ, Augustus, 446-D
SCHWARTZE, William, 392-A
SCHWARTZKOFF, M. E., 132-B
SCHWERTZER, Jacob, 163-A
Rachel, 163-A
SCOFIELD, Ulo W., 172-C
SCOTT, Ann, 54-A
Anna E., 81-B
Benjamin F., 33-C
Charles Edward, 33-C
Dorothea E., 33-C
Edgar Arthur, 33-C
Eliza Jane, 14-B
Elizabeth, 54-A
Frances J., 81-B
Horace R., 54-A
James R., 31-B
Jas. R., 81-B
Jeamie A., 88-B
John G., 14-B
Joseph W., 33-C
Maggie A., 81-B
Mary, 101-A
Mary E., 33-C
Mary Elizabeth, 33-C
Mary F., 11-D
Mary R., 54-A
Mary V., 227-A
Rosanna, 33-C
Saml. G. M., 54-A

SCOTT, Stuart S., 11-D
Walter M., 81-B
Wm. R., 81-B
Wm. W., 81-B
SEABROOK, Eliz A., 214-B
SEACHMAN, C., 468-A
Chas. W., 468-A
J., 468-A
SEAMAN, Edwd., 155-D
SEATON, Margaret, 207-B
Mary T., 207-B
Wm. S., 207-B
SEBASTIAN, Frank, 30-A
SEDDICUM, John, 371-A
SEDICUM, Elizabeth, 371-A
John S., 371-A
Matilda, 371-A
SEDICUMB, Edwd. T., 371-A
Wm. G., 371-A
SEEBO, Lemie C., 216-B
SEELEY, Wm., 284-A
SEEVERS, Annie, 24-B
SEGARS, Emma, 84-B
SEGUIN, Charles H., 352-A
Mary E., 352-A
R. L. J., 352-A
SEGUM, Mary E., 352-A
SELBY, Alice T., 83-B
John A., 83-B
John T., 83-B
SELET, Cath., 56-A
SELLERS, Henry, 70-B
Maria Emily, 4-B
Naomi E., 4-B
SELLY, John W., 313-A
Nellie, 313-A
William, 313-A
SEMISTON, Rhoda, 369-A
SEMMIS, Eliza, 131-B
SEMMON, Martha E., 198 1/2-A
SEMONOIDS, Matthew W., 137-B
SEMONT, Amelia, 146-B
SENFT, Charlotte, 25-D
SEREENY, Elnor B., 264-D
SERFS, Blanch, 149-A
SERIO, Frank, 82-C
Gertrude A., 82-C
Gertrude Alice, 82-C
SEVERSON, Eliza, 327-A
John, 327-A
Margt., 327-A
SEWELL, Eliza H., 188-A
Ely, 422-A
Elya P., 243-A
Garrison, 308-D
Geo. W., 308-D
Geo. Washington, 308-D
James, 67
Jas. F., 243-A

SEWELL, John, 188-A
Maria, 198 1/2-A
Mary H., 243-A
Mary J., 243-A
Sarah A., 243-A
Thos. H., 243-A
Thos., Rev., 67
Willhelmna, 308-D
William A., 308-D
SEYER, Eliz., 136-A
SEYMOUR, Geo., 129-C
Laura, 129-C
SHAFFER, Chas., 148-B
Chas. C., 148-B
Danl., 193-A
Frances, 148-B
Geo. E., 148-B
Grace E., 148-B
W., Mrs., 488-D
SHAFFNER, Isabel R. D., 41-B
Rebecca, 41-B
SHAGOGUE, Jas., 5-D
SHANAHAN, Sarah E., 317-A
SHANE, Amelia M., 151-A
Catherine G., 151-A
George R., 151-A
Joseph, 68
Joseph, Mrs., 151-A
Joseph, Rev., 151-A
Maria M., 151-A
Marie, 151-A
Susan M., 151-A
Sussannah M., 151-A
Sussannah P., 151-A
SHANKS, Mary, 106-A
SHANNAHAN, Mary, 317-A
SHANNON, Geo. M., 201-D
Ida A., 201-D
John A., 201-D
SHANT, Mary, 35-A
SHARBACHER, Fannie C., 140-B
SHAULIS, Anthony, 299-A
SHAW, (?), 226-A
Arthur, 311-A
Augustine, 35-A
Bessie L., 156-B
Callie, 156-B
Edward, 156-B
Edwd., 39-D
Elizabeth, 156-B
Ernest, 156-B
George, 437-A
John H., 198-A
Lucy, 156-B
Margt. A., 198-A
Mary L., 156-B
Montez, 39-D
Priscilla, 40-A
Rachel, 156-B

SHAW, Ruel, 156-B
Ruel M., 156-B
Silvanus, 156-B
Thos., 311-A
Wm. E., 437-A
SHEA, Daniel, 86-B
SHEARER, John J., 217-D
Maria L., 217-D
Willie M., 217-D
SHEARS, C. M., 229-A
Herman, 229-A
Rebecca, 136-A
Susan, 229-A
SHECKELLS, Annie M., 100-C
Charles R., 100-C
Chas. W., 128-C
John R., 100-C
Lena D., 128-C
Magdalene, 128-C
Robert L., 100-C
Vernon E., 100-C
SHECKELS, Richard W., 196-B
Sarah E., 196-B
SHECKETS, Wm., 139-A
SHECKLES, John, 385-D
SHEETS, Eliza, 136-A
John, 136-A
SHELDON, Chas. H., 486-A
James, 486-A
John, 486-A
Margaret, 189-A
Maria L., 486-A
Rachel, 53-B
SHELLHAUS, Anna F., 149-B
Clara M., 149-B
Mary, 149-B
Wm. H., 149-B
SHELLHAUSE, W. H., 149-B
SHELLOR, (?), 35-A
SHELTON, Arthur L., 26-D
Sarah, 521-D
SHEPPARD, Albert, 203-A
Annita, 214-B
Blanch C., 203-A
Chas. W., 203-A
Edward, 190-A
Edwin Thomas, 190-A
Frank, 203-A
Franklin A., 190-A
Fred., 203-A
H. M., 190-A
Ida, 190-A
Ida W., 190-A
Isabella, 190-A
Jennie, 190-A
John T., 190-A
Margaret, 203-A
Margt., 203-A
Mary E., 190-A

SHEPPARD, Mary Elma, 97-C
Mary G., 190-A
Mary J., 190-A
N. A., 190-A
Nicholas, 190-A
Nicholas A., 190-A
Viola, 203-A
William, 203-A
Wm. J., 190-A
SHERMAN, Geo. N., 29-D
SHERWOOD, Mary R., 162-B
SHICKSETS, Mary, 139-A
SHIFLETT, Catharine M., 30-A
SHINNICK, Blanch W., 272-A
Chas., 411-A
Geo., 216-A
George, 272-A
Grace C., 272-A
Jacob, 216-A, 272-A
Jacob A., 272-A
Jacob A. H., 272-A
Kenneth, 272-A
Lillian, 272-A
Margt., 272-A
Martha, 272-A
Thos. E., 272-A
Walter H., 272-A
SHIPLEY, Anne E., 41-A
Arthur W., 122-B
C., 66
Clarence, 204-B
Columbus, 204-B
Cordelia E., 97-A
E., 204-B
Ella H., 7-D
Ella Hahn, 41-A
Ezekiel, 17-D
Ezexiel, 10-D
Francis M., 204-B
Grace, 428-D
Harry I., 15-C
Ida Adair, 204-B
Issac, 7-D
Jno. T., 97-A
Jno. W., 97-A
John, 66
John T., 97-A
John W., 97-A
Laura, 17-D
Leroy, 204-B
Mary E., 204-B
Mary J., 97-A
Maud, 204-B
Maude R., 15-C
Medora, 97-A
Otho A., 41-A
Owen H., 204-B
Parkin Kerr, 17-D
Sarah, 204-B

SHIPLEY, Sarah J., 97-A
  Willie, 123-B
  Wilma, 41-A
  Wilson G., 428-D
SHIVERS, E. Nillie, 363-D
  Emma, 363-D
  Nicholes, 363-D
  Wm. A., 363-D
SHOEMAKER, Chas. A., 88-A
  Georgana, 88-A
  Jno. H., 88-A
  Jno. W., 88-A
  John, 88-A
  John H., 88-A
  John T., 88-A
  Mary M., 88-A
SHORT, Cora Lee, 464-A
  Upton, 195-A
SHRINER, Annetta, 460-D
SHRIVER, Nicholas, 365-D
SHRODES, Edgar D., 127-C
  Ethel L., 127-C
SHROTE, Elizabeth J., 232-A
  Ellen F., 232-A
  John, 232-A
  Laura I., 232-A
  Margt. J., 138-B
SHUCK, Adam, 133-B
SHULTZ, John T., 162-B
  M. J., Mrs., 162-B
SICER, J. F., 91-A
SICK, Chas., 385-A
SICKE, Chas., 385-A
SICKLIN, Wm., 300-A
SICKLINE, Margt., 300-A
SILBERZAHN, Geo. W., 163-B
  May, 163-B
SILVER, Carroll M., 154-B
SIM, Arthur, 143-C
  Thelma L., 143-C
SIMERING, Alice, 33-B
  Amelia, 33-B
  Christian, 33-B
  J. C., 33-B
  M. Kate, 33-B
  Margt., 33-B
  Rose D., 33-B
SIMICK, Thos., 183-A
SIMKIN, Adeline G., 75-A
  Ann, 75-A
  George, 75-A
  Josephine G., 75-A
  Lemuel T., 75-A
  Wm. J., 75-A
SIMMEOUS, Eliza, 131-B
SIMMERING, Wm., 192-B
SIMMOIT, Elizabeth C., 26-D
  Harry, 26-D
SIMMONDS, Margt. T., 203-A

SIMMONS, Charles E., 68
  Eliza, 131-B
  Elizabeth, 23-A
  Frank G., 131-B
  Sarah M., 131-B
SIMMONT, Mary E., 146-B
SIMMORT, Chas. I., 26-D
  Clarence, 26-D
  David, 26-D
  David F., 26-D
  David T., 26-D
  Margt. F., 26-D
  Wm. T., 26-D
SIMMS, Emeline T., 48-B
SIMONT, Marie, 235-D
SIMPSON, Andrew, 32-D
  Annie, 17-A
  Chas. H., 67-C
  Florence G., 67-C
  Francis, 118-B
  Luther R., 54-A
SINCLAIR, Louise A., 285-A
  Mary A. F., 285-A
SINDOFF, Eliza, 21-D
SKINNER, Beulah, 304-D
  Catherine, 304-D
  Howard P., 304-D
  Leonard O., 304-D
  Malcolm, 33-D
  Mary, 304-D
  Thos. W., 304-D
SKIRVEN, Charles D., 4-C
  Emma, 74-B
  Eva, 4-C
  Flora, 74-B
  James A., 4-C
  Mildred, 4-C
SLACK, John H., 202-A
SLADE, John A., 305-D
  Mary E., 305-D
  Willie, 305-D
SLADKY, Rudolph, 44-B
SLATER, Esther V., 144-A
SLAUGHTER, Amanda, 391-A
SLAYSMAN, Anna M., 398-D
  Mahlon, 398-D
  Margaret, 398-D
SLOCUM, Giorgeanna, 88-B
SLUSS, Madeline J., 98-C
SMALL, Harriet I., 509-D
SMELTZER, Chas., 136-B
  Chas. A., 136-B
  Clara E., 136-B
SMILEY, (?), 448-A
  Ann, 79-A
  Cath., 273-A
  Fannie A., 79-A
  Harry H., 79-A
  Isabell, 79-A

SMILEY, James, 79-A
Jonth. P., 79-A
Joseph, 79-A
Joseph P., 79-A
L., 79-A
Laura V., 79-A
M. M., 79-A
Maggie, 79-A
Margt., 79-A
Peter Robert, 79-A
Robert, 79-A, 273-A
Robert, Jr., 273-A
Wm., 79-A
SMITH, (?), 35-A, 257-A
(?), Mrs., 53-A
A. W., 152-B
Albert, 329-D
Albert L., 36-A
Alda G., 231-A
Alice, 25-D
Andrew, 62-C
Ann, 152-B, 175-A
Ann E., 44-A
Annie, 207-B
Annie A., 159-D
Annie E., 47-A
Asbury, Rev., 17-C
Belle, 361-D
Benj. B., 257-A
Bernnett H., 68
Bertha V., 36-A
Bertie G., 329-D
Catherine, 591-D
Charles, 257-A
Charlotte E., 62-C
Chas. I., 46-A
Clara A., 25-D
David, 46-A
David C., 97-A
Delia H., 329-D
E., 334-A
Elijah B., 93-B
Eliz, 392-D
Elizabeth P., 246-D
Elizabeth Rogers, 156-A
Ella, 160-D
Ellen, 44-A
Ellen F., 160-D
Emily R., 185-A
Emma S., 93-B
Esther, 246-D
Ethel Belle, 37-C
Evelyn E. F., 160-D
Florence, 25-D
Florence B., 97-A
Florence E., 7-D
Florence G., 229-B
Frances, 96-B
Geden B., Dr., 95-A

SMITH, Geo. A., 44-A
Geo. Z., 44-A
George E., 37-C
George F., 185-A
George W., 231-A
Gideon B., 95-A
Girden B., Dr., 95-A
Grace T. (JOHNSON), 289-A
H., 334-A
Harry J., 160-D
Harry P., 246-D
Helen R., 90-B
Henry, 67
Herbert, 7-D
Isabella C., 361-D
James, 67, 190-A
Jas., 204-B, 286-A
Jennie F., 246-D
John, 25-D, 465-A
John C., 46-A
John E., 126-A
John G., 46-A
John H., 185-A
John M., 465-A
Julia A., 44-A
Julie Ann, 139-D
Kate, 257-A
Katharine G., 37-C
Lee M., 25-D
Lewis, 159-D
Lewis J., Capt., 159-D
Louis W., 25-D
Lulia L., 46-A
Lulla May, 36-A
M. A., 152-A
Mahon, 159-D
Margt., 190-A
Margt. B., 368-D
Martha A., 3-D
Martha F., 517-D
Martha J., 465-A
Mary, 25-D, 30-B, 207-B
Mary E., 25-D, 139-D
Mary J., 46-A, 274-D, 330-D
Mary L., 30-B
Maud E., 62-C
Minnie L., 25-D
Oliver T., 329-D
R., 25-D
R. Henry, 44-A
Rachel, 180-A
Rebecca, 331-D
Richard H., Jr., 44-A
Rosemarie, 25-D
S. J., 68
S. J., Rev., 67, 68
Sallie E., 152-B
Samuel F., 3-D
Sarah, 190-A, 274-D

SMITH, Sarah A., 175-A, 471-D
Sarah E., 96-C, 493-A
Sarah Jane, 44-A
Saranna, 40-A
Susan, 95-A
Susan E., 46-A
Thos., 110-A, 152-B
Thos. F., 152-B
Thos. H., 361-D
Wallis T., 46-A
Walter F., 46-A
William, 96-C
William E., Sr., 96-C
William Edward, 96-C
William J., 229-B
William P., 229-B
Wm., 4-D, 93-B, 175-A
Wm. E., 289-A
Wm. H., 246-D
Wm. J., 465-A
Wm. T., 46-A
Zacharias, 175-A
SMUCK, L. Merce, 154-A
Lillie G., 154-A
Samuel V., 154-A
SNEDLEY, Mary E., 155-D
SNEED, Elizabeth, 195-A
Jno. T., 201-A
Robert, 201-A
William, 201-A
SNELLING, Ida M., 157-C
Ida Mae, 157-C
Norris W., 157-C
SNETHEN, Theodore, 491-A
SNIAT, J. Harman, 90-B
SNIVELY, Adam, 82-B
SNIVERLY, Adam, 489-A
Ann, 489-A
Jacob, 489-A
SNYDER, Ellen, 44-A
Henrietta Carroll, 530-D
Henrietta S., 530-D
Howard K., 17-D
Isaac W., 530-D
Jane R., 44-A
Lydia A., 530-D
Margt., 44-A
Mary, 44-A
Mary V., 530-D
Peter, Dr., 44-A
Thos. W., 530-D
SOAPER, Edward W., 48-C
Helen Ruth, 48-C
Myrtle, 48-C
SOCKRITTER, Edw., 179-C
Edward Tensall, 179-C
Sarah (DAVIS), 179-C
SODLER, Charlotte, 91-B
SOHN, Henry, 21-D

SOLAN, Clara, 529-D
SOLISBURN, A. G., Mrs., 72-C
SOLZE, Caroline, 141-A
John, 141-A
John M., 141-A
Julius, 141-A
SOMENIG, Alice, 238-A
Jacob, 238-A
Jann, 238-A
Mary, 238-A
SOMMERS, Wm., 462-D
SONDERSTRAM, Geo. A., 133-D
SOPER, Annie M., 89-A
Geo. A., 89-A
SORENSON, Andrew M., 58-D
Peter, 58-D
SOWERS, Cora, 33-D
SPAIGHT, Jeremiah, 415-A
SPALDING, (?), 295-A
SPANGLER, J. N., 68
SPARROW, Henry C., 33-D
SPEDDEN, (?), Mrs., 107-B
Alfred E., 107-B
Ann R., 178-B
Ann Rebecca, 178-B
Annie E., 72-C
Charles P., 72-C
Clarence C., 128-B
Daniel, 326-A
David B., 326-A
Edward P., 178-B
Emily A., 326-A
Emma, 326-A
J., 178-B
M., 178-B
Maggie E., 128-B
Mary G., 128-B
Rebecca, 107-B
Thomas, 178-B
Thomas H., 178-B
Vincent P., 107-B
Wm. A, 110-A
Wm. H., 128-B
Z. Taylor, 178-B
SPEDDON, Clarence, 128-B
Lydia, 128-B
Margaret J. G., 128-B
Margt. G., 128-B
Wm. A., 128-B
SPEEDEN, Wm. H. C., 107-B
SPELLMAN, Jno. W., 107-A
SPENCE, John E., 19-D
Lydia, 484-A
Marg. E., 19-D
Mary E., 19-D
Seldon, 19-D
Wm. S., 19-D
SPENCER, E. A., 112-A
E. Virginia, 112-A

SPENCER, Nance, 100-A
  Peregrine, 48-A
  Susan, 48-A
SPICER, Clara N., 191-A
  Hiram K., 191-A
  J. Fenton, 91-A
  Janah, 110-A
  Rebecca C., 91-A
  Rebecca G., 91-A
  Thos., 91-A
SPIDDEN, Chas. E., 165-B
  Eliz, 165-B
SPIEGEL, Frederick, 397-D
  Frederick J., 397-D
  Hilma, 397-D
SPIEKERMAN, August C., 173-C
  Emma (MADDOX), 173-C
SPIES, Eliza, 89-A
  Elizabeth, 89-A
  John, 89-A
SPIGNER, Mary E., 130-C
SPILLMAN, Andrew J., 22-C
  Daisey, 107-B
  F., Sergt., 39-A
  Margaret, 22-C
  Marguerite, 22-C
  William B., 22-C
SPILMAN, Frances, 39-A
SPINK, Annie, 366-A
  George W., 366-A
SPIRES, Ann, 316-A
  Mary A., 316-A
  Mary J., 316-A
SPNCET, Edith, 35-A
SPOERKE, Henry Otto, 128-C
SPRIGG, Chas. H., 347-A
  Harriet G. C., 309-A
  Harriot G. E., 309-A
  Henson W., 347-A
  Horace, 309-A
  Margt. R., 347-A
  Mary, 347-A
  Mary E., 347-A
  Nathaniel, 309-A
  Rebecca, 309-A
  Singleton, 347-A
  T., 201-A
SPRIGGS, James W., 347-A
  Jas. W., 347-A
SQUIRES, Jane C., 313-A
  Mary (GEISLER), 113-C
  Wm., 113-C
STACK, Emma, 87-A
STAFFORD, Jas., 32-D
STAGGE, Christian, 299-D
  Christian H., 299-D
  Frank W., 299-D
  Louisa, 299-D
  Wm. J., 299-D

STAGMAN, June, 288-A
STAKETT, Elizabeth A., 160-A
STALLINGS, Bessie M., 8-D
  Carroll, 8-D
  Naoma, 8-D
STANDIFORD, Mary C., 134-A
STANFIELD, Louise Barlow, 46-B
STANG, August, Jr., 120-B
  Louise Phillips, 120-B
STANLEY, Elizabeth A., 245-A
  Viola, 41-C
  Walter, 41-C
  Wm. W., 245-A
STANLY, Aly, 245-A
STANP, Elizabeth, 452-A
  Thos., 452-A
  Thos. H., 452-A
  Wm. W., 452-A
STANSBERY, Jane W., 254-A
STANSBURY, Ann E., 2-B
  Ann Eliz., 2-B
  Charles B., 254-A
  Charles F., 2-B
  Daniel, 67
  Daniel R., 2-B
  Elizabeth H., 2-B
  J. T., 68
  James C., 2-B
  Joseph C., 2-B
  Joseph R., 2-B
  Samuel, 2-B
STANTUZER, Elizabeth, 234-A
STARLING, Archabold, 306-A
  Cath., 351-A
  Thos., 359-A
STARR, Emory W., 22-B
  George, 22-B
  George E., Dr., 22-B
  H., Dr., 133-D
  Vallura, 22-B
START, J. W., 68
STATEN, James, 425-A
STAUM, Christian, 67, 129-A
  Clyd Estelle, 129-A
  Clyde E., 129-A
  Elan E., 129-A
  Elizabeth, 129-A
  John, 129-A
  John E., 129-A
STAYLOR, Frank, 267-D
  Margt., 267-D
STAYTON, David, 425-A
STAZTON, Elizabeth, 425-A
STEEL, M. Emily, 246 1/2-A
STEFFE, Esther M., 58-C
  Roland M., 58-C
STEFFEE, Jose., 235-D
STEGMAN, Myrtle, 289-A
STEIFFE, Sophia, 42-A

STEIN, Helen J. Childs, 36-C
  Sallie, 72-A
STEINFORD, I., 39-A
  John, 39-A
  M., 39-A
STEINHAUSER, Blanche E., 162-B
STEINWEDIC, Christian, 66
STEMBLER, Chas., 142-B
  Ecelia, 142-B
  Ella G., 142-B
  Emma (FAGER), 142-B
  Geo. W., 142-B
  Maggie G., 142-B
  Mary C. (or E.), 142-B
  Sarah A., 142-B
  Wm. B., 142-B
  Wm. H., 142-B
STENACKER, E., 214-B
  H. W., 214-B
  Hen, 214-B
STEPHENS, Danl., 66
  Edgar, 7-D, 57-D
  Philip R., 208-D
  Susan R., 7-D
  Upton C., 7-D
STERLING, Alces L., 108-B
STEUART, Edith A., 200-A
  George A., 200-A
  Sarah, 200-A
STEVENS, Edwd. E., 208-D
  Jas. A., 446-A
  Mary, 446-A
STEVERS, Emma C., 310-D
  Harry D., 310-D
  Samuel, 310-D
  Wesley, 310-D
  Wesley B., 310-D
  Wesley W., 310-D
  Willie F., 310-D
STEWART, Annie K., 471-A
  Bessie, 306-A
  Charlotte, 139-B
  Elizabeth M., 239-A
  Emeline, 51-B
  Emma, 203-A
  Emma E., 451-D
  Fannie Reese, 106-B
  Geo. H., 451-D
  George A., 200-A
  George D., 239-A
  George Washington, 239-A
  Howard R., 106-B
  Ida R., 106-B
  Isabell, 471-A
  James F., 451-D
  Jessie R., 51-B
  John, 6-D, 203-A
  John D., 471-A
  Lillie M., 107-A

STEWART, Lydia, 330-A
  Mable R., 451-D
  Margaret, 167-B
  Marion D., 107-A
  Martha, 471-A
  Martha H., 306-A
  Mary C., 126-B
  Mary Elizabeth, 239-A
  Mary J., 239-A, 486-D
  Merreen Q., 107-A
  O. (or C.) F., 203-A
  Richard H., 133-D
  Sarah C., 451-D
  Thos. R., 451-D
  W. Clarence, 106-B
  Washington, 99-A
  Willie, 203-A
  Willie F., 306-A
STIDHAM, Ann, 96-A
  Annie B., 96-A
  Edger J., 96-A
  Geo. W., 96-A
  James, 96-A
  Jane, 96-A
  Jno. A., 96-A
  Nannie, 96-A
  Rebecca, 96-A
  Sallie V., 96-A
  Saml., 96-A
STIER, Josephus, 536-D
  L., Mrs., 536-D
  William, 536-D
STINCHCOMB, Aaron A., 51-B
  Ann, 51-A
  Isabella, 51-B
  James, 53-B
  Jas. H., 51-B
  John, 53-B
  John A., 51-A
  Len, 53-B
  Mary A., 53-B
  Saml., 51-A
  Susan, 53-B
  Susan A., 53-B
STIRLING, William Edward, 465-D
  Wm. E., 465-D
STOCKET, (?), 104-B
STOCKETT, Anne, 244-A
  Bettie, 318-A
  Clintonia, 318-A
  Emily L., 244-A
  Joseph T., 244-A
  Louisa, 244-A
STOCKMAN, (?), 396-A
  Jane T., 396-A
STOELTZER, John T., 80-A
STOKES, Alfred G., Sr., 289-A
  Alverta May, 288-A
  Jeanette Catherine, 289-A

STOKES, Joyce P., 288-A
STOLL, E. Wilbur, 50-C
STOLTZ, Chas., 21-D
STONE, Ann, 239-A
  Caroline, 360-A
  Carrie V., 360-A
  George, 74-B
  Jean, 425-A
  Johannah, 360-A
  Joshua, 360-A
  Sarah, 370-A
  William, 239-A, 360-A
  Wm. B., 360-A
  Wm. T., 360-A
STONER, Chas. Lee, 413-D
  Clarence F., 68-C
  Clarence, Mrs., 68-C
  Grace G., 68-C
STOTTELMYER, J. F., 30-A
STOVER, Brokie, 112-B
STOWMAN, Charles H., Sr., 220-D
  Gertrude E., 220-D
STRAUSE, Hannah (BERLINER), 171-C
  Myer, 171-C
STRAWBRIDGE, Robert, 67
STREET, Maria E., 170-A
  S. K. I., 170-A
STRIDE, John H., 89-B
STRIGEL, Gertrude, 467-A
  Laura, 467-A
STRINGER, Edwin, 46-A
  Maber H., 46-A
STRITCH, Lydia, 439-D
STROM, Wm. C., 183-D
STRONG, James E., 335-D
STUARD, R. Ernest, Mrs., 235-A
STUBBS, Ida May, 123-D
STULTZ, Mary J., 33-D
STUMP, Mary A., 105-B
STURGES, Julia A., 51-A
  Mary A., 51-A
  Nancy, 51-A
  Oliver, 51-A
  Reuben, 51-A
STURGESS, Julia, 51-A
STURGIS, Ruth, 42-A
STURTZ, Guy S., 24-C
SUCKLEY, Hannah, 26-A
SUKE, Chas., 385-A
SULLAVIN, Abbie, 212-A
  Abigil, 212-A
  E., 446-D
  George M., 212-A
  H., 446-D
  Hariet, 212-A
  Jane R., 212-A
  John, 212-A
  Louise K., 212-A

SULLAVIN, Mary, 212-A
  William, 212-A
  William M., 212-A
  William Mansfield, 212-A
  Willie, 23-B
SULLIVAN, (?), 2-C
  Arlene, 274-A
  Charles E., 209-D
  Dorothy, 12-A
  Estella, 4-C
  Frederick C., 4-C
  Grace S., 193-B
  Ida M., 274-A
  John, 25-B
  John B., 88-B
  Martha, 225-B
  Nancy, 25-B
  William, 12-A
SUMALT, Theodore, 29-D
SUMMERS, (?), 445-A
  Mary, 350-A
  Mary G., 110-A
  Rose L., 235-A
  Ruth A., 256-A
  Thos. D., 256-A
  Thos. N., 256-A
  William, 235-A
SUMMERVILLE, Elizabeth, 11-D
  John, 11-D
  Lydia E., 11-D
  R., 13-D
  Thos., 11-D
SUMUALT, George W., 25-A
SUMWALT, C. K. R., 108-A
  Carrie M., 108-A
  Clara Naomi, 29-D
  Cordelia P., 108-A
  Jas. H., 108-A
  Mary A., 108-A
  Mary Ann, 108-A
  Sarah K., 131-B
SUNDERLAND, Gideon, 115-B
SUTCH, John, 33-D
SUTER, Eliza, 442-A
  George, 442-A
  George R., 224-A
  Lillian, 224-A
  Mary, 224-A
SUTTON, Alice White, 155-A
  Ida B., 142-A
  Jno. W., 328-A
  John W., 142-A
  Jos. R., 321-A
  M. R., 142-A
  Mary R., 142-A
SUWALL, Katherine, 33-B
SWAHLEN, John, 68
SWAN, (?), 79-B
  Elizabeth Baker, 7-C

SWAN, Jane (DURFFIELD), 7-C
  John N., 7-C
  Sadie, 146-B
SWANN, Elizabeth K., 7-C
  Thomas H., 7-C
  Thomas Hadden, 7-C
SWEENY, David, 108-A
  Mary, 108-A
TABB, Christopher W., 102-A
  Cora K., 102-A
  Mary A., 102-A
  Mary Dolores, 102-A
  Wm. K., 102-A
TABBALBS, Susan, 21-A
TABBOTT, Mary M., 36-C
TABLER, Jacob, 78-A
TAFFAN, Maggie, 443-D
  Wm. C., 443-D
  Wm., Dr., 443-D
TALBERT, Isabell, 23-D
TALBOT, Alice T., 196-B
  Gertrude, 114-C
  J. T., 87-B
TALBOTT, (?), 288-A
  Alice T., 196-B
  Clarence Elmer, 36-C
  Edna M., 36-C
  Jane, 342-A
  Jas. A. C., 196-B
  Joseph, 342-A
  Kate, 293-A
  S. C., 232-A
  Sophia L., 147-A
  Thos., 293-A
  Walter B., 36-C
TALL, Wm., 244-A
TANELEY, Geo., 134-B
TARR, Lillie L., 84-B
  Mary Alice, 45-C
  Odna L., 26-C
  Oliva S., 164-A
TASE, Lawrence C., 44-C
  Margaret E., 44-C
TATHAM, Amanda M., 391-A
  Joht., 48-A
  Martha, 224-A
TATTLE, Aaron, 453-D
TAUGHINBAUGH, Rose A., 41-A
TAYLER, Alice V., 88-B
  Geo., 84-B
TAYLOR, (?), 400-A, 473-A
  Alelia, 378-A
  Alice, 224-A
  Amanda, 378-A
  Ann, 361-A, 378-A
  Ann E., 485-D
  Ann G., 386-A
  Betty, 186-B
  Chas., 186-B
TAYLOR, Clarence E., 461-A
  Eliza, 186-B
  Elizabeth, 359-A, 378-A
  Ellen, 224-A
  Frances M., 151-A
  Francis, 483-A
  George M., 386-A
  George T., 380-A
  Grace, 386-A
  Irvin, 380-A
  Jacob, 66
  John T., 235-A
  Margaret, 459-D
  Margt. I., 272-D
  Martha A., 380-A
  Mary, 26-D, 66
  Minnie V., 146-B
  Nancy P., 380-A
  Rich. H., 483-A
  Richard, 21-D
  S. B., 459-D
  Saml., 84-B
  Sarah Ann, 386-A
  Sarah E., 317-A
  Sarah R., 89-B
  Sedney B., Jr., 459-D
  Sophia, 383-A
  Thos., 380-A
  Wm., 186-B, 378-A
TAYMOR, Wm. S., 186-B
TEAL, George, 68
TEALE, Ellis S., 68
TENNEMAN, Frank W., 9-D
TERRELL, George W., 83-B
  Mary E., 83-B
TERRY, Annie, 159-A
  Hannah, 159-A
  Isaiah, 159-A
  Isaih, 159-A
  John W., 159-A
  Josephine Anderson, 159-A
  Margt. M., 159-A
  Martha A., 159-A
  Sarah, 159-A
  Tho. W., 159-A
TEULTE, John T., 211-D
TEVES, Edw. W., 109-B
  George Edward William, 109-B
  Wm., 109-B
THAW, Samuel, 214-D
  Sarah E., 214-D
THOMAS, Alice, 43-B
  Annie B., 57-D
  Annie R., 284-A
  Bereuiet, 43-B
  Cara R. Kellinger, 8-B
  Carrie C., 129-B
  Daniel E., 252-A
  David, 252-A

THOMAS, Delaware C., 32-D
Edwd. C., 129-B
Elizabeth, 56-B
Ely, 252-A
Emily, 5-D
Florence M., 37-D
George, 190-A
George R., 35-B
George W., 53-A
Georgia A., 35-B
Gladys F., 30-A
Grace, 252-A
Harold C., 129-B
Henry P., 284-A
Howard M., 81-B
Johanna C., 582-D
Laura, 137-B
Laura N., 129-B
M. V., 366-A
Margt. A., 43-B
Mary A., 35-B
Mary Adeline, 35-B
Mary Alice, 43-B
Mary G., 129-B
Mattie H., 129-B
Millicent G., 35-B
Nancy, 67-B
S. Daw (or Dew), 35-B
S. Dewa (or Dawa), 35-B
Sadie G., 129-B
Saml. H., 366-A
Saml. K., 328-A
Samuel, 35-B
Samuel, Mrs., 35-B
Sidney, 8-B
Susan B. Sweetser, 252-A
Wm. A., 582-D
Wm. B., 252-A
THOMMA, Bessie E., 49-C
THOMPSON, Carrie, 36-D
Edud., 245-A
Edud. E., 245-A
Elizabeth, 245-A
James, 432-A
John, 340-A
Margt., 173-D
Mary, 406-A
Robt. L., 266-D
Sarah, 340-A
William T., 36-D
Wm. P., 36-D
THOMSON, Dollie, 245-A
THON, Christian, 499-D
Louisa, 499-D
Mary, 499-D
Methilda, 26-C
THORN, August, 499-D
Wm., 499-D
THRIFT, Anne H., 48-A

TICKLE, Alice Ann, 45-C
TILLINGS, Cath., 81-A
Rachael, 81-A
TILYARD, Chas. B., 166-B
Nora Greenfield, 166-B
TIMANUS, Eliza, 182-A
Frank E., 182-A
Jacob, 182-A
Jacob H., 182-A
John, 182-A
TINDLE, Henry, 133-D
TIPPETT, Charles T., 68
M., 392-D
Rachel, 392-D
TITTLE, Sarah A., 112-A
Thomas, 112-A
Thos., 112-A
TODD, Charles Hill, 21-D
TOFT, Cath., 196-B
Ellen, 196-B
Fannie E., 196-B
John, 196-B
TOLBERT, Isabella, 23-D
TOLLING, Elizabeth, 81-A
TOLSON, George, 481-A
TOMPKINS, Annie E., 84-C
Edward C., 87-C
Walter W., Jr., 84-C
Walter W., Sr., 84-C
TONTZ, Sarah, 179-C
TOOL, Elizabeth, 467-D
Mary, 467-D
TOOY, Marcus, 73-A
Mary D., 73-A
Mary E., 73-A
Mary P. V., 73-A
TOWNSEND, Annie, 81-D
Edward C., 30-D
Emma, 81-B
James, 13-A, 81-D
John, 81-D
Rebecca, 13-A
TOWSON, Chas., 52-B
Joshua, Mrs., 309-D
TRAFFNBERG, Wm., 188-A
TRAINOR, E., 393-A
Geo. M., 18-D
John R., 393-A
TRAUGHT, Easter, 41-B
TRAVERS, Charles F., 59-C
TRAVIS, Audrey Muller, 14-C
TREADWAY, Achsah E., 373-D
TREADWELL, Hilton F., 47-C
Jennie, 47-C
Jennie (GRAHAM), 47-C
John, 47-C
John F., 47-C
Mary Elizabeth, 161 1/2-D
TREAKEL, Emma, 55-D

TREAS, John, 583-D
M. E., 583-D
TREE, John, 162-B
Mary, 162-B
TREHERNE, Leonard C., 86-B
TREMPER, Mary A., 348-A
TRESS, Wm. D., 583-D
TREULTE, Jacob, 211-D
Maggie C., 211-D
Nicholas, 211-D
TRICKLE, Margt., 514-D
TRIMPER, Herman, 348-A
TRIPP, Mary W., 95-B
TROMAN, G., 200-A
TROUGHT, Wm. E., 520-D
TRUDERNIVE, Andrew, 112-A
Carrie M., 112-A
TRUMBO, Alice A., 73-D
TSCHUDY, Victor P., 233-A
TUCKER, Anne B., 139-A
Benj., 152-A
E. B., 171-D
Elizabeth, 152-A
Erastus B., 171-D
Florence, 86-B
Isac, 85-A
J. L., 171-D
Laura, 171-D
Laura H., 171-D
Mary, 152-A
Robert S., 171-D
Sarah A., 85-A
Wm. L., 171-D
Wm. W., 171-D
TUCKEY, Elisha, 580-D
Florence E., 94-B
Susan J., 580-D
TURNER, Alta May, 5-C
Beatrice Evans, 188-D
Chas. H., 244-A
Eleanor Maynard, 17-A
Frank T., 195-A
George H., 5-C
Jas. M., 17-A
Lillie Pearl, 195-A
Mary S., 36-A
Wm. B., 17-A
TWEEDELL, Thos., 126-A
TWEEDY, Augustus, 24-A
Cath., 24-A
Celiea Caroline, 24-A
Elizabeth, 24-A
Elizabeth C., 24-A
Saml., 24-A
TWILLER, George W., 21-D
TYLER, Alice V., 88-B
Blanche, 191-B
Ella M., 191-B
Geo. B., 191-B

TYLER, Isabella, 191-B
Mary, 134-A
Sarah A., 386-A
TYLOR, Isabelle, 191-B
TYSINGER, Alice E., 105-A
Chas. Osburn, 105-A
Lewis, 105-A
Margt. E., 105-A
Mary, 105-A
Wm. L., 105-A
UHRBROCK, George, 215-D
UKRBROCK, Jas. F., 215-D
Kate M., 215-D
ULLRICK, A. Mary, 44-B
Clara J., 279-A
Wm., 44-B
Wm. H., 44-B
ULRICK, Christen, 44-B
UNDERWOOD, Enock, 443-D
John, 189-A
John J., 443-D
Jos. B., 443-D
Louisa, 189-A
Louisa J., 189-A
Mary, 443-D
Sarah, 443-D
UPEMAN, Louis, 168-B
UPMAN, Henry G., 168-B
Sallie E., 168-B
VAIN, August, 70-D
VALIENT, Martha, 21-D, 381-A
VAN ARSDALE, Hezekiah, 67
VAN ORDER, Laura V., 10-A
VAN SANT, Benjamin F., 1-C
Emma L., 137-B
John A., 137-B
Thomas A., 1-C
VAN SKIVER, Annie Elizabeth, 102-C
Doris A., 102-C
Edward, 102-C
Kathryn, 102-C
William H., 102-C
VAN WERDER, John F., 21-D
VAN WORT, Ella, 85-A
VAN ZANT, John R., Jr., 137-B
VANCE, Lulu, 142-D
VANDERFRIFT, Ada E., 294-A
VANDERGRIF, Jno. M., 294-A
VANDERGRIFT, Benj., 294-A
Carrie V., 294-A
John M., 294-A
Mary A., 294-A
VANDIFORD, Abraham, 590-D
Kate, 590-D
Viola, 590-D
VANORSDALE, Hezekiah, 125-B
Mary, 125-B
VANSANT, Caroline, 134-A

VANSANT, Caroline E., 134-A
  Ellinor, 134-A
  Frank, 134-A
  John, 134-A
  Margt., 134-A
  Ronda, 134-A
  Emma R., 137-B
  John, 134-A
VARNER, Lucy C., 21-D
VEASEY, Chas. R., 199-B
  John M., 199-B
  Loretta, 218-B
  Margt., 199-B
  Rose, 218-B
VEAYCE, Myrele, 173-D
VEEDER, Harriet, 119-B
VENZIE, Howard W., 173-D
VERMILLER, Eliabeth, 108-B
VERNEY, David, 204-B
  Elisha T., 204-B
  Jas. E., 204-B
  John, 204-B
  Lola M., 204-B
  Lottie, 204-B
  Margt. A., 204-B
  Marion, 204-B
VERNON, John, 128-A
  John A., 128-A
VERTIN, Louisa, 232-A
VICK, Carrie V., 489-D
  Eliza, 489-D
  Emma B., 115-C
  Frank T., 489-D
  Harriet C., 489-D
  Harry Penn, 489-D
  James C., 489-D
  James Cordy, 115-C
  James L., 489-D
  John W., 489-D
  Mary L., 489-D
  W. P., 489-D
  William L., 489-D
VICKERY, Elizabeth, 15-A
  Hazeltire, 15-A
  Mary A., 15-A
  Maryman, 15-A
  Stephen J., 15-A
  Thomas, 15-A
VINCENT, Alexander, 88-B
VINTON, Juliet, 102-B
  Juliet M., 102-B
  R. S., Rev., 102-B
  R. Spencer, 67
  Robert S., Rev., 102-B
VODEN, Saml., 26-D
VOGEL, Julia A., 150-B
VOGELMAN, Edward L., 115-C
  Mary F., 115-C
VOHDEN, Barbara, 400-D

VOHDEN, Maggie, 400-D
  Mamie, 400-D
  Saml., 400-D
VOLANDT, Lydie J., 341-D
VOLZ, Anthony F., 88-C
  Bertha Maye, 88-C
  Maye B., 88-C
VON LINDENBURGER, Bertha McKeever, 90-B
VORSTEG, Joseph H., 203-B
VOYCE, Amanda, 6-D
  Bernard F., 6-D
  Hannah, 462-A
  Myrtle M., 6-D
  Thos., 6-D
  Thos. S., 6-D
WACHTEL, M. V. B., 372-D
WADE, Florence, 35-A
  John L., 35-A
WAGNER, (?), Mrs., 21-D
  Bertha M., 73-C
  Caroline, 4-D
  Chas., 497-D
  Etta L., 497-D
  George A., 73-C
  Mildred E., 25-D
WAIN, Beatrice I., 209-D
  George H., 188-A
WAITE, Laura V., 385-A
WALKER, Annie, 189-A
  Annie T., 168-B
  Claude, 460-A
  Eliz. M., 308-A
  Elizabeth, 189-A
  Ella M., 168-B
  Ellen J., 168-B
  Geo., 57-D
  Georgie E., 339-A
  Harrison S., 238-A
  Harry, 238-A
  James L., 21-D
  Jas., 138-D
  Jas. B., 238-A
  Jas. R., 168-B
  Jas. W., 238-A
  John H., 339-A
  John Harry, 308-A
  Kate E., 138-D
  Margt., 213-D
  Margt. S., 168-B
  Mary, 68-C, 198-A, 238-A
  Mary A., 238-A
  Mathias, 238-A
  Matthias T., 238-A
  Patience T., 168-B
  Salvina, 168-B
  Saml. T., 339-A
  Sarah E., 175-A
  Sarah R., 339-A

WALKER, Sarah S., 339-A
WALL, Annie M., 1-D
  Carrie L., 128-B
  Carrie S., 38-A
  Carrie Wright, 128-B
  Chas. A., 128-B
  Chas. P., 38-A
  Eddie, 28-B
  Eliza, 182-A
  Elizabeth, 110-B
  Ellen, 110-B
  Hannah, 182-A
  Jacob, 182-A
  John P., 110-B
  John R., 28-B
  John T., 1-D, 377-A
  Leana, 28-B
  Lena, 28-B
  Mary C., 529-D
  Mary E., 110-B
  Wm. F., 110-B
WALLACE, Ethel, 453-A
  Geo. W., 454-D
  George N., 346-A
  Hanson, 346-A
  Harry E., 454-D
  James, 441-A
  John A., 346-A
  John O., 454-D
  Larina, 441-D
  Maggie W., 168-B
  Martha, 13-A
  Mary E., 454-D
  Mathew, 13-A
  Merison, 346-A
  Susan, 346-A
  Susan E., 346-A
  William, 346-A, 444-A
  Willie, 45-A
WALLEN, John, 140-A
WALTER, Gertrude, 24-C
  Gertrude F. (HUGHES), 15-C
  Harry D., 15-C
  Harry O., 24-C
  Henry M., Dr., 24-C
  Ruth, 112-B
WALTERS, Emma J., 100-C
  Fannie, 40-B
  William, 100-C
WALTHAM, Elizabeth, 320-A
  John, 320-A
  William, 320-A
WALTON, Agnes, 213-D
  Ann, 439-D
  Chas. H., 361-A
  Clara D., 361-A
  Daniel W., 43-B
  Elizabeth, 198-A
  Emma, 213-D

WALTON, Frank C., 198-A
  Henrietta C., 43-B
  Henry, 518-D
  J., 83-A
  John E., 361-A
  Katherine, 43-B
  Mani, 13-A
  Marg. E., 14-B
  Wm. E., 439-D
WALTZ, Annie, 204-D
  Grover C., 204-D
  Samuel E., 204-D
  Susan, 204-D
WARD, Annie C., 108-B
  Annie T., 19-A
  Catherine, 140-A
  Doris M., 89-C
  Edna Lee, 393-A
  Edward J., 463-A
  Edwd. J., 19-A
  Edwd. T., 19-A
  Eleanor Kate, 19-A
  Florence, 103-A
  Grace A., 61-C
  Grace E., 19-A
  Marion E., 19-A
  Martha T., 413-D
  Mary E., 19-A
  Philip G. W., 130-B
  Preston C., 89-C
  Robert J., 463-A
  Robert R., Capt., 61-C
  Saml., 18-A
  Sarah, 18-A
  V. Haues, 108-B
WARE, Catherine, 578-D
  James, 578-D
  Joseph, 578-D
  Julia, 251-A
  Mary (Ida), 251-A
  Willye B., 251-A
  Wm. B., 251-A
WAREHAM, Mary, 21-D
WARFIELD, Adelaide E., 268-A
  Alice E., 197-A
  Ann, 197-A
  Annie R., 197-A
  Chas. E., 284-A
  Elizabeth, 197-A
  Emily, 197-A
  George W., 284-A
  Jennie, 274-A
  Mary, 197-A
  Mary E., 284-A
  Rachel, 197-A
  Sarah A., 197-A
  Susannah, 197-A
  Thomas, 197-A
WARMA, Chas., 110-A

WARNER, Frances W., 44-B
 Thos. J., 7-D
WARREN, Ada, 93-B
WARRING, Spencer M., 21-A
WARRY, John T., 482-A
 Sarah, 482-A
WARTHEM, Henriette A., 234-A
WARWICK, Mary E., 161-D
WASHEY, Hattie B., 393-A
WASTENN, Wesley M. S., 234-A
WATERS, (?), 40-B
 Annie C., 40-B
 Caroline E., 111-A
 Charles E., 17-A
 Charles E., Jr., 17-A
 Eliza, 176-D
 John H., 176-D
 Laura, 137-B
 Sarah, 137-B
 Susie I., 91-B
 Wargaret VanCatt, 176-D
 Wm. D., 137-B
 Wm. H., 45-A, 137-B
WATERTON, George, 386-A
 Sarah A., 386-A
WATERWORTH, Annie M., 164-B
 James S., 164-B
 Jane, 164-B
 Jas. M., 164-B
 Jennie, 164-B
 Samuel, 164-B
WATKINS, (?), 146-B
 A. W., 25-A
 Adelia, 187-A
 Ann, 240-A, 417-A
 Annie, 25-A
 Archibald, 25-A
 C. B., 25-A
 Catherine L., 246 1/2-A
 Chas. B., 25-A
 Eliza, 186-B
 Elizabeth, 25-A
 Elizabeth A., 25-A
 Emma, 246 1/2-A
 Fannie, 179-B, 186-B
 Gassaway, 246 1/2-A
 H. R., 160-A
 Harry W., 246 1/2-A
 Henry B., 246 1/2-A
 Jas. A., 25-A
 John Q. A., 25-A
 John Wesley, 246 1/2-A
 Jos., 240-A
 Kate H., 25-A
 Maria, 246 1/2-A
 Mary A., 25-A
 Mary C., 25-A
 Mortimer S., 246 1/2-A
 Nicholas A., 68

WATKINS, Nicholas W., 160-A
 Robert P., 246 1/2-A
WATSON, Alfred G., 271-D
 Chas., 134-A
 John W., 271-D
 Mable S., 167-B
 Maggie, 134-A, 271-D
 Thos. C., 271-D
WATTERS, Beatrice, 144-A
 John, 42-B
 John L., 40-B
 Mary, 42-B
WATTES, Kath., 84-B
WATTS, Geo., 83-A, 99-A
 George, 107-A
 Mary E., 107-A
 Mary F., 107-A
 Mary R., 421-D
 Sarah, 22-A
WAUGH, A. T., 99-B
 Alex H., 99-B
 Alexander T., 194-A
 Beverly, 99-B
 Beverly Bishop, 67
 Beverly R., Sgt., 99-B
 Catherine, 99-B
 Eliz., 99-B
 Jas. B., 99-B
 John W., 99-B, 194-A
 John Wesley, 194-A
 Kate F., 194-A
 Margt. A., 194-A
 Mary D., 99-B
 Mary E., 99-B
 Mary V., 99-B
 William B., 194-A
WAY, Walter, 44-A
WEATHERLY, G. Frank, Mrs., 80-B
WEAVER, Casper, 335-A
 Daniel, 488-A
 Danl., 237-A
 Dedrick C., 30-D
 Elena, 237-A
 Ellen, 237-A
 Emma J., 30-D
 F. T., Sr., 82-C
 Frederick, 82-C
 Frederocl T., Jr., 82-C
 H. L., Jr., 61-C
 Hannah, 237-A
 Hannah R., 237-A
 Herbert L., Rev., 61-C
 Herbert Lee, 61-C
 Jacob, 441-A
 John L., Jr., 61-C
 Mary A., 30-D
 Myrtle L., 82-C
 Myrtle V., 61-C
 Patricia Ann (CARE), 82-C

WEAVER, Virginia, 61-C
  Virginia T., 61-C
  Virginia Thomas, 61-C
  Wm. E., Mrs., 136-B
WEB(?), Julia May, 21-D
WEBALS, Zas, 85-A
WEBB, Chas. W., 264-D
  Katie E., 66
WEBER, Ananuphalus, 484-A
  Barbara, 33-D
  Cecil, 88-C
  Guyon, 484-A
  Myrtle, 88-C
  William C., 88-C
WEBSTER, Algernon, 101-B
  Alice, 21-D, 101-B
  Ann, 181-B
  Annie L., 101-B
  Bertha Jos., 101-B
  Eunna E., 181-B
  Florence (?), 101-B
  Geo., 202-B
  George E., 101-B
  Harriet E., 101-B
  Henry, 181-B
  J. J., 68
  John, 202-B
  Jos., 101-B
  Martha, 181-B
  Moses, 101-B
  Saml. H., 101-B
  Wm., 181-B
WECKERSTENS, Chas. G., 195-A
WEDEMAN, Edith B., 98-C
WEDGE, Emily, 15-A
  Wm. S., 15-A
WEEKES, Agnes, 531-D
  Blanche E., 531-D
  Charles C., 531-D
  John Y., 531-D
  Matilda, 531-D
  Maud S., 531-D
  Sealy, 531-D
WEEKS, Blanche, 531-D
  Robt. J., 173-A
  S. F., 173-A
  Sarah, 173-A
WEEMS, C. H. W., 368-D
  Ida B., 24-D
  Margt. B., 24-D
  Theopolis N., 368-D
  Thos. A., 368-D
WEHN, Chas. H., 222-B
  Elizabeth, 222-B
  Geo., 222-B
  Philip, 222-B
  Wm. H., 227-B
WEIGAND, Ann S., 75-A
  Edwd., 75-A

WEIKEL, Maud, 459-D
WEIRTLING, Alice, 596-D
  David B., 596-D
WELCH, (?), 392-A
  Elizabeth, 192-A
  John W., 133-D
  Wm. O., 192-A
WELLBOURNE, Florida, 195-B
  John E., 195-B
  Lucy H., 195-B
WELLER, Paul L., 499-D
  Pauline, 499-D
  Wilbur, 499-D
WELLS, John, 493-D
  Joseph, 204-A
  Lillian M., 13-A
  Lilyan M., 107-B
  Robert T., 493-D
  Sadie M., 13-A
WELMOT, (?), 199-D
WELSH, Benj. F., 189-B
  Charles I., 80-B
  Eliza, 192-A
  Emory T., 209-A
  Grace L., 209-A
  Harriett, 67
  Isabell, 189-B
  Jos. A., 85-A
  Lydia, 80-B
  Robert, 67
WENDLER, Alice V., 207-D
  Harry B., 207-D
WENTWORTH, Estella A., 497-D
WESLEY, (?), 152-B
  Cath., 422-A
  Chas., 44-A
  George, 11-D
  J., 14-A
  Lewis, 11-D
  Mary A., 422-A
  Wm. H., 422-A
WESSELLS, Asa, 11-A
  Elmira, 11-A
  Wilber, 11-A
  Wm. D., 11-A
WEST, Benj., 100-A
  Clara A., 295-A
  Clara W., 295-A
  Ketty, 462-A
  Lucy A., 295-A
WESTAWAY, Lillian C. (Ray), 95-B
WESTWAY, Harry J., 95-B
  Lillian Ray, 95-B
WESTWOOD, H. H., 68
WHALAND, Robert M., 220-D
WHALEN, Eliz., 139-B
  Ida, 152-B
  Washington B., 463-A

WHALENS, (?), 152-B
WHALEY, Harriet, 442-A
WHARRY, Amanda M., 482-A
  Chas. S., 482-A
  Thos. S., 482-A
WHEAT, Alice E., 386-D
  Clara, 386-D
  Eliz., 386-D
  Elizabeth D., 386-D
  John, 386-D
  John A., 386-D
WHEELER, (?), 168-B
  Benj., 398-A
  Chas. H., 26-D
  Chas., Mrs., 17-D
  Edw. P., 168-B
  Edwd. L., 398-A
  Ella M., 398-A
  Hannah S., 168-B
  Howard F., 25-C
  James, 336-A, 398-A
  Jas., 23-A
  Jas. A., 336-A
  Jessie L., 336-A
  Mary, 201-A
  Mary L., 101-B
  Maude C., 25-C
  Mollie E., 336-A
  Nellie B., 201-A
  Robert Allen, 25-C
  Robert B., 25-C
  Sallie M., 398-A
  Sarah A., 23-A
  Virginia A., 341-D
WHEKOM, Clement, 1-B
  Ella, 1-B
  Thelius, 1-B
WHELAN, Oliver P., 139-B
WHELER, Elizabeth, 416-A
WHEN, Clara E., 227-B
  Georganna, 227-B
  Willie, 227-B
  Wm. H., 227-B
WHILTON, C. W., 98-A
WHIPPS, George W., 98-A
WHISTLER, D. E., 72-D
  David E., Sr., 72-D
  Edwin E., 138-A
  Mary C., 72-D
WHITAKER, Charles M., 261-A
  Margt., 188-A
  Sarah A., 261-A
  Wm. G., 188-A
  Wm. J., 188-A
  Wm. S., 188-A
WHITE, (?), 53-A
  (?), Mrs., 243-A
  Bertie, 84-B
  Charles, 71-C

WHITE, Claire, 217-A
  Clarence, 144-A
  Edmond C., 155-A
  Edna L., 53-A
  Edward C., 155-A
  Elaine, 217-A
  Elaum Va., 250-A
  Evelyn (CHALMERS), 192-B
  J. T., 175-B
  Joseph, 67
  Lillie Jane, 113-C
  Maneta R., 217-A
  Martha R., 217-A
  Mary A., 155-A
  Mary Ann, 391-A
  Mary E., 54-B
  Milcha, 280-A
  Nora, 71-C
  Norris, 217-A
  Saml. W., 217-A
  Samuel B., 144-A
  Sarah, 54-B, 437-D
  Sarah C., 54-B
  Sarah E., 54-B
  Thos., 133-D
  W. E., 210-B
  W. J., Sr., 192-B
  Wallace J., Jr., 192-B
  Weightell M., 113-C
  William H., 54-B
  Willie, 54-B
WHITEFORD, Henrietta, 193-B, 209-D
  Jas. H., 209-D
  Jennie, 274-A
  Wallace J., 209-D
WHITEHAM, Margt., 338-D
WHITEHORN, Ella L., 338-D
  Emily L., 338-D
  Laura, 338-D
  Margt., 338-D
  Revere, 338-D
WHITEHORNE, Charlotte, 338-D
WHITEHURST, Ellen C., 291-A
  Henry W., 291-A
  John, 252-D
WHITNEY, Annie E., 539-D
  Florence, 539-D
WHITSON, Almina, 136-A
  David, 136-A
  George M., 136-A
  Jane, 136-A
  Jane A., 136-A
  John, 136-A
  Mary, 136-A
WHITTER, Beulah, 210-B
  Crofton S., 210-B
  Irene A., 210-B
  J., 210-B

WHITTER, Mary, 210-B
 W., 210-B
 Wm. E., 210-B
WICKERS, Charles H., 42-A
 Emma, 42-A
 Harry N., 42-A
WICKES, William, 67
WIDERKIND, Elizabeth, 438-D
WIEDEFELD, Mary A., 245-D
 Thos., 245-D
WIEGAND, Ann, 75-A
 Herman, 75-A
 Paul, 75-A
WIGHTMAN, Alice B., 126-B
 Fannie, 126-B
 Geo., 126-B
 Grace, 126-B
 Henrietta, 126-B
 Jane, 126-B
 Wm. H., 126-B
WILCOX, Emma I., 40-A
 Louis N., 40-A
 Louisa N., 40-A
 Maria A., 415-D
 Martha (Matie) D., 40-A
 Sarah, 300-A
 Sarah Ann, 467-D
 Thos. L., 415-D
WILDE, Alice Ann (TICKLE), 45-C
 Robert, 45-C
WILDER, Annie E., 154-B
 Elsie E., 154-B
 Mabel M., 154-B
 Mynete, 154-B
 Ruth, 154-B
WILEY, Joseph, 4-B
WILHELM, Susan A., 193-A
 Thos. F., 193-A
 Virginia, 193-A
 Virginia D., 193-A
 William, 193-A
 Wm., 193-A
WILK, Joseph, 204-A
WILKENS, Chas., 34-B
 Jacob, 155-D
 Thomas D., 43-B
WILKES, Anna, 14-C
 Harry R., Rev., 14-C
WILKINS, George W., 432-A
 Sarah, 432-A
 Thomas, 432-A
 Thos., 432-A
WILKINSON, Albert N., 74-C
 Alma L., 74-C
 Alma Lillian, 74-C
 Elizabeth T., 220-A
 Hiram H., 11-A
 James L., 74-C
 Jerome S., 74-C

WILKINSON, John H. H., 11-A
 Jos., 11-A
 Joseph C., 11-A
 Margt. E., 11-A
 Mary, 11-A
 Thos., 55-A
 Willie, 55-A
WILLEN, Howard V., 311-D
 Samuel J., 311-D
WILLETT, Elizabeth, 119-D
 John, 11-A
 Sarah, 119-D
WILLEY, Jos., 349-A
 Joseph, 188-B
 Susan, 153-B
WILLIAMS, (?), 190-A, 370-A
 Andrew, 154-A
 Annie, 163-D
 Annie R., 121-D
 Betty Busey, 159-B
 Chas. C., 154-A
 Chas. D., 56-A
 Chas. E., 84-B, 154-A, 200-A
 Clayland A., 154-C
 Edith, 200-A
 Edward, 223-B
 Edward T. (or F.), 154-A
 Elanor, 241-D
 Elizabeth, 96-B
 Emma, 593-D
 Eugene C., 416-D
 Eugene H., 416-D
 Eva, 416-D
 George W., 333-A
 Georgiano, 135-B
 Georiana C., 152-B
 Gertrude M. J., 154-C
 Grace Dixon, 154-A
 Hamilton, 164-B
 Harriet, 76-A
 Henry S., 164-B
 J. J., Dr., 159-B
 J. T., 376-A
 James, 243-D, 244-A
 Jno., 333-A
 John, 155-D
 Jone V., 376-A
 Louisa, 154-A
 Margaret A., 164-B
 Margt., 46-A
 Maria, 154-A
 Mary J., 154-A
 N., 53-B
 Nannie M., 517-D
 Olivia, 416-D
 Sarah, 313-A
 Susan, 223-B, 357-A
 Susan B., 357-A
 Thomas, 154-A

WILLIAMS, Walter, 154-A
Wm. LaFayette, 154-A
Wm. P., 154-A
Wm. T., 357-A
WILLING, Willi, 74-B
WILLIS, Alvin M., 189-A
  Edward, 189-A
  Geneva M., 189-A
  Lillian B., 189-A
  Mary E., 189-A
  Mary L., 189-A
  Tamsie W., 189-A
WILLS, Anna Jane, 151-B
  Emily, 151-B
  Francis W., 10-D
  John Thomas, 151-B
  Wm. G., 151-B
WILLY, E., 153-B
WILMOT, Elizabeth, 199-D
WILSON, (?), 80-A, 164-B
  (?), Mrs., 109-B
  Ada, 155-D
  Anna Viola, 602-D
  Annie E., 602-D
  Annie L., 89-D
  Annie L. (NGE), 89-D
  Augustus E., 52-A
  Bell, 366-A
  Bessie, 418-D
  Catherine, 103-D
  Chas., 264-D
  Cordelia Howard, 116-B
  Edith, 598-D
  Edward, 89-D
  Eliz, 425-D
  Elizabeth, 418-D
  Emma F., 52-A
  Henry, 160-B
  James, 456-A
  James H., 103-D
  James J., 52-A
  Jno. T., 461-A
  Johana, 436-A
  Kate, 19-B
  Laura, 526-D
  Lettie, 45-A
  Lilly, 418-D
  Lilly M., 366-A
  M. R., Mrs., 159-B
  Margt. R., 160-B
  Martha, 456-A, 598-D
  Mary E., 526-D
  Mary L., 160-B
  Miliah D., 160-B
  Noris, 301-D
  S. Louesa, 160-B
  Sarah, 19-B
  T. H., 598-D
  Theresa M., 14-C

WILSON, Wilbur, 159-B
  William H., 67
  Wm., 155-D
  Wm. H., 159-B
  Wm. H., Rev., 159-B
WINCHESTER, Geo. E., 237-D
  Roy, 237-D
WINDER, Margt. A., 117-B
WINDLE, Lillie, 264-D
WINKELMAN, Charles Edward, 140-A
  Chas., 140-A
  Chas. E., 140-A
  Eliza A., 140-A
  Susanna, 140-A
  Thos., 55-A
WINKLEMAN, Alice A., 140-A
  Ann, 140-A
  Ann E., 140-A
  Annie, 140-A
  Elizabeth, 140-A
  Sophia, 140-A
  Susannah, 140-A
WINKLER, (?), Mrs., 200-A
  Ann E., 200-A
  Chas. R., 298-A
  Clarence E., 178-D
  Edwd., 200-A
  Emma M., 178-D
  Lloyd H., 178-D
WINKS, (?), 34-C
WINN, Mollie M., 23-D
WINSATT, Frances A., 301-A
WINSETT, Frances F., 301-A
WINTERSON, Washington, 186-B
WIRT, Evelyn Pearl, 102-C
  Tyler C., 102-C
WISE, (?), 281-A
  Chas. L., 275-D
  Elizabeth, 187-A
  John L., 275-D
  Sarah, 275-D
WISTHER, Peter, 21-D
WITENBAKER, Chas. E., 210-A
WOCKENFUSS, Emil, 24-C
  Ida Martha, 24-C
  Margaret C., 23-C
  Margaretha, 24-C
  William E., 23-C
WOLF, Anne F. (FALK), 88-C
  Arabella, 303-A
  Araminta L., 192-A
  Cath. A., 303-A
  Daisy G., 192-A
  Geo. E., 192-A
  Geo. H., 192-A
  Isaac T., 192-A
  Mary, 453-D
  Mary E., 192-A

WOLF, Wm. E., 192-A
  Wm. I., 88-C
WOLFSHEIMER, Georgia, 142-C
  Georgia B., 142-C
  Joel H., 142-C
WOLLEN, Elizabeth, 43-A
  James, 43-A
WOLLSLAGER, Kathleene, 177-B
WOOD, Arthur S., 83-A
  Charlotte, 241-A
  Charlotte R., 224-B
  Danl. P., 52-A
  Eleanora, 224-B
  Eliz J., 205-A
  George H., 52-A
  Hester A., 52-A
  Hester G., 52-A
  John C., 224-B
  John O., 224-B
  Raymond R., 24-B
  Thos. N., 75-A
  Walter, 196-A
  Walter F., 224-B
  William T., 200-A
  Willie J., 76-B
  Wm., 56-B
  Wm. J., 134-B
WOODALL, (?), 235-A
  Alfred, 232-A
  Dorothy M., 32-C
  Edith, 134-B
  Fannie W., 232-A
  Guy L., 21-D
  Harry, 32-C
  Harry W., 134-B
  Henry C. (or E.), 232-A
  Jas., 134-B
  John, 134-B
  Margt. A., 232-A
  Mary C., 134-B
  Rose, 134-B
  Samuel T., 232-A
  W. W., 134-B
  Washington, 134-B
  William E., 232-A
WOODBURY, Vera A., 286-A
WOODEN, Assian, 353-A
WOODFORD, George, 362-A
WOODMAN, Jno. W., 369-A
  John, 369-A
  Mary Ann, 369-A
WOODS, (?), 429-A
  Ann B., 205-A
  Ann Berry, 205-A
  D., 192-A
  Elizabeth, 75-A, 192-A
  Elizabeth A., 448-A
  Elizabeth H., 205-A
  Elizabeth M., 448-A

WOODS, G. B., 192-A
  George W., 448-A
  Harriet, 204-A
  Jane, 432-A
  Jno. W., 419-A, 448-A
  Jos. S., 318-A
  Mary, 597-D
  Matilda, 597-D
  Michael, 597-D
  Pracilla C., 75-A
  Pracilla E., 75-A
  Robert A., 448-A
  Sarah A., 75-A
  Thos., 75-A
  Thos. M., 75-A
  William, 205-A
  Wm., 192-A
WOODWARD, Ellen, 161-A
  Frank M., 401-A
  James, 161-A
  Julia A., 401-A
  Mary, 161-A
  Virginia (?), 161-A
  Wm., 161-A
  Wm. H., 401-A
  Wm. W., 161-A, 401-A
WOOLEN, Elizabeth, 43-A
  Jas., 43-A
WOOLERY, Ella M., 41-D
  James H., 41-D
WOOLF, Chas., 341-A
WOOTEN, (?), 28-A
  Clara V., 450-D
WORKING, Elizabeth, 364-A
  Henry, 364-A
WORTEN, Chas., 448-D
  Howard D., 448-D
WORTH, Melvin H., 199-B
WORTHINGTON, Chas. T., 193-A
  Harriett, 193-A
  Henrietta, 193-A
  Nicholas, 193-A
  Richard, 392-A
  Sarah, 193-A
  Thomas, 193-A
  Thomas J., 193-A
  Willie A., 193-A
  Wm. G., 193-A
WRIGHT, Amos P., 46-C
  Angeline, 447-A
  Anna S., 88-B
  Annie, 128-B
  Annie S., 128-B
  Caroline, 38-A
  Elizabeth A., 37-C
  Elsie M., 46-C
  Fannie E., 301-D
  Frederick Wm., Mrs., 73-B
  Geo. S., 301-D

WRIGHT, George, 454-A, 457-A
George S., 358-A
George T., 55-A
Georgie E., 301-D
James, 128-B
James B., 454-A
Joan Luetta, 131-C
Johanna, 454-A
John J., 51-B
Jos. M., 155-B
Lillie A., 385-A
Lorenzo A., 201-D
Mary A., 224-B
S., 385-A
Saml., 447-A, 454-A
Samuel, 454-A
Sarah T., 55-A
Walter E., 454-A
Wilbur T., 37-C
WRITRIDGE, Andrew, Mrs., 84-B
WROTEN, Evelyn H., 450-D
Hannah, 96-B
Mary, 450-D
WYANT, Mary A., 14-B
YEAGER, Elizabeth M., 48-C
Estelle R., 48-C
George F., Jr., 48-C
YEAGGER, George F., Sr., 48-C
YEARLEY, Alexander, 97-B
Anne, 97-B
Aramenta, 97-B
Clifton K., 1-C
Fanny V., 1-C
John T., 97-B
Saml. I., 97-B
YEATES, H. P. P., Dr., 422-D
YEWELL, Norma F., 142-C
Sarah, 142-C
Sarah Georgiana, 142-C
Thomas Oliver, 142-C
YOECKEL, Fannie, 222-B
Geo., 222-B
YOUNG, Anna, 18-D
C. M., 48-D
Chas. H., 18-D
Chas. M., 48-D
E. P., 32-A
Edwd. R., 218-B
Elmer V., 18-D
Florence, 32-A
Frank C., 18-D
George W., 239-A
Grace E., 514-D
Jas., 92-B
John R., 18-D
Laura M., 345-A
Lillie, 32-A
Lucretta, 98-A, 239-A
Mabel B., 45-B

YOUNG, Margaret (HARRINGTON), 18-D
Mary, 18-D
Mary L., 48-D
Mary W., 18-D
Sarah, 18-D
Thomas, 32-A
William, 18-D
William G., 18-D
Wm., 74-B
Wm. G., 18-D
Wm. H., 32-A
Wm. S., 18-D
YOUNGER, Bertha E., 70-C
Charles W., 70-C
George, 70-C
Susan, 21-D
William, 70-C
YUNDT, Leonard, 15-B
Mary, 15-B
Rebecca, 15-B
Samuel, 15-B
Sarah M., 15-B
ZALAUKA, Hannah E., 396-D
Minnie A., 396-D
ZEANNERET, E. E., 396-A
ZEGLER, Frank A., 250-A
ZEIGLER, Edith M., 250-A
ZELANKA, Richard, 396-D
ZELL, Hattie, 90-B
ZELLER, Mary, 139-A
Sarah, 139-A
ZELLIS, Maggie, 139-A
ZEMIER, (?), 523-D
ZENNERET, Zelin, 396-A
ZENTGRAF, John Mrs., 216-B
ZEULLIN, Gertrude, 380-A
ZIEGLER, Joseph, 164-B
Mary E., 164-B
Nannie J., 164-B
William E., 154-B
ZIMMERMAN, (?), 274-A
Annie B., 55-A
Annie E., 127-B
Christian, 20-A
Emma C., 20-A
George, 20-A
George E., 20-A
George J., 20-A
George, Rev., 20-A
Harry A., 20-A
Isabell, 20-A
Kate, 84-B
Mabel H., 220-D
Mary, 42-A, 181-A
Mary E., 20-A
Sarah E., 369-A
V. Benjaman, 55-A
Wm., 20-A

ZIMMERMAN, Wm. L., 127-B
ZINKER, (?), 219-B
ZITTLE, Josephine, 286-A
 Marlin S., 286-A
 Otho J., 286-A